THE OXFORD HANDBOOK OF

BAYESIAN ECONOMETRICS

THE OXFORD HANDBOOK OF BAYESIAN ECONOMETRICS

Edited by

JOHN GEWEKE, GARY KOOP,

and

HERMAN VAN DIJK

OXFORD
UNIVERSITY PRESS

OXFORD
UNIVERSITY PRESS

Great Clarendon Street, Oxford, OX2 6DP,
United Kingdom

Oxford University Press is a department of the University of Oxford.
It furthers the University's objective of excellence in research, scholarship,
and education by publishing worldwide. Oxford is a registered trade mark of
Oxford University Press in the UK and in certain other countries

First Edition published in 2011
First published in paperback 2013
Impression: 1

Published in the United States of America by Oxford University Press
198 Madison Avenue, New York, NY 10016, United States of America

British Library Cataloguing in Publication Data
Data available

ISBN 978-0-19-955908-4 (hbk)
ISBN 978-0-19-968133-4 (pbk)

Printed in Great Britain on acid-free paper by
Ashford Colour Press Ltd. Gosport, Hampshire

Contents

List of Figures

List of Tables

List of Contributors

Greg Allenby is the Helen C. Kurtz Chair in Marketing in the Fisher College of Business, The Ohio State University.

Gary Chamberlain is the Louis Professor of Economics at Harvard University.

Siddhartha Chib is the Harry C. Hartkopf Professor of Econometrics and Statistics at the Olin Business School, Washington University in St Louis.

Marco Del Negro is Assistant Vice President in the Macroeconomic and Monetary Studies Function of the Research and Statistics Group of the Federal Reserve Bank of New York.

John Geweke is Co-Director and Distinguished Research Professor in the Centre for the Study of Choice at the University of Technology, Sydney. He is co-editor of the *Journal of Econometrics*, a Fellow of the Econometric Society and the American Statistical Association, and past president of the International Society for Bayesian Analysis.

Paolo Giordani is an Advisor at the Swedish Central Bank.

Jim Griffin is a Lecturer in Statistics at the University of Kent. He has worked extensively on Bayesian nonparametric methods, including the development of regression and time series models and their application to econometric problems such as efficiency measurement and volatility estimation.

Eric Jacquier is Associate Professor of Finance at MIT Sloan, on leave from the Finance Department at HEC Montreal.

Robert Kohn is a Scientia Professor in the School of Economics at the School of Banking and Finance at the Australian School of Business in the University of New South Wales.

Gary Koop is a Professor of Economics at the University of Strathclyde.

Mingliang Li is an Associate Professor of Economics in the Department of Economics at the State University of New York at Buffalo.

Michael Pitt is Associate Professor in Economics at the University of Warwick. He has worked extensively on Bayesian methodology, particularly for latent time series models. He has a particular interest in particle filters and their application in financial econometric models such as stochastic volatility.

Dale J. Poirier is Professor of Economics at the University of California, Irvine. He is a Fellow of the Econometric Society, the American Statistical Association, and the *Journal of Econometrics*. He has been on the editorial boards of the *Journal of Econometrics* and *Econometric Theory* and was the founding editor of *Econometric Reviews*.

Nicholas Polson is Professor of Econometrics and Statistics at the Booth School of Business at the University of Chicago. He is currently an associate editor for the *Journal of Econometrics*, the *Journal of Financial Econometrics*, and the *Journal of the American Statistical Association*.

Fernando Quintana is a Professor, Departamento de Estadistica, Pontificia Universidad Católica de Chile. Most of his work has focused on Bayesian nonparametric methods and their multiple applications.

Peter Rossi is the James Collins Professor of Marketing at the UCLA Anderson School of Management. A fellow of the American Statistical Association and the *Journal of Econometrics*, Rossi is the founding editor of *Quantitative Marketing and Economics*, past associate editor for the *Journal of the American Statistical Association*, the *Journal of Econometrics*, and the *Journal of Business and Economic Statistics*.

Frank Schorfheide is a Professor of Economics at the University of Pennsylvania. He is also affiliated with the National Bureau of Economic Research (NBER) and the Centre for Economic and Policy Research (CEPR). Schorfheide is a Visiting Scholar at the Federal Reserve Banks of New York and Philadelphia.

Mark Steel is a Professor of Statistics at the University of Warwick. His research interests focus on theoretical and applied Bayesian statistics and econometrics. He is editor of *Bayesian Analysis* and associate editor of the *Journal of Econometrics*, the *Journal of Productivity Analysis*, and the *Central European Journal of Economic Modelling and Econometrics*, and has previously served as associate editor of the *Journal of the Royal Statistical Society, Series B*, the *Journal of Business and Economic Statistics*, and *Econometric Theory*.

Justin Tobias is a Professor in the Economics Department at Purdue University.

Herman van Dijk is director of the Tinbergen Institute and professor of Econometrics with a Personal Chair at Erasmus University, Rotterdam.

INTRODUCTION

JOHN GEWEKE, GARY KOOP, AND
HERMAN VAN DIJK

1 Introduction

Bayesian econometrics has expanded enormously in recent years. This expansion has occurred not only in econometric theory, but also in empirical work. Many applied fields have seen a large increase in the use of Bayesian econometric methods. Researchers interested in learning the basics of Bayesian econometrics have available a wide range of textbooks, from the classic textbook of Zellner (1971) through the influential contributions of Poirier (1995) and Bauwens, Lubrano, and Richard (1999) to the recent burgeoning of graduate textbooks such as Geweke (2005), Koop (2003), Koop, Poirier, and Tobias (2007), Lancaster (2004), and Rossi et al. (2005). However, there is no single source for researchers and policymakers wanting to learn about Bayesian methods in specialized fields, or for graduate students seeking to make the final step from textbook learning to the research frontier. The purpose of this *Handbook* is to fill this gap.

Although each chapter in this *Handbook* deals with a set of issues distinct to its topic, there are some unifying themes that run through many of the chapters. The first of these is the use of computationally intensive posterior simulation algorithms. In Bayesian econometrics, the simulation revolution has been so overwhelming that almost all of the chapters in this book have a substantial computation component. The development of more powerful computers and more sophisticated simulation algorithms have gone hand in hand, leading to a virtuous cycle where Bayesian econometric methods and model development have become complementary. Indeed, with some models (e.g. dynamic stochastic general equilibrium (DSGE) models), Bayesian methods have become predominant. In the case of DSGE models, there are several factors which account for this Bayesian predominance. But one of these factors is the availability of powerful simulation tools which allow the researcher to uncover features of the high-dimensional, irregular posterior distributions that arise.

A second theme that runs through many of the chapters is heterogeneity. In cross-sectional and panel data sets this is manifest at the individual level. That is, even after controlling for observable characteristics, individuals may still differ to such an extent that use of standard regression-based methods assuming slope coefficients which are common across individuals is inappropriate. In marketing, different groups of consumers may respond to a change in the price of a product differently. In labor economics, different individuals may have different returns to schooling. In time series econometrics, heterogeneity takes the form of time-varying parameters. For instance, in macroeconomics, parameters may follow stochastic processes permitting their gradual evolution, or they may follow Markov switching models permitting different values in expansions and contractions. Although the precise treatment of heterogeneity differs between macroeconomic time series applications and microeconomic panel data applications, the general issues which arise are the same. The researcher must seek to model this heterogeneity in some manner and this is most conveniently done in a Bayesian framework using hierarchical priors. For instance, in Chapter 8 ("Bayesian Applications in Marketing"), heterogeneity relates to the issue of clustering of related groups of consumers using a mixture of normals model. In macroeconomic applications, the mixtures of normals and the Markov switching components both can be interpreted as hierarchical priors, suggesting a Bayesian treatment.

A third, related, theme of much modern Bayesian econometrics arises from problems caused by proliferation of parameters. Many modern models either directly have high-dimensional parameter spaces (e.g. vector autoregressive (VAR) models and the non-linear extensions of VARs used in macroeconomics and finance) or depend on latent variables of high dimension (e.g. the states in state space models are unobserved latent variables and are often of high dimension). In such models, hierarchical priors address concerns about over-fitting in the context of high-dimensional parameter spaces. That is, if the research simply says a parameter, θ_i, varies with i, then the parameter space proliferates regardless of whether i indexes individuals in a panel data exercise or indexes time in a time series exercise. By assuming θ_i for $i = 1, .., N$ to be drawn from a common distribution (i.e. by using a hierarchical prior), we retain a model that allows for individual heterogeneity, but in a much more parsimonious manner. The precise choice of a hierarchical prior (allowing for an adequate degree of heterogeneity, but not so much as to make the model over-parameterized) is crucial and several chapters in this *Handbook* describe the various choices that are coming to be seen as empirically sensible. For the Bayesian, the treatment of such issues is simple and straightforward. The recent advances in Bayesian computation typically mean that Markov chain Monte Carlo (MCMC) methods allow the researcher to integrate out latent variables or nuisance parameters.

Another theme of the *Handbook* will be immediately apparent to anyone who studied Bayesian econometrics 25 years ago. Before the availability of abundant computer power, Bayesian econometrics was mainly limited to models, such as the normal linear regression model with natural conjugate prior, for which analytical results are available. Now, the range and level of complication of models have greatly increased. Of particular note is the development of flexible parametric and nonparametric Bayesian approaches. For instance, in many decision problems in economics, the importance of allowing for asymmetric risk functions has led to econometric models where the use of symmetric distributions such as the normal is inappropriate. In the normal linear regression model, Bayesians are no longer wedded to either normality or linearity, but have developed methods that can relax either or both of these assumptions. Many of the chapters in this *Handbook* include flexible or nonparametric models appropriate to the specific chapter topic. In addition, we think this topic of such importance that we have devoted an entire chapter to it.

Finally, econometrics is distinguished from statistics by its combination of economic theory with statistics. From the analysis of DSGE models through marketing models of consumer choice, we often have models which are strongly infused with economic theory and decision-theoretic issues are important. Bayesian methods have enjoyed an increasing popularity in such cases. Such models are often parameterized in terms of structural parameters with an economic interpretation and attendant prior information. Many of the chapters in this *Handbook* are characterized by their careful linking of statistical with economic theory and their close attention to prior elicitation. Furthermore, features of interest to policymakers facing decision problems can be directly calculated using output from an MCMC algorithm.

This book is organized in three parts addressing principles, methods, and applications, respectively. In the following sections of this Introduction, we offer brief summaries of the contributions of this *Handbook* in each of these areas.

2 Principles

This section contains two chapters on principles of Bayesian analysis especially relevant in econometrics.

Chapter 1 on "Bayesian Aspects of Treatment Choice" by Gary Chamberlain offers a Bayesian approach to decision theory, focusing on the case of an individual deciding between treatments. An important focus of this chapter is the role of information that is available about other individuals through a propensity score. The chapter shows how the propensity score does not appear in the likelihood function, but does appear in the prior. The chapter discusses various priors in this context. It takes up the extension to the case of treatment selection based on unobservables (including a case where an instrumental variable is available) and provides a comparison with the related literature.

Dale Poirier, in Chapter 2 on "Exchangeability, Representation Theorems, and Subjectivity", turns to the foundations of statistical inference rooted in the representation theorems of Bruno de Finetti. He refers to his chapter as a "subjectivist primer" and shows how different assumptions about the joint distribution of the observable data lead to different parametric models defined by prior and likelihood function. Thus, parametric models arise as an implication of the assumptions the researcher makes about observables. Parameters are merely convenient mathematical fictions which serve, in his words, as "lubricants for fruitful communication and thinking". The chapter presents many extensions and offers a clear exposition of the subjectivist attitude which underlies much of Bayesian econometrics.

3 Methods

The second part of the *Handbook* contains three chapters about Bayesian methods that are important in their own right and are used in most of the remaining chapters.

Chapter 3 on "Time Series State Space Models" by Paolo Giordani, Michael Pitt, and Robert Kohn provides a description of the time series methods that underpin much of modern macroeconomics and finance. In these fields, state space methods are commonly used. For instance, various regime switching and change-point models (e.g. Markov switching or time-varying parameter VARs) are state space models, as is the popular dynamic factor model. Stochastic volatility is a state space model. Various treatments of outliers, breaks, and jumps in time series involve state space models. This chapter discusses a variety of posterior simulation algorithms and illustrates their use in a range of models such as those just listed. It is worth noting the extensive discussion of particle filtering methods in this chapter. The particle filter is a very useful tool in the Bayesian analysis of the kinds of complicated nonlinear state space models which are increasingly being used in macroeconomics and finance. The very practical discussion of the advantages and disadvantages of each algorithm provided in this chapter will be of use to the reader wanting to use these methods in empirical work.

The burgeoning use by Bayesians of models far more flexible than the simple parametric models of the past was noted above. Chapter 4 on "Flexible and Nonparametric Modelling" by Jim Griffin, Fernando Quintana, and Mark Steel serves to take the reader to the research frontier in the use of these models. The chapter divides into two parts. The first part considers flexible parametric models while the latter is purely nonparametric. For the Bayesian, nonparametric models are those where the dimension of the parameter space is unfixed and unbounded. Within the class of flexible parametric models, the authors discuss ways of making distributions more flexible than the normal, first in terms of fat tails and then in terms of skewness. A brief discussion of finite mixture models opens the way to the nonparametric part of the chapter. The most popular Bayesian nonparametric approach involves the use of Dirichlet processes and results in an infinite mixture representation for the data. The chapter discusses Dirichlet processes in detail, describes various posterior simulation algorithms for Bayesian nonparametric models, and illustrates their usefulness in empirical illustrations. The chapter also contains a discussion of methods for flexibly estimating the conditional mean in a regression model, including splines, Gaussian processes, and smoothing priors. The concluding part of the chapter ties the previous parts together in a discussion of fully nonparametric (or flexible parametric) regression modelling. That is, it considers the case where both the conditional mean of the regression is given a nonparametric (or flexible parametric) treatment and the p.d.f. (probability density function) of the regression error is estimated nonparametrically (or with a flexible parametric finite mixture model). In short, this chapter provides a detailed discussion of both theory and computation for the reader interested in flexible treatment of distributions or functional forms or both.

Chapter 5 is an "Introduction to Simulation and MCMC Methods" by Siddhartha Chib. As discussed above, posterior simulation methods have revolutionized Bayesian econometrics. This chapter begins with an intuitive exposition of the ideas and concepts which underlie popular algorithms such as importance sampling and the Metropolis-Hastings algorithm, before moving on to multi-block algorithms (e.g. the Gibbs sampler). These algorithms are used in almost every other chapter of this book, so the reader unfamiliar with posterior simulation should first read Chapter 5. This chapter also discusses state-of-the-art algorithms that are not yet in the textbooks. For instance, in Bayesian analysis of DSGE models, the posterior is potentially of a complicated form and no natural blocking of the parameters for an MCMC algorithm suggests itself. An empirical illustration using a DSGE model shows the usefulness of tailored randomized block Metropolis-Hastings algorithms. Finally, the chapter offers extensive discussion of marginal likelihood calculation using posterior simulator output.

4 Applications

The chapters in the third part of the book show how the computational methods and modelling ideas of the earlier chapters are being used by Bayesian econometricians. The aims of these chapters are twofold. First, each chapter's goal is to provide an overview of a field which is as broad as possible. Second, each chapter aims to familiarize the reader with the most recent research in the relevant field.

Chapter 6, on "Bayesian Methods in Microeconometrics" by Mingliang Li and Justin Tobias, surveys a broad range of models used by microeconometricians. Beginning with the regression model, this chapter considers extensions such as heteroskedasticity and the hierarchical linear model (both of which draw on ideas from Chapter 4) and provides a discussion of Bayesian treatments of endogeneity problems. A large number of models can be expressed as linear regression models in which the dependent variable is a suitably defined latent variable. Examples include probit and logit. Such nonlinear hierarchical models form the basis of much of this chapter which, after a general treatment, provides several examples and extensions of multivariate models. As part of the latter, multinomial and multivariate probit models are discussed extensively as are treatment effects models, which have played an important role in recent policy debates (see also Chapter 1). Bayesian methods have proved popular with nonlinear hierarchical models since MCMC methods involving data augmentation (discussed in Chapter 6) can typically be used. Furthermore, Bayesian methods allow the researcher to go beyond a study of model parameters and uncover the posterior of any feature of interest; for example, in a policy study such features might be the effects of treatment on the treated or a local average treatment effect, both of which are much more informative than simply presenting parameter estimates. The chapter concludes with a discussion of duration models. It is replete with many empirical examples and advice for the reader interested in using Bayesian methods in practice.

In recent years, Bayesian methods have enjoyed particular success in macroeconomics. Two main reasons for this are: (i) the fact that macroeconomic models often involve high-dimensional parameter spaces (e.g. as in VARs) and (ii) macroeconomists often desire to incorporate economic theory (e.g. as in the Bayesian estimation of DSGE models). As discussed previously, these are two of the themes that run throughout this *Handbook*—but they run particularly strongly in macroeconomics. Chapter 7 on "Bayesian Macroeconometrics" by Marco Del Negro and Frank Schorfheide emphasizes these points repeatedly. The introduction to their chapter, with its "challenges for inference and decisionmaking" in macroeconomics and response, offers a succinct justification for the use of Bayesian methods in macroeconomics. Much of the chapter deals with multivariate time series models such as VARs and vector error correction models which are so popular in the field. But many macroeconomists may find the clear exposition of Bayesian DSGE modelling of greatest interest. DSGE modelling is a field where Bayesian methods are enjoying great popularity, but little in the way of textbook exposition exists. This chapter takes the reader through both linear and nonlinear DSGE models, describing the practical issues that arise when implementing these methods.

Macroeconomists often find that parameters change. Models that fit well in the 1970s may not fit well now. Models that fit well in recessions may not fit well in expansions. This challenge of building models that allow for the right amount and sort of change (but not too much change or change of the wrong sort, since then the model can be over-parameterized) lies at the heart of much current macroeconomic research. This chapter takes the reader through many of the approaches (e.g. time-varying parameter VARs, Markov switching models, and even DSGE models with Markov switching) that are currently being used by macroeconometricians.

Chapter 7 also has a discussion of the challenges that arise since macroeconomists are often working in data-rich environments. It shows how Bayesian methods have been empirically successful in responding to these challenges. The chapter concludes with a discussion of model uncertainty (often an important issue in macroeconomics) and decision-making with multiple models.

Bayesian methods have been used increasingly in marketing, as emphasized in Chapter 8 by Peter Rossi and Greg Allenby on "Bayesian Applications in Marketing". This chapter describes various discrete choice models of consumers who may be heterogeneous both in terms of their preferences and in their sensitivities to marketing variables such as price. This poses a distinct set of challenges that are addressed in this chapter, often through the use of hierarchical priors. Nonparametric and flexible parametric models involving Dirichlet processes and other mixtures are also accepted and favored in marketing. Building on Chapter 4, Chapter 8 describes how and why such methods are used in marketing. Computational issues are important when dealing with large marketing data sets and this chapter is full of useful advice to the practitioner on how to implement posterior simulation methods in marketing models. Of particular interest is the authors' package of R computer code (*bayesm*) which can be used to implement the various models described in the chapter (Rossi and McCulloch, 2008).

Chapter 9, on "Bayesian Methods in Finance" by Eric Jacquier and Nicholas Polson offers a thorough survey of the usefulness of Bayesian methods in finance. It covers all the major topics in finance (from asset allocation and portfolio management to option pricing and everything in between). Building on earlier chapters in the *Handbook* (especially Chapters 3 and 5), it describes the MCMC and particle filtering algorithms that lie at the heart of modern Bayesian financial econometrics. Many of the other themes in modern Bayesian econometrics, including the use of shrinkage (e.g. with hierarchical priors), the interaction between theory and econometrics, and the desire to obtain posteriors for complicated nonlinear functions of model parameters, run throughout this chapter.

5 Conclusion

This *Handbook* is intended as a resource for readers with a textbook-level knowledge of Bayesian econometrics who wish to move to the research frontier. With this goal in mind, we have striven to produce a volume that is characterized by both breadth and accessibility. That is, one of our aims has been to cover a broad range of the methods and models used by Bayesian econometricians in a wide variety of fields. A second aim has been to have chapters written in a manner so as to allow a student to use the methods and models described in the chapter to do empirical work. As editors, we are grateful to the authors of the chapters in this book. We feel that they have admirably achieved the goals we set out for them—and we hope the readers of this book will feel the same.

References

Bauwens, L., Lubrano, M. and Richard, J.-F. (1999). *Bayesian Inference in Dynamic Econometric Models*. Oxford: Oxford University Press.

Geweke, J. (2005). *Contemporary Bayesian Econometrics and Statistics*. New York: John Wiley and Sons.

Koop, G. (2003). *Bayesian Econometrics*. Chichester: John Wiley and Sons.

—— Poirier, D.J., and Tobias, J.L. (2007). *Bayesian Econometric Methods*. Cambridge: Cambridge University Press.

Lancaster, T. (2004). *An Introduction to Modern Bayesian Econometrics*. Oxford: Blackwell.

Poirier, D. (1995). *Intermediate Statistics and Econometrics: A Comparative Approach*. Cambridge, Mass.: MIT Press.

Rossi, P.E., Allenby, G. and McCulloch, R. (2005). *Bayesian Statistics and Marketing*. Chichester: John Wiley and Sons.

Rossi, P.E. and McCulloch, R. (2008). *Bayesm: Bayesian Inference for Marketing/Microeconometrics. R package version 2.2.2.* <http://faculty.chicogogsb.edu/peter.rossi/research/bsm.html>

Zellner, A. (1971). *An Introduction to Bayesian Inference in Econometrics*. New York: John Wiley and Sons.

PART I

PRINCIPLES

CHAPTER 1

BAYESIAN ASPECTS OF TREATMENT CHOICE

GARY CHAMBERLAIN

1 Introduction

An individual is making a choice between two treatments. Data are available in which other individuals have received one of the treatments and an outcome was recorded. In addition, the data set contains various characteristics of the individuals. For example, the choice could be between two medical treatments. The characteristics could include gender, age, body mass index, blood pressure, lipid profile, smoking history, medical history, and some information on medical history of relatives. The individual making the choice knows his values on all of these variables.

We shall consider three types of data. They differ in how the treatments were assigned to the individuals in the data set. The first case is simple random assignment. For example, there could be a clinical trial in which a group of subjects is selected and then a coin flip determines whether an individual is assigned treatment 0 or treatment 1. A central question here is the use of the possibly extensive data on individual characteristics. One possibility is that the decision maker look only at the subset of the data that exactly matches his values on these characteristics. There may, however, be only a few such matches, even if the data set has a large number of individuals.

In the second type of data, the assignment probability may depend upon individual characteristics, and we work with the assumption of random assignment conditional on the measured characteristics. Within a group of individuals with the same measured characteristics, the assumption is that assignment is as if determined by a coin flip, where the probability of heads may depend upon the measured characteristics. This could correspond to an observational study in which data are collected on characteristics, treatment, and outcome for a group of individuals. This conditional assignment probability was called "propensity score" by Rosenbaum and Rubin (1983). They showed that random assignment conditional on the measured characteristics implies random assignment conditional on the propensity score. Suppose that the propensity score is known. If the object of interest is an average treatment effect, averaging over the measured characteristics, then the Rosenbaum-Rubin result suggests the possibility of a simpler analysis, in which one conditions only on the propensity score and not on the full set of measured characteristics. But the counterpart of a treatment effect for our decision maker is a conditional treatment effect, conditional on the measured characteristics being equal to her values, so there is a question of what role, if any, a known propensity score should play. A related issue is that it may be appropriate to do the analysis conditional on treatment assignment and on the measured characteristics. This analysis can resemble a classical regression problem, where one might argue that the distribution of the regressors is irrelevant, perhaps appealing to a notion of ancillarity. Then the joint distribution of assignment and measured characteristics would not be relevant, and so the propensity score, which gives the assignment distribution conditional on measured characteristics, would not be relevant. We shall be working in a likelihood framework, and the role of the propensity score is a central question for us.

In the third type of data, treatment assignment depends upon unobservables, but an instrumental variable is available. In a clinical trial, for example, an intended treatment could be determined by simple random assignment, but individuals may not comply with the intended treatment. Then the intended treatment could serve as an instrumental variable. A key issue here is the lack of identification, and how to deal with it in the context of a decision maker who has to make a choice.

Now I shall introduce some notation and describe the problem in more detail. Data are available on N individuals. For individual i, we observe a vector of discrete characteristics, which is coded as $X_i \in \{1, \ldots, K\}$. There is assignment to one of two treatments: $D_i \in \{0, 1\}$. There is a discrete outcome, which is coded as $Y_i \in \{1, \ldots, J\}$. Let $Z_i = (X_i, D_i, Y_i)$ and let $Z = (Z_1, \ldots, Z_N)$. So Z is observed.

An individual, call him α, needs to choose between $D_\alpha = 0$ and $D_\alpha = 1$. This individual knows his value for the characteristics X_α. Let $Y_{\alpha 0}$ denote the outcome if $D_\alpha = 0$, and let $Y_{\alpha 1}$ denote the outcome if $D_\alpha = 1$. The uncertainty the individual faces is over the values of the decision outcomes $Y_{\alpha 0}$ and $Y_{\alpha 1}$. The goal of this chapter is to provide guidance on how to advise the individual on making his choice.

We shall work in an expected utility framework:

$$\text{choose } D_\alpha = 1 \quad \text{if} \quad E[u_1(Y_{\alpha 1}) \mid Z] > E[u_0(Y_{\alpha 0}) \mid Z]. \tag{1.1}$$

The notation allows for additional consequences of the choice that are known to the decision maker, such as costs c_0 and c_1. Then we could have $u_l(\cdot) = u(\cdot, c_l)$ for $l = 0, 1$. We shall take the utility function $(u_0(\cdot), u_1(\cdot))$ for α as given, and focus on the expectation. So we need to construct conditional distributions for $Y_{\alpha 0}$ and for $Y_{\alpha 1}$, conditional on the observation Z.

An immediate issue is that we do not observe (Y_{i0}, Y_{i1}) for the individuals in the data set $(i = 1, \ldots, N)$. Suppose that i is sufficiently similar to α so that we can think about

i making a choice between the two treatments, even though the actual assignment of D_i may not have been through such a choice. For example, the actual value of D_i may have been randomly assigned. Define Y_{i0} as the outcome if i chooses treatment 0, and Y_{i1} as the outcome if i chooses treatment 1. We think about these decision outcomes in the same way that we think about $Y_{\alpha 0}$ and $Y_{\alpha 1}$ in the decision maker's problem. Now it becomes a key assumption that if $D_i = 0$, then $Y_i = Y_{i0}$, regardless of how this assignment of $D_i = 0$ came to be. So we are saying that the outcome that is observed when i is assigned to treatment 0 is the same as the outcome that would be observed if i had chosen treatment 0. With a corresponding assumption for treatment 1, we have

$$Y_i = (1 - D_i)Y_{i0} + D_i Y_{i1}.$$

To appreciate the force of these assumptions, suppose that immediately after treatment assignment, individual i can at some cost change the assignment. This is not relevant for unconstrained choice, but if i is assigned to treatment 0 when he would have chosen treatment 1, then this option may become relevant and the observed outcome may differ from Y_{i0}. More generally, if i is assigned a treatment that differs from what he would have chosen, then various actions may become relevant, even though they are not relevant for the unconstrained choice of the decision maker α.

In the literature on evaluating treatment effects, the term "potential outcome" is often used, in the sense that if $D_i = 0$, the problem is missing data on the potential outcome that would have been observed under $D_i = 1$. Likewise, if $D_i = 1$, the problem is missing data on the potential outcome that would have been observed under $D_i = 0$. We could refer to Y_{i0} and Y_{i1} as potential outcomes, but I want to stress that the problem, if $D_i = 0$, is not just that Y_{i1} is not observed. It is a key assumption that the decision outcome, Y_{i0}, defined to correspond to $Y_{\alpha 0}$ for the decision maker, is observed under $D_i = 0$. Likewise, it is a key assumption that the decision outcome Y_{i1} is observed under $D_i = 1$.

Section 2 develops a likelihood function for the case of random assignment conditional on observed characteristics, and then makes the stronger assumption of simple random assignment in setting up prior distributions. If the number of values K for X_i is large, with a small number of observations in a typical $X_i = k$ cell, then the prior distribution plays an important role and is not dominated by the data. Section 3 relaxes the assumption of simple random assignment, maintaining selection on observables. This does not affect the likelihood function but does affect the prior distributions. A question here is whether there is a value in knowing the propensity score. When we condition on X and D, the propensity score does not appear in the likelihood, but it does appear in the prior distribution. So there is a value to knowing the propensity score if the prior is not dominated by the data. This would be the case if the number of values for X_i is large, with a small number of observations in a typical $X_i = k$ cell.

Section 4 considers selection on unobservables. We simplify notation by dropping the X variable. Either there are no observable characteristics for the data individuals or we work with a subset that matches the decision maker. There is, however, an additional vector of discrete variables, which is coded as $W_i \in \{1, \ldots, M\}$. W_i plays the role of an instrumental variable. The prior distribution is not dominated by the data. We make a particular suggestion, in which the undominated part of the prior shows up in the choice of a functional form, which is then combined with a maximum-likelihood approximation to obtain a decision rule. We discuss the role of extrapolation in this decision rule by making a connection with compliers, always-takers, and never-takers in the local average treatment effect developed by Imbens and Angrist (1994).

Section 5 makes connections with the literature.

2 Simple Random Assignment

Let $Z_i^* = (X_i, D_i, Y_{i0}, Y_{i1})$. Suppose that the label i conveys no information, so that the joint distribution of $(Z_1^*, \ldots, Z_N^*)$ is exchangeable. If this is to hold for arbitrary N, then conditional on some distribution F^*, the Z_i^* are independent and identically distributed according to F^*. We can decompose F^* into a distribution for (Y_{i0}, Y_{i1}) conditional on (X_i, D_i), a distribution for D_i conditional on X_i, and a marginal distribution for X_i. We shall condition throughout on $X = (X_1, \ldots, X_N)$, so the marginal distribution for X_i will not play a role. The observation is $Z = (Z_1, \ldots, Z_N)$, with $Z_i = (X_i, D_i, Y_i)$. In order to form a likelihood function for the observation Z, we do not need the joint distribution of (Y_{i0}, Y_{i1}) conditional on (X_i, D_i), just the two margins: Y_{i0} conditional on (X_i, D_i) and Y_{i1} conditional on (X_i, D_i). Because the distributions are discrete, we can use the following notation:

$$\Pr(Y_{i0} = j \mid X_i = x_i, D_i = d_i; \pi, \eta) = \pi_{0j}(x_i, d_i),$$
$$\Pr(Y_{i1} = j \mid X_i = x_i, D_i = d_i; \pi, \eta) = \pi_{1j}(x_i, d_i) \qquad (j = 1, \ldots, J),$$

where the functions π_{0j} and π_{1j} map $\{1, \ldots, K\} \times \{0, 1\}$ to the interval $[0, 1]$ and satisfy

$$\sum_{j=1}^{J} \pi_{0j}(k, d) = 1, \quad \sum_{j=1}^{J} \pi_{1j}(k, d) = 1 \qquad (k = 1, \ldots, K;\ d = 0, 1).$$

Our notation for the distribution of D_i conditional on X_i is

$$\Pr(D_i = 1 \mid X_i = x_i; \pi, \eta) = 1 - \Pr(D_i = 0 \mid X_i = x_i; \pi, \eta) = \eta(x_i),$$

where the function η maps $\{1, \ldots, K\}$ to the interval $[0, 1]$. So the parameter space is $\Theta = \Theta_1 \times \Theta_2$, with

$$\Theta_1 = \{\pi : \pi_l(k, d) = (\pi_{l1}(k, d), \ldots, \pi_{lJ}(k, d)) \in \mathcal{S}_{J-1};\ l = 0, 1;\ k = 1, \ldots, K;\ d = 0, 1\}$$
$$= \mathcal{S}_{J-1}^{4K},$$

$$\Theta_2 = \{\eta : \eta(k) \in [0, 1],\ k = 1, \ldots, K\} = [0, 1]^K,$$

where $\mathcal{S}_{J-1}$ is the unit simplex of dimension $J - 1$ in $\mathcal{R}^J$.

2.1 Likelihood Function

Let z denote the realization of the random variable Z, with $z_i = (x_i, d_i, y_i)$ and $z = (z_1, \ldots, z_N)$, and let $\theta = (\pi, \eta)$. The likelihood function for the observation Z is

$$\begin{aligned}
f_{Z\mid X}(z \mid x; \theta) &= \Pr(Z = z \mid X = x; \theta) \\
&= \prod_{i=1}^{N} \Pr(Y_i = y_i \mid X_i = x_i, D_i = d_i; \pi) \cdot \Pr(D_i = d_i \mid X_i = x_i; \eta) \\
&= \prod_{i=1}^{N} \Big(\prod_{k=1}^{K} \prod_{j=1}^{J} \pi_{0j}(k,0)^{1(d_i=0)1(x_i=k)1(y_i=j)} \pi_{1j}(k,1)^{1(d_i=1)1(x_i=k)1(y_i=j)} \\
&\qquad \times \prod_{k=1}^{K} [1-\eta(k)]^{1(d_i=0)1(x_i=k)} \eta(k)^{1(d_i=1)1(x_i=k)} \Big) \\
&= \prod_{k=1}^{K} \prod_{j=1}^{J} \pi_{0j}(k,0)^{n(0,k,j)} \pi_{1j}(k,1)^{n(1,k,j)} \times \prod_{k=1}^{K} (1-\eta(k))^{n(0,k)} \eta(k)^{n(1,k)} \\
&= f_{Y\mid X,D}(y \mid x, d; \pi) f_{D\mid X}(d \mid x; \eta),
\end{aligned} \tag{1.2}$$

where

$$n(0,k,j) = \sum_{i=1}^{N} 1(d_i = 0)1(x_i = k)1(y_i = j), \quad n(1,k,j) = \sum_{i=1}^{N} 1(d_i = 1)1(x_i = k)1(y_i = j),$$

$$\begin{aligned}
n(0,k) &= \sum_{i=1}^{N} 1(d_i = 0)1(x_i = k) = \sum_{j=1}^{J} n(0,k,j), \quad n(1,k) = \sum_{i=1}^{N} 1(d_i = 1)1(x_i = k) \\
&= \sum_{j=1}^{J} n(1,k,j).
\end{aligned}$$

The value of X_α for the decision maker is τ. Suppose that the following sequence of random variables is exchangeable:

$$((Y_{\alpha 0}, Y_{\alpha 1}), (Y_{i0}, Y_{i1}) : X_i = \tau).$$

Then the F^* distribution of Y_{i0} conditional on $X_i = \tau$ is relevant for the decision maker, and we shall assume that:

$$\begin{aligned}
\Pr(Y_{\alpha 0} = j \mid X_\alpha = \tau; \theta) &= \Pr(Y_{i0} = j \mid X_i = \tau; \theta) \\
&= (1 - \eta(\tau))\pi_{0j}(\tau, 0) + \eta(\tau)\pi_{0j}(\tau, 1).
\end{aligned}$$

Likewise,

$$\begin{aligned}\Pr(Y_{\alpha 1} = j \mid X_\alpha = \tau; \theta) &= \Pr(Y_{i1} = j \mid X_i = \tau; \theta) \\ &= (1 - \eta(\tau))\pi_{1j}(\tau, 0) + \eta(\tau)\pi_{1j}(\tau, 1).\end{aligned}$$

Then, conditional on θ, the decision rule is to choose $D_\alpha = 1$ if

$$\sum_{j=1}^{J} u_1(j)[(1 - \eta(\tau))\pi_{1j}(\tau, 0) + \eta(\tau)\pi_{1j}(\tau, 1)] > \sum_{j=1}^{J} u_0(j)[(1 - \eta(\tau))\pi_{0j}(\tau, 0) + \eta(\tau)\pi_{0j}(\tau, 1)]. \tag{1.3}$$

We need to obtain a distribution on Θ conditional on the observation Z, in order to go from (1.3) to a decision rule that conditions only on the observation, as in (1.1).

Note that the likelihood function depends upon π only through $(\pi_{0j}(k, 0), \pi_{1j}(k, 1))$ for $j = 1, \ldots, J$ and $k = 1, \ldots, K$. So there is no direct information in the data on the terms $\pi_{0j}(\tau, 1)$ and $\pi_{1j}(\tau, 0)$ in (1.3). A tractable special case restricts the F^* distribution so that the treatment assignment D_i is independent of the decision outcomes (Y_{i0}, Y_{i1}) conditional on the measured characteristics X_i. In that case, we have

$$\begin{aligned}&\pi_{0j}(k, 0) = \pi_{0j}(k, 1) \equiv \pi_{0j}(k), \\ &\pi_{1j}(k, 0) = \pi_{1j}(k, 1) \equiv \pi_{1j}(k) \qquad (j = 1, \ldots, J;\ k = 1, \ldots, K),\end{aligned} \tag{1.4}$$

and

$$\Theta_1 = \{\pi \colon \pi_l(k) = (\pi_{l1}(k), \ldots, \pi_{lJ}(k)) \in \mathcal{S}_{J-1};\ l = 0, 1;\ k = 1, \ldots, K\} = \mathcal{S}_{J-1}^{2K}. \tag{1.5}$$

Now the decision rule in (1.3) becomes: conditional on θ,

$$\text{choose } D_\alpha = 1 \quad \text{if} \quad \sum_{j=1}^{J} u_1(j)\pi_{1j}(\tau) > \sum_{j=1}^{J} u_0(j)\pi_{0j}(\tau). \tag{1.3$'$}$$

In order to examine the assumption in (1.4), suppose that

$$D_i = 1(E_i[u_1(Y_{i1})] > E_i[u_0(Y_{i0})]),$$

where the operator E_i provides the expectation with respect to the personal (subjective) distribution of individual i. The assumption in (1.4) will hold if $(E_i[u_0(Y_{i0})], E_i[u_1(Y_{i1})])$ is independent of (Y_{i0}, Y_{i1}) conditional on X_i and π. For example, we could have

$$D_i = 1\Big(\sum_{j=1}^{J} u_1(j)\pi_{1j}(X_i) > \sum_{j=1}^{J} u_0(j)\pi_{0j}(X_i)\Big).$$

More generally, (1.4) will hold if the information available to individual i is independent of (Y_{i0}, Y_{i1}) conditional on X_i and π. The assumption in (1.4) is commonly referred to as "random assignment conditional on X" or "selection on observables." We shall use those terms, but note that although X is observable, we are also conditioning on π. This conditioning on π will play an important role when we discuss prior distributions.

2.2 Limited Information

Let $\pi_l(k) = (\pi_{l1}(k), \ldots, \pi_{lJ}(k))$ and $\pi_l = (\pi_l(1), \ldots, \pi_l(K))$ for $l = 0, 1$. The task of specifying a prior distribution will be easier if we can work with the marginal distributions for π_0 and π_1 without specifying the joint distribution for $\pi = (\pi_0, \pi_1)$. We can do this by adopting a limited information approach. Let

$$Y_i^{(0)} = \begin{cases} Y_i, & \text{if } D_i = 0; \\ \text{missing}, & \text{if } D_i = 1 \end{cases}$$

and

$$Y_i^{(1)} = \begin{cases} \text{missing}, & \text{if } D_i = 0; \\ Y_i, & \text{if } D_i = 1. \end{cases}$$

Let $Z_i^{(l)} = (X_i, D_i, Y_i^{(l)})$ and let $Z^{(l)} = (Z_1^{(l)}, \ldots, Z_N^{(l)})$ for $l = 0, 1$. We shall condition on $Z^{(0)}$ in forming a (predictive) distribution for $Y_{\alpha 0}$ and condition on $Z^{(1)}$ in forming a (predictive) distribution for $Y_{\alpha 1}$. So our limited information decision rule is

$$\text{choose } D_\alpha = 1 \quad \text{if} \quad E[u_1(Y_{\alpha 1}) \,|\, Z^{(1)}] > E[u_0(Y_{\alpha 0}) \,|\, Z^{(0)}]. \tag{1.1$'$}$$

The likelihood function for $Z^{(0)}$ is

$$\begin{aligned} f_{Z^{(0)} \,|\, X}(z^{(0)} \,|\, x; (\pi_0, \eta)) &= \Pr(Z^{(0)} = z^{(0)} \,|\, X = x; (\pi_0, \eta)) \\ &= \prod_{k=1}^{K} \prod_{j=1}^{J} \pi_{0j}(k)^{n(0,k,j)} \times \prod_{k=1}^{K} (1 - \eta(k))^{n(0,k)} \eta(k)^{n(1,k)} \\ &= f_{Y^{(0)} \,|\, X,D}(y^{(0)} \,|\, x, d; \pi_0) f_{D \,|\, X}(d \,|\, x; \eta), \end{aligned} \tag{1.6}$$

and the likelihood function for $Z^{(1)}$ is

$$\begin{aligned} f_{Z^{(1)} \,|\, X}(z^{(1)} \,|\, x; (\pi_1, \eta)) &= \Pr(Z^{(1)} = z^{(1)} \,|\, X = x; (\pi_1, \eta)) \\ &= \prod_{k=1}^{K} \prod_{j=1}^{J} \pi_{1j}(k)^{n(1,k,j)} \times \prod_{k=1}^{K} (1 - \eta(k))^{n(0,k)} \eta(k)^{n(1,k)} \\ &= f_{Y^{(1)} \,|\, X,D}(y^{(1)} \,|\, x, d; \pi_1) f_{D \,|\, X}(d \,|\, x; \eta). \end{aligned} \tag{1.7}$$

Next we shall develop prior distributions that allow us to go from (1.3′) to decision rules that depend only on the observation Z and the prior distribution.

2.3 Prior Distributions

We shall begin with a prior distribution that leads to a closed-form expression for the decision rule. Impose the restriction in (1.4) on the likelihood function, corresponding to random assignment conditional on X. Let

$$\Theta_{10} = \{\pi_0 \colon \pi_0(k) = (\pi_{01}(k), \ldots, \pi_{0J}(k)) \in \mathcal{S}_{J-1};\ k = 1, \ldots, K\} = \mathcal{S}_{J-1}^{K},$$
$$\Theta_{11} = \{\pi_1 \colon \pi_1(k) = (\pi_{11}(k), \ldots, \pi_{1J}(k)) \in \mathcal{S}_{J-1};\ k = 1, \ldots, K\} = \mathcal{S}_{J-1}^{K},$$

so that $\Theta_1 = \Theta_{10} \times \Theta_{11}$. Let T_0 denote a random variable that has the prior distribution on Θ_{10} and let T_1 denote a random variable that has the prior distribution on Θ_{11}. We shall use the limited information approach, so that we only specify the marginal distributions for T_0 and for T_1, and do not specify a joint distribution for $T = (T_0, T_1)$. Let $X = (X_1, \ldots, X_N)$, $D = (D_1, \ldots, D_N)$, and $Y^{(0)} = (Y_1^{(0)}, \ldots, Y_N^{(0)})$. We shall work with the distribution of $Y^{(0)}$ conditional on (X, D), so the distribution of D conditional on X will not play a role, and we can set the parameter space equal to Θ_{10}. We shall combine the distribution of $Y^{(0)}$ conditional on $(X = x, D = d; T_0 = \pi_0)$ with a distribution for T_0 conditional on $(X = x, D = d)$, to obtain a distribution for T_0 conditional on $(X = x, D = d, Y^{(0)} = y^{(0)})$. Likewise, we shall combine the distribution of $Y^{(1)}$ conditional on $(X = x, D = d; T_1 = \pi_1)$ with a distribution for T_1 conditional on $(X = x, D = d)$, to obtain a distribution for T_1 conditional on $(X = x, D = d, Y^{(1)} = y^{(1)})$.

The distributions for T_0 and T_1 conditional on $(X = x, D = d)$ are restricted to not depend upon (x, d). This corresponds to simple random assignment. The assumption that (Y_{i0}, Y_{i1}) is independent of D_i conditional on X_i is implicitly conditioning on $T = \pi$. If we do not condition on $T = \pi$, then D_i and (Y_{i0}, Y_{i1}) can fail to be independent conditional on X_i because D helps to predict T. For example, if

$$D_i = 1\Big(\sum_{j=1}^{J} u_1(j) T_{1j}(X_i) > \sum_{j=1}^{J} u_0(j) T_{0j}(X_i)\Big),$$

then (Y_{i0}, Y_{i1}) is independent of D_i conditional on $(X = x, T = \pi)$, but D_i is not independent of $T(k)$ conditional on $X_i = k$.

We shall assume simple random assignment, so that D is independent of T_l conditional on X for $l = 0, 1$, and we assume in addition that T_l is independent of X. With

$$\Pr(D_i = 1 \,|\, X_i = x_i; \pi, \eta) = 1 - \Pr(D_i = 0 \,|\, X_i = x_i; \pi, \eta) = \eta(x_i),$$

the key is that the randomization probabilities $(\eta(1), \ldots, \eta(K))$ are fixed by design in such a way that the decision maker is confident in assessing T_l independent of η in his personal distribution; for example, $\eta(k) = 1/2$ for $k = 1, \ldots, K$. The distribution of T_l has density p_l which specifies that $(T_l(k) \colon k = 1, \ldots, K)$ are mutually independent with distributions in the Dirichlet family, where $T_l(k) = (T_{l1}(k), \ldots, T_{lJ}(k))$ for $l = 0, 1$:

$$p_l(\pi_l \mid x, d; \beta_l) = p_l(\pi_l \mid \beta_l) = \prod_{k=1}^{K} h_{\mathrm{Dir}}(\pi_{l1}(k), \ldots, \pi_{lJ}(k) \mid \beta_{l1}(k), \ldots, \beta_{lJ}(k)), \quad (1.8)$$

where $\beta_{lj}(k) > 0$ and $h_{\mathrm{Dir}}(\cdot \mid \zeta)$ is the Dirichlet density with parameter ζ:

$$h_{\mathrm{Dir}}(w_1, \ldots, w_J \mid \zeta_1, \ldots, \zeta_J) = \frac{\Gamma(\sum_{j=1}^{J} \zeta_j)}{\prod_{j=1}^{J} \Gamma(\zeta_j)} \prod_{j=1}^{J} w_j^{(\zeta_j - 1)},$$

for $(w_1, \ldots, w_J)$ in the simplex $\mathcal{S}_{J-1}$ and $\zeta_j > 0$.

The conditional density of T_l given $Z^{(l)} = z^{(l)}$ is

$$\bar{p}_l(\pi_l \mid z^{(l)}; \beta_l)$$
$$= f_{Y^{(l)} \mid X,D}(y^{(l)} \mid x, d; \pi_l) p_l(\pi_l \mid x, d; \beta_l) \Big/ \int_{\Theta_{1l}} f_{Y^{(l)} \mid X,D}(y^{(l)} \mid x, d; \pi_l) p_l(\pi_l \mid x, d; \beta_l)\, d\pi_l.$$

Inspecting the product of $f_{Y^{(l)} \mid X,D}(y^{(l)} \mid x, d; \pi_l)$ from (1.6) and (1.7) with $p_l(\pi_l \mid x, d; \beta_l)$ from (1.8) shows that the conditional density is a product of Dirichlet densities:

$$\bar{p}_l(\pi_l \mid z^{(l)}; \beta_l) = \prod_{k=1}^{K} h_{\mathrm{Dir}}(\pi_{l1}(k), \ldots, \pi_{lJ}(k) \mid \bar{\beta}_{l1}(k), \ldots, \bar{\beta}_{lJ}(k)) \qquad (l = 0, 1), \quad (1.9)$$

where

$$\bar{\beta}_{lj}(k) = \beta_{lj}(k) + n(l, k, j) \quad \text{with} \quad n(l, k, j) = \sum_{i=1}^{N} 1(d_i = l) 1(x_i = k) 1(y_i = j).$$

Applying iterated expectations, we can go from the decision rule in (1.3′) to the limited information rule in (1.1′), that depends only upon the observation and the prior distribution:

choose $D_\alpha = 1$ if

$$\sum_{j=1}^{J} u_1(j) E[T_{1j}(\tau) \mid Z^{(1)} = z^{(1)}; \beta_1] > \sum_{j=1}^{J} u_0(j) E[T_{0j}(\tau) \mid Z^{(0)} = z^{(0)}; \beta_0]. \quad (1.10)$$

If $(W_1, \ldots, W_J)$ has a Dirichlet distribution with parameter $(\zeta_1, \ldots, \zeta_J)$, then $E(W_j) = \zeta_j / (\zeta_1 + \ldots + \zeta_J)$. So evaluating the conditional expectations in (1.10) gives the decision rule:

choose $D_\alpha = 1$ if

$$\sum_{j=1}^{J} u_1(j) \frac{\beta_{1j}(\tau) + n(1, \tau, j)}{\sum_{j=1}^{J} [\beta_{1j}(\tau) + n(1, \tau, j)]} > \sum_{j=1}^{J} u_0(j) \frac{\beta_{0j}(\tau) + n(0, \tau, j)}{\sum_{j=1}^{J} [\beta_{0j}(\tau) + n(0, \tau, j)]}. \quad (1.11)$$

Note that this decision rule uses only the data on the subset of individuals with $X_i = \tau$—the individuals who exactly match the decision maker α on the measured characteristics. This aspect of the decision rule arises from the prior specification that $\pi_0(k)$ are mutually independent for $k = 1, \ldots, K$ and, likewise, that $\pi_1(k)$ are mutually independent. We shall consider an alternative prior distribution below that relaxes this independence.

A potential approximation to the decision rule in (1.11) is

$$\text{choose } D_\alpha = 1 \text{ if}$$

$$\sum_{j=1}^{J} u_1(j) \frac{n(1,\tau,j)}{\sum_{j=1}^{J} n(1,\tau,j)} > \sum_{j=1}^{J} u_0(j) \frac{n(0,\tau,j)}{\sum_{j=1}^{J} n(0,\tau,j)}. \tag{1.12}$$

Here the conditional probabilities that $Y_{0\alpha} = j$ and $Y_{1\alpha} = j$ in (1.3′) are replaced by sample frequencies. For a given utility function (u_0, u_1), the approximation in (1.12) coincides with the rule in (1.11) if $\beta_{lj}(\tau)/n(l,\tau,j)$ is sufficiently small ($l = 0, 1$; $j = 1, \ldots, J$). On the other hand, for given values of $\beta_l(\tau)/n(l,\tau) = \sum_{j=1}^{J} \beta_{lj}(\tau)/\sum_{j=1}^{J} n(l,\tau,j)$, there can, depending on the utility function, be extreme sensitivity to the prior distribution. Suppose, for example, that $n(0,\tau) = n(1,\tau) \equiv n(\tau)$, so that there are the same number of observations with $D_i = 0$ and with $D_i = 1$ in the cell with $X_i = \tau$. Then

$$\frac{\bar{\beta}_{1j}(\tau)}{\bar{\beta}_1(\tau)} - \frac{\bar{\beta}_{0j}(\tau)}{\bar{\beta}_0(\tau)} = \frac{1}{n(\tau)} \left(\frac{\beta_{1j}(\tau) + n(1,\tau,j)}{\frac{\beta_1(\tau)}{n(\tau)} + 1} - \frac{\beta_{0j}(\tau) + n(0,\tau,j)}{\frac{\beta_0(\tau)}{n(\tau)} + 1} \right).$$

If $\beta_0(\tau)/n(\tau)$ and $\beta_1(\tau)/n(\tau)$ are sufficiently small, then the sign of this term is determined by the sign of

$$\beta_{1j}(\tau) - \beta_{0j}(\tau) + n(1,\tau,j) - n(0,\tau,j) \tag{1.13}$$

(provided that (1.13) is nonzero). If there are no observations with $X_i = \tau$ and $Y_i = j$, then $n(0,\tau,j) = n(1,\tau,j) = 0$ and, if $\beta_{0j}(\tau) \neq \beta_{1j}(\tau)$, the sign is determined by

$$\beta_{1j}(\tau) - \beta_{0j}(\tau).$$

If the absolute value of $u_1(j)$ is sufficiently large relative to $|u_1(j) - u_0(j)|$, then this sign will determine whether the decision rule in (1.11) chooses $D_\alpha = 1$ or $D_\alpha = 0$. This could correspond to a rare but catastrophic event.

The prior distribution we have been using specifies that $(\pi_l(1), \ldots, \pi_l(K))$ are mutually independent conditional on β (for $l = 0, 1$). We can relax this independence by following Good (1965: p. 28) in putting a prior distribution on the Dirichlet parameter β. A simple version restricts $\beta_{lj}(k)$ to be constant across k: $\beta_{lj}(k) = \beta_{lj}$. Let $\beta_l = (\beta_{l1}, \ldots, \beta_{lJ})$ for $l = 0, 1$. Following our limited information approach, we shall only need the marginal distribution for β_l and not the joint distribution for (β_1, β_2). As β_l varies, we generate a set of distributions for $Y^{(l)}$ conditional on $(X = x, D = d)$. The densities of these conditional distributions form a Type II likelihood function (in Good's terminology) for β_l:

$$g_{Y^{(l)}\,|\,X,D}(y^{(l)}\,|\,x,d;\beta_l) = \int_{\Theta_{1l}} f_{Y^{(l)}\,|\,X,D}(y^{(l)}\,|\,x,d;\pi_l)p_l(\pi_l\,|\,x,d;\beta_l)\,d\pi_l \tag{1.14}$$

$$= \prod_{k=1}^{K} \frac{\Gamma(\sum_{j=1}^{J}\beta_{lj})}{\prod_{j=1}^{J}\Gamma(\beta_{lj})} \frac{\prod_{j=1}^{J}\Gamma(\beta_{lj}+n(l,k,j))}{\Gamma(\sum_{j=1}^{J}(\beta_{lj}+n(l,k,j)))}$$

$$= \prod_{k=1}^{K} \frac{\prod_{j=1}^{J}\left(1(n(l,k,j)=0)+1(n(l,k,j)\neq 0)\prod_{m=0}^{n(l,k,j)-1}(\beta_{lj}+m)\right)}{1(n(l,k)=0)+1(n(l,k)\neq 0)\prod_{m=0}^{n(l,k)-1}[(\sum_{j=1}^{J}\beta_{lj})+m]}.$$

The (Type II) parameter space is

$$\Lambda_l = \{\beta_l = (\beta_{l1},\ldots,\beta_{lJ}) \in \mathcal{R}_+^J\} = \mathcal{R}_+^J \quad (l=0,1),$$

where $\mathcal{R}_+$ is the positive real line.

Let Q_l denote a random variable that has the prior distribution on Λ_l. Suppose that the prior density ψ_l for Q_l conditional on $(X=x, D=d)$ does not depend upon (x,d): $\psi_l(\beta_l\,|\,x,d) = \psi_l(\beta_l)$. Then the conditional density for Q_l given $Z^{(l)} = z^{(l)}$ is

$$\bar{\psi}_l(\beta_l\,|\,z^{(l)}) = g_{Y^{(l)}\,|\,X,D}(y^{(l)}\,|\,x,d;\beta_l)\psi_l(\beta_l) \Big/ \int_{\Lambda_l} g_{Y^{(l)}\,|\,X,D}(y^{(l)}\,|\,x,d;\beta_l)\psi_l(\beta_l)\,d\beta_l, \tag{1.15}$$

which can be combined with (1.11) to form the decision rule

$$\text{choose } D_\alpha = 1 \quad \text{if} \sum_{j=1}^{J} u_1(j)\int_{\Lambda_1}\frac{\beta_{1j}+n(1,\tau,j)}{\sum_{j=1}^{J}[\beta_{1j}+n(1,\tau,j)]}\bar{\psi}_1(\beta_1\,|\,z^{(1)})\,d\beta_1$$

$$> \sum_{j=1}^{J} u_0(j)\int_{\Lambda_0}\frac{\beta_{0j}+n(0,\tau,j)}{\sum_{j=1}^{J}[\beta_{0j}+n(0,\tau,j)]}\bar{\psi}_0(\beta_0\,|\,z^{(0)})\,d\beta_0. \tag{1.16}$$

A potential approximation to this rule can be based on the maximum-likelihood (Type II) estimate of β_l:

$$\hat{\beta}_l = \arg\max_{\beta_l\in\Lambda_l} g_{Y^{(l)}\,|\,X,D}(y^{(l)}\,|\,x,d;\beta_l).$$

If $\bar{\psi}_l(\cdot\,|\,z^{(l)})$ is concentrated around $\hat{\beta}_l$, then an approximation to the decision rule in (1.16) is

choose $D_\alpha = 1$ if

$$\sum_{j=1}^{J} u_1(j)\frac{\hat{\beta}_{1j}+n(1,\tau,j)}{\sum_{j=1}^{J}[\hat{\beta}_{1j}+n(1,\tau,j)]} > \sum_{j=1}^{J} u_0(j)\frac{\hat{\beta}_{0j}+n(0,\tau,j)}{\sum_{j=1}^{J}[\hat{\beta}_{0j}+n(0,\tau,j)]}. \tag{1.17}$$

The restriction that $\beta_{lj}(x_i)$ does not vary with x_i can be replaced by a parametric model: $\beta_{lj}(x_i) = h_{lj}(x_i;\gamma)$, where h_{lj} is a given function and γ is a parameter vector. Suppose, for example, that we start with M binary variables and, allowing for all possible interactions, let X_i take on $K = 2^M$ values. Then we could consider parametric models that allow for main effects but restrict the interactions. The parametric model plays the role of a prior distribution that can be dominated by the data.

3 Random Assignment Conditional on Measured Characteristics

Now consider relaxing the restriction that the prior distribution on Θ_{1l} conditional on $(X, D) = (x, d)$ does not depend upon (x, d) for $l = 0, 1$. We will maintain the assumption in (1.4) of selection on observables, so that the assignment D_i is independent of the potential outcomes (Y_{0i}, Y_{1i}) conditional on the measured characteristics X_i and on π. The parameter space for $\theta_l = (\pi_l, \eta)$ is $\Theta_l = \Theta_{1l} \times \Theta_2 = \mathcal{S}_{J-1}^K \times [0,1]^K$. Let (T_l, S) denote a random variable that has the prior distribution on $\Theta_{1l} \times \Theta_2$. We shall continue to use the limited information approach, in order to avoid having to specify a joint distribution for $T = (T_1, T_2)$. The assumption of selection on observables is implicitly conditioning on π as well as X. If we do not condition on $T = \pi$, then D_i and (Y_{i0}, Y_{i1}) can fail to be independent conditional on X_i because D helps to predict S, which is related to T. D and T are independent conditional on X and S, but in general we want to allow T and S to be correlated.

So we specify that the distribution of T_l conditional on $(X = x, D = d; S = \eta)$ does not depend upon (x, d) but may depend upon η. The distribution has density $p_{T_l \mid S}$ which specifies that $(T_l(k) : k = 1, \ldots, K)$ are mutually independent with distributions in the Dirichlet family, where $T_l(k) = (T_{l1}(k), \ldots, T_{lJ}(k))$:

$$p_{T_l \mid S}(\pi_l \mid x, d; \eta, \beta_l) = p_{T_l \mid S}(\pi_l \mid \eta, \beta_l)$$
$$= \prod_{k=1}^{K} h_{\text{Dir}}(\pi_{l1}(k), \ldots, \pi_{lJ}(k) \mid \beta_{l1}(k, \eta(k)), \ldots, \beta_{lJ}(k, \eta(k))) \qquad (1.18)$$

for $l = 0, 1$, where $\beta_{lj}(k, \cdot)$ is a function mapping $[0,1]$ into the positive real line, and $h_{\text{Dir}}(\cdot \mid \zeta)$ is the Dirichlet density with parameter ζ.

As above, the conditional density of T_l given $(Z^{(l)} = z^{(l)}; S = \eta)$ is a product of Dirichlet densities:

$$\bar{p}_{T_l \mid S}(\pi_l \mid z^{(l)}; \eta, \beta_l) = \prod_{k=1}^{K} h_{\text{Dir}}(\pi_{l1}(k), \ldots, \pi_{lJ}(k) \mid \bar{\beta}_{l1}(k, \eta(k)), \ldots, \bar{\beta}_{lJ}(k, \eta(k))) \qquad (1.19)$$

for $l = 0, 1$, where

$$\bar{\beta}_{lj}(k, \cdot) = \beta_{lj}(k, \cdot) + n(l, k, j) \quad \text{with} \quad n(l, k, j) = \sum_{i=1}^{N} 1(d_i = l)1(x_i = k)1(y_i = j).$$

The corresponding decision rule, given (β_0, β_1, η), is

$$\text{choose } D_\alpha = 1 \quad \text{if} \quad \sum_{j=1}^{J} u_1(j)(\bar{\beta}_{1j}(\tau, \eta(\tau))/\bar{\beta}_1(\tau, \eta(\tau))) > \sum_{j=1}^{J} u_0(j)(\bar{\beta}_{0j}(\tau, \eta(\tau))/\bar{\beta}_0(\tau, \eta(\tau))), \tag{1.20}$$

with

$$\bar{\beta}_0(k, \cdot) = \sum_{j=1}^{J} \bar{\beta}_{0j}(k, \cdot), \quad \bar{\beta}_1(k, \cdot) = \sum_{j=1}^{J} \bar{\beta}_{1j}(k, \cdot) \qquad (k = 1, \ldots, K).$$

We can still consider using the decision rule in (1.12) as an approximation, in which the conditional probabilities that $Y_{0\alpha} = j$ and $Y_{1\alpha} = j$ in (1.3′) are replaced by sample frequencies. For a given utility function (u_0, u_1), the approximation in (1.12) coincides with the rule in (1.20) if $\beta_{lj}(\tau, \eta(\tau))/n(l, \tau, j)$ is sufficiently small ($l = 0, 1$; $j = 1, \ldots, J$).

3.1 Known Propensity Score

Now suppose that the prior is not dominated by the data. There may, for example, be a large number K of values for X_i, with a small number of observations in a typical $X_i = k$ cell. We shall assume initially that η is known, so that the propensity score,

$$\Pr(D_i = 1 \mid X_i = x_i; \eta) = \eta(x_i),$$

is given. Then we can build on the results for this case when we introduce a prior distribution for η.

Suppose that $\beta_{lj}(k, \cdot)$ does not depend upon k and has the following form:

$$\beta_{lj}(k, u) = \beta_{lj}(u) = \exp\left(\sum_{m=1}^{O} \beta_{lj}^{(m)} r_{lj}^{(m)}(u)\right) \quad (l = 0, 1; j = 1, \ldots, J; \; k = 1, \ldots, K; \; 0 \le u \le 1),$$

where $r_{lj}^{(m)}(\cdot)$ is a given function mapping $[0, 1]$ into $\mathcal{R}$. For example, we could have a polynomial, with $r_{lj}^{(m)}(u) = u^{m-1}$. If O is sufficiently large, then this specification can be very flexible. Let $\beta_l = \{\beta_{lj}^{(m)} : j = 1, \ldots, J; \; m = 1, \ldots, O\}$ for $l = 0, 1$. We can form a Type II likelihood function for β_l:

$$g_{Y^{(l)} \mid X, D}(y^{(l)} \mid x, d; \eta, \beta_l) = \int_{\Theta_{1l}} f_{Y^{(l)} \mid X, D}(y^{(l)} \mid x, d; \pi_l) p_{T_l \mid S}(\pi_l \mid x, d; \eta, \beta_l)\, d\pi_l \tag{1.21}$$

$$= \prod_{k=1}^{K} \frac{\Gamma(\sum_{j=1}^{J} \beta_{lj}(\eta(k)))}{\prod_{j=1}^{J} \Gamma(\beta_{lj}(\eta(k)))} \frac{\prod_{j=1}^{J} \Gamma(\beta_{lj}(\eta(k)) + n(l, k, j))}{\Gamma(\sum_{j=1}^{J} (\beta_{lj}(\eta(k)) + n(l, k, j)))}$$

for $l = 0, 1$. The (Type II) parameter space is

$$\Lambda_l = \{\beta_{lj}^{(m)} \in \mathcal{R}: j = 1, \ldots, J;\ m = 1, \ldots, O\} = \mathcal{R}^{JO}.$$

Given a prior distribution for β_l, we can form a decision rule. A potential approximation to that rule can be based on the maximum-likelihood (Type II) estimate of β_l:

$$\hat{\beta}_l = \arg\max_{\beta_l \in \Lambda_l} g_{Y^{(l)} \mid X, D}(y^{(l)} \mid x, d; \eta, \beta_l).$$

Let

$$\hat{\pi}_{lj}(k) = \frac{\exp(\sum_{m=1}^{O} \hat{\beta}_{lj}^{(m)} r_{lj}^{(m)}(\eta(k)) + n(l,k,j))}{\sum_{j=1}^{J} [\exp(\sum_{m=1}^{O} \hat{\beta}_{lj}^{(m)} r_{lj}^{(m)}(\eta(k)) + n(l,k,j)]} \qquad (l = 0, 1;\ j = 1, \ldots, J;\ k = 1, \ldots, K).$$

The approximation to the decision rule is

$$\text{choose } D_\alpha = 1 \quad \text{if} \quad \sum_{j=1}^{J} u_1(j)\hat{\pi}_{1j}(\tau) > \sum_{j=1}^{J} u_0(j)\hat{\pi}_{0j}(\tau). \tag{1.22}$$

When the propensity score is given, it does not play a role through the likelihood function, which is based on the conditional density for the distribution of Y given (X, D). That likelihood function depends only upon π. The propensity score enters through the prior distribution for π. If the prior distribution is dominated by the data, then there would not be value in knowing the propensity score. This corresponds to limit results in Hahn (1998). But if the asymptotic approximation has K increasing as well as N, then knowing the propensity score could have value in the limit results.

3.2 Correlated Random Effects

This section examines the role of the propensity score in a random effects model with normal distributions for the outcomes and the random effects. Some of the issues raised in Section 3.1 show up here in a particularly simple form.

Suppose that

$$Y_{i1} \mid X = x, D = d; \pi, \eta, \sigma \overset{\text{ind}}{\sim} \mathcal{N}(\pi(x_i), \sigma^2),$$

$$D_i \mid X = x; \pi, \eta, \sigma \overset{\text{ind}}{\sim} \text{Bern}(\Phi(\eta(x_i))) \qquad (i = 1, \ldots, N),$$

where the discrete characteristics are coded as $X_i \in \{1, \ldots, K\}$ and Φ is the standard normal cdf (cumulative distribution function). Let $Y_i = D_i * Y_{i1}$ and $Z_i = (X_i, D_i, Y_i)$. We observe $Z = (Z_1, \ldots, Z_N)$. (There could be a parallel analysis in which we observe Y_{i0} if $D_i = 0$.)

The correlated random effects model is

$$\begin{pmatrix} \pi(k) \\ \eta(k) \end{pmatrix} \mid X = x; \mu, \Sigma \quad \overset{\text{i.i.d.}}{\sim} \quad \mathcal{N}(\mu, \Sigma) \qquad (k = 1, \ldots, K),$$

with

$$\mu = \begin{pmatrix} \mu_1 \\ \mu_2 \end{pmatrix}, \quad \Sigma = \begin{pmatrix} \sigma_{11} & \sigma_{12} \\ \sigma_{12} & \sigma_{22} \end{pmatrix}.$$

The decision maker, α, is interested in the distribution of $Y_{\alpha 1}$ conditional on the data Z. The decision maker knows her value, τ, for the characteristics. Assume that

$$Y_{\alpha 1} \mid Z; \pi, \eta, \sigma \quad \sim \quad \mathcal{N}(\pi(\tau), \sigma^2).$$

Suppose that the propensity score is given, so that

$$\eta(k) = \Phi^{-1}(\Pr(D_i = 1 | X_i = k))$$

is given, for $k = 1, \ldots, K$. Then the decision maker can use the distribution of $Y_{\alpha 1}$ conditional on η and Z. Define

$$\rho = \sigma_{12}/\sigma_{22}, \quad \tilde{\mu}_1 = \mu_1 - \rho\mu_2, \quad \tilde{\sigma}_{11} = \sigma_{11} - \sigma_{12}^2/\sigma_{22},$$

and let $\beta = (\sigma, \rho, \tilde{\mu}_1, \tilde{\sigma}_{11})$. Define

$$n(\tau) = \sum_{i=1}^{N} 1(X_i = \tau, D_i = 1), \quad \bar{Y}(\tau) = n(\tau)^{-1} \sum_{i=1}^{N} 1(X_i = \tau, D_i = 1) Y_i \quad (\text{if } n(\tau) \neq 0)$$

and set $\bar{Y}(\tau) = 0$ if $n(\tau) = 0$. Then we have

$$\pi(\tau) \mid \eta, Z; \beta \quad \sim \quad \mathcal{N}(c_1(\beta), c_2(\beta)),$$

where

$$c_1(\beta) = \frac{(n(\tau)/\sigma^2)\bar{Y}(\tau) + \tilde{\sigma}_{11}^{-1}[\tilde{\mu}_1 + \rho\eta(\tau)]}{(n(\tau)/\sigma^2) + \tilde{\sigma}_{11}^{-1}},$$

$$c_2(\beta) = [(n(\tau)/\sigma^2) + \tilde{\sigma}_{11}^{-1}]^{-1}.$$

The corresponding distribution for $Y_{\alpha 1}$ is

$$Y_{\alpha 1} \mid \eta, Z; \beta \quad \sim \quad \mathcal{N}(c_1(\beta), c_2(\beta) + \sigma^2).$$

Let z denote the realization of the random variable Z, with $z_i = (x_i, d_i, y_i)$ and $z = (z_1, \ldots, z_N)$. The random effects likelihood function is

$$g_{Y \mid X,D}(y|x, d; \eta, \beta) = \prod_{k:n(k) \geq 1} (2\pi)^{-n(k)/2} [\det \Omega(\beta)]^{-1/2}$$

$$\times \exp\{-\frac{1}{2}[y(k) - (\tilde{\mu}_1 + \rho\eta(k))\mathbf{1}]'[\Omega(\beta)]^{-1}[y(k) - (\tilde{\mu}_1 + \rho\eta(k))\mathbf{1}]\},$$

where $n(k)$ is the number of observations with $(x_i = k, d_i = 1)$, $y(k)$ is the $n(k) \times 1$ matrix formed from the y_i with $(x_i = k, d_i = 1)$,

$$\Omega(\beta) = \tilde{\sigma}_{11}\mathbf{1}\mathbf{1}' + \sigma^2 I,$$

$\mathbf{1}$ is an $n(k) \times 1$ matrix of ones, and I is the identity matrix of order $n(k)$.

A potential approximation for the predictive distribution of $Y_{\alpha 1}$ conditional on η and Z is

$$Y_{\alpha 1} \mid \eta, Z \quad \overset{a}{\sim} \quad \mathcal{N}(c_1(\hat{\beta}), c_2(\hat{\beta}) + \hat{\sigma}^2),$$

where $\hat{\beta}$ maximizes the random-effects likelihood function:

$$\hat{\beta} = \arg\max_{\beta} g_{Y \mid X,D}(y|x, d; \eta, \beta)$$

(and $\hat{\sigma}$ is the first element of $\hat{\beta}$).

We can extend the correlated random effects specification so that the constant mean μ is replaced by a parametric model $h(x_i; \gamma)$:

$$\begin{pmatrix} \pi(k) \\ \eta(k) \end{pmatrix} \mid X = x; \gamma, \Sigma \quad \overset{\text{ind}}{\sim} \quad \mathcal{N}(h(k; \gamma), \Sigma) \qquad (k = 1, \ldots, K),$$

where $h(\cdot\,;\,\cdot)$ is a given function and γ is a parameter vector. Suppose, for example, that the underlying characteristics for individual i are in the variables $W_i = (W_{i1}, \ldots, W_{iM})$, and that $X_i = k$ corresponds to the value $W_i = w^{(k)} = (w_1^{(k)}, \ldots, w_M^{(k)})$. Then we could have

$$h(k, \gamma) = w_1^{(k)}\gamma_1 + \ldots + w_M^{(k)}\gamma_M$$

(where $w_m^{(k)}$ is scalar and γ_m is 2×1).

3.3 Unknown Propensity Score

Now suppose that the propensity score is not given. We return to the model in Section 3.1, where we have prior distributions for T_0 and for T_1 conditional on $X = x, S = \eta$. Suppose that the prior distribution for S conditional on $X = x$ does not depend upon x. It has density p_S which specifies that $(S(k) : k = 1, \ldots, K)$ are mutually independent with distributions in the beta family:

$$p_S(\eta \mid x; \gamma) = p_S(\eta \mid \gamma) = \prod_{k=1}^{K} h_{\text{Be}}(\eta(k) \mid \gamma_1(k), \gamma_2(k)),$$

where $\gamma_1(k) > 0, \gamma_2(k) > 0$, and $h_{\text{Be}}(\cdot \mid \zeta_1, \zeta_2)$ is the beta density with parameter (ζ_1, ζ_2):

$$h_{\text{Be}}(w \mid \zeta_1, \zeta_2) = \frac{\Gamma(\zeta_1 + \zeta_2)}{\Gamma(\zeta_1)\Gamma(\zeta_2)} w^{\zeta_1 - 1}(1 - w)^{\zeta_2 - 1},$$

for $w \in [0, 1]$ and $\zeta_1 > 0, \zeta_2 > 0$.

For $l = 0, 1$, this prior distribution for S can be combined with the prior distribution for T_l conditional on (X, S) to obtain the prior distribution for (T_l, S) conditional on $X = x$ (which in fact does not depend upon x). This prior distribution for (T_l, S) conditional on X can be combined with the joint distribution for $(Y^{(l)}, D)$ conditional on $(X = x; T_l = \pi_l, S = \eta)$ in (1.6) and (1.7) to obtain the posterior distribution for (T_l, S) conditional on $Z^{(l)} = z^{(l)}$. The posterior density factors over k, so that $((T_l(k), S(k)) : k = 1, \ldots, K)$ are mutually independent conditional on $Z^{(l)} = z^{(l)}$:

$$\bar{p}_{T_l,S}(\pi_l, \eta \mid z^{(l)}; \beta_l, \gamma) = \prod_{k=1}^{K} \bar{p}_{T_l(k),S(k)}(\pi_l(k), \eta(k) \mid z^{(l)}; \beta_l, \gamma),$$

and

$$\bar{p}_{T_l(k),S(k)}(\pi_l(k), \eta(k) \mid z^{(l)}; \beta_l, \gamma) = \bar{p}_{T_l(k) \mid S(k)}(\pi_l(k) \mid z^{(l)}; \eta(k), \beta_l)\bar{p}_{S(k)}(\eta(k) \mid z^{(l)}; \beta_l, \gamma).$$

The posterior density for $T_l(k)$ conditional on $S(k) = \eta(k)$ is

$$\bar{p}_{T_l(k) \mid S(k)}(\pi_l(k) \mid z^{(l)}; \eta(k), \beta_l) = h_{\mathrm{Dir}}(\pi_{l1}(k), \ldots, \pi_{lJ}(k) \mid \bar{\beta}_{l1}(k, \eta(k)), \ldots, \bar{\beta}_{lJ}(k, \eta(k))),$$

where

$$\bar{\beta}_{lj}(k, u) = \beta_{lj}(u) + n(l, k, j)$$

with

$$\beta_{lj}(u) = \exp(\sum_{m=1}^{O} \beta_{lj}^{(m)} r_{lj}^{(m)}(u)) \quad \text{and} \quad n(l, k, j) = \sum_{i=1}^{N} 1(d_i = l)1(x_i = k)1(y_i = j).$$

The posterior density for $S(k)$ is

$$\bar{p}_{S(k)}(\eta(k) \mid z^{(l)}; \beta_l, \gamma) = \frac{\Gamma(\sum_{j=1}^{J} \beta_{lj}(\eta(k)))}{\prod_{j=1}^{J} \Gamma(\beta_{lj}(\eta(k)))} \frac{\prod_{j=1}^{J} \Gamma(\beta_{lj}(\eta(k)) + n(l, k, j))}{\Gamma(\sum_{j=1}^{J}(\beta_{lj}(\eta(k)) + n(l, k, j)))}$$
$$\times h_{\mathrm{Be}}(\eta(k) \mid \bar{\gamma}_1(k), \bar{\gamma}_2(k))/c^{(l)}(k; \beta_l, \gamma),$$

where

$$\bar{\gamma}_1(k) = \gamma_1(k) + \sum_{i=1}^{N} 1(d_i = 1)1(x_i = k), \quad \bar{\gamma}_2(k) = \gamma_2(k) + \sum_{i=1}^{N} 1(d_i = 0)1(x_i = k),$$

and

$$c^{(l)}(k; \beta_l, \gamma) = \int_{[0,1]} \left(\frac{\Gamma(\sum_{j=1}^{J} \beta_{lj}(u))}{\prod_{j=1}^{J} \Gamma(\beta_{lj}(u))} \frac{\prod_{j=1}^{J} \Gamma(\beta_{lj}(u) + n(l, k, j))}{\Gamma(\sum_{j=1}^{J}(\beta_{lj}(u) + n(l, k, j)))} \right. \tag{1.23}$$
$$\left. \times h_{\mathrm{Be}}(u \mid \bar{\gamma}_1(k), \bar{\gamma}_2(k)) \right) du \qquad (l = 0, 1).$$

To evaluate the decision rule, we can use iterated expectations:

$$E(T_{lj}(k) \mid Z^{(l)} = z^{(l)}; \beta_l, \gamma) = E[E(T_{lj}(k) \mid Z^{(l)} = z^{(l)}; S(k), \beta_l) \mid Z^{(l)} = z^{(l)}; \beta_l, \gamma]$$

$$= \int_{[0,1]} \left(\left[\bar{\beta}_{lj}(k, \eta(k)) / \sum_{j=1}^{J} \bar{\beta}_{lj}(k, \eta(k)) \right] \bar{p}_{S(k)}(\eta(k) \mid z^{(l)}; \beta_l, \gamma) \right) d\eta(k).$$

This only requires one-dimensional numerical integration, which can be done by quadrature. Then, given (β_l, γ), the decision rule is

choose $D_\alpha = 1$ if

$$\sum_{j=1}^{J} u_1(j) E(T_{1j}(\tau) \mid Z^{(1)} = z^{(1)}; \beta_1, \gamma) > \sum_{j=1}^{J} u_0(j) E(T_{0j}(\tau) \mid Z^{(0)} = z^{(0)}; \beta_0, \gamma). \quad (1.24)$$

Let $L^{(l)}(\beta_l, \gamma)$ denote the Type II likelihood function for (β_l, γ):

$$L^{(l)}(\beta_l, \gamma) = g_{Y^{(l)}, D \mid X}(y^{(l)}, d \mid x; \beta_l, \gamma)$$

$$= \int_{\Theta_{1l}} \int_{\Theta_2} f_{Y^{(l)} \mid X, D}(y^{(l)} \mid x, d; \pi_l) f_{D \mid X}(d \mid x; \eta) p_{T_l \mid S}(\pi_l \mid \eta, \beta_l) p_S(\eta \mid \gamma) \, d\pi_l \, d\eta.$$

It is given by

$$L^{(l)}(\beta_l, \gamma) = \prod_{k=1}^{K} c^{(l)}(k; \beta_l, \gamma) \frac{\Gamma(\gamma_1(k) + \gamma_2(k))}{\Gamma(\gamma_1(k))\Gamma(\gamma_2(k))} \frac{\Gamma(\bar{\gamma}_1(k))\Gamma(\bar{\gamma}_2(k))}{\Gamma(\bar{\gamma}_1(k) + \bar{\gamma}_2(k))},$$

where $c^{(l)}(k; \beta_l, \gamma)$ is in (1.23). The evaluation of this likelihood at any point (β_l, γ) only requires the calculation of one-dimensional numerical integrals (there are K of them), which can be done by quadrature.

Suppose that $\gamma_1(k)$ and $\gamma_2(k)$ do not vary with k:

$$\gamma_1(k) = \gamma_1, \quad \gamma_2(k) = \gamma_2 \qquad (k = 1, \ldots, K).$$

Then the (Type II) parameter space is

$$\Lambda_l = \{(\beta_l, \gamma) \colon \beta_{lj}^{(m)} \in \mathcal{R}, \, j = 1, \ldots, J; \, m = 1, \ldots, O; \, (\gamma_1, \gamma_2) \in \mathcal{R}_+ \times \mathcal{R}_+\} = \mathcal{R}^{JO} \times \mathcal{R}_+^2,$$

which has dimension $JO + 2$. A prior distribution on Λ_l can be combined with the (Type II) likelihood function $L^{(l)}(\beta_l, \gamma)$ to obtain a posterior distribution. Then we can integrate

$$M_j^{(l)}(\beta_l, \gamma) \equiv E(T_{lj}(\tau) \mid Z^{(l)} = z^{(l)}; \beta_l, \gamma)$$

with respect to this posterior distribution to obtain

$$E(T_{lj}(\tau) \mid Z^{(l)} = z^{(l)}) \qquad (l = 0, 1),$$

and the decision rule

$$\text{choose } D_\alpha = 1 \quad \text{if} \quad \sum_{j=1}^{J} u_1(j)E(T_{1j}(\tau)\,|\,Z^{(1)} = z^{(1)}) > \sum_{j=1}^{J} u_0(j)E(T_{0j}(\tau)\,|\,Z^{(0)} = z^{(0)}). \tag{1.25}$$

A potential approximation to this decision rule can be based on the maximum-likelihood (Type II) estimate of (β_l, γ):

$$(\hat{\beta}_l, \hat{\gamma}^{(l)}) = \arg \max_{(\beta_l,\gamma)\in\Lambda_l} L^{(l)}(\beta_l, \gamma) \qquad (l = 0, 1).$$

The approximation is

$$\text{choose } D_\alpha = 1 \quad \text{if} \quad \sum_{j=1}^{J} u_1(j)\hat{\pi}_{1j}(\tau) > \sum_{j=1}^{J} u_0(j)\hat{\pi}_{0j}(\tau) \tag{1.26}$$

with $\hat{\pi}_{lj}(\tau) = M_j^{(l)}(\hat{\beta}_l, \hat{\gamma}^{(l)})$.

Another possibility is to use a separate limited-information approach for S, basing its posterior distribution on (X, D), so that

$$\bar{p}_S(\eta\,|\,x, d; \gamma) = \prod_{k=1}^{K} h_{\text{Be}}(\eta(k)\,|\,\gamma_1 + n(1,k), \gamma_2 + n(0,k)),$$

where

$$n(l,k) = \sum_{i=1}^{N} 1(d_i = l)1(x_i = k).$$

We can form a Type II likelihood function for γ:

$$\begin{aligned} g_{D\,|\,X}(d\,|\,x; \gamma) &= \int_{\Theta_2} f_{D\,|\,X}(d\,|\,x; \eta) p_S(\eta\,|\,x; \gamma)\, d\eta \\ &= \prod_{k=1}^{K} \frac{\Gamma(\gamma_1+\gamma_2)}{\Gamma(\gamma_1)\Gamma(\gamma_2)} \frac{\Gamma(\gamma_1 + n(1,k))\Gamma(\gamma_2 + n(0,k))}{\Gamma(\gamma_1+\gamma_2+n(1,k)+n(0,k))}. \end{aligned}$$

The maximum-likelihood (Type II) estimate of $\gamma = (\gamma_1, \gamma_2)$ is

$$\hat{\gamma} = \arg \max_{\gamma\in\mathcal{R}_+^2} g_{D\,|\,X}(d\,|\,x; \gamma). \tag{1.27}$$

Given γ, we can form a Type II likelihood function for β_l, based on the distribution of $Y^{(l)}$ conditional on (X, D):

$$
\begin{aligned}
L^{(l)}(\beta_l) &= g_{Y^{(l)}\,|\,X,D}(y^{(l)}\,|\,x,d;\beta_l,\gamma) \\
&= \int_{\Theta_{1l}}\int_{\Theta_2} f_{Y^{(l)}\,|\,X,D}(y^{(l)}\,|\,x,d;\pi_l)p_{T_l\,|\,S}(\pi_l\,|\,\eta,\beta_l)\bar{p}_S(\eta\,|\,x,d;\gamma)\,d\pi_l\,d\eta \\
&= \prod_{k=1}^{K} c^{(l)}(k;\beta_l,\gamma) \qquad (l=0,1),
\end{aligned}
$$

where $c^{(l)}(k;\beta_l,\gamma)$ is in (1.23). Set $\gamma=\hat{\gamma}$ from (1.27) and obtain

$$\hat{\beta}_l^* = \arg\max_{\beta_l\in\mathcal{R}^{J_O}} \prod_{k=1}^{K} c^{(l)}(k;\beta_l,\hat{\gamma}).$$

Then a potential approximation for the decision rule in (1.25) is

$$\text{choose } D_\alpha = 1 \quad \text{if} \quad \sum_{j=1}^{J} u_1(j)M_j^{(1)}(\hat{\beta}_1^*,\hat{\gamma}) > \sum_{j=1}^{J} u_0(j)M_j^{(0)}(\hat{\beta}_0^*,\hat{\gamma}). \tag{1.28}$$

4 Selection on Unobservables

Now we are going to drop the assumption of selection on observables. For individual i, we observe a vector of discrete variables, which is coded as $W_i \in \{1,\dots,M\}$. W_i will play the role of an instrumental variable. As before, there is assignment to one of two treatments: $D_i \in \{0,1\}$. There is a discrete outcome, which is coded as $Y_i \in \{1,\dots,J\}$. We shall simplify notation by dropping the X variable. Either there are no observable characteristics for the data individuals, or we work with the subset that matches the decision maker. Using individuals who do not match the decision maker involves issues similar to those discussed above. Let $Z_i = (W_i, D_i, Y_i)$ and let $Z = (Z_1,\dots,Z_N)$. So Z is observed.

Let $W = (W_1,\dots,W_N)$. We shall condition throughout on W, so its distribution will not play a role. The model for treatment assignment uses a latent variable $V = (V_1,\dots,V_N)$. Conditional on $W = w = (w_1,\dots,w_N)$, we have

$$D_i = 1(\lambda(w_i) - V_i > 0),$$

where the function λ maps $\{1,\dots,M\}$ into $[0,1]$ and the V_i are independently and identically distributed with a uniform distribution on the interval $[0,1]$. So the distribution for D_i conditional on W is

$$\Pr(D_i = 1\,|\,W = w;\lambda) = 1 - \Pr(D_i = 0\,|\,W = w;\lambda) = \Pr(V_i \le \lambda(w_i)) = \lambda(w_i).$$

This distribution is unrestricted if λ is unrestricted, so that $\lambda(m)$ can be any value in the interval $[0,1]$ $(m = 1,\dots,M)$.

For example, we could have

$$D_i = 1(c(w_i) + E_i[u_1(Y_{i1})] - E_i[u_0(Y_{i0})] > 0),$$

where the operator E_i provides the expectation with respect to the personal (subjective) distribution of individual i, and the function c maps $\{1, \ldots, M\}$ into $\mathcal{R}$. Let $U_i = E_i[u_0(Y_{i0})] - E_i[u_1(Y_{i1})]$ and suppose that $(U_1, \ldots, U_N)$ are independent and identically distributed with distribution function G, which is continuous and strictly increasing. Then

$$V_i = G(U_i), \quad \lambda(w_i) = G(c(w_i)), \tag{1.29}$$

and we want to allow V_i to be correlated with (Y_{i0}, Y_{i1}).

We shall assume that W_i is randomly assigned in that (Y_{i0}, Y_{i1}, V_i) is independent of W_i. Then (Y_{i0}, Y_{i1}) is independent of (W_i, D_i) conditional on V_i. As before, in order to form a likelihood function, we do not need the joint distribution of (Y_{i0}, Y_{i1}), just the two margins. We shall use the following model:

$$\Pr(Y_{i0} = j \mid W_i = w_i, D_i = d_i, V_i = v_i; \beta) = h_{0j}(v_i; \beta),$$
$$\Pr(Y_{i1} = j \mid W_i = w_i, D_i = d_i, V_i = v_i; \beta) = h_{1j}(v_i; \beta) \qquad (j = 1, \ldots, J),$$

where $h_{0j}(\cdot\,; \beta)$ and $h_{1j}(\cdot\,; \beta)$ are functions that map $[0, 1]$ into $[0, 1]$ and satisfy

$$\sum_{j=1}^{J} h_{0j}(v; \beta) = 1, \quad \sum_{j=1}^{J} h_{1j}(v; \beta) = 1 \qquad (v \in [0, 1]).$$

The functions h_{0j} and h_{1j} are given up to a parameter β. We could specify

$$h_{l1}(v; \beta) = \frac{1}{1 + \sum_{j=2}^{J} \exp(\sum_{k=1}^{O} \beta_{lj}^{(k)} r_{lj}^{(k)}(v))}, \tag{1.30}$$

$$h_{lj}(v; \beta) = \frac{\exp(\sum_{k=1}^{O} \beta_{lj}^{(k)} r_{lj}^{(k)}(v))}{1 + \sum_{j=2}^{J} \exp(\sum_{k=1}^{O} \beta_{lj}^{(k)} r_{lj}^{(k)}(v))} \qquad (l = 0, 1;\ j = 2, \ldots, J),$$

where $r_{lj}^{(k)}(\cdot)$ is a given function mapping $[0, 1]$ into $\mathcal{R}$. For example, we could have a polynomial, with $r_{lj}^{(k)}(v) = v^{k-1}$. If O is sufficiently large, then this specification can be very flexible. The parameter space is $\Theta = \Theta_1 \times \Theta_2$ with

$$\Theta_1 = \{\beta : \beta_{lj} = (\beta_{lj}^{(1)}, \ldots, \beta_{lj}^{(O)}) \in \mathcal{R}^O;\ l = 0, 1;\ j = 2, \ldots, J\} = \mathcal{R}^{2O(J-1)},$$
$$\Theta_2 = \{\lambda : \lambda(m) \in [0, 1],\ m = 1, \ldots, M\} = [0, 1]^M.$$

Let z denote the realization of the random variable Z, with $z_i = (w_i, d_i, y_i)$, and let $\theta = (\beta, \lambda)$. The likelihood function for the observation Z is

$$\begin{aligned}
f_{Z\,|\,W}(z\,|\,w;\theta) &= \Pr(Z = z\,|\,W = w;\theta) \qquad (1.31)\\
&= \prod_{i=1}^{N} \int_0^1 \Pr(Y_i = y_i\,|\,W_i = w_i, D_i = d_i, V_i = v_i;\beta)\cdot\\
&\qquad \Pr(D_i = d_i\,|\,W_i = w_i, V_i = v_i;\lambda)\,dv_i\\
&= \prod_{i=1}^{N} \int_0^1 \Bigg(\prod_{j=1}^{J} h_{0j}(v_i;\beta)^{1(d_i=0)1(y_i=j)} h_{1j}(v_i;\beta)^{1(d_i=1)1(y_i=j)}\\
&\qquad \times \prod_{m=1}^{M} 1(\lambda(m) - v_i \le 0)^{1(d_i=0)1(w_i=m)} 1(\lambda(m) - v_i > 0)^{1(d_i=1)1(w_i=m)}\Bigg)\,dv_i\\
&= \prod_{l=0}^{1}\prod_{m=1}^{M}\prod_{j=1}^{J} q(l,m,j;\beta,\lambda)^{n(l,m,j)},
\end{aligned}$$

where

$$q(0,m,j;\beta,\lambda) = \int_{\lambda(m)}^{1} h_{0j}(v;\beta)\,dv,$$

$$q(1,m,j;\beta,\lambda) = \int_{0}^{\lambda(m)} h_{1j}(v;\beta)\,dv,$$

and

$$n(l,m,j) = \sum_{i=1}^{N} 1(d_i = l)1(w_i = m)1(y_i = j).$$

Suppose that the decision maker α is exchangeable with the data individuals in that the following sequence of random variables is exchangeable:

$$(Y_{\alpha 0}, Y_{\alpha 1}), (Y_{10}, Y_{11}), \ldots, (Y_{N0}, Y_{N1}).$$

Then the marginal distributions of Y_{i0} and Y_{i1} are relevant for the decision maker, and we shall assume that:

$$\Pr(Y_{\alpha 0} = j\,|\,\beta) = \Pr(Y_{i0} = j\,|\,\beta) = \int_0^1 h_{0j}(v;\beta)\,dv,$$

$$\Pr(Y_{\alpha 1} = j\,|\,\beta) = \Pr(Y_{i1} = j\,|\,\beta) = \int_0^1 h_{1j}(v;\beta)\,dv.$$

Then, conditional on β, the decision rule is to choose $D_\alpha = 1$ if

$$\sum_{j=1}^{J} u_1(j) \int_0^1 h_{1j}(v;\beta)\,dv > \sum_{j=1}^{J} u_0(j) \int_0^1 h_{0j}(v;\beta)\,dv. \qquad (1.32)$$

More generally, the decision maker could use some other distribution Q_α and the decision rule

$$\text{choose } D_\alpha = 1 \quad \text{if} \quad \sum_{j=1}^{J} u_1(j) \int_0^1 h_{1j}(v;\beta)\, dQ_\alpha(v) > \sum_{j=1}^{J} u_0(j) \int_0^1 h_{0j}(v;\beta)\, dQ_\alpha(v). \tag{1.33}$$

Suppose that i has a personal distribution H for (Y_{i0}, Y_{i1}, R_i), observes the signal R_i that is related to (Y_{i0}, Y_{i1}), and then forms $E_i[u_0(Y_{i0})]$ and $E_i[u_1(Y_{i1})]$ by using H to form the conditional distribution of Y_{i0} given R_i and the conditional distribution of Y_{i1} given R_i. Suppose this holds for $i = 1, \ldots, N$ and for the decision maker $i = \alpha$, with the same personal distribution H. Before conditioning on Z, the decision maker observes R_α and forms $E_\alpha[u_0(Y_{\alpha 0})]$ and $E_\alpha[u_1(Y_{\alpha 1})]$ by using H to form the conditional distribution of $Y_{\alpha 0}$ given R_α and the conditional distribution of $Y_{\alpha 1}$ given R_α. Suppose that (Y_{i0}, Y_{i1}, R_i) are independent and identically distributed according to some (unknown) distribution P, for $i = \alpha, 1, \ldots, N$. This implies that $U_i \equiv E_i[u_0(Y_{i0})] - E_i[u_1(Y_{i1})]$ is independent and identically distributed, and as above we let G denote the distribution function and assume it is continuous and strictly increasing. Let $V_i = G(U_i)$ for $i = \alpha, 1, \ldots, N$. Then, conditional on P, we have (Y_{i0}, Y_{i1}, V_i) independent and identically distributed, with V_i uniform on $[0, 1]$. P implies a conditional distribution for (Y_{i0}, Y_{i1}) given V_i, and we assume, as above, that this implies

$$\begin{aligned} \Pr(Y_{i0} = j \mid V_i = v_i; \beta) &= h_{0j}(v_i; \beta), \\ \Pr(Y_{i1} = j \mid V_i = v_i; \beta) &= h_{1j}(v_i; \beta) \qquad (i = \alpha, 1, \ldots, N) \end{aligned} \tag{1.34}$$

for some $\beta \in \Theta_1$. Then Q_α would be the decision maker's posterior distribution for V_α. Note that V_α depends upon U_α and G. The decision maker knows U_α but he does not know G. Furthermore, G does not appear in the likelihood function, so there is no direct information on G in the data. In addition, this approach requires a detailed specification of what people knew and when they knew it. So a limited information approach may be appropriate, simply setting Q_α equal to the uniform distribution.

A prior distribution for (β, λ) can be combined with the likelihood function in (1.31) to obtain a posterior distribution. The corresponding decision rule is obtained by integrating both sides of the inequality in (1.32) with respect to the posterior distribution for β. In general the prior distribution will not be dominated by the data. Nevertheless, it may be useful to have a reference decision rule that does not involve a numerical specification for the prior. One way to do this is to replace β in (1.32) by $\hat{\beta}$, a maximum-likelihood estimate:

$$(\hat{\beta}, \hat{\lambda}) = \arg \max_{(\beta,\lambda) \in \Theta_1 \times \Theta_2} f_{Z \mid W}(z \mid w; (\beta, \lambda)).$$

Note that

$$\sum_{j=1}^{J} q(0, m, j; \beta, \lambda) = 1 - \lambda(m), \quad \sum_{j=1}^{J} q(1, m, j; \beta, \lambda) = \lambda(m).$$

Then $q(l,m,j;\beta,\lambda) \geq 0$ and

$$\sum_{l=0}^{1}\sum_{j=1}^{J} q(l,m,j;\beta,\lambda) = 1$$

imply that

$$\prod_{l=0}^{1}\prod_{j=1}^{J} q(l,m,j;\beta,\lambda)^{n(l,m,j)} \leq \prod_{l=0}^{1}\prod_{j=1}^{J}[n(l,m,j)/n(m)]^{n(l,m,j)} \qquad (m = 1,\ldots,M),$$

where

$$n(m) = \sum_{l=0}^{1}\sum_{j=1}^{J} n(l,m,j).$$

Hence

$$\max_{(\beta,\lambda)\in\Theta_1\times\Theta_2} f_{Z\mid W}(z\mid w;(\beta,\lambda)) \leq \prod_{l=0}^{1}\prod_{m=1}^{M}\prod_{j=1}^{J}[n(l,m,j)/n(m)]^{n(l,m,j)}.$$

So, if we can solve the following equations, we will obtain maximum-likelihood estimates:

$$q(l,m,j;\hat{\beta},\hat{\lambda}) = n(l,m,j)/n(m) \qquad (l = 0,1;\ m = 1,\ldots,M;\ j = 1,\ldots,J).$$

An equivalent set of equations is

$$\hat{\lambda}(m) = \frac{n(1,m)}{n(m)},$$

$$\frac{q(0,m,j;\hat{\beta},\hat{\lambda})}{1-\hat{\lambda}(m)} = \frac{1}{1-\hat{\lambda}(m)}\int_{\hat{\lambda}(m)}^{1} h_{0j}(v;\hat{\beta})\,dv = \frac{n(0,m,j)}{n(0,m)},$$

$$\frac{q(1,m,j;\hat{\beta},\hat{\lambda})}{\hat{\lambda}(m)} = \frac{1}{\hat{\lambda}(m)}\int_{0}^{\hat{\lambda}(m)} h_{1j}(v;\hat{\beta})\,dv = \frac{n(1,m,j)}{n(1,m)},$$

where

$$n(l,m) = \sum_{j=1}^{J} n(l,m,j) \qquad (l = 0,1;\ m = 1,\ldots,M;\ j = 1,\ldots,J).$$

Here we obtain $\hat{\lambda}(m)$ by forming the subgroup whose value for the instrumental variable is $W_i = m$, and then calculating the fraction of this subgroup for which the treatment assignment is $D_i = 1$. We then form the subgroup with $W_i = m$ and $D_i = l$, and calculate the fraction of this subgroup with $Y_i = j$. With $\hat{\lambda}(m)$ already determined, we try to solve for $\hat{\beta}$ by matching the model's probabilities to these fractions.

Consider, for example, the specification for h_{lj} in (1.30). We set $\hat{\lambda}(m) = n(1,m)/n(m)$ and try to solve

$$\frac{1}{1-\hat{\lambda}(m)} \int_{\hat{\lambda}(m)}^{1} \frac{\exp(\sum_{k=1}^{O} \hat{\beta}_{0j}^{(k)} r_{0j}^{(k)}(v))}{1+\sum_{j=2}^{J} \exp(\sum_{k=1}^{O} \hat{\beta}_{0j}^{(k)} r_{0j}^{(k)}(v))}\, dv = \frac{n(0,m,j)}{n(0,m)},$$

$$\frac{1}{\hat{\lambda}(m)} \int_{0}^{\hat{\lambda}(m)} \frac{\exp(\sum_{k=1}^{O} \hat{\beta}_{1j}^{(k)} r_{1j}^{(k)}(v))}{1+\sum_{j=2}^{J} \exp(\sum_{k=1}^{O} \hat{\beta}_{1j}^{(k)} r_{1j}^{(k)}(v))}\, dv = \frac{n(1,m,j)}{n(1,m)} \quad (m=1,\ldots,M;\, j=2,\ldots,J).$$

For each $l \in \{0,1\}$ and $j \in \{2,\ldots,J\}$ there are M equations and O unknowns in $(\hat{\beta}_{lj}^{(1)},\ldots,\hat{\beta}_{lj}^{(O)})$. So we do not expect a unique solution when O is greater than M. The nonuniqueness does not affect how well we "fit" the data, but different solutions for β imply different decision rules.

One possibility is to set $\beta_{lj}^{(k)} = 0$ for $M < k \leq O$. Then the prior is reflected in a careful choice of the basis elements $r_{lj}^{(k)}(\cdot)$ for $k = 1,\ldots,M$. It may be useful to consider prior distributions on the coefficients $\beta_{lj}^{(k)}$, particularly if some of the cell counts $n(l,m,j)$ are small. Also, a prior distribution on the coefficients could downweight the contribution of later basis elements, without the need for a sharp cutoff that sets $\beta_{lj}^{(k)} = 0$ for $k > M$. We shall leave the development of such prior distributions on the coefficients for future work. The main point here is that given the lack of identification, there will be aspects of the prior that are not dominated by the data.

To get a sense of the extrapolation that the model provides, we can make a connection with the role of compliers, always-takers, and never-takers in the local average treatment effect developed by Imbens and Angrist (1994). Note that

$$\Pr(D_i = 0, Y_i = j \mid W_i = m; \beta, \lambda) = \int_{\lambda(m)}^{1} h_{0j}(v;\beta)\, dv.$$

Suppose that $\lambda(m') < \lambda(m'')$. Then we have

$$\frac{\Pr(D_i = 0, Y_i = j \mid W_i = m'; \beta,\lambda) - \Pr(D_i = 0, Y_i = j \mid W_i = m''; \beta,\lambda)}{\Pr(D_i = 0 \mid W_i = m'; \lambda) - \Pr(D_i = 0 \mid W_i = m''; \lambda)} \tag{1.35}$$

$$= \frac{1}{\lambda(m'') - \lambda(m')} \int_{\lambda(m')}^{\lambda(m'')} h_{0j}(v;\beta)\, dv$$

$$= \Pr(Y_{i0} = j \mid \lambda(m') < V_i < \lambda(m''); \beta, \lambda).$$

The condition that $\lambda(m') < V_i < \lambda(m'')$ corresponds to the compliers. There is a direct estimate of the probability that $Y_{i0} = j$ for compliers, in which the probabilities of observable events in (1.35) are replaced by sample frequencies:

$$\frac{\dfrac{n(0,m',j)}{n(m')} - \dfrac{n(0,m'',j)}{n(m'')}}{\dfrac{n(0,m')}{n(m')} - \dfrac{n(0,m'')}{n(m'')}}.$$

We also have

$$\Pr(Y_i = j \mid D_i = 0, W_i = m''; \beta, \lambda) = \frac{1}{1 - \lambda(m'')} \int_{\lambda(m'')}^{1} h_{0j}(v; \beta)\, dv$$
$$= \Pr(Y_{i0} = j \mid \lambda(m'') < V_i; \beta, \lambda).$$

The condition that $\lambda(m'') < V_i$ corresponds to the never-takers. There is a direct estimate of the probability that $Y_{i0} = j$ for never-takers, using sample frequencies:

$$\frac{n(0, m'', j)}{n(0, m'')}.$$

No direct estimate, however, is available for

$$\frac{1}{\lambda(m')} \int_{0}^{\lambda(m')} h_{0j}(v; \beta)\, dv, \tag{1.36}$$

which is the probability that $Y_{i0} = j$ for always-takers. The role of the model is to provide an extrapolation for this term. An estimate of β is obtained by fitting the sample frequencies, and then $h_{0j}(v; \hat{\beta})$ can be used to evaluate the integral in (1.36). Likewise, no direct estimate is available for

$$\frac{1}{1 - \lambda(m'')} \int_{\lambda(m'')}^{1} h_{1j}(v; \beta)\, dv, \tag{1.37}$$

which is the probability that $Y_{i1} = j$ for never-takers. The model provides an extrapolation for this term, using $h_{1j}(v; \hat{\beta})$ to evaluate the integral in (1.37).

5 Connections with the Literature

Dehejia (2005) applies Bayesian decision theory to program evaluation. The Greater Avenues for Independence (GAIN) program began operating in California in 1986 with the aim of increasing employment and earnings among welfare (AFDC) recipients. Dehejia considers a caseworker choosing whether to assign a welfare recipient into GAIN or AFDC. The caseworker knows a list of characteristics of the individual, including age, ethnicity, educational attainment, score on reading and mathematics tests, sex, an indicator for previous participation in other training programs, and pre-assignment earnings history. The caseworker has access to data on welfare recipients in which half were randomly assigned into the GAIN program and the other half were assigned to a control group that was prohibited from receiving GAIN services. An earnings outcome is observed for the treatment group and the control group, as well as the list of characteristics. So the caseworker's decision problem resembles the one I have developed in Section 2, using random assignment. Dehejia uses diffuse priors for the parameters of his model. In the discrete data case I consider, this could correspond to the decision rule in (1.12). Dehejia goes on to consider the implications for social welfare of different assignment mechanisms, such as making all assignments to GAIN, or all to AFDC, or having the caseworker make assignments for each individual based on comparing the individual's (predictive) distribution of future earnings under GAIN with his distribution of future earnings under AFDC.

Manski (2004) considers a planner who wants to maximize population mean welfare. The planner observes a list of discrete covariates for each person and can design treatment rules that differentiate between persons based on their covariate values. The planner has access to a data set in which individuals were randomly assigned a treatment, and values were recorded for covariates, treatment, and outcome. Manski focuses on conditional empirical success rules, in which conditional expectations are replaced by sample averages and treatments are chosen to maximize empirical success. He notes that conditioning tends to diminish the statistical precision of sample averages and that conditioning on only some part of the observed covariates may be preferable when making treatment choices. He uses a minimax regret criterion and develops bounds which give sufficient conditions on sample size in order for it to be optimal to condition treatment choices on all observed covariates. This corresponds to my decision rule in (1.12), which does not use Good's (1965) Type II likelihood function. Stoye (2009) obtains exact results on minimax regret rules. In assigning treatment to an individual with covariate value x, only the subset of the data which matches that covariate value is used, no matter how small the subset. As the number of values that the discrete covariate can take on increases, a minimax regret rule approaches a no data rule.

Angrist and Hahn (2004) are motivated by the result in Hahn (1998) that knowledge of the propensity score does not lower the semiparametric efficiency bound for the average treatment effect. They say that (p. 58): "In short, conventional asymptotic arguments would appear to offer no justification for anything other than full control for covariates in estimation of average treatment effects." They argue (p. 58) that "... because covariate cells may be small or empty, in finite samples there is a cost to covariate matching, even if covariates are discrete and exact matching is feasible." They work with a multinomial covariate that takes K possible values, and they develop an alternative asymptotic approximation where cell sizes are fixed but the number of cells becomes infinitely large. They refer to this as "panel asymptotics," because of the similarity to large cross-section, small time-series asymptotics used with panel data models. Their treatment-assignment mechanism has a constant propensity score, so random assignment. They consider an estimator with full control for covariates (covariate matching) and one which ignores the covariates (matching on the propensity score, which is constant). In analogy with random effects estimators for panel data, they also consider a linear combination of these estimators, which is more efficient than either one under their asymptotic sequence. Their focus is on estimating an average treatment effect, whereas the decision problem in my chapter is more related to a treatment effect for a particular covariate cell. Nevertheless, their panel data analogy is relevant for my chapter and the Type II likelihood function can be given a random effects interpretation, as I have done in Section 3.2.

Hirano and Porter (2009) develop an asymptotic theory explicitly for treatment choice. They establish an asymptotic optimality for Manski's (2004) conditional empirical success rule, in the case where a multinomial covariate takes on K possible values, where K is fixed as sample size N tends to infinity. It would be of interest to have results here under the Angrist-Hahn (2004) asymptotic sequence, where cell sizes are fixed and K tends to infinity.

Rubin (1978) discusses the role of randomization in Bayesian inference for causal effects. In the case of selection on observables, where the treatment assignment D_i is independent of the decision outcomes (Y_{i0}, Y_{i1}) conditional on the measured characteristics X_i (as in (1.4)), it follows from Rosenbaum and Rubin (1983) that this independence holds conditional on the propensity score. Rubin (1985) notes that (p. 463): "It has often been argued that randomization probabilities in surveys or experiments are irrelevant to a Bayesian statistician." This issue is also discussed in Robins and Ritov (1997). Rubin (1985) argues for a limited information approach in which the analysis proceeds as if only the propensity score and not X_i had been observed. Robins and Ritov (1997) relate the use of the propensity score to a minimax criterion. They have a discussion of dependent priors (Section 6) that relates to the dependence on η that I allow for in specifying a prior for π in (1.18). Sims (2006) discusses an example from Wasserman (2004). The arguments that Sims gives for dependence in Section III of his paper (Dependence: Direct Approach) are similar to my motivation for allowing for dependence on η in the prior for π when there is selection on observables. Sims (2006) also discusses a limited information approach.

The latent variable model of selection in Section 4 follows Heckman and Vytlacil (1999, 2005). The connection with the Imbens and Angrist (1994) model is developed in Vytlacil (2002). Manski (1990, 1996) discusses the lack of point identification for average treatment effects, and Manski (2000) discusses implications for decision making.

My use of expected utility maximization is motivated by the Savage (1972) axioms for rational behavior. Some of the decision rules I have provided can be used as "automatic" reference rules in a range of contexts, without needing any additional specification. So risk functions can be calculated for these rules. Chamberlain (2000) discusses the role of risk robustness and regret risk in decision making.

References

Angrist, J., and Hahn, J. (2004). "When to Control for Covariates? Panel Asymptotics for Estimates of Treatment Effects," *The Review of Economics and Statistics*, 86: 58–72.

Chamberlain, G. (2000). "Econometrics and Decision Theory," *Journal of Econometrics*, 95: 255–83.

Dehejia, R. (2005). "Program Evaluation as a Decision Problem," *Journal of Econometrics*, 125: 141–73.

Good, I.J. (1965). *The Estimation of Probabilities: An Essay on Modern Bayesian Methods.* Cambridge, Mass.: The MIT Press.

Hahn, J. (1998). "On the Role of the Propensity Score in Efficient Semiparametric Estimation of Average Treatment Effects," *Econometrica*, 66: 315–31.

Heckman, J., and E. Vytlacil, (1999). "Local Instrumental Variables and Latent Variable Models for Identifying and Bounding Treatment Effects," *Proceedings of the National Academy of Sciences*, 96: 4730–34.

——— (2005). "Structural Equations, Treatment Effects, and Econometric Policy Evaluation," *Econometrica*, 73: 669–738.

Hirano, K., and Porter, J. (2009). "Asymptotics for Statistical Treatment Rules," *Econometrica*, 77: 1683–701.

Imbens, G., and Angrist, J. (1994). "Identification and Estimation of Local Average Treatment Effects," *Econometrica*, 62: 467–75.

Manski, C. (1990). "Nonparametric Bounds on Treatment Effects," *The American Economic Review Papers and Proceedings*, 80: 319–23.

——— (1996). "Learning about Treatment Effects from Experiments with Random Assignment of Treatments," *The Journal of Human Resources*, 31: 709–33.

——— (2000). "Identification Problems and Decisions under Ambiguity: Empirical Analysis of Treatment Response and Normative Analysis of Treatment Choice," *Journal of Econometrics*, 95: 415–42.

——— (2004). "Statistical Treatment Rules for Heterogeneous Populations," *Econometrica*, 72: 1221–46.

Robins, J., and Ritov, Y. (1997). "Toward a Curse of Dimensionality Appropriate (CODA) Asymptotic Theory for Semi-Parametric Models," *Statistics in Medicine*, 16: 285–319.

Rosenbaum, P., and Rubin, D. (1983). "The Central Role of the Propensity Score in Observational Studies for Causal Effects," *Biometrika*, 70: 41–55.

Rubin, D. (1978). "Bayesian Inference for Causal Effects: The Role of Randomization," *The Annals of Statistics*, 6: 34–58.

——— (1985). "The Use of Propensity Scores in Applied Bayesian Inference," in J. Bernardo, M. DeGroot, D. Lindley, and A. Smith (eds.), *Bayesian Statistics*, 2. Amsterdam: North-Holland.

Savage, L. J. (1972). *The Foundations of Statistics*. New York: Dover Publications.

Sims, C. (2006). "On an Example of Larry Wasserman," unpublished manuscript, Department of Economics, Princeton University.

Stoye, J. (2009). "Minimax Regret Treatment Choice with Finite Samples," *Journal of Econometrics*, 151: 70–81.

Vytlacil, E. (2002). "Independence, Monotonicity, and Latent Index Models: An Equivalence Result," *Econometrica*, 70: 331–41.

Wasserman, L. (2004). *All of Statistics: A Concise Course in Statistical Inference*. New York: Springer.

CHAPTER 2

EXCHANGEABILITY, REPRESENTATION THEOREMS, AND SUBJECTIVITY

DALE J. POIRIER

1 Introduction

In his popular notes on the theory of choice, (Kreps 1988: 145) opines that Bruno de Finetti's Representation Theorem is the fundamental theorem of statistical inference. De Finetti's theorem characterizes likelihood functions in terms of symmetries and invariance. The conceptual framework begins with an infinite string of $\{Z_n\}_{n=1}^{n=\infty}$ observable random quantities taking on values in a sample space Z. Then it postulates symmetries and invariance for probabilistic assignments to such strings, and finds a likelihood with the prescribed properties for finite strings of length N. This theorem, and its generalizations: (i) provide tight connections between Bayesian and frequentist reasoning, (ii) endogenize the choice of likelihood functions, (iii) prove the existence of priors, (iv) provide an interpretation of parameters which differs from that usually considered, (v) produce Bayes' Theorem as a corollary, (vi) produce the Likelihood Principle (LP) and Stopping Rule Principle (SRP) as corollaries, and (vii) provide a solution to Hume's problem of induction. This is a large number of results. Surprisingly, these theorems are rarely discussed in econometrics.

De Finetti developed subjective probability during the 1920s independently of Ramsey (1926). De Finetti was an ardent subjectivist. He is famous for the aphorism: "Probability does not exist." By this he meant that probability reflects an individual's beliefs about reality, rather than a property of reality itself. This viewpoint is also "objective" in the sense of being operationally measurable, for example, by means of betting behavior or scoring rules. For example, suppose your true subjective probability of some event A is p and the scoring rule is quadratic $[\mathbf{1}(A) - \tilde{p}]^2$, where $\mathbf{1}(A)$ is the indicator function and $\tilde{\text{p}}$ is your announced probability of A occurring. Then minimizing the expected score implies $\tilde{\text{p}} = p$. See Lindley (1982) for more details.

This subjectivist interpretation is close to the everyday usage of the term "probability." Yet appreciation of the subjectivist interpretation of probability is not widespread in economics. Evidence is the widely used Knightian distinction between risk ("known" probabilities/beliefs) and uncertainty ("unknown" probabilities/beliefs). For the subjectivist, individuals "know" their beliefs; whether these beliefs are well calibrated (i.e. in empirical agreement) with reality or easily articulated are different issues. Subjectivist theory takes such knowledge as a primitive assumption, the same way rational expectations assumes agents know the "true model." However, unlike frequentists, subjectivists are not assuming knowledge of a property of reality, rather only knowledge of their own perception of reality.[1] This distinction is fundamental.

How knowledge of a subjectivist's beliefs is obtained is not addressed here, although there is a substantial literature on elicitation (Garthwaite et al. 2005; O'Hagan et al. 2006). More importantly, de Finetti showed that agreement among Bayesian researchers concerning some aspects of prior beliefs for observables can imply agreement over the likelihood function. In terms of Poirier (1988, 1995), intersubjective agreement among a bevy of Bayesians leads them to a common parametric window through which to view the observable world, and a willingness to "agree to disagree" over their priors.

De Finetti's approach is instrumentalist in nature: past observations are used to make predictions about future observables. Likelihoods, parameters, and random sampling are neither true nor false. They are merely intermediate fictions, that is, mathematical constructs. In contrast, realists seek the "true" data generating process (DGP).

Given the positive integer N, assume an individual's degrees of belief for N quantities of interest are derived from the specification of a subjective joint cumulative distribution function (cdf) $P(z_1, z_2, \ldots, z_N)$ which is representable in terms of a joint probability density function (pdf) $p(z_1, z_2, \ldots, z_N)$ (understood as a mass function in the discrete case), where "z_n" denotes a realization of the corresponding random quantity "Z_n." $P(\cdot)$ and $p(\cdot)$ (and later $F(\cdot)$ and $f(\cdot)$) are used in a generic sense, rather than specifying particular functions. For example, Hume's problem of induction (why should one expect the future to resemble the past?) requires the predictive pdf of some future observables $\{Z_n\}_{n=N+1}^{n=N+M}$ conditional on having observed $\{Z_n = z_n\}_{n+1}^{n=N}$, i.e.

$$p(Z_{N+1}, Z_{N+2}, \ldots, Z_{N+M} | Z_1, Z_2, \ldots, Z_N) = \frac{p(Z_1, Z_2, \ldots, Z_{N+M})}{p(Z_1, Z_2, \ldots, Z_N)}. \tag{2.1}$$

[1] Fuchs and Schack (2004) draw analogies with quantum theory. Is a quantum state an actual property of the system it describes? The Bayesian view of quantum states is that it is not. Rather it is solely a function of the observer who contemplates the predictions or actions he might make with regard to quantum measurements.

The essential building block is $P(\cdot)$ for a variety of arguments. The theorems discussed later put restrictions on $P(\cdot)$. The need for at least some restrictions is obvious since arbitrarily long finite strings will be discussed. But seemingly weak conditions on arbitrarily long finite strings can deliver striking results for finite strings, and computation of (2.1) only involves finite strings of data.

Predictive pdf (2.1) provides a family of solutions to Hume's problem. The only restriction that $P(\cdot)$ must satisfy is *coherence*, that is, use of $P(\cdot)$ avoids being made a sure loser regardless of the outcomes in any betting situation (also known as avoiding *Dutch Book*).[2] This implies that $P(\cdot)$ obeys the axioms of probability (at least up to finite additivity). Whether (2.1) leads to good out-of-sample predictions is a different question for which there is no guaranteed affirmative answer.

Beyond coherence I consider a variety of restrictions to facilitate construction of $P(\cdot)$. Again, such restrictions should not be thought of as "true" or "false." They are not meant to be properties of reality; rather, they are restrictions on one's beliefs about reality. Other researchers may or may not find a particular restriction compelling. Part of the art of empirical work is to articulate restrictions that other researchers are at least willing to entertain if not outright adopt, that is, to obtain intersubjective agreement among a bevy of Bayesians. The simplest such restriction, exchangeability, is the topic of the next section.

2 Exchangeability

De Finetti assigned a fundamental role to the concept of exchangeability. Given a finite sequence $\{Z_n\}_{n=1}^{n=N}$ suppose an individual makes the subjective judgment that the subscripts are uninformative in the sense that the individual specifies the same marginal distributions for the individual random quantities identically, and similarly for all possible pairs, triplets, etc. of the random quantities. Then $P(\cdot)$ satisfies $P(z_1, z_2, \ldots, z_N) = P(z_{\pi(1)}, z_{\pi(2)}, \ldots, z_{\pi(N)})$ for all positive integers N, where $\pi(n)(n = 1, 2, \ldots, N)$ is a permutation of the elements in $1, 2, \ldots, N$. Such beliefs are said to be *exchangeable*. In terms of the corresponding density/mass function, exchangeability implies $P(z_1, z_2, \ldots, z_N) = P(z_{\pi(1)}, z_{\pi(2)}, \ldots, z_{\pi(N)})$. A sequence is *infinitely exchangeable* iff every finite subsequence is exchangeable.

Exchangeability is one of many instances of the use of symmetry arguments in the historical development of probability (Poirier 1995: 17), and more generally, in mathematics (du Sautoy 2008). It provides an operational meaning to the weakest possible notion of a sequence of "similar" random quantities. It is "operational" in the sense that it only requires probability assignments for observable quantities, albeit arbitrarily long sequences. Exchangeability expresses a symmetric type of ignorance: no additional

[2] Implicitly, de Finetti assumed the utility of money is linear. He and others suggested rationalizations like the "stakes are small." Separation of the concepts of "probability" and "utility" remains a controversial matter (Kadane and Winkler 1988).

information is available to distinguish among the quantities. A sequence of Bernoulli quantities $Z_n(n = 1, 2, \ldots, N)$ in $Z = 0, 1$ is exchangeable iff the probability assigned to particular sequences does not depend on the order of zeros and ones. For example, if $N = 3$ and the trials are exchangeable, then the sequences 011, 101, and 110 are assigned the same probability. For applications of exchangeability in economics, see McCall (1991).

Schervish (1995: 7–8) argued that a judgment of exchangeability is a confession by the observer that he cannot distinguish among the quantities, since he believes they are homogeneous. Gelman et al. (1995: 124) remarked: "In practice, ignorance implies exchangeability. Generally, the less we know about the problem, the more confidently we can make claims about exchangeability." Arguing against an exchangeability assessment is an admission of the existence of non-data-based information on observables for the problem at hand.

Like iid sequences, the quantities in an exchangeable sequence are *identically distributed*. However, unlike in iid sequences, such quantities *need not be independent* for exchangeable beliefs. For example, if the quantities are a sample (without replacement) of size N from a finite population of unknown size $N^* > N$, then they are dependent and exchangeable. Also, the possible dependency in the case of exchangeable beliefs is what enables the researcher to learn from experience using (2.1).

Whereas iid sampling is the foundation of frequentist econometrics, exchangeability is the foundation for Bayesian econometrics. Both serve as the basis for further extensions to incorporate heterogeneity and dependency across observations. For example, in Section 6 exchangeability will be weakened to partial exchangeability and a time series model (a first-order Markov process) arises for the likelihood.

In the Bernoulli case, the sample space Z of $\{Z_n\}_{n=1}^{n=N}$ has 2^N elements, and it takes $2^N - 1$ numbers to specify the probabilities of all possible outcomes. In the case of exchangeability, however, the symmetry reduces this number dramatically. All that are needed are the N probabilities $q_1 = P(Z_1), q_2 = P(Z_1 \cap Z_2), \ldots, q_N = P(Z_1 \cap Z_2 \cap \ldots \cap Z_N)$. By the Inclusion-Exclusion Law (O'Hagan 1994: 113), the probability of any outcome in which r specified Z_is occur and the other $N - r$ do not occur is $\sum_{k=0}^{N-r} (-1)^k \binom{N-r}{k} q_{r+k}$. Therefore, probabilities of all possible outcomes can be expressed in terms of N of the q_ks. The difference $2^N - 1 - N$ grows rapidly as N increases, suggesting the power of the exchangeability assumption. Exchangeability is also applicable to continuous quantities as the following example shows.

Example 1: Suppose the multivariate normal pdf $p(z) = \phi_N(z \mid 0_N, \Sigma_N(\rho))$ captures a researcher's beliefs about $\{Z_n\}_{n-1}^{n=N}$, where $\Sigma_N(\rho) = (1-\rho)I_N + \rho\iota_N\iota_{N'}, \iota_N = [1, 1, \ldots, 1]'$, and $\rho > -(N-1)^{-1}$ is known. It is easy to see that such equicorrelated beliefs are exchangeable. Hereafter assume $\rho > 0$ to accommodate infinite exchangeability. Further suppose these beliefs can be extended across M additional observations $Z^* = [Z_{N+1}, Z_{N+2}, \ldots, Z_{N+M}]'$ so that $[Z', Z^{*\prime}]'$ has pdf $\phi_{N+M}\left([z, z^*]' | 0_{N+M,} \Sigma_{N+M}\right)$, where

$$\sum\nolimits_{N+M}(\rho) = (1-\rho)I_{N+M} + \rho\iota_{N+M}\iota_{N+M}{}' = \begin{bmatrix} \sum_N(\rho) & \rho\iota_N\iota_M{}' \\ \rho\iota_M\iota_N{}' & \sum_M(\rho) \end{bmatrix}.$$

Suppose $Z = z$ is observed. Because beliefs between Z and Z^* are dependent, the initial beliefs $Z^* \sim N_M(0_M, \Sigma_M(\rho))$ are updated to $Z^*|Z = z \sim N_M(\mu_{z^*|z}(\rho), \Sigma_{Z^*|z}(\rho))$, where

$$\mu_{Z\cdot|z}(\rho) = \left(\frac{N\rho}{(N-1)\rho+1}\right)\bar{z}_N\iota_M,$$

$$\Sigma_{Z\cdot|z}(\rho) = \Sigma_M(\rho) - \rho^2\iota_M\iota_{N'}\left[\Sigma_N\right]^{-1}\iota_N\iota_M{}' = (1-\rho)\left[I_M + \left(\frac{\rho}{(N-1)\rho+1}\right)\iota_M\iota_M{}'\right],$$

and $\bar{z}_N = N^{-1}\iota_{N'}z$. The predictive beliefs $Z^*|Z - z$ are also exchangeable, and the predictive means $\mu_{Z^*|z}(\rho)$ are all shrunk identically in the direction of $\bar{z}_N$. Finally, $\bar{z}_N$ serves as a sufficient statistic summarizing the impact of the past data z on beliefs about the future observables Z^*.

3 The Bernoulli Case

De Finetti's Representation Theorem for Bernoulli sequences can be stated formally as follows (Bernardo and Smith 1994: 172–3).

Theorem 1. (de Finetti's Representation Theorem): Let $\{Z_n\}_{n=1}^{n=N}$ be an infinitely exchangeable sequence of Bernoulli random quantities in $Z = \{0,1\}$ with probability measure $P(\cdot)$. Define the sum $S_N = Z_1 + Z_2 + \ldots + Z_N$, and the average number $\bar{Z}_N = S_N/N$ of occurrences in a string of length N. Let $z = [z_1, z_2, \ldots, z_N]'$ denote realized values. Then there exists a cdf $F(\cdot)$ such that the joint mass function $p(z) = P(Z_1 = z_1, Z_2 = z_2, \ldots, Z_N = z_N) = p(z_1, z_2, \ldots, z_N)$ satisfies

$$p(z) = \int_\Omega \mathcal{L}(\theta; Z)\mathrm{d}F(\theta), \tag{2.2}$$

where the observed likelihood function corresponding to $S_N = s$ is $\mathcal{L}(\theta; z) \equiv p(z|\theta) = \binom{N}{s}\theta^s(1-\theta)^{N-s}$, the random variable $\Theta \in \Omega \equiv [0,1]$ is defined by $\Theta =_{N\to\infty}^{\text{Limit}} \bar{Z}_N$ P—almost surely, and $F(\cdot)$ is the cdf of Θ under $P(\cdot)$, i.e. $F(\theta) \equiv_{N\to\infty}^{\text{Limt}} p(\bar{Z}_N \leq \theta)$.

In other words, Theorem 1 implies it is *as if*, given $\Theta = \theta$, $\{Z_n\}_{n=1}^{n=N}$ are iid Bernoulli trials with likelihood function $\mathcal{L}(\theta; z)$, and where the probability Θ of a success is assigned a prior cdf $F(\theta)$ that can be interpreted as the researcher's beliefs about the long-run relative frequency of $Z_N \leq \theta$ as $N \to \infty$. From de Finett's standpoint, both the parameter Θ and the notion of independence are "mathematical fictions" implicit in the researcher's subjective assessment of arbitrarily long sequences of observable successes and failures. The "P—almost surely," or equivalently, "with probability one" qualification on the existence of Θ in Theorem 1 refers to the researcher's predictive beliefs (i.e. the left-hand side of (2.2), which may not be reflected in reality. De Finetti's Theorem commits the researcher to believe almost surely in the existence of Θ in his/her personal world, not necessarily in the physical universe. In standard cases where $F(\theta)$ is absolutely continuous with pdf $f(\theta)$, (2.2) can be replaced with the more familiar form

$$p(z) = \int_{\Omega} \mathcal{L}(\theta; Z) f(\theta) d\theta. \tag{2.3}$$

The pragmatic value of de Finetti's Theorem depends on whether it is easier to assess the left-hand side $p(z)$ of (2.3), which only involves observable quantities, or instead, the integrand on the right-hand side of (3.3) which involves the likelihood, the prior, and the mathematical fiction θ. Most researchers think in terms of the right-hand side. Non-Bayesians implicitly do so with a degenerate distribution that treats Θ as equal to a constant θ_o with probability one, that is, a degenerate "prior" distribution for Θ at the "true value" θ_o. I am promoting an attitude that emerges from the left-hand side of (3.3), but which can be used to help researchers work on the right-hand side of (2.3).

De Finetti's theorem suggests an isomorphism between two worlds, one involving only observables z and the other involving the parameter Θ. De Finetti put parameters in their proper perspective: they are mathematical constructs that provide a convenient index for a probability distribution, they induce conditional independence for a sequence of observables, and they are "lubricants" for fruitful thinking and communication. Their "real-world existence" is a question only of metaphysical importance.

Example 2: Suppose N Bernoulli trials $\{Z_n\}_{n=1}^{n=N}$ yield r ones and $N - r$ zeros. Assume $F(\theta)$ is absolutely continuous with pdf $f(\theta)$. Applying Theorem 1 to the numerator and denominator of (2.1) (see Poirier 1995; 216) with $M = 1$ yields the predictive probability

$$P(Z_{N+1} = Z_{N+1} | N\bar{Z}_N = r) = \begin{Bmatrix} \mathrm{E}(\Theta|z), & \text{if } z_{N+1} = 1 \\ 1 - \mathrm{E}(\Theta|z), & \text{if } z_{N+1} = 0 \end{Bmatrix},$$

where $E(\Theta|z) = \int_{\Omega} \theta f(\theta|z) d\theta$, and

$$\mathrm{f}(\theta|z) = \frac{\mathrm{f}(\theta)\mathcal{L}(\theta; z)}{p(z)}, 0 \leq \theta \leq 1, \tag{2.4}$$

is the posterior pdf of Θ. From (2.4) it is clear that experiments with proportional likelihoods yield the same posterior, implying the Likelihood Principle. The fiction Θ and its posterior mean $\mathrm{E}(\Theta \mid z)$ have a conceptually useful role in updating beliefs about $Z_{N+1} = z_{N+1}$ after observing $N\bar{z}_N = r$ ones in N trials. □

The existence of the prior $F(\cdot)$ is a *conclusion* of Theorem 1, not an *assumption*. The updating of prior beliefs captured in (2.4) corresponds to Bayes' Theorem. Although

$\{Z_n\}_{n=1}^{n=N}$ are conditionally independent given $\Theta = \theta$, unconditional on Θ they are dependent. Putting further restrictions on the observable Bernoulli quantities $\{Z_n\}_{n=1}^{n=\infty}$ beyond infinite exchangeability can help pin down the prior $F(\cdot)$. For example, the assumption that $\{Z_n\}_{n=1}^{n=\infty}$ correspond to draws from a Polya urn process implies the prior $F(\cdot)$ belongs to the conjugate beta family (Freedman 1965).[3] Hill et al. (1987) proved that an exchangeable urn process can only be Polya, Bernoulli iid, or deterministic.

Example 3: Consider the Bernoulli case in Example 2 for a Polya urn. Then for some hyperparameters $\underline{\alpha} > 0$ and $\underline{\delta} > 0$ the implied prior for Θ is the conjugate beta density $f_b(\theta|\underline{\alpha}, \underline{\delta}) = \frac{\Gamma(\underline{\alpha}+\underline{\delta})}{\Gamma(\underline{\alpha})\Gamma(\underline{\delta})}\theta^{\underline{\alpha}-1}(1-\theta)^{\underline{\delta}-1}$. Posterior pdf (2.4) is $f_b(\theta|\overline{\alpha}, \overline{\delta})$ with hyperparameters $\overline{\alpha} = \underline{\alpha} + N\bar{z}_N$ and $\overline{\delta} = \underline{\delta} + N(1 - \bar{z}_N)$. Note that the posterior mean of Θ is $E(\Theta|z) = \frac{\overline{\alpha}}{\overline{\alpha}+\overline{\delta}} = \frac{\underline{\alpha}+N\bar{z}}{\underline{\alpha}+\underline{\delta}+N}$, demonstrating posterior linearity in $\bar{z}$. Diaconis and Ylvisaker (1979: 279–80) prove that the beta family is the unique family of distributions allowing linear posterior expectation of success in exchangeable binomial sampling. Infinite exchangeability for observables is enough to pin down the likelihood, and the addition of the Polya urn interpretation for the observable process identifies a beta prior up to the two free hyperparameters $\underline{\alpha}$ and $\underline{\delta}$. □

While the Polya urn formulation is a predictive argument for a beta prior, there remains the choice of $\underline{\alpha}$ and $\underline{\delta}$. Recall that $S_N \equiv N\bar{z}_N$ is the number of ones. Bayes advocated $P(S_N = s) = (N+1)^{-1}(s = 0, 1, \ldots, N)$, implying $\underline{\alpha} = \underline{\delta} = 1$. Chaloner and Duncan (1983) recommended eliciting $\underline{\alpha}$ and $\underline{\delta}$ predictively by putting additional restrictions on the implied beta-binomial mass function for S_N:

$$
\begin{aligned}
p(S_N = s) &= \int_0^1 \binom{N}{S} \theta^s(1-\theta)^{N-s}\left[\frac{\Gamma(\underline{\alpha}+\underline{\delta})}{\Gamma(\underline{\alpha})\Gamma(\underline{\delta})}\right]\theta^{\underline{\alpha}-1}(1-\theta)^{\underline{\delta}-1}d\theta \\
&= \binom{N}{S}\left[\frac{\Gamma(\underline{\alpha}+\underline{\delta})}{\Gamma(\underline{\alpha})\Gamma(\underline{\delta})}\right]\int_0^1 \theta^{s+\underline{\alpha}-1}(1-\theta)^{N-s+\underline{\delta}-1}d\theta \qquad (2.5) \\
&= \binom{N}{S}\left[\frac{\Gamma(\underline{\alpha}+\underline{\delta})}{\Gamma(\underline{\alpha})\Gamma(\underline{\delta})}\right]\left[\frac{\Gamma(s+\underline{\alpha})\Gamma(N-s+\underline{\delta})}{\Gamma(\underline{\alpha}+\underline{\delta}+N)}\right], \quad s = 0, 1, \ldots, N,
\end{aligned}
$$

with mean $\frac{N\underline{\alpha}}{\underline{\alpha}+\underline{\beta}}$ and variance $\frac{N\underline{\alpha}\underline{\delta}(N+\underline{\alpha}+\underline{\delta})}{(\underline{\alpha})\underline{\beta}^2(\underline{\alpha})+\underline{\delta}+1}$. Specifically, Chaloner and Duncan (1983) argued (assuming $\underline{\alpha} > 1$ and $\underline{\delta} > 1$) for elicitation in terms of the mode $m = \frac{\underline{\alpha}-1}{(\underline{\alpha}+\underline{\delta}-2)}$ of (2.5) and the ratios of probability at m relative to $m-1$ and $m+1$. In contrast, Geisser (1984) discussed "noninformative" priors for θ including two members of the

[3] Suppose an urn initially contains r red and b black balls and that, at each stage, a ball is selected at random, then replaced by two of the same color. Let Z_n be 1 or 0 accordingly as the nth ball selected is red or black. Then the $Z_n (n = 1, 2, 3, \ldots)$ are infinitely exchangeable and comprise a Polya urn process. However, not all urn processes are exchangeable. Neither can all exchangeable processes be represented as urn processes. See Hill et al. (1987).

beta family other than the uniform: the limiting improper prior of Haldane ($\underline{\alpha} = \underline{\delta} = 0$) and the proper prior of Jeffreys ($\underline{\alpha} = \underline{\delta} = 1/2$).

For extension to the multinomial case, see Bernardo and Smith (1994: 176–7). Johnson (1924) gave a predictive argument for the multinomial case, similar to Bayes' argument in the binomial case.

4 Nonparametric Representation Theorem

De Finetti's Representation Theorem has been extended to cover exchangeable beliefs involving random variables more complicated than Bernoulli random variables. The initial nonparametric case for Euclidean spaces was studied by de Finetti (1938). Hewitt and Savage (1955) extended the result to arbitrary compact Hausdorff spaces, and Aldous (1985) extended it to random elements with values in a standard Borel space. Dubins and Freedman (1979) showed that without any topological assumptions, the result need not hold. The following theorem covers the general case for real-valued exchangeable random quantities (Bernardo and Smith 1994: 178–9 outlined its proof).

Theorem 2. (General Representation Theorem): Consider an infinitely exchangeable sequence $\{Z_n\}_{n=1}^{n=\infty}$ of real-valued random quantities with probability measure $P(\cdot)$. Then there exists a probability measure F over $\mathcal{F}$, the space of all distribution functions on $\Re$, such that the joint cdf of $\{Z_n\}_{n=1}^{n=N}$ has the form

$$P(Z_1, Z_2, \ldots, Z_N) = \int_{\mathcal{F}} \prod_{n=1}^{N} Q(Z_n) \mathrm{d}F(Q),$$

where

$$F(Q) =_{N\to\infty}^{\text{limit}} P(Q_N), \tag{2.6}$$

and Q_N is the empirical distribution function corresponding to $\{Z_n\}_{n=1}^{n=N}$. □

In other words, it is *as if* the observations $\{Z_n\}_{n=1}^{n=N}$ are independent conditional on Q, an unknown cdf (in effect an infinite-dimensional parameter), with a belief distribution $F(\cdot)$ for Q, having the operational interpretation in (2.6) of what we believe the empirical distribution function would look like for a large sample.

Theorem 2 is a general existence theorem. Unfortunately, it is of questionable pragmatic value because it is hard to think of specifying a prior on all probabilities on $\Re$. Diaconis and Freedman (1986) discussed the difficulties of specifying priors over infinite dimensional spaces. Also see Sims (1971), Schervish (1995: 52–72) and Ferguson (1974). Therefore, in the next section attention turns to additional restrictions required to specify intermediate familiar finite-dimensional parametric sampling models. Unlike in the simple Bernoulli case of Section 3, however, predictive arguments for choosing particular priors are harder to obtain.

5 Generalizations

Diaconis and Freedman (1981: 205) noted that an equivalent formulation of exchangeability of Bernoulli random quantities is the following. For every N, given the sum $S_N = s$, the joint distribution of $\{Z_n\}_{n=1}^{n=N}$ is uniformly distributed over the $\binom{N}{S}$ sequences having s ones and $(N-s)$ zeros. In other words, $\{Z_n\}_{n=1}^{n=N}$ are exchangeable iff the partial sums are sufficient with an "equiprobable" conditional distribution for $Z_1, Z_2, \ldots, Z_N$ given $S_N = s$. This section explores invariance and sufficiency restrictions that deliver familiar sampling distributions in cases more complicated than Bernoulli variables. In the process, these restrictions on observables will yield parametric families and operationally useful results falling between Theorems 1 and 2.

An example of such a restriction is spherical symmetry. Beliefs regarding z are *spherically symmetric* iff $p(z) = p(Az)$ for any $N \times N$ orthogonal matrix A (i.e. $A^{-1} = A'$) satisfying $A\iota_N = \iota_N$ (i.e. which preserves the unit N-vector ι_N). This restriction amounts to rotational invariance of the coordinate system which fixes distances from the origin. Exchangeability is one form of spherical symmetry since permutation is one form of orthogonal transformation.

Example 4: The exchangeable beliefs captured by $p(z) = \phi_N(z \mid 0_N, \Sigma_N(\rho))$ in Example 1 are characterized by spherical symmetry because $A\Sigma_N(\rho)A' = \Sigma_N(\rho)$ for any $N \times N$ orthogonal matrix A satisfying $A\iota_N = \iota_N$. Even without assuming infinite exchangeability, $p(z)$ has the representation

$$p(z) = \int_{-\infty}^{\infty} \prod_{n=1}^{N} \phi(z_n|\theta, 1-\rho)\phi(\theta|0, \rho)d\theta, \quad z \in \Re^N. \qquad \square$$

Dropping the multivariate normality assumption in Example 1, maintaining $p(z) = p(Az)$ for any $N \times N$ orthogonal matrix A, not requiring $A'\iota_N = \iota_N$, and strengthening the exchangeability assumption to infinite exchangeability, leads to the following theorem (see Schoenberg 1938; Freedman 1962b; Kingman 1972; and Bernardo and Smith 1994: 182).

Theorem 3. (Normal Sampling with zero mean): Consider an infinitely exchangeable sequence, $\{Z_n\}_{n=1}^{n=\infty}$, $Z_n \in \Re$, with cdf $P(\cdot)$. If for any N, $z = [z_1, z_2, \ldots, z_N]'$ is characterized by spherical symmetry, then there exists a distribution $F(\theta)$, $\theta \in \Re_+$, such that

$$p(z) = \int_{0}^{\infty} \prod_{n=1}^{N} \Phi(z_n/\sqrt{\theta})dF(\theta),$$

where $\Phi(\cdot)$ is the standard normal cdf, $\tilde{s}_N^2 = (z_1^2 + z_2^2 + \ldots + z_N^2)/N, \theta \equiv \text{Limit}_{N\to\infty}\ \tilde{s}_n^{-2}$, and

$$F(\theta) = \text{limit}_{N\to\infty} P(s_N^{-2} \le \theta). \qquad \square \quad (2.7)$$

Theorem 3 implies that if predictive beliefs are characterized by infinite exchangeability and spherical symmetry, then it is *as if*, given $\Theta = \theta$, $\{Z_n\}_{n=1}^{n=N}$ are iid $N(0, \theta^{-1})$ with a prior distribution $F(\cdot)$ in (2.7) for the precision θ. $F(\cdot)$ can be interpreted as beliefs about the reciprocal of the limiting means sum of squares of the observations.

Diaconis and Freedman (1981: 209–10) provided the equivalent condition: for every N, given the sufficient statistic $T = \left(\sum_{n=1}^{N} z_n^2\right)^{1/2} = t$, the joint distribution of $\{Z_n\}_{n=1}^{n=N}$ is uniform on the $(N-1)$-sphere of radius t. Arellano-Valle et al. (1994) showed that if the condition $\mathrm{E}(Z_2^2|Z_1) = aZ_1^2 + b$, where $0 < a < 1$ and $b > 0$, is added to the spherical symmetry judgment, then $F(\cdot)$ is the conjugate inverted-gamma distribution. Consequently, the distribution of z is a spherical multivariate Student-t model. Loschi et al. (2003) extended this result to the matrix-variate case. Dawid (1978) considered the multivariate extension of Theorem 3.

If beliefs about $z_1 - \bar{z}_N, z_2 - \bar{z}_N, \ldots, z_N - \bar{z}_N$ possess spherical symmetry, then beliefs about z are said to be characterized by *centered spherical symmetry*. Centered spherical symmetry fixes distances from the mean of the observations, that is, identical probabilities are asserted for all outcomes $z_1, z_2, \ldots, z_N$ leading to the same value of $(z_1 - \bar{z}_N)^2 + (z_2 - \bar{z}_N)^2 + \ldots + (z_N - \bar{z}_N)^2$. When infinite exchangeability is augmented with centered spherical symmetry, then the familiar normal random sampling model with unknown mean and unknown precision emerges in the following theorem of Smith (1981). For a proof, see Bernardo and Smith (1994: 183–5). Also see Eaton et al. (1993: 4) for an important qualification.

Theorem 4. (Centered Normal Sampling): Consider an infinitely exchangeable sequence $\{Z_n\}_{n=1}^{n=\infty}$ of real-valued random quantities with probability measure $P(\cdot)$. If for any N, $z = [z_1, z_2, \ldots, z_N]'$ is characterized by centered spherical symmetry, then there exists a distribution function $F(\theta)$, with $\theta = [\mu, \sigma^{-2}]' \in \Re \times \Re_+$, such that the joint distribution of z has the form

$$P(z) = \int_{\Re\times\Re_+} \prod_{n=1}^{N} \Phi[(z_n - \mu)/\sigma] \mathrm{d}F(\mu, \sigma^{-2}),$$

where $\mathbf{\Phi}(\cdot)$ is the standard normal cdf,

$$F(\mu, \sigma^{-2}) = \text{limit}_{N\to\infty} P[(\bar{z}_N \le \mu) \cap (s_N^{-2} \le \sigma^{-2})], \qquad (2.8)$$

$$\mu \equiv \text{Limit}_{N\to\infty} \bar{z}_N, \qquad (2.9)$$

where $s_N^2 = [(z_1 - \bar{z}_N)^2 + (z_2 - \bar{z}_N)^2 + \ldots + (z_N - \bar{z}_N)^2]/N$, and

$$\sigma^2 \equiv \text{Limit}_{N\to\infty} s_N^2. \qquad \square \quad (2.10)$$

Theorem 4 implies that if predictive beliefs are characterized by infinite exchangeability and centered spherical symmetry, then it is *as if* $\{Z_n\}_{n=1}^{n=N}$ are iid $N(\mu, \sigma^2)$ given μ and σ^{-2} defined in (2.9) and (2.10), and with prior distribution $F(\cdot)$ in (2.8). As in the Bernoulli case, adding the restriction of linearity of the poster mean in terms of $\bar{z}_N$ implies a conjugate normal-gamma prior.

Example 5: Under the conditions of Theorem 4 and a conjugate normal-gamma prior density

$$f(\mu, \sigma^{-2}) = \phi(\mu|\underline{\mu}, \underline{q}\sigma^2) f_g(\sigma^{-2}|\underline{v}/2, 2/\underline{vs}^2), \quad \underline{\mu} \in \Re, \underline{q}, \underline{s}, \underline{v} > 0,$$

(2.3) is the centered spherically symmetric multivariate-t pdf $f_t^N(y|\underline{\mu}, \underline{s}^2(I_N + \underline{q}\iota_N\iota_N')]^{-1}, \underline{v})$. □

The multivariate analog of Theorem 4 follows (see Bernardo and Smith 1994: 186 and Diaconis et al. 1992).

Theorem 5. (Multivariate Normal Sampling): Consider an infinitely exchangeable sequence $\{Z_n\}_{n=1}^{n=\infty}$ of real-valued random vectors in $\Re^K$ with cdf $P(\cdot)$, such that for any N and $c \in \Re^K$, the random quantities $c'Z_1, c'Z_2, \ldots, c'Z_N$ are characterized by centered spherical symmetry. Then the predictive beliefs $P(z)$ are *as if* $\{Z_n\}_{n=1}^{n=N}$ were iid multivariate normal vectors, conditional on a random mean μ and covariance matrix Σ, with a distribution over μ and Σ induced by $P(\cdot)$, where

$$\mu \equiv \operatorname*{Limit}_{N\to\infty} \bar{z}_N,$$

$$\sum \equiv \operatorname*{Limit}_{N\to\infty} \frac{1}{N} \sum_{n=1}^{N} (z_n - \bar{z}_N)(z_n - \bar{z}_N)'. \qquad \square$$

Additional results based on infinite exchangeability and particular invariance properties yield other familiar sampling models. Two examples of characterizations of discrete distributions over nonnegative integers are:

(a) Freedman (1962b) showed that if for every N, the joint distribution of $\{Z_n\}_{n=1}^{n=N}$, given the sum S_N is multinomial on N-tuples with uniform probabilities equal to N^{-1} (the Maxwell-Boltzman distribution), then it is *as if* $\{Z_n\}_{n=1}^{n=N}$ are iid Poisson random variables.

(b) Diaconis and Freedman (1981: 214) noted that if for every N, the joint distribution of $\{Z_n\}_{n=1}^{n=N}$, given S_N, is uniform on N-tuples with uniform probabilities equal to J^{-1}, where J is the total number of N-tuples with sums S_N, then it is *as if* $\{Z_n\}_{n=1}^{n=N}$ are iid geometric random variables.

Five examples of characterizations of continuous distributions are:

(c) Suppose for every N, the joint distribution of $\{Z_n\}_{n=1}^{n=N}$, given $M_N \equiv \max\{Z_1, Z_2, \ldots, Z_N\}$, are independent and uniform over the interval $[0, M_N]$. Diaconis and Freedman (1981: 210) noted that this condition is necessary and sufficient for the representation that $\{Z_n\}_{n=1}^{n=N}$ are iid uniform over the interval $[0, \Theta]$, with a prior distribution for Θ.

(d) Diaconis and Freedman (1987) showed that if for every N, given the sum $S_N = s$, the joint distribution of $\{Z_n\}_{n=1}^{n=N}$ is uniformly distributed over the simplex $\{Z_n \geq 0, s\}$, then it is *as if* $\{Z_n\}_{n=1}^{n=N}$ are iid exponential random variables.[4]

(e) Singpurwalla (2006: 54) noted that if for every N, given the sum $S_N = s$, the joint distribution of $\{Z_n^{\Theta_1}\}_{n=1}^{n=N}$ is uniformly distributed over the simplex $\{Z_n \geq 0, s\}$, then it is *as if* $\{Z_n\}_{n=1}^{n=N}$ are iid gamma random variables with pdf $p(z_n) = \Theta_2^{\Theta_1} z_n^{\Theta_1 - 1} \exp(\Theta_2 z_n)/\Gamma(\Theta_1)$.

(f) Singpurwalla (2006: 55) noted that if the uniformity in (e) is over the simplex $\{Z_n \geq 0, \sum_{n=1}^{N} Z_n^{\Theta_1}\}$, then it is *as if* $\{Z_n\}_{n=1}^{n=N}$ are iid Weibull random variables.

Further restrictions on $\{Z_n\}_{n=1}^{n=\infty}$ to analytically derive the prior distributions are difficult to find once we leave the Bernoulli sample space of Section 3. A more common approach is to elicit moments and quantiles for the left-hand side of (2.3), and assuming a parametric family for $f(\cdot)$ (usually conjugate), to then back-out a prior on the right-hand side of (2.3). Usually the process is iterative.[5] Rationalization for restricting attention to conjugate priors is provided by Diaconis and Ylvisaker (1979), who characterized conjugate priors through the property that the posterior expectation of the mean parameter of Z_n, $\mathrm{E}[\mathrm{E}(Z_n \mid \Theta = \theta) \mid Z_n = z_n]$, is linear in z_n. While not analytical, the approach is predictively motivated.

There are many other representation theorems available. Bernardo and Smith (1994: 215–16) outline how two-way ANOVA (analysis of variation) specifications and hierarchical specifications can be rationalized. But these are only partly predictively motivated. Bernardo and Smith (1994: 219–22) cover binary choice models, growth curves, and regression. In these extensions, the parameter Θ becomes a function of the regressors, but the specification of $\Theta(\cdot)$ is done in an ad hoc manner to provide common specifications instead of providing transparent restrictions on observables for the left-hand side of a representation theorem. Diaconis et al. (1992) characterize normal models for regression and ANOVA in terms of symmetry or sufficiency restrictions. Arnold (1979) considered multivariate regression models with exchangeable errors.

Finally, although de Finetti's theorem does not hold exactly for finite sequences, it does hold approximately for sufficiently large finite sequence. Diaconis and Freedman (1980) showed that for a binary exchangeable sequence of length K which can be extended to an exchangeable sequence of length N, then de Finetti's theorem

[4] Alternative formulations are possible. For example, Diaconis and Ylvisaker (1985) showed that in the case of an infinitely exchangeable sequence $\{Z_n\}_{n=1}^{n=\infty}$ of positive real quantities with probability measure $P(\cdot)$ that exhibit a certain "lack of memory" property with respect to the origin, then $p(\cdot)$ has a representation as a mixture of iid exponential random quantities. A similar result holds for an infinitely exchangeable sequence of positive integers leading to a representation as a mixture of iid geometric random quantities. In both of the latter cases, the predictive "lack of memory" property is reminiscent of similar properties for the parametric exponential and geometric distributions. See Bernardo and Smith (1994: 187–90) for more details.

[5] Indeed the method of Chaloner and Duncan (1983), discussed in Example 3, is an example.

"almost" holds in the sense that the total variation distance between the distribution of $Z_1, Z_2, \ldots, Z_K$ and the approximating mixture is $\leq 2K/N$. Diaconis et al. (1992: 292) provided a finite version of Dawid (1978). Diaconis and Freedman (1987) discussed numerous extensions with K/N continuing to play a key role. Finite versions of de Finetti's theorem for Markov chains are given by Diaconis and Freedman (1980) and Zaman (1986).

6 Partial Exchangeability

Exchangeability involves complete symmetry in beliefs. Often such beliefs are not warranted across all observables, but are reasonable for subsets. This leads to *partial exchangeability*. Partial exchangeability takes on a variety of guises (see de Finetti 1938; Aldous 1981; and Diaconis and Freedman 1980, 1981), but an essential ingredient is that the sequence $\{Z_n\}_{n=1}^{n=\infty}$ is broken down into exchangeable subsequences. For example, suppose $\{Z_n\}_{n=1}^{n=\infty}$ are the employment status after undergoing job training. If both males and females are included, one might be reluctant to make a judgment of exchangeability for the entire sequence of results. However, within subsequences defined by gender, an assumption of exchangeability might be reasonable.

Alternatively, consider the case of Markov chains for Bernoulli quantities as initially studied by de Finetti (1938) and then Freedman (1962a). Consider three subsequences: the first observation, observations following a zero, and observations following a one. Two binary sequences are said to be *equivalent* if they begin with the same symbol and have the same number of transitions from 0 to 0, 0 to 1, 1 to 0, and 1 to 1. A probability on binary sequences is partially exchangeable iff it assigns equal probability to equivalent strings. Freedman (1962a) showed that a stationary partially exchangeable process is a mixture of Markov chains. Diaconis and Freedman (1980) eliminated the stationary assumption. To get a mixture of Markov chains in this case, infinitely many returns to the starting state are needed. Extensions to countable situations are straightforward, but extensions to more general spaces are more complex (see Diaconis 1988).

Yet another form of partial exchangeability is described by Bernardo and Smith (1994: 211). The M infinite sequences of 0–1 random quantities $Z_{m1}, Z_{m2}, \ldots$ $(m = 1, 2, \ldots, M)$ are *unrestrictedly infinitely exchangeable* iff each sequence is infinitely exchangeable and, in addition, for all $n_m \leq N_m$ and $z_m(n_m) = [z_{m1}, z_{m2}, \ldots, z_{mn_m}]'(m = 1, 2, \ldots, M)$,

$$p[z_1(n_1), \ldots, z_M(n_M)|w_1(N_1), \ldots, w_M(N_M)] = \prod_{m=1}^{M} p[z_m(n_m)|w_m(N_m)],$$

where $w_m(N_m) = z_{m1} + z_{m2} + \ldots + z_{mN_m}$ is the number of successes in the first N_m observation from the mth sequence $(m = 1, 2, \ldots, M)$. In other words, unrestrictedly infinite exchangeability adds to infinite exchangeability the requirement that, given

$w_m(N_m)(m = 1, 2, \ldots, M)$, only the total for the mth sequence is relevant for beliefs about the outcomes of any subset of n_m of the N_m observations from that sequence. Therefore, unrestrictedly infinite exchangeability involves a conditional irrelevance judgment. With this definition in hand, the following theorem of Bernardo and Smith (1994: 212–13) can be proved.

Theorem 6. (Representation Theorem for Several Sequences of 0–1 Random Quantities): Suppose $\{Z_{mn}\}_{n=1}^{n=\infty}(m = 1, \ldots, M)$ are unrestrictedly infinitely exchangeable sequences of $\{0, 1\}$ random quantities with joint probability measure $P(\cdot)$. Then there exists a cdf $F(\cdot)$ such that

$$p[z_1(n_1), \ldots, z_M(n_M)] = \int_{[0,1]^M} \prod_{m=1}^{M} \prod_{j=1}^{n_m} \theta_m^{z_{mj}} (1 - \theta_m)^{1-z_{mj}} dF(\theta),$$

where $w_m(n_m) = z_{m1} + z_{m2} + \ldots + z_{mn_m} (m = 1, 2, \ldots, M)$, and

$$F(\theta) = \lim_{\substack{n_m \to \infty \\ (m = 1, \ldots, M)}} P\left[\left(\frac{w_1(n_1)}{n_1} \leq \theta_1\right) \cap \ldots \cap \left(\frac{w_M(n_M)}{n_M} \leq \theta_M\right)\right]. \qquad \square$$

To appreciate Theorem 6, consider the case of $M = 2$ subsequences as do Bernardo and Smith (1994: 214, 223). Then Theorem 6 implies we can proceed *as if* (i) the $\{Z_{mn}\}_{n=1}^{n=N}(m = 1, 2)$ are judged to be independent Bernoulli random quantities conditional on $\Theta_m (m = 1, 2)$, (ii) Θ_1 and Θ_2 have bivariate cdf $F(\theta_1, \theta_2)$, and according to the SLLN, $\Theta_m = \text{Limit}_{n_m \to \infty} \bar{W}_{n_m}/n_m (m = 1, 2)$ P-almost surely. Specification of $F(\theta_1, \theta_2)$ depends on the application at hand. Four possibilities are: (i) belief that knowledge of the limiting relative frequency for one of the sequences will not change beliefs about the other sequence (prior beliefs about Θ_1 and Θ_2 are independent), (ii) belief that the limiting relative frequency of the second sequence is necessarily greater than for the first sequence implies $F(\theta_1, \theta_2)$ is zero outside of $0 \leq \theta_1 < \theta_2 \leq 1$, (iii) belief that there is a positive non-unitary probability that the limits of the two sequences are the same, and (iv) belief that the long-run frequencies $\Theta_m (m = 1, 2)$ are themselves exchangeable, leading to a hierarchical model.

The mathematics behind de Finetti's Theorem and its generalizations has many cousins. Diaconis and Freedman (1981) discussed the mathematical similarity to statistical-mechanical studies of "Gibbs states". Lauritzen (1988) developed extreme point models in the language of projective systems. Ladha (1993) used de Finetti's Theorem to relax Condorcet's assumption of independent voting while preserving the result that a majority of voters is more likely than any single voter to choose the better of two alternatives. The mathematics of representation theorems is both deep and broad.

7 Conclusions

> ... one could say that for him (de Finetti) Bayesianism represents the crossroads where pragmatism and empiricism meet subjectivism. He thinks one needs to be Bayesian in order to be subjectivist, but on the other hand subjectivism is a choice to be made if one embraces a pragmatist and empiricist philosophy.
>
> (Galavotti 2001: 165)

I believe the case has been made for Bayesianism in the sense of de Finetti. I have promoted a subjective attitude emerging from the left-hand side of (2.3), but which can be used to help researchers work on the more customary right-hand side. This change of emphasis from parameters to observables puts the former in a subsidiary role. Less fascination with parameters can be healthy. The prior $f(\cdot)$, which is implied (not assumed) by a representation theorem, is always proper. This rules out the usual priors used in *objective Bayesian analysis* (see Berger 2004). But interestingly, exchangeability, which is an admission of no additional information regarding otherwise similar observable quantities, implies the use of a *proper* prior for the mathematical fiction Θ. To pin down this prior further requires additional assumptions about observable sequences (e.g. the Polya urn assumption in Example 3).

If the researcher finds it more convenient to think in terms of the right-hand side of (2.3) (say, because the researcher has a theoretical framework in which to interpret Θ), then by all means elicit a personal prior for Θ or consider the sensitivity of the posterior with respect to professional viewpoints of interest defined parametrically. But given that most people find prior choice difficult, a representation theorem provides an alternative way to use subjective information about observables to facilitate prior choice for Θ.

Even when a representation theorem is not available for a given parametric likelihood (say, because it is unclear what restrictions on the left-hand side of (2.3) would be sufficient to imply this choice of likelihood), the spirit of this discussion has hopefully not been lost on the reader. Representation theorems reflect a healthy attitude toward parametric likelihoods: they are not intended to be "true" properties of reality, but rather useful windows for viewing the observable world, communicating with other researchers, and making inferences regarding future observables.

References

Aldous, D. (1981). "Representations for Partially Exchangeable Arrays of Random Variables". *Journal of Multivariate Analysis*, 11: 581–98.

—— (1985). "Exchangeability and Related Topics", in P. L. Hennequin (ed.), *Ècole d'Èté de Probabilités de Saint-Flour XIII—1983*. Berlin: Springer, 1–198.

Arellano-Valle, R. B., Bolfarine, H., and Iglesias, P. (1994). "A Predictivistic Interpretation of the Multivariate t Distribution". Test, 3: 221–36.

Arnold, S. F. (1979). "Linear Models with Exchangeably Distributed Errors". *Journal of the American Statistical Association*, 74: 194–9.

Berger. J. O. (2004). 'The Case for Objective Bayesian Analysis'. *Bayesian Analysis*, 1: 1–17.

Bernardo, J. M., and Smith, A. F. M. (1994). *Bayesian Theory*. New York: Wiley.

Chaloner, K. M., and Duncan, G. T. (1983). "Assessment of a Beta Prior Distribution: PM Elicitation". *Statistician*, 32: 174–80.

Dawid, A. P. (1978). "Extendibility of Spherical Matrix Distributions," *Journal of Multivariate Analysis*, 8: 559–66.

de Finetti, B. (1938). "Sur la Condition d'équivalence Partielle". *Actualités Scientifiques et Industrielles*, 739. Paris: Herman and Cii.

Diaconis, P. (1988). "Recent Progress on de Finetti's Notions of Exchangeability", in J. M. Bernardo, M. H. DeGroot, D. V. Lindley, and A. F. M. Smith (eds.), *Bayesian Statistics*, iii. Oxford: Oxford University Press, 111–25.

—— Eaton, M. L. and Lauritzen, S. L. (1992). "Finite de Finetti Theorems in Linear Models and Multivariate Analysis". *Scandinavian Journal of Statistics*, 19: 289–315.

—— and Freedman, D. (1980). "de Finetti's Theorem for Markov Chains". *Annals of Probability*, 8: 115–30.

—— —— (1981). "Partial Exchangeability and Sufficiency", in J. K. Ghosh and J. Roy (eds.), *Proceedings of the Indian Statistical Institute Golden Jubilee International Conference on Statistics: Applications and New Directions*. Calcutta: Indian Statistical Institute, 205–36.

—— —— (1986). "On the Consistency of Bayes Estimates (with discussion)". *Annals of Statistics*, 14: 1–67.

—— —— (1987). "A Dozen de Finetti-style Results in Search of a Theory". *Annals of the Institute Henri Poincaré*, 23: 394–423.

—— and Ylvisaker, D. (1979). "Conjugate Priors for Exponential Families". *Annals of Statistics*, 7: 269–81.

—— —— (1985). "Quantifying Prior Opinion" (with discussion), in J. M. Bernardo, M. H. DeGroot, D. V. Lindley, and A. F. M. Smith (eds.), *Bayesian Statistics*, ii. Amsterdam: North-Holland, 133–56.

du Sautoy, M. (2008). *Finding Moonshine: A Mathematician's Journey through Symmetry*. London: Fourth Estate.

Dubins, L. E., and Freedman, D. A. (1979). "Exchangeable Processes Need Not be Mixtures of Independent Identically Distributed Random Variables". *Zeitschrift für Wahrscheinlichkeitstheorie und verwandte Gebiete*, 48: 115–32.

Eaton, M. L., Fortini, S., and Regazzini, E. (1993). "Spherical Symmetry: An Elementary Justification". *Journal of the Italian Statistical Association*, 1: 1–16.

Ferguson, T. S. (1974). "Prior Distributions on Spaces of Probability Measures". *Annals of Statistics*, 2: 615–29.

Freedman, D. (1962a). "Mixtures of Markov Processes". *Annals of Mathematical Statistics*, 33: 114–18.

—— (1962b). "Invariants under Mixing which Generalize de Finetti's Theorem". *Annals of Mathematical Statistics*, 33: 916–23.

—— (1965). "Bernard Friedman's Urn". *Annals of Mathematical Statistics*, 36: 956–70.

Fuchs, C. A., and Schack, R. (2004)."Unknown Quantum States and Operations, a Bayesian View", in M. G. A. Paris and J. Řeháček (eds.), *Quantum Estimation Theory*. Berlin: Springer.

Galavotti, M. C. (2001). "Subjectivism, Objectivism and Objectivity in Bruno de Finetti's Bayesianism". in D. Cornfield and J. Williamson (eds.), *Foundations of Bayesianism*. Dordrecht: Kluwer, 161–74.

Garthwaite, P. H., Kadane, J. B., and O'Hagan, A. (2005). "Statistical Methods for Eliciting Probability Distributions". *Journal of the American Statistical Association*, 100: 680–700.

Geisser, S. (1984). "On Prior Distributions for Binary Trials (with discussion)". *American Statistician*, 38: 244–51.

Gelman, A., Carlin, J. B., Stern, H. S., and Rubin, D. B. (1995). *Bayesian Data Analysis*. London: Chapman & Hall.

Hewitt, E., and Savage, L. J. (1955). "Symmetric Measures on Cartesian Products". *Transactions of the American Mathematical Society*, 80: 470–501.

Hill, B., Lane, D., and Suddreth, W. (1987). "Exchangeable Urn Processes". *Annals of Probability*, 15: 1586–92.

Johnson, W. E. (1924). *Logic, Part III: The Logical Foundations of Science*, Cambridge: Cambridge University Press.

Kadane, J. B., and Winkler, R. L. (1988). "Separating Probability Elicitation from Utilities". *Journal of the American Statistical Association*, 83: 357–63.

Kingman, J. F. C. (1972). "On Random Sequences with Spherical Symmetry". *Biometrika*, 59: 492–4.

Kreps, D. M. (1988). *Notes on the Theory of Choice*. Boulder, Colo.: Westview Press.

Ladha, K. K. (1993). "Condorcet's Jury Theorem in Light of de Finetti's Theorem: Majority-Rule Voting with Correlated Votes". *Social Choice and Welfare*, 10: 69–85.

Lauritzen, S. L. (1988). "Extremal Families and Systems of Sufficient Statistics", *Lecture Notes in Statistics*, 49. New York: Springer.

Lindley, D. V. (1982). "Scoring Rules and the Inevitability of Probability". *International Statistical Review*, 50: 1–26.

Loschi, R. H., Iglesias, P. L., and Arellano-Valle, R. B. (2003). "Predictivistic Characterizations of Multivariate Student-t Models". *Journal of Multivariate Analysis*, 85: 10–23.

McCall, J. J. (1991). "Exchangeability and its Economic Applications". *Journal of Economic Dynamics and Control*, 15: 549–68.

O'Hagan, A. (1994). *Kendall's Advanced Theory of Statistics, Vol. 2B, Bayesian Inference*. London: Halsted Press.

—— Buck, C. E., Daneshkhah, A., Eiser, J. R., Garthwaite, P. H., Jenkinson, D. J., Oakley, J. E., and Rakow, T. (2006). *Uncertain Judgements: Eliciting Experts' Probabilities*. New York: Wiley.

Poirier, D. J. (1988). "Frequentist and Subjectivist Perspectives on the Problems of Model Building in Economics (with discussion)". *Journal of Economic Perspectives*, 2: 121–70.

—— (1995). *Intermediate Statistics and Econometrics: A Comparative Approach*. Cambridge, Mass.: MIT Press.

Ramsey, F. P. (1926). "Truth and Probability", in Ramsey (1931), *The Foundations of Mathematics and other Logical Essays*, Ch. VII, ed. R. B. Braithwaite, London: Kegan, Paul, Trench, Trubner & Co. (New York: Harcourt, Brace and Company), 156–98.

Schervish, M. J. (1995). *Theory of Statistics*. New York: Springer-Verlag.

Schoenberg, I. J. (1938). "Metric Spaces and Positive Definite Functions". *Transactions of the American Mathematical Society*, 44: 522–36.

Sims, C. A. (1971). "Distributed Lag Estimation When the Parameter Space is Explicitly Infinite-Dimensional". *Annals of Mathematical Statistics*, 42: 1622–36.
Singpurwalla, N. (2006). *Reliability and Risk: A Bayesian Perspective.* Chichester: Wiley.
Smith, A. F. M. (1981). "On Random Sequences with Centred Spherical Symmetry". *Journal of the Royal Statistical Society*, 43, Series B: 208–9.
Zaman, A. (1986). "A Finite Form of de Finetti's Theorem for Stationary Markov Exchangeability". *Annals of Probability*, 14: 1418–27.

PART II

METHODS

CHAPTER 3

BAYESIAN INFERENCE FOR TIME SERIES STATE SPACE MODELS

PAOLO GIORDANI, MICHAEL PITT, AND ROBERT KOHN

1 Introduction

This chapter considers state space models for time series, with particular emphasis on some important developments occurring in the last decade. We made this choice because a large number of models fit within this framework and a reasonably unified treatment is possible. Many of the methods discussed in the chapter can be applied to general time series models.

The state space representation of a dynamic system assumes that the density of the observations depends on a vector of parameters and a sequence of latent states so that the observations and states are assumed to be jointly Markovian, that is, they have a one-period memory. The observations and the states can be continuous or discrete. This allows the construction of efficient filtering procedures to evaluate the likelihood and predictive densities. A general framework for inference is obtained by coupling these filtering algorithms with modern simulation methods such as Markov chain Monte Carlo (MCMC) simulation and the particle filter.

Bayesian simulation methods are especially useful for time series space space models as they can deal with models having high-dimensional and non-Gaussian latent states, for example, factor stochastic volatility models, as well as non-standard models such as continuous time models observed discretely, where it is difficult to write the likelihood analytically. Bayesian simulation methods are powerful because they help overcome the "curse of dimensionality" of latent variables and parameters in two ways. First, they allow computational problems to be divided into a number of tractable subproblems which are solved iteratively. Second, they allow latent variables and in some cases parameters to be integrated out.

The chapter is organized into nine sections. Section 2 introduces the state space framework and explains the main ideas behind filtering, smoothing, and likelihood computation. These are the main building blocks for carrying out inference, prediction, and diagnostic analysis. This section shows that many of the important properties of state space models can be derived without assuming a specific structure for the model. Section 3 discusses Gaussian linear state space models that allow for analytical solutions to filtering, smoothing, and likelihood computation that are straightforward to implement computationally. Some simple examples and applications are given, including the local level model, measurement errors, and autoregressive moving average (ARMA) models, missing observations, and time-varying parameter models. Section 4 deals with conditionally Gaussian state space models, that is models that can be made Gaussian by conditioning on a set of latent variables. Section 4.1 deals with conditionally Gaussian state space models which are discrete mixtures of Gaussian state space models, and are Gaussian models after conditioning on a sequence of discrete, possibly unobserved, variables. We first discuss models in which the discrete unobserved variables can be sampled in one block conditional on the states in an MCMC scheme. These include Markov switching autoregressive (AR) models and mixture models, models with additive outliers, and an accurate approximation of a standard stochastic volatility model. We then discuss cases in which the latent variables must be drawn with the states integrated out, including regression models with random shifts of random magnitude in conditional mean or conditional variance, local level models with random shifts in the signal-to-noise ratio, that is, where the signal to noise ratio may change through time, and stochastic volatility models with shifts in the mean. Issues associated with forecasting with conditionally Gaussian models are also discussed. Section 4.2 considers non-Gaussian state space models, such as binary state space models that can be made Gaussian by introducing auxiliary latent variables. Section 5 generalizes Sections 3 and 4.1 to multivariate state space models, like time varying parameter vector autoregressive models, Markov switching vector autoregressive models, vector autoregressive models with structural breaks, and dynamic factor models.

Section 6 discusses non-Gaussian state space models that are still tractable to estimation using MCMC methods. Inference for such non-Gaussian state space models is less efficient in general than for Gaussian and conditionally Gaussian state space models, although efficient procedures are available for some special cases.

Sections 7 and 8 introduce the particle filter as a general approach for estimating state space models. Section 7 considers the case where the parameters are known and Section 8 discusses parameter estimation. Particle filtering is an important and developing research area of time series that has the potential to make computation in general state space models tractable. Section 9 deals with model selection, model averaging, and model diagnostics.

This chapter does not provide an extensive discussion on how to generate fixed parameters within an MCMC scheme nor how to set priors for them. One reason is that in most cases there is little that is insightful in terms of time series that we can say, over and above what is usually written about setting priors for general models. The second reason is that when a careful specification of priors is necessary, this is usually done in the context of specific applications. See, for example, the careful treatment of priors for Bayesian Macroeconometric models in Del Negro and Schorfheide (Chapter 7 in this volume).

There are three chapters in this volume that have particular relevance to our chapter. The first is the chapter on general Bayesian computational methods by Chib (Chapter 5). The second is the chapter on Bayesian macroeconometrics by Del Negro and Schorfheide (Chapter 7). This chapter gives a detailed treatment of priors, parameter generation, and state generation for some of the models considered in general terms in the present chapter. The third is the chapter on Bayesian econometrics in finance by Jacquier and Polson (Chapter 9), which is also concerned with some of the issues addressed in the present chapter.

2 The general state space framework

This section presents many of the qualitative features of filtering, smoothing, and likelihood computation that hold generally within a state space framework. To carry out numerical work, it is necessary to make further assumptions, which we do in later sections. Section 2.2 discusses the general filtering equations, Section 2.3 shows how the general filtering equations are used to compute the likelihood, Section 2.4 discusses smoothing, and Section 2.5 discusses the generalization of the previous three sections when there are missing observations.

We use the same symbol to denote a random variable and its realization. For any univariate or multivariate random variable y_t, define $y_{s:t} = \{y'_s, \ldots, y'_t\}'$ for $s \leq t$.

2.1 Assumptions

The general state space framework considered in this chapter satisfies, for $t \geq 1$,

$$p(y_t|x_{1:t}, y_{1:t-1}; \theta) = p(y_t|x_t; \theta) \tag{3.1a}$$

$$p(x_{t+1}|x_{1:t}, y_{1:t}; \theta) = p(x_{t+1}|x_t, y_t; \theta) \tag{3.1b}$$

where y_t is the observation and x_t is the state vector at time t, and θ is an unknown parameter vector. Equation (3.1a) is called the "observation" or "measurement" equation. Equation (3.1b) is called the "state transition" equation. Equations (3.1a) and (3.1b) imply that the sequence $\{(y_t, x_t), t \geq 1\}$ is Markovian in the sense that $p(y_{t+1}, x_{t+1}|y_{1:t}, x_{1:t}; \theta) = p(y_{t+1}, x_{t+1}|y_t, x_t; \theta)$. For many models, equation (3.1b) simplifies to

$$p(x_{t+1}|x_t, y_t; \theta) = p(x_{t+1}|x_t; \theta). \tag{3.2}$$

Initial conditions on x_1 are discussed in Section 3.6. In most, but not all, applications, x_t is an unobserved vector of latent variables.

The stochastic volatility (SV) model

$$y_t = \exp(x_t/2)\varepsilon_t, \qquad x_{t+1} = \mu + \phi(x_t - \mu) + \sigma_v v_t \tag{3.3}$$

is an example of a state space model which is often used to model asset returns y_t, with x_t the log of the volatility at time t which evolves as a first-order autoregressive process with persistence parameter ϕ. The disturbance vector $u_t = (\varepsilon_t, v_t)'$ is an independent bivariate normal sequence with $u_t \sim N_2(0, \Sigma)$ and Σ is a correlation matrix, with its (1,2) element ρ being the correlation between ε_t and v_t. The model parameters are $\theta = (\mu, \phi, \sigma_v, \rho)$.

If $\rho = 0$, then ε_t and v_t are independent and (3.2) holds. If the correlation $\rho \neq 0$, then (3.3) is said to be an SV model with leverage.

In many state space models we can think of the state transition equation as a prior on the evolution of the states. For example, in the SV model at (3.3), the state transition equation can be thought of as a prior on the evolution of the log volatility.

Some references to state space models in the literature are Harrison and West (1997), chapter 4 of Harvey (1993), and Durbin and Koopman (2001).

To simplify the notation for the rest of this section, we usually omit to show dependence on the unknown parameters θ unless it is instructive to do so.

2.2 Filtering

Filtering evaluates the densities $p(x_t|y_{1:t})$ for $t \geq 1$. The filtering densities provide a measure of uncertainty about the current state x_t given all the observations available up to time t. The filtering densities are evaluated recursively through time for $t = 1, 2, \ldots$. Explicit computations using the Kalman filter are given in Section 3.1 for the Gaussian linear state space model and by the particle filter in Section 7 for more general models.

The Markov structure of $\{y_t, x_t, t \geq 1\}$ allows the following sequential solution to filtering for a given set of parameters θ, assuming that the distribution $p(x_1|\theta)$ is specified. For $t \geq 1$ the filtering equations are

$$\begin{aligned} p(x_{t+1}|y_{1:t}) &= \int p(x_{t+1}|x_t, y_t)p(x_t|y_{1:t})dx_t \\ p(x_{t+1}|y_{1:t+1}) &\propto p(y_{t+1}|x_{t+1})p(x_{t+1}|y_{1:t}). \end{aligned} \tag{3.4}$$

The filtering equations can also be used for prediction. Thus, suppose that we have $p(x_T|y_{1:T})$. Then the one step ahead predictive densities for x_{T+1} and y_{T+1} are

$$
\begin{aligned}
p(x_{T+1}|y_{1:T}) &= \int p(x_{T+1}|x_T, y_T)p(x_T|y_{1:T})dx_T \\
p(y_{T+1}|y_{1:T}) &= \int p(y_{T+1}|x_{T+1})p(x_{T+1}|y_{1:T})dx_{T+1}.
\end{aligned}
\tag{3.5}
$$

These equations can be used for one step ahead prediction as new observations come in, that is, as T increases.

Multistep ahead forecasts are obtained similarly. Suppose the predictive density $p(x_{T+i}, y_{T+i}|y_{1:T})$ is computed for $i = 1, \ldots, j$. Then,

$$
\begin{aligned}
p(x_{T+j+1}|y_{1:T}) &= \int p(x_{T+j+1}|x_{T+j}, y_{T+j})p(x_{T+j}, y_{T+j}|y_{1:T})dx_{T+j}dy_{T+j} \\
p(y_{T+j+1}|y_{1:T}) &= \int p(y_{T+j+1}|x_{T+j+1})p(x_{T+j+1}|y_{1:T})dx_{T+j+1}.
\end{aligned}
\tag{3.6}
$$

We can also simulate the future states and observations from their predictive distributions using

$$
p(x_{T+1:T+j}, y_{t+1:T+j}|y_{1:T}) = \prod_{i=1}^{j} p(x_{T+i}|x_{T+i-1}, y_{T+i-1})p(y_{T+i}|x_{T+i}) \tag{3.7}
$$

with x_T generated from $p(x_T|y_{1:T})$.

The filtering and prediction equations obtained in this section are general and can often be simplified in many applications. In the Gaussian case, the filtering equations are evaluated efficiently using the Kalman filter as in Section 3.1. In many other cases, we can also carry out filtering conditional on some latent variables. The particle filter described in Section 7 makes it possible to evaluate these equations, at least approximately, for a large set of models.

Usually, the equations at (3.4)–(3.7) also depend on an unknown parameter vector θ which can be integrated out using MCMC methods.

2.3 Likelihood computation

Evaluating the likelihood, that is, the density of the observations, when it is possible to do so, is an important calculation for both frequentist and Bayesian analysis.

Suppose that we have a vector of observations $y = y_{1:T}$, with T the sample size, from a state space model satisfying the equations at (3.1a) and (3.1b). The likelihood can be written as

$$
\begin{aligned}
p(y|\theta) &= p(y_1|\theta)\prod_{t=1}^{T-1} p(y_{t+1}|y_{1:t};\theta), \qquad \text{where} \\
p(y_{t+1}|y_{1:t},\theta) &= \int p(y_{t+1}|x_{t+1};\theta)p(x_{t+1}|y_{1:t};\theta)dx_{t+1}.
\end{aligned}
\tag{3.8}
$$

The filtering equations at (3.4) allow the computation of the likelihood in $O(T)$ operations, at least in principle, by which we mean that we just outline the structure of the calculation, and do not imply that it is feasible in practice nor do we say anything about the constant in the $O(T)$ calculation. Explicit evaluation of these equations is possible in the Gaussian case and some other special cases and the particle filter allows the approximation of the likelihood more generally.

2.4 Smoothing

Evaluating the state densities $p(x_t|y_{1:T})$ based on all the data is called smoothing and shows the uncertainty in x_t based on all the data. For example, for the stochastic volatility model, we may wish to know the uncertainty of the volatilities based on all the data. Smoothing by simulation is also important in MCMC Bayesian computation.

Smoothing can also be done, at least principle, in $O(T)$ operations by first filtering to obtain the densities $p(x_t|y_{1:t})$ for $t = 1, \dots, T$. This means in particular that $p(x_T|y_{1:T})$ is available. For $t = T - 1, \dots, 1$,

$$p(x_t|y_{1:T}, x_{t+1:T}) = p(x_t|x_{t+1}, y_{1:t}) \propto p(x_{t+1}|x_t, y_{1:t})p(x_t|y_{1:t}). \tag{3.9}$$

To show (3.9), for $t = T - 1, \dots, 1$, we note that for $t = T - 1$, $p(x_{T-1}|y_{1:T}, x_T) \propto p(y_T|x_T)p(x_{T-1}|x_T, y_{1:T-1})$. To obtain the result for general t, it is sufficient to show that $p(x_t|y_{1:T}, x_{t+1:T}) = p(x_t|x_{t+1:T-1}, y_{1:T-1})$, because the result then follows by an induction argument. Now, for $t < T - 1$,

$$p(x_t|y_{1:T}, x_{t+1:T}) \propto p(y_T|x_T)p(x_T|y_{T-1}, x_{T-1})p(x_t|y_{1:T-1}, x_{1:T-1}) \propto p(x_t|y_{1:T-1}, x_{1:T-1}).$$

Starting with $p(x_T|y_{1:T})$, the general smoothing equations for $t = T - 1, \dots, 1$ are

$$\begin{aligned} p(x_t|y_{1:T}) &= \int p(x_t|x_{t+1}, y_{1:t})p(x_{t+1}|y_{1:T})dx_{t+1} \\ &\propto p(x_t|y_{1:t}) \int p(x_{t+1}|x_t, y_t)p(x_{t+1}|y_{1:T})dx_{t+1}. \end{aligned} \tag{3.10}$$

To obtain the first line of (3.10), we note that

$$\begin{aligned} p(x_t|y_{1:T}) &= \int p(x_t|y_{1:T}, x_{t+1:T})p(x_{t+1:T}|y_{1:T})dx_{t+1:T} \\ &= \int p(x_t|x_{t+1}, y_{1:t})p(x_{t+1:T}|y_{1:T})dx_{t+1:T} \\ &= \int p(x_t|x_{t+1}, y_{1:t})p(x_{t+1}|y_{1:T})dx_{t+1}. \end{aligned}$$

We can also generate a sample from the smoothing density $p(x_{1:T}|y_{1:T})$ by using

$$p(x_{1:T}|y_{1:T}) = \prod_{t=1}^{T-1} p(x_t|y_{1:t}, x_{t+1})p(x_T|y_{1:T}), \tag{3.11}$$

which follows from (3.9). Thus, starting with $x_T \sim p(x_T|y_{1:T})$, suppose that we have generated $x_{t+1:T}$. Then, we generate x_t from $p(x_t|y_{1:t}, x_{t+1})$.

Usually, equations (3.10) and (3.11) depend on the unknown parameter vector θ which can be integrated out using MCMC methods.

2.5 Missing y_t

We have assumed till now that there are no missing or partially missing y_t, but it is straightforward to deal with missing y_t within the state space framework if we assume that the missing y_t are generated by the same state space model as the y_t that are available.

Let $y_t^{(o)}$ and $y_t^{(u)}$ be the observed and unobserved parts of y_t and let $y_{1:t}^{(o)}$ be the subvector of $y_{1:t}$ that is observed. Then the filtering equations (3.4) become

$$\begin{aligned} p(x_{t+1}|y_{1:t}^{(o)}) &= \int p(x_{t+1}|x_t, y_t^{(u)}, y_t^{(o)})p(y_t^{(u)}|y_t^{(o)}, x_t)p(x_t|y_{1:t}^{(o)})dx_t dy_t^{(u)} \\ p(x_{t+1}|y_{1:t+1}^{(o)}) &\propto p(y_{(t+1)}^{(o)}|x_{t+1})p(x_{t+1}|y_{1:t}^{(o)}) \end{aligned} \tag{3.12}$$

It is straightforward to derive these equations from (3.1a) and (3.1b).

The likelihood equations (3.8) become

$$\begin{aligned} p(y_{1:T}^{(o)}|\theta) &= p(y_1^{(o)}|\theta)\prod_{t=1}^{T-1} p(y_{t+1}^{(o)}|y_{1:t}^{(o)};\theta), \text{ where} \\ p(y_{t+1}^{(o)}|y_{1:t}^{(o)};\theta) &= \int p(y_{t+1}^{(o)}|x_{t+1};\theta)p(x_{t+1}|y_{1:t}^{(o)};\theta)dx_{t+1}, \end{aligned} \tag{3.13}$$

with $p(x_{t+1}|y_{1:t}^{(o)};\theta)$ available from filtering.

The smoothing equations (3.10) also generalize, with $p(x_T|y_{1:T}^{(o)})$ available from filtering. Similarly to (3.9),

$$p(x_t|y_{1:T}^{(o)}, x_{t+1:T}) = p(x_t|x_{t+1}, y_{1:t}^{(o)}) \propto p(x_{t+1}|x_t, y_{1:t}^{(o)})p(x_t|y_{1:t}^{(o)}).$$

Furthermore, starting with $p(x_T|y_{1:T}^{(o)})$, the general smoothing equations for $t = T-1, \ldots, 1$ are now,

$$\begin{aligned} p(x_t|y_{1:T}^{(o)}) &= \int p(x_t|x_{t+1}, y_{1:t}^{(o)})p(x_{t+1}|y_{1:T}^{(o)})dx_{t+1} \\ &\propto p(x_t|y_{1:t}^{(o)})\int p(x_{t+1}|x_t, y_t^{(o)})p(x_{t+1}|y_{1:T}^{(o)})dx_{t+1}. \end{aligned}$$

It is also possible to generate $x_{1:T}$ as a block from $p(x_{1:T}|y_{1:T}^{(0)})$.

An alternative approach for dealing with missing observations is to embed the filtering and smoothing within an MCMC scheme, with the missing observations generated conditional on the states and then filtering and smoothing carried out on all the y_t. This approach is less efficient statistically than integrating out the missing observations, and this is so in particular when there are many missing observations. For a further discussion of missing observations in state space models, see section 12.3 of Brockwell and Davis (2009).

3 Gaussian linear state space models

The Gaussian linear state space model (e.g. Harrison and West 1997: 102) is used in many applications and is also an important building block of many other state space models, and in particular discrete and continuous mixtures of Gaussian linear state space models. We write the Gaussian linear state space model as

$$y_t = g_t + H_t x_t + G_t u_t, \tag{3.14a}$$

$$x_{t+1} = f_{t+1} + F_{t+1} x_t + \Gamma_{t+1} u_t. \tag{3.14b}$$

The vectors f_t, g_t, and the matrices H_t, G_t, F_t, Γ_t may be functions of a parameter vector θ as well as covariates, and $u_t \sim N(0, \Sigma_t)$ is a independent sequence with Σ_t also a function of θ. There is some redundancy in our notation, because if G_t and Γ_t are present, then Σ_t can be set as I. However, this redundancy allows for a more flexible notation.

Equation (3.14a) is the "observation" equation and equation (3.14b) is the "state transition" equation. It is clear that given θ, if $p(x_1|\theta)$ is Gaussian, then $p(x_{1:T}, y_{1:T}|\theta)$ is Gaussian so that the filtering densities $p(x_t|y_{1:t};\theta)$, $t = 1, \ldots, T$, the likelihood, $p(y_{1:T}|\theta)$, and the smoothing densities $p(x_t|y_{1:T};\theta)$, $t = 1, \ldots, T$, are Gaussian. This means that it is straightforward to carry out filtering, likelihood evaluation, and smoothing using $O(T)$ algorithms that are available in the literature and reviewed below.

An example of a Gaussian linear state space model is the local level model

$$\begin{aligned} y_t &= x_t + e_t, \quad x_{t+1} = x_t + v_t, \\ u_t &= (e_t, v_t)' \sim N(0, \Sigma), \quad \Sigma = \begin{pmatrix} \sigma_e^2 & 0 \\ 0 & \sigma_v^2 \end{pmatrix}, \end{aligned} \tag{3.15}$$

where x_t is the level or mean of the time series y_t at time t. In (3.15), x_t is the state at time t, the parameters are $\theta = (\sigma_e^2, \sigma_v^2)$, and e_t and v_t are independent; $G_t = \Gamma_t = 1$ and $\Sigma_t = \Sigma$ for all t. We can think of the state transition equation at (3.15) as a joint prior for $x_{1:T}$ which tries to capture the idea that the x_t evolve smoothly. It is called a smoothness prior in the time series literature (e.g. Kitagawa and Gersch 1996) and is closely related to spline smoothing in the nonparametric regression literature (e.g. Wahba 1990).

A second example of a Gaussian linear state space model is an autoregressive moving average model with one autoregressive and one moving average lag, called an ARMA(1,1) model,

$$y_t = \phi y_{t-1} + e_t - \omega e_{t-1}, \quad e_t \sim N(0, \sigma_e^2), \tag{3.16}$$

with e_t an independent $N(0, \sigma_e^2)$ sequence. We assume that $|\phi| < 1$ so the autoregression is stationary. The state space representation for (3.16) is

$$\begin{aligned} &y_t = Hx_t, \quad x_{t+1} = Fx_t + \Gamma u_t, \quad u_t = e_{t+1}, \\ &H = \begin{pmatrix}1\ 0\end{pmatrix}, \quad F = \begin{pmatrix}\phi & -\omega \\ 0 & 0\end{pmatrix}, \quad \Gamma = \begin{pmatrix}1 \\ 1\end{pmatrix}, \quad \Sigma = \sigma_e^2 . \end{aligned} \tag{3.17}$$

The state vector $x_t = (y_t, e_t)'$ is stationary, so the distribution of x_1 is normal with zero mean. The variance of y_1 is $\sigma_e^2(1 + \omega^2 - 2\omega\phi)/(1 - \phi^2)$ and the covariance between y_1 and e_1 is σ_e^2, which gives us the covariance matrix of x_1.

We note that there are alternative ways of writing equations (3.14a) and (3.14b). In general, the state space representation is not unique. Let $e_t = G_t u_t \sim N(0, G_t \Sigma_t G_t')$ and $v_t = \Gamma_t u_t \sim N(0, \Gamma_t \Sigma_t \Gamma_t')$. Then we can write

$$y_t = g_t + H_t x_t + e_t, \tag{3.18a}$$

$$x_{t+1} = f_{t+1} + F_{t+1} x_t + v_t, \tag{3.18b}$$

with e_t and v_t independent if and only if $\text{cov}(e_t, v_t) = G_t \Sigma_t \Gamma_t' = 0$. If e_t and v_t are independent, then there is also no loss in generality in writing (3.18b) as $x_t = f_t + F_t x_{t-1} + v_t$, and we will sometimes use these alternative representations in the chapter.

3.1 Filtering

To simplify notation, we do not show dependence on θ. The filtered densities $p(x_t|y_{1:t})$ for $t \geq 1$ are Gaussian because the observations and states at equations (3.14a) and (3.14b) are jointly Gaussian. It is therefore sufficient to compute the means and covariance matrices of these densities to know their distributions. The general filtering equations at (3.4) also show that the filtered densities are Gaussian and very importantly that the means and variances of the filtered densities can be evaluated iteratively in $O(T)$ operations. Although it is possible to obtain the filtered iterations from (3.4), it is more convenient to do so directly as outlined below because we deal with conditional means and variances.

The computations are done efficiently in $O(T)$ operations using the Kalman filter (Kalman, 1960) by transforming the observations $y_{1:T}$ into an equivalent independent sequence $\varepsilon_{1:T}$ called the innovations, which are defined by $\varepsilon_1 = y_1 - E(y_1)$ and $\varepsilon_{t+1} = y_{t+1} - E(y_{t+1}|y_{1:t})$ for $t = 1, \ldots, T-1$. We note that for any t, $\varepsilon_{1:t}$ is a one to one transformation of $y_{1:t}$ so that conditioning on $y_{1:t}$ is the same as conditioning on $y_{1:t-1}, \varepsilon_t$. Let $R_t = \text{var}(y_t|y_{1:t-1}) = \text{var}(\varepsilon_t)$ be the tth innovation variance. We use the notation $x_{t|s} = E(x_t|y_{1:s})$ and $S_{t|s} = \text{var}(x_t|y_{1:s})$ for any $s \geq 0$ and $t \geq 1$, with $x_{t|0} = E(x_t)$ and $S_{t|0} = \text{var}(x_t)$.

The version of the Kalman filter given below assumes the general representation (3.14a) and (3.14b), whereas most other treatments assume independence of the error terms in (3.18a) and (3.18b).

Algorithm 1 (Kalman Filter). For $t = 1, \ldots, T$,

$$\varepsilon_t = y_t - H_t x_{t|t-1} - g_t \tag{3.19a}$$

$$R_t = H_t S_{t|t-1} H_t' + G_t \Sigma_t G_t' \tag{3.19b}$$

$$x_{t|t} = x_{t|t-1} + S_{t|t-1} H_t' R_t^{-1} \varepsilon_t \tag{3.19c}$$

$$S_{t|t} = S_{t|t-1} - S_{t|t-1} H_t' R_t^{-1} H_t S_{t|t-1} \tag{3.19d}$$

$$x_{t+1|t} = f_{t+1} + F_{t+1} x_{t|t} + \Gamma_{t+1} \Sigma_t G_t' R_t^{-1} \varepsilon_t \tag{3.19e}$$

$$\begin{aligned} S_{t+1|t} = {} & F_{t+1} S_{t|t} F_{t+1}' + \Gamma_{t+1}(\Sigma_t - \Sigma_t G_t' R_t^{-1} G_t \Sigma_t)\Gamma_{t+1}' \\ & - F_{t+1} S_{t|t-1} H_t' R_t^{-1} G_t \Sigma_t \Gamma_{t+1}' - \Gamma_{t+1} \Sigma_t G_t' R_t^{-1} H_t S_{t|t-1} F_{t+1}' \end{aligned} \tag{3.19f}$$

We now outline a geometric derivation of the Kalman filter as it gives useful insights into the structure of the linear Gaussian state space model. By geometric we mean that we regard conditional expectations as projections on subspaces and zero correlation or independence as orthogonality. We note that from (3.19a), $\varepsilon_t = H_t(x_t - x_{t|t-1}) + G_t u_t$ and equation (3.19b) follows. Next, we note that $x_{t|t} = E(x_t|y_{1:t-1}, \varepsilon_t) = x_{t|t-1} + \text{cov}(x_t, \varepsilon_t) R_t^{-1} \varepsilon_t$ because ε_t is orthogonal to $y_{1:t-1}$ and equation (3.19c) follows. From equation (3.19c), $x_t - x_{t|t} + S_{t|t-1} H_t' R_t^{-1} \varepsilon_t = x_t - x_{t|t-1}$. Equation (3.19d) follows because $x_t - x_{t|t}$ is orthogonal to $y_{1:t}$ and hence to ε_t. Next we note that $x_{t+1|t} = f_{t+1} + F_{t+1} x_{t|t} + \Gamma_{t+1} E(u_t|y_{1:t-1}, \varepsilon_t)$ and $E(u_t|y_{1:t-1}, \varepsilon_t) = E(u_t|\varepsilon_t) = \Sigma_t G_t' R_t^{-1} \varepsilon_t$, giving equation (3.19e). To obtain (3.19f), we note that $x_{t+1} - x_{t+1|t} = F_{t+1}(x_t - x_{t|t}) + \Gamma_{t+1}(u_t - E(u_t|\varepsilon_t))$ and the result follows after save algebra.

It is instructive to link up the Kalman filter to the Cholesky decomposition of the covariance matrix of the observations $y_{1:T}$. It is sufficient to consider the case of y_t univariate with zero mean. We can write $\text{var}(y_{1:T}) = LDL'$, where L is a lower triangular matrix with ones on the diagonal and D is a diagonal matrix. Let $\eta = L^{-1}y$. Then the sequence $\eta_t, t = 1, \ldots, T$, is independent with $\eta_t \sim N(0, D_t)$, with D_t the tth diagonal element of D. It is straightforward to deduce that $\varepsilon_t = \eta_t$ and $R_t = D_t$ for all t. Thus, the Kalman filter performs the operation $L^{-1}y_{1:T}$. However, the Cholesky decomposition is $O(T^3)$, whereas the Kalman filter is $O(T)$ because it takes into account the state space structure. Conversely, we can perform filtering and smoothing in Gaussian linear state space models using standard matrix operations, although at a greater cost.

3.2 Missing y_t

Section 2.5 provides a general approach to handling missing y_t. However, it is straightforward to generalize the filtering equations for the Gaussian linear state space model to handle missing y_t. Let J_t be the selector matrix such that $y_t^{(o)} = J_t y_t$, where $y_t^{(o)}$ is the subvector of y_t observed at time t. Then the observation equation in the Gaussian linear state space becomes $y_t^{(o)} = J_t(g_t + H_t x_t + G_t u_t)$ and the Kalman filter equations follow by replacing g_t by $J_t g_t$, etc. In particular, if none of y_t is observed, then J_t is null and $x_{t|t} = x_{t|t-1}, S_{t|t} = S_{t|t-1}$.

By using the idea of filtering with missing y_t, it is straightforward to apply the filtering algorithms to obtain one-step and multi-step ahead predictive densities for the states and future observations. Thus, if we have observations $y_{1:T}$ and treat $y_{T+1:T+j}$ as missing, then the filtering algorithm for $i = 1, \ldots, j$ is

$$\begin{aligned}
x_{T+i|T} &= f_{T+i} + F_{T+i} x_{T+i-1|T} \\
S_{T+i|T} &= F_{T+i} S_{T+i-1|T} F'_{T+i} + \Gamma_{T+i} \Sigma_{T+i-1|T} \Gamma'_{T+i} \\
y_{T+i|T} &= g_{T+i} + H_{T+i} x_{T+i|T} \\
\text{var}(y_{t+i}|y_{1:T}) &= H_{T+i} S_{T+i|T} H'_{T+i} + G_{T+i} \Sigma_{t+i} G'_{T+i}
\end{aligned}$$

3.3 Likelihood computation

The likelihood is computed in $O(T)$ evaluations, using the Kalman filter, by noting that $p(y_{1:T}|\theta) = p(\varepsilon_{1:T}|\theta)$ so that the ε_t are independent and

$$\begin{aligned}
p(y_{1:T}|\theta) &= \prod_{t=1}^{T} p(\varepsilon_t|\theta) \\
&= \prod_{t=1}^{T} (\det(2\pi R_t))^{-\frac{1}{2}} \exp\left(-\frac{1}{2}\epsilon_t' R_t^{-1} \epsilon_t\right),
\end{aligned}$$

with the obvious modification when there are missing observations.

3.4 Smoothing

Section 2.4 outlined general smoothing algorithms for state space models. Similarly to the filtering equations, the smoothing equations can be obtained explicitly and more directly for the Gaussian linear state space model case. The smoothing algorithm is given by

Algorithm 2 (Smoothing). $x_{T|T}$ and $S_{T|T}$ are available from the Kalman filter. For $t = T-1, \ldots, 1$.

$$x_{t|T} = x_{t|t} + S_{t|t} F'_{t+1} S^{-1}_{t+1|t} (x_{t+1|T} - x_{t+1|t}) \tag{3.20a}$$

$$S_{t|T} = S_{t|t} - S_{t|t} F'_{t+1} S^{-1}_{t+1|t} (S_{t+1|t} - S_{t+1|T}) S^{-1}_{t+1|t} F_{t+1} S_{t|t} \tag{3.20b}$$

It is again instructive to derive the algorithm using a geometric argument. From (3.9), $p(x_t|y_{1:T}, x_{t+1:T}) = p(x_t|y_{1:t}, x_{t+1}) = p(x_t|y_{1:t}, x_{t+1} - x_{t+1|t})$, and we note that $y_{1:t}$ and $x_{t+1} - x_{t+1|t}$ are orthogonal. To obtain $x_{t|T}$ we note that

$$E(x_t|y_{1:t}, x_{t+1}) = x_{t|t} + S_{t|t}F'_{t+1}S^{-1}_{t+1|t}(x_{t+1} - x_{t+1|t}), \text{ implying that}$$

$$x_{t|T} = x_{t|t} + S_{t|t}F'_{t+1}S^{-1}_{t+1|t}(x_{t+1|T} - x_{t+1|t}).$$

To obtain $S_{t|T}$ we note that

$$x_t - x_{t|T} + S_{t|t}F'_{t+1}S^{-1}_{t+1|t}(x_{t+1|T} - x_{t+1|t}) = x_t - x_{t|t}$$

and that $x_t - x_{t|T}$ is orthogonal to $y_{1:T}$ and so it is orthogonal to $x_{t+1|T} - x_{t+1|t}$. Hence,

$$S_{t|T} = S_{t|t} - S_{t|t}F'_{t+1}S^{-1}_{t+1|t}\text{var}(x_{t+1|T} - x_{t+1|t})S^{-1}_{t+1|t}F_{t+1}S_{t|t}.$$

The expression for $S_{t|T}$ follows by writing $x_{t+1} - x_{t+1|t} = x_{t+1} - x_{t+1|T} + x_{t+1|T} - x_{t+1|t}$ and noting that $x_{t+1} - x_{t+1|T}$ is orthogonal to $y_{1:T}$ while $x_{t+1|T} - x_{t+1|t}$ is a linear function of $y_{1:T}$. This implies that $S_{t+1|t} = S_{t+1|T} + \text{var}(x_{t+1|T} - x_{t+1|t})$.

3.5 Inclusion of covariates

It is straightforward to handle covariates in the observation or state equations. Thus we could have $g_t = w_t'\beta$ and $f_t = w_t'\delta$ where w_t is a vector of covariates at time t and β and δ are regression coefficients. However, this embeds the regression coefficients within the state space structure. An alternative approach dealing with a linear regression model with errors that have a Gaussian linear state space form is given by Kohn and Ansley (1985). Their approach is likely to be computationally more efficient than dealing directly with covariates in the state space model, but there is an initial setup cost.

3.6 Initial conditions for the state vector

The filtering and smoothing algorithms require an initial distribution for x_1. In some problems this distribution is well defined. For example, we obtained the distribution of x_1 in the state space representation of the ARMA(1,1) model at (3.16). In other problems, the distribution of x_1 may not be well defined in which case we may regard x_1 as having a noninformative prior distribution or having a diffuse prior. By a diffuse prior we mean that $x_1 \sim N(0, kI)$, with $k \to \infty$. For example, in the local level model (3.15), it may be sensible to assume that the initial level x_1 is an unknown constant or diffuse. In some problems, we may wish to take the initial conditions as partially diffuse, which means that some elements of x_1 have a diffuse distribution, while the rest have a proper distribution. For example, suppose that y_t is a time series whose first difference $\widetilde{y}_t = y_t - y_{t-1}$ is the first order stationary autoregression $\widetilde{y}_t = \phi \widetilde{y}_{t-1} + e_t$, with $|\phi| < 1$ and $e_t \sim N(0, \sigma_e^2)$. Then y_t can be written in state space form with a two dimensional state vector x_t such that $x_{1t} = y_t$ and $x_{2t} = \widetilde{y}_t$. The observation equation is $y_t = (1, 0)x_t$ and the state transition equation is the pair of equations $x_{1t} = x_{1,t-1} + x_{2t}$ and $x_{2t} = \phi x_{2,t-1} + e_t$. The distribution of $x_{2,1} \sim N(0, \sigma_e^2/(1-\phi^2))$ is well defined, while we may wish to take $x_{1,1}$ as diffuse or at least let it have a zero mean and a large variance. If $x_{1,1}$ is diffuse, the covariance between the first two elements of x_1 is usually taken as zero with no loss of generality.

Ansley and Kohn (1985) show how to generalize the filtering and smoothing algorithms for Gaussian linear state space models to allow for diffuse or partially diffuse initial conditions. They also show how to define the likelihood and compute it efficiently using the generalized filtering algorithm. Kohn and Ansley (1986) apply the ideas in Ansley and Kohn (1985) to univariate ARIMA models with partially diffuse initial conditions. Ansley and Kohn (1990) simplify the general approach of Ansley and Kohn (1985). De Jong (1989) and Koopman (1997) give alternative algorithmic approaches to the same problem.

3.7 Bayesian inference

We have already seen that the Kalman filter computes the likelihood $p(y|\theta)$ for the Gaussian linear state space model and so is the solution to the, typically very high dimensional, integral

$$p(y|\theta) = \int p(y|x;\theta)p(x|\theta)dx.$$

In this case, $p(x|\theta) = p(x_1|\theta)\prod_{t=2}^{T} p(x_t|\theta; x_{t-1})$ is the state transition density and $p(y|x;\theta) = \prod_{t=1}^{T} p(y_t|\theta; x_t)$ is the measurement density for all the observations. Formally, Bayesian inference for the Gaussian linear state space model is obtained by placing a prior $p(\theta)$ on the unknown parameters θ and computing the likelihood $p(y|\theta)$ via the Kalman filter to obtain the posterior density of θ,

$$p(\theta|y) = p(y|\theta)p(\theta)/p(y). \tag{3.21}$$

For the Gaussian linear state space model, the two terms in the numerator are available explicitly. Typically, even for the Gaussian linear state space model, the marginal likelihood, which is also the normalizing constant in the expression in (3.21), is unknown analytically but is given by,

$$p(y) = \int p(y|\theta)p(\theta)d\theta.$$

Working with the numerator of (3.21) is a relatively straightforward problem requiring MCMC methods. The dimension of the parameters θ is often quite small relative to the dimensions of the states over which we have integrated, x. When we move beyond the Gaussian linear state space model, it is no longer possible to analytically obtain the likelihood $p(y|\theta)$ and this approach is no longer directly applicable.

An alternative approach, which is relatively straightforward to generalize to more general non-Gaussian state space models, is to augment the posterior with the states. That is, we consider the joint posterior,

$$p(\theta; x|y) = \frac{p(y|x;\theta)p(x|\theta)p(\theta)}{p(y)}. \tag{3.22}$$

It is important to note that the marginal inference from this joint density $p(\theta|y) = \int p(\theta; x|y)dx$ is the same as in (3.21). We use MCMC to sample under (3.22) resulting in samples $\{\theta^{(j)}; x^{(j)}, j \geq 1\}$, as discussed below, with $\{\theta^{(j)}, j \geq 1\}$ a sample from $p(\theta|y)$.

The posterior density (3.22) also delivers the posterior densities of functionals of the states. For example, in the local level model (3.15), it is of interest to estimate the local mean at a given time point t within the sample (a smoothing problem) as well as to predict the level into the future (a filtering problem), with the parameters integrated out to take into account parameter uncertainty.

The joint posterior $p(x;\theta|y)$ in (3.22) is typically high dimensional as the dimension of x is proportional to the length T of the time series. This means that numerical methods or importance sampling methods are difficult to apply for non-Gaussian state space models. The great advantage of MCMC in high dimensions is that it is possible to reduce the dimension of the problem by considering the full conditional densities arising from the density of interest. For the Gaussian linear state space model, we may consider two of the full conditional densities arising from (3.22). These are,

$$p(x|y;\theta) \propto p(y|x;\theta)p(x|\theta) \quad \text{and} \quad p(\theta|y;x) \propto p(y|x;\theta)p(x|\theta)p(\theta).$$

In practice, it may be difficult to obtain the posterior densities of interest analytically and simulation based approaches are used. For the Gaussian linear state space model, a general Gibbs-type simulation approach is

Algorithm 3 (Simulation smoother). Let $x = x_{1:T}, y = y_{1:T}$. Let $\theta^{(0)}$ be the initial value of θ. For $j \geq 1$,

(1) Generate $x^{(j)} \sim p(x|y;\theta^{(j-1)})$ as a block.
(2) Generate $\theta^{(j)} \sim p(\theta|y, x^{(j-1)})$.

To carry out step 1 of the simulation smoother, we first obtain the conditional means $x_{t|t}$ and covariance matrices $S_{t|t}$ for $t = 1, \ldots, T$ using the Kalman filter. The states are generated as a block as in (3.11). The distribution $p(x_t|y_{1:t}, x_{t+1};\theta)$ is normal with mean $x_{t|t} + S_{t|t}F_t'S_{t+1|t}^{-1}(x_{t+1} - x_{t+1|t})$ and conditional covariance matrix $S_{t|t} - S_{t|t}F_t'S_{t+1|t}^{-1}S_{t+1|t}^{-1}F_tS_{t|t}$ using the same geometric arguments as in Section 3.4.

The block method of generating the states is proposed by Carter and Kohn (1994) and Frűwirth-Schnatter (1994). De Jong and Shephard (1995) call this method the simulation smoother; it is also known as forward filtering and backward smoothing. Alternative implementations of simulation smoothing, with all the states generated as a block, are proposed by De Jong and Shephard (1995) and Durbin and Koopman (2002).

Conditional on the states, the parameters θ in step 2 are usually generated by standard MCMC methods, either as a single block or in blocks. See Section 3.5 of Chib (Chapter 5 this volume) for a general discussion of the choice of proposal densities in MCMC sampling. For example, in the local level model (3.15), it is straightforward to generate σ_e^2 and σ_v^2 from the conditional density $p(\sigma_e^2, \sigma_v^2|y, x) \propto p(y|x, \sigma_e^2)p(x|\sigma_v^2)p(\sigma_e^2)p(\sigma_v^2)$. The point we make here, and elsewhere in the chapter, is that unless we state otherwise, there is no specific time series insight about the way that the parameters are generated.

The simulation smoother (algorithm 3) for obtaining the posterior distributions of both the parameters and the states works well for many cases. However, in some models, the parameter iterates and the state iterates are highly dependent, which makes such a sampling scheme inefficient, and the algorithm requires a large number of iterates to converge and to obtain reliable estimates of posterior functionals. A general approach to overcome this problem is to generate the parameters with the states integrated out as it is straightforward to obtain the likelihood for a Gaussian linear state space model as in Section 3.3. The parameters are then generated using general MCMC methods as in Chib (Chapter 5 this volume). See, for example, Kim et al. (1998), who generate the parameters in an SV model with the states integrated out by forming proposals based on iterating to the mode, while Giordani and Kohn (2010) use adaptive Metropolis Hastings sampling to generate the parameters.

4 Conditionally Gaussian Models

4.1 Discrete mixtures of Gaussian state space models

This section considers a generalization of the Gaussian linear state space model to a discrete mixture of Gaussian linear state space models, with K_t determining the mixture component at time t. Formally, suppose that $K_t, t \geq 1$, is a sequence of discrete random variables so that

$$p(y_t|x_{1:t}, y_{1:t-1}, K_{1:t}; \theta) = p(y_t|x_t, K_t; \theta) \tag{3.23a}$$

$$p(x_{t+1}|x_{1:t}, y_{1:t}, K_{1:t+1}) = p(x_{t+1}|x_t, y_t, K_{t+1}) \tag{3.23b}$$

$$p(K_{t+1}|x_{1:t}, y_{1:t}, K_{1:t}; \theta) = p(K_{t+1}|K_t; \theta). \tag{3.23c}$$

Equation (3.23a) is the "observation" equation, equation (3.23b) is the "state transition" equation and equation (3.23c) is the transition equation for the discrete variables K_t which is assumed to be Markov.

Although (x_t, K_t) can be treated as a single state vector consisting of discrete and continuous components, the treatment is more transparent if we consider them separately.

We assume that $p(x_{t+1}|x_t, y_t, K_t; \theta)$ and $p(y_t|x_t, K_t; \theta)$ are linear and Gaussian and of the form

$$\begin{aligned} y_t &= g_{K_t} + H_{K_t} x_t + G_{K_t} u_t \\ x_{t+1} &= f_{K_{t+1}} + F_{K_{t+1}} x_t + \Gamma_{K_{t+1}} u_t, \end{aligned} \tag{3.24}$$

with $u_t \sim N(0, \Sigma_t)$ an independent sequence. The terms $g_{K_t}, H_{K_t}, G_{K_t}, f_{K_t}, F_{K_t}, \Gamma_{K_t}$ depend on K_t and θ. There are a number of applications that fit into this framework.

Markov switching regression model Suppose that K_t takes the values 1 and 2,

$$y_t = w_t' \beta_{K_t} + \sigma_{K_t} e_t \quad e_t \sim N(0, \sigma^2) \tag{3.25}$$

and the K_t are Markov with transition probabilities $p(K_{t+1}|K_t; \pi)$ that are functions of parameters π. The w_t are the covariates at time t and (β_1, σ_1^2) and (β_2, σ_2^2) are the parameter vectors in regimes 1 and 2. In this model, $g_{K_t} = w_t' \beta_{K_t}$ and the state vector x_t is null.

Flexible local level model with jumps Consider the local level model

$$y_t = x_t + e_t, \quad x_{t+1} = x_t + K_{t+1} v_t, \tag{3.26}$$

with K_t an independent sequence taking the values 0, 1, and 3 with probabilities π_0, π_1, and $1 - \pi_0 - \pi_1$. The errors $e_t \sim N(0, \sigma_e^2)$ and $v_t \sim N(0, \sigma_v^2)$ are independent sequences that are also independent of each other. This model allows for no change in the trend if $K_t = 0$, a standard stochastic evolution of the trend if $K_t = 1$, and a jump in the trend if $K_t = 3$.

More generally, we can have regression models whose parameters are allowed to stay constant or evolve through time and errors in the observation equation and state transition equation that can be heavy tailed to allow for outliers and level shifts.

4.1.1 Bayesian inference

We now show how to carry out inference by simulation for conditionally Gaussian state space models by generalizing the simulation smoother discussed in Section 3.

Algorithm 4 (Simulation smoother for conditionally Gaussian model). Let $x = x_{1:T}, y = y_{1:T}, K = K_{1:T}$. Let $K^{(0)}$ and $\theta^{(0)}$ be the initial values of K and θ. For $j \geq 1$,

(1) Generate $x^{(j)} \sim p(x|y, K^{(j-1)}; \theta^{(j-1)})$.
(2) Generate $K^{(j)} \sim p(K|y, x^{(j)}; \theta^{(j-1)})$.
(3) Generate $\theta^{(j)} \sim p(\theta|y, x^{(j)}, K^{(j)})$.

Step 1 is carried out by first running the Kalman filter because all the conditional distributions are Gaussian so that it is only necessary to update the conditional means and variances. Suppose that for a given t we have the distribution of $p(x_t|y_{1:t}, K_{1:t}; \theta)$. Then $p(x_{t+1}|y_{1:t}, K_{1:t}; \theta)$ and $p(x_{t+1}|y_{1:t+1}, K_{1:t+1}; \theta)$ are computed in exactly the same way as in Section 3.1. Thus, we have $p(x_t|y_{1:t}, K_{1:t}; \theta)$ for $t = 1, \ldots, T$. We now generate

$x_t, t = T, \ldots, 1$ as in Section 3.7. Step 2 is similar to step 1. We first run a filter to compute $p(K_t|y_{1:t}, x_{1:t}, \theta)$ for $t = 1, \ldots, T$. Thus, suppose that for a given t, we have $p(K_t|y_{1:t}, x_{1:t}, \theta)$. Then, from (3.4) and replacing integration by summation

$$p(K_{t+1}|y_{1:t}, x_{1:t}; \theta) = \sum_{K_t} p(K_{t+1}|K_t; \theta) p(K_t|y_{1:t}, x_{1:t}, \theta)$$
$$p(K_{t+1}|y_{1:t+1}, x_{1:t+1}; \theta) \propto p(y_{t+1}|x_{t+1}, K_{t+1}; \theta) p(K_{t+1}|y_{1:t}, x_{1:t}; \theta), \tag{3.27}$$

where the constant of proportionality in the second equation is evaluated by noting that

$$\sum_{K_{t+1}} p(K_{t+1}|y_{1:t+1}, x_{1:t+1}; \theta) = 1.$$

Once the densities $p(K_t|y_{1:t}, x_{1,t}; \theta)$ are obtained for $t = 1, \ldots, T$, the $K_t, t = T, \ldots, 1$ are generated by simulation smoothing similarly to the way that the x_t are generated in Section 3.7. Thus, K_T is generated from the density $p(K_T|y_{1:T}, x_{1,T}; \theta)$ which is available from the filtering. Now suppose that $K_T, \ldots, K_{t+1}$ have been generated. Then

$$p(K_t|y_{1:T}, x_{1:T}, K_{t+1:T}; \theta) \propto p(K_{t+1}|K_t; \theta) p(K_t|y_{1:t}, x_{1:t}; \theta). \tag{3.28}$$

The density $p(K_t|y_{1:T}, x_{1:T}, K_{t+1:T}; \theta)$ is obtained by evaluating the right side for each value of K_t and normalizing. See Carter and Kohn (1994) for details. Step 3 is carried out by general MCMC methods.

A large number of Markov mixture models can be estimated using this approach. However, in some cases, the iterates of the discrete variables K and the states x are highly dependent when running algorithm 4. In this case algorithm 4 will be inefficient and produce poor results. Consider, for example, the local level model where a given K_t is 0. Then, $x_{t+1} = x_t$ and conversely if $x_{t+1} = x_t$, then K_t must be zero almost surely. This leads to a degenerate sampling scheme as noted by Carter and Kohn (1996). They propose the following sampling scheme that generates the K_t without conditioning on the states.

Algorithm 5 (Reduced conditional sampling). Let $x = x_{1:T}, y = y_{1:T}, K = K_{1:T}$. Let $K^{(0)}, \theta^{(0)}$ be the initial values of K and θ. For $j \geq 1$,

(1) For each $t = 1, \ldots, T$, generate $K_t^{(j)} \sim p(K_t|K_{1:t-1}^{(j)}, K_{t+1:T}^{(j-1)}, y; \theta^{(j-1)})$.
(2) Generate $x^{(j)} \sim p(x|y, K^{(j)}; \theta^{(j-1)})$.
(3) Generate $\theta^{(j)} \sim p(\theta|y, x^{(j)}, K^{(j)})$.

Carter and Kohn (1996) call algorithm 5 a reduced conditional sampling scheme because we can view step 1 as generating both x and K_t as a block with K_t generated as above, and then x generated from $p(x|K_{1:t}^{(j)}, K_{t+1:T}^{(j-1)}, y; \theta^{(j-1)})$. However, it is unnecessary to actually generate x because K_{t+1} is generated without conditioning on x.

Let $K_{\backslash t} = \{K_s, s = 1, \ldots, T, s \neq t\}$. A straightforward implementation of algorithm 5 obtains the density

$$p(K_t | K_{s \neq t}, y, \theta) \propto p(y|K;\theta)p(K_t|K_{\backslash t};\theta) \propto p(y|K;\theta)p(K_t|K_{t-1};\theta)p(K_{t+1}|K_t;\theta)$$

by evaluating $p(y|K;\theta)$ for each value of K_t using the Kalman filter, computing $p(y|K;\theta)$, $p(K_t|K_{t-1};\theta)$, and $p(K_{t+1}|K_t;\theta)$ and then normalizing the probabilities so they sum to 1. This approach requires $O(T)$ operations for each t and hence $O(T^2)$ operations overall to generate all the K_t. Such an approach may be quite slow in large samples and Carter and Kohn (1996) propose an $O(T)$ algorithm for generating all the K_t. An improved $O(T)$ version of algorithm 5 is proposed by Gerlach et al. (2000). Further improvements and applications are given by Giordani and Kohn (2008).

Example: A Markov switching model of US industrial production with outliers and level shifts Giordani et al. (2007) investigate nonlinearities in G7 industrial production (IP) series using a two-regime Markov switching model, extended to allow for structural changes in the mean and in the variance and for additive and innovation outliers. Here we extend their sample of IP growth rates to the period 1950q2 to 2009q2 (the series in Giordani et al. 2007, ends in 2004q1).[1] The model is

$$\begin{aligned}
y_t &= z_t + v_t + \sigma_t K_{\delta t}\delta_t + \sigma_t K_{at} a_t, \\
z_t &= \phi_1 z_{t-1} + \sigma_t K_{et} e_t, \\
v_t &= v_{t-1} + \sigma_t K_{ot} o_t, \\
\sigma_t &= \sigma_1 I_{\{t \leq \tau\}} + \sigma_2 I_{\{t > \tau\}}, \\
\delta_t &= \delta_1 I_{\{t \leq \tau\}} + \delta_2 I_{\{t > \tau\}},
\end{aligned} \tag{3.29}$$

where y_t is the quarterly IP growth rate in annualized percentage points, and a_t, e_t, and o_t are standard normal. Additive and innovation outliers are defined by the values of K_{at} and K_{et} respectively. Switching between the high- and low-growth states is determined by $K_{\delta t} \in \{0, 1\}$, where $K_{\delta,t}$ is a two-state Markov switching process, while $K_{a,t}$, $K_{e,t}$, and $K_{o,t}$ are Bernoulli and independent of each other. For identification purposes we assume $\delta_t < 0$ for all t, such that $K_{\delta t} = 0$ (1) corresponds with the high-growth (low-growth) state. By construction, σ_t^2 and δ_t experience a single structural break, at an unknown point τ. Occasional permanent shifts (of unknown number and size) in the growth rate are captured by the time-varying process v_t. The priors and inference are the same as in Giordani et al. (2007).

The top panel of Figure 3.1 shows the posterior mean probability of a recession state and the bottom panel shows IP growth and $v_t + \sigma_t K_{\delta t}\delta_t$. There is no evidence of time variation in v_t and very strong evidence of outliers. The posterior probabilities of no

[1] The IP series that we use is aggregated from the monthly seasonally adjusted industrial production index. Source: Board of Governors of the Federal Reserve System. Series ID INDPRO, last update 15 May 2009.

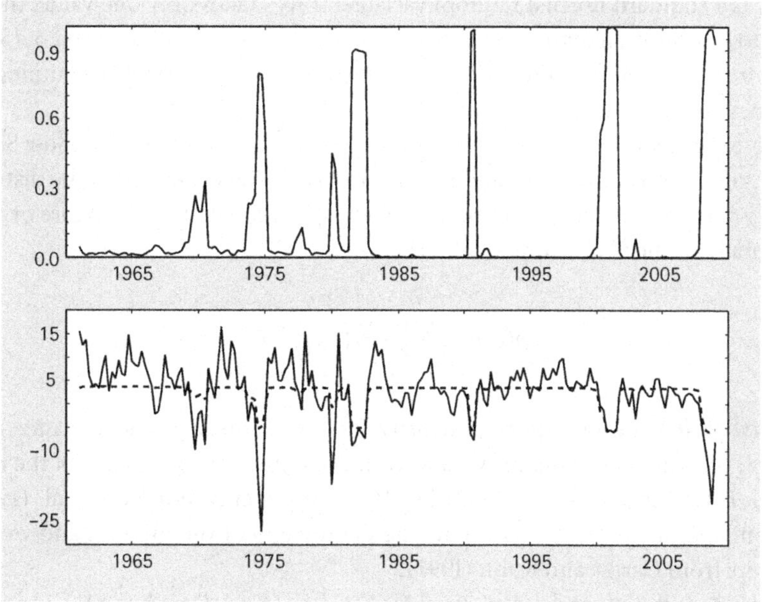

FIGURE 3.1 US industrial production Top panel shows the posterior probability of a recession state. Bottom panel shows IP growth and $v_t + \sigma_t K_{\delta t}\delta_t$.

shift in v_t and no outliers in the sample are 0.54 and $< 10^{-5}$ and the Bayes factors are consistent with this. While Giordani et al. (2007) observe a sizable reduction in the depth of the business cycle after approximately 1980 ($\delta_1\sigma_1 > \delta_2\sigma_2$), based on a sample ending in 2004, the size of the 2008–9 recession reverses this conclusion.

4.1.2 Modeling shifts in innovation variance

McCulloch and Tsay (1993) model shifts in the variance using a state space approach with mixture innovations. Giordani and Kohn (2008) show how to use the more efficient algorithm of Gerlach et al. (2000) once the distribution of the squared residuals is accurately approximated by a mixture of normals, a common practice in the stochastic volatility literature (e.g. Kim et al. 1998).

Let

$$y_t = \sigma_t \epsilon_t, \tag{3.30}$$

where ϵ_t is a standard normal independent sequence. It is straightforward to allow a time-varying conditional mean for y_t as in Giordani and Kohn (2008). Following the stochastic volatility literature, we work with $x_t = \log(\sigma_t^2)$, ensuring that σ_t^2 is always positive. It is then natural to model permanent shifts in σ_t^2 as

$$x_t = x_{t-1} + \sigma_v(K_{2,t})v_t, \tag{3.31}$$

where v_t is a standard normal random variable. If $K_{2,t}$ takes only one value, the model reduces to smoothly changing variances. We can set $\sigma_v(K_{2,t} = 0) = 0$ and $\sigma_v(K_{2,t} = 1) = \sigma_v^* > 0$ for occasional shifts. More complex processes are easily accommodated in this framework.

We note that $\log(y_t^2) = x_t + \zeta_t$, where ζ_t is $\log(\chi_1^2)$ distributed. We follow Shephard (1994), Carter and Kohn (1997), and Kim et al. (1998) who observe that the distribution of a $\log(\chi_1^2)$ random variable can be accurately approximated by a mixture of normals with a small number I of components. That is,

$$p(\zeta_t) \simeq \sum_{i=1}^{I} \pi_i N(\zeta_t; g_i, \gamma_i^2), \tag{3.32}$$

where $N(\zeta; a, b^2)$ means a normal density in ζ with mean a and variance b^2, with $\{\pi_i, g_i, \gamma_i^2\}$ the known weight, mean, and variance of the ith component of the mixture, $i = 1, \ldots, I$. Carter and Kohn (1997) use five components and Kim et al. (1998) use seven components. Both papers report the parameters of the mixture and we use the parameters from Carter and Kohn (1997).

We introduce the latent discrete variables $K_{1,t}, t = 1, \ldots, T$, with the $K_{1,t}$ independent and each $K_{1,t}$ taking the values $1, \ldots, I$ such that

$$\zeta_t | (K_{1,t} = 1) \sim N(\zeta_t; g_i, \gamma_i^2) \quad \text{and} \quad \Pr(K_{1,t} = i) = \pi_i. \tag{3.33}$$

Using the approximation (3.32), we write the model (3.30) and (3.31) in conditionally Gaussian state space form

$$z_t = g_{K_{1,t}} + x_t + \gamma_{K_{1,t}} e_t\,, \quad x_t = x_{t-1} + \sigma_v(K_{2,t}) v_t, \tag{3.34}$$

where $z_t = \log(y_t^2)$, and e_t and v_t are standard normal.

Our experience suggests that the most efficient algorithm draws the $K_{2,t}$ one at a time conditional on the $K_{1:T}$ using the algorithm of Gerlach et al. (2000) and $K_{1:T}$ in one block conditional on the $x_{1:T}$ and $K_{1,1:T}$ as in Carter and Kohn (1994).

Example: Changing mean, dynamics and volatility in US inflation Giordani and Kohn (2008) model US inflation as an AR(1) process with outliers and random breaks in intercept, autoregressive parameter, and residual variance. We use the same model and priors for the updated sample 1960q1–2009q2.[2] The model is

$$y_t = c_t + b_t y_{t-1} + \sigma_t K_{e,t} e_t$$
$$c_t = c_{t-1} + K_{c,t} u_t^c$$

[2] The US inflation data we use is aggregated from the monthly consumer price index for all urban consumers, all items, seasonally adjusted. Source: U.S. Department of Labor: Bureau of Labor Statistics. Series ID: CPIAUCSL. Last updated: 2009-05-15.

$$
\begin{aligned}
b_t &= b_{t-1} + K_{b,t} u_t^b \\
\log(\sigma_t^2) &= \log(\sigma_{t-1}^2) + K_{v,t} v_t \\
p(K_t) &\equiv p(K_{m,t}, K_{v,t}) = p(K_{m,t}) p(K_{v,t}) = p(K_t | K_{s \neq t}),
\end{aligned}
\tag{3.35}
$$

where $K_{m,t} = (K_{e,t}, K_{c,t}, K_{b,t})$. The latent variable $K_{e,t}$ takes the values $(1, 2.5)$, where 1 is a standard observation and 2.5 an innovation outlier; $K_{c,t}$ takes the values $(0, 0.2, 1)$ and $K_{b,t}$ takes the values $(0, 0.5)$. For ease of interpretation, we assume that a break and an outlier cannot occur simultaneously, but we do allow breaks in c_t and b_t to occur both separately and jointly. $K_{v,t}$ can take the values (0, 1.39); $\sigma_t = \sigma_{t-1}$ for $K_{v,t} = 0$, while $K_{v,t} = 1.39$ and $v_t = 1\,(-1)$ imply $\sigma_t/\sigma_{t-1} \simeq 2\,(\sigma_t/\sigma_{t-1} \simeq 0.5)$. The prior probabilities of interventions are fixed and reflect the assumption that breaks in any parameter are rare (the combined probability of a break in c_t and/or b_t is 1%, so the prior mean interval between breaks is 25 years; the probability of a break in variance is also 1%).

Figure 3.2 summarizes the results. The posterior means of c_t, b_t, and σ_t show substantial time variation, with b_t and c_t positively correlated (high inflation is locally more persistent) and σ_t shows the largest shifts, with a dramatic surge at the end of the sample.

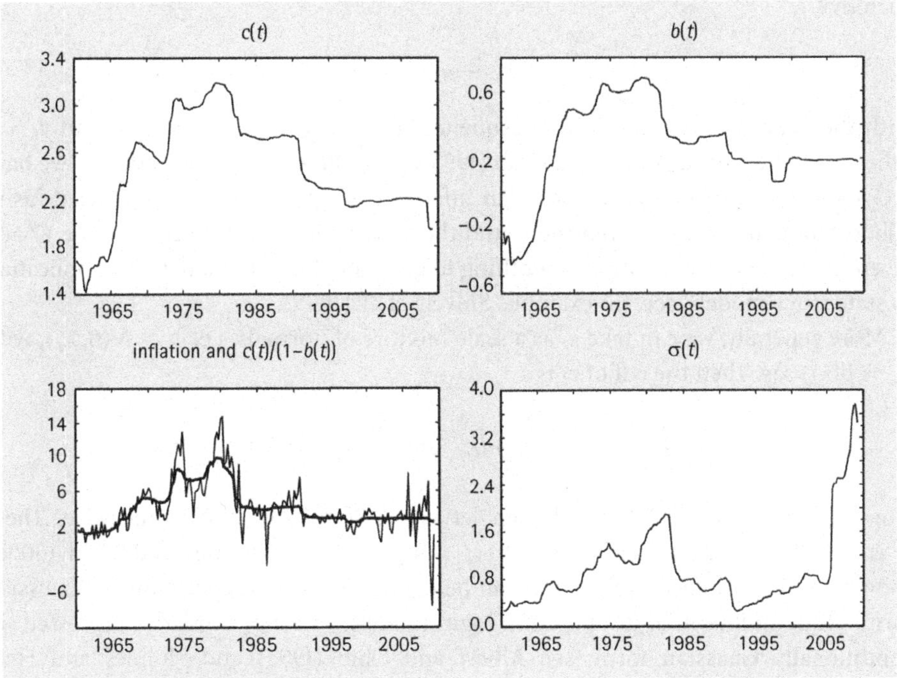

FIGURE 3.2 US inflation data

Notes: Plots of the posterior means of $b_t, c_t, c_t/(1 - b_t)$, and σ_t, together with the inflation data.

4.2 Auxiliary latent variable models

This section discusses non-Gaussian state space models that become Gaussian if we condition on a set of auxiliary latent variables. Such auxiliary variable approaches to non-Gaussian models are particulary important in time series because the dimension of the state vector is $O(T)$. Hence, the methods discussed in this section can be much more efficient than the more general methods considered in Section 6.

One example of such a model is the SV model (3.3). In Section 4.1.2 we approximated this model by the model (3.34), which has an error term in the observation equation that is a mixture of normals. Conditional on the discrete variables $\{K_{1,t}, K_{2,t}, t \geq 1\}$, this becomes a Gaussian state space model.

A second example is the binary probit state space model. Suppose that $y_{1:T}$ are binary observations taking the values 0 and 1, and such that

$$\Pr(y_t = 1|s_t) = \Phi(s_t), \quad s_t = Hx_t, \quad x_{t+1} = f_{t+1} + F_{t+1}x_t + \Gamma_{t+1}v_t \qquad v_t \sim N(0, I), \tag{3.36}$$

where s_t is a univariate signal and $\Phi(\cdot)$ is the standard normal cumulative distribution function (cdf). Following Albert and Chib (1993), we introduce the latent variables y_t^* such that

$$y_t^* = s_t + e_t, \tag{3.37}$$

with the e_t an independent $N(0, 1)$ sequence, and define $y_t = 1$ if $y_t^* > 0$ and $y_t = 0$ otherwise. Then, as in Albert and Chib (1993), y_t satisfies (3.36). Given the y_t^*, we have a Gaussian state space model. Bayesian inference using MCMC now proceeds as in Albert and Chib (1993). Given the s_t and the observations y_t, we generate the y_t^* and given the y_t^* we use simulation smoothing to generate the s_t. For a detailed application to state space models, see, for example, Shively et al. (1999).

More generally, we can take e_t as a scale mixture of normals, i.e. $e_t \sim N(0, \lambda_t)$, with $\lambda_t \sim p(\lambda_t)$ say. Then the cdf of e_t is

$$\Psi(z) = \int \Phi(z/\sqrt{\lambda})p(\lambda)d\lambda \quad \text{and} \quad \Pr(y_t = 1|s_t) = \Psi(s_t).$$

Now define y_t^* as in (3.37) and then let $y_t = 1$ if $y_t^* > 0$ and 0 otherwise. Then, it is straightforward to show that $\Pr(y_t = 1|s_t) = \Psi(s_t)$. Holmes and Held (2006) show that binary logistic regression can be expressed in such conditionally Gaussian form. The multinomial probit and logit models can be similarly expressed in conditionally Gaussian form, see Albert and Chib (1993) and Holmes and Held (2006). Frűwirth-Schnatter and Wagner (2006) and Frűwirth-Schnatter and Wagner (2008) show how to express the Poisson and binomial models in conditionally Gaussian form.

5 Multivariate Gaussian and conditionally Gaussian state space models

The extension of the state space framework to the multivariate case is straightforward in the sense that the general filtering, smoothing, and simulation formulae in Sections 3 and 4.1 are unchanged if y_t is a vector. The use of conjugate priors allows parameter vectors of very large dimensions to be updated in successive Gibbs steps, analogously to the univariate case (see Koop and Korobilis 2009; Del Negro and Schorfheide 2010).[3] The main modeling challenge in the multivariate case is the need to contain the natural quadratic expansion of the number of parameters and states without imposing excessively stringent assumptions on the evolution of the individual series. This can be achieved via smoothness priors or variable selection priors, or via a common factor structure. See for example Cripps et al. (2005) and George et al. (2008) for variable and covariance selection to reduce the dimension of the parameter space of a multivariate regression model.

This section provides an introduction to some of the most common multivariate state space models: local level models, vector autoregressive (VAR) plus noise models, time-varying parameter VAR models, regime switching and change-point VAR models, and dynamic factor models.

5.1 Multivariate local level and VAR plus noise models

The local level model (3.15) is easily generalized to a vector of observables,

$$y_t = x_t + e_t, \quad e_t \sim N(0, \Sigma_e), \quad x_t = x_{t-1} + v_t, \quad v_t \sim N(0, \Sigma_v).$$

Sampling $\Sigma_e|(x, y)$ and $\Sigma_v|x$ is straightforward assuming conditionally conjugate priors, and $x|(y, \Sigma_e, \Sigma_u)$ is updated as in Section 3.7. Harrison and West (1997) provide an early Bayesian treatment. An interesting extension is to assume a VAR process for the local level, so that the observed vector is generated by a VAR process corrupted by white Gaussian noise

$$\begin{aligned} y_t &= y_t^* + e_t \, , \; e_t \sim N(0, \Sigma_e) \\ y_t^* &= c + R_1 y_{t-1}^* + \ldots + R_p y_{t-p}^* + v_t \, , \; v_t \sim N(0, \Sigma_v). \end{aligned}$$

[3] Koop and Korobilis (2009) provide Matlab code for for VARs, TVP-VARs, and factor models at http://personal.strath.ac.uk/gary.koop/bayes_matlab_code_by_koop_and_korobilis.html.

The state vector is $x_t = \{y_t^{*\prime}, \ldots, y_{t-p}^{*\prime}\}'$ and the parameters vector is $\theta = \{\Sigma_\epsilon, c, R_1, \ldots, R_p, \Sigma_v\}$. Sampling of $\theta|x, y$ is again straightforward assuming conditionally conjugate priors. If desired, the stationarity of y_t^* can be enforced with a rejection step. When priors on the unconditional mean of the process are available, we can generalize the VAR with priors on the mean as in Villani (2009) and write the transition equation as

$$y_t^* = \mu + R_1(y_{t-1}^* - \mu) + \ldots + R_p(y_{t-p}^* - \mu) + v_t.$$

5.2 Time-varying parameter VAR models

VAR models with time-varying parameters (TVP-VAR) have been popular in Bayesian econometrics since Doan et al. (1984). The expression "time varying parameters" is, by convention, typically used with the implicit assumption that the transition innovations are Gaussian. Assuming a Gaussian random walk evolution of the parameters, a TVP-VAR(1) is

$$y_t = c_t + (I \otimes y_{t-1}')\beta_t + e_t\,, \qquad e_t \sim N(0, \Sigma_e)$$

$$x_t = x_{t-1} + v_t\,, \qquad v_t \sim N(0, \Sigma_v)$$

$$x_t = \begin{pmatrix} c_t \\ \beta_t \end{pmatrix}$$

Relaxing the fixed parameter assumption is appealing as economic environments are often thought to evolve through time because of a variety of factors including technology, institutional changes, preferences, and learning. A different interpretation of parameter variation is proposed by Harrison and West (1997) who argue that parameter variation can approximate un-modeled nonlinearities and omitted variables, and is therefore a useful tool for forecasting or as a first step in building nonlinear models, at least as long as the nonlinear behavior implies VAR coefficients with high persistency.

Inference by Gibbs sampling for TVP-VARs is straightforward assuming Wishart priors on Σ_e and Σ_v, and a normal prior on β_0 (see Koop and Korobilis 2009; Del Negro and Schorfheide, Chapter 7 this volume). However, convergence and mixing of the Gibbs chain, which can be slow even in the univariate case, should be carefully monitored. Moreover, the large number of states and parameters to estimate can quickly lead to overfitting (often a problem even in fixed parameter VARs), so thoughtful and parsimonious priors are recommended, as in Doan et al. (1984) or Amisano and Federico (2005).

A drawback of TVP-AR and VAR models is the difficulty in imposing non-exploding behavior or other constraints when the states $\beta_{1:T}$ are updated in one block. One option is to express the transition equation as in Doan et al. (1984):

$$\beta_t = \alpha\overline{\beta} + (1 - \alpha)\beta_{t-1} + v_t.$$

The stationarity of β_t can then be imposed by constraining $|\alpha| < 1$. However, the possibility of explosive y_t at some time point is not ruled out, in the sense that, for some t, $E(y_{t+j}|y_{1:t})$ and $\text{var}(y_{t+j}|y_{1:t})$ may both grow exponentially with j. However, the acceptance rates may be very low. Updating $\beta_t|\beta_{\neq t}$ one at a time can solve this problem but at the expense of increased computational costs and slower mixing. See Koop and Potter (2008) for a discussion.

Koop et al. (2009) construct a nonlinear VAR using a dynamic mixture state space approach, extending the model of Primiceri (2005) along the lines suggested by Giordani and Kohn (2008). Their model nests a time-varying parameter VAR but makes the state innovations, i.e. the innovations to the VAR linear coefficients, mixtures of normals, with the restriction that all linear coefficients shift at the same time, and also allows for time-varying residual log variances and correlations.

5.3 Regime switching and multiple change-point VARs

A VAR with regime switching is written as

$$y_t = c_{K_t} + B_{K_t} z_t + \Sigma_{K_t}^{1/2} e_t,$$

where $z_t = \{y'_{t-1}, \ldots, y'_{t-p}\}'$ and K_t is a Markov discrete latent variable.

Inference by Gibbs sampling is in principle simple for this model, even when the number of parameters is large. Given all parameters, $K|y, \theta$ can be updated in one block as in the univariate case. Given the discrete states K, the VAR parameters in each state have standard normal inverse gamma posteriors. Use of filtering and smoothing recursions is unnecessary, so inference is fast even in large dimensions. However, multiple modes and slow mixing can make inference problematic in practice (Sims et al., 2008).

Chib (1998) models multiple change-points (also called breaks, or shifts), with large efficiency gains over previous samplers, by framing change-point problems as regime-switching problems, with transition probabilities constrained so that regimes come in a non-reversible sequence.

Regime switching and change-point models invariably assume that all parameters change at the same time (unless some are forced to be constant at all time points). Without this restriction, a change-point model would need to keep track of M^p regimes, where $M - 1$ is the maximum number of breaks in each parameter and p is the number of parameters that are allowed to change, implying at least $O(nM^p)$ operations to draw the break dates. When the number of series and parameters is large, forcing all parameters to shift jointly can reduce the chances of finding genuine shifts. Andersson and Karlsson (2008) find that, in simulated samples of the size normally encountered in macroeconomics, the determination of the correct number of change-points is considerably more difficult if redundant lags are included in the VAR. They suggest that this is due to redundant variables leading to overfitting. We propose the alternative interpretation that since redundant variables make the detection of shifts harder because they are in fact associated with parameter values that, being near zero in all regimes, can in fact be considered constant. The problem is of course aggravated if the shifts only affect a subset of the variables.

5.4 Dynamic factor models

Dynamic factor models (DFM) are used to parsimoniously model multivariate conditional densities. Consider, for example, the following Gaussian dynamic factor model,

$$y_t = \mu + Ax_t + e_t, \qquad e_{jt} \sim N(0, \sigma_j^2),\ j = 1, \dots, p$$

$$x_t = R_1 x_{t-1} + \dots + R_p x_{t-p} + v_t\,, \qquad v_t \sim N(0, V).$$

The possibly high-dimensional vector y_t depends linearly on a smaller number of latent variables x_t (the *common factors*) and on idiosyncratic noise e_t, where $E(x_t e_{t-i}) = 0$ for all i. The model can be extended to make each e_{jt} an AR process or simplified by assuming that the common factors evolve independently of each other (i.e. $R_i, i = 1, \dots, p$ and V are diagonal). The elements of the $p \times l$ matrix A are called *factor loadings* and are identified only up to an orthonormal rotation. The most common identifying restrictions set the upper $l \times l$ block of A to a lower triangular matrix with unit diagonal, which helps interpret the factors but also makes inference on all predictive distributions depend on the ordering of the variables within the vector y_t.

Inference by Gibbs sampling is straightforward assuming conjugate priors. Given the system parameters $\mu, A, R_1, \dots, R_p, \sigma_1^2, \dots, \sigma_p^2, V$, the simulation smoother of Section 3.7 is used to draw $x_{1:T}$, and all the parameters can be updated conditional on y and x. However, since in general the computing time for the Kalman filter is quadratic in p, a fully Bayesian analysis is only feasible in small and moderate dimensions. In some cases, the Kalman filter can be speeded up by exploiting known structure (such as diagonality) in the state space matrices. See Koopman and Durbin (2000).

Factor models with no dynamics in x_t and e_t require no filtering and can be analyzed even with p in the thousands (see Carvalho et al. 2008 for work on variable selection on the factor loadings).

Conditionally, Gaussian DFM are obtained by making the system vectors and matrices g_t, H_t, G_t, f_t, F_t, and Γ_t depend on discrete latent variables K_t. Kim and Nelson (1999) apply Markov switching DFM to business cycle analysis. Pitt and Shephard (1999c), Aguilar and West (2000), and Chib et al. (2006) model heteroskedastic multivariate data by letting the factors follow stochastic volatility processes. Del Negro and Otrok (2008) study the evolution of the international business cycle using a dynamic factor model with stochastic volatility in both the latent factors and idiosyncratic components, as well as time-varying factor loadings in the form of a univariate random walk for the free elements of $\text{vec}(A_t)$.

6 MCMC INFERENCE FOR GENERAL STATE SPACE MODELS

This section develops inference for general non-Gaussian state space models. In some cases, it is possible to obtain more efficient exact or approximate sampling schemes by introducing auxiliary variables as discussed in Section 4.2. However, this is not always possible to do in an efficient manner. For the purposes of this section the latent states x_t are Markov so that (3.1b) reduces to $p(x_{t+1}|x_t, y_t; \theta) = p(x_{t+1}|x_t; \theta)$ as in (3.2).

The stochastic volatility model at equation (3.3) is an example of a non-Gaussian state space model. Within the econometrics literature, this model is seen as a generalization of the Black-Scholes model for option pricing that allows for volatility clustering in returns, as discussed in Shephard (1996). There have been different methodologies proposed in the context of parameter estimation for such models. Harvey et al. (1994) advocate a Quasi Maximum Likelihood procedure, whereas Jacquier et al. (1994) used MCMC methods in order to construct a Markov chain that draws directly from the posterior distributions of the model parameters and unobserved volatilities. More recent literature considers leverage and jumps, making the model more nonlinear.

As a second example, we consider a state space model with a Poisson observation equation,

$$y_t \sim Po\{\exp(x_t)\} \qquad x_{t+1} = \mu(1-\phi) + \phi x_t + \sigma_v v_t, \;\; t = 1, \ldots, T. \tag{3.38}$$

The log intensity x_t follows a first-order autoregressive process. This model may represent for instance the number of trades or transactions taking place within an hour. It is also used to model credit risk (e.g. Lando 1998). The binary model at equation (3.36) is also an example of the non-Gaussian state space model we consider in this section.

The aim of MCMC inference is to sample from the joint distribution $p(\theta, x_{1:T}|y_{1:T})$ for the general state space model (3.1a) and (3.1b) and where the state equation is Markov as $p(x_{t+1}|x_t; \theta)$. The Bayesian inference problem is identical to that discussed in Section 3.7. Again a general approach, although not necessarily the optimal approach, to MCMC for such models is to break the MCMC sweep into two main Gibbs-type stages.

Algorithm 6 (Non-Gaussian MCMC). Assume that we have the sample $\theta^{(j)}$ and $x_{1:T}^{(j)}$ for the jth iteration of the MCMC scheme. We then cycle through:

(1) Sample $\theta^{(j+1)} \sim p(\theta|y_{1:T}; x_{1:T}^{(j)})$.
(2) Sample $x_{1:T}^{(j+1)} \sim p(x_{1:T}|y_{1:T}; \theta^{(j+1)})$.

This is similar to algorithm 3 in Section 3.7. The purpose of algorithm 6 is to qualitatively suggest the type of MCMC sampling we may need to undertake for non-Gaussian state space models. In practice, in both Steps 1 and 2 the parameters and states may be sampled in blocks using either Gibbs or Metropolis Hastings steps. This is in contrast to Section 3.7, in which simulation in Step 2 can be performed exactly by applying the simulation smoother.

The approach of algorithm 6 can lead to slow mixing in the resulting Markov chain, which can be measured by the inefficiency factors defined in Section 6.1. The issue of parameterization is considered in Section 6.2. Closed form analytic results for the inefficiency of different parameterisations are difficult to establish in general. However, the closed form results which exist for the linear Gaussian state space models may indicate parameterization principles for more general models. In Section 6.3, it is argued that single move methods (which move a single state at a time) generally perform poorly. Analytic results may be obtained for simple state space models which again shed light on convergence behavior in more general models. To combat the slow mixing of single move methods, the blocking method (which moves large blocks of states) is considered in Section 6.4.

6.1 Inefficiency and convergence problems

The issue of efficiency in the output of MCMC is discussed in more detail in Section 3.4 of Chib (Chapter 5, this volume). Consider the estimation of the moments of $\{\theta^{(j)}\}$. The asymptotic variance of an estimate of $E(g(\theta)|y)$ is a product of the inefficiency τ_g times what is obtained if independent sampling could be used, where the inefficiency τ_g depends on g and is defined as

$$\tau_g = \sum_{k=-\infty}^{\infty} \rho_k = 1 + 2\sum_{k=1}^{\infty} \rho_k,$$

and ρ_k is the autocorrelation function of the chain $g(\theta^{(j)})$. The interpretation of the inefficiency factor is that in order to get the same accuracy for $E(g(\theta)|y)$ as, say, 100 independent draws, the MCMC scheme needs to be run for $100 \times \tau_g$ iterations. In practice, using N samples from the Markov chain, τ is estimated using the correlogram and a Parzen kernel (see e.g. Priestley 1981). An alternative estimator is given in Section 3.4 of Chapter 5.

6.2 Inefficiency analysis: Parameterization

Parameterization is important when applying MCMC to latent statistical models. A very simple change of parameterization can make the difference between a very slow Markov chain and one which is close to independent. Further, the computational cost or coding intricacy involved in a reparameterization is frequently very low.

Our discussion follows Pitt and Shephard (1999a) who examine the issue of the effect parameterization has on MCMC inference for state space form models. Pitt and

Shephard (1999a) extend the work of Gelfand et al. (1995) and Roberts and Sahu (1997) who consider the issue of parameterization for hierarchical linear models.

Pitt and Shephard (1999a) consider the AR(1) plus noise model

$$y_t = \mu + x_t^* + \sigma_e e_t, \qquad x_{t+1}^* = \phi x_t^* + \sigma_v v_t. \tag{3.39}$$

The error terms e_t and v_t are independent standard Gaussian. The parameters σ_e^2, σ_v^2, and ϕ are known and $|\phi| < 1$ so the model is stationary. The only unknown parameter is the unconditional mean μ of the observations. The parameterization (3.39) is called uncentered (see Roberts and Sahu 1997). An equivalent centered parameterization is

$$y_t = x_t + \sigma_e e_t, \qquad x_{t+1} = \mu(1-\phi) + \phi x_t + \sigma_v v_t. \tag{3.40}$$

In either case, it is straightforward to apply the Gibbs sampler. In the centered model, this consists of sampling from $p(\mu|y_{1:T}; x_{1:T})$, which has closed form if a conjugate Gaussian prior is used, and then generating $x_{1:T}$ from $p(x_{1:T}|y_{1:T}; \mu)$ using a simulation smoother (see (3.11)). The mean μ and $x_{1,T}^*$ are similarly sampled for the noncentred parameterization. The marginal variance for the states in both models is $\sigma_x^2 = \sigma_v^2/(1-\phi^2)$, but the two chains exhibit radically different behavior.

Pitt and Shephard (1999a) show that as $T \to \infty$ (and this is also true for moderate T in practice), the relative efficiency (the ratio of the inefficiencies from Section 6.1) of the centered parameterization to the uncentered parameterization for the parameter μ lies in the interval,

$$\left(\frac{1}{2} \frac{\sigma_x^2}{\sigma_e^2} \frac{(1+\phi)}{(1-\phi)}, 2\frac{\sigma_x^2}{\sigma_e^2} \frac{(1+\phi)}{(1-\phi)} \right), \tag{3.41}$$

which can give dramatic differences in performance as $\phi \to 1$. Consider a persistent, tightly observed process, for example $\sigma_x^2 = 2$, $\sigma_e^2 = 0.1$, and $\phi = 0.99$. The signal to noise ratio, σ_x^2/σ_e^2, is large. In this case, the centered parameterization (which gives close to independent samples) is approximately 8,000 times more efficient than the uncentered parameterization. In other words, if we wished to estimate $E(\mu|y_{1:T})$, we would require 800,000 iterations of the Gibbs sampler applied to the uncentered parameterization to get the same precision as 100 iterations from the centered parameterization. Importantly, Pitt and Shephard (1999a) show that as $\phi \to 1$, the autocorrelation associated with the Gibbs output for the centered parameterization tends to 0, whilst for the uncentered parameterization, the corresponding autocorrelation tends to 1. See also Frűhwirth-Schnatter (2004) for a detailed discussion of these issues.

This intuition carries over into models that have a Gaussian state transition equation and an observation equation that belongs to the exponential family, so that the observation is unimodal and log-concave in the state vector. For example, Pitt and Shephard (1999a) show that the centered SV model in (3.3) delivers substantial gains over the uncentered SV model

$$y_t = \epsilon_t \beta \exp(x_t^*/2), \quad x_{t+1}^* = \phi x_t^* + \sigma_v v_t, \tag{3.42}$$

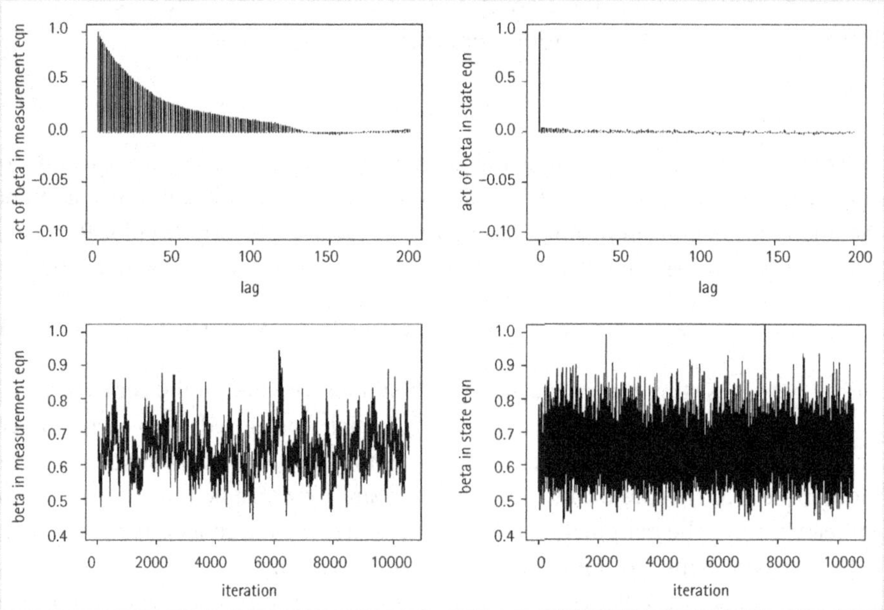

FIGURE 3.3 Stochastic Volatility (SV) model

Notes: The correlograms and sample paths for 10,000 MCMC samples of $\beta = \exp(\mu/2)$ with other parameters fixed as $\phi = 0.98$ and $\sigma_v^2 = 0.02$. Left: uncentered parameterization. Right: centered parameterization.

particularly in estimating $\beta = \exp(\mu/2)$. This is illustrated in Figure 3.3. Similar remarks apply to the Poisson model, which is given in its centred form by (3.38). The uncentered form is given by $y_t \sim Po\{\beta \exp(x_t^*)\}$ where $x_{t+1}^* = \phi x_t^* + \sigma_v v_t$. We note that for the SV model, the signal to noise ratio is typically moderate (as each observation is not very informative). However, as the persistence goes up ($\phi \to 1$), quite substantial gains are obtained for the centered parameterization. Although this is an artificial model where Bayesian inference can be carried out more efficiently by alternative methods, the example is informative in that the parameterization issue arising here also occurs in more complex models.

For non-Gaussian non-linear models, the signal to noise ratio, σ_x^2/σ_e^2, is again important. In a non-Gaussian model, such as an SV model, it is curvature of $\log p(y_t|x_t)$ that can be used instead of σ_e^2. Specifically, we can use the following, conditional information, measure

$$V = -E_{p(x_t)} \left\{ \left[E_{p(y_t|x_t)} \left(\frac{\partial^2 \log p(y_t|x_t)}{\partial x_t^2} \right) \right]^{-1} \right\}. \tag{3.43}$$

For the AR(1) plus noise model of either equations (3.39) and (3.40), we have $V = \sigma_e^2$ as expected. For the stochastic volatility model (for either parameterization), $V = 2$. We may use V instead of σ_e^2 in equation (3.41) to gain an impression of the benefit in using an alternative parameterization in the general case. Figure 3.3 shows the gains of using a centered rather than an uncentered parameterization for the SV model (with $T = 1,000$). For illustration, just the single parameter $\beta = \exp(\mu/2)$ is sampled (holding the other two fixed). A block sampler for the states in step 2 of Algorithm 6, described later in Section 6.4, is also used (average block size is 100). It may be seen that the gains are quite substantial. Generally, if the measurement is highly informative or if the process is very persistent, there are large gains from having a centered parameterization.

This section shows that how the state space model is parameterized can affect convergence substantially, and that in general reparameterization procedures are quite simple, involve no computational overhead, and can deliver very substantial gains in performance. It is also possible to switch between different parameterizations during an MCMC run if it is unclear which parameterization works best.

6.3 Inefficiency analysis: single move state updating

Step 2 of the Gibbs-type algorithm 6, where the simulation of $x_{1:T}^{(j+1)}$ from $p(x_{1:T}|y_{1:T};\theta)$ is required, is usually the more complicated of the two steps and certainly the most high dimensional as it involves the entire time series $x_{1:T}$. Several strategies are possible.

One way to sample from $p(x_{1:T}|y_{1:T};\theta)$ is to do Gibbs (or Metropolis within Gibbs) steps, sampling each state conditional on all the others, the observations and the parameters. That is, sample from $p(x_t|x_{\setminus t}, y_{1:T};\theta)$ for $t = 1, .., T$ where $x_{\setminus t} = \{x_{1:t-1}, x_{t+1:T}\}$. It was first observed by Carlin et al. (1992) that for the state space model with observation equation (3.1a) and state transition equation (3.2),

$$\begin{aligned} p(x_t|x_{\setminus t}, y_{1:T};\theta) &\propto p(y_t|x_t;\theta)p(x_t|x_{t-1};\theta)p(x_{t+1}|x_t;\theta) \quad t \neq 1, T \\ &\propto p(y_t|x_t;\theta)p(x_t|x_{t-1}, x_{t+1};\theta), \end{aligned} \tag{3.44}$$

with the obvious modification for $t = 1$ and $t = T$. Equation (3.44) follows from the Markov property of the state transition equation. Thus, the conditional distribution (3.44) of x_t only depends on the immediate neighbors x_{t-1}, x_{t+1}, the observation y_t, and the parameters and so $p(x_t|x_{\setminus t}, y_{1:T};\theta) = p(x_t|x_{t-1}, x_{t+1}, y_t;\theta)$. The state is updated according to $p(x_t^{(j+1)}|x_{t-1}^{(j+1)}, x_{t+1}^{(j)}, y_t;\theta)$ for $t = 2, \ldots, T-1$. The end conditions are dealt with as $p(x_1^{(j+1)}|x_2^{(j)}, y_1;\theta)$ and $p(x_T^{(j+1)}|x_{T-1}^{(j+1)}, y_T;\theta)$. The density of (3.44) is low dimensional (the dimension of the state), which makes forming proposals relatively straightforward. However, the mixing properties of the resulting Markov chain may be poor.

This can be seen in the simple and analytically tractable model at (3.40). Suppose that the parameters $\theta = (\mu, \phi, \sigma_v^2, \sigma_e^2)$ are fixed and that we are only interested in the posterior of the states $p(x_{1:T}|y_{1:T};\theta)$. If we use the univariate, in this case Gaussian, updating scheme of (3.44), then we obtain a linear VAR(1) (see Roberts and Sahu 1997) in the output of the Gibbs sampler so that $E(x_{1:T}^{(j+1)}|x_{1:T}^{(j)}) = C + Ax_{1:T}^{(j)}$. In this case, it is the spectral radius $\rho(A)$ (the largest eigenvalue) of the persistence matrix A, that determines the efficiency of the slowest mixing component of $x_{1:T}$. Pitt and Shephard (1999a) show that the persistence ρ of the Gibbs chain satisfies,

$$\lim_{T\to\infty} \rho = 4\frac{\phi^2}{(1+\phi^2+(1-\phi^2)\sigma_x^2\sigma_e^{-2})^2}, \tag{3.45}$$

where $\sigma_x^2 = \sigma_v^2/(1-\phi^2)$ and $\sigma_x^2\sigma_e^{-2}$ is again the signal to noise ratio. If ρ is close to 1, then the convergence is slow. From (3.45), $\rho \to 1$ (from below) as $|\phi| \to 1$ (from below). Whilst this closed form result only applies to a Gaussian linear state space model, the same intuition applies to other models. If the signal to noise ratio $\sigma_x^2\sigma_e^{-2}$ is already quite low, then ρ moves close to 1 rapidly as $\phi \to 1$. This is a severe problem in discrete time models with high persistence, such as SV models. It is particularly problematic for models in continuous time which are approximated by finely discretized discrete time systems (by using an Euler scheme, for instance Kloeden and Platen (1992)). For more general models, ρ in (3.45) can intuitively be seen as a lower bound to the rate of convergence as we usually have a Metropolis rejection step as we also sample the parameters θ. In more general statistical models, Liu et al. (1994) suggest that a key feature to improve the speed of convergence is to use blocking.

6.4 State simulation in blocks

Both in theory as well as practice single-move methods can result in slowly mixing MCMC chains. We now follow the MCMC methodology of Shephard and Pitt (1997) who sample blocks of states efficiently for the model

$$y_t \sim p(y_t|s_t), \quad s_t = Hx_t, \quad x_{t+1} = f + Fx_t + \Gamma u_t, \tag{3.46}$$

which has a linear and Gaussian state transition equation. The signal s_t is assumed to be univariate so that H is a row vector. The vectors H and f and the matrices F and Γ are indexed by the unknown parameter θ and $u_t \sim N(0, I)$. The observation equation at (3.46) can be non-Gaussian and nonlinear but the methods described below work best when $\log p(y_t|s_t) = l(s_t)$ is a concave function of the univariate signal s_t, which includes the SV and Poisson time series models.

Section 6.4.1 describes how to randomly place the fixed states and signals for each sweep of the method. Section 6.4.2 describes how to form the proposal density to approximate the true conditional density of a block of states between two knots. Section 6.4.3 shows how this proposal density can be seen as a Gaussian linear state space model and therefore easy to sample from. The expansion points for the signals are usually chosen as the mode of the conditional density and are described in Section 6.4.4. Finally, the construction of the overall Metropolis method for deciding whether to update a block of states is detailed in Section 6.4.5.

We note that the block sampling methods reduce to single move sampling if each block consists of a single state.

6.4.1 *Stochastic knots*

A fixed number, $\mathcal{K}$, of states, widely spaced over the time domain, are randomly chosen to remain fixed for one sweep of the MCMC method. These states, known as "knots", ensure that as the sample size increases, the algorithm does not fail due to excessive numbers of rejections. Since the knots are selected randomly, the points of conditioning change over the iterations. We work with a collection of stochastic knots, at times $\kappa = (\kappa_1, \ldots, \kappa_{\mathcal{K}})'$. These are a sample without replacement from $\{1, 2, 3, .., T\}$. The corresponding $\mathcal{K}$ states are $(x'_{\kappa_1}, \ldots, x'_{\kappa_{\mathcal{K}}})'$ and the the corresponding signals $(s_{\kappa_1}, \ldots, s_{\kappa_{\mathcal{K}}})$ are also regarded as fixed.

The selection of the knots is carried out randomly and independently of the outcome of the MCMC process. In this chapter, we use the scheme

Algorithm 7 (Stochastic knot selection). For $i = 1, \ldots, \mathcal{K}$,
Set $\kappa_i = \text{int}\{T \times (i + U_i)/(\mathcal{K} + 2)\}$ where U_i is uniform on $(0, 1)$. If $\kappa_i \leq \kappa_{i-1}$ then draw U_i again until $\kappa_i > \kappa_{i-1}$.

In Algorithm 7, int$(\cdot)$ means rounded to the nearest integer. For given $\kappa_i, i = 1, \ldots, \mathcal{K}$, the blocks of states that are sampled are $x_{\kappa_{(i-1)}} + 1_{\kappa_{i-1}}, i = 1, \ldots, \mathcal{K}$, with $\kappa_0 = 0$. For example, for a time series of length $T = 1,000$, we could have $\mathcal{K} = 10$ (knots) states which remain fixed (for a single MCMC sweep). The average size of the blocks to update between these states is 99. Single move sampling is a special case where $K = T - 1$, and where we usually generate $x_t, t = 1, \ldots, T$ in that order.

6.4.2 *The proposal density*

Let $x_{t:t+k}$ be the block of states that we wish to generate. The MCMC method uses a proposal density based on a quadratic approximation of the conditional density

$$\begin{aligned}
\log p(x_{t:t+k} \mid x_{t-1}, x_{t+k+1}, y_{t:t+k}) &= -\frac{1}{2}u'_{t:t+k}u_{t:t+k} + \sum_{i=t}^{t+k} l(s_i), \quad \text{where} \\
x_{i+1} &= f + Fx_i + \Gamma u_i, \quad \text{and} \quad s_i = Hx_i \\
&\simeq -\frac{1}{2}u'_{t:t+k}u_{t:t+k} + \sum_{i=t}^{t+k}\Bigg(l(\widehat{s}_i) + (s_i - \widehat{s}_i)^T l'(\widehat{s}_i) + \\
&+ \frac{1}{2}(s_i - \widehat{s}_i)^T D_i(\widehat{s}_i)(s_i - \widehat{s}_i)\Bigg) \\
&= \log g(x_{t:t+k} \mid x_{t-1}, x_{t+k+1}, y_{t:t+k}),
\end{aligned} \tag{3.47}$$

around some preliminary estimate $\widehat{x}_{t:t+k}$ of $x_{t:t+k}$ made by conditioning on x_{t-1}, x_{t+k+1} and $y_t, \ldots, y_{t+k}$. The corresponding estimate of $s_{t:t+k} = (s_t, \ldots, s_{t+k})$ is $\widehat{s}_{t:t+k}$. In (3.47),

$l(s_t) = \log f(y_t|s_t)$ with $l'(s_t)$ and $l''(s_t)$ its first and second derivatives. The innovations u_t are regarded as implicit functions of the states. We assume that the (as yet unspecified) matrix $D_i(s)$ is everywhere strictly negative definite as a function of s. Typically, we take $D_i(\widehat{s}_i) = l''(\widehat{s}_i)$ so that the approximation is a second-order Taylor series expansion. This is convenient in the vast majority of cases. For l concave for example, which covers the SV, Poisson, and binomial models, l'' is everywhere strictly negative. However, we allow for the possibility that D_i is not the second derivative to cover the non-concave cases.

An attractive feature of this expansion is that the ratio f/g, used in the Metropolis step, involves only the difference between $l(s_i)$ and $\widetilde{l}(s_i) = l(\widehat{s}_i) + (s_i - \widehat{s}_i)^T l'(\widehat{s}_i) + \frac{1}{2}(s_i - \widehat{s}_i)^T D_i(\widehat{s}_i)(s_i - \widehat{s}_i)$, not the transition density $u'_{t:t+k}u_{t:t+k}$. This suggests that the algorithm should not become significantly less effective as the dimension of x_i increases. This is contrasted with other approaches, such as the numerical integration routines used in Kitagawa (1987), whose effectiveness usually deteriorates as the dimension of x_t increases.

We note that the approach above may need to be modified if $\sum_{i=t}^{t+k} l(s_i)$ has a non-standard shape, for example if it is multimodal. We do not pursue this issue here.

6.4.3 *Block generation using the Gaussian linear state space model*

The density g defined by (3.47) is highly multivariate Gaussian but there is some hope that it is a good approximation. Now,

$$\begin{aligned}\log g &= -\frac{1}{2}u'_{t:t+k}u_{t:t+k} + \sum_{i=t}^{t+k}\left(l(\widehat{s}_i) + (s_i - \widehat{s}_i)^T l'(\widehat{s}_i) + \frac{1}{2}(s_i - \widehat{s}_i)^T D_i(\widehat{s}_i)(s_i - \widehat{s}_i)\right)\\ &= c - \frac{1}{2}u'_{t:t+k}u_{t:t+k} - \frac{1}{2}\sum_{i=t}^{t+k}(\widehat{y}_i - s_i)^T V_i^{-1}(\widehat{y}_i - s_i), \end{aligned} \tag{3.48}$$

where $\widehat{y}_i = \widehat{s}_i + V_i l'(\widehat{s}_i)$, $\quad i = t, \ldots, t+k$, and $V_i^{-1} = -D_i(\widehat{s}_i)$ are obtained by equating coefficients of powers of s_i in (3.48). This approximating density can be viewed as a Gaussian linear state space model consisting of the Gaussian measurement density with pseudo measurements $\widehat{y}_i$ and the standard linear Gaussian Markov chain prior on the states. So the approximating joint density of $x_{t:t+k}|x_{t-1}, x_{t+k+1}, y_{t:t+k}$ can be calculated by writing:

$$\begin{aligned}\widehat{y}_i &= s_i + \varepsilon_i, \quad \varepsilon_i \sim \mathsf{N}(0, V_i)\\ s_i &= Hx_i, \quad i = t, \ldots, t+k,\\ x_{i+1} &= f + Fx_i + \Gamma u_i, \quad u_i \sim \mathsf{NID}(0, I).\end{aligned} \tag{3.49}$$

The knots are fixed by setting $\widehat{y}_i = x_i$, $i = t-1$, and $i = t+k+1$ and by making the measurement equation $\widehat{y}_i = x_i + \varepsilon_i$, $\varepsilon_i \sim \mathsf{N}(0, \delta I)$, where δ is extremely small, at the positions of these knots, $i = t-1$ and $i = t+k+1$. This is a Gaussian linear state space model and it is possible to simulate from $x_{t:t+k} \mid x_{t-1}, x_{t+k+1}, \widehat{y}$ using a simulation smoother on the constructed set of pseudo-measurements $\widehat{y}_{t:t+k}$.

We have now outlined how to generate from a Gaussian proposal density. It is straightforward to modify this proposal density to generate from a multivariate t density with the same mean and covariance matrix and with a small number of degrees of freedom to give a heavier tailed proposal.

6.4.4 *Finding* $\widehat{s}_t, \ldots, \widehat{s}_{t+k}$

It is important to select sensible values for the sequence $\widehat{s}_{t:t+k}$, the points at which the quadratic expansion is carried out. The most straightforward choice is to take them as the mode of $f(s_{t:t+k}|x_{t-1}, x_{t+k+1}, y_{t:t+k})$. To do so we first expand around some arbitrary starting value of $\widehat{s}_{t:t+k}$ to obtain (3.49), set $\widehat{s}_{t:t+k}$ to the means from the resulting expectation smoother and then expand $\widehat{s}_{t:t+k}$ again, and so on. This ensures that we obtain $\widehat{s}_{t:t+k}$ as the mode of $f(s_{t:t+k}|x_{t-1}, x_{t+k+1}, y_{t:t+k})$. This is a very efficient Newton-Raphson method (since it avoids explicitly calculating the Hessian) using analytic first and second derivatives on a concave objective function. Thus, the approximations presented here can be interpreted as Laplace approximations to a very high-dimensional density function. We note that the adequacy of the approximation used will affect the efficiency of the MCMC scheme, but not its validity, because the approximation is used as a proposal density rather than as an end in itself. In practice, we often find that after a small number of iterations, e.g. 3 iterations, of the smoothing algorithm we usually obtain a sequence $\widehat{s}_{t:t+k} = (\widehat{s}_t, \ldots, \widehat{s}_{t+k})$ which is extremely close to the mode, where convergence to the mode is monitored in the usual way. Such fast convergence is very important in practice since the expansion is performed for each iteration of the proposed MCMC sampler.

6.4.5 *Metropolis acceptance probability*

This section describes the construction of the Metropolis-Hastings acceptance probabilities for generating the states in blocks. Let $x^o_{t:t+k}$ be the current value of the block of states $x_{t:t+k}$ and $x^n_{t:t+k}$ the proposed value, with corresponding signals $s^o_{t:t+k}$ and $s^n_{t:t+k}$. The blocks are drawn from $g(x_{t:t+k} \mid x_{t-1}, x_{t+k+1}, y_{t:t+k})$. The probability of accepting $x^n_{t:t+k}$ is

$$\Pr(x^o_{t:t+k} \to x^n_{t:t+k}) = \min\left\{1, \frac{\omega(s^n_{t:t+k})}{\omega(s^o_{t:t+k})}\right\}, \tag{3.50}$$

where

$$\omega(s_{t:t+k}) = \exp\{l(s_{t:t+k}) - \widetilde{l}(s_{t:t+k})\} = \exp\left(\sum_{i=t}^{t+k} \{l(s_i) - \widetilde{l}(s_i)\}\right).$$

In many problems, $\omega(s_{t:t+k})$ will be close to 1, resulting in high acceptance probabilities in both stages. All the blocks between the fixed knots are sampled in this way which defines a complete MCMC sweep through the states.

6.5 Simulation illustration: single versus multi-move for the SV model

Ideally, all the states are proposed without any knots from $\log g(x_{1:T} \mid y_{1:T})$. This works well for small T, but the probability of acceptance falls rapidly as T increases. In practice, small block sizes (many knots) result in high acceptance probabilities but there is more posterior correlation between these small blocks. Large blocks result in low posterior correlation but the acceptance probability is low. Generally, there is a tradeoff between these criteria to achieve good mixing.

It is also important to note that in highly persistent problems, for which single site methods work very poorly, we can take very large blocks because the quadratic terms from the state equation dominate the log-posterior. For problems with low persistence we cannot take large blocks, but mixing is less of a problem.

The simulated data allow two sets of parameters, designed to reflect typical problems for weekly and daily financial data sets for the SV model at (3.3), but without leverage. In the weekly case, $\mu = 0, \sigma_u^2 = 0.1$, and $\phi = 0.9$, while in the daily case $\mu = 0, \sigma_u^2 = 0.01$, and $\phi = 0.99$. The MCMC method is carried out for the simulated SV model, noting efficiency gains over the single-move algorithm with the states generated systematically. Table 3.1 reports some results from a simulation using $T = 1,000$. For the simulation we keep the parameters fixed and report the inefficiency, estimated via the Parzen kernel for the middle state, x_{500}. Reported is the ratio of the inefficiency for the single move method relative to the blocking method for various block sizes (number of knots). In all cases, the multi-move sampler outperforms the single move sampler. When the number of knots is 0, so all the states are sampled simultaneously, the gains for the weekly parameter case are not that great, whilst for the daily parameters they are substantial. This is because the Gaussian approximation is better for the daily parameters since the Gaussian AR(1) prior dominates for this persistent case. This is important, because it is in persistent cases where the single move method does particularly badly. There are two competing considerations here. If the number of knots is large, then the blocks are small and the Gaussian approximation is good since it is over a low dimension and so the Metropolis method will accept frequently. On the other hand, we will be retaining a lot of states from the previous MCMC sweep, leading to correlation over sweeps. In this example the multi-move method does not appear to be too sensitive to block size but the best number of knots for these simulations appears to be about ten.

7 The particle filter with known parameters

This section takes the parameters as known in the state space model

$$y_t \sim p(y_t|x_t),\ x_{t+1} \sim p(x_{t+1}|x_t)\ ,\ t = 1, \ldots, T \tag{3.51}$$

Table 3.1: Relative efficiency of block sampler to single-move Gibbs sampler

Weekly parameters	$\mathcal{K}=0$	$\mathcal{K}=1$	$\mathcal{K}=3$	$\mathcal{K}=5$	$\mathcal{K}=10$	$\mathcal{K}=20$	$\mathcal{K}=50$	$\mathcal{K}=100$	$\mathcal{K}=200$
	1.7	4.1	7.8	17	45	14	12	4.3	3.0
Daily parameters	$\mathcal{K}=0$	$\mathcal{K}=1$	$\mathcal{K}=3$	$\mathcal{K}=5$	$\mathcal{K}=10$	$\mathcal{K}=20$	$\mathcal{K}=50$	$\mathcal{K}=100$	$\mathcal{K}=200$
	66	98	98	85	103	69	25	8.5	2.5

Notes: $\mathcal{K}$ is the number of stochastic knots used. The figures are the ratio of the computed variances, and so reflect efficiency gains. The variances are computed using 10,000 lags and 100,000 iterations in all cases except for the single-move sampler on daily parameter cases. For that problem, 100,000 lags and 1,000,000 iterations are used. In all cases, the burn-in period is the same as the number of lags.

which are (3.1a) and (3.2) in our general state space formulation. The parameters are suppressed from the notation for simplicity. Section 8 deals with the particle filter when the parameters are also estimated.

The particle filter was introduced by Gordon et al. (1993) as a general approach to sequentially obtain a sample from the filtering distribution through time. That is, we require $x_t^i \sim p(x_t|y_{1:t})$ for $i = 1, \ldots, M$ and for $t = 1, \ldots, T$. In the basic Sampling Importance Resampling (SIR) filter of Gordon et al. (1993), the only requirement on the system (3.51) is that it is possible to simulate from the transition density $p(x_{t+1}|x_t)$ and evaluate the measurement density $p(y_t|x_t)$. This is clearly more general than for the MCMC methods described above where it is typically necessary to calculate $p(x_{t+1}|x_t)$.

One simple approach to filtering is to independently sample from $p(x_{1:t}|y_{1:t})$ for each $t = 1, \ldots, T$ using MCMC. This results in an $O(T^2)$ algorithm which is prohibitively costly for large T. For this reason we employ a particle filter which is $O(T)$.

7.1 Sampling Importance Resampling

We first describe the SIR algorithm of Gordon et al. (1993), but slightly modify its implementation to involve a single resampling step (without the so-called boosting used in the original SIR paper). This relates to observations made by Carpenter et al. (1999). The algorithm was independently proposed by Kitagawa (1996). A particular advantage of the SIR method, in addition to its simplicity, is that it is only necessary to draw samples from the Markov transition density $p(x_{t+1}|x_t)$. It is not necessary to evaluate the density $p(x_{t+1}|x_t)$, which can be complicated for some classes of models

The basic SIR algorithm is outlined below. We start at $t = 0$ with samples from $x_0^k \sim p(x_0)$, $k = 1, \ldots., M$, which is generally a stationary distribution, if it exists (e.g. in the stochastic volatility model). See the discussion on initial values in Section 3.6.

Algorithm 8 (SIR). For $t = 0, .., T-1$:
We have samples $x_t^k \sim p(x_t|y_{1:t})$ for $k = 1, \ldots, M$.

(1) For $k = 1$: M, sample $\widetilde{x}_{t+1}^k \sim p(x_{t+1}|x_t^k)$.
(2) For $k = 1$: M, calculate normalized weights,

$$\omega_{t+1}^k = p(y_{t+1}|\widetilde{x}_{t+1}^k), \qquad \pi_{t+1}^k = \frac{\omega_{t+1}^k}{\sum_{i=1}^M \omega_{t+1}^i}.$$

(3) For $k = 1$: M, sample (from the mixture) $x_{t+1}^k \sim \sum_{i=1}^M \pi_{t+1}^i \delta(x_{t+1} - \widetilde{x}_{t+1}^i)$.

The particles $\{x_{t+1}^k, k = 1, \ldots, M\}$ represent the filtering density at time $t+1$. In standard notation, $\delta(z)$ is the Dirac delta density. The $x_{t+1}^k \sim p(x_{t+1}|y_{1:t+1})$ are obtained after Step 3 which involves sampling the indices k with probability π_{t+1}^k and is therefore a univariate problem regardless of the state dimension. Such multinomial sampling is sometimes referred to as the weighted bootstrap, see Rubin (1988) and is computationally $O(M)$. The multinomial procedure is described in Section 7.2. The justification for importance resampling is found in Rubin (1988) and Smith and Gelfand (1992).

Note that step 3 involves sampling x_{t+1}^k from the approximating filtering density at time $t+1$ given by

$$\tilde{p}_M(x_{t+1}|y_{1:t+1}) = \sum_{i=1}^{M} \pi_{t+1}^i \delta(x_{t+1} - \tilde{x}_{t+1}^i). \tag{3.52}$$

Typically, summary statistics are recorded through time as output from Algorithm 8. To estimate a moment $\Psi = E[g(x_{t+1})|y_{1:t+1}]$ it is possible to use either

$$\widehat{\Psi} = \frac{1}{M}\sum_{k=1}^{M} g(x_{t+1}^k) \quad \text{or} \quad \widetilde{\Psi} = \sum_{i=1}^{M} \pi_{t+1}^i g(\tilde{x}_{t+1}^i).$$

The estimator $\widehat{\Psi}$ uses the samples x_{t+1}^k arising from step 3 of algorithm 8. The Rao-Blackwellized estimator $\widetilde{\Psi}$ takes the expectation of $g(x_{t+1})$ under (3.52). Whilst the expectation of the two estimators is the same since x_{t+1}^k arise from (3.52), the Rao-Blackwellized estimator has smaller variance and is preferable.

The steps in the SIR algorithm parallel the updates in the standard Kalman filter described in Sections 2.2 and 3.1. The description by Pitt and Shephard (1999b) of the SIR method is informative in explicitly comparing the prediction and update stages. They term the mixture

$$\widehat{p}_M(x_{t+1}|y_{1:t}) = \frac{1}{M}\sum_{i=1}^{M} p(x_{t+1}|x_t^i), \tag{3.53}$$

where $x_t^i \sim p(x_t|y_{1:t})$, as the empirical prediction density, is the density we sample from in step 1 of the SIR algorithm. It is an approximation to the true prediction density $p(x_{t+1}|y_{1:t}) = \int p(x_{t+1}|x_t)p(x_t|y_{1:t})dx_t$.

The corresponding empirical filtering density is given by

$$\widehat{p}(x_{t+1}|y_{1:t+1}) \propto p(y_{t+1}|x_{t+1})\widehat{p}(x_{t+1}|y_{1:t}), \tag{3.54}$$

and this is the density from which we need to sample x_{t+1}. This is achieved in steps 2 and 3 and is then a standard resampling procedure used in Bayesian updating (see Smith and Gelfand 1992 and Rubin 1988). We already have samples from $\widehat{p}(x_{t+1}|y_{1:t})$ which we can reweight with respect to the measurement density $p(y_{t+1}|x_{t+1})$. We resample via a weighted bootstrap, Rubin (1988), as in step 3 of the SIR algorithm.

The analysis of the SIR algorithm in this way is instructive. Not only does the updating parallel the widely used Kalman filter but we can also think about when the procedure will fail. By examining (3.54) we can see that we are generating samples from the second term on the right-hand side and reweighting with respect to the first term, the measurement density. If we have a highly peaked or informative measurement (as a function of x_{t+1}) relative to $\widehat{p}(x_{t+1}|y_{1:t})$, then the method will perform badly. We will have only very few samples of x_{t+1} with appreciable weight π_{t+1} in step 2 of the method. As a consequence, in step 3 we will only be resampling very few of these. This may become a severe problem if there is an outlier or if the model is badly specified. This problem may be circumvented to a large extent by the auxiliary particle filter discussed in Section 7.4.

Before proceeding to the auxiliary particle filter, it is useful reintroduce the parameter θ and note that the log-likelihood

$$\begin{aligned} \log L(\theta) &= \sum_{t=0}^{T-1} \log p(y_{t+1}|\theta; y_{1:t}), \quad \text{with} \\ p(y_{t+1}|\theta; y_{1:t}) &= \int p(y_{t+1}|x_{t+1};\theta)p(x_{t+1}|y_{1:t};\theta)dx_{t+1} \end{aligned} \tag{3.55}$$

and $p(y_{t+1}|y_{1:t};\theta)$ is estimated by

$$\widehat{p}_M(y_{t+1}|\theta; y_{1:t}) = \frac{1}{M}\sum_{i=1}^{M} \omega_{t+1}^i, \tag{3.56}$$

from step 2 of the algorithm. This is first noted by Kitagawa (1996). Thus, an estimate of the likelihood can be obtained at any parameter ordinate as a free by-product of the algorithm. It is also important to note that the resulting estimate of the likelihood function is not a continuous function of θ even if both the random numbers used in steps 1 and 3 are fixed because the multinomial sampling scheme in step 3 gives rise to discontinuities. As θ is changed, the weights of step 2 alter and this can lead to quite different choices of the states x_{t+1}^i in step 3.

The computational complexity of the SIR algorithm is of total order $O(T \times M)$. Note that it is unnecessary to resample at each time point. We could simply propagate the weights in the algorithm sampling at, say, every tenth time step. This remains true of particle filters in general. This idea was proposed by Liu and Chen (1995). Of course, if we only resample once, at time T, then we have a standard importance sampler operating over the whole dimension of T in the states. For the SIR algorithm this scheme rapidly deteriorates, as T becomes larger, as we would be sampling from the transition density and resampling, at the end, with weights proportional to the product of all the measurement densities from $t = 1, \ldots, T$.

As an example, consider the stochastic volatility model at (3.3) without leverage applied to the continuously compounded daily returns on the US dollar against UK sterling from the first day of trading in 1997 and for the next 200 days of active trading. This data is discussed in more detail in Pitt and Shephard (1999c), where the parameters of the model were estimated using Bayesian methods. The parameters are fixed as $(\phi, \mu, \sigma_\eta) = (0.9702, -1.02, 0.178)$, the posterior means of the model for a long time series of returns up until the end of 1996. Figure 3.4 shows the standard SIR particle filter, resampling at each time step, applied to the stochastic volatility model. The quantiles associated with the filtered standard deviation are displayed. The figure also shows that

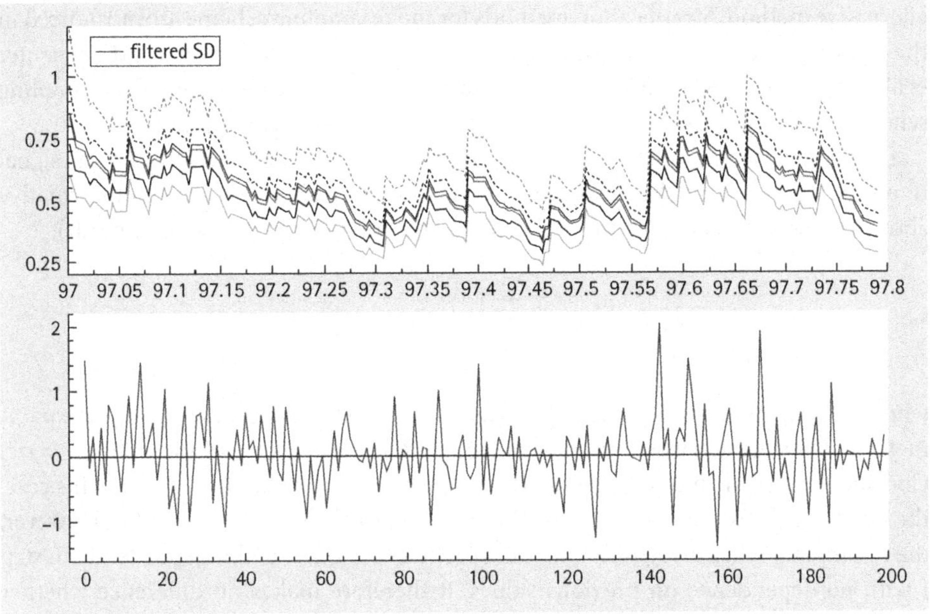

FIGURE 3.4 Results for the daily returns of the US dollar against UK sterling

Notes: The bottom graph shows the daily returns on the dollar against UK sterling from the first day of trading in 1997 for 200 trading days. The top graph shows the posterior filtered mean (heavy line) of $\exp(x_t/2)|y_{1:t}$, together with the 5, 20, 50, 80, 95 percentage points of the distribution. Notice the median is always below the mean. $M = 5,000$.

the filtered volatility jumps up more quickly than it tends to go down. This is typical, reflecting the fact that the volatility is modeled on the log scale.

7.2 Multinomial sampling

A common feature of all of the particle filter methods described in the section is the need to resample. This is true for the SIR approach of Gordon et al. (1993) presented in algorithm 8 and also for the algorithms introduced in Sections 7.4 and 7.5. Whilst this is a technical aspect, it is nonetheless important. The standard approach is to sample from the multinomial distribution. An important aspect of the resampling mechanism is that it works on the indices associated with the particles and is therefore a univariate operation, like a standard bootstrap, even if the state dimension is high.

7.3 Stratified sampling

Stratified sampling methods apply to the resampling stage so that the multinomial sampling in step 3 in algorithm 8 of Gordon et al. (1993) is replaced by a stratified alternative method. Stratification methods for the resampling scheme are introduced in the context of particle filtering by Kitagawa (1996), Liu and Chen (1998), and Carpenter et al. (1999). The gains in using stratified sampling, together with the auxiliary sampling scheme discussed in Section 7.4, are discussed in Pitt and Shephard (2001).

The main advantage of the stratified approaches appears in problems where the signal to noise ratio is low, so the measurement equation in (3.1a) is relatively uninformative about the state. As a simple example, consider the following AR(1) + noise model,

$$y_t = x_t + e_t$$

$$x_{t+1} = \phi x_t + \sqrt{1-\phi^2} v_t,$$

where e_t, v_t are independent Gaussian with variances σ_e^2 and σ_v^2 respectively. We parameterize the state equation for convenience so that the variance of the state $\sigma_x^2 = \sigma_v^2$. Consider first algorithm 8 applied to the case where $\phi = 0$ and $\sigma_e^2 \to \infty$. In this case, the weights are equal in step 2 of algorithm 8 and the probabilities $\pi_{t+1}^k = 1/M$. However, the resampling scheme is irrelevant as the particles are generated independently in step 1 with no dependence on previous values. It therefore makes no difference whether stratified or standard multinomial resampling is used.

If, however, we consider $\phi \to 1$ (from below) and again $\sigma_e^2 \to \infty$, then the states are highly dependent through time (approximately constant). This of course becomes a static Bayesian problem in which we are updating the posterior of the mean x_t. Again, in step 2 we have $\pi_{t+1}^k = 1/M$. In this case in step 3 of algorithm 8, if we use standard multinomial sampling, we will unnecessarily throw away about a third of our values, and then in step 1 there will be no regeneration. Therefore the particle filter will collapse rapidly. This illustrates that when the weights are even and the system is highly persistent, we wish to use a stratified scheme in step 3 of algorithm 8. Either of the approaches of Kitagawa (1996) or Carpenter et al. (1999) would ensure that all of the samples in step 3 are retained. Though this is an artificial problem, the same sort of difficulty arises when we discretize continuous time systems via, for instance, an Euler scheme discussed in Kloeden and Platen (1992) and Elerian et al. (2001).

By using a combination of auxiliary particle filters, introduced in Section 7.4, to accommodate outliers and highly informative measurements and stratification in the resampling procedure, it is possible to have an extremely robust procedure.

Measuring performance Liu (1996) introduced a measure of effective sample size (ESS). This is similar in motivation to the inefficiency measures for MCMC but may be applied to the resampling algorithm. The measure for time t is,

$$ESS_t = \frac{1}{\sum_{i=1}^{M} \left(\pi_t^i\right)^2}.$$

Clearly, if we have $\pi_t^i = 1/M$ for $i = 1, \ldots, M$ then this yields an ESS of M. The greater the variability of the weights, the greater the reduction from this optimal value.

7.4 Auxiliary particle filter

The auxiliary particle filter includes the SIR particle filter as a special case, but allows greater flexibility in the way proposals are made. In particular, it allows us to avoid the blind (blind because we ignore the contribution of y_{t+1}) proposals for (3.54) based upon $\widehat{p}(x_{t+1}|y_{1:t})$ in (3.53). Consider (3.54) again, which may be expressed more fully as,

$$\widehat{p}_M(x_{t+1}|y_{1:t+1}) \propto p(y_{t+1}|x_{t+1}) \sum_{k=1}^{M} p(x_{t+1}|x_t^k). \tag{3.57}$$

Clearly, we wish to sample x_{t+1} from $\widehat{p}(x_{t+1}|y_{1:t+1})$. We have already argued that if we ignore the term $p(y_{t+1}|x_{t+1})$ in making proposals (as in the SIR method), then if $p(y_{t+1}|x_{t+1})$ is very informative we will perform badly. A natural proposal might be another mixture density $g(x_{t+1})$, say, from which we can easily simulate. However, when we correct (using a Metropolis Hastings, a rejection sampling, or a resampling procedure) for the approximation we will have an $O(M^2)$ algorithm because for each of the M proposed samples we will have to evaluate (3.57) as the numerator over $g(x_{t+1})$ for the denominator. Of course, in Gordon et al. (1993), by using

$$g(x_{t+1}) = \frac{1}{M} \sum_{k=1}^{M} p(x_{t+1}|x_t^k)$$

as the proposal, the summation vanishes in the ratio $\widehat{p}(x_{t+1}|y_{1:t+1})/g(x_{t+1})$ and so this does not arise.

The main insight of Pitt and Shephard (1999b) is that if we write down a joint density,

$$\widehat{p}(x_{t+1}; x_t^k|y_{1:t+1}) \propto p(y_{t+1}|x_{t+1})p(x_{t+1}|x_t^k), \tag{3.58}$$

then its marginal density in x_{t+1} is $\widehat{p}(x_{t+1}|y_{1:t+1})$ of (3.57). This is straightforward to verify and allows us to make general proposals but now in the expanded space of the index k for $k = 1, \ldots, M$. Whatever our proposal $g(x_{t+1}; k)$, we will no longer have M summation terms in the numerator (or denominator) when we resample (or use a Metropolis or rejection algorithm). The remainder of our discussion is based on effective ways of choosing the proposal $g(x_{t+1}; k)$, which we call the auxiliary particle filter. For further material on the auxiliary particle filter, see Pitt and Shephard (1999b) and Pitt and Shephard (2001). The theoretical properties of the auxiliary particle filter are examined by Douc et al. (2008).

Fully adapted proposals In some cases when going a single time step ahead, it is possible to form an optimal proposal. We note that it is always true that

$$p(y_{t+1}|x_{t+1})p(x_{t+1}|x_t) = p(y_{t+1}|x_t)p(x_{t+1}|x_t, y_{t+1}). \tag{3.59}$$

If, in addition, the observation equation is conjugate to the state transition equation, then it is possible to generate x_{t+1} from $p(x_{t+1}|x_t, y_{t+1})$ and evaluate $p(y_{t+1}|x_t)$. We call this the "fully adapted" case. An example of this is a non-linear Gaussian system observed with noise

$$y_t = x_t + \sigma_e e_t \,, \; x_{t+1} \sim N\left(a(x_t); b^2(x_t)\right). \tag{3.60}$$

This happens, for example, when a crude Euler approximation (see Kloeden and Platen 1992; Elerian et al. 2001, for a discussion of Euler approximations) to a stochastic differential equation in x_t is used and x_t is observed subject to some noise.

We have

$$\widehat{p}(x_{t+1}; x_t^k|y_{1:t+1}) \propto p(y_{t+1}|x_{t+1})p(x_{t+1}|x_t^k) = p(y_{t+1}|x_t^k)p(x_{t+1}|x_t^k; y_{t+1}).$$

We set $g(x_{t+1}; k) = g(k)g(x_{t+1}|k)$, with

$$g(k) = \left\{ \frac{p(y_{t+1}|x_t^k)}{\sum_{j=1}^M p(y_{t+1}|x_t^j)} \right\} \quad \text{and} \quad g(x_{t+1}|k) = p(x_{t+1}|x_t^k; y_{t+1}).$$

There is no approximation in this case as $\widehat{p}(x_{t+1}; x_t^k|y_{1:t+1}) = g(x_{t+1}; k)$. The following algorithm again starts at $t = 0$ with samples from $x_0^k \sim p(x_0)$, $k = 1, \ldots, M$, which is generally the prior stationary distribution of the x_t (see Section 3.6).

Algorithm 9 (Fully adapted auxiliary particle filter).

For $t = 0, \ldots, T - 1$:

We have samples $x_t^k \sim p(x_t|y_{1:t})$ for $k = 1, \ldots, M$.

(1) For $k = 1$: M, compute

$$\omega_{t|t+1}^k = p(y_{t+1}|x_t^k) \text{ and } \pi_{t|t+1}^k = \frac{\omega_{t|t+1}^k}{\sum_{i=1}^M \omega_{t|t+1}^i}.$$

(2) For $k = 1 : M$, sample $\widetilde{x}_t^k \sim \sum_{i=1}^M \pi_{t|t+1}^i \delta(x_t - x_t^i)$.

(3) For $k = 1 : M$, sample $x_{t+1}^k \sim p(x_{t+1}|\widetilde{x}_t^k; y_{t+1})$.

Note that in step 1 the samples x_t^k with mass $\pi_{t|t+1}^k$ arise from $p(x_t|y_{1:t+1})$. In step 2, these are resampled to produce an equally weighted sample $\widetilde{x}_t^k$ from this density. Step 3 therefore delivers an equally weighted sample from $p(x_{t+1}|y_{1:t+1})$.

At each time t, the predictive likelihood may be estimated by,

$$p(y_{t+1}|y_{1:t}) \simeq \frac{1}{M}\sum_{k=1}^M p(y_{t+1}|x_t^k) = \frac{1}{M}\sum_{k=1}^M \omega_{t|t+1}^k. \tag{3.61}$$

When it is possible to adapt completely, as described at equation (3.59) and below it, considerable gains in efficiency are possible, both in estimating filtering moments, for example $\widehat{x}_{t|t} = E(x_t|y_{1:t})$, and in estimating the likelihood at a particular parameter ordinate θ,

$$p(y_{1:T}|\theta) = p(y_1)\prod_{t=1}^{T-1} p(y_{t+1}|y_{1:t};\theta).$$

The efficiency gains depend on the signal to noise ratio. For example, if σ_e^2 is very small in (3.60), so that the signal to noise ratio is very high, then the gains are considerable. The weights in the fully adapted algorithm above, which are proportional to $p(y_{t+1}|x_t^k)$, will be much less variable than those from the Gordon et al. (1993) SIR algorithm, which are proportional to $p(y_{t+1}|x_{t+1}^k)$. As a consequence, the estimate of the likelihood (in both cases, these weights are used) will be much more accurate for the completely adapted method. The samples in step 3 above from $p(x_{t+1}|\widetilde{x}_t^k; y_{t+1})$ will be greatly influenced by y_{t+1}, whereas in the SIR method of Gordon et al. (1993) we are sampling blindly from $p(x_{t+1}|x_t^i)$ without taking into account y_{t+1}. It is almost always better to use a completely adapted method if possible. The gains may be modest when the signal to noise ratio is low, but are substantial when this ratio is high. Indeed, the gains in efficiency are unbounded as $\sigma_e^2 \to 0$, in which case only a single sample (from M) will have appreciable weight in the Gordon et al. (1993) SIR algorithm, whereas for the adapted method we will have equal weights and so an effective sample size of M.

We now illustrate the benefits of stratification and full adaptation for a simple state space model.

7.4.1 Example: AR(1) model with noise

To illustrate the performance of stratification and adaptation when using the auxiliary particle filter, we consider the AR(1) plus noise model at equation (3.40) in Section 6.2. We choose the parameterization to be similar to that typically found in an SV model $\phi = 0.975$, $\mu = 0.5$, and $\sigma_v^2 = 0.02$. The two errors e_t and v_t are standard normal and uncorrelated. In this case, it is straightforward to see that full adaptation is possible as $p(y_{t+1}|x_t)$ can be evaluated and we can simulate from the Gaussian density $p(x_{t+1}|x_t, y_{t+1})$. We can therefore apply algorithm 9 from the previous section. To study the performance of various different particle filters, we consider $\sigma_e^2 = 2, 0.2$, and 0.02. The case where $\sigma_e^2 = 2$ is similar to the information in the SV model as shown at equation (3.43) in Section 6.2.

We examine the standard SIR particle filter of algorithm 8 both with and without the stratification of Section 7.3, then the fully adapted procedure of algorithm 9, both with and without stratification. We impose two outliers at times 10 and 30, taking $T = 50$. The true filtering solution, given by the Kalman filter, is $x_t|y_{1:t} \sim N(\widehat{x}_{t|t}; S_{t|t})$. We perform $N = 100$ replications of the four particle filters for $M = 1,000$ particles. We can generally represent the estimate of the filter mean based on the sample M as $\widetilde{x}_{t|t}$ where the truth, from the Kalman filter, is $\widehat{x}_{t|t} = E(x_t|y_{1:t})$. We are taking single time series and we record the bias, for each particle filter, over time as

$$\text{bias}_t = \widehat{x}_{t|t} - \frac{1}{N}\sum_{i=1}^{N}\widetilde{x}_{t|t}^{(i)}.$$

The optimal mean squared error (MSE), if we had independent samples from the Kalman filtering density, would be $S_{t|t}/M$. We record the actual MSE as

$$\text{MSE}_t = \frac{1}{N}\sum_{i=1}^{N}(\widetilde{x}_{t|t}^{(i)} - \widehat{x}_{t|t})^2.$$

We record the logarithm of the ratio of MSE_t to the optimal $S_{t|t}/M$ (so a value of 0 is very good, but we expect positive values typically). Figures 3.5, 3.6, and 3.7 display the results for $\sigma_\varepsilon^2 = 2$, 0.2, and 0.02 respectively. We note that looking at the bias and MSE gives us information over and above that in the equivalent sample size, because they give an overall measure of performance of the particle filter, whereas ESS is more a measure of one step ahead performance.

The results are informative. For the weak signal, $\sigma_\varepsilon^2 = 2$, of Figure 3.5, stratification is more important than (full) adaptation for both MSE and bias. Full adaptation does slightly better than no adaptation, but the difference is small. This is because the weights in algorithm 8 have low variance and the simple proposal (without taking into account y_{t+1}) is adequate. Stratification is important, since as the weights have low variance, we do not want to unnecessarily discard particles. For the medium signal, $\sigma_\varepsilon^2 = 0.2$, of Figure 3.6, stratification appears to do better than no stratification and

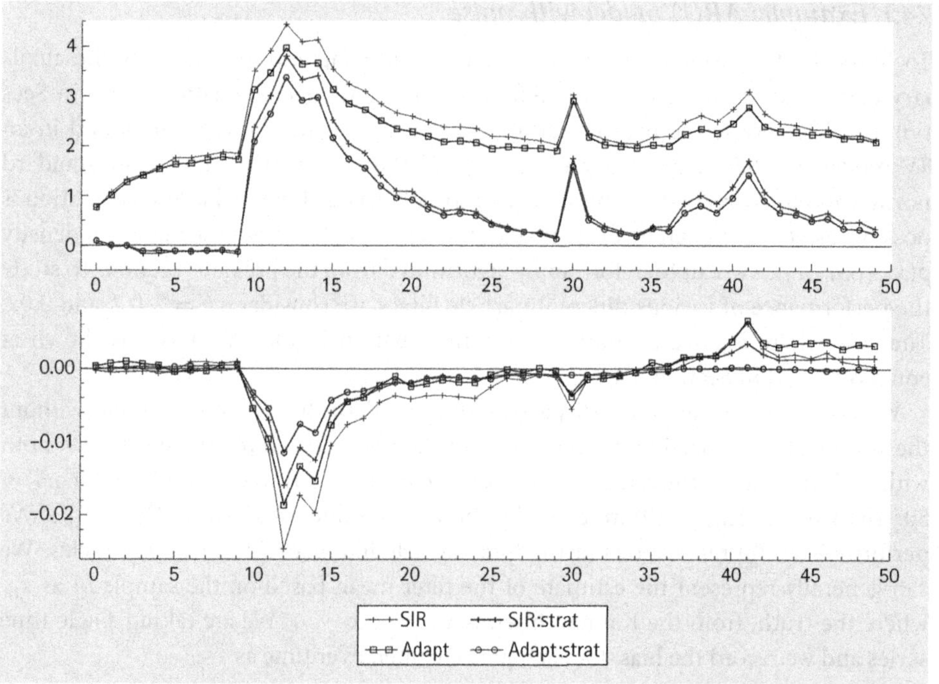

FIGURE 3.5 Weak signal case: $\sigma_\varepsilon^2 = 2$

Notes: Bias and MSE for the four particle filters based on $N = 100$ replications where the PF size is $M = 1,000$. *Top*: log of the ratio of MSE to optimal MSE from KF. *Bottom*: bias relative to the KF mean.

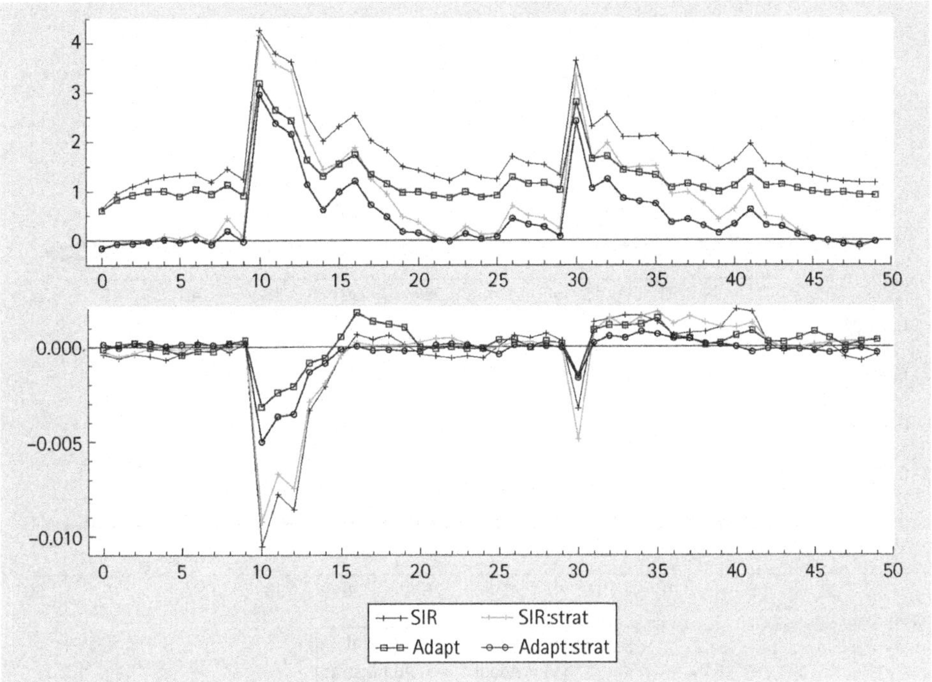

FIGURE 3.6 Medium signal case: $\sigma_\varepsilon^2 = 0.2$

Notes: Bias and MSE for the four particle filters based on $N = 100$ replications where the PF size is $M = 1,000$. *Top*: log of the ratio of MSE to optimal MSE from KF. *Bottom*: bias relative to the KF mean.

is the most important factor for the majority of observations. However, for the two outliers we introduced at times 10 and 30, adaptation is much more important, with both the adapted particle filters resulting in lower bias and smaller MSE than the non-adapted particle filters. This pattern is more pronounced for the strong signal, $\sigma_\varepsilon^2 = 0.02$, of Figure 3.7, where both fully adapted particle filters substantially outperform the standard particle filters not only for the two outliers but for the other observations also.

In general, it appears that combining stratification with adaptation is optimal. Stratification is helpful when the signal to noise ratio is low, and so the variance of the weights in algorithm 8 is low, as the standard multinomial sampler is unnecessarily throwing away particles, whereas the stratified sampler retains the majority of them. As the signal to noise ratio increases, it is apparent that (full) adaptation becomes increasingly crucial as we are guiding our proposals in algorithm 9 taking into account the, very informative, y_{t+1}.

Whilst there are some models which allow full adaptation, this is not the general case. However, we still wish to take into account the future observation y_{t+1} and be as close as possible to the fully adapted case. This means that we employ approximations to allow for good proposals leading to the general auxiliary particle filter.

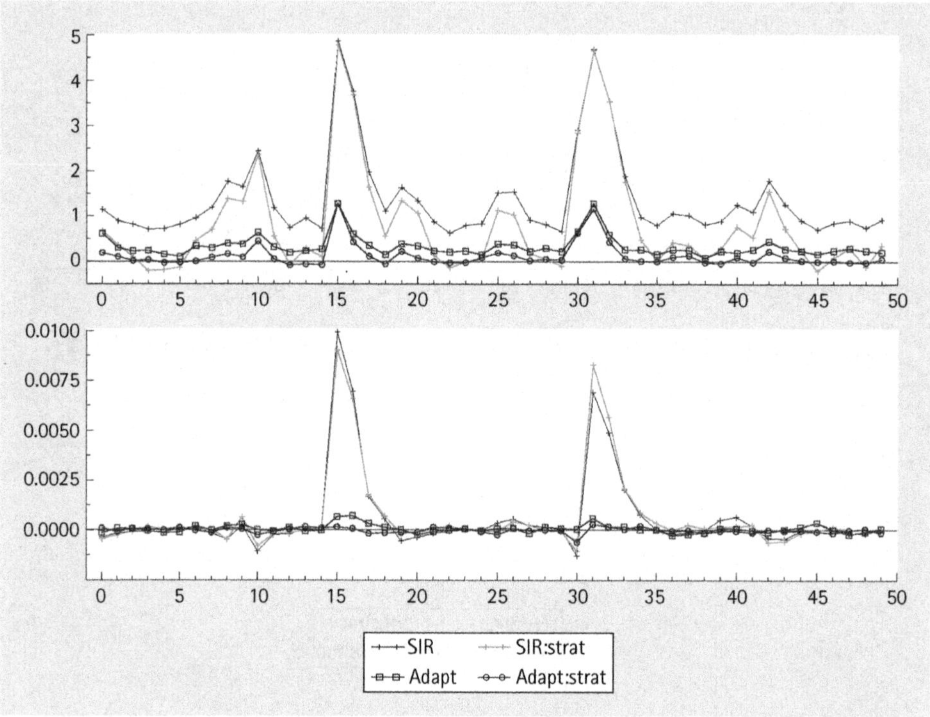

FIGURE 3.7 Strong signal case: $\sigma_\varepsilon^2 = 0.02$

Notes: Bias and MSE for the four particle filters based on $N = 100$ replications where the PF size is $M = 1,000$. *Top*: log of the ratio of MSE to optimal MSE from KF. *Bottom*: bias relative to the KF mean.

7.5 General auxiliary particle filter

For now we assume that we have formed the approximations,

$$g(y_{t+1}|x_t) \simeq p(y_{t+1}|x_t) \quad \text{and} \quad g(x_{t+1}|x_t, y_{t+1}) \simeq p(x_{t+1}|x_t, y_{t+1}), \tag{3.62}$$

where we can evaluate $g(y_{t+1}|x_t)$, simulate from $g(x_{t+1}|x_t, y_{t+1})$, and evaluate the ratio of $p(y_{t+1}|x_{t+1})p(x_{t+1}|x_t)/g(y_{t+1}|x_t)g(x_{t+1}|x_t, y_{t+1})$. We note from (3.59) and (3.62) that

$$g(y_{t+1}|x_t)g(x_{t+1}|x_t, y_{t+1}) \simeq p(y_{t+1}|x_{t+1})p(x_{t+1}|x_t). \tag{3.63}$$

We first outline the general auxiliary particle filter algorithm and then discuss various methods of constructing the approximations at (3.62). The choice of these approximations is crucial for the efficiency of the general auxiliary particle filter.

In this section the representation of the filter density $p(x_t|y_{1:t})$ consists of the pairs $\{x_t^k, \pi_t^k\}$ for $k = 1, \ldots, M$. The term π_t^k represents the mass at x_t^k.

For the following algorithm we again start at $t = 0$ with samples from $x_0^k \sim p(x_0)$, $k = 1, \ldots, M$, which is generally the stationary distribution of the x_t, with $\pi_0^k = 1/M$ as this is an equally weighted sample.

Algorithm 10 (General auxiliary particle filter). For $t = 0, .., T-1$: We have $\{x_t^k, \pi_t^k\} \sim p(x_t|y_{1:t})$ for $k = 1, \ldots, M$.

(1) For $k = 1{:}\ M$, compute

$$\omega_{t|t+1}^k = g(y_{t+1}|x_t^k)\pi_t^k, \qquad \pi_{t|t+1}^k = \frac{\omega_{t|t+1}^k}{\sum_{i=1}^M \omega_{t|t+1}^i}.$$

(2) For $k = 1{:}\ M$, sample $\widetilde{x}_t^k \sim \sum_{i=1}^M \pi_{t|t+1}^i \delta(x_t - x_t^i)$.

(3) For $k = 1{:}\ M$, sample $x_{t+1}^k \sim g(x_{t+1}|\widetilde{x}_t^k; y_{t+1})$.

(4) For $k = 1{:}\ M$, compute

$$\omega_{t+1}^k = \frac{p(y_{t+1}|x_{t+1}^k)p(x_{t+1}^k|\widetilde{x}_t^k)}{g_{x_t}(y_{t+1}|x_{t+1}^k)g(x_{t+1}^k|\widetilde{x}_t^k)}, \qquad \pi_{t+1}^k = \frac{\omega_{t+1}^k}{\sum_{i=1}^M \omega_{t+1}^i}.$$

The fully adapted particle filter and the SIR particle filter are two important special cases. In the fully adapted case, the approximations in (3.62) are exact, step 4 becomes unnecessary because $\pi_{t+1}^k = 1/M$, and the algorithm reduces to algorithm 9.

Another special case arises when we use $g(y_{t+1}|x_t) = 1$ and $g(x_{t+1}|x_t, y_{t+1}) = p(x_{t+1}|x_t)$. The algorithm reduces to the SIR method of Gordon et al. (1993) in algorithm 8.

In general, the aim is to make the weights in step 4 as constant as possible, or equivalently to make the joint approximation as close to the true joint as possible in equation (3.63). If we achieve this, then we hope to inherit many of the strengths of full adaptation.

In step 4, the samples x_{t+1}^k with mass π_{t+1}^k together represent the filtered density $p(x_{t+1}|y_{1:t+1})$ and so the moments may be estimated as described in Section 7.1.

The likelihood can be estimated efficiently as a by-product of the algorithm 10 procedure just as it was for algorithm 8 and the fully adapted auxiliary particle filter of algorithm 9. The estimate of the likelihood is

$$\widehat{p}(y_{t+1}|y_t) = \left\{\frac{1}{M}\sum_{k=1}^M \omega_{t|t+1}^k\right\}\left\{\frac{1}{M}\sum_{k=1}^M \omega_{t+1}^k\right\}, \tag{3.64}$$

where $\omega_{t|t+1}$ and ω_{t+1} are the weights of step 2 and step 4 respectively in algorithm 10. The derivation of (3.64) is in Pitt (2002). For the SIR method, the first sum in (3.64) is 1 and the weights in the second sum are $\omega_{t+1}^k = p(y_{t+1}|x_{t+1}^k)$. Hence (3.64) reduces to (3.56) as expected. For the fully adapted case, the second summation becomes 1 and the weights in the first sum are $\omega_{t|t+1}^k = p(y_{t+1}|x_t^k)$ and the estimator for the likelihood reduces to that given in (3.61).

Many different approximations are available, for example, in Pitt and Shephard (1999b), Pitt and Shephard (2001), and Smith and Santos (2006). The simplest, and most generally applicable, approximation is introduced by Pitt and Shephard (2001). As an illustration, we consider the following class of models for which the transition density is conditionally Gaussian,

$$y_t \sim p(y_t|x_t), \quad x_{t+1} \sim N\left(a(x_t); b^2(x_t)\right). \tag{3.65}$$

This model is similar to the model at (3.60) but with a general measurement density which we write as $p(y_{t+1}|x_{t+1}) = \exp\left(l(x_{t+1})\right)$. We assume that $l(x_{t+1})$ is log concave in x_{t+1} for simplicity and approximate $l(x_{t+1})$ by the second-order approximation

$$\widehat{l}_{x_t}(x_{t+1}) = l(\widehat{x}_{t+1}) + (x_{t+1} - x_{t+1})l'(\widehat{x}_{t+1}) + \frac{1}{2}(x_{t+1} - x_{t+1})^2 l''(\widehat{x}_{t+1}) \tag{3.66}$$

around the point $\widehat{x}_{t+1}$ which can be a function of x_t. In this example, a good candidate is $\widehat{x}_{t+1} = E(x_{t+1}|x_t) = a(x_t)$. Then $g_{x_t}(y_{t+1}|x_{t+1}) = \exp(\widehat{l}_{x_t}(x_{t+1}))$ is an approximation to $p(y_{t+1}|x_{t+1})$ and it is clear that we can write $g_{x_t}(y_{t+1}|x_{t+1})p(x_{t+1}|x_t)$ as $g(y_{t+1}|x_t)g(x_{t+1}|x_t, y_{t+1})$ with $g(x_{t+1}|x_t, y_{t+1})$ Gaussian in x_{t+1}. Details are in Pitt and Shephard (2001). Smith and Santos (2006) apply this idea for the stochastic volatility model. There is no reason why a first-order (or zero-th order) expansion cannot be used in (3.66), although the approximation may be worse. Extended Kalman filter (Anderson and Moore 1979: 194) steps may also be used to provide effective proposals.

7.6 Particle filtering for conditionally Gaussian state space models

A useful reduction in the number of particles may be achieved by considering again the special case of the conditionally Gaussian state space model (3.24) (which is a finite mixture of Gaussian state space models) in Section 4.1. This is an interesting case because the particles do not have to be the states x_t but can represent sufficient information more generally. In practice, these methods should require far fewer particles than the standard SIR method of Gordon et al. (1993) for a given level of precision.

Consider again the mixture state space form representation where we have (as earlier),

$$y_t = H_{K_t} x_t + G_{K_t} u_t, \quad u_t \sim N(0, \Sigma_t) \tag{3.67a}$$

$$x_{t+1} = F_{K_{t+1}} x_t + \Gamma_{K_{t+1}} u_t. \tag{3.67b}$$

The intercept terms in both equations are omitted for simplicity. The mixture variables K_t, $t = 1, \ldots, T$ have associated probabilities q_l for $l = 1, .., L$ and are considered independently drawn at each time point (it is straightforward to relax this assumption). Chen and Liu (2000) introduce efficient procedures for this case. A similar problem is considered in Andrieu and Doucet (2002), where a state space form is observed with non-Gaussian error. The crucial aspect of these papers is that we propagate the sufficient terms I_t^j, π_t^j, for $j = 1, .., M$. Here, as we have a mixture of state space models,

I_t^j represents the sufficient moments of the Kalman filter recursions $I_t^j = \{\widehat{x}_{t|t}^j; S_{t|t}^j\}$ and π_t^j is the attached probability, where the π_t^j sum to 1 for each t. Hence,

$$p(x_t|I_t^j) = N(x_t; \widehat{x}_{t|t}^j, S_{t|t}^j).$$

The filter density is therefore represented as

$$p(x_t|y_{1:t}) = \sum_{j=1}^{M} \pi_t^j N(x_t; \widehat{x}_{t|t}^j, S_{t|t}^j).$$

The transition density (conditional upon the component K_{t+1}) is also Gaussian and of the form

$$p(x_{t+1}|I_t^j; K_{t+1}) = N(x_{t+1}; \widehat{x}_{t+1|t,K_{t+1}}^j, S_{t+1|t,K_{t+1}}^j), \tag{3.68}$$

where we show dependence on K_{t+1}. Similarly, the measurement density is of the form

$$p(y_{t+1}|x_{t+1}, K_{t+1}) = N(y_{t+1}; H_{K_{t+1}} x_{t+1}, G_{K_{t+1}} \Sigma_{t+1} G'_{K_{t+1}}). \tag{3.69}$$

Before describing the particle filter for this problem, we note that the one step update of the Kalman filter (conditional upon K_{t+1}) can be used to obtain,

$$p(y_{t+1}|x_{t+1}, K_{t+1}) p(x_{t+1}|I_t^j; K_{t+1}) = p(y_{t+1}|I_t^j, K_{t+1}) p(x_{t+1}|I_t^j; y_{t+1}, K_{t+1}),$$

where, using (3.68) and(3.69),

$$p(y_{t+1}|I_t^j, K_{t+1}) = N\left(y_{t+1}; H_{K_{t+1}} \widehat{x}_{t+1|t,K_{t+1}}^j, R_{t+1,K_{t+1}}^j\right)$$
$$p(x_{t+1}|I_t^j, y_{t+1}, K_{t+1}) = N\left(x_{t+1}; \widehat{x}_{t+1|t,K_{t+1}}^j, S_{t+1|t+1,K_{t+1}}^j\right)$$

with

$$R_{t+1,K_{t+1}}^j = G_{K_{t+1}} \Sigma_{t+1} G'_{K_{t+1}} + H_{K_{t+1}} S_{t+1|t,K_{t+1}}^j H'_{K_{t+1}}$$
$$\widehat{x}_{t+1|t+1,K_{t+1}}^j = \widehat{x}_{t+1|t,K_{t+1}}^j + S_{t+1|t,K_{t+1}}^j H'_{K_{t+1}} (R_{t+1,K_{t+1}}^j)^{-1} (y_{t+1} - H_{K_{t+1}} \widehat{x}_{t+1|t,K_{t+1}}^j)$$
$$S_{t+1|t+1,K_{t+1}}^j = S_{t+1|t,K_{t+1}}^j - S_{t+1|t,K_{t+1}}^j H'_{K_{t+1}} \left(R_{t+1,K_{t+1}}^j\right)^{-1} H_{K_{t+1}} S_{t+1|t,K_{t+1}}^j.$$

These are the Kalman filter equations given in Section 3.1.

We now present the particle filter. Consider,

$$p(x_{t+1}|y_{1:t+1}) \propto \sum_{K_{t+1}=1}^{L} p(y_{t+1}|x_{t+1}; K_{t+1}) \left\{ \sum_{j=1}^{M} p(x_{t+1}|I_t^j; K_{t+1}) \pi_t^j \right\} q_{K_{t+1}}.$$

Similarly to the auxiliary particle filter, consider the corresponding joint density,

$$\begin{aligned} p(x_{t+1}, j, K_{t+1}|y_{1:t+1}) &\propto p(y_{t+1}|x_{t+1}; K_{t+1})p(x_{t+1}|I_t^j; K_{t+1})\pi_t^j q_{K_{t+1}} \\ &= p(x_{t+1}|I_t^j; y_{t+1}, K_{t+1}) \times p(y_{t+1}|I_t^j, K_{t+1})\pi_t^j q_{K_{t+1}}, \end{aligned} \tag{3.70}$$

using the Kalman filter update equations in algorithm 1.

It is now straightforward to use the particle filter. Explicitly, we may sample the particle j and the mixture component K_{t+1} using probability π_t^j and q_k respectively. We do this for $i = 1, \ldots, M$ obtaining j^i and $K_{t+1} = k_{t+1}^i$. Having sampled (j^i, k_{t+1}^i) from the joint, $\pi_t^j q_k$, we now reweight to get

$$\pi_{t+1}^i \propto p(y_{t+1}|I_t^{j^i}, k_{t+1}^i),$$

with $\widehat{x}_{t+1|t+1}^i = \widehat{x}_{t+1|t+1,k_{t+1}^i}^{j^i}$ and $S_{t+1|t+1}^i = S_{t+1|t+1,k_{t+1}^i}^{j^i}$.

Chen and Liu (2000) note that the proposal can be improved by incorporating information about y_{t+1}. We observe that the term $p(x_{t+1}|I_t^j; y_{t+1}, k_{t+1})$ in (3.70) is quite separate in that the particle filter does not depend on it. For each sample (j^i, k_{t+1}^i) we can reconstruct the Gaussian density $p(x_{t+1}|I_t^{j^i}; y_{t+1}, k_{t+1}^i)$, resulting in a Rao-Blackwellization where we are essentially recording mixtures of Gaussians for the filter. This leads to much more efficient inference (for a given number of particles) as demonstrated by Chen and Liu (2000) and Andrieu and Doucet (2002).

8 Particle filtering with parameter estimation

Particle filters are extremely successful as pure filters. If designed well, they provide a very accurate representation of $p(x_t|y_{1:t}; \theta)$ for all t. For some, relatively benign, models such as the basic SV model, the simple method of Gordon et al. (1993) is sufficient to produce reliable results (in the absence of extreme outliers). When used to estimate the smoothed path $p(x_{1:t}|y_{1:t}; \theta)$ or to estimate parameters sequentially as $p(\theta|y_{1:t})$, the results are mixed. A variety of techniques have appeared recently in the literature.

There are two main approaches to inference on fixed parameters using particle filters. The first, most ambitious, approach, which is described in Section 8.1, is on-line inference. This approach attempts to draw jointly from the evolving density $p(\theta; x_t|y_{1:t})$. There are problems (typically degeneracy problems) associated with approaches of this type. The second, less ambitious approach, is presented in Section 8.2 where the goal is inference given all of the available data $p(\theta|y_{1:T})$.

8.1 Online parameter estimation

For online inference, the first attempts (e.g. Liu and West 2001) quite naturally included the unknown parameters as part of the states, using the augmented state space model

$$y_t \sim p(y_t|x_t;\theta),\ x_{t+1} \sim p(x_{t+1}|x_t;\theta_t),\ \theta_{t+1} = \theta_t, \quad t = 1, \ldots, T.$$

Clearly, the combined system $\alpha_t = (x_t', \theta_t')'$ is an evolving unobserved state. However, the lack of noise in the evolution of θ_t leads to a deterioration of the representation of $p(\theta|y_{1:t})$ through time and as t becomes large, the particle filter representation moves further away from the true density $p(\theta|y_{1:t})$ and becomes degenerate as $t \to \infty$.

8.1.1 Sufficient statistics updates

Storvik (2002) presents a sequential updating scheme which does not rely on augmenting the parameters to the state equation. Similar concepts are proposed by Berzuini et al. (1997) and explored by Fearnhead (2002). This idea is developed and improved by Polson et al. (2008). For both the fully adapted auxiliary particle filter and the mixture state space form approach, the efficient techniques rely on conjugacy and integrating out unnecessary quantities. In the former case of Section 7.4, this means integrating out the corresponding state x_{t+1} to obtain $p(y_{t+1}|x_t)$ and in the latter case of Section 7.6, the states are integrated out to give

$$p(y_{t+1}|I_t^j; K_t).$$

This leads to greater efficiency. A similar idea is employed by Storvik (2002).

Before discussing parameter estimation, we consider filtering again. In performing particle filtering, a weighted sample x_t^k is obtained, with attached probabilities π_t^k for $k = 1, \ldots, M$ generated from $p(x_t|y_{1:t};\theta)$. However, we may also think about this as being a weighted sample of the entire trajectory $x_{1:t}^k$ for $k = 1, \ldots, M$, with attached probabilities π_t^k as a representation of $p(x_{1:t}|y_{1:t};\theta)$. For example, we may think of this being the result of algorithm 8, where, importantly, x_{t-1}^k is the "parent" of the sample x_t^k. That is the point at time $t-1$ from which we derived x_t^k. Similarly, x_{t-2}^k is the "parent" of the sample x_{t-1}^k and so on through time until we obtain the original parent x_1^k for $k = 1, \ldots, M$. The important aspect to note is that the standard particle filter methods may be very effective at producing samples from $p(x_t|y_{1:t};\theta)$, with many distinct samples and fairly even weights π_t^k. However, the number of distinct parents goes down as we move backwards in time from t to $t-1$ to $t-2$ etc. If t is reasonably large, we may have very few distinct samples of x_1^k for $k = 1, \ldots, M$. Indeed, we could have simply M identical copies of the same point. So the trajectory $x_{1:t}^k$ for $k = 1, \ldots, M$ with probabilities π_t^k provides a good representation at time t for $p(x_t|y_{1:t};\theta)$, but an increasingly poor representation as we go h periods back in time for $p(x_{t-h}|y_{1:t};\theta)$. See Figure 1 in Andrieu et al. (2005). This observation relates closely to the sufficient statistics updating method described presently.

Let us assume that the density of the parameters given the entire history of the states and the observations $p(\theta|x_{1:t}, y_{1:t})$ is available in closed form. We shall go further and assume that the dependence can be captured by a fairly low-dimensional sufficient statistic $T(x_{1:t}, y_{1:t})$. So we have $p(\theta|x_{1:t}, y_{1:t}) = p(\theta|T(x_{1:t}, y_{1:t}))$. An example of this is the stochastic volatility model where the log-volatility evolves as

$$x_{t+1} = \mu^* + \phi x_t + \sigma_\eta \eta_t,$$

η_t is standard Gaussian, and for simplicity we assume the initial condition $x_0 \sim N(0, 1)$. In this case, we have a linear model formulation and so the updating distribution $p(\theta|x_{1:t})$, is a standard Gaussian-gamma (e.g. Koop 2003). We assume conjugacy (although we may be able to relax this by using importance sampling) to be able to directly update as

$$\begin{aligned} p(\theta|T(x_{1:t+1}, y_{1:t+1})) &= \frac{p(y_{t+1}, x_{t+1}|\theta; x_{1:t}, y_{1:t})p(\theta|T(x_{1:t}, y_{1:t}))}{p(y_{t+1}, x_{t+1}|x_{1:t}, y_{1:t})} \\ &= \frac{p(y_{t+1}|x_{t+1}; \theta)p(x_{t+1}|x_t; \theta)p(\theta|T(x_{1:t}, y_{1:t}))}{p(y_{t+1}, x_{t+1}|x_{1:t}, y_{1:t})}. \end{aligned} \tag{3.71}$$

Consider now the SIR particle filter applied to this problem. We will, however, use the auxiliary particle filter manner of expressing this problem. Suppose that at time t, we have particles $\{x_t^k, T_{1:t}^k\}$ with associated mass π_t^k for $k = 1, \ldots, M$ where $T_{1:t}^k = T(x_{1:t}^k;, y_{1:t})$.

$$p(x_{1:t+1}; \theta; k|y_{1:t+1}) \propto p(y_{t+1}|x_{t+1}; \theta)p(x_{t+1}|x_t^k; \theta)p(\theta|T_{1:t}^k)\pi_t^k.$$

Note that $T_{1:t}^k$ are the low-dimensional sufficient statistics that we have recorded. We may now rearrange this expression, from which we wish to sample, as

$$\begin{aligned} p(x_{1:t+1}; \theta; k|y_{1:t+1}) &\propto p(y_{t+1}|x_{t+1}; \theta)p(x_{t+1}|x_t^k; \theta)p(\theta|T_{1:t}^k)\pi_t^k \\ &= p(y_{t+1}, x_{t+1}|x_{1:t}^k; y_{1:t})p(\theta|T_{1:t}^k; x_{t+1}, y_{t+1})\pi_t^k. \end{aligned}$$

So on the jth draw the particle filter works by sampling $k = k^j$ say with probability π_t^k then sampling $\theta^j \sim p(\theta|T_{1:t}^k)$ and $x_{t+1}^j \sim p(x_{t+1}|x_t^k; \theta)$. The weights are then computed as,

$$\pi_{t+1}^j = \frac{p(y_{t+1}|x_{t+1}^j; \theta^j)}{\sum_{i=1}^M p(y_{t+1}|x_{t+1}^i; \theta^i)}.$$

We augment the sufficient statistics via

$$T_{1:t+1}^j = T(x_{1:t}^{k^j}, x_{t+1}^j, y_{1:t+1}).$$

We now have that the posterior for

$$p(\theta|y_{1:t+1}) \simeq \sum_{j=1}^{M} p(\theta|T^j_{1:t+1})\pi^j_{t+1}. \tag{3.72}$$

The algorithm proceeds in a straightforward manner through the next time step.

It may be useful to think of the Storvik filter as applying to a modified state space form for which the parameters have been integrated out. The particle filter is then essentially applied to the system

$$p(y_t, x_t|x_{1:t-1}) = \int p(y_t|x_t;\theta)p(x_t|x_{t-1};\theta)p(\theta|x_{1:t-1})d\theta.$$

If the measurement equation does not involve θ (e.g. in the SV model) so that $p(y_t|x_t;\theta) = p(y_t|x_t)$, then,

$$p(y_t, x_t|x_{1:t-1}) = p(y_t|x_t)p(x_t|x_{1:t-1}),$$

$$p(x_t|x_{1:t-1}) = \int p(x_t|x_{t-1};\theta)p(\theta|x_{1:t-1})d\theta.$$

The particle filter, for instance algorithm 8, is applied to this system and the moving posterior for θ is recorded separately as described. It is also straightforward to consider an auxiliary particle filter applied to this system.

The great advantage of this approach is that rather than propagating and reweighting particles which are the parameters themselves, say θ^j, we are instead propagating the sufficient summary quantities associated with these parameters. We can therefore never collapse to a single point for θ as we always have a mixture representation.

The disadvantage relates to the point made at the beginning of this section. Particle filters provide poor representations of smoothing densities. Implicitly, the sufficient statistic $T^j_{1:t+1}$ is a function of the past trajectory $x^j_{1:t+1}$ and whilst there may be many distinct copies of x^j_{t+1} for $j = 1, \ldots, M$, there will be very few distinct copies of x^j_{t-h} as h becomes large. As a consequence, for a single run of this filter the left-hand side of (3.72) becomes too tight and centered at the wrong value relative to $p(\theta|y_{1:t+1})$ as t becomes large. How quickly this degeneracy happens depends upon the length of the times series and the signal to noise ratio. Figures 3.2 and 3.3 of Andrieu et al. (2005) provide a good illustration of the degeneracies associated with this methodology which may occur through time.

In Lopes et al. (2010), the propagation of sufficient statistics for the parameters, together with conditional state space form models, is considered. In this chapter, it is argued that for many time series models of realistic length encountered in econometrics the degeneracy just described is not apparent.

8.2 MCMC with particle filters

This section discusses how to perform Bayesian inference using MCMC combined with standard SIR particle filtering. They will also hold for more general auxiliary particle filters. Let $\widehat{p}_M(y|\theta)$ be the particle filter estimate of the likelihood for a given θ and number of particles M. We will also refer to $\widehat{p}_M(y|\theta)$ as the simulated likelihood. Proposition 7.4.1 of Del Moral (2004) shows that the simulated likelihood is unbiased,

$$E\left(\widehat{p}_M(y|\theta)\right) = p(y|\theta), \tag{3.73}$$

for any M and for standard multinomial sampling and the stratified methods outlined in Section 7.3. The expectation at equation (3.73) is with respect to all the random numbers generated in the particle filter both for the state propagation and for the resampling. These correspond to steps 1 and 3 of algorithm 8.

The unbiasedness property is particularly useful for constructing MCMC methods using particle filters. The results of Andrieu et al. (2007) suggest that importance sampling estimates can be placed into a Metropolis algorithm with the result that we still get the correct invariant distribution. Andrieu et al. (2010) show how the true likelihood can be formulated as the marginal arising from an auxiliary density based on the particle filter likelihood whose invariant distribution is still correct. Explicitly, we can write down the simulated likelihood as $g_M(y|\theta; u) = \widehat{p}_M(y|\theta)$, where u represents the stream of random numbers, arising from the density $g_M(u)$, say. Thus, we can write (3.73) as

$$\int g_M(y|\theta; u) g_M(u) du = p(y|\theta). \tag{3.74}$$

We note that the random numbers u are generated from $g_M(u)$, which means that the same random numbers u should not be used for different θ or even the same θ as then (3.74) will not hold.

Let $p(\theta)$ be the prior for θ. Then,

$$g_M(\theta, u|y) \propto g_M(y|\theta; u) p(\theta) g_M(u)$$

is the joint posterior for (θ, u), with the marginal posterior for θ given by

$$g_M(\theta|y) \propto g_M(y|\theta) p(\theta) \propto p(\theta|y).$$

That is, the marginal density $g_M(\theta|y)$ of $g_M(\theta, u|y)$ is the target density $p(\theta|y)$.

We can therefore set up an MCMC scheme operating on the joint density $g_M(\theta, u|y)$. Suppose we propose a move from $\theta^{(j)}$ to $\theta^{(j+1)}$ from the conditional density $q(\theta^{(j+1)}|\theta^{(j)})$ in a Metropolis Hastings scheme, accepting the move with probability,

$$\alpha(\theta^{(j)} \to \theta^{(j+1)}) = \min\left\{1, \frac{g_M(y_{1:T}|\theta^{(j+1)}; u^{(j+1)}) p(\theta^{(j+1)})}{g_M(y_{1:T}|\theta^{(j)}; u^{(j)}) p(\theta^{(j)})} \frac{q(\theta^{(j)}|\theta^{(j+1)})}{q(\theta^{(j+1)}|\theta^{(j)})}\right\}. \tag{3.75}$$

Note that $u \sim g_M(u)$ is drawn independently across Metropolis draws and does not appear in the Metropolis Hastings ratio at (3.75) because it cancels out. The invariant distribution for this MCMC scheme is $p(\theta|y) \propto p(y|\theta)p(\theta)$. Thus, even though we use the approximate (simulated) likelihood in our MCMC algorithm, the draws arise from the correct posterior density based on the correct likelihood $p(y|\theta)$. This is a powerful result as it allows likelihood inference on previously intractable models even for high-dimensional states.

Silva et al. (2009) implement particle filter MCMC for the stochastic volatility model with leverage at (3.3) and for the Poisson time series model at (3.38). The proposal density $q(\theta|\theta') = q(\theta)$ is obtained through adaptive sampling. The reported results show that particle filter MCMC is feasible without using an excessively large number of particles.

Summary Particle filter MCMC has the potential to greatly extend the range of time series models that can be fully analyzed. It also has the potential to simplify Bayesian computational work in general state space models because the simulated likelihood is a noisy integral of the states, so that the MCMC involves particle filtering (which is now standard), together with the generation of the parameters.

However, the ideas involved in particle filter MCMC are quite new and it is still necessary to learn how to to obtain practical MCMC simulation algorithms. The following are some of the issues that require further work. (a) How many particles should be used in the particle filter. In principle, (3.73) holds for even one particle, that is, $M = 1$. In practice, a small number of particles M will give a very noisy estimate $\widehat{p}_M(y|\theta)$ of $p(y|\theta)$, which will result in very high rejection rates in the Metropolis Hastings step and the chain is also likely to get stuck frequently, and even catastrophically. By "stuck catastrophically", we mean that for a given $\theta = \theta^*$ we may get a realization of u such that $\widehat{p}_M(y|\theta^*) = g_M(y\theta^*, u)$ is much larger than $p(y|\theta^*)$. At the next step of the chain, the Metropolis Hastings ratio at (3.75) is likely to be very small so the chain will get stuck at that θ^* for a very large number of iterations. (b) Building good proposals $q(\cdot)$ without excessive computational cost is challenging because the likelihood is noisy so it is not feasible to use methods requiring derivatives of the likelihood. (c) We need to study how the methods scale up with the dimension of θ and the state vector.

9 Model selection, model averaging, and model diagnostics

Model selection, model averaging, and model diagnostics are important issues in the Bayesian analysis of time series data, but most of the discussion about these issues applies more generally to any Bayesian analysis. In this section, our discussion focuses mostly on those aspects that are specific to time series models.

9.1 Model selection and model averaging

Suppose we consider fitting $M > 1$ models $\mathcal{M}_1, \ldots, \mathcal{M}_M$ to the data. Model selection chooses one of these models. For example, we may consider fitting dynamic factor models (see Section 6.2 of Chapter 7 in this volume, by Del Negro and Schorfheide, and Section 5.4 of this chapter) with one to four factors, so that we have four models to choose from. A popular Bayesian method for carrying out model choice is to use the model having the highest posterior probability. Chib (Chapter 5 in this volume), Section 7, discusses model selection in the Bayesian context and the central role played by the marginal likelihood in Bayesian model selection. In particular, if the prior model probabilities are equal, then choosing a model with maximum posterior probability is the same as choosing the model with maximum marginal likelihood. The marginal likelihood of model $\mathcal{M}_k$ is

$$m(y; \mathcal{M}_k) = \int p(y|\theta_k; \mathcal{M}_k) p(\theta_k; \mathcal{M}_k) d\theta_k, \tag{3.76}$$

where θ_k is the vector of parameters in model $\mathcal{M}_k$ and $p(\theta_k; \mathcal{M}_k)$ is its prior.

The computation of the marginal likelihood is often more challenging in state space models because of the presence of the high-dimensional state vector. One approach to evaluate the marginal likelihood is to use the methods of Chib (1995) and Chib and Jeliazkov (2001), who express the marginal likelihood of model $\mathcal{M}$ with parameter vector θ as

$$m(y; \mathcal{M}) = \frac{p(y|\theta^*; \mathcal{M}) p(\theta^*; \mathcal{M})}{p(\theta^*|y; \mathcal{M})}, \tag{3.77}$$

where θ^* is a value of θ with a high value for the ordinate $p(\theta^*|y; \mathcal{M})$ such as the posterior mean or componentwise posterior median. We refer to Chib (1995), Chib and Jeliazkov (2001), and Chapter 5 in this volume for methods of estimating the denominator of (3.77) using MCMC methods and discuss the evaluation of the numerator.

We note that $\theta = \theta^*$ is fixed in the denominator so that the likelihood evaluation is at a fixed parameter value independent of the size of the parameter space. A general expression for the likelihood of a state space model is given in Section 2.3. For some simple state space models, such as the Gaussian linear state space, the likelihood can be evaluated explicitly (see Section 3.3). In general, the likelihood cannot be evaluated explicitly, but as discussed in Section 8.2, the particle filter provides an unbiased estimate $p(y|\theta^*; \mathcal{M})$, with the variance of the estimator going to zero as the number of particles increases. As an example, see Kim et al. (1998) for an application to an SV model and Chib et al. (2006) for an application to factor SV models.

We now discuss a second approach to model selection that is particularly useful when the models under consideration are submodels of a general model which can be expressed in additive form. Consider the additive model

$$y_t \sim p(y_t|s_t), \quad s_t = f_{1t} + f_{2t} + f_{3t}, \tag{3.78}$$

where the f_{it} are independent and each can be expressed in state space form. An example of such a model is a time series model, with f_{1t} a random walk trend, f_{2t} is the seasonal, and f_{3t} a stationary noise with an autoregressive structure. Suppose now that we wish to select between the full model (3.78) and all its possible sub-models. Thus, we can consider model selection between eight possible models, that is, each of the three components can be in or out. Instead of estimating each of the eight models separately, it is possible to use variable selection ideas to compute the posterior probabilities of all the eight models simultaneously. This approach will work well if (3.78) can be expressed in Gaussian or conditionally Gaussian form as in Section 4. See Shively et al. (1999) for further discussion and examples.

Model averaging Suppose that we wish to evaluate some entity g that is common to all models under consideration, conditional on $y = y_{1:T}$, for example, the expected value of the future observation $g = y_{T+1}$. One approach to doing so is to first carry out model selection to obtain a model $\mathcal{M}_k$ say, and then estimate the expected value based on the selected model and y. A second approach is to take a weighted average of expected values of all the models, with the weights being the posterior model probabilities. Such an approach is called model averaging. See Hoeting et al. (1999) for a general discussion of Bayesian model averaging.

9.2 Model Diagnostics

In addition to model fitting and model selection, we may wish to compute model diagnostics to see if a particular model fits the data. This section outlines an approach to model diagnostics assuming a univariate and continuous dependent variable y_t. Suppose first that we have a state space model whose parameter vector θ is known, and let $F(y_t|x_t;\theta)$ be the cumulative distribution function of y_t conditional on x_t and $F(y_t|y_{1:t-1};\theta)$ the cumulative distribution function of y_t conditional on $y_{1:t-1}$. Then, for $t = 1, \ldots, T$,

$$F(y_t|y_{1:t-1};\theta) = \int F(y_t|x_t;\theta)p(x_t|y_{1:t-1};\theta)dx_t. \tag{3.79}$$

Suppose that the model is correctly specified and θ is the true value of the parameter. It then follows from Smith (1985) that $\zeta_{t,\theta} = F(y_t|y_{1:t-1};\theta), t = 1, \ldots, T$, is a sequence of independent and uniformly distributed random variables on $[0, 1]$ and one can use the $\zeta_{t,\theta}$ to form diagnostics, for example, by transforming them to standard normal random variables. In practice, θ is unknown so that an estimate of $\widehat{\theta}$ of θ if often plugged into (3.79). The $\zeta_{t,\theta}, t = 1, \ldots, T$ can be evaluated explicitly for some state space models such as the Gaussian linear state space model. The particle filter provides a general approach for estimating the $\zeta_{t,\theta}$; see Kim et al. (1998) for an application to SV models.

Instead of plugging an estimate of θ into $\zeta_{t,\theta}$, it is possible to integrate out θ. See Geweke and Amisano (2010) for an application. However, this usually requires running a separate MCMC simulation for each t, which may be very expensive for some models.

Gerlach et al. (1999) propose an importance sampling approach to integrating out θ for each t, to make the computations tractable, and apply this idea to the conditionally Gaussian state space models in Section 4.

References

Aguilar, O., and West, M. (2000), "Bayesian Dynamic Factor Models and Variance Matrix Discounting for Portfolio Allocation," *Journal of Business and Economic Statistics*, 18: 338–57.

Albert, J., and Chib, S. (1993), "Bayesian Analysis of Binary and Polychotomous Response Data," *Journal of the American Statistical Association*, 88: 669–79.

Amisano, G., and Federico, L. (2005), "Alternative Time-Varying Parameter Specifications for Bayesian VAR Models," in M. Mazzoli and F. Arcelli (eds.), *Atti della Prima " Lezione Mario Arcell "*, Soveria Mannelli, Italy: Rubbettino, 13–65.

Anderson, B., and Moore, J. (1979), *Optimal Filtering*, Englewood Cliffs, NJ: Prentice-Hall.

Andersson, M., and Karlsson, S. (2008), "Bayesian Forecast Combination for VAR Models," *Bayesian Econometrics Advances in Econometrics*, 23, Amsterdam: Elsevier, pp. 501–24.

Andrieu, C. and Doucet, A. (2002), "Particle Filtering for Partially Observed Gaussian State Space Models," *Journal of the Royal Statistical Society, Series B*, 64: 827–36.

——— and Holenstein, R. (2010), "Particle Markov Chain Monte Carlo (with discussion)," *Journal of the Royal Statistical Society, Series B*, 269–342.

——— and Roberts, G. (2007), "The Expected Auxiliary Variable Method for Monte Carlo Simulation," Unpublished paper.

——— and Tadic, V. (2005), "On-line Parameter Estimation in General State-Space Models," in *44th IEEE Conference on Decision and Control, 2005 and 2005 European Control Conference. CDC-ECC'05*, pp. 332–37.

Ansley, C., and Kohn, R. (1985), "Estimation, Filtering and Smoothing in State Space Models with Incompletely Specified Initial Conditions," *Annals of Statistics*, 13: 1286–316.

——— (1990), "Filtering and Smoothing in State Space Models with Partially Diffuse Initial Conditions," *Journal of Time Series Analysis*, 11: 275–93.

Berzuini, C., Best, N., Gilks, W., and Larizza, C. (1997), "Dynamical Conditional Independence Models and Markov Chain Monte Carlo Methods," *Journal of the American Statistical Association*, 92: 1403–12.

Brockwell, P., and Davis, R. (2009), *Time Series: Theory and Methods*, 2nd edn., New York: Springer.

Carlin, B. P., Polson, N. G., and Stoffer, D. S. (1992), "A Monte Carlo Approach to Nonnormal and Nonlinear State-Space Modelling," *Journal of the American Statistical Association*, 87: 493–500.

Carpenter, J. R., Clifford, P., and Fearnhead, P. (1999), "An Improved Particle Filter for Nonlinear Problems," *IEE Proceedings on Radar, Sonar and Navigation*, 146: 2–7.

Carter, C., and Kohn, R. (1994), "On Gibbs Sampling for State-Space Models," *Biometrika*, 81: 541–53.

——— (1996), "Markov Chain Monte Carlo in Conditionally Gaussian State Space Models," *Biometrika*, 83: 589–601.

——— (1997), "Semiparametric Bayesian inference for Time Series with Mixed Spectra," *Journal of the Royal Statistical Society, Series B*, 255–68.

Carvalho, C., Chang, J., Lucas, J., Nevins, J., Wang, Q., and West, M. (2008), "High-Dimensional Sparse Factor Modelling: Applications in Gene Expression Genomics," *Journal of the American Statistical Association*, 103: 1438–56.

Chen, R. and Liu, J., (2000), "Mixture Kalman filters," *Journal of the Royal Statistical Society, Series B*, 62: 493–508.

Chib, S. (1995), "Marginal Likelihood from the Gibbs Output," *Journal of the American Statistical Association*, 90: 1313–21.

——— (1998), "Estimation and Comparison of Multiple Change-Point Models," *Journal of Econometrics*, 86: 221–41.

—— and Jeliazkov, I. (2001), "Marginal Likelihood from the Metropolis-Hastings Output," *Journal of the American Statistical Association*, 96: 270–81.

—— Nardari, F., and Shephard, N. (2006), "Analysis of High Dimensional Multivariate Stochastic Volatility Models," *Journal of Econometrics*, 134: 341–71.

Cripps, E., Carter, C., and Kohn, R. (2005), "Variable Selection and Covariance Selection in Multivariate Regression Model," in D. Dey and C. Rao (eds.), *Handbook of Statistics: Bayesian Thinking: Modeling and Computation*, vol. 25, Amsterdam: Elsevier Science.

De Jong, P. (1989), "The Diffuse Kalman Filter," *Annals of Statistics*, 19: 1073–83.

—— and Shephard, N. (1995), "The Simulation Smoother for Time Series Models," *Biometrika*, 82: 339–50.

Del Moral, P. (2004), *Feynman-Kac Formulae: Genealogical and Interacting Particle Systems with Applications*, New York: Springer Verlag.

Del Negro, M. and Otrok, C. (2008), "Dynamic Factor Models with Time-Varying Parameters: Measuring Changes in International Business Cycles," Technical Report 326, Federal Reserve Bank of New York Staff Reports, available at http://papers.ssrn.com/sol3/papers.cfm?abstract_id=113616.

Doan, R., Litterman, R., and Sims, C. (1984), "Forecasting and Conditional Projection using Realistic Prior Distributions," *Econometric Reviews*, 3: 1–100.

Douc, R., Moulines, E., and Olsson, J. (2008), "Optimality of the Auxiliary Particle Filter," *Probabability and Mathematical Statistics*, 28: 1–28.

Durbin, J. and Koopman, S. J. (2001), *Time Series Analysis by State Space Methods*, The Oxford Statistical Science Series, Oxford: Oxford University Press.

——— (2002), "A Simple and Efficient Simulation Smoother for State Space Time Series Analysis," *Biometrika*, 89: 603–16.

Elerian, O., Chib, S., and Shephard, N. (2001), "Likelihood Inference for Discretely Observed Nonlinear Diffusions," *Econometrica*, 69: 959–93.

Fearnhead, (2002), "MCMC, Sufficient Statistics Particle Filter," *Journal of Computational and Graphical Statistics*, 11: 848–62.

Frűwirth-Schnatter, S. (1994), "Data Augmentation and Dynamic Linear Models," *Journal of Time Series Analysis*, 15: 183–202.

—— (2004), "Efficient Bayesian parameter estimation," in A. Harvey, S. Koopman, and N. Shephard, eds. *State space and Unobserved Component Models*, Cambridge: Cambridge University Press, 123–51.

—— and Wagner, H. (2006), "Auxiliary Mixture Sampling for Parameter-Driven Models of Time Series of Counts with Applications to State Space Modeling," *Biometrika*, 93: 827–41.

——— (2008), "Marginal Likelihoods for Non-Gaussian Models using Auxiliary Mixture Sampling," *Computational Statistics and Data Analysis*, 52: 4608–24.

Gelfand, A. E., Sahu, S. K., and Carlin, B. P. (1995), "Efficient Parameterisations for Normal Linear Mixed Models," *Biometrika*, 82: 479–88.

George, E. I., Ni, S., and Sun, D. (2008), "Bayesian Stochastic Search for VAR Model Restriction," *Journal of Econometrics*, 142: 553–80.

Gerlach, R., Carter, C., and Kohn, R. (1999), "Diagnostics for Time Series Analysis," *Journal of Time Series Analysis*, 20: 309–30.

——— ——— ——— (2000), "Efficient Bayesian Inference for Dynamic Mixture Models," *Journal of the American Statistical Association*, 95: 819–28.

Geweke, J., and Amisano, G. (2010), "Comparing and Evaluating Bayesian Predictive Distributions of Asset Returns," *International Journal of Forecasting*, 26: 216–30.

Giordani, P., and Kohn, R. (2008), "Efficient Bayesian Inference for Multiple Change-Point and Mixture Innovation Models," *Journal of Business and Economic Statististics*, 26: 66–77.

——— ——— (2010), "Adaptive Independent Metropolis-Hastings by Fast Estimation of Mixture of Normals," *Journal of Computational and Graphical Statistics*: see http://pubs.amstat.org/doi/abs/10.1198/jcgs.2009.07174.

——— ——— and van Dijk, D. (2007), "A Unified Approach to Nonlinearity, Structural Change, and Outliers," *Journal of Econometrics*, 137: 112–33.

Gordon, N. J., Salmond, D., and Smith, A. (1993), "A Novel Approach to Nonlinear and Non-Gaussian Bayesian State Estimation," *IEE-Proceedings F*, 140: 107–13.

Harrison, J., and West, M. (1997), *Bayesian Forecasting and Dynamic Models*, New York: Springer-Verlag.

Harvey, A. (1993), *Time Series Models*, New York: Harvey Wheatsheaf.

——— Ruiz, E., and Shephard, N. (1994), "Multivariate Stochastic Variance Models," *Review of Economic Studies*, 61: 247–64.

Hoeting, J., Madigan, D., Raftery, A., and Volinsky, C. (1999), "Bayesian Model Averaging," *Statistical Science*, 14: 382–401.

Holmes, C., and Held, L. (2006), "Bayesian Auxiliary Variable Models for Binary and Multinomial Regression," *Bayesian Analysis*, 1: 145–68.

Jacquier, E., Polson, N. G., and Rossi, P. E. (1994), "Bayesian Analysis of Stochastic Volatility Models (with Discussion)," *Journal of Business and Economic Statististics*, 12, 371–417.

Kalman, R. (1960), "A New Approach to Linear Filtering and Prediction Problems," *Transactions ASME Journal of Basic Engineering*, D82: 35–45.

Kim, C., and Nelson, C. (1999), *State Space Models with Regime Switching: Classical and Gibbs-Sampling Approaches with Applications*, Cambridge, Mass. MIT Press.

Kim, S., Shephard, N., and Chib, S. (1998), "Stochastic Volatility: Likelihood Inference and Comparison with ARCH Models," *Review of Economic Studies*, 65: 361–94.

Kitagawa, G. (1987), "Non-Gaussian State Space Modelling of Non-Stationary Time Series," *Journal of the American Statistical Association*, 82: 503–14.

——— (1996), "Monte Carlo Filter and Smoother for Non-Gaussian Nonlinear State Space Models," *Journal of Computational and Graphical Statistics*, 5: 1–25.

Kitagawa, G., and Gersch, W. (1996), *Smoothness Priors Analysis of Time Series*, New York: Springer Verlag.

Kloeden, P., and Platen, E. (1992), *Numerical Solutions to Stochastic Differential Equations*, New York: Springer.

Kohn, R., and Ansley, C. F. (1985), "Efficient Estimation and Prediction in Time Series Regression Models," *Biometrika*, 72: 694–7.

——— ——— (1986), "Estimation, Prediction and Interpolation for ARIMA Models with Missing Data," *Journal of the American Statistical Association*, 81: 751–61.

Koop, G. (2003), *Bayesian Econometrics*, Chichester: Wiley Interscience.

——— and Korobilis, D. (2009), "Bayesian Multivariate Time Series Methods for Empirical Macroeconomics," available at http://personal.strath.ac.uk/gary.koop/kk3.pdf.

——— Leon-Gonzalez, R., and Strachan, R. (2009), "On the Evolution of Monetary Policy," *Journal of Economic Dynamics and Control*, 33: 997–1017.

——— and Potter, S. (2008), "Time Varying VARs with Inequality Restrictions," available at http://personal.strath.ac.uk/gary.koop/koop_potter14.pdf.

Koopman, S. (1997), "Exact Initial Kalman Filtering and Smoothing for Non-stationary Time Series Models," *Journal of the American Statistical Association*, 92: 1630–38.

——— and Durbin, J. (2000), "Fast Filtering and Smoothing for Multivariate State Space Models," *Journal of Time Series Analysis*, 21: 281–96.

Lando, D. (1998), "On Cox Processes and Credit Risky Securities," *Review of Derivatives Research*, 2: 99–120.

Liu, J. S. (1996), "Metropolized Independent Sampling with Comparison to Rejection Sampling and Importance Sampling," *Statistics and Computing*, 6: 113–19.

——— and Chen, R. (1995), "Blind Deconvolution via Sequential Imputation," *Journal of the American Statistical Association*, 90: 567–76.

——— ——— (1998), "Sequential Monte Carlo methods for Dynamic Systems," *Journal of the American Statistical Association*, 93: 1032–44.

——— and West, M. (2001), "Combined Parameter and State Estimation in Simulation-Based Filtering," *Sequential Monte Carlo Methods in Practice*, 197–223.

——— Wong, W. H., and Kong, A. (1994), "Covariance Structure of the Gibbs Sampler with Applications to the Comparison of Estimators and Augmentation Schemes," *Biometrika*, 81: 27–40.

Lopes, H., Carvalho, C., Johannes, M., and Polson, N. (2010), "Particle Learning for Sequential Bayesian Computation," *Bayesian Statistics*, 9: 709–40.

McCulloch, R., and Tsay, R. (1993), "Bayesian Inference and Prediction for Mean and Variance Shifts in Autoregressive Time Series," *Journal of the American Statistical Association*, 88: 968–78.

Pitt, M. K. (2002), "Smooth particle filters for likelihood maximisation," Available at http://www.warwick.ac.uk/fac/soc/economics/staff/academic/pitt/publications/smoothfilter.pdf.

——— and Shephard, N. (1999a), "Analytic Convergence Rates and Parametrization Issues for the Gibbs Sampler and State Space Models," *Journal of Time Series Analysis*, 20: 63–85.

——— ——— (1999b), "Filtering via Simulation: Auxiliary Particle Filter," *Journal of the American Statistical Association*, 94: 590–9.

——— ——— (1999c), "Time Varying Covariances: A Factor Stochastic Volatility Approach (with Discussion)," in J. M. Bernardo, J. O. Berger, A. Dawid, and A., Smith, (eds.), *Bayesian Statistics 6*, Oxford: Oxford University Press, 547–70.

——— ——— (2001), "Auxillary Variable based Particle filters," in *Sequential Mante Carlo Methods in Practice*, eds. de Frcitas, N., Doucet, A., and Gordon, N.J., New York: Springer-valag, pp. 273–293.

Polson, N., Stroud, J., and Muller, P. (2008), "Practical Filtering with Sequential Parameter Learning," *Journal of the Royal Statistical Society: Series B (Statistical Methodology)*, 70: 413–28.

Priestley, M. B. (1981), *Spectral Analysis and Time Series*, London: Academic Press.

Primiceri, G. (2005), "Time Varying Structural Vector Autoregressions and Monetary Policy," *Review of Economic Studies*, 72: 821–52.

Roberts, G. O., and Sahu, S. K. (1997), "Updating Schemes, Correlation Structure, Blocking and Parameterization for the Gibbs Sampler," *Journal of the Royal Statistical Society, Series B*, 59: 291–317.

Rubin, D. B. (1988), "Using the SIR Algorithm to Simulate Posterior Distributions," in J. M. Bernardo, M. H. DeGroot, D. V. Lindley, and A. F. M. Smith, (eds.), *Bayesian Statistics 3*, Oxford: Oxford University Press Press, 395–402.

Shephard, N. (1994), "Partial Non-Gaussian State Space." *Biometrika*, 81: 115–31.

—— (1996), "Statistical Aspects of ARCH and Stochastic Volatility," in D. R. Cox, D. V. Hinkley, and O. E. Barndorff-Nielse (eds.), *Models in Econometrics, Finance and Other Fields*, London: Chapman and Hall.

—— and Pitt, M. K. (1997), "Likelihood Analysis of Non-Gaussian Measurement Time Series," *Biometrika*, 84: 653–67.

Shively, T., Kohn, R., and Wood, S. (1999), "Variable Selection and Function Estimation in Additive Nonparametric Regression Using a Data-based Prior," *Journal of the American Statistical Association*, 94: 777–94.

Silva, R., Giordani, P., Kohn, R., and Pitt, M. (2009), "Particle Filtering within Adaptive Metropolis Hastings Sampling," avilable at http://arxiv.org/abs/0911.0230.

Sims, C. A., Waggoner, D. F., and Zha, T. (2008), "Methods for Inference in Large Multiple-equation Markov-switching Models," *Journal of Econometrics*, 146: 255–74.

Smith, A. F. M., and Gelfand, A. (1992), "Bayesian Statistics without Tears: A Sampling-resampling Perspective," *American Statistican*, 46: 84–8.

Smith, J., and Santos, A. (2006), "Second-Order Filter Distribution Approximations for Financial Time Series With Extreme Outliers," *Journal of Business and Economic Statistics*, 24: 329–37.

Smith, J. Q. (1985), "Diagnostic Checks of Non-standard Time Series Models," *Journal of Forecasting*, 4: 283–91.

Storvik, G. (2002), "Particle Filters in State Space Models with the Presence of Unknown Static Parameters," *IEEE Transactions on Signal Processing*, 50: 281–9.

Villani, M. (2009), "Steady State Priors for Vector Autoregression," *Journal of Applied Econometrics*, 24: 630–50.

Wahba, G. (1990), *Spline Models for Observation Data*, Philadelphia: Society for Industrial and Applied Mathematics (SIAM).

CHAPTER 4

FLEXIBLE AND NONPARAMETRIC MODELING

JIM GRIFFIN, FERNANDO QUINTANA, AND MARK STEEL

1 Introduction

The standard distributional assumptions, such as normality, typically have the advantage of simplicity in deriving theoretical results and inference. However, it is often the case that such assumptions do not really fit the data at hand. In that case, we will need to sacrifice some computational and analytical convenience in order to obtain an acceptable fit to the data by using more flexible distributions. This chapter deals with two approaches to this problem. One is to remain in the parametric realm, and to use a more flexible, yet fully parametric, model (often a parametric extension of the standard model). A simple example is the Student-t model, which has an extra degrees of freedom parameter that induces more flexible tail behavior than the normal, and the normal can be seen as the limiting case when the degrees of freedom parameter tends to infinity. Another approach is to adopt nonparametric models, which in a Bayesian context, implies models with an infinite-dimensional parameterization. The latter implies we are dealing with the specification of probability measures in functional spaces (see Bernardo and Smith 1994 and Müller and Quintana 2004), or random probability measures. Thus, we are using a prior over distributions with a very wide support (typically, the space of all distributions), and this allows us to robustify the analysis with respect to parametric assumptions (such as unimodality, symmetry, moment existence). Of course, this comes at a cost in terms of both additional computational effort and also often less interpretability. Thus, such a fully nonparametric analysis is sometimes used as a way to explore the data within a very wide distributional setting and to suggest more adequate parametric models. As an example, the use of a nonparametric inefficiency distribution in the context of stochastic frontiers in Griffin and Steel (2004) directly inspired the use of mixtures of generalized gamma distributions in Griffin and Steel (2008).

Often, flexible modeling is more important in certain aspects of a model than in others. For example, we may be happy with a normal distribution for the measurement error in a stochastic frontier model, but not with a gamma distribution on the inefficiency error term, as the latter is more contentious and also happens to be of central interest in these models. Then we often only use nonparametric distributions for these selected parts of the model (which are difficult to model and/or of particular interest), while retaining parametric assumptions for the rest, leading to so-called semiparametric models.

Sections 2 and 3 of this chapter deal with flexible parametric modeling and nonparametric modeling, respectively, with applications to regional growth data and semiparametric estimation of binomial proportions.

The most commonly used model in econometrics is the linear regression model, which is analysed in detail in the chapter by Li and Tobias on "Bayesian Methods in Microeconometrics" (Chapter 6). Often, the main interest in using such models is the way in which a set of regressors (x) influences the response variable, y. Rather than the linear or polynomial effects typically assumed in standard linear regression models, we can investigate more flexible ways of associating y with x, by for example making the conditional mean of y a flexible function of x. Section 4 of this chapter reviews methods for such flexible mean regression, using either basis functions, such as splines, or Gaussian processes. Applications to the prestige of occupations as a function of income and a cost function for electricity distribution are discussed.

One step further is to free up the entire conditional distribution, and use flexible or nonparametric methods for both the regression function and the error distribution simultaneously. This is a fairly new and burgeoning area, which is briefly discussed in Section 5 of this chapter, with applications to the same prestige data as in the previous section.

The final section concludes and lists some freely available software which can accommodate many of the methods discussed in this chapter. The latter is an excellent way for applied users to familiarize themselves with these techniques in the context of their particular application areas of interest.

2 Flexible parametric modeling

In this section, we will focus on approaches that model extra flexibility, such as skewness, fat tails, bimodality etc., through parametric families of distributions. In econometric modelling, we often start from normal linear regression, which is a convenient assumption for the sampling model, but it may not be a close fit with the observed data. A first deviation from this Gaussian assumption that is often required in practice has to do with the tails: observed data frequently display thicker tails than those under normality.

2.1 Fat tails

It is commonly accepted that normal tails are often too thin in many empirical settings. This goes back at least to Jeffreys (1961), while a maximum-likelihood analysis for models with Student-t sampling was given in Maronna (1976) and Lange et al. (1989). Geweke (1993) provided a Bayesian analysis of the linear regression model with Student-t errors. West (1984) considered the wider class of scale mixtures of normals. Let us now consider this class in the context of a linear regression model. Thus, we assume the observations $y_i \in \Re$ $(i = 1, \ldots, n)$ to be generated from

$$y_i = \boldsymbol{x}_i'\boldsymbol{\beta} + \sigma\varepsilon_i, \tag{4.1}$$

where the k-dimensional vector $\boldsymbol{x}_i$ groups the explanatory variables and $\varepsilon_1, \ldots, \varepsilon_n$ are i.i.d. (independent and identifically distributed) random variables distributed as a scale mixture of normals. This implies that

$$\varepsilon_i \stackrel{d}{=} z_i/\lambda_i^{1/2}, \tag{4.2}$$

where z_i is a standard normal random variable and λ_i an independent random variable with some probability distribution P_{λ_i} on $(0, \infty)$, which is often parameterized by one or more unknown parameters. By choosing different mixing distributions P_{λ_i} we generate the entire class of scale mixtures of normals, covering for example Student-t (a gamma $\mathrm{G}(\nu/2, 2/\nu)$ mixing distribution leads to a Student-t with ν degrees of freedom), Laplace, and symmetric stable distributions. Table 1 of Fernández and Steel (2000) gives a fairly comprehensive summary of known distributions in this class. Scale mixtures of normals are continuous, symmetric, and unimodal and are the only spherical distributions that can always be interpreted as the marginals of higher-dimensional spherical distributions.

The sampling model is thus characterized by the density function

$$p(y_i|\boldsymbol{\beta}, \sigma) = \int_0^\infty \frac{\lambda_i^{1/2}}{(2\pi)^{1/2}\sigma} \exp\left\{-\frac{\lambda_i}{2\sigma^2}(y_i - \boldsymbol{x}_i'\boldsymbol{\beta})^2\right\} \mathrm{d}P_{\lambda_i}. \tag{4.3}$$

Independent replications from (4.3) will constitute the sampling information regarding the model parameters. We usually group the explanatory variables into an $n \times k$ matrix $X = (\boldsymbol{x}_1, \ldots, \boldsymbol{x}_n)'$ which is assumed to be of full column rank (and thus $n \geq k$). In addition, we define $\boldsymbol{y} = (y_1, \ldots, y_n)'$ as the vector of observations.

We now consider the prior structure. The parameters introduced in (4.1) are the regression coefficients $\boldsymbol{\beta} \in \Re^k$ and the scale $\sigma > 0$. A common choice for a non-informative prior distribution is the "independence" Jeffreys' prior given by

$$p(\boldsymbol{\beta},\sigma) \propto \sigma^{-1}. \tag{4.4}$$

The prior in (4.4) is also the reference prior in the sense of Berger and Bernardo (1992a) for any regular distribution on ε_i as shown in Fernández and Steel (1999).

Since the prior distribution in (4.4) is not proper, the existence of the posterior distribution (defined as the conditional distribution of the parameters given the observables) is not guaranteed. The results in Mouchart (1976) imply that such a conditional distribution exists only when the predictive distribution is σ-finite, that is, $p(y) \equiv \int p(y|\boldsymbol{\beta},\sigma)p(\boldsymbol{\beta},\sigma)\mathrm{d}\boldsymbol{\beta}\mathrm{d}\sigma < \infty$ except possibly on a set of y's of Lebesgue measure zero in $\Re^n$. In the context of the model (4.3)–(4.4), Fernández and Steel (2000) prove the following result concerning the feasibility of Bayesian inference:

Theorem 7. Propriety of posterior
Under the prior in (4.4) and with n independent observations from (4.3), the conditional distribution of $(\boldsymbol{\beta},\sigma)$ given y exists if and only if $n \geq k+1$, for any choice of the mixing distribution P_{λ_i}.

Proof: see Fernández and Steel (2000).

Note that the condition $n \geq k+1$ is both necessary and sufficient, and does not involve any properties of the mixing distribution. Thus, for any scale mixture of normals in (4.3) a Bayesian analysis can be conducted on the basis of a sample of at least $k+1$ observations, and, perhaps surprisingly, the wide range of tails accommodated within the class of scale mixtures of normals has no influence whatsoever on the existence of the posterior. □

Inference in these models can naturally exploit the scale mixture representation above through a Gibbs sampler, as first discussed in Geweke (1993) for the special case of the Student-t model. The MCMC sampler now also includes the vector of λ_i's. This is an example of data augmentation as explained in Section 4.1 of Chapter 5 in this volume by Chib. For the Student-t, as mentioned before, P_{λ_i} is $G(\nu/2, 2/\nu)$, and the relevant distribution of the vector of mixing variables is easily drawn from, as each λ_i is independently distributed as $G((\nu+1)/2, 2/\{\nu+\sigma^{-2}(y_i - x_i'\boldsymbol{\beta})^2\})$ in the conditional posterior.[1] Fernández and Steel (2000) briefly discuss MCMC strategies for other members of the class.

2.2 Skewness

Another major concern when dealing with actual data is the usual assumption of symmetry. An important contribution is the skew-normal class of Azzalini (1985), which was formed by multiplying a normal density function by a normal cumulative distribution function (cdf) for $\epsilon \in \Re$:

[1] Of course, this Gibbs sampler is not necessarily the most efficient MCMC strategy, but it is easily implemented and does not require any choice of proposal distribution, such as with Metropolis-Hastings strategies. One additional advantage of this Gibbs sampling strategy is that we conduct inference on individual λ_i's, which immediately informs us on outlying observations.

$$p(\epsilon|\alpha) = 2\phi(\epsilon)\Phi(\alpha\epsilon), \tag{4.5}$$

where $\phi(\cdot)$ and $\Phi(\cdot)$ are the standard normal probability density function (pdf) and cdf, respectively, and the skewness parameter α takes values in $\Re$. For $\alpha = 0$ we retain the usual normal, and for $\alpha \to \infty$ the distribution tends to the positive half-normal. Right and left skewness can be exchanged by changing the sign of α, since $p(\epsilon|\alpha) = p(-\epsilon| - \alpha)$. Location and scale generalizations are immediate. Interestingly, this distribution was used as a prior in O'Hagan and Leonard (1976). The distribution is always unimodal and has a "hidden truncation" representation as follows: if (X, Y) has a bivariate normal distribution with standard marginals and correlation ρ then X given $Y > 0$ has a skew-normal distribution as in (4.5), with α a one-to-one function of ρ. More general classes of hidden truncation models are discussed in Arnold and Beaver (2002). An application in economics where this skew-normal distribution appears naturally is in stochastic frontier modeling, where the composed error term adds together a symmetric measurement error and a one-sided error; if these are, respectively, chosen to be normal and half-normal, the resulting composed error has the skew-normal form of (4.5). The basic idea in (4.5) has also been applied to other settings, such as Student-t distributions in Azzalini and Capitanio (2003) and has been generalized in for example Genton and Loperfido (2005). Inference with even the simple skew normal model in (4.5) can actually be surprisingly challenging. For example, the likelihood resulting from an i.i.d. sample can easily be shown to be monotonic in α when all the ϵ_i have the same sign. Of course, in practice, adding an unknown location parameter to the model would often solve this, but it does highlight some problems with the behavior of the likelihood. In addition, Azzalini (1985) shows that the Fisher information matrix is singular for $\alpha = 0$. This makes maximum likelihood inference very difficult to defend.[2] Liseo (2004) discusses this in some detail and examines Bayesian inference with such distributions, using Jeffreys' priors.[3]

A different approach to inducing skewness was examined and implemented in a Bayesian analysis in Fernández and Steel (1998). They start from a symmetric univariate pdf $f(\cdot)$ with a single mode at zero and introduce inverse scale factors in the positive and negative orthants. This generates the following class of skewed distributions, indexed by a positive scalar γ:

$$p(\epsilon|\gamma) = \frac{2}{\gamma + \frac{1}{\gamma}} \left\{ f\left(\frac{\varepsilon}{\gamma}\right) I_{[0,\infty)}(\varepsilon) + f(\gamma\varepsilon) I_{(-\infty,0)}(\varepsilon) \right\}. \tag{4.6}$$

This leads to a skewed distribution for $\gamma \neq 1$ which retains the unique mode at zero. Clearly, $p(\varepsilon|\gamma) = p(-\varepsilon|1/\gamma)$. It is easy to see that γ controls the mass on both sides of the mode, through

[2] Azzalini (1985) does propose a different parameterization to avoid some of these problems. See also Pewsey (2000).

[3] Interestingly, this problem is one of the very rare examples with a proper Jeffreys' prior for a parameter with unbounded support. In particular, the Jeffreys' prior for the skewness parameter α is proper.

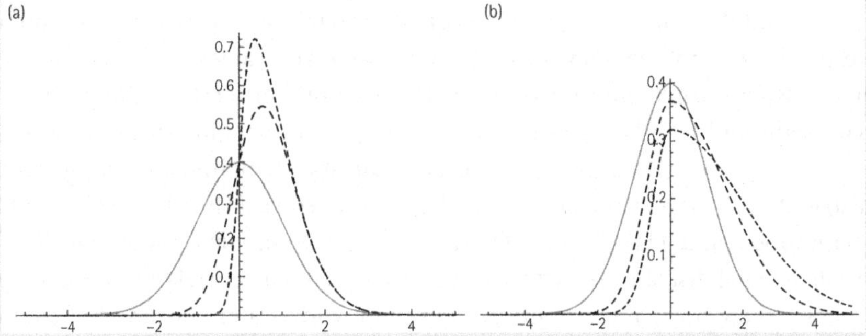

FIGURE 4.1 Examples of skew-normal distributions. Panel (a) displays the Azzalini skew-normal of (4.5) for $\alpha = 0, 1.5, 5$ and panel (b) shows the normal with inverse scaling as in (4.6) for $\gamma = 1, 1.5, 2$ with larger values of α and γ corresponding to shorter dashes. The solid grey line in both graphs is the standard normal corresponding to $\alpha = 0$ and $\gamma = 1$.

$$\frac{P(\varepsilon \geq 0|\gamma)}{P(\varepsilon < 0|\gamma)} = \gamma^2, \tag{4.7}$$

irrespective of the choice of $f(\cdot)$. This implies that γ immediately translates into the measure of skewness introduced in Arnold and Groeneveld (1995)[4] as follows

$$\text{AG}(\epsilon|\gamma) = \frac{\gamma^2 - 1}{\gamma^2 + 1}. \tag{4.8}$$

Thus, AG is a strictly increasing function of γ and by changing γ we can cover the entire range of AG values. Clearly, for $\gamma > 1$ we generate positive (right) skewness while $\gamma < 1$ leads to negative (left) skewness. Expressions for moments are derived in Fernández and Steel (1998).

To illustrate the previous two methods for introducing skewness, Figure 4.1 plots some examples of skewed versions of the normal, displaying various degrees of positive skewness. The same amount of negative skewness would be generated by changing the sign of α in (a) and inverting γ in (b). This clearly shows the difference in the skewing mechanism: whereas the Azzalini approach keeps the right tail unchanged, it squeezes the left tail. This makes the mode shift to the right as α increases. The inverse scaling approach simply applies inverse scale factors to both tails and shifts mass around while maintaining the mode always in the same place.

While the skewing method in (4.6) works for any symmetric unimodal $f(\cdot)$, the analysis in Fernández and Steel (1998) focuses on a Student-t choice for $f(\cdot)$ with unknown degrees of freedom ν. They adopt a regression context as in (4.1) and use a product prior structure with the improper prior in (4.4) and any proper prior on

[4] The Arnold and Groeneveld measure of skewness for unimodal distributions is defined as one minus twice the probability mass to the left of the mode. This measure, denoted here by AG, takes values in $(-1, 1)$ and is zero for symmetric distributions.

ν and γ. They prove that skewness does not affect the existence of the posterior or posterior moments on the regression and scale parameters, and that properness of the posterior is obtained under exactly the same conditions as Theorem 7. A Gibbs sampler for inference is given in some detail in Fernández and Steel (1998), who show that this skew-t distribution can provide a good predictive fit to skewed data, even when the latter are generated from a skewed stable distribution with extremely fat tails.

Jones (2004) introduced the class of skewed distributions based on order statistics. Jones (2004) remarks that a generalized version of distributions based on order statistics "... is also the result of applying the inverse probability integral transformation to the beta distribution". Indeed, if we define $F(\cdot)$ to be the cdf of a symmetric and unimodal $f(\cdot)$ as defined above, and X as some random variable with a distribution P on (0,1), then we can consider $Y = F^{-1}(X)$, which is the usual inverse probability integral transformation for a uniform choice of P. Jones (2004) considers instead the wider class of beta distributions, so that P is a beta distribution parameterized by $\boldsymbol{\psi} = (\psi_1, \psi_2) \in \Re^2_+$. The class of distributions generated by this framework is also denoted by the generalized class (Amoroso 1925). Ferreira and Steel (2007a) suggested the use of a restricted parameterization $\boldsymbol{\psi} = (\varphi, 1/\varphi)$, $\varphi \in \Re_+$. Such a parameterization will always lead to a unimodal distribution for Y with many common choices of F. In addition, it greatly aids in prior elicitation and imposes that the only choice of P resulting in symmetry is the uniform.

A more general approach was taken in Ferreira and Steel (2006), who consider the inverse probability integral transformation above with any distribution P on (0,1), which they call the skewing mechanism. Starting from any symmetric distribution with cdf F, this leads to skewed distributions S with pdf

$$s(y|F,P) = f(y)p[F(y)], \tag{4.9}$$

where we denote pdfs with lower case letters, and caps denote either distributions or their cdfs. We can immediately see that S equals F only when P is uniform, and obtaining a symmetric S for any F is equivalent to P being symmetric around 1/2. Furthermore, when F has a unique mode and P is unimodal with mode at 1/2, then S has the same unique mode as F. The moment existence of S in the left and right tails is the same as for F if $p(\cdot)$ has a finite nonzero limit at $x = 0$ and $x = 1$, respectively. All three previously described ways of skewing distributions are special cases of this framework, leading to implicit choices for P. Ferreira and Steel (2006) construct a skewing mechanism P that has the following characteristics:

- P does not depend on F, giving both distributions clear and distinct interpretations, and facilitating inference and prior elicitation.
- The only P that leads to symmetry is the uniform.
- The unique mode of S equals the mode of F.
- Moment existence of S is the same as for F.
- Any AG skewness in $(-1, 1)$ can be achieved and the AG skewness measure does not depend on F.

They specify two parametric classes of P: one class accommodates only skewness around the mode (parameterized by a scalar parameter δ), assuming equal tail behavior, and the other class allows for a proportionality factor in the tails, leading both to skewness in the central part of the distribution (parameterized by δ) and in the tails (parameterized by a scalar r). Use of these classes in regression modeling is illustrated, using all the different skew mechanisms described above, where the priors on the skewness parameters are matched by relating them to a common prior on the AG measure of skewness (prior matching).

Elal-Olivero et al. (2009) formulate an extension of the framework set out in Azzalini and Capitanio (1999) to include bimodal distributions. They use a Bayesian model with point masses in the prior corresponding to the special cases of symmetry and unimodality. Comparison with other model specifications is conducted using pseudo-Bayes factors based on conditional predictive ordinates, as in Chen et al. (2000).

Whereas the previously defined skewed classes are all parametric, Quintana et al. (2009) use the constructive representation in (4.9) and introduce flexible classes of skewed distributions by nonparametric modeling of either P or F. A nonparametric skewing mechanism is based on Bernstein densities, which are defined as the following mixtures of Beta densities

$$p(x \mid m, w^m) = \sum_{j=1}^{m} w_j^m f_b(x \mid j, m-j+1), \tag{4.10}$$

where m is a positive integer and the weight vector w^m is constrained by $w_j^m \geq 0$ for all $1 \leq j \leq m$ and $\sum_{j=1}^m w_j^m = 1$, and we use the Beta pdfs

$$f_b(x \mid j, m-j+1) = \frac{m!}{(j-1)!(m-j)!} x^{j-1}(1-x)^{m-j}, \qquad 0 \leq x \leq 1.$$

For $m = 1$ and for any m when $w_i^m = 1/m,\ i = 1, \ldots, m$, we get a uniform P and reproduce F.[5] In general, multimodality is easily accommodated, especially for large m. In the case where F is a Student-t distribution with ν degrees of freedom, it can be shown that the largest existing moments can be multiplied by an integer factor $k+1$ by restricting the k weights at the end to zero ($w_1^m = \cdots = w_k^m = 0$ for the left tail and $w_{m-k+1}^m = \cdots = w_m^m = 0$ for the right tail). Thus, the prior specification on these weights puts point masses on zero for the end points, and uses Dirichlet distributions for the unconstrained weights. Various choices for the Dirichlet parameters are discussed in Quintana et al. (2009). This Bernstein skewing mechanism works well for density estimation as it can accommodate quite flexible shapes. However, if we wish to conduct regression modeling, we often want to impose unimodality and control the mode. For this reason, a second flexible class is proposed, by using as a skewing mechanism the parametric construct (with proportional tails) of Ferreira and Steel (2006), which

[5] This is easily verified in simple examples. Take $m = 3$, for instance, for which (4.10) leads to $p(x \mid 3, w^3) = w_1^3 f_b(x \mid 1, 3) + w_2^3 f_b(x \mid 2, 2) + w_3^3 f_b(x \mid 3, 1) = 3w_1^3(1-x)^2 + 6w_2^3 x(1-x) + 3w_3^3 x^2$, which equals one if all three weights are equal.

imposes that S has the same unique mode as F. To model F in a flexible manner, we use the representation of symmetric densities with a unique mode at zero as mixtures of uniform distributions:

$$f(y) = \int_0^\infty \frac{1}{2\theta} I\{y \in (-\theta, \theta)\}\, dG(\theta), \tag{4.11}$$

as discussed in Brunner and Lo (1989), where $I\{\cdot\}$ is the indicator function and where G is a distribution function on the positive real numbers. In particular, for G in (4.11) we adopt a stick-breaking prior distribution (as explained in Section 3.1 of this chapter) with a finite number of terms. This means that G can be expressed as

$$G(\cdot) = \sum_{i=1}^{N} w_i \delta_{\theta_i}(\cdot), \tag{4.12}$$

where δ_θ denotes a point mass at θ. For independent Beta distributed random variables $V_1, \ldots, V_{N-1}$ with $V_i \sim \text{Be}(a_i, b_i)$ and known a_i and b_i, we then set $w_1 = V_1$ and $w_k = V_k \prod_{j=1}^{k-1}(1 - V_j)$ for $k = 2, \ldots, N$, and $V_N = 1$, which guarantees $P(\sum_{i=1}^{N} w_i = 1) = 1$. Furthermore, $\theta_1, \ldots, \theta_N$ are i.i.d. draws from some absolutely continuous centering probability measure G_0 on the positive real numbers, and independent of the weights w_i. Under this specification, the resulting G will be centered around G_0 for any given N, in the sense that for any Borel measurable subset of $\Re^+$, $\text{E}(G(B)) = G_0(B)$. Skewness properties of the resulting distributions are parametric, and thus easily controlled and estimated.

2.3 Mixtures

In the previous section, distributions were usually constrained to be unimodal, with the exception of the bimodal model of Elal-Olivero et al. (2009) and the flexible class with Bernstein skewing mechanism of Quintana et al. (2009). Whereas this is typically a good idea for modelling residual distributions, it may not be ideal when modeling observables. In particular, when heterogeneity of location or scale is present in the population, a mixture model could be more appropriate. Often, a very useful representation of such models is as a hierarchical latent variable model, where the distribution of the observable y_i depends on a latent discrete indicator variable S_i, say, which assigns observation i to one of the components. In particular, we can write for $\boldsymbol{y} = (y_1, \ldots, y_n)'$ given $\mathbf{S} = (S_1, \ldots, S_n)'$

$$p(\boldsymbol{y}|\mathbf{S}, \boldsymbol{\theta}) = \prod_{i=1}^{n} p(y_i|S_i, \boldsymbol{\theta}) = \prod_{i=1}^{n} p(y_i|\boldsymbol{\theta}_{S_i}), \tag{4.13}$$

where the different components of the mixture are distinguished by different parameter values; depending on the context, these could for example be different location, regression, and/or scale parameters. If the number of possible components is K, then each S_i takes values in the set $\{1, 2, \ldots, K\}$, and often we assume the S_i's to be independent and categorically distributed with parameter vector, say, $\boldsymbol{\eta} = (\eta_1, \ldots, \eta_K)'$. This is a multivariate generalization of a Bernoulli distribution, which is characterized by $P(S_i = j) = \eta_j, j = 1, \ldots, K$. Integrating out S, the model for each observation can then be written as

$$p(y_i|\boldsymbol{\theta}) = \sum_{j=1}^{K} \eta_j p(y_i|\boldsymbol{\theta}_j), \tag{4.14}$$

independently for $i = 1, \ldots, n$. These types of models are discussed in Everitt and Hand (1981), Titterington et al. (1985) and a recent contribution with lots of emphasis on Bayesian implementation and computational ideas is Frühwirth-Schnatter (2006).

Bayesian inference with such mixture models was discussed in some detail by Richardson and Green (1997), who focus on univariate mixtures of normals with an unknown number of components K. Because the dimension of the parameter space is not constant (as K changes), they consider reversible jump MCMC methods (Green 1995), while Stephens (2000a) and Phillips and Smith (1996) propose alternative samplers that move between models. In cases where K is unlikely to be large, a simple approach is to fit the model for different values of K and then compute Bayes factors in order to decide which number of clusters performs best, as in Bensmail et al. (1997), Frühwirth-Schnatter and Kaufmann (2008), and Raftery (1996). This approach can be particularly useful in cases where the clusters have a specific interpretation, as inference given a chosen number of components is then immediately available. On the other hand, often a mixture model is simply used as a flexible modeling tool, and the components will lack any real interpretation. Geweke (2007) provides some interesting econometric examples of this situation.

One particular issue that occurs in mixture modeling is the labeling problem. Mixture distributions are naturally invariant with respect to simply relabeling their components, which induces a lack of identifiability and can cause problems in estimation. A simple example can illustrate this: consider a mixture of two normals $p(y|\boldsymbol{\theta}) = \eta_1\phi(y|\mu_1, \sigma_1^2) + \eta_2\phi(y|\mu_2, \sigma_2^2)$; in this case, clearly the likelihood is exactly the same for parameter vector $\boldsymbol{\theta} = (\mu_1, \sigma_1^2, \mu_2, \sigma_2^2, \eta_1, \eta_2)$ as it is for $\boldsymbol{\theta} = (\mu_2, \sigma_2^2, \mu_1, \sigma_1^2, \eta_2, \eta_1)$, which is obtained by simply changing the labels of the components. If the prior is also invariant with respect to relabeling, the posterior distribution will be characterized by symmetry with respect to the $K!$ possible ways of labelling the components. A simple approach to this consists of imposing a labeling by ordering parameters that were well separated between the components, for example the means or the weights, as in Diebolt and Robert (1994) and Richardson and Green (1997). In contrast, Celeux et al. (2000) and Stephens (2000b) propose decision-theoretical criteria. Casella et al. (2004) suggest a method based on an appropriate partition of the space of augmented variables. Casella et al. (2002) introduce a perfect sampling scheme, which is not easily extended to non-exponential families. Using the analytical structure of the posterior distribution, Frühwirth-Schnatter (2001) proposes a random permutation scheme, while Geweke (2007) introduces the permutation-augmented simulator, a deterministic modification of the usual MCMC sampler. Comprehensive discussions of this issue are found in Jasra et al. (2005), Frühwirth-Schnatter (2006), and Geweke (2007).

Also, as remarked by for example Diebolt and Robert (1994), the use of improper priors on the component parameters is excluded if we allow for situations where not enough observations are allocated to each component to lead to a proper posterior on all parameters. Thus, they implicitly use a prior on S which excludes such allocations.

2.4 Multivariate modeling

The class of elliptical distributions, as presented for example by Kelker (1970), has been the predominant framework for multivariate continuous random quantities. This class of distributions is quite well studied and we refer the interested reader to for example Fang et al. (1990). However, in a substantial number of situations, elliptical distributions have been found to be too restrictive. Such is certainly the case for problems where the random quantity exhibits skewness, our main focus in this section.

A multivariate extension of the Azzalini skew-normal distribution was proposed in Azzalini and Dalla Valle (1996) for a random vector $\boldsymbol{\epsilon} \in \Re^p$

$$p(\boldsymbol{\epsilon}|\boldsymbol{\alpha}) = 2\phi_p(\boldsymbol{\epsilon}|0, \Omega)\Phi(\boldsymbol{\alpha}'\boldsymbol{\epsilon}), \tag{4.15}$$

where Ω is a correlation matrix and $\boldsymbol{\alpha} \in \Re^p$ is now a vector of skewness parameters. Marginal distributions from this class are univariate skew normals as in (4.5). This distribution can again be interpreted as arising from a hidden truncation model. Such conditioning models have been generalized further. Still conditioning on one unobserved variable, Branco and Dey (2001) introduced a class of multivariate skew-elliptical distributions. They essentially start from the class of elliptically contoured distributions[6] and use the same hidden truncation idea underlying (4.15) to generate more general classes of multivariate skewed distributions with flexibility regarding tail behavior. Arnold and Beaver (2002) made these models more general by allowing for non-elliptical skew distributions. Within the class of hidden truncation models, but conditioning on as many arguments as observed variables, Sahu et al. (2003) generate a very general class of multivariate skew-elliptical distributions. They start from

$$\boldsymbol{\varphi} = (\boldsymbol{\psi}', \boldsymbol{\epsilon}')', \boldsymbol{\mu} = (\boldsymbol{\mu}^{*'}, 0_p')' \text{ and } \Sigma = \begin{pmatrix} \Sigma^* & 0 \\ 0 & I_p \end{pmatrix},$$

[6] These continuous distributions are characterized by a pdf for the random variable $\boldsymbol{\epsilon} \in \Re^p$ of the form $g\left\{(\boldsymbol{\epsilon} - \boldsymbol{\mu})'\Sigma^{-1}(\boldsymbol{\epsilon} - \boldsymbol{\mu})\right\}$, with $\boldsymbol{\mu} \in \Re^p$ and Σ a PDS matrix of dimension $p \times p$ while $g(\cdot)$ is some nonincreasing function from $\Re_+$ to $\Re_+$ such that the density integrates to unity. The density generator g will determine tail behavior with the contours being ellipsoids.

where $\boldsymbol{\psi}, \boldsymbol{\epsilon}$, and $\boldsymbol{\mu}^*$ are in $\Re^p$, $\mathbf{0}_p$ is the p-dimensional zero vector, Σ^* is a $p \times p$ covariance matrix, and I_p denotes the p-dimensional identity matrix. Further, let $\boldsymbol{\varphi}$ have an elliptically contoured distribution as in footnote 6 with parameters μ and Σ. By defining

$$\boldsymbol{\eta} = D\boldsymbol{\epsilon} + \boldsymbol{\psi},$$

where $D = \text{diag}(\boldsymbol{\delta})$, $\boldsymbol{\delta} \in \Re^p$, the random variable $\boldsymbol{\eta}$ given that $\boldsymbol{\epsilon} > \mathbf{0}_p$ has a multivariate skewed distribution as proposed by Sahu et al. (2003). For specific examples of elliptically contoured distributions (multivariate normal and Student-t), Sahu et al. (2003) derive closed-form expressions for the sampling density, and for Bayesian inference they adopt an MCMC sampler which also generates values for the latent variable $\boldsymbol{\epsilon}$ (data augmentation).

A different approach to multivariate skewed distributions was proposed by Jones (2002): starting from spherical symmetry, this approach replaces the marginal distribution of some of the variables by a skewed distribution. This method is particularly interesting when only one variable is to have a skewed marginal, as several options for univariate skewed distributions are available in the literature.

An alternative methodology for constructing multivariate skewed distributions is through affine linear transformations of univariate random variables with skewed distributions. Ferreira and Steel (2007b) consider p independent potentially skewed random variables ϵ_j in a vector $\boldsymbol{\epsilon}$ and form a new random variable $\boldsymbol{\eta} \in \Re^p$ through

$$\boldsymbol{\eta} = A'\boldsymbol{\epsilon} + \boldsymbol{\mu}, \tag{4.16}$$

where A is a $p \times p$ nonsingular matrix and $\mu \in \Re^p$. This generates a general class of multivariate skewed distributions, with a very simple expression for the pdf (in contrast to the approach of Sahu et al. (2003)). In particular, the pdf for $\boldsymbol{\eta}$ is given by

$$p(\boldsymbol{\eta}|\boldsymbol{\mu}, A, \gamma_1, \ldots, \gamma_m) = \|A\|^{-1} \prod_{j=1}^{m} p_j[(\boldsymbol{\eta} - \boldsymbol{\mu})' A_{\cdot j}^{-1} | \gamma_j], \tag{4.17}$$

where $A_{\cdot j}^{-1}$ denotes the jth column of A^{-1}, $\|A\|$ denotes the absolute value of the determinant of A, and $p_j(\cdot|\gamma_j)$ is the pdf of the skewed distribution of ϵ_j with its own parameterization γ_j (which typically includes skewness and possibly other parameters to govern tail behavior etc.). Ferreira and Steel (2007b) show that, in contrast to elliptically contoured distributions, knowledge of $A'A$ is not sufficient. They use a unique decomposition of the nonsingular matrix $A = LO$, where O is a $p \times p$ orthogonal matrix and L is a $p \times p$ real lower triangular matrix with strictly positive diagonal elements. Keeping the same $A'A$ matrix, but changing O, we can generate very different distributions. In particular, the choice of A (as opposed to $A'A$) will determine the basic axis $e_j, j = 1, \ldots, p$, where e_j is defined as the axis along which the distribution is a linear combination of $p - j + 1$ independent univariate skewed distributions. These axes define the direction of the skewness of the distribution. Changing the orthogonal matrix O is then equivalent to rotating or reflecting the basic axes. The specification of the skewed univariate distributions of ϵ_j can be chosen freely. In Ferreira and Steel (2007b), these distributions are defined using the method proposed by Fernández and Steel (1998). The multivariate skewed distributions generated in this way have a number of interesting characteristics, such as the dependence of the existence of moments on the existence of moments of the univariate distributions alone, and the possibility of unrestricted modeling of mean, variance, and skewness. The latter provides flexibility in modeling skewed multivariate data. An econometric application of this modeling approach (with a slightly restricted specification of A for simplicity and interpretability, where the lower triangular matrix L in the decomposition $A = LO$ is replaced by a diagonal matrix) can be found in Ferreira and Steel (2007a). They use the multivariate skewed distribution in (4.17) (with various choices of the marginal distributions on the components ϵ_j) to model the composed error in a multi-output stochastic frontier model. Priors on skewness parameters are matched between various choices for $p_j(\epsilon_j|\gamma_j)$ by making sure they all imply the same prior on the AG skewness measure (see footnote 4). Bayesian inference is conducted through MCMC with the main complication being the drawing of orthogonal matrices required for A (Ferreira and Steel 2007b, section 7.1).

The skewed distribution of Azzalini and Dalla Valle (1996) or Sahu et al. (2003) introduces skewness into symmetric distributions along the coordinate axes. Bauwens and Laurent (2005) use a regression framework with a linear transformation as in (4.16), where $\boldsymbol{\epsilon}$ has a similar distribution as the one used in Ferreira and Steel (2007b), but fix $A = \Sigma^{1/2}$, the spectral decomposition of Σ. The latter formulation does not allow for a separate choice of the directions of the asymmetry of the distribution (i.e. the basic axes), and fixes it to be a function of Σ.

2.5 Applications

2.5.1 Regional growth data

We consider annual per-capita GDP growth rates from 258 NUTS2 European regions, for the period 1996–2004.[7] These data cover 21 European countries. We define the growth of region i from time $t-1$ to t as $y_{it} = \log(z_{it}/z_{it-1})$, where z_{it} is the per-capita GDP of region i at time t. Thus, we end up with a balanced panel with $T = 9$ time periods and $m = 258$ regions.

To get an initial idea of the distribution of growth rates, we can simply forget about the panel structure of the data and treat each observation as independently generated from some unknown distribution. If we use the Bernstein skew model (4.10) from Subsection 2.2, we obtain the results in Figure 4.2. This is not very revealing, and only shows us a

[7] The NUTS Classification (Nomenclature des Unités Territoriales Statistiques) was introduced by Eurostat in order to provide a single uniform breakdown of territorial units. NUTS2 units are of intermediate size and roughly correspond to regional level.

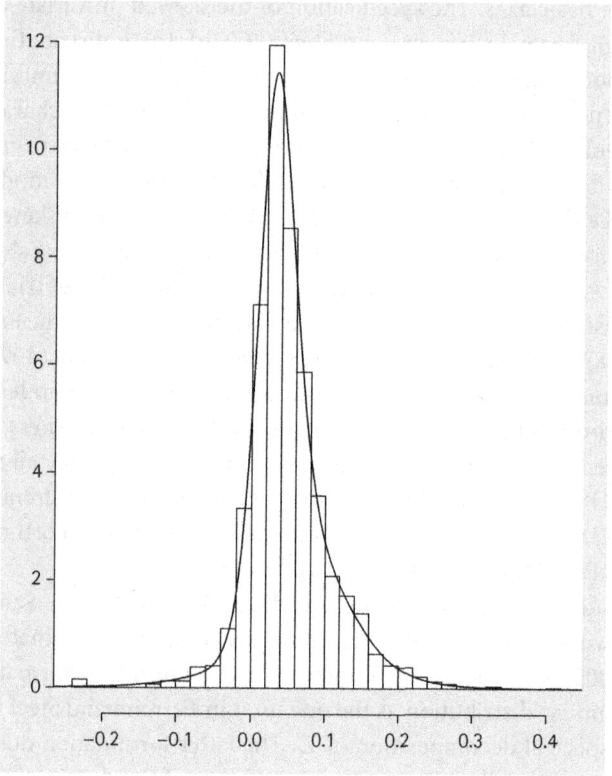

FIGURE 4.2 NUTS2 GDP growth data: histogram of the observed growth rates over all years and regions, and posterior predictive plot based on the Bernstein skew model

positively skewed distribution of growth rates with a fairly large spread (and a negative "outlier"). Predicting a region's growth rate on the basis of this analysis is unlikely to lead to extremely useful results.

A perhaps more satisfying approach to modeling these data takes both the dynamics and the panel structure seriously and attempts to accommodate both in a simple first-order autoregressive model:

$$y_{it} = \beta_i (1 - \alpha) + \alpha y_{i t-1} + (1 - \alpha)\boldsymbol{\mu}' \boldsymbol{x}_{it} + \lambda^{-\frac{1}{2}} \varepsilon_{it}, \tag{4.18}$$

where the errors ε_{it} are independent and identically distributed random quantities with mode at zero and unit precision, α is the parameter governing the dynamic behavior of the panel and $\boldsymbol{\mu} = (\mu_1, \ldots, \mu_p)'$ is a vector of coefficients related to p explanatory variables in $\boldsymbol{x}_{it}$. We standardize these covariates to have mean zero and unit variance for each region. We assume that the process is stationary, that is, $|\alpha| < 1$ (strictly speaking, stationarity only holds for the model without explanatory variables). The parameters β_i are individual effects. Since the error distribution has zero mode, these individual effects can be interpreted as reflecting differences in the long-run modal tendencies for the corresponding individuals.[8] In addition, the individual effects are assumed to be related according to $\beta_i \sim N(\beta_i|\beta, \tau^{-1})$, which is a commonly used normal random effects specification, found for example in Liu and Tiao (1980) and Nandram and Petruccelli (1997), where β is a common mean and τ the precision. Within a Bayesian framework, this is merely a hierarchical specification of the prior on the β_i's, which puts a bit more structure on the problem and allows us to parameterize the model in terms of β and τ, rather than all m individual effects. See also Section 2.4 of the chapter by Tobias and Li for a similar hierarchical model structure. Finally, we condition throughout on the initial observed values, y_{i0}.

For the error distribution in (4.18), we assume the skew-t distribution of Fernández and Steel (1998), that is, (4.6), with $f(\cdot)$ a Student-t distribution with unknown degrees of freedom, ν. Recall that γ is the skewness parameter and for $\gamma = 1$ we recover the symmetric Student-t distribution. An alternative flexible distribution for such models was introduced in Geweke and Keane (2000), who use a mixture of three normal distributions, which also allows for a relatively simple MCMC strategy.

The model in (4.18) assumes that all regions follow similar patterns, and this may well be too strong an assumption. Therefore, Juárez and Steel (2010) consider a mixture model as in Subsection 2.3 allowing for model-based clustering of regions, with cluster-specific values of $\{\alpha, \beta, \boldsymbol{\mu}\}$ in (4.18). Thus, if region i corresponds to cluster j, the model becomes

$$y_{it} = \beta_i (1 - \alpha^j) + \alpha^j y_{it-1} + (1 - \alpha^j)(\boldsymbol{\mu}^j)' \boldsymbol{x}_{it} + \lambda^{-\frac{1}{2}} \varepsilon_{it}, \tag{4.19}$$

with $|\alpha^j| < 1$ and $\beta_i \sim N(\beta_i|\beta^j, \tau^{-1})$. The same skew-$t$ distribution as described above for (4.18) is chosen and the number of clusters is left unknown.

The prior distribution is chosen to be a "benchmark" prior that will represent a reasonable reflection of prior ideas in many applied settings. A standard improper prior on λ is used (for which properness of the posterior is shown), while τ requires a proper prior, which is selected in line with the data by making the prior dependent on an aspect of the observed data.[9] The prior on γ is induced by a uniform prior on the AG skewness measure and for ν two different proper priors are used, a G(2,10) and a hierarchical prior which is obtained by putting an exponential prior on the scale parameter of a gamma prior with shape parameter 2. The latter prior does not allow for a mean and has the pdf

$$p(\nu) = 2d \frac{\nu}{(\nu + d)^3}, \tag{4.20}$$

[8] This is exactly true for symmetric ε_{it} and approximately true for the skewed distribution used in the sequel.

[9] This is strictly in violation of Bayesian principles, where the prior can not depend on observed data, but when priors for scale parameters have to be chosen and no convenient scale-invariant improper prior can be chosen, we often need to resort to slightly data-dependent priors to make sure they are properly calibrated. A prior that is not in line with the data can have a large unintended effect on the posterior results.

where $d > 0$ controls the mode $(d/2)$ and the median $((1+\sqrt{2})d)$. Interestingly, this prior has the same right tail as the Jeffreys' prior for the Student-t regression model derived in Fonseca et al. (2008). The probabilities η of cluster assignment in (4.14) are given a Dirichlet prior with parameter vector $(1/2, \ldots, 1/2)$ (which is a Jeffreys' type prior: see Berger and Bernardo 1992b). We need a carefully elicited proper prior on cluster-specific parameters since we often want to compare (using Bayes factors) models with different numbers of components. If β^j's and/or $\boldsymbol{\mu}^j$'s are cluster-specific, we can not put a flat improper prior on these parameters, as Bayes factors would no longer be defined. Of course, any proper prior on the cluster-specific parameters will give us Bayes factors, but we need to be very careful that the prior truly reflects reasonable prior assumptions, since the Bayes factors will depend crucially on the particular prior used.

Within each cluster, the dynamics parameter α gets a rescaled Beta prior (on $(-1,1)$), and we make the hyperparameters of this Beta distribution random, with equal gamma priors. This hierarchical structure of the prior on α^j leads to more flexibility. In particular, we adopt

$$p(\alpha^j|a_\alpha, b_\alpha) = \frac{2^{1-a_\alpha-b_\alpha}}{B(a_\alpha, b_\alpha)}\left(1+\alpha^j\right)^{a_\alpha-1}\left(1-\alpha^j\right)^{b_\alpha-1} \qquad |\alpha^j| < 1, \tag{4.21}$$

with

$$a_\alpha \sim \mathrm{G}(2,10) \qquad \text{and} \qquad b_\alpha \sim \mathrm{G}(2,10). \tag{4.22}$$

The implied marginal prior on α^j is roughly bell-shaped with $\mathrm{P}(|\alpha^j| < 0.5) = 0.65$ and $\mathrm{P}(|\alpha^j| > 0.9) = 0.03$, in line with reasonable prior beliefs for this (and many) applications. In the clustering model, the dynamics parameters of the different clusters are assigned independent and identical priors.

Given the standardization of the covariates $\boldsymbol{x}_{it}$ in the model, the β^j's can be interpreted as long-run equilibrium levels associated with each cluster. We may well possess some prior information about these levels. Juárez and Steel (2010) propose the following multivariate normal prior for $\boldsymbol{\beta} = (\beta^1, \ldots, \beta^K)'$:

$$\boldsymbol{\beta} \sim \mathrm{N}_K(\boldsymbol{\beta}|m\boldsymbol{\iota}, c^2\left[(1-a)I + a\,\boldsymbol{\iota}\boldsymbol{\iota}'\right]), \tag{4.23}$$

where $\boldsymbol{\iota}$ is a vector of ones, $c > 0$ and $-1/(K-1) < a < 1$. The prior in (4.23) generates an equicorrelated prior structure for $\boldsymbol{\beta}$ with prior correlation a throughout. Thus, if $a = 0$, we have independent normally distributed β^j's, but if $a \to 1$, they tend to perfect positive correlation. Note that (4.23) implies that $\beta^j \sim \mathrm{N}(m, c^2), j = 1, \ldots, K$ and $\beta^i - \beta^j \sim \mathrm{N}(0, 2c^2(1-a)), i \neq j,\ i,j = 1, \ldots, K$. Thus, for $a = 0$ the prior variance of the difference between the equilibrium levels of two clusters would be twice the prior variance of the level of any cluster. This would seem counterintuitive, and positive values of a would be closer to most prior beliefs. In fact, $a = 3/4$, leading to $\mathrm{Var}(\beta^i - \beta^j) = (1/2) \times \mathrm{Var}(\beta^j)$ might be more reasonable. We can go one step further and put a prior on a. This implies an additional level in the prior hierarchy and would allow us to learn about a from the data. We put a Beta prior on a, rescaled to the interval $(-1/(K-1), 1)$, and posterior inference on a then provides valuable information regarding the assumption that all β^j's are equal. In particular, if we find a lot of posterior mass close to one for a, that would imply that a model with $\beta^j = \beta, j = 1, \ldots, K$ (where only the α^j's and μ^j's differ across clusters) might be preferable to the model with cluster-specific β^j's.

A similar prior structure is used for the coefficients μ^j. Standardizing each of the p covariates to have mean zero and variance one for each individual unit will help the interpretation of these coefficients. The K cluster-specific coefficients of regressor l, grouped in $\boldsymbol{\mu}_l = (\mu_l^1, \ldots, \mu_l^K)'$, are then assigned the prior

$$\boldsymbol{\mu}_l \sim \mathrm{N}_K(\boldsymbol{\mu}_l | \mathbf{0}, c_l^2 \left[(1 - a_l) I + a_l \boldsymbol{\iota}\boldsymbol{\iota}'\right]), \quad l = 1, \ldots, p, \tag{4.24}$$

where we choose $c_l > 0$ and we specify a rescaled Beta prior for each $a_l \in (-1/(K-1), 1)$.

This hierarchical prior structure on cluster-specific parameters will reduce the sensitivity of the Bayes factors to prior assumptions. For example, in the model with cluster-specific β^j's, Bayes factors between models with different K depend on the prior on $\boldsymbol{\beta}$ mostly through the implied prior on the contrasts $\beta^i - \beta^j$. By changing a we can thus affect model choice, and making a largely determined by the data reduces the dependence of Bayes factors on prior assumptions.

Inference is conducted through Markov chain Monte Carlo (MCMC) methods using the permutation sampler of Frühwirth-Schnatter (2001) and the labeling problem (as discussed in Subsection 2.3) is overcome by imposing an identifiability constraint (simply assigning labels in accordance with an inequality on one of the parameters; for example, the component with smallest α^j is always called cluster 1). Model comparison is done through Bayes factors, for which the marginal likelihoods are computed using the bridge sampler of Meng and Wong (1996). See DiCiccio et al. (1997) and Frühwirth-Schnatter (2006) for comprehensive discussions of this method.

Applied to the NUTS2 data with a single covariate (the standardized lagged level of Gross Domestic Product (GDP)), the best model by far is the one with two clusters. We use an identifiability constraint through the dynamics parameter α and assign labels to the clusters by imposing that $\alpha^1 < \alpha^2$. Figure 4.3 indicates the prior and posterior densities for the model parameters, suggesting that while skewness is not very strong (the log Savage-Dickey density ratio[10] in favor of $\gamma = 1$ is 1.7, providing mild evidence in favor of the symmetric model), the tails of the error distribution are very fat: posterior

[10] The Savage-Dickey density ratio is the ratio of the posterior and the prior density values at the restriction (see Verdinelli and Wasserman 1995) which defines a nested model. For example, the Bayes factor in favor of a symmetric model over its skewed counterpart will be $p(\gamma = 1|\text{data})/p(\gamma = 1)$. Section 4.2.5 of Koop (2004) provides a good explanation. This way of computing Bayes factors is typically easier and can be more precise than using other methods for estimating the marginal likelihoods, but is not always applicable.

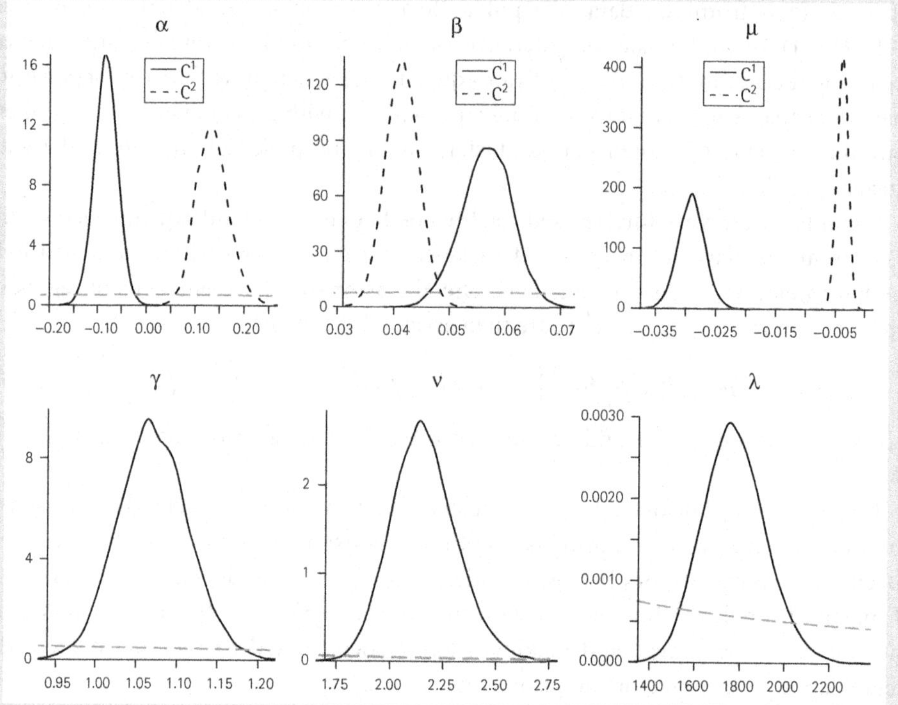

FIGURE 4.3 NUTS2 GDP growth data: prior (long dashes) and posterior (as in legend) densities for parameters of the model with $K = 2$. For the cluster-specific parameters, C^i indicates cluster i

inference on ν is quite concentrated on small values. In addition, convergence is fairly rapid (values of $|\alpha|$ are far from one), and we have a small club of regions with small negative first-order growth autocorrelation (i.e. those with a small negative value of α) and a larger subset with small positive first-order autocorrelation, as indicated in the top left graph of Figure 4.3. The posterior mean relative cluster sizes are $\{0.28, 0.72\}$. Inference on the β's shows us that the regions with alternating growth dynamics (first cluster) correspond to a higher long-run growth rate of around 5.9%, while the second group has a long-run growth rate of about 4.1%.

Figure 4.4 shows the individual membership probabilities with the regions ordered in ascending order according to initial GDP level. This illustrates that the first cluster tends to consist of regions with relatively low GDP in 1995. In particular, it groups emerging regions such as all of the Polish regions in the sample and most of the Czech regions, but also includes for example Inner London and Stockholm with high probability, which experience a similar, somewhat erratic, growth pattern.

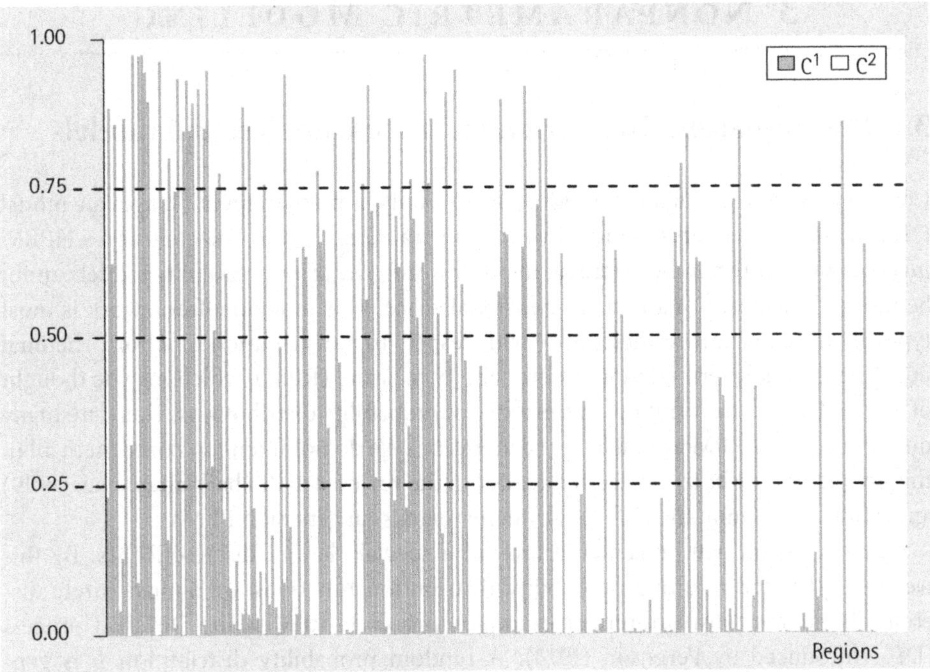

FIGURE 4.4 NUTS2 GDP growth data: membership probabilities for the model with $K = 2$. The 258 units (regions) are ordered according to initial GDP level. Bars indicate the posterior probability of belonging to cluster 1 for each region

For the regions in cluster 1, μ tends to take large negative values, implying a fairly substantial negative trend of growth over time (the covariate is standardized lagged GDP, which is negative for the early years, thus having a positive effect on growth and positive for the later years, thus reducing growth). For the second cluster, this effect is much smaller. Indeed, observed growth rates for cluster 1 tend to go down over the sample period, while those for cluster 2 remain almost unaffected. In addition, the time pattern of growth rates for cluster 2 is more stable, with the negative value of α for cluster 1 reflected in a more unstable growth pattern. This is in line with cluster 1 grouping mostly emerging economies, which are growing more rapidly at the beginning of the sample period. Interestingly, observed growth rates suggest convergence in growth between the two clusters by the end of the sample period.

2.5.2 Some other applications in econometrics

An application similar to the one described above is discussed in Frühwirth-Schnatter and Kaufmann (2008). In addition, other recent applications of flexible parametric modeling include Ferreira and Steel (2004), who examine the distribution of firm sizes, Bauwens and Laurent (2005), focusing on GARCH modeling in finance, and Griffin and Steel (2008) for flexible mixture modeling in the context of stochastic frontiers.

3 Nonparametric Modeling

3.1 Preliminaries: The Dirichlet Process and related models

Contrary to what the name would seem to imply, a nonparametric Bayesian model (NPBM) does not refer to a model with "no parameters". Quite the contrary, a NPBM involves an infinite number of them. In other words, the prior probability model cannot be indexed by means of a finite dimensional space. This modeling framework is most typically used to express uncertainty with respect to a distribution function. The final outcome is usually termed random probability measure (RPM), which may be thought of as a probability distribution on the space of probability distributions. There are many different types of RPM available in the literature. We do not intend to cover them all in this chapter. We refer the interested reader to the review articles by Walker et al. (1999) and Müller and Quintana (2004) for further details on general NPBMs.

Our discussion will be centered around a special class of discrete RPMs. By this we mean that the resulting probability distribution functions are almost surely discrete. By far the most prominent example of discrete RPM is the Dirichlet process (DP) introduced by Ferguson (1973). A random probability distribution F is generated by a DP if for any measurable partition $B_1, \ldots, B_k$ of the sample space, the vector of random probabilities $\{F(B_i) : i = 1, \ldots, k\}$ follows a Dirichlet distribution: $(F(B_1), \ldots, F(B_k)) \sim D(M \cdot F_0(B_1), \ldots, M \cdot F_0(B_k))$. We denote this by $F \sim \mathcal{D}(M, F_0)$. It is clear that this definition involves two parameters: the *total mass* parameter M, and the *baseline measure* F_0. It follows that $E(F(B)) = F_0(B)$ for any Borel set B in the sample space, which shows the role of F_0 as a centering distribution for the DP. On the other hand, it also follows that $\text{Var}(F(B)) = F_0(B)(1 - F_0(B))/(1 + M)$. This means that M plays the role of a concentration parameter, which weighs the prior uncertainty we have on our centering distribution F_0. Generally speaking, large values for M imply more prior certainty on F_0, and in the limit case $M \to \infty$, $\text{Var(F(B))} \to 0$.

A central motivation for the DP construction is that the DP is conjugate under i.i.d. sampling, that is, for the model

$$y = y_1, \ldots, y_n | F \overset{\text{iid}}{\sim} F, \qquad \text{and} \qquad F \sim \mathcal{D}(M, F_0), \tag{4.25}$$

the posterior distribution is $F \mid y \sim \mathcal{D}(M + n, (M + n)^{-1}[M \cdot F_0 + \sum_{i=1}^{n} \delta_{y_i}(\cdot)])$, where $\delta_y(\cdot)$ denotes a point mass at y. A posteriori we then have that

$$E(F(B) \mid y) = \left\{\frac{M}{M+n}\right\} F_0(B) + \left\{\frac{n}{M+n}\right\} \frac{1}{n} \sum_{i=1}^{n} \delta_{y_i}(B),$$

that is, a convex combination of the centering measure $F_0(B)$ and the empirical distribution from the observed data $\frac{1}{n} \sum_{i=1}^{n} \delta_{y_i}(B)$. In other words, the posterior DP is centered at a combination between the prior guess at the unknown distribution, F_0, and a standard classical nonparametric estimate of the unknown distribution, with weights proportional to M and the sample size n. This also illustrates why M is sometimes referred to as the prior sample size parameter.

Another key property of the DP is that its support includes the set of all distribution functions that are absolutely continuous with respect to F_0, in a sense that is made precise in Ferguson (1973). Therefore, the choice of F_0 is crucial, not only because it is the center of the DP in the sense described earlier, but also because the wide support property requires a distribution having a probability density function supported on the whole sample space. See also the discussion after (4.27) below.

The above two properties (analytical tractability and wide support) are key considerations for the study and development of virtually all RPMs that have been proposed in the literature. Being the most popular one within this class, the DP has been widely studied and many of its properties have been reported. We limit our account to two additional properties. Of special relevance for computational purposes is the Pólya urn representation by Blackwell and MacQueen (1973). Under model (4.25) it follows that y are marginally exchangeable with joint distribution given by

$$P(y \in (B_1 \times \cdots \times B_n)) = \prod_{i=1}^{n} \left\{ \frac{MF_0(B_i) + \sum_{j<i} \delta_{y_j}(B_i)}{M + i - 1} \right\}, \tag{4.26}$$

for Borel sets $B_1, \ldots, B_n$ in the sample space. Blackwell and MacQueen (1973) showed that the distribution in (4.26) can be described by means of a Pólya urn scheme with colors that are drawn from F_0. Specifically, imagine an urn that initially contains only the baseline measure F_0 and its weight M. In the first stage we then sample one value, y_1 from F_0, return F_0 to the urn, and add a point mass at y_1. Next time we either choose y_1 with probability proportional to one or again F_0 with probability proportional to M. Then y_2 is either equal to y_1 in the former case, or another value sampled from F_0 in the latter. Before continuing to the next stage, we return all sampled elements, together with another point mass at y_2. The process continues in the same fashion. A colorful alternative description of (4.26) has been termed the "Chinese restaurant process" in Arratia et al. (1992). As we can see, the sample y admits ties with positive probability, and the "new", fresh values are drawn from F_0, with probability proportional to M. From a theoretical viewpoint, (4.26) expresses that the DP is the mixing measure in de Finetti's representation theorem for an infinite exchangeable sequence of Pólya draws with a continuum of colors. Finally, (4.26) is very useful for computational purposes, as will be seen in Section 3.3.

Another very useful result is the construction by Sethuraman (1994), which states that any $F \sim \mathcal{D}(M, F_0)$ can be represented as an infinite mixture

$$F(B) = \sum_{i=1}^{\infty} w_i \delta_{y_i}(B), \tag{4.27}$$

where $y_1, y_2, \ldots \overset{\text{iid}}{\sim} F_0$ and the mixture weights satisfy $w_1 = V_1$, $w_k = \prod_{j<k}(1 - V_j)V_k$, if $k \geq 2$, for $V_1, V_2, \cdots \overset{\text{iid}}{\sim} \text{Be}(1, M)$. In other words, samples from the DP can be represented as infinite mixtures of point masses drawn from F_0 with random weights generated through a "stick-breaking" procedure.[11] This also shows that the DP is an almost surely discrete RPM. In practice, it is customary to choose F_0 as having a probability density function, because this ensures the point masses $\{y_i\}$ to be different with probability one. Again, it is important for F_0 to be supported on the whole sample space. Otherwise, the point masses in (4.27) will not "cover" the whole sample space and we would lose the wide support property. For further general properties of the DP, we refer the interested reader to Diaconis and Kemperman (1996), Cifarelli and Melilli (2000), and references within.

Several extensions of the DP have been studied. Ishwaran and James (2001) proposed the stick-breaking priors. These consist of a mixture representation as in (4.27), but with weights expressed as $w_1 = V_1$, $w_k = \prod_{j<k}(1 - V_j)V_k$, if $k \geq 2$, where now $V_1, V_2, \cdots$ are independent and Beta distributed with $V_j \sim \text{Be}(a_j, b_j)$. This representation is well-defined provided that $\sum_{j=1}^{\infty} \log(1 + a_j/b_j) = \infty$. It is evident that the DP is a special case of a stick-breaking prior for which $a_j = 1$ and $b_j = M$ for all $j \geq 1$. It is also possible to generate a finite stick-breaking prior, with N components say. Indeed, this is achieved by letting $V_N = 1$, which guarantees that $\sum_{k=1}^{N} w_k = 1$ surely. Another special case is the Poisson-Dirichlet process of Pitman and Yor (1997), which results from taking $a_j = 1 - a$, $b_j = b + ja$, for $j \geq 1$, where $0 \leq a < 1$ and $b > -a$. The DP also follows from the Poisson-Dirichlet process (take $a = 0$ and $b = M$).

3.2 Semiparametric mixture modeling

In practice, however, the discreteness is one disadvantage of the models discussed in Section 3.1 for general purpose modeling. Indeed, it would seem inappropriate to directly model quantities that are expected to have a continuous behavior using a discrete RPM prior for their (unknown) distribution. It is precisely the presence of ties with positive probability, for example as expressed in (4.26), that creates this awkward situation. We will circumvent this difficulty with the help of *mixture models*. By this we mean that the marginal distribution of responses y_i will be expressed in the form

$$y_i \sim \int p(y_i \mid \theta)\, dF(\theta), \qquad i = 1, \ldots, n, \tag{4.28}$$

for some conveniently chosen absolutely continuous kernel density $p(\cdot \mid \theta)$, and where F is one of the RPM models described in Section 3.1. Here, the chosen density is

[11] The name refers to the idea that we start with a stick of length one (the total probability mass) and break off pieces that are then assigned as weights to the point masses. So the first point mass gets weight V_1, leaving $(1 - V_1)$ to be distributed. The second point mass gets $(1 - V_1)V_2$, etc.

mixed over the (possibly vector-valued) index θ, which could, for instance, represent location-scale parameters or some other quantity of interest related to p. An immediate consequence of (4.28) is that the resulting distribution of y_i is almost surely absolutely continuous, regardless of the discrete nature of F, and in fact, it is easily seen that ties occur with probability zero. Moreover, by the Sethuraman (1994) representation, this marginal distribution corresponds almost surely to an infinite mixture of absolutely continuous distributions and is therefore absolutely continuous itself.

When F in (4.28) is taken to be the DP, the resulting model is usually termed a "Dirichlet process mixture" (DPM). In the specific case of density estimation, it has been shown that the resulting posterior is consistent, in a sense that is made precise in various articles. The interested reader may seek details in Ghosal et al. (1999), Lijoi et al. (2005), and in Ghosal and van der Vaart (2007) and references therein. Thus, from a technical viewpoint there are strong reasons (wide support and posterior consistency) to use models based on DPs.

From both practical and conceptual viewpoints, it is often convenient to break the mixture (4.28) by introducing latent parameters $\boldsymbol{\theta} = (\theta_1, \ldots, \theta_n)$, where θ_i is the parameter associated with y_i. By doing so, the mixture model can be hierarchically expressed as

$$y_i \mid \theta_i \sim p(y_i \mid \theta_i), \qquad \theta_i \mid F \sim F, \qquad F \sim \text{RPM}. \tag{4.29}$$

Under (4.29), the undesired discreteness problem is transferred to the parameters $\boldsymbol{\theta}$. In fact, an additional benefit of this modeling line is that responses sharing a common parameter value are typically interpreted as *clusters*, which are viewed as internally homogeneous. The number of such clusters $N(\boldsymbol{\theta})$ is random, with a distribution that is controlled by the specific RPM assumptions. It can be shown that for the case $F \sim \mathcal{D}(M, F_0)$, we have a priori

$$E(N(\boldsymbol{\theta})) = \sum_{i=1}^{n} \frac{M}{M+i-1} \approx M \log\left(\frac{M+n}{M}\right),$$

and

$$Var(N(\boldsymbol{\theta})) = \sum_{i=1}^{n} \frac{M(i-1)}{(M+i-1)^2} \approx M\left\{\log\left(\frac{M+n}{M}\right) - 1\right\},$$

where the approximations to mean and variance work well for moderate to large values of n. See, for example, Liu (1996). The above formulas for the mean and variance of the number of clusters may be useful for the purpose of eliciting prior information on M in terms of the clustering structure. See an illustration of this method in Kottas et al. (2005). A further refinement of this idea appears in Jara et al. (2007).

3.3 Computational aspects

The advent of Markov chain Monte Carlo (MCMC) technology revolutionized the way Bayesian inference was conducted. The availability of such simulation-based methods helped to solve problems that were otherwise intractable. As an example, it is increasingly common to find situations where the standard parametric conjugate posterior analysis is replaced by the use of richer families of prior distributions that reflect subjective beliefs and/or prior information more accurately. To fix ideas, and in the spirit of Section 3.2, let us consider the following generic hierarchical model:

$$y_i \mid \theta_i \sim f(y_i \mid \theta_i), \qquad \theta_1, \ldots, \theta_n \mid F \overset{\text{iid}}{\sim} F, \qquad F \sim \mathcal{D}(M, F_0). \tag{4.30}$$

Here, the θ_i parameters are defined on a certain parametric space Θ, typically a subset of some Euclidean space. In some cases, a realistic model may require the use of additional parameters and/or levels in the hierarchy stated in (4.30). We focus here on the special updating process required for the parameters $\boldsymbol{\theta} = (\theta_1, \ldots, \theta_n)$ using Gibbs sampling, as the updating of the remaining ones (if any) relies only on routine techniques, possibly including Metropolis-Hastings steps (Chib, Chapter 5, this volume).

A standard practice when dealing with a model like (4.30) is to first marginalize with respect to the RPM F. This is possible by virtue of the Pólya urn representation (4.26), leading to a joint marginal distribution for data y and parameters $\boldsymbol{\theta}$ of the form

$$P(y, \boldsymbol{\theta}) \propto \prod_{i=1}^{n} f(y_i \mid \theta_i) \times \prod_{i=1}^{n} \{M f_0(\theta_i) + \sum_{j<i} \delta_{\theta_j}(\theta_i)\},$$

where f_0 is the density function associated with F_0. At first sight, it seems strange to get rid of the RPM via the above marginalization. This has been historically motivated by the fact that generating draws from a DP is a nontrivial problem. Although some methods are available, for example, Doss (1994) and Papaspiliopoulos and Roberts (2008), we will limit our discussion to the marginalized methods.

The key part is the updating of the $\boldsymbol{\theta}$ parameters in (4.30). In the context of estimating normal means using a DP-based model, Escobar (1994) derived a posterior simulation scheme based on Gibbs sampling. In our generic model, implementation of this algorithm reduces to sampling from the conditional distributions

$$\theta_i \mid \boldsymbol{\theta}_{-i}, y, \qquad \text{for } i = 1, \ldots, n,$$

where $\boldsymbol{\theta}_{-i} = (\theta_1, \ldots, \theta_{i-1}, \theta_{i+1}, \ldots, \theta_n)$. From the Pólya urn representation (4.26), it follows that

$$p(\theta_i \mid \boldsymbol{\theta}_{-i}, y) \propto \sum_{j \neq i} f(y_i \mid \theta_j) \delta_{\theta_j}(\theta_i) + M \left\{ \int_{\Theta} f(y_i \mid \theta) f_0(\theta)\, d\theta \right\} p(\theta_i \mid y_i), \tag{4.31}$$

i.e. a mixture of point masses at the currently imputed parameters, weighted by the likelihood factor, and a continuous distribution corresponding to the posterior under a parametric model $y \mid \theta \sim f(y \mid \theta)$ and $\theta \sim f_0(\theta)$, weighted by the marginal likelihood $\int_\Theta f(y_i \mid \theta) f_0(\theta)\, d\theta$. Mathematically, (4.31) expresses that the resulting conditional distribution is a mixture of discrete and continuous components. The first part on the right-hand side of (4.31) is the discrete component that accounts for the recycling of already existing parameters and accommodates the clustering, and the second part corresponds to the continuous component that brings in the "fresh" cluster values. If additional hyperparameters are included in the likelihood and/or in the prior, (4.31) is simply reinterpreted as conditional on those extra hyperparameters. Sampling from (4.31) is feasible provided that $\int_\Theta f(y_i \mid \theta) f_0(\theta)\, d\theta$ can be evaluated analytically and $p(\theta_i \mid y_i)$ is easy to sample from. This is typically the case when likelihood $f(y \mid \theta)$ and centering density $f_0(\theta)$ are in conjugate form. Assume for now this is indeed the case. The posterior simulation scheme can then be represented as

Algorithm 1.

(a) update $\theta_1, \dots, \theta_n$ from the corresponding conditional distributions (4.31).
(b) update any other hyperparameters from their corresponding complete conditionals.

A drawback of Algorithm 1 is that, in practice, every iteration changes only a few of the currently imputed θ_i values, and these values may stay for many iterations, leading to an inefficient posterior simulation scheme. This "sticky clusters" problem can be solved by using the resampling step introduced in Bush and MacEachern (1996). To understand the fix, we introduce some additional notation. Because there are ties among the components of $\boldsymbol{\theta}$, denote by $\boldsymbol{\theta}^* = (\theta_1^*, \dots, \theta_k^*)$ the corresponding set of unique values, also known as *locations*. Recall we had earlier assumed that F_0 has density function f_0, which guarantees that the elements of $\boldsymbol{\theta}^*$ are different with probability 1. Here, $k \equiv k(n)$ is the number of clusters among the n parameter values, but if clear from the context, we drop the dependence on n to simplify notation. Next, let the *cluster memberships* $\mathbf{s} = (s_1, \dots, s_n)$ be the set of indicators showing which unique value each parameter is equal to, that is, $s_1 = 1$ and $s_i = j$ if $\theta_i = \theta_j^*$ for $i = 1, \dots, n$. Note that $\theta_i = \theta_{s_i}^*$, and that $\boldsymbol{\theta}$ can be alternatively represented by $(\boldsymbol{\theta}^*, \mathbf{s})$. Finally, denote the k clusters as $S_1, \dots, S_k$, where $S_j = \{i : s_i = j\}$. Step (a) in Algorithm 1 is now replaced by (a') and (a'') as follows:

Algorithm 2.

(a') update $\theta_1, \dots, \theta_n$ from the corresponding conditional distributions (4.31).
(a'') the updated $\boldsymbol{\theta}$ parameters from (a) implicitly define a new set of cluster memberships $\mathbf{s}$ and locations $\boldsymbol{\theta}^*$. Keep $\mathbf{s}$, drop $\boldsymbol{\theta}^*$, and resample new $\boldsymbol{\theta}^*$ values from their complete conditional distributions:

$$\theta_j^* \mid \mathbf{s}, \mathbf{y} \propto \left\{ \prod_{i \in S_j} p(y_i \mid \theta_j^*) \right\} f_0(\theta_j^*), \tag{4.32}$$

which amounts to sampling from the posterior distribution under a parametric model with likelihood $p(y|\theta)$ and prior $f_0(\theta)$, applied to data corresponding to subjects in the jth cluster.

(b) update any other hyperparameters from their corresponding complete conditionals.

Steps (a') and (a'') together update the entire parameter vector $\boldsymbol{\theta}$, making sure the entire set of unique values is updated at every Gibbs scan. This generates a much more efficient algorithm, as the resulting Markov chain traverses the parameter space $\boldsymbol{\Theta}$ much faster than when only (a) in Algorithm 1 is considered. See the details in Bush and MacEachern (1996).

3.4 Examples

3.4.1 *Semiparametric estimation of binomial proportions*

Liu (1996) considered semiparametric estimation of success probabilities for binomial data. The specific data considered were generated by Beckett and Diaconis (1994) and consisted of the number of times a thumbtack landed pointing up (labeled "success") when rolled nine times consecutively. Starting with each tack pointing down, the tack was flicked or hit with the fingers from the exact place where it last landed. There were a total of 16 tacks, ten surfaces, and the tacks were flicked by each of Beckett and Diaconis, to yield 320 counts of successes out of a sequence of nine trials. The 320 counts are available in Beckett and Diaconis (1994) and in Liu (1996).

To model these data, it seems reasonable to assume sequence-specific success probabilities, because of the "flicker", tack, and surface effect. Doing so results in a straightforward parametric model of the form

$$y_i \mid \theta_i \sim \text{Bin}(9, \theta_i), \qquad \theta_i \overset{\text{iid}}{\sim} \text{Be}(a, b),$$

where $\text{Bin}(n, p)$ denotes a binomial distribution with n trials and success probability p and we assume known hyperparameters a and b. A slight refinement of this model would assign a hierarchical prior distribution to a and b. However, any of these models would indeed force all success probabilities to be almost surely different. There is no cluster structure among the θ_i's, and one basically ends up drawing inferences about each θ_i from a binomial sample with nine trials. Despite the differences in the data-generating mechanisms, one may argue that there are not enough observations to effectively distinguish the 320 numbers, and some pooling of sequences may help improve the estimation. On the other hand, a model for which we impose every sequence of trials to have the same success rate, that is, $\theta_1 = \cdots = \theta_{320} = \theta$, would seem too restrictive and unrealistic.

With $n = 320$, we consider the model in Liu (1996)

$$y_i \mid \theta_i \sim \text{Bin}(9, \theta_i), \qquad \theta_1, \ldots, \theta_n \mid F \overset{\text{iid}}{\sim} F, \qquad F \sim \mathcal{D}(M, F_0), \tag{4.33}$$

where F_0 is the Be(a, b) distribution. From our previous discussion, model (4.33) means that the distribution of success rates is treated as unknown, and assigned a DP distribution, centered on a certain parametric model, namely, that defined by a beta distribution. Given the cluster structure underlying the DP assumption in (4.33), the model supports both extreme clustering cases, that is, all θ_i parameters identical, or all of them different, in the sense of assigning a positive prior probability to each of these. In fact, it also supports all the intermediate configurations, and therefore, the pooling is determined from the evidence carried by the data.

While many specific features of the model may be of interest, we will here focus on obtaining the density of a new success probability θ_{n+1} corresponding to a hypothetical next sequence of trials. The Bayes estimate of this density is the posterior predictive distribution $p(\theta_{n+1} \mid y)$, which can be expressed as

$$p(\theta_{n+1} \mid y) = \int p(\theta_{n+1} \mid \boldsymbol{\theta}, y) p(\boldsymbol{\theta} \mid y)\, d\boldsymbol{\theta} = \int p(\theta_{n+1} \mid \boldsymbol{\theta}) p(\boldsymbol{\theta} \mid y)\, d\boldsymbol{\theta}, \tag{4.34}$$

where the last equality follows from the conditional independence assumption in (4.33), and the prior predictive distribution $p(\theta_{n+1} \mid \boldsymbol{\theta})$ follows from the Pólya urn representation (4.26).

The posterior distribution $p(\boldsymbol{\theta} \mid y)$ is quite complicated, as it involves a summation over all possible partitions of the set $\{1, \ldots, n\}$. A similar consideration holds for the posterior predictive distribution (4.34). Therefore, we will use an MCMC posterior simulation scheme to approximate it, focusing on Algorithm 2. The key step in the implementation is the set of conditionals (4.31). In our case, the binomial likelihood is conjugate with the beta baseline distribution, and so we get, after simplifying

$$\begin{aligned}\theta_i \mid \boldsymbol{\theta}_{-i}, y \propto &\sum_{j \neq i} \theta_j^{y_i} (1 - \theta_j)^{9 - y_i} \delta_{\theta_j}(\theta_i) \\ &+ M \left\{ \frac{B(a + y_i, b + 9 - y_i)}{B(a, b)} \right\} \text{Be}(\theta_i \mid a + y_i, b + 9 - y_i), \quad i = 1, \ldots, n, \end{aligned} \tag{4.35}$$

where $B(a, b) = \Gamma(a)\Gamma(b)/\Gamma(a + b)$ is the beta function evaluated at a and b. As mentioned earlier, this is indeed a mixture between point masses (weighted by the binomial likelihood factor evaluated at the various locations θ_j) and the posterior distribution $p(\theta_i \mid y_i)$, weighted by the marginal density of y_i times the total mass parameter. After drawing from (4.35) for $i = 1, \ldots, n$, the implied cluster structure $(S_1, \ldots, S_k)$ is retained and new locations are drawn from (4.32) which in this case reduces to

$$\theta_j^* \mid s, y \sim \text{Be}\left(\theta_j^* \mid a + \sum_{i \in S_j} y_i, b + \sum_{i \in S_j} \{9 - y_i\} \right), \qquad j = 1, \ldots, k. \tag{4.36}$$

It is interesting to point out that after cycling through $1, \ldots, n$ in a given iteration of (4.35), the number of clusters k could change. Keeping track of these values yields an approximation of the posterior distribution of the number of clusters.

The complete version of Algorithm 2 then becomes

(a') For $i = 1, \ldots, n$ update θ_i from (4.35). Let k denote the number of implied clusters, keep the cluster memberships s and drop the locations $\boldsymbol{\theta}^*$.
(a'') Generate new locations by drawing θ_j^* from (4.36) for $j = 1, \ldots, k$.

Note that (b) in Algorithm 2 is actually not needed in this case. Finally, we observe that

$$\theta_{n+1} \mid \boldsymbol{\theta} \sim \frac{1}{M+n} \sum_{j=1}^{k} n_j \delta_{\theta_j^*}(\theta_{n+1}) + \frac{M}{M+n} \mathrm{Be}(\theta_{n+1} \mid a, b), \tag{4.37}$$

where $n_j = |S_j| = \sum_{i=1}^{n} I\{s_i = j\}$, that is, the number of elements in cluster j. In other words, (4.37) means that θ_{n+1} is simply the next draw in the Pólya urn sequence started by the elements of $\boldsymbol{\theta}$. Samples from the posterior predictive distribution $p(\theta_{n+1} \mid y)$ can then be generated from the MCMC output by drawing from (4.37) for every imputed vector $\boldsymbol{\theta}$. These samples can be used to construct an approximation to $p(\theta_{n+1} \mid y)$ itself. Alternatively, one can also consider a Rao-Blackwellized approximation to this predictive distribution by evaluating

$$\frac{1}{M+n} \sum_{j=1}^{k} n_j I\{\theta = \theta_j^*\} + \frac{M\theta^{a-1}(1-\theta)^{b-1}}{(M+n)B(a,b)},$$

for all elements θ in a suitable grid over $\Theta = (0, 1)$, and averaging over MCMC iterations.

Applying the above method to the tack data in Beckett and Diaconis (1994) with $a = b = 1$, that is, the centering measure F_0 is the uniform distribution on $(0, 1)$, yields the results shown in Figure 4.5. The left panel shows the marginal posterior distribution of the number of clusters. The posterior predictive distribution $p(\theta_{n+1} \mid y)$ is plotted in the right panel. We basically see a bimodal distribution that could be reflecting the effect of the two flicking hands in the experiment. We remark here that none of these results would be possible under the extreme model versions discussed above.

3.4.2 *Autoregressive panel data models*

We revisit the annual per-capita GDP growth rates data introduced in Section 1.2.5, considering now a semiparametric model. Given the strong evidence supporting the bimodality of the individual effects β_i, we investigate whether the data support more than two clusters. One possible approach would be to replace the two-component mixture adopted in Section 1.2.5 with a k-component mixture with unknown k. A posterior simulation scheme based on reversible jumps, as in, for example Richardson and Green (1997), is well suited to such a problem. We assume instead a DP prior for the

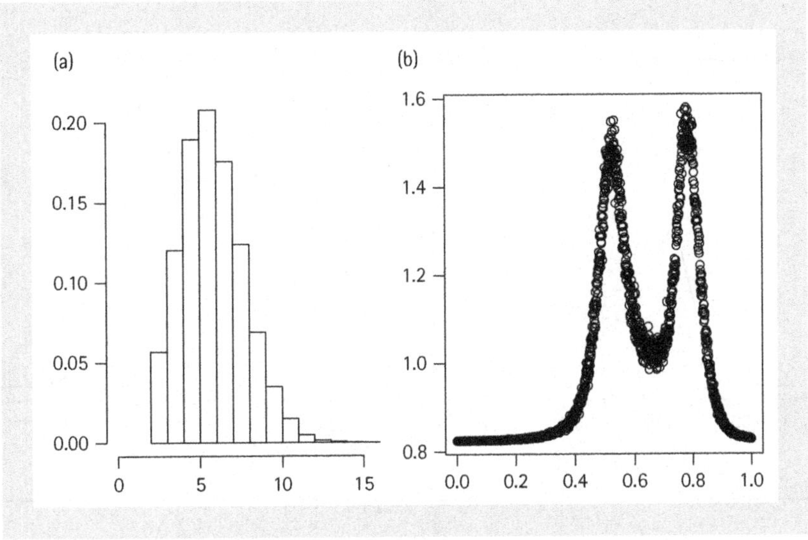

FIGURE 4.5 Tack data example. Panel (a) shows the posterior distribution of k, the number of clusters. Panel (b) presents the posterior predictive distribution of θ_{n+1}

β_is, which has the conceptual advantage of automatically taking care of the unknown number of components, and the practical convenience that the posterior simulation schemes (such as Algorithms 1 and 2 above) automatically avoid transdimensional issues as well.

We consider again the GDP growth in region i from time $t-1$ to t, defined as y_{it}, and the likelihood (4.18), with two changes. First, we assume $\beta_1, \ldots, \beta_m \overset{i.i.d.}{\sim} F$ and $F \sim \mathcal{D}(M, F_0)$, where $F_0(\beta_i) = N(\beta_i \mid \beta, \tau^{-1})$. This extends the earlier two-component mixture by allowing a priori essentially any clustering of the β_i parameters, with a Pólya urn-style probability model, controlled by parameter M. Furthermore, we assume $M = 1$, which means that, a priori, for the number of clusters N we assume $P(N > 2) = 0.9712$, $E(N) \approx 5.56$, and $\text{var}(N) \approx 4.56$, using the earlier approximations. Therefore, we encourage through the prior the formation of (more than two) clusters. Alternatively, we could treat M itself as unknown and choose a prior distribution on it. A common such choice is a $G(M \mid a, b)$ distribution, for which a closed-form sampling method is available, as explained in Escobar and West (1995). Secondly, we simplify the error assumptions to just $\varepsilon_{it} \sim N(0, 1)$. In doing so, we shift the model flexibility from the errors to the individual effects. We use vague proper priors on the other model parameters: $\lambda^{-1} \sim G(\lambda \mid 0.01, 100)$, $\alpha \sim N(\alpha \mid 0, 10^4)$, $\beta \mid \tau \sim N(\beta \mid 0, \tau)$, $\tau^{-1} \sim G(\tau \mid 0.01, 100)$, and $\mu \sim N(0, 10^4)$.

Figure 4.6 shows the marginal posterior distribution of parameters controlling the likelihood model. The posterior distributions for α, β, and μ are mostly away from zero, suggesting a significant autoregression and lagged GDP effect, and a positive centering parameter for individual effects. The precision parameter λ is now concentrated on

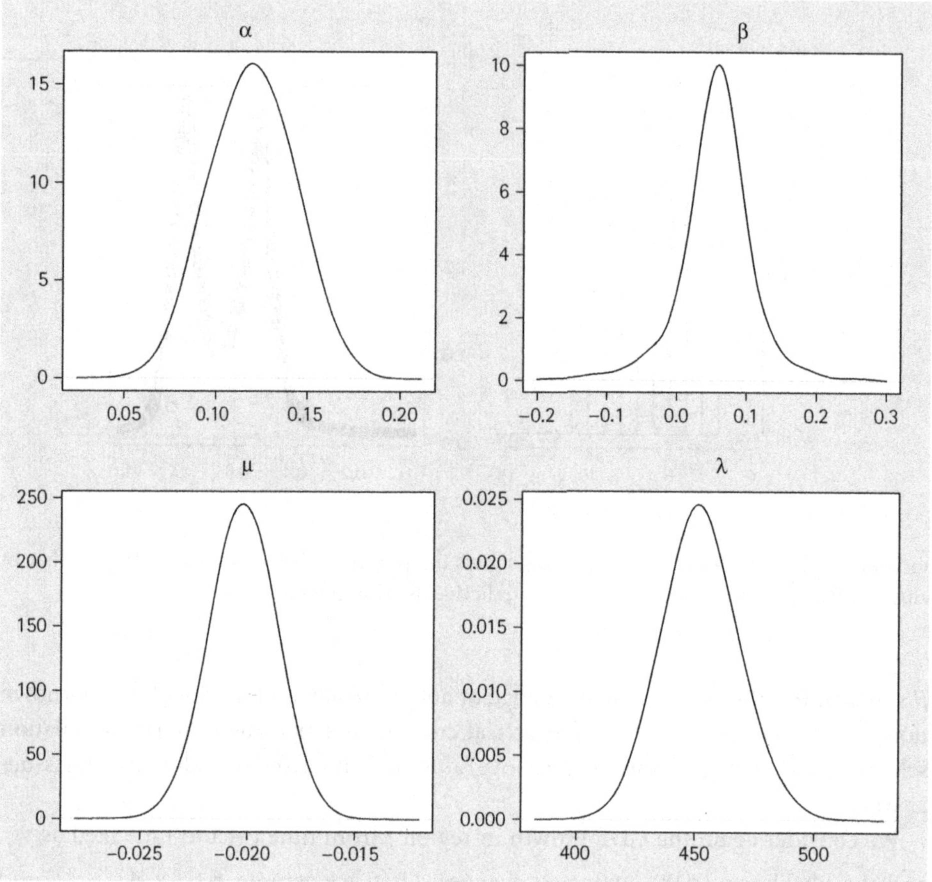

FIGURE 4.6 Posterior inference under the semiparametric model for NUTS2 growth rates

much smaller values. We note though that λ is here a precision parameter for a normal error term, and the parametric analysis was conducted with an error term with Student tails with small degrees of freedom (around 2), so this is not surprising.

Inference on cluster-related quantities is reported in Figure 4.7. The left panel shows the prior distribution of the number of clusters, while the posterior is shown in the right panel. The posterior mean, mode, and variance of this distribution are, respectively, 4.72, 4, and 2.99. The posterior gives higher weight to smaller number of clusters than the prior, but the data still strongly suggest the existence of more than two clusters.

Finally, we note that a slightly more complicated model was discussed in Hirano (2002), which allowed arbitrary clusters of region–time (i, t) pairs. While such an approach is even more flexible than the analysis here, it has the drawback that the clustering is not easy to interpret. Here clusters correspond to groups of regions with the same individual effects (corresponding here to the long-run mean growth under stationarity in the case without covariates).

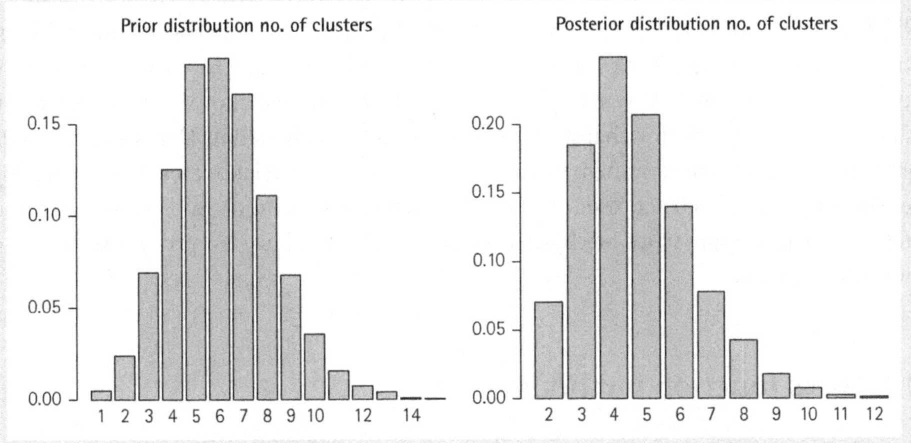

FIGURE 4.7 Prior (left panel) and posterior (right panel) distribution of the number of clusters under semiparametric model for NUTS2 growth rates

3.4.3 *Other applications in the econometrics literature*

Some other examples of applications of nonparametric methods as discussed in this section can be found in Chib and Hamilton (2002) (for longitudinal data treatment models), Griffin and Steel (2004), who analyse stochastic frontier models, and Koop (2008), who focuses on equilibrium job search models.

4 Flexible mean regression modeling

In the previous section, we considered nonparametric and semiparametric specifications of distributions. If covariates are also observed, it would be natural to consider how the distribution of the response changes with covariates. This is a challenging problem from a Bayesian perspective since a prior must be specified across distributions at all covariate values and this will be discussed in Section 5. However, allowing only a few aspects of the distribution, such as the mean and/or the variance, to change with the covariates defines a simpler set of models and may well be an adequate representation of many data sets. A natural starting point is nonlinear regression with homoskedastic errors. In this case, we assume the observations are generated by

$$y_i = g(x_i) + \epsilon_i, \qquad i = 1, 2, \ldots, n \tag{4.38}$$

where the errors $\epsilon_1, \epsilon_2, \ldots, \epsilon_n$ are i.i.d. from some parametric distribution, say $N(0, \sigma^2)$. The model could be extended to also include additional regressors $z_1, \ldots, z_n$ which are assumed to have a linear effect so that

$$y_i = g(x_i) + z_i'\eta + \epsilon_i,$$

where η is a vector of regression coefficients. This chapter will concentrate on problems without these additional regressors, z_i, but the methods could be easily extended to cover this case. Many Bayesian approaches have been proposed for this problem and it is beyond the scope of this chapter to review all methods in detail (Denison et al. 2002 provide a book-length treatment of the subject). We will restrict ourselves to reviewing several methods which represent the most widely used methods in econometrics and statistics. These approaches are basis function methods, Gaussian process priors, and smoothing priors.

4.1 Basis function methods

Basis function methods assume that we can express the unknown function in (4.38) as the linear combination

$$g(x) = \sum_{k=1}^{K} \beta_k \phi_k(x), \tag{4.39}$$

where $\phi_1(x), \phi_2(x), \ldots, \phi_K(x)$ are a collection of basis functions and $\beta_1, \beta_2, \ldots, \beta_K$ are real-valued parameters. Many examples of basis functions exist in the statistics literature. The method of polynomial regression expresses the unknown function $f(x)$ as a qth-order polynomial

$$g(x) = \sum_{k=0}^{q} \beta_k^* x^k$$

for some regression coefficients $\beta_0^*, \beta_2^*, \ldots, \beta_q^*$. This can be represented in the form of (4.39) if $\phi_k(x) = x^{k-1}$ and $K = q + 1$. Such polynomial expansions offer a flexible way to express a function. However, other collections of basis functions, defined through a collection of points on the real line, have become more popular recently. The points are known as knot points and each knot point is associated with a basis function. The idea is that the function close to a knot point is modeled by the respective basis function. Examples include the pth-order polynomial regression spline basis which is given by $\{1, x, x^2, \ldots, x^p, (x - \zeta_1)_+^p, (x - \zeta_2)_+^p, \ldots, (x - \zeta_{K-p-1})_+^p\}$ where $\zeta_1, \zeta_2, \ldots, \zeta_{K-p-1}$ are the knot points and

$$(x)_+ = \begin{cases} x \text{ if } x > 0 \\ 0 \text{ otherwise} \end{cases},$$

and radial basis functions where the value of the basis at a given point only depends on its distance from the knot, that is, $\phi_k(x) = \phi(|x - \zeta_k|)$. The most widely used example of a radial basis function in econometrics is the thin plate spline basis $\{1, x, |x - \zeta_1|, \ldots, |x - \zeta_{K-2}|\}$ where $\zeta_1, \zeta_2, \ldots, \zeta_{K-2}$ are knot points. Both spline bases include an intercept term (4.1), polynomial terms (linear for the thin plate spline basis and up to p-th order for the p-th order polynomial regression spline basis) and functions defined by the knot points. Several suggestion have been made for the position of the knot points. If there are J knot points, they can be chosen to be the $\frac{1}{J+1}$-th, $\frac{2}{J+1}$-th, $\ldots$, $\frac{J}{J+1}$-th percentiles of the observed covariates (Smith and Kohn 1996) or chosen to be placed at all observed covariate values where $J = n$ and the knots are $x_1, x_2, \ldots, x_n$ (Denison et al. 2002). If J is large, we have a very flexible specification of the unknown function. However, this substantial flexibility can potentially lead to overfitting and a large literature, both Bayesian and non-Bayesian, has proposed methods to avoid this problem.

Reviews of Bayesian approaches are provided by Kohn et al. (2001) and Denison et al. (2002). Using the basis function representation in (4.39), the model in (4.38) is a linear model in the basis functions and so standard Bayesian variable selection methods (Brown et al. 1998; Chipman et al. 2001; George and McCulloch 1993; Mitchell and Beauchamp 1988; Raftery et al. 1997) can be applied to avoid overfitting. This approach assumes that some regression coefficients can be set to zero which effectively removes some basis functions from (4.39). The removed basis functions do not substantially increase the fit of the model to the data. However, there will be uncertainty about which regression coefficients should be set to zero and this can be straightforwardly included in the inference using a Bayesian approach.

The method is most clearly explained in hierarchical form introducing an indicator γ_i which is 1 if the i-th basis function is included in the model and 0 if it is excluded. Model (4.38) can then be written in a linear regression form

$$y = X_\gamma \boldsymbol{\beta}_\gamma + \boldsymbol{\epsilon}$$

where $\boldsymbol{\epsilon}$ is an n dimensional vector of i.i.d. $\mathrm{N}(0, \sigma^2)$ random variables and X_γ is a data matrix whose (i,j)-th element is $\phi_k(x_i)$ if $\gamma_k = 1$ and $\sum_{l=1}^{k} \gamma_l = j$. The Bayesian hierarchical model is completed by defining priors for σ^2, $\boldsymbol{\beta}_\gamma$, and $\boldsymbol{\gamma} = (\gamma_1, \gamma_2, \ldots, \gamma_K)$. Often σ^{-2} is given the improper prior $p(\sigma^2) \propto 1/\sigma^2$ or the proper choice $\sigma^{-2} \sim \mathrm{Ga}(a_0, 1/b_0)$, where a_0 is a shape parameter and σ^{-2} has prior mean a_0/b_0, and $\gamma_1, \gamma_2, \ldots, \gamma_K$ are assumed a priori independent with $p(\gamma_i = 1) = p_i$. The probability p_i represents our prior belief that the i-th basis function should be included in the model. Usually, an intercept term is included by defining $\phi_1(x) = 1$ and $p_1 = 1$ so that it is always included in the model. Similarly, there are often polynomial terms, for example, $x, x^2, \ldots, x^p$ in the polynomial regression spline basis, which are often assumed always to be included in the model and so $p_i = 1$ for those basis functions. Finally, it seems natural to assume that all other basis functions (which depend on knot points) should be equally likely, with probability p, to be included in the model. The value of p represents a prior guess at the proportion of these basis functions that are needed to model the data. There has been substantial work and disagreement about the choice of prior specification for β (Denison et al. 2002; Holmes and Mallick 1998; Kohn et al. 2001). The standard choices are the so-called "ridge prior" which is

$$\boldsymbol{\beta}_\gamma|\sigma^2 \sim \mathrm{N}(\mathbf{0}, c\sigma^2 I), \tag{4.40}$$

where I is the identity matrix with the same dimension as $\boldsymbol{\beta}_\gamma$ and the g-prior which is

$$\boldsymbol{\beta}_\gamma|\sigma^2 \sim \mathrm{N}(\mathbf{0}, c\sigma^2 (X'_\gamma X_\gamma)^{-1}). \tag{4.41}$$

The g-prior specification is invariant to changes of scale of the covariates and to changes of scale of the responses and we will restrict attention to the g-prior specification in this chapter with the default value $c = n$ as suggested by Kohn et al. (2001). In each case, the prior for $\boldsymbol{\beta}_\gamma$ depends on σ^2, which leads to closed-form expressions for $p(y|\boldsymbol{\gamma})$. This is useful for computational reasons and for studying the properties of the posterior distribution of $\boldsymbol{\gamma}$.

There has been substantial work on computational methods for these models using MCMC methods. A Gibbs sampling approach was proposed by Kohn et al. (2001) and a reversible jump approach was described in Holmes and Mallick (1998). We present the simplest versions of these computational strategies which will be the easiest to implement but which may not be the most efficient computationally. Both methods use the integrated likelihood $p(y|\boldsymbol{\gamma})$ which is available analytically if the prior in (4.41) is used. Then

$$p(y|\boldsymbol{\gamma}) = (1+c)^{-q_\gamma/2}(S(\gamma) + 2b_0)^{-n/2+a_0}$$

where $a_0 = b_0 = 0$ if the improper prior for σ^2 is used, q_γ is the number of basis functions included in $\boldsymbol{\gamma}$ (i.e. $\sum_{i=1}^K \gamma_i$) and $S_\gamma = \boldsymbol{y}'\boldsymbol{y} - \frac{c}{c+1}\boldsymbol{y}'X_\gamma(X'_\gamma X_\gamma)^{-1}X'_\gamma \boldsymbol{y}$.

The simplest Gibbs sampling approach updates γ_i from its full conditional distribution $p(\gamma_i|y, \gamma_j, j \neq i)$ for $i = 1, 2, \ldots, K$. The full conditional distribution is

$$p(\gamma_i = 1|y, \gamma_j, j \neq i) = \frac{p(y|\boldsymbol{\gamma}^{(i,1)})p_i}{p(y|\boldsymbol{\gamma}^{(i,1)})p_i + p(y|\boldsymbol{\gamma}^{(i,0)})(1-p_i)}$$

$$p(\gamma_i = 0|y, \gamma_j, j \neq i) = \frac{p(y|\boldsymbol{\gamma}^{(i,0)})(1-p_i)}{p(y|\boldsymbol{\gamma}^{(i,1)})p_i + p(y|\boldsymbol{\gamma}^{(i,0)})(1-p_i)}$$

where $\boldsymbol{\gamma}^{(i,k)}$ is formed by keeping $\gamma_j, j \neq i$ fixed and setting $\gamma_i = k$.

The simplest Metropolis-Hasting sampling scheme updates the model by proposing to change the model in several ways: addition of a basis function, deletion of a basis function, or the swapping of one basis function included in the model for one currently excluded from the model (swap). The first two moves (addition and deletion) are proposed with the same probability p_{AD} and the swap move with probability $1 - 2p_{AD}$ where $0 < p_{AD} < 0.5$. The proposed model is accepted with probability

$$\min\left\{1, \frac{p(y|\boldsymbol{\gamma}')p(\boldsymbol{\gamma}')}{p(y|\boldsymbol{\gamma})p(\boldsymbol{\gamma})}\right\}$$

where

$$p(\gamma) = \prod_{i=1}^{K} p_i^{\gamma_i}(1-p_i)^{1-\gamma_i}.$$

To illustrate this method of nonparametric regression, we re-analyse an example measuring the relationship between average income and prestige of 102 occupations using the 1971 Canadian census (Fox 1997). The prestige of the jobs was measured through a social survey and will be treated as the response with average income as the covariate. Figure 4.8 shows the results of applying a thin-plate spline model using the prior in (4.41) to the data with $K = 30$ and the knots placed equidistantly at the percentiles of the observed covariate values. The hyperparameters $a_0 = 0$ and $b_0 = 0$. It shows that prestige increases with income but that the relationship is not linear. There seems to be some evidence that the rate changes at around \$10,000 and the prestige of high income jobs is relatively constant. The credibility interval becomes wider for covariate values around which there is less data, which represents greater uncertainty about the function. The function can be fitted by a relatively small number of basis functions. The posterior distribution is shown in Figure 4.8(b) and indicates that the modal number is 4, with values between 1 and 8 well-supported by the data.

The methods described so far are restricted to a univariate covariate. However, it is often necessary to assume that the function depends on more than one covariate and use the model

$$y_i = g(x_{i1}, x_{i2}, \ldots, x_{ip}) + \epsilon_i,$$

where $x_{i1}, x_{i2}, \ldots, x_{ip}$ is a p-dimensional vector of regressors, as a generalization of (4.38). The approach developed for univariate covariates could be extended directly to

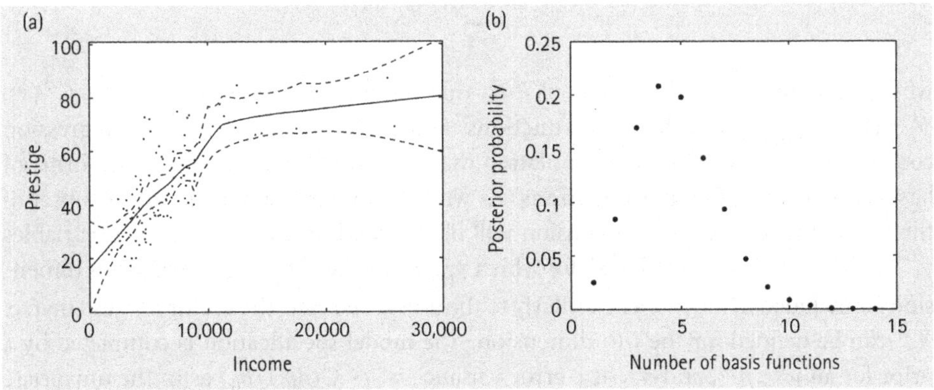

FIGURE 4.8 Prestige data using spline regression with parametric errors. (a) The data and the posterior median of $f(x)$ (solid line) with a 95% credibility interval (dashed lines) and (b) the posterior distribution of the number of basis functions

higher dimensions by defining a collection of basis functions in p-dimensions, which is trivial for the radial basis function. For example, the thin-plate spline can be written generally as

$$\phi_k(x) = \begin{cases} \| x - \tilde{x}_k \|^{2m-p} \log(\| x - \tilde{x}_k \|) & 2m - p \text{ is even} \\ \| x - \tilde{x}_k \|^{2m-p} & 2m - p \text{ is odd} \end{cases}$$

where m is an integer-valued parameter giving the order of the spline and $\| x - y \| = \sum_{i=1}^{p}(x_i - y_i)^2$ is the Euclidean distance between x and y. The function $g(x_1, x_2, \ldots, x_p)$ can be expressed as a linear function of the basis function, as in (4.39), and the methodology extended (see Holmes and Mallick 1998; Smith and Kohn 1997). However, there is a potential problem with blindly following this approach. As the dimension of p grows, the data become increasingly sparse and the predictive ability of the spline model can be adversely affected, which is known as the curse of dimensionality. This has led to an interest in simpler multivariate models.

The simplest multivariate extension is the additive model where it is assumed that the function can be expressed as the sum of functions for each dimension so that

$$g(x_1, x_2, \ldots, x_p) = \sum_{i=1}^{p} g_i(x_i). \tag{4.42}$$

The multiple linear regression model fits in this class for the linear function $g_i(x) = x\beta_i$ and so the additive model allows nonlinear effects for each covariate. In practice, we may want to restrict some functions to be parametric (linear or quadratic), whilst allowing others to be modeled nonparametrically. Each function, g_i, to be modeled nonparametrically can be given a basis function representation as in equation (4.39) and so

$$g_i(x_i) = \sum_{k=1}^{K_i} \beta_k^{(i)} \phi_k^{(i)}(x_i)$$

where, for the i-th dimension, K_i is the number of basis functions, $\phi_1^{(i)}(x)$, $\phi_2^{(i)}(x), \ldots, \phi_{K_i}^{(i)}(x)$ are the basis functions, and $\beta_1^{(i)}, \beta_2^{(i)}, \ldots, \beta_{K_i}^{(i)}$ are the regression coefficients. This is a general formulation that allows different numbers and forms of basis function in different dimensions. As with the univariate model, only a subset of the basis functions for any dimension will be included in the model and so variables $\gamma_1^{(i)}, \gamma_2^{(i)}, \ldots, \gamma_{K_i}^{(i)}$ are introduced, for which $\gamma_j^{(i)} = 1$ if the j-th basis function for dimension i is included in the model. Similarly to the univariate case, the vector $\beta_\gamma^{(i)}$ and matrix $X_\gamma^{(i)}$ can be defined for the i-th dimension. The model specification is completed by a prior for all $\gamma^{(i)}, \beta^{(i)}$, and σ^2. The error variance $\sigma^2 \sim \mathrm{G}(a_0, 1/b_0)$ as in the univariate model and $\gamma^{(i)}, \beta^{(i)}$ is assumed independent of $\gamma^{(j)}, \beta^{(j)}$ for $i \neq j$. Finally, the prior for $\gamma^{(i)}, \beta^{(i)}$ can be chosen in the same way as the univariate model. The model can be fitted using extensions of the previous algorithms (Smith and Kohn 1996).

As an example of fitting an additive model, we consider fitting a cost function for the distribution of electricity (Yatchew 2003). The model allows the costs to depend on some factors in a nonlinear way. The model is

$$\text{tc} = g_1(\text{cust}) + g_2(\text{wage}) + \beta_1\,\text{pcap} + \beta_2\,\text{PUC} + g_3(\text{kwh}) + g_4(\text{life}) + g_5(\text{lf}) + g_6(\text{kmwire}) + \epsilon,$$

where tc is the log of total cost per customer, cust is the log of the number of customers, wage is the log wage rate, pcap is the log price of capital, PUC is a dummy variable for public utility commissions, life is the log of the remaining life of distribution assets, lf is the log of the load factor, and kmwire is the log of kilometres of distribution wire per customer. The data consist of 81 municipal distributors in Ontario, Canada during 1993. This generalizes the Cobb-Douglas cost function, which assumes that the cost of each factor depends linearly on the factor level. Each function $g_1, g_2, \ldots, g_6$ is modeled using a thin-plate spline with $K = 30$. The prior given in (4.41) is used for $\beta_\gamma^{(i)}$ and $a_0 = b_0 = 0$ in the prior for σ^{-2}. Figure 4.9 shows summaries of the posterior for each function. The graph shows the posterior median of $g_i(x)$ and a 95% credible interval which were each plotted against the variable minus its mean. The model is identified by setting $g_i(0) = 0$ (which can be achieved by appropriately adjusting the function values recorded at each iteration of the MCMC sampler) so each curve measures the difference in cost from an "average" firm where all variables take their mean value. As noted by

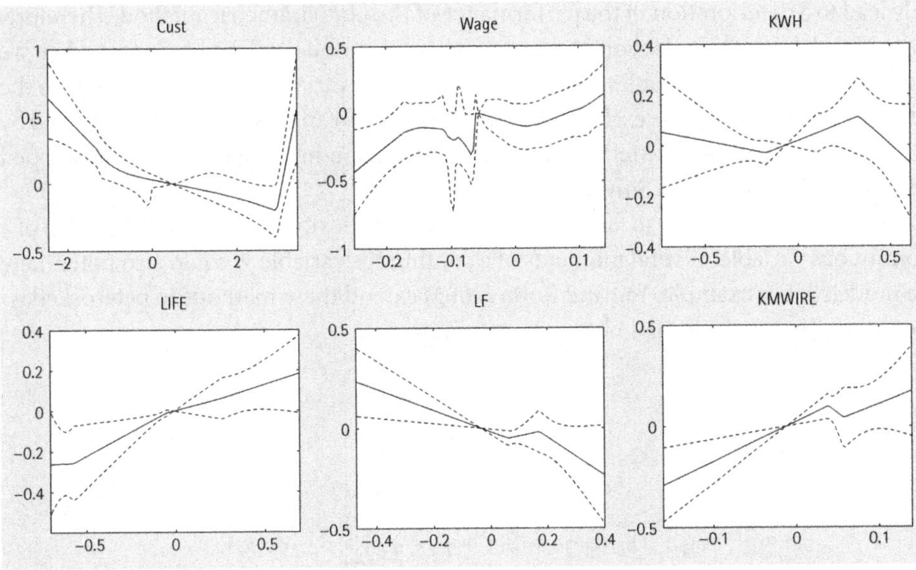

FIGURE 4.9 The contribution of some covariates to the cost function (the covariates are plotted with their means subtracted) for electricity production. Solid lines denote the posterior median and dashed lines indicate the 95% credible interval

Yatchew (2003), the most interesting variable is cust, which has a nonlinear effect on cost. However, we also find some evidence that wages and kwh enter in a nonlinear way. We have not imposed monotonicity on the function, but most other covariates enter in a monotonic way. However, several regressors do show rather nonlinear effects. This example illustrates the flexibility of these models, but also shows a potential drawback. Usually, the researcher would want to assume regularity conditions, implying that costs will either increase or decrease with some of the factors, which implies that we would require some $g_i(x)$ to be monotone. This simple model estimated above makes no such assumption. An alternative approach is the use of Müntz-Satz series expansions as basis functions by Barnett, Geweke, and Wolfe (1991) in the context of asymptotically ideal models (AIM) for production. This particular choice of basis function simplifies the imposition of economic regularity conditions, which is particularly important in the area of production modeling.

We could extend equation (4.42) to

$$g(x_1, x_2, \ldots, x_p) = \sum_{i=1}^{p} g_i(x_i) + \sum_{i=1}^{p} \sum_{j=1; j \neq i}^{k} g_{ij}(x_i, x_j),$$

where g_{ij} is a bivariate function which can be modeled using a linear combination of bivariate basis functions (such as the bivariate thin-plate spline). This relaxes the assumption that $g(x_1, x_2, \ldots, x_p)$ is the sum of functions for each dimension and so allows greater flexibility. The model can be fitted using extensions of the methods already described. It is important to note that the inclusion of more flexibility may actually lead to a deterioration in the performance of the nonparametric method. Therefore, variable selection and selection of the structure of the model will be important when we have more than a few variables. We may find that some variables do not contribute to the fit of the model and can be excluded or that their effects can be satisfactorily modeled by simple parametric forms. Methods for variable selection in these models are developed in Wood et al. (2002) and Shively et al. (1999).

In this section, we have so far restricted attention to flexible modeling of the mean of a continuous variable. Several moments of a continuous variable y_i could also potentially be modeled. For example, Yau and Kohn (2003) extend these methods to heteroskedastic errors. The model for the observations is now

$$y_i = g(x_i) + \sigma(x_i)\epsilon_i,$$

where $\epsilon_i \sim \mathrm{N}(0, 1)$. They assume that

$$\log \sigma^2(x_i) = \gamma + \tilde{\beta}_1 x + \tilde{\beta}_2 x + \sum_{j=1}^{r} \tilde{\beta}_{j+2} \tilde{\phi}_j(x_i),$$

where $\tilde{\beta}_1, \tilde{\beta}_2, \ldots, \tilde{\beta}_{r+2}$ are regression coefficients and $\phi_1(x), \phi_2(x), \ldots, \phi_r(x)$ are thin-plate splines. The variance, through the log transform, is then modeled in a flexible way. The interested reader is referred to Yau and Kohn (2003) for a description of the methodology.

We may want to model binary or multinomial observations or model higher moments of continuous observations. Extending spline regression models to binary or continuous data is discussed by Wood and Kohn (1998) and Kohn et al. (2003). In the binary case, observations, y_i, fall into two classes which are given the label 0 and 1 and it is assumed that

$$P(y_i = 1) = \Phi(g(x_{i1}, x_{i2}, \ldots, x_{ip})) \tag{4.43}$$

where Φ represents the cumulative distribution function of a normal distribution. The unknown function g can be modeled using the spline basis function explained in this chapter. The computational approaches can be directly extended using the data augmentation approach of Albert and Chib (1993), which introduces latent variables $z_1, z_2, \ldots, z_n$ and the model is expressed as

$$y_i = \begin{cases} 0 & z_i < 0 \\ 1 & z_i > 0 \end{cases}$$

$$z_i = g(x_{i1}, x_{i2}, \ldots, x_{ip}) + \epsilon_i, \qquad \epsilon_i \sim \mathrm{N}(0, 1).$$

Integrating $z_1, z_2, \ldots, z_n$ from the model returns us to the original model in (4.43).

4.2 Gaussian processes and smoothing priors

Gaussian processes have a long history as priors for nonparametric function estimation in Bayesian analysis. Rasmussen and Williams (2006) give a recent book-length treatment of their use in regression problems. A Gaussian process prior for a function g is parameterized by a mean function $m(\cdot)$ and a covariance function $\kappa(\cdot, \cdot)$. It assumes that, for points $x_1, x_2, \ldots, x_n$, the function values $g(x_1), g(x_2), \ldots, g(x_n)$ have a joint normal distribution with mean $m(x_1), m(x_2), \ldots, m(x_n)$ and the covariance of $g(x_i)$ and $g(x_j)$ is $\kappa(x_i, x_j)$. The choice of κ is not arbitrary but must define a positive semi-definite covariance matrix for $g(x_1), g(x_2), \ldots, g(x_n)$, with any choice of $x_1, x_2, \ldots, x_n$ and any n. This ensures that the Gaussian process exists but it can be difficult to check for an arbitrary choice of $\kappa(\cdot, \cdot)$.

The Gaussian process can be used for inference in the regression model in (4.38) where

$$y_i = g(x_i) + \epsilon_i, \qquad i = 1, 2, \ldots, n$$

where $\epsilon_1, \epsilon_2, \ldots, \epsilon_n$ are i.i.d. and $\epsilon_i \sim \mathrm{N}(0, \sigma^2)$. The unknown function g is given a Gaussian process prior with the mean function taken to be zero, that is, $m(x) = 0$ for all x, which implies that the joint prior distribution of $\mathbf{g} = (g(x_1), g(x_2), \ldots, g(x_n))'$ is $\mathrm{N}(\mathbf{0}, \Sigma_0)$ where $\mathbf{0}$ is an $(n \times 1)$-dimensional vector with all entries 0 and Σ_0 is an

$(n \times n)$-dimensional matrix with (i,j)-th entry $\kappa(x_i, x_j)$. The posterior distribution, conditional on σ^2, is available in closed form. The joint posterior distribution of g is normal with mean μ_n and variance Σ_n where

$$\mu_n = \Sigma_0(\sigma^2 I + \Sigma_0)^{-1} y$$

and

$$\Sigma_n = \sigma^2(\sigma^2 I + \Sigma_0)^{-1}\Sigma_0.$$

Inference about the function at an unobserved point x_{n+1} can also be made in closed form. The Gaussian process prior for g implies that $g(x_1), g(x_2), \ldots, g(x_n), g(x_{n+1})$ have a multivariate normal distribution and so

$$g(x_{n+1})|g \sim \mathrm{N}(k'\Sigma_0^{-1}g, \kappa(x_{n+1}, x_{n+1}) - k'\Sigma_0^{-1}k),$$

where k is an n-dimensional vector with elements $k_i = \kappa(x_{n+1}, x_i)$. This result combined with the normal posterior distribution for g implies that the posterior distribution of $g(x_{n+1}), g(x_{n+1})|y$, is $\mathrm{N}(\mu^*, \sigma^{*2})$, where

$$\mu^* = k'(\sigma^2 I + \Sigma_0)^{-1} y$$

and

$$\sigma^{*2} = \kappa(x_{n+1}, x_{n+1}) - k'(\sigma^2 I + \Sigma_0)^{-1} k.$$

The mean, μ^*, is a linear combination of the observations $y_1, y_2, \ldots, y_n$ where the weight given to each observation is determined by the vector $k'(\sigma^2 I + \Sigma_0)^{-1}$. This vector will give more weight to observations that are closer to x_{n+1} than those further away. The posterior predictive variance can be expressed as the prior predictive variance $\kappa(x_{n+1}, x_{n+1})$ less the factor $k'(\sigma^2 I + \Sigma_0)^{-1}k$, which measures the amount that our prior uncertainty is reduced by observing the data.

The prior covariance function $\kappa(\cdot,\cdot)$ encodes our prior beliefs about the unknown function. However, it can be difficult to check that an arbitrary $\kappa(\cdot,\cdot)$ defines a covariance function and so, in practice, the covariance function will often be chosen from a list of standard choices. Often, the covariance functions are stationary, meaning that $\kappa(x_i, x_j) = h(|x_i - x_j|)$ is only a function of $|x_i - x_j|$ where $|\cdot|$ is a distance measure. Some popular choices include: the Gaussian kernel $h(d) = \exp\{-d^2\}$, the Laplace or exponential kernel $h(d) = \exp\{-d\}$ and the Matèrn class of covariance functions

$$h(d) = \frac{1}{2^{\tau-1}\Gamma(\tau)} d^\tau \mathcal{K}_\tau(d),$$

where $\mathcal{K}_\tau$ is the modified Bessel function of order τ and the parameter $\tau > 0$ is a smoothness parameter. For $\tau = 1/2$, we retrieve the exponential covariance structure.

In practice, the inference described so far has assumed that σ^2 is known. If σ^2 is unknown, then the posterior distribution of σ^2 and the posterior distribution of $g(x_{n+1})$

are available in closed form if it is assumed that the covariance $\kappa(\cdot,\cdot) = \sigma^2\tilde{\kappa}(\cdot,\cdot)$, so that the prior covariance matrix is scaled by the regression error variance, and $\sigma^{-2} \sim G(a_0, 1/b_0)$. In this case,

$$\sigma^{-2}|y \sim G(a^*, 1/b^*),$$

where

$$a^* = a_0 + n/2, \qquad b^* = b_0 + (y'y - y'(I + \tilde{\Sigma}_0)^{-1}y)/2$$

and the (i, j)-th element of $\tilde{\Sigma}_0$ is $\tilde{\kappa}(x_i, x_j)$. The posterior distribution of $g(x_{n+1})$ has the density

$$\frac{\Gamma(a^* + 1/2)}{\Gamma(a^*)} \frac{1}{\sqrt{2\pi \tilde{A} b^*}} \left(1 + \frac{(g(x_{n+1}) - \tilde{\mu}^*)^2}{2\tilde{A}b^*}\right)^{-(a^*+1/2)}$$

where

$$\tilde{\mu}^* = \tilde{k}'(I + \tilde{\Sigma}_0)^{-1}y$$

and

$$\tilde{A} = \tilde{\kappa}(x_{n+1}, x_{n+1}) - \tilde{k}'(I + \tilde{\Sigma}_0)^{-1}\tilde{k},$$

where $\tilde{k}$ is an n-dimensional vector with j-th element $\tilde{\kappa}(x_{n+1}, x_j)$. Clearly, the marginal posterior distribution of $g(x_{n+1})$ is a Student-t distribution; in particular, $g(x_{n+1})|y \sim t(\tilde{\mu}^*, 1/(2\tilde{A}b^*), 2a^*)$ which has mean $\tilde{\mu}^*$ if $a^* > 1/2$ (assured if $n > 1$) and variance $\{b^*/(a^* - 1)\}\tilde{A}$ provided $a^* > 1$ (always the case if we have two or more observations).

The Gaussian process places a prior directly on the unknown function. Alternatively, suppose that g is a univariate function. Prior information could be placed on the other aspects of the unknown function. Shiller (1984) describes "smoothness priors" which place prior information on the second derivative of the function. The idea is that the slope of the derivatives does not change quickly for a smooth function. A realization of the integral of Brownian motion is used as a prior for the function. Slope of the derivative of the function will change slowly if the increments of the Brownian motion have small variances. It will be assumed that $x_1 < x_2 < \cdots < x_n$ so that there are no common values of the covariates (Shiller (1984) discusses the case where there are common values). The model is most easily expressed through an $(n-2) \times n$-dimensional matrix R with the form

$$R_{ij} = \begin{cases} \Delta_i^{-1}, & i = j \\ -(\Delta_i^{-1} + \Delta_{i+1}^{-1}), & i = j - 1 \\ \Delta_{i+1}^{-1}, & i = j - 2 \\ 0 & \text{otherwise} \end{cases}$$

where $\Delta_i = x_{i+1} - x_i$. The i-th element of the vector Rg is the difference in slope between a line connecting $(x_i, g(x_i))$ to $(x_{i+1}, g(x_{i+1}))$ and a line connecting $(x_{i+1}, g(x_{i+1}))$ to $(x_{i+2}, g(x_{i+2}))$. The prior for $g = (g(x_1), g(x_2), \ldots, g(x_n))$ is $\mathrm{N}(\mathbf{0}, \sigma^2 k R' H^{-1} R)$ where k is an prior scale parameter and H is an $(N-2) \times (N-2)$ matrix whose elements are

$$H_{ij} = \begin{cases} (\Delta_i + \Delta_{i+1})/3 & i = j \\ \Delta_{i+1}/6 & i = j-1 \\ \Delta_i/6 & i = j+1 \\ 0 & \text{otherwise} \end{cases}.$$

Therefore the prior is a Gaussian process with a specific choice of covariance matrix. However, it will be sparse since many elements will be zero which will allow faster computation than general Gaussian processes. If σ^2 is given the improper prior $p(\sigma^2) \propto \sigma^{-2}$, the posterior distribution of g is available in closed form

$$p(g) \propto \left[n - 2 + \hat{\sigma}^{-2}(g - g^*)'(I + k^2 R' H^{-1} R)(g - g^*)\right]^{-(n-1)}$$

where $g^* = (I + k^2 R' H^{-1} R)^{-1} y$ and

$$\hat{\sigma}^2 = [(y - g^*)'(y - g^*) + k^2 g^{*'} R' R g^*]/(n-2).$$

A similar approach is developed by Koop and Poirier (2004) who argue that a prior should be placed on the first differences $g(x_2) - g(x_1), g(x_3) - g(x_2), \ldots, g(x_n) - g(x_{n-1})$, where the observations are ordered according the values of x. This will place prior mass on functions without rapid changes. A normal prior for the differences is introduced so that

$$Dg \sim \mathrm{N}(\mathbf{0}, \sigma^2 V(\eta)),$$

where D is the first difference matrix and $V(\eta)$ is a positive-definite matrix which depends on the hyperparameters η. The choice of a normal prior for the differences encourages shrinkage of $g(x_i)$ towards $g(x_{i-1})$ and $g(x_{i+1})$. If σ^{-2} is given the improper prior, $p(\sigma^2) \propto \sigma^{-2}$, posterior moments of g are available

$$\mathrm{E}[g|y] = [I + D' V(\eta)^{-1} D]^{-1} y$$

and

$$\mathrm{V}[g|y] = [I + D' V(\eta)^{-1} D]^{-1}.$$

Koop and Poirier (2004) discuss other possible choices. This approach can be extended to higher-order differencing. Applications to wages and labour participation are considered by Koop and Tobias (2006). Koop et al. (2005) extend these methods to multiple equation models and apply a two-equation structural model to returns to schooling.

5 Fully non/semiparametric regression modeling

The previous section concentrated on flexible modeling of the mean, whilst assuming that the errors in the regression model were normal. There is often no particular reason for making this assumption other than simplicity and tradition. Potentially, the errors could be drawn from a distribution which is, for example, heavy tailed, skewed, or bimodal. If this is the case, choosing an arbitrary distribution and making posterior inference could lead to misleading inference about quantities of interest such as the conditional mean. This section considers using nonparametric methods to specify flexible error distributions in a regression model and, more generally, defining nonparametric priors which allow the unknown distribution to depend upon covariates.

A natural approach to semiparametric regression models combines a flexible specification of the mean with a nonparametric prior for the distribution of the errors. The most straightforward example assumes that the error distribution is a nonparametric mixture of normals, as in (4.29). The model can be written as

$$y_i = g(\mathbf{x}_i) + \epsilon_i, \quad \epsilon_i \mid \theta_i \sim \mathrm{N}(\epsilon_i \mid \mu_i, \sigma_i^2), \quad (\mu_i, \sigma_i^2) \mid F \sim F, \quad F \sim \mathrm{RPM}, \tag{4.44}$$

where the RPM for F has a centering distribution $H(\mu, \sigma^2)$ with density $h(\mu, \sigma^2) = h(\mu)h(\sigma^2)$. The density $h(\mu)$ is chosen to be a zero mean distribution (which is often chosen to be normal). The model was initially studied by Bush and MacEachern (1996) when analyzing randomized block designs where $g(\mathbf{x}_i)$ is assumed to be linear, that is, $g(\mathbf{x}_i) = \mathbf{x}_i'\boldsymbol{\beta}$. More recently, the model where $g(\mathbf{x}_i)$ is flexibly modeled through a spline basis has been considered by Chib and Greenberg (2009) and Leslie et al. (2007). Leslie et al. (2007) use regression splines whereas Chib and Greenberg (2009) use cubic splines and pay particular attention to prior elicitation and model selection, using the approximation of marginal likelihoods of Dirichlet process mixture models introduced by Basu and Chib (2003). The model can be fitted using a Gibbs sampler. The parameters of the mixture model conditional on $g(\mathbf{x}_i)$ can be updated using standard methods since $y_i - g(\mathbf{x}_i)$ follows a nonparametric mixture model and the errors $\epsilon_1, \epsilon_2, \ldots, \epsilon_n$ conditional on the allocation variables used in MCMC methods for nonparametric mixtures will be normal and so the methods developed in the previous section can be used to update the parameters of the nonlinear regression function $g(\mathbf{x}_i)$.

The interpretation of $g(\mathbf{x}_i)$ in the regression model in (4.44) is complicated since the mean of $\epsilon_i|F$ is no longer 0 (as in standard parametric models). There are several potential solutions to this problem. First, we can assume that $g(\mathbf{x}_i)$ does not include an intercept and allow F to be centred over a distribution with a non-zero mean. The mean of F can then be interpreted as the intercept. Secondly, the problem can be effectively ignored since the distribution of $\mathrm{E}[\epsilon_i|F]$ will often be tightly concentrated around zero if F is centered over a zero-mean distribution for sensible choices of the RPM.

Alternatively, Brunner (1995) and Kottas and Gelfand (2001) suggest using a median regression model

$$y_i = g(\mathbf{x}_i) + \epsilon_i, \qquad \epsilon_i \mid \theta_i \sim \mathrm{U}(\epsilon_i \mid -\theta_i, \theta_i), \qquad \theta_i \mid F \sim F, \qquad F \sim \mathrm{RPM}, \quad (4.45)$$

where $\mathrm{U}(a, b)$ represents a uniform distribution on (a, b). The distribution of $\epsilon_i|F$ follows a mixture of uniform distributions which can represent any symmetric, unimodal distribution (Brunner and Lo 1989; Feller 1971) and always has median zero. This allows $g(\mathbf{x})$ to be interpreted as the conditional median of y given $\mathbf{x}$. This idea, including MCMC methodology, is developed by Kottas and Krnjajic (2009) for general quantile regression.

The model in (4.44) is flexible but makes the assumption that the errors are homoskedastic, which may not be supported by the data. A simple extension is considered by Leslie et al. (2007), who assume

$$y_i = g(\mathbf{x}_i) + \exp\{z_i'\boldsymbol{\delta}\}\epsilon_i, \qquad \epsilon_i \mid \theta_i \sim \mathrm{N}(\epsilon_i \mid \theta_i), \qquad \theta_i \mid F \sim F, \qquad F \sim \mathrm{RPM},$$

where z_i is a vector of covariates which may have some elements in common with $\mathbf{x}_i$ and $\boldsymbol{\delta}$ is a vector of parameters. The error variance is now be modeled as a function of the covariates by $\exp\{z_i'\boldsymbol{\delta}\}$. The function $g(\mathbf{x})$ can be modeled using spline basis functions, Gaussian processes, or smoothing priors. The model can be fitted using MCMC methods in a Gibbs sampling framework using the same approach as the one described for the model in (4.44).

Figure 4.10 shows the results of applying the model in (4.44) to the prestige data discussed in the previous section, with $g(x)$ again modeled through first-order thin-plate splines with $K = 30$ and the knots set at the percentiles of the observed covariates. The prior for the nonparametric part is taken from Griffin (2010), who uses a simplification of the model in (4.44) by assuming

$$y_i = g(\mathbf{x}_i) + \epsilon_i, \qquad \epsilon_i \mid \theta_i \sim \mathrm{N}(\epsilon_i \mid \mu_i, a\sigma^2), \qquad \mu_i \mid F \sim F, \qquad F \sim \mathrm{DP}(MH),$$

where F is centered over a normal distribution, with mean μ_0 and variance $(1 - a)\sigma^2$, $0 < a < 1$, and $g(\mathbf{x}_i)$ is assumed not to include an intercept term. The distribution of $\epsilon_i|\mu_0, \sigma^2, a$ is $\mathrm{N}(\mu_0, \sigma^2)$ and so the model is naturally centered over a regression model with normal errors where the intercept is μ_0 and σ^2 is the regression error variance. The parameter a is interpreted as a measure of the distance between the distribution of ϵ_i and that normal distribution. If a is close to 1, these distributions are very similar but become increasingly dissimilar as a decreases to 0. The model specification is completed by choosing the improper prior $p(\mu_0, \sigma^2) \propto \sigma^{-2}$ and $a \sim \mathrm{U}(0, 1)$. At each iteration of the MCMC sampler, the samples are adjusted so that the expectation of ϵ has zero mean which makes the results comparable to those for the model with a normal error distribution, assumed in the analysis in Section 4.1.

Figure 4.10 shows results for the analysis. The posterior predictive distribution of ϵ is plotted in Figure 4.10 (a) (the posterior predictive distribution of ϵ from the model with normal errors is shown for comparison). The posterior predictive distribution for the

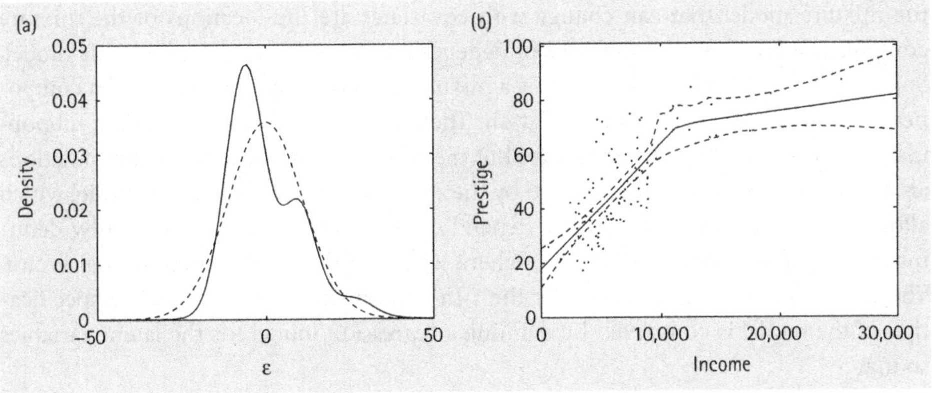

FIGURE 4.10 Prestige data using spline regression with nonparametric errors. (a) the posterior predictive distribution of the errors with the nonparametric model (4.44) (solid line) and the normal regression model (dashed line), (b) The data and the posterior median of $g(x)$ (solid line) with a 95% credibility interval (dashed lines)

nonparametric model is far from normal and shows both skewness and some evidence of bimodality. The estimates of the regression curve are shown in panel Figure 4.10 (b) and indicate a similar relationship to our previous analysis but with a tighter 95% credibility interval for incomes in the range 0 to 10,000 Canadian dollars. This illustrates that making fewer assumptions about the data does not necessarily lead to greater posterior uncertainty, but can in fact lead to greater certainty if the parametric model is violated, as in this case.

The model in (4.44) assumes that the distribution of the regression errors does not depend on the covariates. In other words, although the mean (and perhaps the variance) change with the covariate, all the other characteristics such as multimodality and skewness are unchanged by the covariates. This may be a reasonable assumption for many modeling purposes but, in reality, it usually won't be true and so models that allow distributions to change with the covariates become useful. In order to construct such a general modeling framework it is assumed that the unknown distribution is now indexed by the covariate values which will be written $F_{\mathbf{x}_i}$ and a prior is placed directly on $\{F_{\mathbf{x}}\}_{\mathbf{x}\in\mathcal{X}}$, where $\mathcal{X}$ is the space of the covariates. Several specifications have been developed in the literature. This section will concentrate on methods that extend either the finite mixture model or the semiparametric mixture models in Section 3.1.

In finite mixture modeling, Geweke and Keane (2007) suggested a smoothly mixing regression model which has the following form for y_i

$$p(y_i|s_i = j, \mathbf{x}_i, r_i) \sim \mathrm{N}(\mathbf{x}_i'\boldsymbol{\beta}_j, \sigma_j^2), \quad j = 1, \ldots, m.$$

Here, s_i indicates to which regression y_i is allocated and $\mathbf{x}_i$ is a vector of covariates (possibly basis expansions). If $P(s_i = j) = \pi_j$ then the model will reduce to a regression where the distribution of the residual is a finite mixture model. The only features of the mixture model that can change with covariates are the locations of the mixture components. However, some forms of dependence cannot be captured by this model. Suppose that the distribution $p(y|x)$ is a mixture of two components and each component represents a different subpopulation. The model allows the means of the subpopulations to change with the covariates but the relative sizes of the two subpopulations are fixed. This restriction is addressed by the smoothly mixing regression model which allows the probability that $s_i = j$ to depend on covariates. This is achieved by defining latent parameters $w_1, w_2, \ldots, w_n$ where w_i is a real-valued k-dimensional vector. The i-th observation is allocated to the j-th component if $w_{ij} \geq w_{ik}$. The specification of the model is completed by defining a regression model for the latent variables so that

$$w_i = \Gamma z_i + \zeta_i, \qquad \zeta_i \sim \mathrm{N}(0, I_K)$$

where Γ is a $K \times p$-dimensional matrix and z_i is a vector of covariates, which is not necessarily different from x_i. The regression modeling of the allocation s_i allows a further level of flexibility to the model.

Villani et al. (2009) suggest extending this model by allowing the variance of each normal component to depend on covariates

$$p(y_i|s_i = j, x_i, r_i) \sim \mathrm{N}\left(x_i'\beta_j, \sigma_j^2 \exp\{\delta_j' r_i\}\right),$$

where r_i is another vector of covariates. This allows the heteroskedastic spline regression model of Ruppert, Wand, and Carroll (2003) to be nested within this model (it arises if $m = 1$). They also suggest using an alternative method of allowing the allocations s_i to depend on covariates,

$$p(s_i = j|z_i) = \frac{\exp\{\varphi_j' z_i\}}{\sum_{k=1}^{m} \exp\{\varphi_k' z_i\}}, \qquad j = 1, 2, \ldots, m,$$

where φ_j is a vector of regression coefficients. In practice, it is not always necessary to use the full model in an application and some parameters can be set to zero a priori. Villani et al. (2009) illustrate this point in their examples. The model can be fitted by MCMC methods, but some care is need in the construction of the sampler to achieve an efficient method. Possible schemes are discussed by Geweke and Keane (2007) and Villani et al. (2009).

The structure of the model is determined by the number of components m and the choice of which parameters vary with the covariates or differ between the components. The usual approach to these problems in a Bayesian framework is model averaging, which needs the evaluation of the marginal likelihood. Unfortunately, this is difficult for these models and Villani et al. (2009) suggest using a B-fold cross-validation of the log-predictive density score to compare models. The data is divided into a test data set y_b and a training data set y_{-b} and the score is calculated by

$$B^{-1}\sum_{b=1}^{B}\log p(y_b|y_{-b},x).$$

In the recent literature, semiparametric mixture models such as the one given in (4.29) are often extended to the more general

$$y_i \mid \theta_i \sim p(y_i \mid \theta_i), \qquad \theta_i \mid F_x \sim F_x, \qquad F_x \sim \text{DRPM},$$

where DRPM denotes a Dependent Random Probability Measure, represented as

$$F_x = \sum_{i=1}^{\infty} w_i(x)\delta_{\phi_i(x)}, \tag{4.46}$$

with $\sum_{i=1}^{\infty} w_i(x) = 1$ for all x. The problem then reduces to constructing priors for $w_1(x), w_2(x), \ldots$ and $\phi_1(x), \phi_2(x), \ldots$. These models have typically appeared in the statistics literature rather than the econometrics literature. However, we assume that these methods will be much more widely used and studied by econometricians over the coming years. In a similar way to nonparametric priors for density estimation without covariates, the priors need: (1) to have a large support, (2) suitable methods for posterior inference, and (3) to lead to sensible statistical procedures. Furthermore, the dependence of the prior should be simple to specify. An approach with these properties was initially proposed by MacEachern (1999), who suggested the idea of dependent Dirichlet processes. A natural method to maintain good statistical properties is to specify a prior which induces F_x to have a standard nonparametric prior for each value of x. Many priors also assume that either $w_1(x), w_2(x), w_3(x), \ldots$ or $\phi_1(x), \phi_2(x), \phi_3(x), \ldots$ do not depend on x to make priors simpler to specify and posterior inference (usually with MCMC methods) simpler.

The simplest method is the so-called *single p* dependent Dirichlet process, which sets $w_j(x) = w_j$ for all x. The model is completed by specifying a stochastic process for $\phi_j(x)$ with $x \in \mathcal{X}$. Then the marginal prior of F_x is a mixture of the distribution of ϕ_j at x. For example, if ϕ_j is chosen to be a Gaussian process, then the marginal distribution of $\phi_j(x)$ is a normal distribution and the marginal prior of F_x is a mixture of normal distributions. The construction was suggested by MacEachern (1999) and applied to spatial statistics (Gelfand et al. 2005) and quantile regression (Kottas and Krnjajic 2009). The model was applied to ANOVA problems where the covariates only take a finite number of values by De Iorio et al. (2004).

These models can be fitted using a simple extension of computational methods for Dirichlet process mixture models. The model can be expressed using equation (4.46) with $w_i(x) = w_i$ for all x so that the weightings do not depend on the covariates x. The prior for $w_1, w_2, w_3, \ldots$ is chosen to follow the Dirichlet process with

$$w_j = V_j \prod_{k<j}(1 - V_k),$$

where $V_1, V_2, V_3, \ldots$ are an infinite sequence of independent Be(1, M) random variables and $\phi_1(x), \phi_2(x), \phi_3(x), \ldots$ are independent and identically distributed where $\phi_i(x)$ is a Gaussian process with a zero mean function and covariance function $\kappa(x_i, x_j)$. Indicator variables $s_1, s_2, \ldots, s_n$ showing the allocation of points to the clusters of the Dirichlet process are introduced and the model can be re-expressed as

$$y_i \mid s_i \sim \mathrm{N}(\phi_{s_i}, \sigma^2_{s_i}), \qquad p(s_i = j) = w_j,$$

$\sigma_1^2, \sigma_2^2, \sigma_3^2, \ldots$ are i.i.d. from a distribution with density $h(\sigma^2)$, and the covariance function for ϕ_j is $\sigma_j^2 \tilde{\kappa}(\cdot,\cdot)$. The model can be fitted using a simple extension of the Gibbs sampler for Dirichlet process mixture models. The conditional distribution of $s_i \mid s_{-i}$ can be sampled using the Pólya urn scheme representation of the Dirichlet process. At any point in the algorithm, the data is divided into K clusters which contain $n_1, n_2, \ldots, n_K$ data points. It is also useful to define K_{-i} and $n_1^{-i}, n_2^{-i}, \ldots, n_{K_{-i}}^{-i}$, which represent the same quantities excluding the i-th observation. The algorithm is

(a) For $i = 1, \ldots, n$, update s_i from the discrete distribution

$$p(s_i = j) \propto a_j, \qquad j = 1, \ldots, K_{-i} + 1.$$

The values $a_1, a_2, \ldots, a_{k_{-i}}$ are calculated using the formula

$$a_j = n_j^{-i}\mathrm{N}\left(y_i \,\middle|\, \mu_j^*, \sigma_j^{*2}\right),$$

where $\mathrm{N}(y_i|\mu, \sigma^2)$ represents the density value of y_i for a normal distribution with mean μ and variance σ^2

$$\mu_j^* = k_j'(I + \tilde{\Sigma}_{0,j})^{-1} y_{(j)}^{-i},$$

and

$$\sigma_j^{*2} = \sigma_j^2 \left(1 + \tilde{\kappa}(x_i, x_i) - k_j'(I + \tilde{\Sigma}_{0,j})^{-1} k_j\right).$$

The quantities are defined as follows. Let $S_j^{-i} = \{k | s_k = j, k \neq i\}$ be the indices of the observations allocated to cluster j (excluding the i-th observation), then k_j is an n_j^{-i}-dimensional vector with elements $\tilde{\kappa}(x_i, x_l)$ where $l \in S_j^{-i}$, $y_{(j)}^{-i}$ is an n_j^{-i}-dimensional vector with elements y_l where $l \in S_j^{-i}$, and $\tilde{\Sigma}_{0,j}$ is an $n_j^{-i} \times n_j^{-i}$-dimensional covariance matrix for the observations indexed by S_j^{-i}. The value $a_{K_{-i}+1}$ is given by

$$a_{K_{-i}+1} = \int \mathrm{N}(y_i | 0, \sigma^2(1 + \tilde{\kappa}(x_i, x_i))) h(\sigma^2)\, d\sigma^2.$$

If $K_{-i} + 1$ is selected, then a new cluster is formed and $\sigma^2_{K_{-i}+1}$ is drawn with a density proportional to

$$h(\sigma^2)\sigma^{-1}\exp\left\{-\frac{1}{2}\sigma^{-1}\left[y_i^2 - y_i^2(1+\tilde{\kappa}(x_i,x_i))^{-1}\right]\right\}.$$

(b) For $j = 1, 2, \ldots, K$, the full conditional distribution of σ_j^2 is proportional to

$$h(\sigma_j^2)\sigma_j^{-n}\exp\left\{-\frac{1}{2}\sigma_j^{-1}\left[y_{(j)}'y_{(j)} - y_{(j)}'(I+\tilde{\Sigma}_{0,j})^{-1}y_{(j)}\right]\right\}.$$

Here, let $S_j = \{k|s_k = j\}$ be the indices of the observations allocated to cluster j, then $y_{(j)}$ is an n_j-dimensional vector with elements y_l where $l \in S_j$ and $\tilde{\Sigma}_{0,j}$ is an $n_j \times n_j$-dimensional covariance matrix for the observations indexed by S_j.

A second simplification is setting $\phi_j(x_i) = \phi_j$ for all x_i which leads to so-called "single-θ" models. Many models have been proposed within this framework which often use the stick-breaking representation of the Dirichlet process or stick-breaking priors (described in Section 3.1) as a starting point. We will briefly review some of the most prominent examples. Griffin and Steel (2006) suggest writing

$$w_i(x) = \sum_{i=1}^{\infty} V_{\pi_i(x)} \prod_{j<i}\left(1 - V_{\pi_j(x)}\right),$$

where $\pi_1(x), \pi_2(x), \pi_3(x), \ldots$ is a permutation of $\{1, 2, 3, \ldots\}$ and $V_1, V_2, V_3, \ldots$ is an infinite sequence of independent Be$(1, M)$ random variables. The dependence between two random probability measures can be measured by the correlation between the mass that the measures $F_y(B)$ and $F_x(B)$ assign to a measurable set B. It is generally true that if $\phi_1, \phi_2, \phi_3, \ldots$ are independent of $w_1(x), w_2(x), w_3(x), \ldots$, then this correlation will not depend on the set B and represents a simple summary of the dependence between two distributions. Griffin and Steel (2006) showed that this correlation is simply related to the dependence between $\pi_1(x_1), \pi_2(x_1), \pi_3(x_1), \ldots$ and $\pi_1(x_2), \pi_2(x_2), \pi_3(x_2), \ldots$ where x_1 and x_2 are two possible values of x. Defining a stochastic process of infinite permutations is difficult, but a method is developed, based around point processes, which leads to a simple expression for the correlation. These methods have been applied to several problems in econometrics, for example Griffin and Steel (2006) describe fitting a nonparametric model to financial data. Alternatively, the value of V_i in the stick-breaking prior can be allowed to depend on the covariate x so that

$$w_i(x) = \sum_{i=1}^{\infty} V_i(x) \prod_{j<i}(1 - V_j(x)).$$

Several authors have suggested modeling $V_j(x) = V_j k(x, \tau_j)$, where $k(x, \tau_j)$ is a kernel function for which $k(\tau_j, \tau_j) = 1$ and $k(x, \tau_j)$ decreases as the distance between x and τ_j increases. Then $V_j(x)$ will be close to zero if x is far from τ_j and will have a small mixture weight. This allows components to have an effect only in a region around τ_j. Possible specifications are discussed by Dunson and Park (2008) and Reich and Fuentes (2007).

An interesting special case occurs when $k(x, \tau_j) = 1$ if $|x - \tau_j| < r_j$ for some distance r_j and distance measure $|\cdot|$ (Chung and Dunson 2007; Griffin and Steel 2010).

5.1 Applications

These methods have been applied to earnings distributions by Geweke and Keane (2007), to US inflation by Villani et al. (2009), stock returns (Geweke and Keane 2007; Villani et al. 2009), finance (Griffin and Steel 2006), and scale economies in electricity distribution (Griffin and Steel 2010).

6 Concluding Remarks

6.1 Summary

In this chapter we have discussed methods for avoiding the use of frequently made distributional assumptions, which are convenient, but may be at great odds with the data at hand. We have reviewed fully parametric solutions to this issue, which involve the use of more flexible distributions that often constitute a parametric extension of the usual classes of distribution. Allowing for non-Gaussian (fatter than Gaussian) tails and skewness is seen to be fairly simple to implement, and typically leads to very straightforward computational strategies using MCMC. Another popular approach is to use mixtures modeling, which can lead to very flexible structures indeed, at the cost of slightly more computational effort. Finally, flexible parametric models have been proposed for a multivariate context, but it is perhaps here that most additional research is still required. It is not trivial to find general classes of multivariate distributions that combine a sufficient amount of flexibility with ease of implementation and nice theoretical properties (such as leading to well-known and easily interpreted marginal distributions). Perhaps the use of copulas in econometrics can be an interesting approach to this modelling issue. Such methods allow for separate modeling of the marginal distributions and the dependence. They have been used extensively in finance and risk management (Cherubini et al. 2004; McNeil et al. 2005), but until now only rarely in other areas in econometrics: see Zimmer and Trivedi (2006) and Pitt et al. (2006).

A second strand of methods that we discuss deals with nonparametric approaches. Computationally, such models are a bit more demanding, but they do allow for a lot more flexibility than parametric models, as the classes of distributions they cover are very large indeed. There has been a lot of research regarding the specification and computational implementation of such models, and they are slowly starting to become part of the toolbox of the Bayesian econometrician. Often such nonparametric approaches are combined with parametric methods for other parts of the model, leading to semi-parametric models.

In the context of regression models, the use of basis expansions and Gaussian process priors allows us to specify flexible forms for the regression function. This flexible modeling of the mean function can be combined with nonparametric methods for the regression error term.

Even more general classes of models allow for both the regression function and the distribution of the error term to vary flexibly with covariates. Such models can be represented as generalized mixture models, where both the weights and the atoms (parameter values) can depend on covariates. Finite mixture models have recently been discussed by Geweke and Keane (2007) and Villani et al. (2009), and infinite dimensional mixture models have been proposed, using a variety of ideas (Dunson and Park 2008; Gelfand et al. 2005; Griffin and Steel 2006). The development of new modeling and computational methods and the incorporation of these methods into applied modeling is an area of active research, as there is an obvious interest in models where all aspects are potentially varying over covariates (and time could, of course, be one of these covariates), especially for applications as complex as the ones typically used in econometrics.

6.2 Some available software

One of the traditional issues preventing massive use of flexible methods of a semi- or non-parametric nature was the perceived difficulty in computational implementation of such methods. While this perception is perhaps somewhat exaggerated, it is also true that many researchers and some practitioners tended to write their own code for personal use. Fortunately, nowadays there are a few publicly available sources of code that are designed to implement some specific models. We next describe some of these alternatives.

bayesm: This package is described in the book by Rossi et al. (2005) and is extensively used in Chapter 8 of this volume by Rossi and Allenby on "Marketing". It is a contributed package to the R system and considers inference for many important models used in econometrics. Most of them are of a parametric nature, but the package includes density estimation and hierarchical multinomial logits based on the DP.

DPpackage: Written by Alejandro Jara and discussed in Jara (2007), this is also part of the contributed packages to the R system. It provides posterior simulation for a number of interesting models, including multivariate density estimation, mixed effects linear and generalized linear models, and models based on item-response, among others. The package includes models based not only on DPs but also on Pólya trees and Bernstein polynomials.

WinBUGS: This is a general purpose software for implementing Bayesian inference using Gibbs sampling, described in Lunn et al. (2000). Based on Congdon (2001), an implementation of a model involving a truncated version (i.e. $F(B) = \sum_{i=1}^{N} w_i \delta_{\theta_i}(B)$) of the stick-breaking representation (4.27) is provided at http://www.mrc-bsu.cam.ac.uk/bugs/winbugs/examples/eye-tracking.txt. The main advantage of this code is that it can be extended using the flexible facilities provided in WinBUGS. On the other hand, the code only considers a truncation, not the full infinite mixture, and increasing N may result in very slow performance.

References

Albert, J., and Chib, S. (1993). "Bayesian Analysis of Binary and Polychotomous Response Data", *Journal of the American Statistical Association*, 88: 669–79.

Amoroso, L. (1925). "Ricerche intorno alla curva dei redditi", *Annali de Mathematica*, 2: 132–59.

Arnold, B. C., and Beaver, R. J. (2002). "Skewed Multivariate Models Related to Hidden Truncation and/or Selective Reporting (with discussion)", *Test*, 11: 7–54.

—— and Groeneveld, R. A. (1995). "Measuring Skewness with Respect to the Mode", *The American Statistician*, 49: 34–8.

Arratia, R., Barbour, A. D., and Tavaré, S. (1992). "Poisson Process Approximations for the Ewens Sampling Formula", *The Annals of Applied Probability*, 2(3): 519–35.

Azzalini, A. (1985). "A Class of Distributions which Include the Normal Ones", *Scandinavian Journal of Statistics*, **12**: 171–8.

—— and Capitanio, A. (1999). "Statistical Applications of the Multivariate Skew Normal Distribution", *Journal of the Royal Statistical Society, B* 61: 579–602.

—— —— (2003). "Distributions Generated by Perturbations of Symmetry with Emphasis on a Multivariate Skew-*t* Distribution", *Journal of the Royal Statistical Society, B* 65: 367–89.

—— and Dalla Valle, A. (1996). "The Multivariate Skew-normal Distribution", *Biometrika*, 83: 715–26.

Barnett, W., Geweke, J., and Wolfe, M. (1991). "Seminonparametric Bayesian Estimation of the Asymptotically Ideal Production Model", *Journal of Econometrics*, 49: 5–50.

Basu, S., and Chib, S. (2003). "Marginal Likelihood and Bayes Factors for Dirichlet Process Mixture Models", *Journal of the American Statistical Association*, **98**: 224–35.

Bauwens, L., and Laurent, S. (2005). "A New Class of Multivariate Skew Densities, with Application to Generalized Autoregressive Conditional Heteroscedasticity Models", *Journal of Business and Economic Statistics*, 23: 346–54.

Beckett, L., and Diaconis, P. (1994). "Spectral Analysis for Discrete Longitudinal Data", *Advances in Mathematics*, 103(1): 107–28.

Bensmail, H., Celeux, G., Raftery, A. E., and Robert, C. P. (1997). "Inference in Model-Based Cluster Analysis", *Statistics and Computing*, 7: 1–10.

Berger, J. O., and Bernardo, J. M. (1992a). "On the Development of the Reference Prior Method (with Discussion)", in J. M. Bernardo, J. O. Berger, A. P. Dawid and A. F. M. Smith (eds.), *Bayesian Statistics 4*, Oxford: Oxford University Press, 35–60.

—— —— (1992b). "Ordered Group Reference Priors with Application to the Multinomial Problem", *Biometrika*, 79: 25–37.

Bernardo, J. M., and Smith, A. F. M. (1994). *Bayesian Theory*, Chichester: Wiley.

Blackwell, D., and MacQueen, J. B. (1973). "Ferguson Distributions via Pólya Urn Schemes", *The Annals of Statistics*, 1: 353–5.

Branco, M. D., and Dey, D. K. (2001). "A General Class of Multivariate Skew-Elliptical Distributions", *Journal of Multivariate Analysis*, 79: 99–113.

Brown, P. J., Vannucci, M., and Fearn, T. (1998). "Multivariate Bayesian Variable Selection and Prediction", *Journal of the Royal Statistical Society, B* 60: 627–42.

Brunner, L. J. (1995). "Bayesian Linear Regression with Error Terms that have Symmetric Unimodal Densities", *Journal of Nonparametric Statistics*, 4: 335–48.

____ and Lo, A. Y. (1989). "Bayes Methods for a Symmetric Unimodal Density and its Mode", *Annals of Statistics*, 17: 1550–66.

Bush, C. A., and MacEachern, S. N. (1996). "A Semiparametric Bayesian Model for Randomised Block Design", *Biometrika*, 83: 275–85.

Casella, G., Mengersen, K. L., Robert, C. P., and Titterington, D. M. (2002). "Perfect Samplers for Mixtures of Distributions", *Journal of the Royal Statistical Society, B* 64: 777–90.

____ Robert, C. P., and Wells, M. T. (2004). "Mixture Models, Latent Variables and Partitioned Important Sampling", *Statistical Methodology*, 1: 1–18.

Celeux, G., Hurn, M., and Robert, C. P. (2000). "Computational and Inferential Difficulties with mixture posterior distributions", *Journal of the American Statistical Association*, 95: 957–70.

Chen, M. H., Shao, Q. M., and Ibrahim, J. G. (2000). *Monte Carlo Methods in Bayesian Computation*, New York: Springer.

Cherubini, U., Vecchiato, W., and Luciano, E. (2004). *Copula Methods in Finance*, Chichester: Wiley.

Chib, S., and Greenberg, E. (2009). "Additive Cubic Spline Regression with Dirichlet Process Mixture Errors", *Technical report*, Olin Business School, Washington University in St Louis.

____ and Hamilton, B. H. (2002). "Semiparametric Bayes Analysis of Longitudinal Data Treatment Models", *Journal of Econometrics*, **110**(1): 67–89.

Chipman, H., George, E. I., and McCulloch, R. E. (2001). "The Practical Implementation of Bayesian Model Selection", *Model selection*, vol. 38 of *IMS Lecture Notes Monograph Series*, Institute of Mathematical Statistics, Beachwood, OH, 65–134.

Chung, Y., and Dunson, D. B. (2007). "The Local Dirichlet Process", *Technical Report 07-04*, ISDS, Duke University.

Cifarelli, D. M., and Melilli, E. (2000). "Some New Results for Dirichlet Priors", *The Annals of Statistics*, **28**(5): 1390–413.

Congdon, P. (2001). *Bayesian Statistical Modelling*, Chichester: Wiley.

De Iorio, M., Muller, P., Rosner, G. L., and MacEachern, S. N. (2004). "An ANOVA Model for Dependent Random Measures", *Journal of the American Statistical Association*, 99: 205–15.

Denison, D. G. T., Holmes, C. C., Mallick, B. K., and Smith, A. F. M. (2002). *Bayesian Methods for Nonlinear Classification and Regression*, Chichester: Wiley.

Diaconis, P., and Kemperman, J. (1996). "Some New Tools for Dirichlet Priors", in J. M. Bernardo, J. O. Berger, A. P. David, and A. F. M. Smith (eds.), *Bayesian statistics* 5, Oxford: Oxford University Press 97–106.

DiCiccio, J., Kass, R. E., Raftery, A. E., and Wasserman, L. (1997). "Computing Bayes Factors by Combining Simulations and Asymptotic Approximations", *Journal of the American Statistical Association*, 92: 903–15.

Diebolt, J., and Robert, C. P. (1994). "Estimation of Finite Mixture Distributions through Bayesian Sampling", *Journal of the Royal Statistical Society, B* 56: 363–75.

Doss, H. (1994). "Bayesian Nonparametric Estimation for Incomplete Data via Successive Substitution Sampling", *The Annals of Statistics*, 22(4): 1763–86.

Dunson, D. B., and Park, J. H. (2008). "Kernel Stick-Breaking Processes", *Biometrika*, 95: 307–23.

Elal-Olivero, D., Gómez, H., and Quintana, F. (2009). "Bayesian Modeling Using a Class of Bimodal Skew-Elliptical Distributions", *Journal of Statistical Planning and Inference*, 139: 1484–92.

Escobar, M. D. (1994). "Estimating Normal Means with a Dirichlet Process Prior", *Journal of American Statistics Associations*, 89(425): 268–77.

—— and West, M. (1995). "Bayesian Density Estimation and Inference Using Mixtures", *Journal of the American Statistical Association*, 90(430): 577–88.

Everitt, B. S., and Hand, D. J. (1981). *Finite Mixture Distributions*, London: Chapman and Hall.

Fang, K. T., Kotz, S., and Ng, K. W. (1990). *Symmetric Multivariate and Related Distributions*, London: Chapman and Hall.

Feller, W. (1971). *An Introduction to Probability Theory and its Applications*, vol. 2, New York: Wiley.

Ferguson, T. S. (1973). "A Bayesian Analysis of some Nonparametric Problems", *The Annals of Statistics*, 1: 209–30.

Fernández, C., and Steel, M. F. J. (1998). "On Bayesian Modeling of Fat Tails and Skewness", *Journal of the American Statistical Association*, 93: 359–71.

———— (1999). "Reference Priors for the General Location-Scale Model", *Statistics and Probability Letters*, 43: 377–84.

———— (2000). "Bayesian Regression Analysis with Scale Mixtures of Normals", *Econometric Theory*, 16: 80–101.

Ferreira, J. T. A. S., and Steel, M. F. J. (2004). "Bayesian Multivariate Skewed Regression Modelling with an Application to Firm Size", in M. G. Genton (ed.), *Skew-Elliptical Distributions and their Applications: A Journey beyond Normality*, Boca Raton, Fla.: CRC Chapman & Hall.

———— (2006). "A Constructive Representation of Univariate Skewed Distributions", *Journal of the American Statistical Association*, 101: 823–9.

———— (2007a). "Model Comparison of Coordinate-Free Multivariate Skewed Distributions with an Application to Stochastic Frontiers", *Journal of Econometrics*, 137: 641–73.

———— (2007b). "A New Class of Skewed Multivariate Distributions with Applications to Regression Analysis", *Statistica Sinica*, 17: 505–29.

Fonseca, T. C. O., Ferreira, M. A. R., and Migon, H. (2008). "Objective Bayesian Analysis for the Student-t Regression Model", *Biometrika*, 95: 325–33.

Fox, J. (1997). *Applied Regression Analysis, Linear Models, and Related Methods*, Thousand Oaks, Calif.: Sage.

Frühwirth-Schnatter, S. (2001). "Markov Chain Monte Carlo Estimation of Classical and Dynamic Switching and Mixture Models", *Journal of the American Statistical Association*, 96: 194–209.

—— (2006). *Finite Mixtures and Markov Switching Models*, New York: Springer.

—— and Kaufmann, S. (2008). "Model-Based Clustering of Multiple Time Series", *Journal of Business and Economic Statistics*, 26: 78–89.

Gelfand, A. E., Kottas, A., and MacEachern, S. N. (2005). "Bayesian Nonparametric Spatial Modeling with Dirichlet Process Mixing", *Journal of the American Statistical Association*, 100: 1021–35.

Genton, M. G., and Loperfido, N. (2005). "Generalized Skew-Elliptical Distributions and their Quadratic Forms", *Annals of the Institute of Statistical Mathematics*, 57: 389–401.
George, E. I., and McCulloch, R. E. (1993). "Variable Selection via Gibbs Sampling", *Journal of the American Statistical Association*, 88: 881–9.
Geweke, J. (1993). "Bayesian Treatment of the Independent Student-*t* Linear Model", *Journal of Applied Econometrics*, 8: S19–S40.
____(2007). "Interpretation and Inference in Mixture Models: Simple MCMC Works", *Computational Statistics & Data Analysis*, 51: 3529–50.
____and Keane, M. (2000). "An Empirical Analysis of Earnings Dynamics among Men in the PSID: 1968–1989", *Journal of Econometrics*, 96: 293–356.
____ ____(2007). "Smoothly Mixing Regressions", *Journal of Econometrics*, 138: 291–311.
Ghosal, S., Ghosh, J. K., and Ramamoorthi, R. V. (1999). "Posterior Consistency of Dirichlet Mixtures in Density Estimation", *The Annals of Statistics*, 27(1): 143–58.
____and van der Vaart, A. (2007). "Posterior Convergence Rates of Dirichlet Mixtures at Smooth Densities", *The Annals of Statistics*, 35(2): 697–723.
Green, P. J. (1995). "Reversible Jump Markov Chain Monte Carlo Computation and Bayesian Model Determination", *Biometrika*, 82: 7H–32.
Griffin, J. E. (2010). "Default Priors for Density Estimation with Mixture Models", *Bayesian Analysis*, 5: 847–66.
____and Steel, M. F. J. (2004). "Semiparametric Bayesian Inference for Stochastic Frontier Models", *Journal of Econometrics*, 123(1): 121–52.
____ ____(2006). "Order-Based Dependent Dirichlet Processes", *Journal of the American Statistical Association*, 101: 179–94.
____ ____(2008). "Flexible Mixture Modelling of Stochastic Frontiers", *Journal of Productivity Analysis*, 29: 33–50.
____ ____(2010). "Bayesian Nonparametric Modelling with the Dirichlet Process Regression Smoother", *Statistica Sinica*, 20: 1507–27.
Hirano, K. (2002). "Semiparametric Bayesian Inference in Autoregressive Panel Data Models", *Econometrica*, 70(2): 781–99.
Holmes, C. C., and Mallick, B. K. (1998). "Radial Basis Functions of Variable Dimension", *Neural Computation*, 10: 1217–33.
Ishwaran, H., and James, L. F. (2001). "Gibbs Sampling Methods for Stick-Breaking Priors", *Journal of the American Statistical Association*, 96: 161–73.
Jara, A. (2007). "Applied Bayesian Non- and Semi-parametric Inference using DPpackage", *Rnews*, 7(3): 17–26.
____García-Zattera, M. J., and Lesaffre, E. (2007). "A Dirichlet Process Mixture Model for the Analysis of Correlated Binary Responses", *Computational Statistics & Data Analysis*, 51(11): 5402–15.
Jasra, A., Holmes, C. C., and Stephens, D. A. (2005). "Markov Chain Monte Carlo Methods and the Label Switching Problem in Bayesian Mixture Modelling", *Statistical Science*, 20: 50–67.
Jeffreys, H. (1961). *Theory of Probability*, 3rd edn., Oxford: Oxford University Press.
Jones, M. C. (2002). "Marginal Replacement in Multivariate Densities, with Application to Skewing Spherically Symmetric Distributions", *Journal of Multivariate Analysis*, 81: 85–99.
____(2004). "Families of Distributions Arising from Distributions of Order Statistics (with Discussion)", *Test*, 13: 1–43.
Juárez, M., and Steel, M. F. J. (2010). "Model-Based Clustering of Non-Gaussian Panel Data Based on Skew-*t* Distributions", *Journal of Business and Economic Statistics*, 28: 52–66.

Kelker, D. (1970). "Distribution Theory of Spherical Distributions and a Location-Scale Parameter Generalization", *Sankhya*, 32: 419–30.
Kohn, R., Smith, M., and Chan, D. (2001). "Nonparametric Regression using Linear Combinations of Basis Functions", *Statistics and Computing*, 11: 313–22.
—— Wood, S. and Yau, P. (2003). "Bayesian Variable Selection and Model Averaging in High Dimensional Multinomial Nonparametric Regression", *Journal of Computational and Graphical Statistics*, 12: 23–54.
Koop, G. (2004). *Bayesian Econometrics*, Chichester: Wiley.
—— (2008). "Parametric and Nonparametric Inference in Equilibrium Job Search Models", in T. B. Fomby and R. C. Hill (eds.), *Advances in Econometrics*, vol. 23, Binglers, UK: Emerald.
—— and Poirier, D. J. (2004). "Bayesian Variants of some Classical Semiparametric Regression Techniques", *Journal of Econometrics*, 123: 259–82.
—— —— and Tobias, J. (2005). "Semiparametric Bayesian Inference in Multiple Equation Models", *Journal of Applied Econometrics*, 20: 723–47.
—— and Tobias, J. L. (2006). "Semiparametric Bayesian Inference in Smooth Coefficient Models", *Journal of Econometrics*, 134: 283–315.
Kottas, A., and Gelfand, A. E. (2001). "Bayesian Semiparametric Median Regression Modeling", *Journal of the American Statistical Association*, 96: 1458–68.
—— and Krnjajic, M. (2009). "Bayesian Semiparametric Modelling in Quantile Regression", *Scandinavian Journal of Statistics*, 36: 297–319.
—— Müller, P., and Quintana, F. (2005). "Nonparametric Bayesian Modeling for Multivariate Ordinal Data", *Journal of Computational and Graphical Statistics*, 14(3): 610–25.
Lange, K. L., Little, R. J. A., and Taylor, J. M. G. (1989). "Robust Statistical Modeling Using the *T*-Distribution", *Journal of the American Statistical Association*, 84: 881–96.
Leslie, D. S., Kohn, R., and Nott, D. J. (2007). "A General Approach to Heteroscedastic Linear Regression", *Statistics and Computing*, 17: 131–6.
Lijoi, A., Prünster, I., and Walker, S. G. (2005). "On Consistency of Nonparametric Normal Mixtures for Bayesian Density Estimation", *Journal of the American Statistical Association*, 100(472): 1292–6.
Liseo, B. (2004). "Skew-Elliptical Distributions in Bayesian Inference", in M. G. Genton (ed.), *Skew-Elliptical Distributions and their Applications: A Journey beyond Normality*, Boca Raton, Fla.: Chapman & Hall, 153–71.
Liu, J. S. (1996). "Nonparametric Hierarchical Bayes via Sequential Imputations", *The Annals of Statistics*, 24(3): 911–30.
Liu, M. C., and Tiao, G. C. (1980). "Random Coefficient First-Order Autoregressive Models", *Journal of Econometrics*, 13: 305–25.
Lunn, D. J., Thomas, A., Best, N., and Spiegelhalter, D. (2000). "WinBUGS—A Bayesian Modelling Framework: Concepts, Structure, and Extensibility", *Statistics and Computing*, 10: 325–37.
MacEachern, S. N. (1999). "Dependent Nonparametric Processes", *Proceedings of the Section on Bayesian Statistical Science*, American Statistical Association, 50–5.
Maronna, R. (1976). "Robust M-estimators of Multivariate Location and Scatter", *Annals of Statistics*, 4: 51–67.
McNeil, A., Frey, R., and Embrechts, P. (2005). *Quantitative Risk Management: Concepts, Techniques and Tools*, Princeton: Princeton University Press.
Meng, X. L., and Wong, W. H. (1996). "Simulating Ratios of Normalizing Constants via a Simple Identity: A Theoretical Exploration", *Statistica Sinica*, 6: 831–60.

Mitchell, T. J., and Beauchamp, J. J. (1988). "Bayesian Variable Selection in Regression", *Journal of the American Statistical Association*, 83: 1023–36.

Mouchart, M. (1976). "A Note on Bayes Theorem", *Statistica*, 36: 349–57.

Müller, P., and Quintana, F. A. (2004). "Nonparametric Bayesian Data Analysis", *Statistical Science. A Review Journal of the Institute of Mathematical Statistics*, 19(1): 95–110.

Nandram, B., and Petruccelli, J. D. (1997). "A Bayesian Analysis of Autoregressive Time Series Panel Data", *Journal of Business and Economic Statistics*, 15: 328–34.

O'Hagan, A., and Leonard, T. (1976). "Bayes Estimation Subject to Uncertainity about Parameter Constraints", *Biometrika*, 63: 201–3.

Papaspiliopoulos, O., and Roberts, G. O. (2008). "Retrospective Markov Chain Monte Carlo Methods for Dirichlet Process Hierarchical Models", *Biometrika*, 95(1): 169–86.

Pewsey, A. (2000). "Problems of Inference for Azzalini's Skew-Normal Distribution", *Journal of Applied Statistics*, 27: 859–70.

Phillips, D. B., and Smith, A. F. M. (1996). "Bayesian Model Comparison via Jump Diffusions", in W. R. Gilks, S. Richardson, and D. J. Spiegelhalter (eds.), *Markov Chain Monte Carlo in Practice*, Boca Raton, Fla.: Chapman & Hall, 215–40.

Pitman, J., and Yor, M. (1997). "The Two-Parameter Poisson-Dirichlet Distribution Derived from a Stable Subordinator", *The Annals of Probability*, 25(2): 855–900.

Pitt, M., Chan, D., and Kohn, R. (2006). "Efficient Bayesian Inference for Gaussian Copula Regression Models", *Biometrika*, 93: 537–54.

Quintana, F., Steel, M. F. J., and Ferreira, J. T. A. S. (2009). "Flexible Univariate Continuous Distributions", *Bayesian Analysis*, 4: 497–522.

Raftery, A. E. (1996). "Hypothesis Testing and Model Selection", in W. R. Gilks, S. Richardson, and D. J. Spiegelhalter (eds.), *Markov Chain Monte Carlo in Practice*, Boca Raton, Fla.: Chapman & Hall, 163–88.

____ Madigan, D., and Hoeting, J. A. (1997). "Bayesian Model Averaging for Linear Regression Models", *Journal of the American statistical Association*, 92: 179–91.

Rasmussen, C. E., and Williams, C. K. I. (2006). *Gaussian Processes for Machine Learning*, Cambridge, Mass.: MIT Press.

Reich, B. J., and Fuentes, M. (2007). "A Multivariate Nonparametric Bayesian Spatial Framework for Hurricane Surface Wind Fields", *The Annals of Applied Statistics*, 1: 249–64.

Richardson, S., and Green, P. J. (1997). "On Bayesian Analysis of Mixtures with an Unknown Number of Components (with Discussion)", *Journal of the Royal Statistical Society, B* 59: 731–92.

Rossi, P. E., Allenby, G. M., and McCulloch, R. (2005). *Bayesian statistics and marketing*, Wiley Series in Probability and Statistics, Chichester: Wiley.

Ruppert, D., Wand, M. P., and Carroll, R. J. (2003). *Semiparametric Regression*, Cambridge: Cambridge University Press.

Sahu, S., Dey, D. K., and Branco, D. (2003). "A New Class of Multivariate Skew Distributions with Applications to Bayesian Regression Models", *Canadian Journal of Statistics*, 31: 129–50.

Sethuraman, J. (1994). "A Constructive Definition of Dirichlet Priors", *Statistica Sinica*, 4(2): 639–50.

Shiller, R. J. (1984). "Smoothness Priors and Nonlinear Regression", *Journal of the American Statistical Association*, 79: 609–15.

Shively, T., Kohn, R., and Wood, S. (1999). "Model Selection for Additive Nonparametric Regression with Data-Based Priors (with Discussion)", *Journal of the American Statistical Association*, 94: 777–805.

Smith, M., and Kohn, R. (1996). "Nonparametric Regression via Bayesian Variable Selection", *Journal of Econometrics*, 75: 317–44.

——— (1997). "A Bayesian Approach to Nonparametric Bivariate Regression", *Journal of the American Statistical Association*, 92: 1522–35.

Stephens, M. (2000a). "Bayesian Analysis of Mixture Models with an Unknown Number of Components—An Alternative to Reversible Jump Methods", *The Annals of Statistics*, 28: 40–74.

—— (2000b). "Dealing with Label Switching in Mixture Models", *Journal of the Royal Statistical Society, B* 62: 795–809.

Titterington, D. M., Smith, A. F. M., and Makov, U. E. (1985). *Statistical Analysis of Finite Mixture Distributions*, New York: Wiley.

Verdinelli, I., and Wasserman, L. (1995). "Computing Bayes Factors Using a Generalization of the Savage-Dickey Density Ratio", *Journal of the American Statistical Association*, 90: 614–18.

Villani, M., Kohn, R., and Giordani, P. (2009). "Regression Density Estimation Using Smooth Adaptive Gaussian Mixtures", *Journal of Econometrics*, 153: 155–73.

Walker, S. G., Damien, P., Laud, P. W., and Smith, A. F. M. (1999). "Bayesian Nonparametric Inference for Random Distributions and Related Functions (with Discussion)", *Journal of the Royal Statistical Society, B* 61: 485–527.

West, M. (1984). "Outlier Models and Prior Distributions in Bayesian Linear Regression", *Journal of the Royal Statistical Society, B* 46: 431–9.

Wood, S., and Kohn, R. (1998). "A Bayesian Approach to Robust Nonparametric Binary Regression", *Journal of the American Statistical Association*, 93: 203–13.

——— Shively, T., and Jiang, W. (2002). "Model Selection in Spline Nonparametric Regression", *Journal of the Royal Statistical Society, B* 64: 119–39.

Yatchew, A. (2003). *Semiparametric Regression for the Applied Econometrician*, Cambridge: Cambridge University Press.

Yau, P., and Kohn, R. (2003). "Estimation and Variable Selection in Nonparametric Heteroscedastic Regression", *Statistics and Computing*, 13: 191–208.

Zimmer, D. M., and Trivedi, P. K. (2006). "Using Trivariate Copulas to Model Sample Selection and Treatment Effects: Application to Family Health Care Demand", *Journal of Business and Economic Statistics*, 24: 63–76.

CHAPTER 5

INTRODUCTION TO SIMULATION AND MCMC METHODS

SIDDHARTHA CHIB

1 Introduction

The purpose of this chapter is to provide an overview of a class of Monte Carlo methods of generating variates from a target probability distribution which are based on Markov chains whose stationary distribution is the probability distribution of interest. These methods, popularly called Markov chain Monte Carlo (MCMC) methods, are widely used to summarize complicated posterior distributions in Bayesian statistics and econometrics.

Let $p(\mathrm{y}|\boldsymbol{\theta})$ denote the sampling density and $\pi(\boldsymbol{\theta})$ the prior density, where y is a vector of observations and $\boldsymbol{\theta} = (\theta_1, \ldots, \theta_d) \in \Theta \subseteq \Re^d$ is an unknown parameter. Then, the posterior density is given by

$$\pi(\boldsymbol{\theta}|\mathrm{y}) = \frac{p(\mathrm{y}|\boldsymbol{\theta})\pi(\boldsymbol{\theta})}{\int_\Theta p(\mathrm{y}|\boldsymbol{\theta})\pi(\boldsymbol{\theta})\, d\boldsymbol{\theta}} \propto p(\mathrm{y}|\boldsymbol{\theta})\pi(\boldsymbol{\theta})$$

which in most practical problems is a complex distribution of unrecognizable form. The norming constant, or the marginal likelihood,

$$m(\mathrm{y}) = \int_\Theta p(\mathrm{y}|\boldsymbol{\theta})\pi(\boldsymbol{\theta})\, d\boldsymbol{\theta}$$

is also difficult to evaluate. As a result, analysis of the posterior distribution by direct analytical methods, or by numerical quadrature or even classical Monte Carlo methods, is generally not possible. These difficulties, however, can in principle be resolved by MCMC methods. These methods involve the simulation of a Markov sequence

$$\{\boldsymbol{\theta}^{(0)}, \boldsymbol{\theta}^{(1)}, \ldots, \boldsymbol{\theta}^{(g)}, \ldots\}$$

on the state space Θ such that the stationary distribution of the Markov chain is the target distribution of interest. A general method of constructing such chains is by the Metropolis-Hastings method that is due to Metropolis, et al. (1953) and Hastings (1970). The M-H method, as it is called, is quite general and flexible and forms the basis for almost all MCMC methods, including the Gibbs sampling method of Geman and Geman (1984), Tanner and Wong (1987), and Gelfand and Smith (1990). It has been extensively studied and discussed, starting with Tierney (1994) and Chib and Greenberg (1995). Liu (2001), Chib (2001), Roberts and Rosenthal (2004), and Robert and Casella (2004) summarize the theory and provide extensions.

The defining feature of Markov chains is the fact that the future evolution of the chain, depends only on the current value of the chain. Thus, the distribution of $\boldsymbol{\theta}^{(g+1)}$, the $(g+1)$st element of the sequence, given the current and past values of the chain, depends only on $\boldsymbol{\theta}^{(g)}$, and is represented by the one-step transition kernel

$$K(\boldsymbol{\theta}^{(g)}, A|\mathbf{y}) = \Pr\left(\boldsymbol{\theta}^{(g+1)} \in A|\mathbf{y}, \boldsymbol{\theta}^{(g)}\right)$$

where A is any measurable set under $\pi(\boldsymbol{\theta}|\mathbf{y})$. The idea behind MCMC methods is to construct $K(\boldsymbol{\theta}, A|\mathbf{y})$ such that for any starting point $\boldsymbol{\theta}^{(0)}$, the probability that the chain will be in the set A after g steps, given by the g-step transition kernel $K^{(g)}(\boldsymbol{\theta}^{(0)}, A|\mathbf{y})$ and defined as

$$K^{(g)}(\boldsymbol{\theta}^{(0)}, A|\mathbf{y}) = \Pr(\boldsymbol{\theta}^{(g)} \in A|\mathbf{y}, \boldsymbol{\theta}^{(0)})$$

converges to the probability of A under the target, as g becomes large. Once such a $K(\boldsymbol{\theta}, A|\mathbf{y})$ has been constructed, a sequence of variates can be obtained by recursively sampling the transition density in the following way:

$$\begin{aligned}
\boldsymbol{\theta}^{(1)} &\sim K(\boldsymbol{\theta}^{(0)}, \cdot|\mathbf{y}) \\
\boldsymbol{\theta}^{(2)} &\sim K(\boldsymbol{\theta}^{(1)}, \cdot|\mathbf{y}) \\
&\vdots \\
\boldsymbol{\theta}^{(g+1)} &\sim K(\boldsymbol{\theta}^{(g)}, \cdot|\mathbf{y}) \\
&\vdots
\end{aligned}$$

Because the chain was constructed to converge to the posterior density, the G values beyond the first n_0 iterations

$$\{\boldsymbol{\theta}^{(n_0+1)}, \boldsymbol{\theta}^{(n_0+2)}, \ldots, \boldsymbol{\theta}^{(n_0+G)}\}$$

(for suitably large n_0) can be taken as draws from $\pi(\boldsymbol{\theta}|\mathbf{y})$. The initial draws up to n_0, constituting the "burn-in" period, are discarded to allow the effect of the starting value to wear off.

Provided G is large, the sample $\{\boldsymbol{\theta}^{(n_0+1)}, \boldsymbol{\theta}^{(n_0+2)}, \ldots, \boldsymbol{\theta}^{(n_0+G)}\}$ can be used as a surrogate for the posterior density. One can summarize the target with the help of this sample. For instance, one can estimate the expectation of a real-valued function $h(\boldsymbol{\theta})$ that is integrable under $\pi(\boldsymbol{\theta}|\mathrm{y})$ from the sample average

$$\hat{h}_G = G^{-1} \sum_{g=1}^{G} h(\boldsymbol{\theta}^{(g)}), \tag{5.1}$$

as in the case of random samples (here and later the iterates used in the calculations are those beyond the burn-in period). By suitable laws of large numbers for Markov chains, one can show that

$$\hat{h}_G \rightarrow \int_{\Theta} h(\boldsymbol{\theta}) \pi(\boldsymbol{\theta}|\mathrm{y}) d\boldsymbol{\theta},$$

almost surely as the simulation sample size G becomes large. Of course, the sample can be used to construct many other summaries of the target distribution. For example, the sample of draws

$$\theta_l^{(n_0+1)}, \ldots, \theta_l^{(n_0+G)}$$

on the lth component of $\boldsymbol{\theta}$ can be used to summarize the marginal distribution of θ_l

$$\pi(\theta_l|\mathrm{y}) = \int \pi(\boldsymbol{\theta}|\mathrm{y}) d\boldsymbol{\theta}_{-l}$$

where

$$\boldsymbol{\theta}_{-l} = (\theta_1, \ldots, \theta_{l-1}, \theta_{l+1}, \ldots, \theta_d)$$

denotes the components of $\boldsymbol{\theta}$ excluding θ_l. This is because of the result that if a collection of variates is from a joint distribution, then the components of that sample are from the marginal distributions.

Despite the enormous power of the MCMC approach, the actual application of these methods requires considerable care and expertise. In practice, it is possible to construct several different transition densities $K(\boldsymbol{\theta}, \cdot|\mathrm{y})$ for the same target distribution. Some, or all, of these transition densities can produce draws that are heavily correlated, thus providing a poor exploration of the target even with large samples. These problems are particularly acute in high-dimensional problems with parameter constraints, ridges, flat areas, and other complications. Such complications are the norm in the dynamic stochastic general equilibrium (DSGE) models that are discussed in Marco and Schorfeide (Chapter 7, this volume). MCMC procedures have to be carefully designed in state space models (Giordani et al., Chapter 3 this volume), in financial time series models (Jacquier and Polson, Chapter 9, this volume), in hierarchical models (Rossi and Allenby, Chapter 8, this volume), nonparametric problems (Griffin et al., Chapter 4, this volume), in categorical response models (Li and Tobias, Chapter 6, this volume), and essentially in almost any problem where the model is relatively complex in relation to the available data.

1.1 Organization

The rest of the chapter is organized as follows. In Section 2 we summarize two classical Monte Carlo sampling methods, the accept-reject and importance sampling methods, that provide background for the newer MCMC methods. In Section 3 we discuss the M-H method and include the relevant Markov chain theory that justifies simulation by the M-H method. Section 4 deals with some special topics and Section 5 with the calculation of the marginal likelihood. Section 6 has several examples to illustrate the techniques. The last section has some summary comments.

2 Two classical sampling methods

We begin by briefly presenting two classical Monte Carlo methods. These methods share with MCMC methods the concept of a source or proposal density which is used to supply candidate draws and a randomization step or an acceptance condition to determine if the candidate draw should be accepted. As in the case of MCMC methods, as we will see later, the reliability or efficiency of the methods depends vitally on the match between the proposal and the target. Unlike MCMC methods, however, the two methods we present next produce independent samples from the target density (unless correlation is deliberately introduced as a variance reduction device).

2.1 Accept-reject method

The accept-reject method is the basis for many of the well-known univariate random number generators that are provided in software programs. This method is characterized by a source density $q(\boldsymbol{\theta}|\mathrm{y})$ which is used to supply candidate values and a constant c such that for all $\boldsymbol{\theta} \in \Theta$

$$\pi(\boldsymbol{\theta}|\mathrm{y}) \leq cq(\boldsymbol{\theta}|\mathrm{y}).$$

Thus, $c = \sup_{\theta\in\Theta} \{\pi(\boldsymbol{\theta}|\mathrm{y})/q(\boldsymbol{\theta}|\mathrm{y})\}$. Note that the accept-reject method does not require knowledge of the normalizing constant of π because that constant can be absorbed in c. Then, in the accept-reject method, one draws a variate from q, accepting it with probability $\pi(\boldsymbol{\theta}|\mathrm{y})/\{cq(\boldsymbol{\theta}|\mathrm{y})\}$. If the particular proposal is rejected, a new one is drawn and the process continued until one is accepted. The accepted draws constitute an i.i.d (independent and identically distributed) sample from π. The efficiency of this method depends on c which essentially is equal to the expected number of draws from q before one is accepted.

Algorithm: Accept-reject

Step 1: In each iteration g, $g = 1, \ldots, G$,

- **Propose**

$$\boldsymbol{\theta}^\dagger \sim h(\boldsymbol{\theta}^\dagger)\,;\ \text{and independently}\ U \sim \text{Unif}(0,1)$$

- **Accept-reject** Let $\boldsymbol{\theta}^{(g)} = \boldsymbol{\theta}^\dagger$ if

$$U \leq \frac{\pi(\boldsymbol{\theta}^\dagger|\mathrm{y})}{cq(\boldsymbol{\theta}^\dagger|\mathrm{y})}$$

  otherwise go to Propose

Step 2: Return the values $\{\boldsymbol{\theta}^{(g)}\}$.

The idea behind this algorithm may be explained quite simply using Figure 5.1. Imagine drawing random bivariate points in the region bounded above by the function $cq(\boldsymbol{\theta}|\mathrm{y})$ and below by the x-axis. A point in this region may be drawn by first drawing $\boldsymbol{\theta}^\dagger$ from $q(\boldsymbol{\theta}|\mathrm{y})$, which fixes the x-coordinate of the point, and then drawing the y-coordinate of the point as $Ucq(\boldsymbol{\theta}^\dagger)$. Now, if $Ucq(\boldsymbol{\theta}^\dagger|\mathrm{y}) \leq \pi(\boldsymbol{\theta}^\dagger|\mathrm{y})$, the point lies below π and is accepted; but the latter is simply the acceptance condition of the AR method, which completes the justification.

Example: The accept-reject method is sometimes applied to sampling a target density that is truncated to a non-standard region. In that case, one draws from the untruncated distribution. If the draw lies in the truncated region it is accepted; otherwise the process is repeated until a value that satisfies the truncation is found. As a simple example

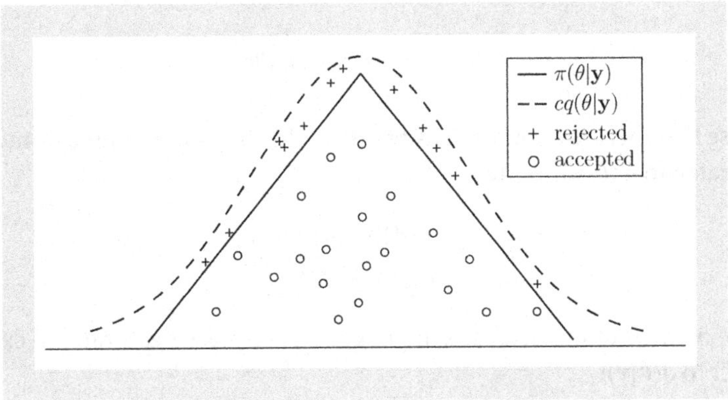

FIGURE 5.1 Accept-reject method

Notes: The x-coordinate of the points below the target density are accepted.

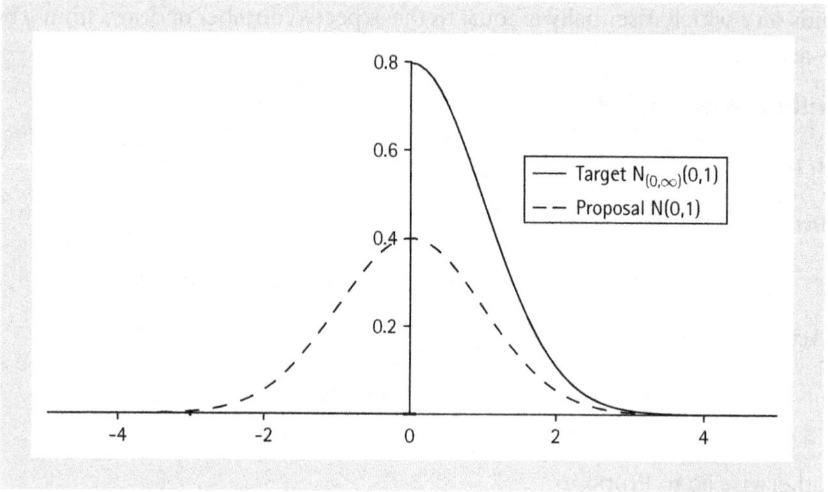

FIGURE 5.2 Half-normal target and the source density for the accept-reject method

of this approach, consider sampling a standard normal distribution that is truncated to $(0, \infty)$. This is the half-normal distribution. If the proposal distribution is taken to be untruncated distribution, as in Figure 5.2, it is clear that the value $c = 2$ times the proposal bounds the target. The problem, however, is that although $2\mathcal{N}(\boldsymbol{\theta}|0, 1)$ perfectly bounds the target on $(0, \infty)$, it is quite badly matched to the target on the interval $(-\infty, 0)$. This is the generic problem with this approach to sampling a truncated distribution.

2.2 Importance sampling

Suppose that one is interested in calculating the value of the integral

$$I = \int_{\Theta} h(\boldsymbol{\theta})\pi(\boldsymbol{\theta}|\mathrm{y})d\boldsymbol{\theta}$$

and suppose that there is a source density $q(\boldsymbol{\theta}|\mathrm{y})$ that is easy to sample from and which is a close match to $\pi(\boldsymbol{\theta}|\mathrm{y})$. Write

$$I = \frac{\int_{\Theta} h(\boldsymbol{\theta})p(\mathrm{y}|\boldsymbol{\theta})\pi(\boldsymbol{\theta})d\boldsymbol{\theta}}{\int_{\Theta} p(\mathrm{y}|\boldsymbol{\theta})\pi(\boldsymbol{\theta})d\boldsymbol{\theta}}.$$

Then in the method of importance sampling, we re-express I as a ratio of expectations with respect to $q(\boldsymbol{\theta}|\mathrm{y})$:

$$I = \frac{\mathbb{E}_q[h(\boldsymbol{\theta})p(\mathrm{y}|\boldsymbol{\theta})\pi(\boldsymbol{\theta})/q(\boldsymbol{\theta}|\mathrm{y})]}{\mathbb{E}_q[p(\mathrm{y}|\boldsymbol{\theta})\pi(\boldsymbol{\theta})/q(\boldsymbol{\theta}|\mathrm{y})]},$$

then take a large number of draws $\{\boldsymbol{\theta}^{(1)}, \ldots, \boldsymbol{\theta}^{(G)}\}$ from $q(\boldsymbol{\theta}|\mathrm{y})$ and estimate I as

$$\hat{I} = G^{-1} \sum_{g=1}^{G} h(\boldsymbol{\theta}^{(g)}) w(\boldsymbol{\theta}^{(g)}, \mathrm{y})$$

where

$$w(\boldsymbol{\theta}^{(g)}, \mathrm{y}) = \frac{p(\mathrm{y}|\boldsymbol{\theta}^{(g)})\pi(\boldsymbol{\theta}^{(g)})/q(\boldsymbol{\theta}^{(g)}|\mathrm{y})}{G^{-1}\sum_{l=1}^{G} p(\mathrm{y}|\boldsymbol{\theta}^{(l)})\pi(\boldsymbol{\theta}^{(l)})/q(\boldsymbol{\theta}^{(l)}|\mathrm{y})}, \quad g = 1, 2, \ldots, G$$

are the so-called *importance weights*. For this method to work (in particular for $\hat{I}$ to have finite Monte Carlo variance) these importance weights must be bounded as a function of $\boldsymbol{\theta}$. Importance sampling was first discussed in an econometric setting by Kloek and Van Dijk (1978). Further details about the importance sampling approach for evaluating integrals and assessing the approximation error are given in Geweke (1989 and 2005).

Sampling importance re-sampling Over the last decade or so, the scope of importance sampling methods has broadened to include the sampling of the target density itself. Now since

$$\pi(\boldsymbol{\theta}|\mathrm{y}) = \frac{\pi(\boldsymbol{\theta}|\mathrm{y})}{q(\boldsymbol{\theta}|\mathrm{y})} q(\boldsymbol{\theta}|\mathrm{y})$$

it follows that if $\{\boldsymbol{\theta}^{(1)}, \ldots, \boldsymbol{\theta}^{(G)}\}$ are draws from $q(\boldsymbol{\theta}|\mathrm{y})$, then the target can be expressed as the discrete distribution

$$\hat{\pi}(\boldsymbol{\theta}|\mathrm{y}) = w(\boldsymbol{\theta}^{(g)}, \mathrm{y})\delta_{\boldsymbol{\theta}^{(g)}}(\boldsymbol{\theta}),$$

where $w(\boldsymbol{\theta}^{(g)}, \mathrm{y})$, which is defined above, is the probability mass attached to the point $\boldsymbol{\theta}^{(g)}$ and $\delta_{\boldsymbol{\theta}^{(g)}}(\boldsymbol{\theta})$ is the indicator function which takes the value 1 if $\boldsymbol{\theta} = \boldsymbol{\theta}^{(g)}$ and the value zero otherwise. The variates $\boldsymbol{\theta}^{(g)}$ are called *particles*.

Given this representation, it follows that to get the particles $\{\boldsymbol{\theta}^{*(1)}, \ldots, \boldsymbol{\theta}^{*(L)}\}$ from $\pi(\boldsymbol{\theta}|\mathrm{y})$ (where L is likely much smaller than G), we sample $\hat{\pi}(\boldsymbol{\theta}|\mathrm{y})$. This amounts to re-sampling $\{\boldsymbol{\theta}^{(1)}, \ldots, \boldsymbol{\theta}^{(G)}\}$ with replacement with probabilities $\{w(\boldsymbol{\theta}^{(g)}, \mathrm{y})\}$.

That this method works is easily checked. Under $\hat{\pi}(\boldsymbol{\theta}|\mathrm{y})$, and for any measurable set A,

$$\begin{aligned}
\Pr(\boldsymbol{\theta} \in A|\mathrm{y}) &= \sum_{g=1}^{G} w(\boldsymbol{\theta}^{(g)}, \mathrm{y}) I[\boldsymbol{\theta}^{(g)} \in A] \\
&\to \frac{\int_{\Theta} p(\mathrm{y}|\boldsymbol{\theta})\pi(\boldsymbol{\theta})/q(\boldsymbol{\theta}|\mathrm{y}) I[\boldsymbol{\theta} \in A] q(\boldsymbol{\theta}|\mathrm{y}) d\boldsymbol{\theta}}{\int_{\Theta} p(\mathrm{y}|\boldsymbol{\theta})\pi(\boldsymbol{\theta})/q(\boldsymbol{\theta}|\mathrm{y}) q(\boldsymbol{\theta}|\mathrm{y}) d\boldsymbol{\theta}} \\
&= \frac{\int_{A} p(\mathrm{y}|\boldsymbol{\theta})\pi(\boldsymbol{\theta}) d\boldsymbol{\theta}}{\int_{\Theta} p(\mathrm{y}|\boldsymbol{\theta})\pi(\boldsymbol{\theta}) d\boldsymbol{\theta}} = \int_{A} \pi(\boldsymbol{\theta}|\mathrm{y}) d\boldsymbol{\theta}
\end{aligned}$$

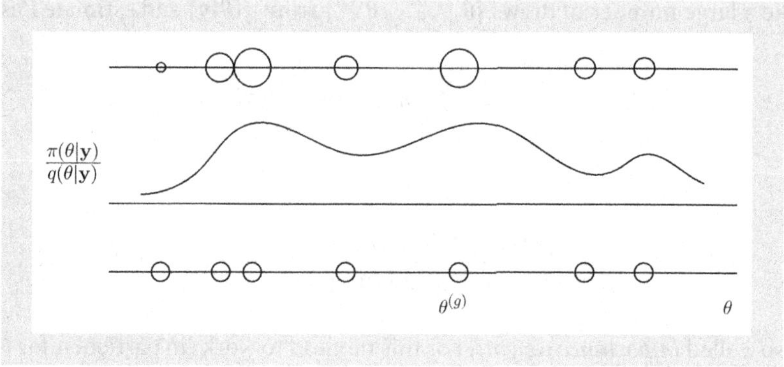

FIGURE 5.3 SIR method

Notes: Incoming particles are reweighted (resampled) according to probabilities proportional to the ratio of the target to the proposal density.

as L and G both increase with L/G going to zero and provided the expectations are bounded. Rubin (1988) has called this the sampling importance re-sampling or SIR method.

We illustrate this method in Figure 5.3 which shows how the particle $\boldsymbol{\theta}^{(g)}$ gets weights according to the importance of the ratio of the target to the proposal.

The SIR approach is now also heavily used in nonlinear state-space models where it is referred to as particle filtering, a method that was introduced into econometrics in Kim et al. (1998). Particle filtering is discussed in several recent papers, for example, Del Moral et al. (2006) and is extensively discussed in Giordani et al. (Chapter 3, this volume).

3 Metropolis-Hastings Algorithm

Suppose that we are interested in sampling the target density $\pi(\boldsymbol{\theta}|\mathrm{y})$, where $\boldsymbol{\theta}$ is the parameter vector and $\pi(\boldsymbol{\theta}|\mathrm{y})$ is a continuous density. The idea behind the M-H algorithm is to simulate a convenient transition density $q(\boldsymbol{\theta},\boldsymbol{\theta}^{\dagger}|\mathrm{y})$, where $(\boldsymbol{\theta},\boldsymbol{\theta}^{\dagger})$ are any two points, and then to modify the transition density to ensure that the modified Markov chain has the correct limiting distribution. The source density $q(\boldsymbol{\theta},\boldsymbol{\theta}^{\dagger}|\mathrm{y})$ is called the candidate generating density or proposal density.

To define the M-H algorithm, let $\boldsymbol{\theta}^{(g)}$ be the current value. Then the next value $\boldsymbol{\theta}^{(g+1)}$ is produced by a two-step process consisting of a "proposal step" and a "move step."

Algorithm: Metropolis-Hastings

Step 1: Initialize $\boldsymbol{\theta}^{(0)}$

Step 2: In each iteration g, $g = 1,\ldots,n_0 + G$,

- **Propose:** Sample a proposal value $\boldsymbol{\theta}^{\dagger}$ from $q(\boldsymbol{\theta}^{(g)}, \boldsymbol{\theta}|\mathrm{y})$ and calculate the quantity (the *acceptance probability* or the *probability of move*)

$$\alpha(\boldsymbol{\theta}^{(g)}, \boldsymbol{\theta}^{\dagger}|\mathrm{y}) = \min\left\{1, \frac{\pi(\boldsymbol{\theta}^{\dagger}|\mathrm{y})}{\pi(\boldsymbol{\theta}^{(g)}|\mathrm{y})} \frac{q(\boldsymbol{\theta}^{\dagger}, \boldsymbol{\theta}^{(g)}|\mathrm{y})}{q(\boldsymbol{\theta}^{(g)}, \boldsymbol{\theta}^{\dagger}|\mathrm{y})}\right\} \tag{5.2}$$

- **Move:** Set

$$\boldsymbol{\theta}^{(g+1)} = \begin{cases} \boldsymbol{\theta}^{\dagger} & \text{with prob } \alpha(\boldsymbol{\theta}^{(g)}, \boldsymbol{\theta}^{\dagger}|\mathrm{y}) \\ \boldsymbol{\theta}^{(g)} & \text{with prob } 1 - \alpha(\boldsymbol{\theta}^{(g)}, \boldsymbol{\theta}^{\dagger}|\mathrm{y}) \end{cases}$$

Step 3: Discard the draws from the first n_0 iterations and save the subsequent G draws $\boldsymbol{\theta}^{(n_0+1)}, \ldots, \boldsymbol{\theta}^{(n_0+G)}$

Note that the probability $\alpha(\boldsymbol{\theta}^{(g)}, \boldsymbol{\theta}^{\dagger}|\mathrm{y})$ does not require knowledge of the norming constant of the posterior density $\pi(\boldsymbol{\theta}|\mathrm{y})$. Also if the proposal density satisfies the condition $q(\boldsymbol{\theta}, \boldsymbol{\theta}^{\dagger}|\mathrm{y}) = q(\boldsymbol{\theta}^{\dagger}, \boldsymbol{\theta}|\mathrm{y})$, then $\alpha(\boldsymbol{\theta}^{(g)}, \boldsymbol{\theta}^{\dagger}|\mathrm{y})$ reduces to

$$\min\left\{1, \frac{\pi(\boldsymbol{\theta}^{\dagger}|\mathrm{y})}{\pi(\boldsymbol{\theta}^{(g)}|\mathrm{y})}\right\}.$$

This simplication is a feature of the random-walk version of the M-H algorithm that is discussed below.

3.1 Derivation of the M-H algorithm

The M-H algorithm has been derived by Chib and Greenberg (1995) from the logic of reversible Markov chains. Their derivation is helpful in understanding the M-H algorithm.

To start, we need some definitions. A Markov transition density $K(\boldsymbol{\theta}, \boldsymbol{\theta}^{\dagger}|\mathrm{y})$ is reversible for $\pi(\boldsymbol{\theta}|\mathrm{y})$ if for every $(\boldsymbol{\theta}, \boldsymbol{\theta}^{\dagger})$ in the support of the target distribution

$$\pi(\boldsymbol{\theta}|\mathrm{y})K(\boldsymbol{\theta}, \boldsymbol{\theta}^{\dagger}|\mathrm{y}) = \pi(\boldsymbol{\theta}^{\dagger}|\mathrm{y})K(\boldsymbol{\theta}^{\dagger}, \boldsymbol{\theta}|\mathrm{y}). \tag{5.3}$$

If a chain is reversible it is also invariant. Invariance refers to the property that

$$\pi(\boldsymbol{\theta}^{\dagger}|\mathrm{y}) = \int K(\boldsymbol{\theta}, \boldsymbol{\theta}^{\dagger}|\mathrm{y})\pi(\boldsymbol{\theta}|\mathrm{y})d\boldsymbol{\theta} \tag{5.4}$$

which means that once convergence is achieved, a subsequent value $\boldsymbol{\theta}^{\dagger}$ drawn from the transition density is also from the target density. To see that reversibility implies invariance one simply integrates both sides of (5.3) over $\boldsymbol{\theta}$. This leads to the invariance condition since $\int K(\boldsymbol{\theta}^{\dagger}, \boldsymbol{\theta}|\mathrm{y})d\boldsymbol{\theta} = 1$ by virtue of being a transition density.

Now consider the Markov chain induced by the proposal density $q(\boldsymbol{\theta}, \boldsymbol{\theta}^\dagger|\mathrm{y})$. Suppose that for a pair of points $(\boldsymbol{\theta}, \boldsymbol{\theta}^\dagger)$ it is true that

$$\pi(\boldsymbol{\theta}|\mathrm{y})q(\boldsymbol{\theta}, \boldsymbol{\theta}^\dagger|\mathrm{y}) > \pi(\boldsymbol{\theta}^\dagger|\mathrm{y})q(\boldsymbol{\theta}^\dagger, \boldsymbol{\theta}|\mathrm{y}), \tag{5.5}$$

which means informally that the process moves from $\boldsymbol{\theta}$ to $\boldsymbol{\theta}^\dagger$ too frequently and too rarely in the reverse direction. We can correct this situation by reducing the flow from $\boldsymbol{\theta}$ to $\boldsymbol{\theta}^\dagger$ by introducing probabilities $\alpha(\boldsymbol{\theta}, \boldsymbol{\theta}^\dagger|\mathrm{y})$ and $\alpha(\boldsymbol{\theta}^\dagger, \boldsymbol{\theta}|\mathrm{y})$ of making the moves in either direction so that

$$\pi(\boldsymbol{\theta}|\mathrm{y})q(\boldsymbol{\theta}, \boldsymbol{\theta}^\dagger|\mathrm{y})\alpha(\boldsymbol{\theta}, \boldsymbol{\theta}^\dagger|\mathrm{y}) = \pi(\boldsymbol{\theta}^\dagger|\mathrm{y})q(\boldsymbol{\theta}^\dagger, \boldsymbol{\theta}|\mathrm{y})\alpha(\boldsymbol{\theta}^\dagger, \boldsymbol{\theta}|\mathrm{y}). \tag{5.6}$$

We now set $\alpha(\boldsymbol{\theta}^\dagger, \boldsymbol{\theta}|\mathrm{y})$ to be as high as possible, namely equal to one. Solving for $\alpha(\boldsymbol{\theta}, \boldsymbol{\theta}^\dagger|\mathrm{y})$, we then get that

$$\alpha(\boldsymbol{\theta}, \boldsymbol{\theta}^\dagger|\mathrm{y}) = \frac{\pi(\boldsymbol{\theta}^\dagger|\mathrm{y})\, q(\boldsymbol{\theta}^\dagger, \boldsymbol{\theta}|\mathrm{y})}{\pi(\boldsymbol{\theta}|\mathrm{y})\, q(\boldsymbol{\theta}, \boldsymbol{\theta}^\dagger|\mathrm{y})}$$

This quantity is less than one because we started from (5.5). On the other hand, if we reverse the inequality in (5.5), a similar argumentation leads to the conclusion that $\alpha(\boldsymbol{\theta}, \boldsymbol{\theta}^\dagger|\mathrm{y}) = 1$, which produces the expression given in (5.2).

3.2 Transition density of the M-H chain

Because of the fact that the M-H chain can repeat values, the transition density of the M-H chain $K_{MH}(\boldsymbol{\theta}, \boldsymbol{\theta}^\dagger|\mathrm{y})$ has two components—one for the move away from $\boldsymbol{\theta}$ given by

$$\alpha(\boldsymbol{\theta}, \boldsymbol{\theta}^\dagger|\mathrm{y})q(\boldsymbol{\theta}, \boldsymbol{\theta}^\dagger|\mathrm{y})$$

and one for the probability of staying at $\boldsymbol{\theta}$ given by

$$r(\boldsymbol{\theta}|\mathrm{y}) = 1 - \int \alpha(\boldsymbol{\theta}, \boldsymbol{\theta}^\dagger|\mathrm{y})q(\boldsymbol{\theta}, \boldsymbol{\theta}^\dagger|\mathrm{y})d\boldsymbol{\theta}^\dagger.$$

Therefore,

$$K_{MH}(\boldsymbol{\theta}, \boldsymbol{\theta}^\dagger|\mathrm{y}) = \alpha(\boldsymbol{\theta}, \boldsymbol{\theta}^\dagger|\mathrm{y})q(\boldsymbol{\theta}, \boldsymbol{\theta}^\dagger|\mathrm{y}) + \delta_{\boldsymbol{\theta}}(\boldsymbol{\theta}^\dagger)r(\boldsymbol{\theta}|\mathrm{y})$$

where $\delta_{\boldsymbol{\theta}}(\boldsymbol{\theta}^\dagger)$ is the Dirac-function at $\boldsymbol{\theta}$ defined as $\delta_{\boldsymbol{\theta}}(\boldsymbol{\theta}^\dagger) = 0$ for $\boldsymbol{\theta}^\dagger \neq \boldsymbol{\theta}$ and $\int \delta_{\boldsymbol{\theta}}(\boldsymbol{\theta}^\dagger)d\boldsymbol{\theta}^\dagger = 1$. It is easy to check that the integral of this transition density over all possible values of $\boldsymbol{\theta}$ is one, as required.

As shown through the preceding derivation, the first term of $K_{MH}(\boldsymbol{\theta}, \boldsymbol{\theta}^\dagger|\mathrm{y})$ satisfies the reversibility condition by construction. The reversibility condition for the second term

$$\pi(\boldsymbol{\theta}|\mathrm{y})\delta_{\boldsymbol{\theta}}(\boldsymbol{\theta}^\dagger)r(\boldsymbol{\theta}|\mathrm{y}) = \pi(\boldsymbol{\theta}^\dagger|\mathrm{y})\delta_{\boldsymbol{\theta}^\dagger}(\boldsymbol{\theta})r(\boldsymbol{\theta}|\mathrm{y})$$

is trivially confirmed because the left and the right-hand sides in this expression are only non-zero when $\boldsymbol{\theta} = \boldsymbol{\theta}^{\dagger}$. Thus, $K_{MH}(\boldsymbol{\theta}, \boldsymbol{\theta}^{\dagger}|\mathrm{y})$ is reversible and hence invariant.

3.3 Convergence properties

The theoretical properties of the M-H algorithm (in particular, the ergodic behavior of the chain from an arbitrarily specified initial value) requires assumptions about the properties of the Markov chain. The main results are from Tierney (1994), which also has the definition of the terms involved.

Theorem 1. Suppose that the Markov chain $\{\boldsymbol{\theta}^{(g)}\}$ is π-irreducible and has invariant distribution $\pi(\boldsymbol{\theta}|y)$. Then $\pi(\boldsymbol{\theta}|\mathrm{y})$ is the unique invariant distribution. If the chain is π-irreducible, aperiodic, and the invariant distribution is proper, then for π-every $\boldsymbol{\theta}^{(0)}$ and all measurable sets A

$$\| \Pr(\boldsymbol{\theta}^{(g)} \in A|\mathrm{y}, \boldsymbol{\theta}^{(0)}) - \int_A \pi(\boldsymbol{\theta}|\mathrm{y})d\boldsymbol{\theta} \| \to 0$$

as $g \to \infty$, where $\| \cdot \|$ denotes the total variation distance. If the chain is ergodic (π-irreducible, aperiodic, and Harris recurrent), then for all functions $h(\boldsymbol{\theta})$ such that $\int_\Theta |h(\boldsymbol{\theta})|\pi(\boldsymbol{\theta}|\mathrm{y})d\boldsymbol{\theta} < \infty$ and any initial distribution,

$$\hat{h}_G = G^{-1}\sum_{g=1}^{G} h(\boldsymbol{\theta}^{(g)}) \to \int_\Theta h(\boldsymbol{\theta})\pi(\boldsymbol{\theta}|\mathrm{y})d\boldsymbol{\theta} \text{ as } G \to \infty, \text{ a.s.}$$

These powerful results hold under relatively weak conditions (for example, as discussed in Tierney 1994, π-irreducibility of the chain is satisfied if the proposal density is everywhere positive in the support of the posterior density; it is Harris recurrent if it is π-irreducible, has π as it is unique invariant distribution, and the transition kernel is absolutely continuous with respect to π). These provide the basis for MCMC methods. For a given target distribution and MCMC transition density, they allow us to utilize the simulated sample path of that transition kernel to develop simulation-consistent estimates of posterior moments, posterior probabilities, and other summaries of the target.

A central limit theorem for sample-path averages requires a further strengthening of the conditions. One now requires that the chain is also uniformly ergodic. An ergodic chain with invariant distribution π is uniformly ergodic if there exists a non-negative bounded real-valued function $C(\cdot)$ and a positive constant $r < 1$ such that

$$\| K^{(g)}(\boldsymbol{\theta}^{(0)}, A|\mathrm{y}) - \int_A \pi(\boldsymbol{\theta}|\mathrm{y})d\boldsymbol{\theta} \| \leq C(\boldsymbol{\theta}^{(0)})r^g$$

for every $\boldsymbol{\theta}^{(0)}$, g, and measurable sets A. Then we have the following ergodic limit theorem for the sample average $\hat{h}_G$.

Theorem 2. Suppose that the Markov chain $\{\boldsymbol{\theta}^{(g)}\}$ is uniformly ergodic and has invariant distribution $\pi(\boldsymbol{\theta}|y)$. Then for functions $h(\boldsymbol{\theta})$ such that $\int_\Theta h(\boldsymbol{\theta})^2\pi(\boldsymbol{\theta}|\mathrm{y})d\boldsymbol{\theta} < \infty$, and any initial distribution, the sample average $\hat{h}_G$ satisfies the ergodic limit theorem

$$\sqrt{G}\left(\hat{h}_G - \mathrm{E}_\pi h\right) \xrightarrow{d} \mathcal{N}(0, \sigma_h^2)$$

where

$$\mathrm{E}_\pi h = \int_\Theta h(\boldsymbol{\theta})\pi(\boldsymbol{\theta}|\mathrm{y})d\boldsymbol{\theta}$$

$$\sigma_h^2 = \mathrm{Var}_\pi\left(h(\boldsymbol{\theta}^{(1)})\right) + 2\sum_{k=2}^{\infty}\mathrm{Cov}_\pi\left\{h(\boldsymbol{\theta}^{(1)}), h(\boldsymbol{\theta}^{(k)})\right\}$$

and the subscript π indicates that the expectations are calculated under the invariant distribution.

3.4 Numerical standard error and inefficiency factor

In order to understand how accurately $\hat{h}_G$ has estimated $\mathrm{E}_\pi h$, it is necessary to calculate $\mathrm{Var}(\hat{h}_G) = \sigma_h^2/G$, where σ_h^2 is the variance that appears in Theorem 2. The square root of $\mathrm{Var}(\hat{h}_G)$ is called the numerical standard error. One effective way of estimating $\mathrm{Var}(\hat{h}_G)$ is by the method of *batch means* (Ripley 1987). First, we let $Z_g = h(\boldsymbol{\theta}^{(g)}), g = 1, 2, \ldots, G$. Next, we divide the data $\{Z_1, Z_2, \ldots, Z_G\}$ into k non-overlapping batches of length m with means

$$B_i = m^{-1}(Z_{(i-1)m+1} + \ldots + Z_{im}),\ i = 1, 2, \ldots, k$$

where the batch size m is chosen to ensure that the first-order serial correlation of the batch means is less than 0.05. The average of these batch means

$$\bar{B} = \frac{1}{k}\sum_{i=1}^{k} B_i$$

is of course $\hat{h}_G$ and the estimate of the sample variance of $\bar{B}$ by standard calculations is

$$\mathrm{Var}\left(\bar{B}\right) = \frac{1}{k(k-1)}\sum_{i=1}^{k}(B_i - \bar{B})^2.$$

In the batch means method, this variance estimate is taken to be the estimate of $\mathrm{Var}(\hat{h}_G)$. Jones et al. (2006) show that it is a consistent estimate of σ_h^2/G if k and m both increase with G.

Inefficiency factor Once we have an estimate of $\text{Var}(\hat{h}_G)$, a useful quantity to calculate and report is the *inefficiency factor* defined as

$$\text{Ineff}(\hat{h}_G) = \frac{\text{Var}(\hat{h}_G)}{s^2/G}, \tag{5.7}$$

where s^2 is just the sample variance of $\{Z_g\}$. This quantity is the ratio of variance of $\hat{h}_G$ to the variance of $\hat{h}_G$ relevant for the case of independent draws. One way to interpret this quantity is in terms of the *effective sample size*, or ESS, defined as

$$\text{ESS}(\hat{h}_G) = \frac{G}{\text{Ineff}(\hat{h}_G)}. \tag{5.8}$$

With independent sampling, the inefficiency factor is theoretically equal to one, and the effective sample size is G. When the inefficiency factor is greater than one (the typical case with MCMC sampling), the effective sample size is smaller than G.

3.5 Choice of proposal density

There are many ways of formulating the proposal density. We consider two that are popular in practice.

Random walk proposals Given the current value $\boldsymbol{\theta}$, the proposal is drawn as

$$\boldsymbol{\theta}^\dagger = \boldsymbol{\theta} + \mathbf{z},$$

where $\mathbf{z}$ follows some symmetric distribution q such as the multivariate normal with mean of zero and some covariance matrix $\tau\mathbf{V}$, which is adjusted in trial runs to reach some desired acceptance rate (given by the proportion of proposed values that are accepted). Because of the symmetry of the increment distribution it follows that $q(\boldsymbol{\theta}, \boldsymbol{\theta}^\dagger|\mathbf{y}) = q(\boldsymbol{\theta}^\dagger, \boldsymbol{\theta}|\mathbf{y})$ and hence, due to the cancellation of the q terms, the M-H probability of move takes the simplified form

$$\alpha(\boldsymbol{\theta}, \boldsymbol{\theta}^\dagger|\mathbf{y}) = \min\left\{1, \frac{\pi(\boldsymbol{\theta}^\dagger|\mathbf{y})}{\pi(\boldsymbol{\theta}|\mathbf{y})}\right\}$$

as a function solely of the target density, as illustrated in Figure 5.4.

Although the random walk M-H proposal is quite popular in applications, it can be difficult to tune, especially when the dimension of $\boldsymbol{\theta}$ is large. In such cases, it is difficult to generate reasonable acceptance rates and large enough moves to ensure a full exploration of the posterior surface.

Independent proposals Another common strategy is to set $q(\boldsymbol{\theta}, \boldsymbol{\theta}^\dagger|\mathbf{y}) = q(\boldsymbol{\theta}^\dagger|\mathbf{y})$, an *independence M-H chain* in the terminology of Tierney (1994). In this case,

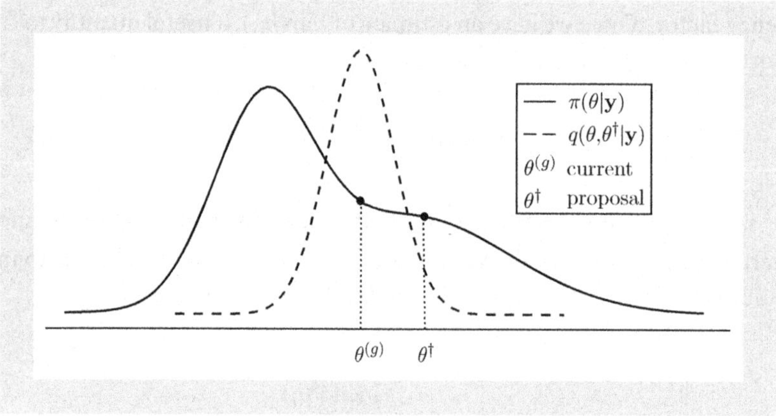

FIGURE 5.4 Random-walk M-H: the two points that determine the probability of move

$$\alpha(\boldsymbol{\theta},\boldsymbol{\theta}^\dagger|\mathrm{y}) = \min\left\{1, \frac{\pi(\boldsymbol{\theta}^\dagger|\mathrm{y})}{\pi(\boldsymbol{\theta}|\mathrm{y})}\frac{q(\boldsymbol{\theta}|\mathrm{y})}{q(\boldsymbol{\theta}^\dagger|\mathrm{y})}\right\},$$

which involves the ratio of targets and the ratio of proposal densities, as shown in Figure 5.5.

One way to implement such chains is by tailoring the proposal density to the target at the mode by a multivariate normal or multivariate-t distribution with location given by the mode of the target and the dispersion given by inverse of the Hessian evaluated at the mode (Chib and Greenberg 1994). Specifically, one can let $q(\boldsymbol{\theta}|\mathrm{y}) = p(\boldsymbol{\theta}|\mathbf{m}, \mathrm{V})$, where p is some multivariate density and the parameters of the proposal density are taken to be

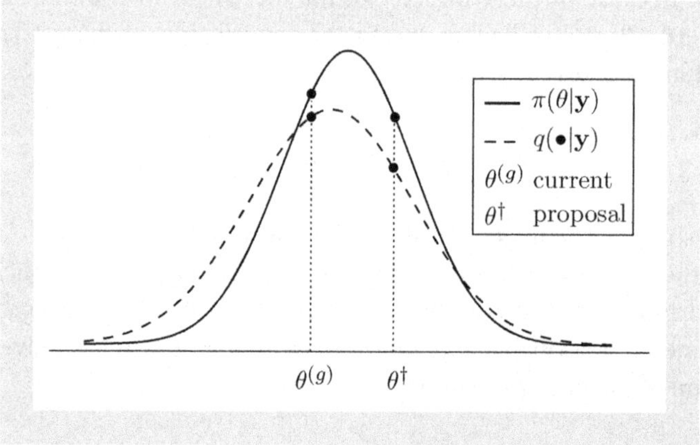

FIGURE 5.5 Independence M-H: the four points that determine the probability of move

$$\mathbf{m} = \max_{\theta} \log \pi(\boldsymbol{\theta}|\mathrm{y}) \text{ and}$$

$$\mathrm{V} = \tau \left\{ -\frac{\partial^2 \log \pi(\boldsymbol{\theta}|\mathrm{y})}{\partial \boldsymbol{\theta} \partial \boldsymbol{\theta}'} \right\}^{-1}_{\theta=\hat{\theta}} \tag{5.9}$$

where τ is again a tuning parameter that (along with $\mathbf{V}$) may have to be adjusted so that the tails of the proposal density are thicker than those of the target. As mentioned above, an equivalent requirement is needed in the importance sampling method. This may be called a tailored M-H chain.

3.6 Multiple-block sampling

When the dimension of $\boldsymbol{\theta}$ is large, sampling of the target in one block (as described in the preceding section) tends not to be efficient. It becomes necessary then to divide the parameters into smaller groups or blocks and then to sample these blocks in turn. To explain this idea, suppose that $\boldsymbol{\theta}$ is split as $(\boldsymbol{\theta}_1, \boldsymbol{\theta}_2)$, with $\boldsymbol{\theta}_k \in \Omega_k \subseteq \Re^{d_k}$. In many problems, this sort of grouping is suggested by the model structure itself. For example, in a regression model, one block may consist of the regression coefficients and the other block may consist of the error variance.

Now let

$$q_1(\boldsymbol{\theta}_1, \boldsymbol{\theta}_1^\dagger|\mathrm{y}, \boldsymbol{\theta}_2);\ q_2(\boldsymbol{\theta}_2, \boldsymbol{\theta}_2^\dagger|\mathrm{y}, \boldsymbol{\theta}_1)$$

denote the proposal densities, one for each block $\boldsymbol{\theta}_k$, where the proposal density q_k may depend on the current value of the remaining block. Versions of either the random-walk or tailored proposal densities are possible, analogous to the single-block case. Also define

$$\alpha_1(\boldsymbol{\theta}_1, \boldsymbol{\theta}_1^\dagger|\mathrm{y},\ \boldsymbol{\theta}_2) = \min\left\{1, \frac{\pi(\boldsymbol{\theta}_1^\dagger|\ \mathrm{y}, \boldsymbol{\theta}_2) q_1(\boldsymbol{\theta}_1^\dagger, \boldsymbol{\theta}_1|\mathrm{y}, \boldsymbol{\theta}_2)}{\pi(\boldsymbol{\theta}_1|\mathrm{y}, \boldsymbol{\theta}_2) q_1(\boldsymbol{\theta}_1, \boldsymbol{\theta}_1^\dagger|\mathrm{y}, \boldsymbol{\theta}_2)}\right\}, \tag{5.10}$$

and

$$\alpha_2(\boldsymbol{\theta}_2, \boldsymbol{\theta}_2^\dagger|\mathrm{y},\ \boldsymbol{\theta}_1) = \min\left\{1, \frac{\pi(\boldsymbol{\theta}_2^\dagger|\ \mathrm{y}, \boldsymbol{\theta}_1) q_2(\boldsymbol{\theta}_2^\dagger, \boldsymbol{\theta}_2|\mathrm{y}, \boldsymbol{\theta}_1)}{\pi(\boldsymbol{\theta}_2|\mathrm{y}, \boldsymbol{\theta}_1) q_2(\boldsymbol{\theta}_2, \boldsymbol{\theta}_2^\dagger|\mathrm{y}, \boldsymbol{\theta}_1)}\right\}, \tag{5.11}$$

as the probability of move for block $\boldsymbol{\theta}_k$ $(k = 1, 2)$ conditioned on the other block. The conditional posterior densities

$$\pi(\boldsymbol{\theta}_1|\mathrm{y}, \boldsymbol{\theta}_2) \text{ and } \pi(\boldsymbol{\theta}_2|\mathrm{y}, \boldsymbol{\theta}_1)$$

that appear in these functions are called the *full conditional densities* and by Bayes' theorem are just proportional to the joint posterior density. For example,

$$\pi(\boldsymbol{\theta}_1|\mathrm{y}, \boldsymbol{\theta}_2) \propto \pi(\boldsymbol{\theta}_1, \boldsymbol{\theta}_2|\mathrm{y}),$$

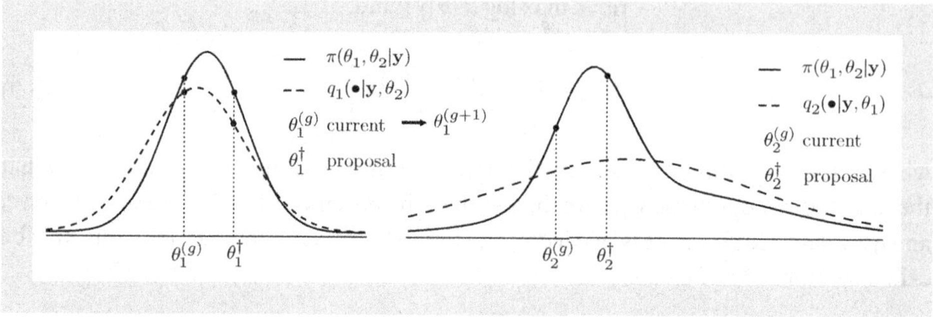

FIGURE 5.6 Multiple-block M-H

Notes: Left panel has the target and proposal densities of the first block and the four points that determine the probability of move; right panel has the same information for the second block.

and, therefore, the probabilities of move in (5.10) and (5.11) can be expressed equivalently in terms of the kernel of the joint posterior density $\pi(\boldsymbol{\theta}_1, \boldsymbol{\theta}_2|\mathbf{y})$ because the normalizing constant of the full conditional density (the norming constant in the latter expression) cancels in forming the ratio. Then in the multiple-block M-H algorithm, one sweep of the algorithm is completed by updating each block, say sequentially in fixed order, using an M-H step with the above probabilities of move, given the most current value of the other block. Thus, at the gth iteration, given the value $\boldsymbol{\theta}_2^{(g)}$ one sweep is completed by the following steps.

Algorithm: Multiple-block M-H

Step 1: Propose

$$\boldsymbol{\theta}_1^\dagger \sim q_1(\boldsymbol{\theta}_1^{(g)}, \boldsymbol{\theta}_1^\dagger|\mathbf{y}, \boldsymbol{\theta}_2^{(g)})$$

and move with probability

$$\alpha_1(\boldsymbol{\theta}_1^{(g)}, \boldsymbol{\theta}_1^\dagger|\mathbf{y},\ \boldsymbol{\theta}_2^{(g)})$$

(otherwise stay at the current value) to produce the value $\boldsymbol{\theta}_1^{(g+1)}$.

Step 2: Given this updated value of the first block, propose

$$\boldsymbol{\theta}_2^\dagger \sim q_2(\boldsymbol{\theta}_2^{(g+1}, \boldsymbol{\theta}_2^\dagger|\mathbf{y}, \boldsymbol{\theta}_1^{(g+1)})$$

and move with probability

$$\alpha_2(\boldsymbol{\theta}_2^{(g)}, \boldsymbol{\theta}_2^\dagger|\mathbf{y},\ \boldsymbol{\theta}_1^{(g+1)})$$

(otherwise stay at the current value) to produce the value $\boldsymbol{\theta}_2^{(g+1)}$.

The ingredients involved in these two steps are illustrated in Figure 5.6.

It is important to note that the Markov chain generated by this multiple-block M-H satisfies the invariance condition but not reversibility. It does, however, satisfy the condition of local reversibility, a concept that is introduced in Chib and Jeliazkov (2001). The assumptions under which such an algorithm is Harris-recurrent are taken up in Roberts and Rosenthal (2006).

Gibbs sampling In many situations, it is the case that each full conditional distribution is of recognizable form and easily sampled. We can use these as the proposal distributions in the multiple-block M-H algorithm. Specifically, let

$$q_1(\boldsymbol{\theta}_1^{(g)}, \boldsymbol{\theta}_1^{\dagger}|\mathrm{y}, \boldsymbol{\theta}_2^{(g)}) = \pi(\boldsymbol{\theta}_1^{\dagger}|\mathrm{y}, \boldsymbol{\theta}_2^{(g)}),$$

and

$$q_2(\boldsymbol{\theta}_2^{(g+1}, \boldsymbol{\theta}_2^{\dagger}|\mathrm{y}, \boldsymbol{\theta}_1^{(g+1)}) = \pi(\boldsymbol{\theta}_2'|\mathrm{y}, \boldsymbol{\theta}_1^{(g+1)}).$$

If we insert these choices into the probabilities of move, an interesting simplification occurs. For instance, for the first block, the probability of move reduces to

$$\begin{aligned}
\alpha_1(\boldsymbol{\theta}_1^{(g)}, \boldsymbol{\theta}_1^{\dagger}|\mathrm{y}, \boldsymbol{\theta}_2^{(g)}) &= \min\left\{1, \frac{\pi(\boldsymbol{\theta}_1^{\dagger}|\, \mathrm{y}, \boldsymbol{\theta}_2^{(g)}) q_1(\boldsymbol{\theta}_1^{\dagger}, \boldsymbol{\theta}_1^{(g)}|\mathrm{y}, \boldsymbol{\theta}_2^{(g)})}{\pi(\boldsymbol{\theta}_1^{(g)}|\mathrm{y}, \boldsymbol{\theta}_2^{(g)}) q_1(\boldsymbol{\theta}_1^{(g)}, \boldsymbol{\theta}_1^{\dagger}|\mathrm{y}, \boldsymbol{\theta}_2^{(g)})}\right\} \\
&= \min\left\{1, \frac{\pi(\boldsymbol{\theta}_1^{\dagger}|\, \mathrm{y}, \boldsymbol{\theta}_2^{(g)}) \pi(\boldsymbol{\theta}_1^{(g)}|\mathrm{y}, \boldsymbol{\theta}_2^{(g)})}{\pi(\boldsymbol{\theta}_1^{(g)}|\mathrm{y}, \boldsymbol{\theta}_2^{(g)}) \pi(\boldsymbol{\theta}_1^{\dagger}|\mathrm{y}, \boldsymbol{\theta}_2^{(g)})}\right\} = 1
\end{aligned}$$

and similarly for the second block, implying that if the proposal values are drawn from their full conditional densities then the proposal values are accepted with probability one. This special case of the multiple-block M-H algorithm (in which *each* block is proposed using its full conditional distribution) is called the Gibbs sampling algorithm.

Algorithm: Gibbs sampling

In each iteration g, $g = 1, \ldots, n_0 + G$,

- Generate $\boldsymbol{\theta}_1^{(g+1)}$ from $\pi(\boldsymbol{\theta}_1|\mathrm{y}, \boldsymbol{\theta}_2^{(g)})$
- Generate $\boldsymbol{\theta}_2^{(g+1)}$ from $\pi(\boldsymbol{\theta}_2|\mathrm{y}, \boldsymbol{\theta}_1^{(g+1)})$

Return the values $\{\boldsymbol{\theta}^{(n_0+1)}, \boldsymbol{\theta}^{(n_0+2)}, \ldots, \boldsymbol{\theta}^{(n_0+G)}\}$.

Metropolis-within-Gibbs In some problems, it is the case that one or more of the full conditional distributions are of recognizable form, but at least one full conditional distribution is not. In that case, the blocks with the tractable full conditional distributions can be sampled directly and the blocks with the intractable full conditional distributions by an M-H step. Such an algorithm is sometimes called the *Metropolis-within-Gibbs* algorithm though the multiple-block M-H terminology is sufficient to cover this special case.

General case The extension of the multiple block method to more than two blocks is straightforward in principle. As a general rule, sets of parameters that are highly correlated should be treated as one block when applying the multiple-block M-H algorithm. Otherwise, it would be difficult to develop proposal densities that lead to large moves through the support of the target distribution. It is also possible in some cases to reduce the number of blocks by the method of composition. For example, suppose that $\boldsymbol{\theta}_1, \boldsymbol{\theta}_2$, and $\boldsymbol{\theta}_3$ denote three blocks and that the distribution $\boldsymbol{\theta}_1|\mathrm{y}, \boldsymbol{\theta}_3$ is tractable (i.e. can be sampled directly). Then, the blocks $(\boldsymbol{\theta}_1, \boldsymbol{\theta}_2)$ can be collapsed by first sampling $\boldsymbol{\theta}_1$ from $\boldsymbol{\theta}_1|\mathrm{y}, \boldsymbol{\theta}_3$ followed by $\boldsymbol{\theta}_2$ from $\boldsymbol{\theta}_2|\mathrm{y}, \boldsymbol{\theta}_1, \boldsymbol{\theta}_3$. This amounts to a two block MCMC algorithm. In addition, if it is possible to sample $(\boldsymbol{\theta}_1, \boldsymbol{\theta}_2)$ marginalized over $\boldsymbol{\theta}_3$ then the number of blocks is reduced to one.

Tailored Randomized Block M-H Despite these general precepts, the question of the number of blocks and the composition of the blocks is not always easy to address especially in nonlinear models (such as DSGE models and arbitrage-free term structure models) where no natural grouping of the parameters is suggested by the model structure. Because incorrect grouping can compromise the mixing of the Markov chain, Chib and Ramamurthy (2010) have explored an extension of the above multiple-block algorithm in which the number of blocks and the composition of the blocks is randomized in each iteration. The proposal density of each of the blocks in each iteration is determined by tailoring. They call the resulting algorithm the TaRB-MH algorithm (for Tailored Randomized Block M-H). The algorithm has the following form.

Algorithm 1. TaRB-MH algorithm

Step 1: Initialize $\boldsymbol{\theta}^{(0)}$

Step 2: In each iteration g, $g = 1, \ldots, n_0 + G$,

- **Randomize:** Randomly generate blocks $(\boldsymbol{\theta}_{g,1}, \boldsymbol{\theta}_{g,2}, \ldots, \boldsymbol{\theta}_{g,p_g})$
- **M-H:** Sample each block $\boldsymbol{\theta}_{g,l}$, $l = 1, \ldots, p_g$, by the multiple-block M-H algorithm with the proposal density of each block found by tailoring to the target density of that block

Step 3: Discard the draws from the first n_0 iterations and save the subsequent G draws $\boldsymbol{\theta}^{(n_0+1)}, \ldots, \boldsymbol{\theta}^{(n_0+G)}$

We illustrate both the fixed blocks and randomized blocks M-H algorithms in the examples.

4 Special topics

4.1 MCMC sampling with latent variables

In sampling a given target distribution, it is sometimes helpful to modify the target distribution by introducing latent variables or auxiliary variables into the sampling. This idea was called data augmentation by Tanner and Wong (1987) in the context of missing data problems. Slice sampling, which we do not discuss in this chapter, is a particular way of introducing auxiliary variables into the sampling, for example see Damien et al. (1999) and Mira and Tierney (2002).

To fix notations, suppose that z denotes a vector of latent variables and let the modified target distribution be $\pi(\boldsymbol{\theta}, \mathbf{z}|\mathbf{y})$. Then, in many cases (see, for example, Li and Tobias, Chapter 6, this volume), the conditional distribution of $\boldsymbol{\theta}$ (or subcomponents of $\boldsymbol{\theta}$) given z are easy to derive. A multiple-block M-H simulation over $\boldsymbol{\theta}$ and z would lead to the sample

$$\left(\boldsymbol{\theta}^{(n_0+1)}, \mathbf{z}^{(n_0+1)}\right), \ldots, \left(\boldsymbol{\theta}^{(n_0+M)}, \mathbf{z}^{(n_0+M)}\right) \sim \pi(\boldsymbol{\theta}, \mathbf{z}|\mathbf{y}).$$

At the end of this process, the sampled draws on $\boldsymbol{\theta}$ are from $\pi(\boldsymbol{\theta}|\mathbf{y})$, which was the original objective.

Early use of this technique, which formed the basis for many subsequent developments, is to be found in Chib (1992) for the Tobit censored regression model, Albert and Chib (1993b) for binary, ordinal, and categorical outcomes, Albert and Chib (1993a) and Chib (1996) for hidden Markov models, and Carlin et al. (1992), Carter and Kohn (1994), and Frühwirth-Schnatter (1994) for state space models.

Example: In the binary probit case, the model is cast in the form

$$\begin{aligned} z_i|\beta &\sim \mathcal{N}(\mathbf{x}_i'\beta, 1), \\ y_i &= I[z_i > 0]\,,\ i \le n, \\ \beta &\sim \mathcal{N}_k(\beta_0, \mathbf{B}_0). \end{aligned} \tag{5.12}$$

Then, the Albert-Chib (1993) algorithm proceeds with the sampling of the full conditional distributions

$$\beta|\mathbf{y}, \{z_i\}\,; \quad \{z_i\}|\mathbf{y}, \beta,$$

where both these distributions are tractable. In particular, the distribution of β conditioned on the latent data becomes independent of the observed data and has the same form as in the Gaussian linear regression model with the response data given by $\{z_i\}$. It is multivariate normal with mean $\hat{\boldsymbol{\beta}} = \mathbf{B}(\mathbf{B}_0^{-1}\beta_0 + \sum_{i=1}^n \mathbf{x}_i z_i)$ and variance matrix $\mathbf{B} = (\mathbf{B}_0^{-1} + \sum_{i=1}^n \mathbf{x}_i\mathbf{x}_i')^{-1}$. Next, the distribution of the latent data conditioned on the data and the parameters factor into a set of n independent distributions, with each depending on the data through y_i:

$$\{z_i\}|\mathbf{y}, \beta \stackrel{d}{=} \prod_{i=1}^{n} z_i|y_i, \beta,$$

where the distribution $z_i|y_i, \beta$ is the distribution $z_i|\beta$ truncated by the knowledge of y_i; if $y_i = 0$, then $z_i \leq 0$ and if $y_i = 1$, then $z_i > 0$. Thus, one samples z_i from $\mathrm{TN}_{(-\infty,0)}(\mathbf{x}_i'\beta, 1)$ if $y_i = 0$ and from $\mathrm{TN}_{(0,\infty)}(\mathbf{x}_i'\beta, 1)$ if $y_i = 1$, where $\mathrm{TN}_{(a,b)}(\mu, \sigma^2)$ denotes the $\mathrm{N}(\mu, \sigma^2)$ distribution truncated to the region (a, b).

5 Estimation of density ordinates

If the full conditional densities are available, then the MCMC output can be used to estimate the posterior marginal density functions (Gelfand and Smith 1990; Tanner and Wong 1987). By definition, the marginal density of $\boldsymbol{\theta}_k$ at the point $\boldsymbol{\theta}_k^*$ is

$$\pi(\boldsymbol{\theta}_k^*|\mathbf{y}) = \int \pi(\boldsymbol{\theta}_k^*|\mathbf{y}, \boldsymbol{\theta}_{-k})\, \pi(\boldsymbol{\theta}_{-k}|\mathbf{y}) d\boldsymbol{\theta}_{-k},$$

where as before $\boldsymbol{\theta}_{-k}$ is $\boldsymbol{\theta}$ excluding $\boldsymbol{\theta}_k$. Provided the normalizing constant of $\pi(\boldsymbol{\theta}_k^*|\mathbf{y}, \boldsymbol{\theta}_{-k})$ is known, the marginal density can be estimated by the sample average

$$\hat{\pi}(\boldsymbol{\theta}_k^*|\mathbf{y}) = G^{-1} \sum_{g=1}^{G} \pi(\boldsymbol{\theta}_k^*|\mathbf{y}, \boldsymbol{\theta}_{-k}^{(g)}).$$

Gelfand and Smith (1990) refer to this as the Rao-Blackwell method because of the connections with the Rao-Blackwell theorem in classical statistics. Chib (1995) extends this method for estimating the posterior density of $\boldsymbol{\theta}_k$, conditioned on one or more of the remaining blocks.

6 Sampler performance and diagnostics

In implementing an MCMC method, it is important to assess the performance of the sampling algorithm to determine the rate of mixing and the size of the burn-in. A large literature is available on this topic, for example, Cowles and Rosenthal (1998), Gamerman and Lopes (2006), Robert and Casella (2004), Fan et al. (2006), and Diaconis et al. (2008).

In practice, convergence (or more properly, lack of convergence) is assessed by informal methods based on the sampled output. For example, one can monitor the autocorrelation plots and the inefficiency factors. Slowly decaying correlations indicate problems with the mixing of the chain. It is also useful in connection with M-H Markov chains to monitor the acceptance rate of the proposal values, with low rates implying "stickiness" in the sampled values and thus a slower approach to the invariant distribution.

The somewhat different issue from assessing non-convergence, that of detecting coding errors, can also be based on the sampled output (Geweke, 2004).

7 Marginal likelihood computation

Computation of the marginal likelihood is of considerable importance in Bayesian statistics because the marginal likelihood is needed for the Bayesian comparison of models (Carlin and Louis, 2008; Congdon, 2006; Geweke, 2005; Robert, 2001).

Consider the situation in which there are K possible models $\mathcal{M}_1, \ldots, \mathcal{M}_K$ for the observed data defined by the sampling densities $\{p(\mathbf{y}|\boldsymbol{\theta}_k, \mathcal{M}_k)\}$ and proper prior densities $\{\pi(\boldsymbol{\theta}_k|\mathcal{M}_k)\}$ and the objective is to find the evidence in the data for the different models. In the Bayesian approach, this question is answered by placing prior probabilities $\Pr(\mathcal{M}_k)$ on each of the K models and using the Bayes calculus to find the posterior probabilities $\{\Pr(\mathcal{M}_1|\mathbf{y}), \ldots, \Pr(\mathcal{M}_K|\mathbf{y})\}$ conditioned on the data but marginalized over the unknowns $\boldsymbol{\theta}_k$. Specifically, the posterior probability of $\mathcal{M}_k$ is given by the expression

$$\begin{aligned}\Pr(\mathcal{M}_k|\mathbf{y}) &= \frac{\Pr(\mathcal{M}_k)m(\mathbf{y}|\mathcal{M}_k)}{\sum_{l=1}^{K}\Pr(\mathcal{M}_l)m(\mathbf{y}|\mathcal{M}_l)} \\ &\propto \Pr(\mathcal{M}_k)m(\mathbf{y}|\mathcal{M}_k)\ , \quad (k \le K)\end{aligned}$$

where

$$m(\mathbf{y}|\mathcal{M}_k) = \int p(\mathbf{y}|\boldsymbol{\theta}_k, \mathcal{M}_k)\pi(\boldsymbol{\theta}_k|\mathcal{M}_k)d\boldsymbol{\theta}_k \tag{5.13}$$

is the marginal density of the data and is called the marginal likelihood of $\mathcal{M}_k$. In words, the posterior probability of $\mathcal{M}_k$ is proportional to the prior probability of $\mathcal{M}_k$ times the marginal likelihood of $\mathcal{M}_k$. The evidence provided by the data about the models under consideration is summarized by the posterior probability of each model.

Often the posterior probabilities are summarized in terms of the posterior odds

$$\frac{\Pr(\mathcal{M}_i|\mathbf{y})}{\Pr(\mathcal{M}_j|\mathbf{y})} = \frac{\Pr(\mathcal{M}_i)}{\Pr(\mathcal{M}_j)}\frac{m(\mathbf{y}|\mathcal{M}_i)}{m(\mathbf{y}|\mathcal{M}_j)},$$

where the first term is the prior odds and the second the Bayes factor of $\mathcal{M}_i$ versus $\mathcal{M}_j$.

Therefore, as part of any complete Bayesian study, it is necessary to get an estimate of the marginal likelihood. The obvious strategy of estimating the marginal likelihood by sampling the prior and averaging the likelihood $p(\mathbf{y}|\boldsymbol{\theta}_k, \mathcal{M}_k)$ tends to be highly inefficient because the prior is rarely concentrated enough in the region where the likelihood has mass. This has led to methods that estimate the marginal likelihood by other means. Green (1995) and Carlin and Chib (1995) first developed methods that involve the joint sampling of parameters and models. Recent applications and developments of these methods include Holmes and Mallick (2003), Dellaportas et al. (2006) and Jasra et al. (2007). These model space methods are particularly useful for the problem of variable selection (Cottet et al., 2008; Lamnisos et al., 2009), but beyond that setting they can be difficult to implement. Here we focus on the method of Chib (1995), which is both general and easy to implement.

For notational simplicity, suppress the model index k. By virtue of the fact that $m(\mathbf{y})$ is the normalizing constant of the posterior density, we can write

$$m(\mathbf{y}) = \frac{p(\mathbf{y}|\boldsymbol{\theta}^*)\pi(\boldsymbol{\theta}^*)}{\pi(\boldsymbol{\theta}^*|\mathbf{y})}, \tag{5.14}$$

for any given point $\boldsymbol{\theta}^*$ (generally taken to be a high density point such as the posterior mode or mean). This implies that we can estimate the marginal likelihood on the log scale as

$$\log m(\mathbf{y}) = \log p(\mathbf{y}|\boldsymbol{\theta}^*) + \log \pi(\boldsymbol{\theta}^*) - \log \hat{\pi}(\boldsymbol{\theta}^*|\mathbf{y}), \tag{5.15}$$

where the first two terms on the right-hand side are generally available in closed form and $\hat{\pi}(\boldsymbol{\theta}^*|\mathbf{y})$ is an estimate of the posterior ordinate. Chib (1995) shows how such an estimate can be found.

Suppose that the MCMC simulation is run with B blocks. Let $\boldsymbol{\Theta}_i = (\boldsymbol{\theta}_1, \ldots, \boldsymbol{\theta}_i)$ and $\boldsymbol{\Theta}^i = (\boldsymbol{\theta}_i, \ldots, \boldsymbol{\theta}_B)$ denote the list of blocks up to i and the set of blocks from i to B, respectively, and let $\mathbf{z}$ denote any latent data that is included in the sampling. Then, we can write

$$\pi(\boldsymbol{\theta}^*|\mathbf{y}) = \pi(\boldsymbol{\theta}_1^*|\mathbf{y}) \times \ldots \times \pi(\boldsymbol{\theta}_i^*|\mathbf{y}, \boldsymbol{\Theta}_{i-1}^*) \times \ldots \times \pi(\boldsymbol{\theta}_B^*|\mathbf{y}, \boldsymbol{\Theta}_{B-1}^*), \tag{5.16}$$

where the typical term is of the form

$$\pi(\boldsymbol{\theta}_i^*|\mathbf{y}, \boldsymbol{\Theta}_{i-1}^*) = \int \pi(\boldsymbol{\theta}_i^*|\mathbf{y}, \ \boldsymbol{\Theta}_{i-1}^*, \boldsymbol{\Theta}^{i+1}, z)\, \pi(\boldsymbol{\Theta}^{i+1}, \mathbf{z}|\, \mathbf{y}, \boldsymbol{\Theta}_{i-1}^*) d\boldsymbol{\Theta}^{i+1} dz.$$

This is the *reduced conditional ordinate* since one is integrating only over $(\boldsymbol{\Theta}^{i+1}, \mathbf{z})$ and the measure is conditioned on $\boldsymbol{\Theta}_{i-1}^*$. One can estimate each of the ordinates in the marginal-conditional decomposition from the output of the full MCMC and suitably designed reduced MCMC runs.

Case 1 Consider first the case where the normalizing constant of each full conditional density is known and MCMC sampling is by the Gibbs algorithm. Then, the first term of (5.16) can be estimated by the Rao-Blackwell method. To estimate the typical reduced conditional ordinate, a reduced MCMC run is set up, consisting of the full conditional distributions

$$\left\{\pi(\boldsymbol{\theta}_i|\mathrm{y},\boldsymbol{\Theta}^*_{i-1},\boldsymbol{\Theta}^{i+1},\mathrm{z});\ \ldots;\ \pi(\boldsymbol{\theta}_B|\mathrm{y},\boldsymbol{\Theta}^*_{i-1},\boldsymbol{\theta}_i,\ldots,\boldsymbol{\theta}_{B-1},\mathrm{z});\ \pi(\mathrm{z}|\mathrm{y},\boldsymbol{\Theta}^*_{i-1},\boldsymbol{\Theta}^i)\right\}, \tag{5.17}$$

where the blocks in $\boldsymbol{\Theta}_{i-1}$ are set equal to $\boldsymbol{\Theta}^*_{i-1}$. By MCMC theory, the draws on $(\boldsymbol{\Theta}^{i+1},\mathrm{z})$ from this run are from the distribution $\pi(\boldsymbol{\Theta}^{i+1},\mathrm{z}|\,\mathrm{y},\boldsymbol{\Theta}^*_{i-1})$ and so the reduced conditional ordinate can be estimated as the average

$$\hat{\pi}(\boldsymbol{\theta}^*_i\,|\,\mathrm{y},\boldsymbol{\Theta}^*_{i-1}) = G^{-1}\sum_{g=1}^{G}\pi(\boldsymbol{\theta}^*_i|\mathrm{y},\boldsymbol{\Theta}^*_{i-1},\boldsymbol{\Theta}^{i+1,(g)},\mathrm{z}^{(g)})$$

over the simulated values of $\boldsymbol{\Theta}^{i+1}$ and z from the reduced run. Each subsequent reduced conditional ordinate that appears in the decomposition (5.16) is estimated in the same way though, conveniently, with fewer and fewer distributions appearing in the reduced runs. Given the marginal and reduced conditional ordinates, the marginal likelihood on the log scale is available as

$$\log\hat{m}(\mathrm{y}|) = \log p(\mathrm{y}|\boldsymbol{\theta}^*) + \log\pi(\boldsymbol{\theta}^*) - \sum_{i=1}^{B}\log\hat{\pi}(\boldsymbol{\theta}^*_i|\mathrm{y},\boldsymbol{\Theta}^*_{i-1}), \tag{5.18}$$

where $p(\mathrm{y}|\boldsymbol{\theta}^*)$ is the density of the data marginalized over the latent data z.

Case 2 Consider next the case where the normalizing constant of one or more of the full conditional densities is not known and sampling is by the M-H algorithm. In that case, the posterior ordinate can be estimated by a modified method developed by Chib and Jeliazkov (2001). If sampling is conducted in one block by the M-H algorithm with proposal density $q(\boldsymbol{\theta}^{(g)},\boldsymbol{\theta}^\dagger|\mathrm{y})$ and probability of move

$$\alpha(\boldsymbol{\theta}^{(g)},\boldsymbol{\theta}^\dagger|\mathrm{y}) = \min\left\{1,\frac{\pi(\boldsymbol{\theta}^\dagger|\mathrm{y})q(\boldsymbol{\theta}^\dagger,\boldsymbol{\theta}^{(g)}|\mathrm{y})}{\pi(\boldsymbol{\theta}^{(g)}|\mathrm{y})q(\boldsymbol{\theta}^{(g)},\boldsymbol{\theta}^\dagger|\mathrm{y})}\right\},$$

then it can be shown that the posterior ordinate is given by

$$\pi(\boldsymbol{\theta}^*|\mathrm{y}) = \frac{\mathbb{E}_1\left\{\alpha(\boldsymbol{\theta},\boldsymbol{\theta}^*|\mathrm{y})q(\boldsymbol{\theta},\boldsymbol{\theta}^*|\mathrm{y})\right\}}{\mathbb{E}_2\left\{\alpha(\boldsymbol{\theta}^*,\boldsymbol{\theta}|\mathrm{y})\right\}},$$

where the numerator expectation $\mathbb{E}_1$ is with respect to the distribution $\pi(\boldsymbol{\theta}|\mathrm{y})$ and the denominator expectation $\mathbb{E}_2$ is with respect to the proposal density $q(\boldsymbol{\theta}^*,\boldsymbol{\theta}|\mathrm{y})$. This leads to the simulation consistent estimate

$$\hat{\pi}(\boldsymbol{\theta}^*|\mathrm{y}) = \frac{G^{-1}\sum_{g=1}^{G}\alpha(\boldsymbol{\theta}^{(g)},\boldsymbol{\theta}^*|\mathrm{y})q(\boldsymbol{\theta}^{(g)},\boldsymbol{\theta}^*|\mathrm{y})}{J^{-1}\sum_{j=1}^{M}\alpha(\boldsymbol{\theta}^*,\boldsymbol{\theta}^{(j)}|\mathrm{y})}, \tag{5.19}$$

where $\boldsymbol{\theta}^{(g)}$ are the given draws from the posterior distribution, while the draws $\boldsymbol{\theta}^{(j)}$ in the denominator are from $q(\boldsymbol{\theta}^*,\boldsymbol{\theta}|\mathrm{y})$, given the fixed value $\boldsymbol{\theta}^*$.

In general, when sampling is done with B blocks, the typical reduced conditional ordinate is given by

$$\pi(\boldsymbol{\theta}_i^*|\mathrm{y}, \boldsymbol{\Theta}_{i-1}^*) = \frac{\mathbb{E}_1\left\{\alpha(\boldsymbol{\theta}_i, \boldsymbol{\theta}_i^*|\mathrm{y}, \boldsymbol{\Theta}_{i-1}^*, \boldsymbol{\Theta}^{i+1}, \mathrm{z})q_i(\boldsymbol{\theta}_i, \boldsymbol{\theta}_i^*|\mathrm{y}, \boldsymbol{\Theta}_{i-1}^*, \boldsymbol{\Theta}^{i+1}, \mathrm{z})\right\}}{\mathbb{E}_2\left\{\alpha(\boldsymbol{\theta}_i^*, \boldsymbol{\theta}_i|\mathrm{y}, \boldsymbol{\Theta}_{i-1}^*, \boldsymbol{\Theta}^{i+1}, \mathrm{z})\right\}}, \quad (5.20)$$

where $\mathbb{E}_1$ is the expectation with respect to $\pi(\boldsymbol{\Theta}^i, \mathrm{z}|\mathrm{y}, \boldsymbol{\Theta}_{i-1}^*)$ and $\mathbb{E}_2$ that with respect to the product measure $\pi(\boldsymbol{\Theta}^{i+1}, \mathrm{z}|\mathrm{y}, \boldsymbol{\theta}_i^*)q_i(\boldsymbol{\theta}_i^*, \boldsymbol{\theta}_i|\mathrm{y}, \boldsymbol{\Theta}_{i-1}^*, \boldsymbol{\Theta}^{i+1})$. The quantity $\alpha(\boldsymbol{\theta}_i, \boldsymbol{\theta}_i^*|\mathrm{y}, \boldsymbol{\Theta}_{i-1}^*, \boldsymbol{\Theta}^{i+1}, \mathrm{z})$ is the M-H probability of move. The two expectations are estimated from the output of the reduced runs in an obvious way.

8 Examples

8.1 Jump-diffusion model

To illustrate use of MCMC methods in a practical problem, we consider an example that is drawn from Chan and Wong (2006). The fitting of this model highlights several interesting MCMC aspects:

- multiple block MCMC sampling in which each block is updated by proposing from its (tractable) full conditional distribution;
- marginalization to improve the efficiency of the sampling;
- treatment of mixture distributions;
- involvement of latent variables to simplify sampling.

In the model we consider, it is assumed that returns (in continuous time) are given by

$$d\log r_t = \mu dt + J_t dN_t + \sigma dW_t$$

where

$$J_t|\boldsymbol{\theta} \sim \mathcal{N}(k, s^2)$$

is the jump component, N_t is a Poisson process with intensity λ, W_t is the Wiener process, and

$$\boldsymbol{\theta} = (\mu, k, \sigma^2, s^2, \lambda)$$

the parameters.

Now suppose that this process is observed at the n equi-spaced time points $t_1, \ldots, t_n$ over the interval $(0, T)$, where $t_{i+1} = t_i + \Delta$ $(i = 0, 1, \ldots, n)$, $t_0 = 0$, $t_n = T$, and $\Delta = T/n$. Then, taking the Euler discretization, we have the model

$$\log r_{t_{i+1}} - \log r_{t_i} = \mu\Delta + J_{t_i}(N_{t_{i+1}} - N_{t_i}) + \sigma(W_{t_{i+1}} - W_{t_i}),$$

which we can denote as

$$y_t = \mu\Delta + J_t \Delta N_t + \varepsilon_t, \tag{5.21}$$

where from the properties of the Poisson and Wiener processes

$$\Delta N_t | \boldsymbol{\theta} \sim \mathcal{B}er(q),$$

a Bernoulli random variable with probability of success $q = \lambda\Delta$ and

$$\varepsilon_t | \boldsymbol{\theta} \sim \mathcal{N}(0, \sigma^2 \Delta).$$

Under these asssumptions, it is obvious that

$$p(y_t | J_t, \Delta N_t, \boldsymbol{\theta}) = \mathcal{N}(y_t | \mu\Delta + J_t \Delta N_t, \sigma^2 \Delta). \tag{5.22}$$

Now given the form of the model in (5.22), it is clear that the prior-posterior analysis will be aided by including $\{J_t\}$ and $\{\Delta N_t\}$ in the sampling. But one has to be careful, because J_t and ΔN_t appear as a product and neither one is observed. As a result, sampling one conditioned on the other is likely to produce highly correlated output. This point is made by Chib et al. (2006) in the context of factor models. The solution is to sample ΔN_t marginalized over J_t. Marginalization over J_t also helps in the sampling of μ, as noted by Chib and Carlin (1999) in the context of panel models where the equivalent of J_t is the random effect. With this in mind, the distribution of y_t marginalized over J_t can be calculated as

$$p(y_t | \Delta N_t, \boldsymbol{\theta}) = \mathcal{N}(y_t | x_t' \boldsymbol{\beta}, V_t), \tag{5.23}$$

where $\boldsymbol{\beta} = (\mu, k)'$,

$$x_t' = (\Delta, \Delta N_t), \text{ and}$$
$$V_t = \sigma^2 \Delta + s^2 \Delta N_t.$$

Here we made use of the fact that $(\Delta N_t)^2 = \Delta N_t$. A final integration over the distribution of ΔN_t shows that the density of y_t is a two-component mixture of normal distributions

$$\begin{aligned} p(y_t | \boldsymbol{\theta}) &= q p(y_t | \Delta N_t = 1, \boldsymbol{\theta}) + (1 - q) p(y_t | \Delta N_t = 0, \boldsymbol{\theta}) \\ &= q \mathcal{N}(y_t | \mu\Delta + k, \sigma^2 \Delta + s^2) + (1 - q) \mathcal{N}(y_t | \mu\Delta, \sigma^2 \Delta). \end{aligned}$$

Therefore, given independently distributed outcomes $\mathrm{y} = (y_1, \ldots, y_n)$, the joint distribution of the outcomes is

$$p(\mathrm{y} | \boldsymbol{\theta}) = \prod_{t=1}^{n} \left\{ q \mathcal{N}(y_t | \mu\Delta + k, \sigma^2 \Delta + s^2) + (1 - q) \mathcal{N}(y_t | \mu\Delta, \sigma^2 \Delta) \right\}. \tag{5.24}$$

Even though this is a mixture model, the usual problem of "label-switching" does not arise here because the first component, which is unambiguously different from the second, occurs with probability q that can be expected to be substantially smaller than $(1-q)$. Thus, the first component, in which $\Delta N_t = 1$, cannot be switched with the second component, in which $\Delta N_t = 0$, without changing the probability distribution of the data.

To show how this model can be estimated, we simulate data from this model under the assumption that $T = 10$ (for ten years), $\Delta = 1/250$ (corresponding to daily data measured in years assuming 250 trading days), $\mu = 0.08$ (corresponding to an 8% annual rate of return), $k = 0$, $s^2 = 0.15$, $\lambda = 5$ (corresponding to five jumps on average every year) and $\sigma = 0.3$ (correspoding to an annual volatility of 30%). The $n = 2,500$ observations that we have simulated are given in Figure 5.7.

For doing inference, suppose that the following prior distribution is appropriate:

$$\boldsymbol{\beta} = (\mu, k)' \sim \mathcal{N}_2(\boldsymbol{\beta}_0, \mathbf{B}_0)$$
$$\sigma^2 \sim \mathcal{IG}(\frac{\nu_0}{2}, \frac{\delta_0}{2})$$
$$s^2 \sim \mathcal{IG}(\frac{\nu_{00}}{2}, \frac{\delta_{00}}{2})$$
$$q \sim \mathcal{B}eta(a_0, b_0),$$

where $\boldsymbol{\beta}_0 = (0.05, 0)$, $\mathbf{B}_0 = \text{diag}(0.01, 0.01)$, $\nu_0 = 12$, $\delta_0 = 1$, $\nu_{00} = 4.889$, $\delta_{00} = 0.058$, $a_0 = 0.9$, and $b_0 = 12.1$. Our MCMC algorithm is defined in terms of four blocks as follows.

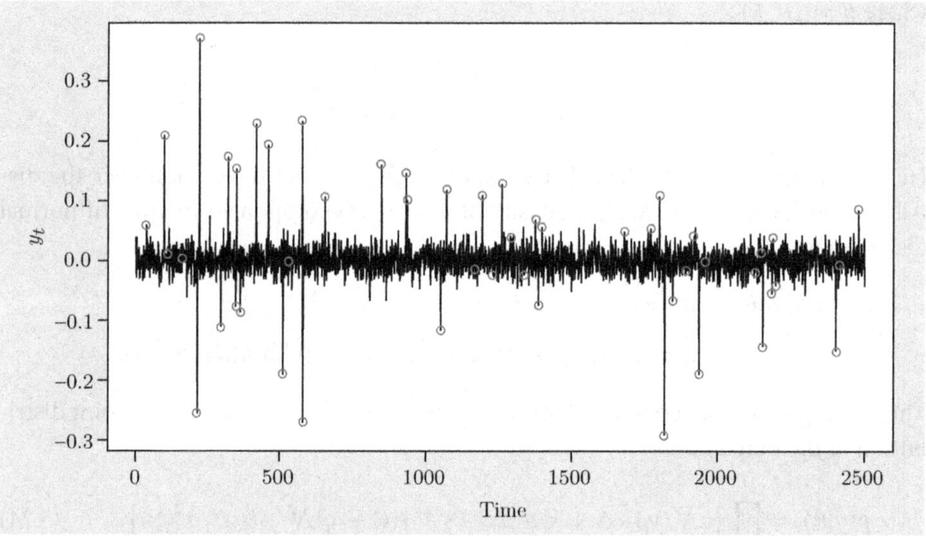

FIGURE 5.7 Simulated data from the jump-diffusion model

Notes: Observations that include the jump component are circled.

(1) Sample $(\boldsymbol{\beta}, q)$ from $\pi(\boldsymbol{\beta}, q|\{y_t\}, \{\Delta N_t\}, \sigma^2, s^2)$. On combining the model in (5.23) with the prior of $\boldsymbol{\beta}$ and q, one sees that $\boldsymbol{\beta}$ and q are a posteriori independent and that

$$\begin{aligned}\pi(\boldsymbol{\beta}, q|\{y_t\}, \{\Delta N_t\}, \sigma^2, s^2) &= \pi(\boldsymbol{\beta}|\{y_t\}, \{\Delta N_t\}, \sigma^2)\pi(q|\{\Delta N_t\}) \\ &= \mathcal{N}_2(\boldsymbol{\beta}|\hat{\boldsymbol{\beta}}, \mathbf{B})\text{Beta}(q|a_0 + n_1, b_0 + (n - n_1))\end{aligned}$$

where

$$\mathbf{B} = \left(\mathbf{B}_0^{-1} + \sum_{t=1}^{n} x_t V_t^{-1} x_t'\right)^{-1}$$

$$\hat{\boldsymbol{\beta}} = \mathbf{B}\left(\mathbf{B}_0^{-1}\boldsymbol{\beta}_0 + \sum_{t=1}^{n} x_t V_t^{-1} y_t\right)$$

and n_1 is the sum of ΔN_t (i.e. the number of jumps in the sample).

(2) Sample ΔN_t from $\Delta N_t|y_t, \boldsymbol{\theta}$ for $t = 1, \ldots, n$. Since ΔN_t takes the values 1 or 0, with prior probabilities q and $(1 - q)$ respectively, it follows by Bayes theorem that the updated probabilities are

$$\Pr(\Delta N_t = 1|y_t, \boldsymbol{\theta}) \propto qp(y_t|\Delta N_t = 1, \boldsymbol{\theta}) \propto q\mathcal{N}(y_t|\mu\Delta + k, \sigma^2\Delta + s^2)$$

$$\Pr(\Delta N_t = 0|y_t, \boldsymbol{\theta}) \propto (1 - q)p(y_t|\Delta N_t = 0, \boldsymbol{\theta}) \propto (1 - q)\mathcal{N}(y_t|\mu\Delta, \sigma^2\Delta).$$

(3) Sample J_t (whenever $\Delta N_t = 1$) from $J_t|y_t, \Delta N_t = 1, \boldsymbol{\theta}$. This distribution can be derived as a regression update from the model

$$y_t - \mu\Delta = J_t + \varepsilon_t.$$

A simple calculation shows that this distribution is

$$\mathcal{N}(\hat{J}_t, Q_t),$$

where

$$Q_t = \left(s^{-2} + \left(\sigma^2\Delta\right)^{-1}\right)^{-1}$$

and

$$\hat{J}_t = Q_t\left(s^{-2}k + \left(\sigma^2\Delta\right)^{-1}(y_t - \mu\Delta)\right).$$

(4) Sample σ^2 and s^2 from $(\sigma^2, s^2)|\{y_t\}, \{\Delta N_t\}, \{J_t\}, \boldsymbol{\beta}, q$. Again by well-known Bayesian calculations it is easily checked that σ^2 and s^2 are independent and that

$$\pi(\sigma^2, s^2|\{y_t\}, \{\Delta N_t\}, \{J_t\}, \boldsymbol{\beta}, q) = \pi(\sigma^2|\{y_t\}, \{\Delta N_t\}, \{J_t\}, \boldsymbol{\beta})\pi(s^2|\{J_t\}, \boldsymbol{\beta})$$

$$= \mathcal{IG}\left(\sigma^2|\frac{\nu_0 + n}{2}, \frac{\delta_0 + \frac{1}{\Delta}\sum(y_t - \mu\Delta - J_t\Delta N_t)^2}{2}\right)\mathcal{IG}\left(s^2|\frac{\nu_{00} + n}{2}, \frac{\delta_{00} + \sum(J_t - k)^2}{2}\right).$$

Table 5.1: Posterior summary: jump-diffusion model

	Prior		Posterior				
	Mean	SD	Mean	SD	Lower	Upper	Ineff.
μ	0.050	0.100	0.042	0.070	-0.095	0.177	1.000
k	0.000	0.100	0.016	0.024	-0.030	0.064	1.000
σ^2	0.100	0.050	0.091	0.003	0.086	0.096	1.000
$s2$	0.040	0.020	0.025	0.006	0.016	0.038	1.200
q	0.050	0.050	0.018	0.003	0.012	0.025	1.997

We run our MCMC algorithm for 21,000 iterations, and drop the first 1,000 as part of the burn-in. We summarize the posterior distribution by calculating the sample mean, standard deviation, and 0.025 and 0.975 quantiles from the sampled draws. These are the MCMC estimates of the corresponding posterior parameters. We also calculate the inefficiency factors from the sampled output. These results, along with the prior mean and prior standard deviations, are given in Table 5.1. These results show that in this problem it is difficult to estimate the parameter μ given the noise in the sample, but that the parameter estimates are still close to the true values that were used to generate the data. The inefficiency factors in the last column of the table are small and show that the sampler has mixed almost as well as a hypothetical independence sample. We also use the sampled output to calculate the marginal posterior densities of the parameters. These are calculated by kernel smoothing and are reported in the top panel of Figure 5.8. The bottom panel of the figure has the autocorrelation functions from the sampled draws. These decline quickly, as one would expect given the small values of the inefficiency factors.

8.2 DSGE model

As another interesting illustration, we consider the application of MCMC methods in the analysis of DSGE models (Del Negro and Schorfheide, Chapter 7, this volume). An interesting feature of DSGE models is that because of the complex process that is used to solve the model, the structural parameters appear in the reduced form model in a highly nonlinear way that cannot be described in closed form. This nonlinearity poses a serious challenge for inference. The method of maximum likelihood does not always deliver parameter estimates that are reasonable on a priori grounds. Interestingly, the Bayesian approach provides a useful alternative to frequentist approaches because the prior distribution can be used to concentrate attention on regions of the parameter space that are economically meaningful.

To demonstrate the issues involved, we consider the relatively small-scale DSGE model in Ireland (2004). The linearized model, derived by log-linearizing the original

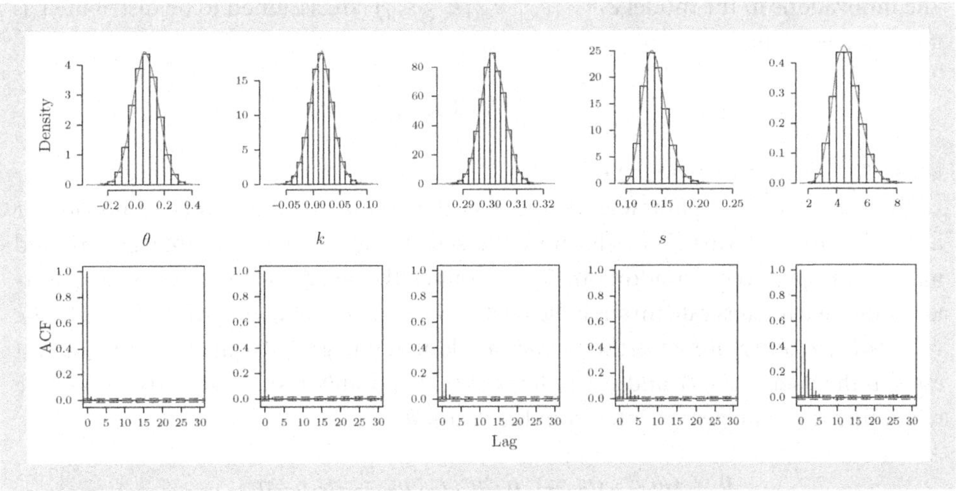

FIGURE 5.8 Jump-diffusion model: marginal posterior densities and acf's of the sampled draws

Notes: Results based on $n_0 = 1,000$, $G = 20,000$.

non-linear model around its deterministic steady state (Ireland, 2004), is expressed by the following system of equations

$$\begin{aligned}
\hat{x}_t &= \alpha_x \hat{x}_{t-1} + (1-\alpha_x)\mathbb{E}_t\hat{x}_{t+1} - (\hat{r}_t - \mathbb{E}_t\hat{\pi}_{t+1}) + (1-\omega)(1-\rho_a)\hat{a}_t \\
\hat{\pi}_t &= \beta\alpha_\pi\hat{\pi}_{t-1} + \beta(1-\alpha_\pi)\mathbb{E}_t\hat{\pi}_{t+1} + \psi\hat{x}_t - \hat{e}_t \\
\hat{g}_t &= \hat{y}_t - \hat{y}_{t-1} + \hat{z}_t \\
\hat{x}_t &= \hat{y}_t - \omega\hat{a}_t \\
\hat{r}_t &= \rho_r\hat{r}_{t-1} + \rho_\pi\hat{\pi}_t + \rho_g\hat{g}_t + \rho_x\hat{x}_t + \varepsilon_{r,t},
\end{aligned} \tag{5.25}$$

where x_t, g_t, π_t, r_t, and y_t denote output gap, output growth, inflation, nominal interest rate, and stochastically detrended output, respectively, and the hats denote log-deviation of the variables from their steady-state or average values; $\mathbb{E}_t$ denotes the expectation of the relevant variables by the agents in this economy, formed under rational expectations; finally, $\hat{a}_t$, $\hat{e}_t$, and $\hat{z}_t$ capture exogenous shifts in preferences, costs of production, and technology, respectively. These equations, in descending order, represent a forward-looking IS curve, a new Keynesian Phillips curve, growth rate of output, growth rate of output gap, and the modified Taylor rule (1993). Further, it is assumed that the exogenous driving processes $\hat{a}_t$, $\hat{e}_t$, and $\hat{z}_t$ evolve independently of one another as

$$\begin{aligned}
\hat{a}_t &= \rho_a\hat{a}_{t-1} + \varepsilon_{a,t} \\
\hat{e}_t &= \rho_e\hat{e}_{t-1} + \varepsilon_{e,t} \\
\hat{z}_t &= \varepsilon_{z,t}.
\end{aligned} \tag{5.26}$$

The innovations in the model $\boldsymbol{\varepsilon}_t = [\varepsilon_{a,t}, \varepsilon_{e,t}, \varepsilon_{z,t}, \varepsilon_{r,t}]'$ are assumed to be distributed as multivariate normal

$$\boldsymbol{\varepsilon}_t \sim \mathcal{N}_4(\mathbf{0}, \Omega),$$

where $\Omega = \text{diag}(\sigma_a^2, \sigma_e^2, \sigma_z^2, \sigma_r^2)$.

There are two other parameters z and π in the nonlinear model (that do not appear in the linearized form) that determine the steady-state values of output growth and inflation, respectively. In addition, β determines the steady-state value of the short-term nominal interest rate through the relation $\bar{r} = z\pi/\beta$. Following Ireland (2004), the values of z, π, and β are set to the average levels of output growth, inflation, and interest rates in the data. Also, ψ and ρ_r are fixed at 0.10 and 1.00, respectively. We collect the remaining 12 parameters of interest in the vector $\boldsymbol{\theta}$

$$\boldsymbol{\theta} = (\omega, \alpha_x, \alpha_\pi, \rho_\pi, \rho_g, \rho_x, \rho_a, \rho_e, \sigma_a, \sigma_e, \sigma_z, \sigma_r).$$

The parameters $(\omega, \alpha_x, \alpha_\pi, \rho_\pi, \rho_g, \rho_x)$, where $\omega, \alpha_x, \alpha_\pi$ are each assumed to be between 0 and 1, and each of ρ_π, ρ_g, and ρ_x are greater than 0, may be called the structural parameters. It is also assumed that (ρ_a, ρ_e) each lie between 0 and 1. Let $\mathcal{S}_L$ denote the subset of $\mathcal{R}^{12}$ satisfying these linear constraints. In addition, one is interested in restricting the parameters to the determinacy region of the solution space. Denote this constraint set by $\mathcal{S}_D$. Finally, the variance parameters σ_i^2 lie in the region $\mathcal{S}_\Omega$ that satisfies the usual positivity and positive definiteness constraints.

It is now assumed that for a given value of $\boldsymbol{\theta}$, the model is solved subject to the determinacy constraint to produce a Markov process in the endogenous variables of the model

$$\mathbf{s}_t = \mathbf{D}(\boldsymbol{\theta})\mathbf{s}_{t-1} + \mathbf{F}(\boldsymbol{\theta})\boldsymbol{\varepsilon}_t, \tag{5.27}$$

where

$$\mathbf{s}_t = [\hat{y}_t, \hat{r}_t, \hat{\pi}_t, \hat{g}_t, \hat{x}_t, \hat{a}_t, \hat{e}_t, \hat{z}_t, \mathbb{E}_t\hat{\pi}_{t+1}, \mathbb{E}_t\hat{x}_{t+1}]'$$

and $\boldsymbol{\varepsilon}_t$ is as defined above. Moreover, the matrices $\mathbf{D}(\boldsymbol{\theta})$ and $\mathbf{F}(\boldsymbol{\theta})$ are awkward implicit functions of the model parameters, obtained (numerically) from the solution.

The data for the fitting are the series of demeaned log-deviations of output growth $\hat{g}_t$, inflation $\hat{\pi}_t$, and the short-term nominal interest rate $\hat{r}_t$ from their steady-state or average values for the period 1980:I to 2003:I, with all three observables measured in decimal units. The resulting measurement equation has the straightforward form

$$\underbrace{\begin{bmatrix} \hat{g}_t \\ \hat{\pi}_t \\ \hat{r}_t \end{bmatrix}}_{\mathbf{y}_t} = \underbrace{\begin{bmatrix} 0&0&0&1&0&0&0&0&0&0 \\ 0&0&1&0&0&0&0&0&0&0 \\ 0&1&0&0&0&0&0&0&0&0 \end{bmatrix}}_{\mathbf{B}} \mathbf{s}_t. \tag{5.28}$$

Table 5.2: Posterior sampling results using the TaRB-MH algorithm for the Ireland (2004) model

	Prior		Posterior			
Parameter	Mean	Standard deviation	Mean	Numerical S.E.	90% interval	Inefficiency factors
ω	0.20	0.10	0.1089	0.0010	[0.0381,0.2036]	5.2791
α_x	0.10	0.05	0.0778	0.0006	[0.0186,0.1669]	2.7625
α_π	0.10	0.05	0.0807	0.0009	[0.0184,0.1819]	4.9731
ρ_π	0.30	0.10	0.5522	0.0023	[0.3341,0.7767]	4.1913
ρ_g	0.30	0.10	0.3747	0.0011	[0.2751,0.4867]	3.9146
ρ_x	0.25	0.0625	0.2001	0.0016	[0.1108,0.3134]	9.2058
ρ_a	0.85	0.10	0.9310	0.0008	[0.8814,0.9662]	15.013
ρ_e	0.85	0.10	0.8674	0.0016	[0.7582,0.9555]	9.7198
$10000\sigma_a^2$	30.00	30.00	15.7994	0.3784	[6.0171,38.228]	15.814
$10000\sigma_e^2$	0.08	1.00	0.0068	0.0000	[0.0041,0.0107]	6.2913
$10000\sigma_z^2$	5.00	15.00	0.7633	0.0030	[0.4785,1.1145]	3.1988
$10000\sigma_r^2$	0.50	2.00	0.0969	0.0005	[0.0635,0.1443]	6.3380

Note: The results reported in this table are based on the prior mean as the starting value. However, the results are insensitive to this choice.

Given this state space representation, the likelihood function is calculated by the usual Kalman filtering recursions. To complete the model, one needs to specify a prior distribution for the parameters, which, as mentioned above, can play an important role in the estimation of DSGE models. We construct our prior by reasoning in terms of the implied distribution of the data. Our prior is summarized in Table 5.2. This prior implies a quarterly deviation, as measured by the 90% interval, of roughly 4.5% for output and the rate of interest, and around 5% in the case of inflation.

Our interest lies in the posterior distribution resulting from the combination of the likelihood function and the prior distribution. We summarize the posterior distribution with the help of the TaRB-MH algorithm of Chib and Ramamurthy (2010). As discussed above, in this algorithm, the parameters are updated in blocks by the M-H algorithm, but the number and composition of the blocks is randomized in every MCMC iteration. The M-H proposal density of each block is in turn obtained by tailoring to the target, as described earlier in the context of the choice of proposal density in Section 3. That is, the proposal density takes the form of a multivariate student-*t* with 15 degrees of freedom and with location and dispersion that are the mode and negative inverse Hessian of the target. In the current problem, the latter quantities are found from the output of simulated annealing, a powerful stochastic optimization method that proves helpful when standard gradient-based optimizers are difficult to implement (for a detailed discussion on the implementation of simulated annealing, the reader is referred to Chib and Ramamurthy, 2010). The TaRB-MH chain is initialized at the prior mean and run for 11,000 iterations. The first 1,000 draws are discarded as part of the burn-in.

The posterior summary from this algorithm is given in Table 5.2. As can be seen from the table, the inefficiency factors are all mostly in the single digits, indicating a well-mixing chain. Figure 5.9 gives the prior-posterior plots and autocorrelation functions for the structural and autoregressive parameters of the model. As can be observed, for most parameters, the likelihood function carries information beyond that contained in the prior. These plots also show that the serial correlations among the draws decay

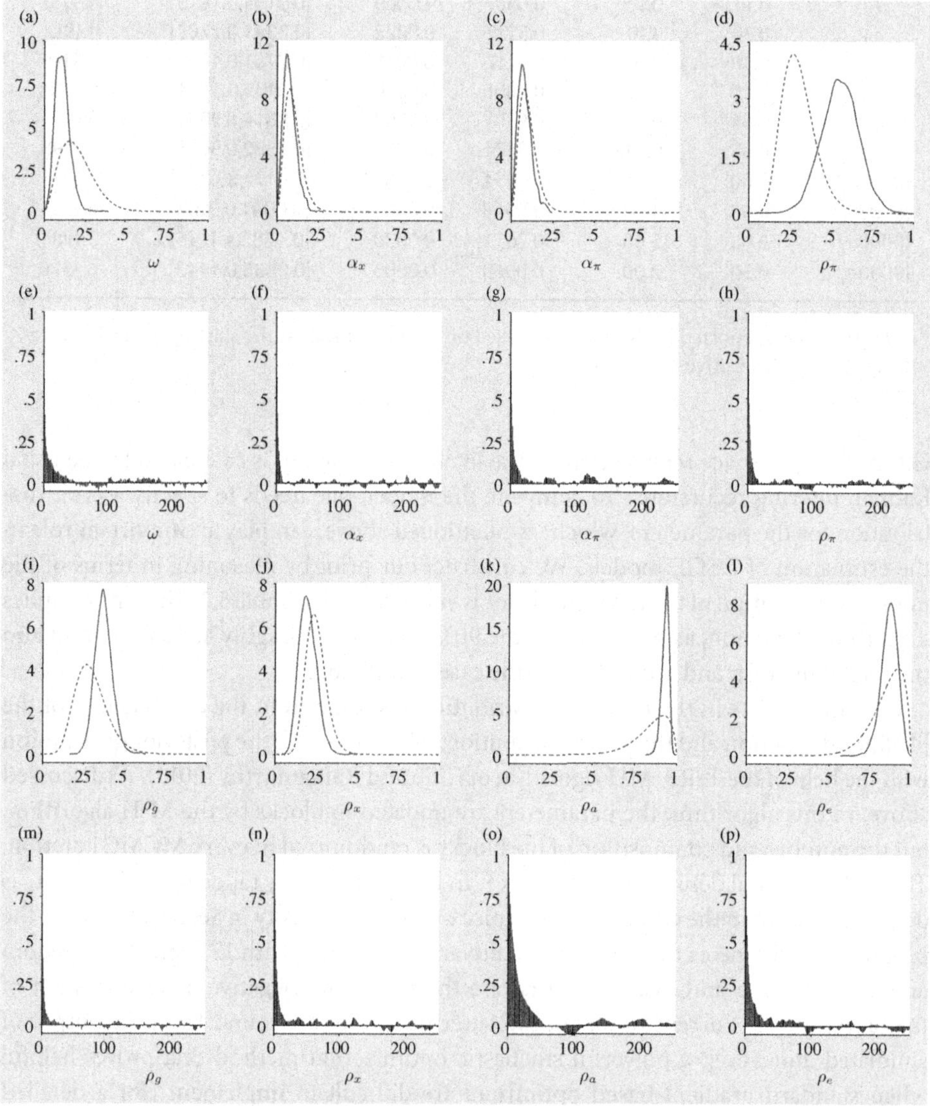

FIGURE 5.9 Sampling results for the Ireland (2004) model using the TaRB-MH algorithm: marginal prior-posterior plots and autocorrelation functions for the structural and autoregressive parameters

quickly to zero. The success of the MCMC sampling is further revealed by the fact that the results are virtually identical, regardless of where the chain is initialized.

9 Concluding remarks

It should be clear from this survey that the importance of MCMC methods for Bayesian statistics and econometrics cannot be overstated. The remarkable growth of Bayesian thinking over the last 20 years has been made possible largely by the innovative use of MCMC methods, as the chapters in this book so amply confirm.

References

Albert, J. H., and Chib, S. (1993a), "Bayes Inference via Gibbs Sampling of Autoregressive Time Series Subject to Markov Mean and Variance Shifts," *Journal of Business and Economic Statistics*, 11, 1–15.

—— —— (1993b), "Bayesian Analysis of Binary and Polychotomous Response Data," *Journal of the American Statistical Association*, 88: 669–79.

Carlin, B. P. and Chib, S. (1995), "Bayesian Model Choice via Markov Chain Monte Carlo Methods," *Journal of the Royal Statistical Society, Series B*, 57: 473–84.

—— and Louis, T. (2008), *Bayes and Empirical Bayes Methods for Data Analysis*, 3rd edn., Boca Raton, Fla.: Chapman & Hall.

—— Polson, N. G., and Stoffer, D. (1992), "A Monte Carlo Approach to Nonnormal and Nonlinear State-Space Modelling," *Journal of the American Statistical Association*, 87: 493–500.

Carter, C. K., and Kohn, R. (1994), "On Gibbs Sampling for State-Space Models," *Biometrika*, 81: 541–53.

Chan, N. H., and Wong, H. Y. (2006), *Simulation Techniques in Financial Risk Management*, New York: John Wiley and Sons.

Chib, S. (1992), "Bayes Inference in the Tobit Censored Regression Model," *Journal of Econometrics*, 51: 79–99.

—— (1995), "Marginal Likelihood from the Gibbs Output," *Journal of the American Statistical Association*, 90: 1313–21.

—— (1996), "Calculating Posterior Distributions and Modal Estimates in Markov Mixture Models," *Journal of Econometrics*, 75: 79–97.

—— (2001), "Markov Chain Monte Carlo Methods: Computation and Inference," in J. J. Heckman and E., Leamer (eds.), *Handbook of Econometrics*, vol. 5, Amsterdam: North-Holland, 3569–649.

—— and Carlin, B. (1999), "On MCMC Sampling in Hierarchical Longitudinal Models," *Statistics and Computing*, 9: 17–26.

—— and Greenberg, E. (1994), "Bayes Inference in Regression Models with ARMA (p,q) Errors," *Journal of Econometrics*, 64: 183–206.

—— —— (1995), "Understanding the Metropolis-Hastings Algorithm," *The American Statistician*, 49: 327–35.

Chib, S. and Jeliazkov, I. (2001), "Marginal Likelihood from the Metropolis-Hastings Output," *Journal of the American Statistical Association*, 96: 270–81.

——— Nardari F., and Shephard, N. (2006), "Analysis of High Dimensional Multivariate Stochastic Volanility Models," *Journal of Econometrics*, 134: 341–71.

——— and Ramamurthy, S. (2010), "Tailored Randomized-block MCMC Methods with Application to DSGE Models," *Journal of Econometrics*, 155: 19–38.

Congdon, P. (2006), *Bayesian Statistical Modelling*, 2nd edn., Chichester: John Wiley & Sons.

Cottet, R., Kohn, R. J., and Nott, D. J. (2008), "Variable Selection and Model Averaging in Semiparametric Overdispersed Generalized Linear Models," *Journal of the American Statistical Association*, 103: 661–71.

Cowles, M. K. and Rosenthal, J. S. (1998), "A Simulation Approach to Convergence Rates for Markov Chain Monte Carlo Algorithms," *Statistics and Computing*, 8: 115–24.

Damien, P., Wakefield, J., and Walker, S. (1999), "Gibbs Sampling for Bayesian Non-conjugate and Hierarchical Models by Using Auxiliary Variables," *Journal of the Royal Statistical Society Series B—Statistical Methodology*, 61: 331–44.

Del Moral, P., Doucet, A., and Jasra, A. (2006), "Sequential Monte Carlo Samplers," *Journal of the Royal Statistical Society Series B—Statistical Methodology*, 68: 411–36.

Dellaportas, P., Friel, N., and Roberts, G. O. (2006), "Bayesian Model Selection for Partially Observed Diffusion Models," *Biometrika*, 93: 809–25.

Diaconis, P., Khare, K., and Saloff-Coste, L. (2008), "Gibbs Sampling, Exponential Families and Orthogonal Polynomials," *Statistical Science*, 23: 151–78.

Fan, Y., Brooks, S. P., and Gelman, A. (2006), "Output Assessment for Monte Carlo Simulations via the Score Statistic," *Journal of Computational and Graphical Statistics*, 15: 178–206.

Frühwirth-Schnatter, S. (1994), "Data Augmentation and Dynamic Linear Models," *Journal of Time Series Analysis*, 15: 183–202.

Gamerman, D., and Lopes, H. F. (2006), *Markov Chain Monte Carlo: Stochastic Simulation for Bayesian Inference*, 2nd edn., Boca Raton, Fla.: Chapman and Hall/CRC.

Gelfand, A. E., and Smith, A. F. (1990), "Sampling-Based Approaches to Calculating Marginal Densities," *Journal of the American Statistical Association*, 85: 398–409.

Geman, S., and Geman, D. (1984), "Stochastic Relaxation, Gibbs Distribution and the Bayesian Restoration of Images," *IEEE Transactions, PAMI*, 6: 721–41.

Geweke, J. (1989), "Bayesian Inference in Econometric Models Using Monte Carlo Integration," *Econometrica*, 57: 1317–39.

——— (2004), "Getting it Right: Joint Distribution Tests of Posterior Simulators," *Journal of the American Statistical Association*, 99: 799–804.

——— (2005), *Contemporary Bayesian Econometrics and Statistics*, Hoboken, NJ: John Wiley & Sons.

Green, P. J. (1995), "Reversible Jump Markov chain Monte Carlo Computation and Bayesian Model Determination," *Biometrika*, 82: 711–32.

Hastings, W. K. (1970), "Monte-Carlo Sampling Methods Using Markov Chains and their Applications," *Biometrika*, 57: 97–109.

Holmes, C. C., and Mallick, B. K. (2003), "Generalized Nonlinear Modeling with Multivariate Free-Knot Regression Splines," *Journal of the American Statistical Association*, 98: 352–68.

Ireland, P. N. (2004), "Technology Shocks in the New Keynesian Model," *The Review of Economics and Statistics*, 86: 923–36.

Jasra, A., Stephens, D. A., and Holmes, C. C. (2007), "Population-Based Reversible Jump Markov Chain Monte Carlo," *Biometrika*, 94: 787–807.

Jones, G. L., Haran, M., Caffo, B. S., and Neath, R. (2006), "Fixed-Width Output Analysis for Markov Chain Monte Carlo," *Journal of the American Statistical Association*, 101: 1537–47.

Kim, S., Shephard, N., and Chib, S. (1998), "Stochastic Volatility: Likelihood Inference and Comparison with ARCH Models," *Review of Economic Studies*, 65: 361–93.

Kloek, T., and Van Dijk, H. K. (1978), "Bayesian Estimates of Equation System Parameters: An Application of Integration by Monte Carlo," *Econometrica*, 46: 1–20.

Lamnisos, D., Griffin, J. E., and Steel, M. F. J. (2009), "Transdimensional Sampling Algorithms for Bayesian Variable Selection in Classification Problems with Many More Variables than Observations," *Journal of Computational and Graphical Statistics*, 18: 592–612.

Liu, J. S. (2001), *Monte Carlo Strategies in Scientific Computing*, New York: Springer.

Metropolis, N., Rosenbluth, A. W., Rosenbluth, M. N., Teller, A. H., and Teller, E. (1953), "Equations of State Calculations by Fast Computing Machines," *Journal of Chemical Physics*, 21: 1087–92.

Mira, A., and Tierney, L. (2002), "Efficiency and Convergence Properties of Slice Samplers," *Scandinavian Journal of Statistics*, 29: 1–12.

Ripley, B. D. (1987), *Stochastic Simulation*, New York: Wiley.

Robert, C. P. (2001), *The Bayesian Choice*, 2nd edn., New York: Springer Verlag.

——— and Casella, G. (2004), *Monte Carlo Statistical Methods*, 2nd edn., New York: Springer Verlag.

Roberts, G. O. and Rosenthal, J. S. (2004), "General State Space Markov Chains and MCMC Algorithms," *Probability Surveys*, 1: 20–71.

——— ——— (2006), "Harris Recurrence of Metropolis-within-Gibbs and Trans-dimensional Markov Chains," *Annals of Applied Probability*, 16: 2123–39.

Rubin, D. B. (1988), "Using the SIR Algorithm to Simulate Posterior Distributions," in J. M. Bernardo, M. H. DeGroot, D. V. Lindley, and A. F. M. Smith (eds), *Bayesian Statistics 3*, Oxford: Oxford University Press, 395–402.

Tanner, M. A., and Wong, W. H. (1987), "The Calculation of Posterior Distributions by Data Augmentation (with Discussion)," *Journal of the American Statistical Association*, 82: 528–50.

Taylor, J.B. (1993), "Discretion versus Policy Rules in Practice," *Carnegie-Rochester Conference Series on Public Policy*, 39: 195–214.

Tierney, L. (1994), "Markov Chains for Exploring Posterior Distributions," *Annals of Statistics*, 22: 1701–28.

PART III

APPLICATIONS

CHAPTER 6

BAYESIAN METHODS IN MICROECONOMETRICS

MINGLIANG LI AND JUSTIN TOBIAS

1 Introduction

This chapter is intended to serve as an introduction to Bayesian analysis of models commonly encountered in microeconomics. In what follows we cover much of the "how" to conduct Bayesian inference in microeconometric applications by discussing, in reasonable detail, the steps involved in posterior simulation via Markov chain Monte Carlo (MCMC) methods in a wide array of models. To a lesser extent we also address issues of "why" one might choose to employ a Bayesian approach for estimating these models over well-established frequentist alternatives. Our answers to the latter types of questions tend to be pragmatic rather than grounded in theory, emphasizing the ease with which simulations from the posterior distribution can be used to calculate exact finite sample point estimates or complete posterior distributions for economically relevant quantities of interest.

The level of presentation of this chapter is quite similar to that provided in recent Bayesian textbooks, including Koop (2003); Lancaster (2004); Geweke (2005); Koop et al. (2007). The reader may, in fact, regard this chapter as an introduction to several of the more specialized chapters that appear elsewhere in this volume. For example, Griffin et al. (Chapter 4) provide flexible alternatives to many of the more restrictive assumptions entertained here, all of which are presented under the assumption of normal sampling. Furthermore, Rossi and Allenby (Chapter 8) also relax some of the distributional and prior assumptions made in the basic hierarchical and multinomial choice frameworks and illustrate the value of such models in marketing applications. Given the broad scope of a chapter like this one, however, our coverage of a representative model will typically be brief rather than fully detailed and, as is necessary, we will provide the reader with references to the literature that extend the basic methodology.

Our approach to this chapter is to teach by example. By this we mean that many of the models considered will contain an actual empirical example to illustrate the use of MCMC methods in practice. In most cases our examples employ data sets that are specific to the model being considered, although the estimation of several different types of models will be illustrated with a common data set on BMI (Body Mass Index) and wage outcomes. Finally, all of our applications are coded in MATLAB and our programs made available to the interested reader for inspection, refinement, and additional modifications.[1]

The outline of this chapter is as follows. Section 2 discusses linear models. We begin this presentation with a review of the normal linear regression model, deriving marginal, conditional, and predictive posterior densities of interest. To illustrate how MCMC methods can be employed to accommodate interesting departures from the standard linear regression framework under "ideal" conditions, we also discuss several generalizations of the basic model, including allowing for parametric heteroscedasticity and incorporating a changepoint into the analysis. Our treatment of linear models then moves on to discuss hierarchical linear models and to review approaches to handling endogeneity problems in the context of a bivariate system of linear equations. Section 3 presents applications and posterior simulation strategies for univariate (nonlinear) latent variable models, including the probit, logit, tobit, and ordered probit specifications. Section 4 extends these approaches to the multivariate case and considers the analysis of treatment effects models and multinomial and multivariate probit models. Finally, Section 5 briefly reviews basic Bayesian approaches to the analysis of duration data, and the chapter concludes with a summary in Section 6.

2 Linear Models

The linear regression model is central to microeconometrics, and so it seems natural to begin our review of Bayesian microeconometrics with an investigation of this model. We start by discussing Bayesian inference in the linear regression model under ideal conditions. While a careful understanding of this model is surely useful in its own right, what is learned from analysis of the linear model will also prove useful when estimating generalized models, like those of Sections 3 and 4, that will be linear in suitably defined latent data.

2.1 Bayesian analysis of the Linear Regression Model

Before discussing such generalizations, we first consider a standard regression model of the form

[1] The code can be obtained from the website: http://web.ics.purdue.edu/~jltobias/handbook.html.

$$y_i = \boldsymbol{x}_i\boldsymbol{\beta} + u_i, \qquad u_i|X,\sigma^2 \overset{iid}{\sim} \mathcal{N}(0,\sigma^2), \quad i = 1,2,\ldots,n, \tag{6.1}$$

where $\boldsymbol{x}_i$ is a $1 \times k$ vector of covariate data, y_i is a scalar outcome of interest, $\boldsymbol{\beta}$ and σ^2 are a $k \times 1$ vector of regression parameters and a scalar variance parameter, respectively, and

$$X \equiv \begin{bmatrix} \boldsymbol{x}_1 \\ \boldsymbol{x}_2 \\ \vdots \\ \boldsymbol{x}_n \end{bmatrix}.$$

The likelihood is derived from (6.1), and specification of the model is completed upon selecting a prior for the parameters $\boldsymbol{\beta}$ and σ^2. To this end, we choose proper priors of the forms:

$$\boldsymbol{\beta}|\sigma^2 \sim \mathcal{N}\left(\boldsymbol{\mu}_\beta, \sigma^2 \mathbf{V}_\beta\right) \tag{6.2}$$

$$\sigma^2 \sim IG\left(\frac{a}{2}, b\right), \tag{6.3}$$

that is, a conditional normal prior for the regression coefficients and an inverse gamma prior for the variance parameter.[2] The hyperparameters $\boldsymbol{\mu}_\beta$, $\mathbf{V}_\beta$, a, and b are known and selected by the researcher.

With respect to the prior, it is often selected to be conjugate (meaning that posteriors in the same distributional family are produced), as will be the case for (6.2)–(6.3), primarily for reasons of computational tractability (see e.g. Bernardo and Smith 1994; Poirier 1995). The adoption of conjugate priors can also be viewed as the addition of "fictitious" sample information to the analysis, which is combined with the data in exactly the same way that additional (real) sample information would have been combined. Thus, conjugate priors enable the researcher to directly assess the informational content of the prior in terms of equivalent sample information—a useful result in practice, if for no other reason than to potentially mitigate concerns about the influence of the prior.

Within a given class of priors it remains, of course, to choose the hyperparameters. This decision can potentially be guided based upon the findings of past research, when available. While it may be difficult in general for the researcher to elicit her prior beliefs regarding unobservable parameters when such information does not exist, a useful exercise is to think about implications of the prior on the prior predictive, $p(\boldsymbol{y}) = \int p(\boldsymbol{y}|\boldsymbol{\beta},\sigma^2)p(\boldsymbol{\beta},\sigma^2)d\boldsymbol{\beta}d\sigma^2$, which is something the researcher is probably informed about. Here, $\boldsymbol{y} = (y_1\, y_2\, \cdots\, y_n)'$ and we will discuss more on the calculation of $p(\boldsymbol{y})$ below. Finally, it may also be tempting to simply use improper priors in practice, as they appear to be the closest approximation to letting the data completely speak for itself.

[2] In this chapter we follow the general conventions of the *Handbook* and parameterize the inverse gamma as follows: $x \sim IG(c,d) \Rightarrow p(x) \propto x^{-(c+1)} \exp(-d/x), c > 0, d > 0, x > 0$. For $c > 1$, it follows that $E(x) = d(c-1)^{-1}$ and, for $c > 2$, $\text{Var}(x) = d^2[(c-1)^2(c-2)]^{-1}$.

Doing so is not without problems, however, as marginal likelihoods are generally no longer well-defined, improper priors can be unexpectedly informative for functions of the parameters, and marginalization paradoxes can occur. In this chapter, we simply employ conjugate (or conditionally conjugate) priors and in the limited space available focus on issues of implementation and posterior simulation rather than prior selection. Interested readers can specify their own priors, of course, and slightly modify the code provided to see how results change.

2.1.1 Marginal posteriors, conditional posteriors, and posterior predictive distributions

The prior and likelihood combine via Bayes' Theorem to yield the joint posterior, up to a constant of proportionality. Applying this general result to our linear regression model, we obtain:

$$p(\boldsymbol{\beta}, \sigma^2 | y) \propto p(\boldsymbol{\beta}, \sigma^2) p(y | \boldsymbol{\beta}, \sigma^2), \tag{6.4}$$

without the conditioning on X explicitly denoted. Though (6.4) will be tailored to the case of linear regression in this section, it also summarizes the general process of Bayesian learning, as priors combine with the likelihood to form posterior distributions for the model parameters. For low dimension problems, the right-hand side of (6.4) can be plotted to visualize how prior beliefs have been updated from the data. When the dimension of the parameter vector is very low, standard numerical integration routines such as Simpson's rule or Gaussian quadrature can be employed to approximate the normalizing constant of (6.4) and thereby plot a proper joint posterior density.

When the dimension of the parameter space is moderate or large and the structure of the posterior distribution is not simple, however, it becomes far more difficult to visualize interesting features of the posterior surface and direct calculation of the normalizing constant using standard methods is no longer possible. As many of the chapters of this volume describe, it is often possible, however, to simulate draws from (6.4) and use these draws to calculate posterior quantities of interest.

In the case of the linear regression model described here, such numerical methods are not required as the priors in (6.2)–(6.3) combine nicely with the likelihood function, and all of the requisite posterior densities are available in closed form. To see this, suppose that the objects of interest happen to be the regression coefficients $\boldsymbol{\beta}$.[3] To this end, one would like to report posterior summary statistics such as posterior means or posterior standard deviations for the elements of the regression coefficient vector.

A step in this direction leads us to consider the posterior conditional density $\boldsymbol{\beta}|\sigma^2, y$. This is obtained upon noting that its density is proportional to that of the joint posterior

[3] Though it is convention in the profession to at least report a table of coefficient posterior means and standard deviations, and we tend to follow this convention in this chapter, parameters themselves rarely tell the whole story. The examples provided in the following subsections illustrate how quantities of interest are commonly functions of the parameters, and how posterior simulations can be easily used to make inference regarding such quantities.

$\boldsymbol{\beta}, \sigma^2 | y$ in (6.4) and then completing the square in $\boldsymbol{\beta}$ to obtain (e.g. Lindley and Smith 1972):

$$\boldsymbol{\beta} | \sigma^2, y \sim \mathcal{N}\left(\boldsymbol{\mu}_{\beta|y}, \sigma^2 V_{\beta|y}\right) \tag{6.5}$$

where

$$V_{\beta|y} = \left(X'X + V_\beta^{-1}\right)^{-1} \quad \text{and} \quad \boldsymbol{\mu}_{\beta|y} = V_{\beta|y}\left(X'y + V_\beta^{-1}\boldsymbol{\mu}_\beta\right). \tag{6.6}$$

The dependence of this density on σ^2 is rather undesirable, however, as we seek to report posterior statistics about $\boldsymbol{\beta}$ that do not require such conditioning on unobservables. The Bayesian prescription is clear: simply marginalize the nuisance parameter out of the problem, or obtain:

$$p(\boldsymbol{\beta}|y) = \int_0^\infty p(\boldsymbol{\beta}|\sigma^2, y) p(\sigma^2|y) d\sigma^2. \tag{6.7}$$

The first term within the integral has been determined, as in (6.5), and it remains to calculate the marginal posterior for the variance parameter, $p(\sigma^2|y)$. This quantity can be obtained by starting with the joint posterior $p(\boldsymbol{\beta}, \sigma^2|y)$ in (6.4), completing the square in $\boldsymbol{\beta}$, recognizing the resulting quadratic form in $\boldsymbol{\beta}$ as being part of a multivariate normal kernel for $\boldsymbol{\beta}$, and then integrating over the multivariate normal. Doing so gives:

$$\sigma^2 | y \sim IG\left(\frac{n+a}{2}, \tilde{b}\right), \tag{6.8}$$

where

$$\tilde{b} = \left[b + \frac{1}{2}\left(SSE + (\boldsymbol{\mu}_\beta - \hat{\beta})'\left[V_\beta + (X'X)^{-1}\right]^{-1}(\boldsymbol{\mu}_\beta - \hat{\beta})\right)\right], \tag{6.9}$$

with

$$\hat{\beta} \equiv (X'X)^{-1}X'y \quad \text{and} \quad SSE \equiv (y - X\hat{\boldsymbol{\beta}})'(y - X\hat{\boldsymbol{\beta}}). \tag{6.10}$$

Equation 6.8, of course, is interesting in its own right as it can be used to calculate marginal posterior statistics for the variance parameter σ^2, using known properties of the inverse gamma distribution. Equations (6.5) and (6.8) also reveal that the prior in (6.2)–(6.3) is *conjugate*, as originally asserted, since the prior and posterior are of the same distributional family. For our purposes here, the result in (6.8) can also be substituted into (6.7) and the necessary integration performed to obtain the marginal posterior for $\boldsymbol{\beta}$. By doing so, we obtain:[4]

$$\boldsymbol{\beta}|y \sim t(\boldsymbol{\mu}_{\beta|y}, [2\tilde{b}V_{\beta|y}]^{-1}, n + a), \tag{6.11}$$

[4] We, again, employ a parameterization of the multivariate t distribution that is consistent with the usage in this *Handbook*. Specifically, for a $k \times 1$ vector x, writing $\boldsymbol{x} \sim t(\boldsymbol{\mu}, V, \nu)$ implies $p(x) \propto [1 + (x - \boldsymbol{\mu})'V(x - \boldsymbol{\mu})]^{-(k+\nu)/2}$.

a multivariate t density with mean $\boldsymbol{\mu}_{\beta|y}$ (for $n+a>1$) and variance $(n+a-2)^{-1}2\tilde{b}V_{\beta|y} = E(\sigma^2|y)V_{\beta|y}$ (for $n+a>2$), with both $\boldsymbol{\mu}_{\beta|y}$ and $V_{\beta|y}$ being defined in (6.6). The parameter $\tilde{b}$ is defined in (6.9) as the second parameter of the IG density. The density in (6.11) can be used to calculate posterior means, posterior standard deviations, optimal point, and interval estimates (see e.g. Poirier 1995: chapters 6 and 9) or other desired quantities for the regression parameters $\boldsymbol{\beta}$.

Apart from estimation, we would also like to use our linear regression framework for two additional purposes: prediction and model comparison. In terms of the latter, marginal likelihoods (see e.g. Chib, chapter 5 of this volume) are often calculated and Bayes factors and/or posterior model probabilities reported to compare models or average model-specific posterior predictions. With the priors employed in (6.2)–(6.3) together with our normal sampling model, the marginal density of the data y is also available analytically (e.g. Poirier 1995):

$$y \sim t\left(X\boldsymbol{\mu}_{\beta}, \left[2b\left(I_n + XV_{\beta}X'\right)\right]^{-1}, a\right). \tag{6.12}$$

Equation (6.12), when evaluated at the observed sample of data y^o, provides the marginal likelihood, which provides a vehicle for model comparison, selection, and averaging. Chib (chapter 5 of this volume) provides many more details surrounding the calculation and use of marginal likelihoods in practice and we refer the interested reader there for further details.

In terms of prediction, consider a future, out-of-sample value y_f, presumed to be generated by the model in (6.1):

$$y_f = x_f\beta + u_f, \quad u_f|X, x_f, \sigma^2 \sim \mathcal{N}(0, \sigma^2). \tag{6.13}$$

The posterior predictive density for y_f (given values of the covariates x_f) is obtained as:

$$p(y_f|x_f, y) = \int_{-\infty}^{\infty} \cdots \int_{-\infty}^{\infty} \int_0^{\infty} p(y_f|x_f, \boldsymbol{\beta}, \sigma^2)p(\boldsymbol{\beta}, \sigma^2|y)d\sigma^2 d\boldsymbol{\beta}, \tag{6.14}$$

noting that the future outcome y_f is independent of the past outcomes y, given the covariates x_f and parameters $\boldsymbol{\beta}$ and σ^2. Methods similar to those used in deriving (6.11) produce:

$$y_f|x_f, y \sim t\left(x_f\boldsymbol{\mu}_{\beta|y}, \left[2\tilde{b}(1 + x_f V_{\beta|y}x_f')\right]^{-1}, n+a\right), \tag{6.15}$$

which can be used to make point, interval, or other predictions regarding out-of-sample outcomes. The following example illustrates how such results can be used in practice.

2.1.2 An illustrative application with (log) wage data

To illustrate how Bayesian calculations are carried out in this simplest specification, we obtain a sample of $n = 1,645$ observations on white males in the US in 1993. Our data, taken from the National Longitudinal Survey of Youth (NLSY), contain information on wage outcomes for all of these respondents. The dependent variable we employ is the natural logarithm of hourly wages received in 1993, measured in 1993 dollars. Other demographic variables, included as right-hand-side covariates in our analysis, include years of schooling completed (EDUCATION), a test score variable (SCORE), years of schooling completed by the respondent's parents (MOMED and DADED), and number of siblings (NUMSIBS) of the respondent. The variable SCORE is constructed from a battery of tests administered to the NLSY participants during the fall and summer of 1980, and is standardized to have a sample mean of zero and sample variance equal to unity.

While analytic results are available for the $\boldsymbol{\beta}$ and σ^2 marginal posteriors, we employ simulation methods to generate draws from the joint posterior $p(\boldsymbol{\beta}, \sigma^2|y)$ and use these simulations to calculate posterior quantities of interest. Sampling is conducted using the method of composition, first drawing from the marginal posterior for the variance parameter, $\sigma^2|y$ in (6.8) and then sampling from the conditional posterior for the regression parameters, $\boldsymbol{\beta}|\sigma^2, y$ in (6.5). This is repeated 25,000 times, producing 25,000 iid (independent and identically distributed) samples from the joint posterior $p(\boldsymbol{\beta}, \sigma^2|y)$. Monte Carlo simulation methods are employed as their use will easily enable us to calculate posterior statistics for economically relevant (nonlinear) hourly wage gaps of the form:

$$\Delta(\boldsymbol{\beta}, \sigma^2; \boldsymbol{x}_l, \boldsymbol{x}_h) = \exp\left(\boldsymbol{x}_h\boldsymbol{\beta} + \frac{\sigma^2}{2}\right) - \exp\left(\boldsymbol{x}_l\boldsymbol{\beta} + \frac{\sigma^2}{2}\right) \tag{6.16}$$

in addition to simple posterior statistics regarding the parameters $\boldsymbol{\beta}$ and σ^2.

Equation (6.16) represents the expected hourly wage gap between persons of characteristics $\boldsymbol{x}_h$ and $\boldsymbol{x}_l$. In practice, the two sets of covariates are distinguished by evaluating $\boldsymbol{x}_h$ at a higher education category and $\boldsymbol{x}_l$ at a lower education category, while the remaining values in both covariate vectors are fixed at sample means. We focus in particular on the BA/high school wage gap, and the Ph.D./high school wage gap. For the first of these cases, $\boldsymbol{x}_h$ sets EDUCATION $= 16$ while in the second, $\boldsymbol{x}_h$ sets EDUCATION $= 20$. For the high school comparison group, $\boldsymbol{x}_l$ sets education equal to 12 each time.

The ease with which our posterior simulations can be used to calculate quantities like (6.16) should not be overlooked, as classical approaches to inference, via delta-method asymptotics or the bootstrap, seem to be significantly more difficult to implement. For example, a point estimate (posterior mean) of (6.16) can be readily calculated as

$$\widehat{\Delta}(\boldsymbol{x}_l, \boldsymbol{x}_h) = \frac{1}{R}\sum_{r=1}^{R} \Delta(\boldsymbol{\beta}^{(r)}, \sigma^{2,(r)}; \boldsymbol{x}_l, \boldsymbol{x}_h), \tag{6.17}$$

with $\boldsymbol{\beta}^{(r)}$ and $\sigma^{2,(r)}$ denoting the rth simulation from the joint posterior and R denoting the total number of simulations. A point estimate of the posterior standard deviation of (6.16) can be calculated in an analogous way, using the simulations produced from the Monte Carlo sampling scheme.

Table 6.1: Posterior statistics from wage data application

Variable / Parameter	Posterior Mean	Posterior Std. Dev.
Constant	1.79	0.102
EDUCATION	0.044	0.007
SCORE	0.096	0.017
MOMED	0.003	0.006
DADED	0.007	0.005
NUMSIBS	0.004	0.006
BA/HS GAP	2.51	0.406
Ph.D./HS GAP	5.51	0.971

Posterior summary statistics associated with two different Δ parameters and the regression coefficients are reported in Table 6.1. These results are obtained upon setting $a = 6, b = 1, \boldsymbol{\mu}_\beta = \mathbf{0}_k$, and $\boldsymbol{V}_\beta = 10\boldsymbol{I}_k$, providing a proper yet reasonably uninformative prior.

The entries of Table 6.1 have the expected signs and posterior means appear reasonable in magnitude, with education and test scores clearly having a meaningful impact on earnings. On average (and in 1993 dollars), those graduating with a four-year degree earn about \$2.51 more per hour than high school graduates, while those with a Ph.D. earn about \$5.51 more per hour than their high school counterparts.

Rather than simply looking at differences in means, one can also obtain entire predictive wage distributions. To illustrate how this is done, Figure 6.1(a) plots posterior predictive hourly wage densities for two different hypothetical individuals—an individual with a high school degree who is otherwise "average" (that is, all other covariates are fixed at sample mean values), and a similarly average individual with a BA degree.

Letting $w_f = \exp(y_f)$ denote the hourly wage for a future or out-of-sample individual with characteristics $\boldsymbol{x}_f$, these figures can be obtained by noting:

$$p(w_f|\boldsymbol{x}_f, y) = \int_{-\infty}^{\infty} \cdots \int_{-\infty}^{\infty} \int_{0}^{\infty} p(w_f|y_f)p(y_f|\boldsymbol{x}_f, \boldsymbol{\beta}, \sigma^2)p(\boldsymbol{\beta}|\sigma^2, y)p(\sigma^2|y)d\sigma^2 d\boldsymbol{\beta} \tag{6.18}$$

where superfluous information has been dropped from the conditioning above, when applicable.

Although evaluation of the multiple integral in (6.18) may seem like a daunting task, it is useful to pause and emphasize how simulation methods can be employed to generate draws from this predictive density. To begin, samples from $p(\sigma^2|y)$ and $p(\boldsymbol{\beta}|\sigma^2, y)$ are obtained by first drawing from (6.8) and then (6.5) immediately after, updating the conditioning in (6.5) to reflect the σ^2 just generated from (6.8). Let us denote this posterior sample at iteration r as $(\sigma^{2,(r)}, \boldsymbol{\beta}^{(r)})$. A log wage simulation $y_f^{(r)}$ is then produced by drawing from the normal sampling model in (6.13), setting $y_f^{(r)} = \boldsymbol{x}_f \boldsymbol{\beta}^{(r)} + \sigma^{(r)} z$, where $z \sim \mathcal{N}(0, 1)$. Finally, an hourly wage simulation $w_f^{(r)}$ is produced by simply

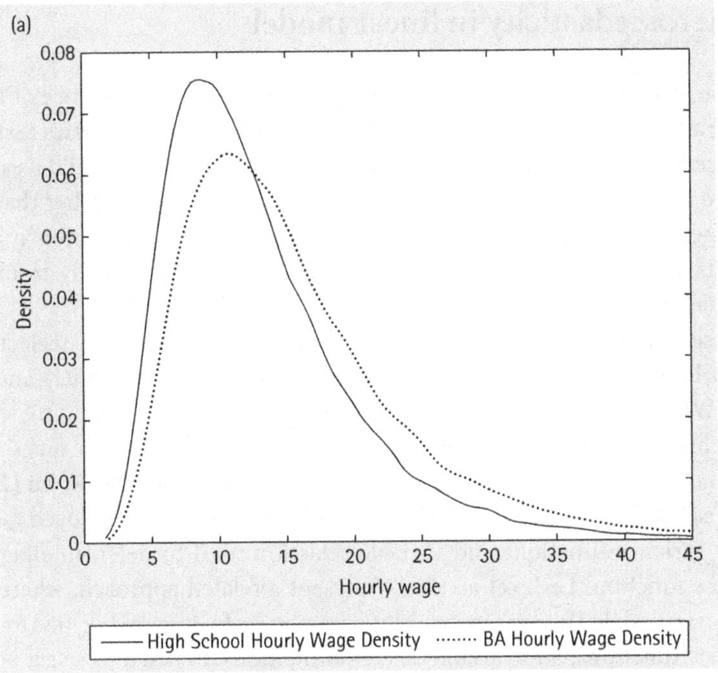

FIGURE 6.1A Posterior predictive hourly wage densities

exponentiating the log wage simulation $y_f^{(r)}$, given that the conditional distribution is degenerate, that is, $p(w_f|y_f) = I(w_f = \exp[y_f])$. This produces a set of draws from the posterior predictive density of hourly wages. Therefore, draws from (6.18) only require a few additional lines of code beyond what has already been written to fit the model, and obtaining them does not require change of variables analytics or large-sample approximations for inference.

In Figure 6.1(a) we generate 25,000 simulations from the posterior predictive density (6.18) in this manner and smooth these simulations via a kernel method to plot the posterior predictive hourly wage densities for the High School graduate and BA groups. In these calculations all covariates other than education are fixed at their sample mean values. The posterior simulations can also be used to directly calculate posterior predictive means, standard deviations, etc., as well as other economically relevant quantities, such as the probability of being in poverty (e.g. Geweke and Keane 2000), and we briefly take up the last of these in the context of our application. Specifically, we calculate $\Pr(w_f < \$5 \,|y, Ed = 12, X_{-Ed} = \overline{X}_{-Ed}) \approx 0.05$ and $\Pr(w_f < \$5 \,|y, Ed = 16, X_{-Ed} = \overline{X}_{-Ed}) \approx 0.025$, where Ed denotes education, X_{-c} denotes all variables other than c, and $\overline{X}$ denotes the sample average. The value \$5 was chosen as an approximate hourly wage consistent with the poverty threshold at full-time employment.[5]

[5] The US Census Bureau reports a 1993 poverty threshold for a two person family with one child less than 18 years of age equal to \$9,960. Using 2,000 hours as the number of annual hours worked for

2.2 Heteroscedasticity in linear models

Despite the prominence of heteroscedasticity in the theory and practice of frequentist econometrics, and its ubiquitousness in classical graduate econometrics texts, the role of heteroscedasticity in Bayesian treatments is comparatively minor, and its appearance as a component of Bayesian empirical work seems the exception rather than the rule. Although several explanations exist for the differential treatment of this issue among frequentists and Bayesians, it remains rather strange, and potentially troubling, that heteroscedasticity seems to garner comparatively little attention.

Of course, the issue of heteroscedasticity has not been completely neglected among Bayesians. Poirier (2008), for example, builds upon Lancaster (2003) and seeks to reconcile White's (1980) heteroscedasticity-robust estimation of the OLS covariance matrix within the Bayesian framework.[6] In a different spirit, which seeks to employ Bayesian methods to flexibly model the variance function, Yau and Kohn (2003) consider analysis of a normal linear regression model, with splines employed for both the mean and variance functions and variable selection used to determine key terms in the variance function. Leslie et al. (2007) present a related approach, where the error distribution is modeled nonparametrically, parameteric forms are specified for the mean and variance functions, and variable selection methods are used to select appropriate covariates in both sets of functions. Villani et al. (2007), based upon an approach similar to the smoothly mixing regression model of Geweke and Keane (2007), describe a nonparametric-type approach to the modeling of heteroscedasticity.

Although these papers offer valuable contributions, the norm in applied work appears to remain one of conditional homoscedasticity. With this in mind, we describe in the following section a simple generalization of this assumption which permits a multiplicative, parametric form of heteroscedasticity. When such a specification is not adequately flexible, the reader is invited to see the references listed above for more advanced alternatives.

2.2.1 Posterior simulation in a model of parametric heteroscedasticity

To provide some initial guidance and a simple first step toward handling linear models in the presence of heteroscedasticity, we consider analysis of the following specification:

$$y_i = \boldsymbol{x}_i\boldsymbol{\beta} + \epsilon_i, \quad \epsilon_i|X, Z, \boldsymbol{\alpha} \stackrel{ind}{\sim} \mathcal{N}[0, \exp(\boldsymbol{z}_i\boldsymbol{\alpha})] \tag{6.19}$$

someone engaged in full-time employment motivates our decision to use \$5 as the approximate hourly wage threshold. This is, admittedly, a simplified calculation and, among other things, assumes no other sources of income for the household.

[6] Interestingly, the first sentence of Poirier (2008) frames the exercise well, as it reads: "Often, researchers find it useful to recast frequentist procedures in Bayesian terms, so as to get a clear understanding of how and when the procedures work."

where it is understood that an intercept is included in z_i and that z_i can be the same as, or potentially different from x_i. We complete the specification of our model in (19) with priors of the forms:

$$\boldsymbol{\beta} \sim \mathcal{N}(\boldsymbol{\mu}_\beta, V_\beta) \tag{6.20}$$

$$\boldsymbol{\alpha} \sim \mathcal{N}(\boldsymbol{\mu}_\alpha, V_\alpha). \tag{6.21}$$

These priors in (6.20) and (6.21) together with the likelihood implied by (6.19) yield a posterior of the form:

$$p(\boldsymbol{\alpha}, \boldsymbol{\beta}|y) \propto p(\boldsymbol{\beta})p(\boldsymbol{\alpha}) \left[\prod_{i=1}^{n} \exp(z_i\boldsymbol{\alpha}) \right]^{-1/2} \exp\left(-\frac{1}{2} \sum_{i=1}^{n} \frac{(y_i - x_i\boldsymbol{\beta})^2}{\exp(z_i\boldsymbol{\alpha})} \right). \tag{6.22}$$

We propose a Metropolis-within-Gibbs algorithm (see Chib, chapter 5 of this volume, for further details) to generate draws from this posterior density.[7]

To this end, we first recognize that:

$$\boldsymbol{\beta}|\boldsymbol{\alpha}, y \sim \mathcal{N}\left(D_\beta d_\beta, D_\beta\right), \tag{6.23}$$

where

$$D_\beta = \left(X'W^{-1}X + V_\beta^{-1}\right)^{-1}, \qquad d_\beta = X'W^{-1}y + V_\beta^{-1}\boldsymbol{\mu}_\beta, \tag{6.24}$$

and

$$W = W(\boldsymbol{\alpha}) \equiv diag\{\exp(z_i\boldsymbol{\alpha})\}. \tag{6.25}$$

As for the sampling of $\boldsymbol{\alpha}|\boldsymbol{\beta}, y$ we note from (6.22),

$$p(\boldsymbol{\alpha}|\boldsymbol{\beta}, y) \propto p(\boldsymbol{\alpha}) \left[\prod_{i=1}^{n} \exp(z_i\boldsymbol{\alpha}) \right]^{-1/2} \exp\left(-\frac{1}{2} \sum_{i=1}^{n} \frac{(y_i - x_i\boldsymbol{\beta})^2}{\exp(z_i\boldsymbol{\alpha})} \right), \tag{6.26}$$

which is not of a known form. We employ a random walk Metropolis-within-Gibbs step to generate draws from (6.26). Specifically, we first sample a candidate $\boldsymbol{\alpha}^*$ from a multivariate normal proposal density:

$$\boldsymbol{\alpha}^* \sim \mathcal{N}(\boldsymbol{\alpha}^{(r)}, c^2\boldsymbol{\Sigma}_\alpha), \tag{6.27}$$

where the (r) superscript denotes the current value of the chain at iteration r. Implementation of our method requires choosing the scale matrix $\boldsymbol{\Sigma}_\alpha$ as well as the "tuning parameter" c^2, the latter of which will be chosen to optimize the mixing of the simulations

[7] Tanizaki and Zhang (2001) provide a similar analysis to the one presented here.

within this scheme for variance parameter simulation. Following Harvey (1976), we select the scale matrix by first noting

$$\frac{\epsilon_i^2}{\exp(z_i\boldsymbol{\alpha})} \equiv \nu_i, \quad \nu_i \sim \chi_1^2, \tag{6.28}$$

suggesting that a point estimate of $\boldsymbol{\alpha}$ can be obtained from a regression of $\log \epsilon_i^2$ (which is known, given $\boldsymbol{\beta}$) on z_i.[8] A reasonable choice for $\boldsymbol{\Sigma}_\alpha$, then, is the variance-covariance matrix from this regression, or,

$$\boldsymbol{\Sigma}_\alpha = 4.93(Z'Z)^{-1}, \tag{6.29}$$

where the value 4.93 denotes the approximate variance of $\log \nu_i$. The candidate $\boldsymbol{\alpha}^*$ generated from the proposal is then accepted with probability

$$\min\left\{1, \frac{p(y|\boldsymbol{\alpha}=\boldsymbol{\alpha}^*, \boldsymbol{\beta}=\boldsymbol{\beta}^{(r)})p(\boldsymbol{\alpha}^*)}{p(y|\boldsymbol{\alpha}=\boldsymbol{\alpha}^{(r)}, \boldsymbol{\beta}=\boldsymbol{\beta}^{(r)})p(\boldsymbol{\alpha}^{(r)})}\right\} \equiv \min\left\{1, \exp[g(\boldsymbol{\alpha}^*, \boldsymbol{\alpha}^{(r)}, \boldsymbol{\beta}^{(r)})]\right\}, \tag{6.30}$$

where

$$\begin{aligned} g(\boldsymbol{\alpha}^*, \boldsymbol{\alpha}^{(r)}, \boldsymbol{\beta}^{(r)}) = -\frac{1}{2}\Big[& \boldsymbol{\iota}_n' Z(\boldsymbol{\alpha}^* - \boldsymbol{\alpha}^{(r)}) + \sum_i (y_i - x_i\boldsymbol{\beta}^{(r)})^2 \left(\exp(-z_i\boldsymbol{\alpha}^*) - \exp(-z_i\boldsymbol{\alpha}^{(r)})\right) \\ & + (\boldsymbol{\alpha}^* - \boldsymbol{\mu}_\alpha)' V_\alpha^{-1} (\boldsymbol{\alpha}^* - \boldsymbol{\mu}_\alpha) - (\boldsymbol{\alpha}^{(r)} - \boldsymbol{\mu}_\alpha)' V_\alpha^{-1} (\boldsymbol{\alpha}^{(r)} - \boldsymbol{\mu}_\alpha)\Big], \end{aligned} \tag{6.31}$$

and $\boldsymbol{\iota}_n$ denotes an $n \times 1$ vector of ones. If the candidate $\boldsymbol{\alpha}^*$ is accepted, then $\boldsymbol{\alpha}^{(r+1)} = \boldsymbol{\alpha}^*$. Otherwise, the chain remains at its current value, setting $\boldsymbol{\alpha}^{(r+1)} = \boldsymbol{\alpha}^{(r)}$.

2.2.2 Adding parametric heteroscedasticity to the log wage data application

Using the algorithm above we estimate the heteroscedastic regression model employing the wage data of Section 2.1.2. All covariates in $\boldsymbol{x}_i$ are included as covariates in z_i and we fit the model by sampling successively from the conditional posteriors in (6.23) and (6.26), discarding the first 10,000 of 100,000 simulations as the burn-in period. For our priors, we set $\boldsymbol{\mu}_\beta = \boldsymbol{\mu}_\alpha = 0_k$ and $V_\beta = V_\alpha = 100I_k$.

The tuning parameter c^2 is set equal to 1/2, which was chosen experimentally and in a rather ad hoc fashion, and results in an acceptance rate of approximately 23% in the M-H (Metropolis-Hastings) step. This roughly matches the rule of thumb of Gelman et al. (1996; Koop 2003: section 5.5.2), suggesting that random walk chain acceptance rates near 25% in large dimension problems may offer reasonable targets. Of course,

[8] In practice, we start the MCMC chain by first running an OLS regression of y_i on $\boldsymbol{x}_i$ to obtain the initial value of $\boldsymbol{\beta}$. We then run the above regression of $\log \epsilon_i^2$ on z_i to obtain an initial value of $\boldsymbol{\alpha}$, adding 1.27 to the intercept parameter. The adjustment to the intercept is due to the fact that the mean of $\log \nu_i$ is (approximately) -1.27 instead of zero.

interest should ultimately center on the numerical precision of the simulation-based estimate (which will vary with different choices of c) as well as its precision relative to what we could have obtained had iid draws been employed. To this end, we report in Table 6.2 inefficiency factors associated with alternate choices of c^2, and specifically consider $c^2 \in \{0.1, 0.5, 1\}$ for illustration purposes. As shown in that table, the 25% target (which we come close to with $c^2 = 0.5$, whereas $c^2 = 0.1$ and $c^2 = 1$ yield acceptance rates of 56% and 10%, respectively) has steered us in the right direction, and produces the lowest inefficiency factors among this set. In terms of the precision of posterior mean estimates of the regression parameters $\boldsymbol{\beta}$, these are largely unaffected by the choice of c and the level of precision essentially equals what we would have obtained with an iid sample of equal size. The numerical precisions of our simulation-based estimates of $E(\alpha_j|y)$ are rather low relative to those obtained under iid sampling, however, as the inefficiency factors with $c^2 = 0.5$ are near 20.[9]

Posterior means and standard deviations of $\boldsymbol{\beta}$ and $\boldsymbol{\alpha}$ are also provided in the table below. As the reader can see, posterior means and standard deviations of the regression parameters are only slightly changed relative to those reported in Table 6.1. In addition, we find some evidence that higher education increases conditional log wage variability, while the other covariates do not appear to play a strong role in explaining variation in log wages.

Like the homoscedastic version of this model in Section 2.1.2, we can also examine posterior distributions of various hourly wage gaps, though now we additionally account for heteroscedasticity. Specifically, we consider:

$$\Delta(\boldsymbol{\beta}, \boldsymbol{\alpha}; x_l, x_h, z_l, z_h) = \exp\left(x_h\beta + \frac{\exp(z_h\alpha)}{2}\right) - \exp\left(x_l\beta + \frac{\exp(z_l\alpha)}{2}\right) \tag{6.32}$$

and obtain posterior means and standard deviations of Δ for the same choices that were made in Section 2.1.2. Table 6.2 reveals that point estimates of the wage gaps increase (relative to those of Table 6.1) when accounting for heteroscedasticity.

Lastly, we present in Figure 6.1(b) a plot of the hourly wage densities obtained within our heteroscedastic regression model, along with those previously reported in Figure 6.1(a) under homoscedasticity. As the figure reveals, for high school graduates, little difference emerges between the posterior predictive densities. For the BA group, however, we begin to see the increased variance associated with the heteroscedastic predictive density, though these two curves are, again, rather similar. Analogous poverty probability calculations also remain nearly the same for the high school graduate group ($\Pr(w_f < \$5\,|y, Ed = 12, X_{-Ed} = \overline{X}_{-Ed}) = 0.047$) and have slightly increased for the BA group ($\Pr(w_f < \$5\,|y, Ed = 16, X_{-Ed} = \overline{X}_{-Ed}) = 0.032$).

[9] This implies that the numerical standard error of the MCMC-based estimate of $\boldsymbol{\alpha}$ is (approximately) $4.64 \approx \sqrt{21.5}$ times as large as the numerical standard error that would have been attained under iid sampling. Said differently, in order to achieve the sample level of numerical precision for the estimated mean of $\boldsymbol{\alpha}$ that we would get with m iid draws, we would need to run the sampler for $M \approx 21.5m$ iterations.

Table 6.2: Heteroscedastic wage application

Variable	β Parameters					α Parameters				
	Post. Mean	Post. Std.	Ineff. Factors (c^2)			Post. Mean	Post. Std.	Ineff. Factors (c^2)		
			0.1	0.5	1			0.1	0.5	= 1
Constant	1.79	0.103	1.12	1.18	1.19	−1.97	0.287	33.83	21.52	28.27
EDUCATION	0.045	0.007	1.09	1.05	1.02	0.047	0.019	34.92	21.56	30.80
SCORE	0.094	0.017	1.10	1.16	1.15	−0.009	0.048	34.00	21.59	30.45
MOMED	0.002	0.006	1.03	1.04	1.05	−0.012	0.016	30.58	19.97	28.37
DADED	0.007	0.005	1.01	1.02	1.00	0.012	0.013	32.27	22.07	28.57
NUMSIBS	0.004	0.007	1.01	1.00	1.00	0.007	0.019	31.20	20.16	28.46
BA / HS GAP	2.97	0.47								
Ph.D. / HS GAP	6.77	1.22								

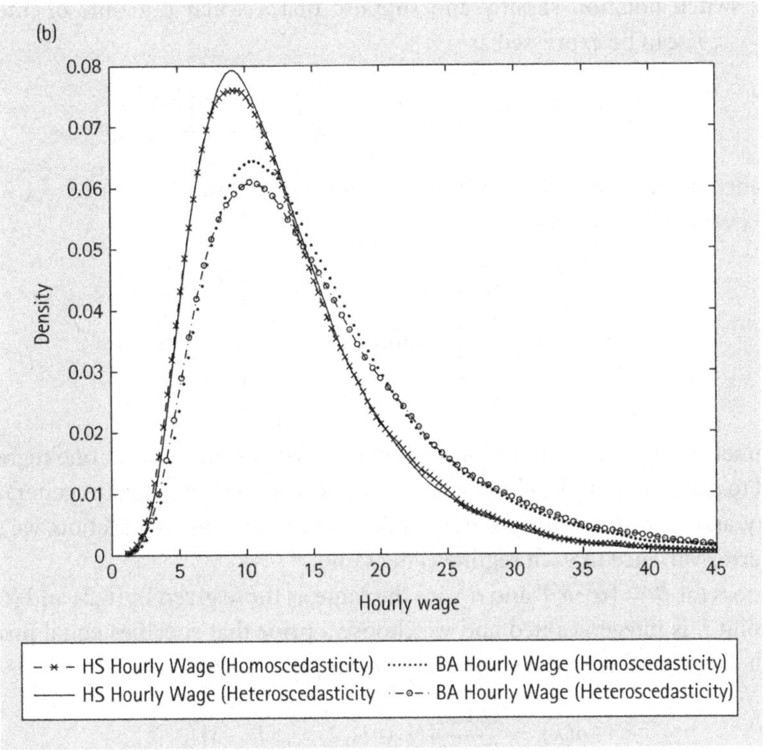

FIGURE 6.1B Posterior predictive hourly wage densities

2.3 A linear model with a changepoint

The previous section illustrated the relative ease with which MCMC methods can be used to accommodate a departure from standard assumptions of the classical linear regression model. Other straightforward extensions include the imposition of inequality restrictions on the elements of $\boldsymbol{\beta}$ (e.g. Geweke 1996b) or analysis of multivariate linear outcomes, such as the Seemingly Unrelated Regressions (SUR) Model (e.g. Zellner 1962; Percy 1992). We do not discuss these particular extensions in this chapter, but turn our attention instead to an alternate generalization by considering a linear regression model with a single, unknown changepoint. The generalizations of such a model frequently appear in time series econometrics (Geweke and Terui 1993). Apart from simply keeping with our theme of generalizing the standard linear model, the methods described in this section also have considerable value in microeconomic applications—for example, in order to allow for jumps and nonlinearities in a regression function, or as a stepping stone toward understanding other related methods for nonparametric regression (e.g. Smith and Kohn 1996), as the resulting posterior simulators are highly similar to the one described here.

Let us switch notation slightly and suppose that a scalar outcome of interest, y_t, $t = 1, 2, \cdots, T$, can be expressed as

$$y_t|\boldsymbol{\alpha}, \boldsymbol{\theta}, \sigma^2, \lambda, X_{1,(\lambda)}, X_{2,(\lambda)} \sim \begin{cases} \mathcal{N}(x_t\boldsymbol{\alpha}, \sigma^2) \text{ if } t \leq \lambda \\ \mathcal{N}(x_t\boldsymbol{\theta}, \sigma^2) \text{ if } t > \lambda, \end{cases} \tag{6.33}$$

where x_t denotes a $1 \times k$ vector of characteristics at time t and $X_{j,(\lambda)}$, for $j = 1, 2$, assembles the covariate data for each "regime":

$$X_{1,(\lambda)} \equiv \begin{bmatrix} x_1 \\ x_2 \\ \vdots \\ x_\lambda \end{bmatrix}, \quad \text{and} \quad X_{2,(\lambda)} \equiv \begin{bmatrix} x_{\lambda+1} \\ x_{\lambda+2} \\ \vdots \\ x_T \end{bmatrix}. \tag{6.34}$$

The parameter λ is a changepoint or breakpoint—for periods until λ, one regression is specified to generate y, and following λ, a new regression is specified to generate y. For simplicity, and with an eye toward our application in the following section, we suppose that the error variance in each regime is the same.

The priors for $\boldsymbol{\beta} = [\boldsymbol{\alpha}' \ \boldsymbol{\theta}']'$ and σ^2 are the same as those given in (6.2) and (6.3). The changepoint λ is integer-valued and we choose a prior that specifies equal probability over each discrete value in the support. For example, one could specify

$$p(\lambda) = \frac{1}{T-1} I(\lambda \in \{1, 2, \ldots, T-1\}), \tag{6.35}$$

which imposes that at least one observation belongs to each regime.

2.3.1 *Posterior Simulation*

Stacking observations over i, we can write:

$$y = X_{(\lambda)}\boldsymbol{\beta} + \epsilon, \quad \epsilon|X, \lambda, \sigma^2 \sim N(0, \sigma^2 I_n), \tag{6.36}$$

where $X_{(\lambda)}$ is a block diagonal matrix with $X_{1,(\lambda)}$ in the upper block and $X_{2,(\lambda)}$ in the lower block. The assumptions of our model imply:

$$p(\boldsymbol{\beta}, \sigma^2, \lambda|y) \propto p(\boldsymbol{\beta}|\sigma^2)p(\sigma^2)p(\lambda)\phi(y|X_{(\lambda)}\boldsymbol{\beta}, \sigma^2 I_n). \tag{6.37}$$

We use the method of composition, as discussed in Section 2.1.2, to directly generate samples from the joint posterior above, following the results of Chin Choy and Broemeling (1980). This proceeds by drawing (in order) from $\lambda|y$, $\sigma^2|\lambda, y$ and $\boldsymbol{\beta}|\sigma^2, \lambda, y$.

With respect to the first of these, one can show:

$$p(\lambda|y) \propto p(\lambda)|D_{(\lambda)}|^{-1/2} \left[b + \frac{1}{2}(y - X_{(\lambda)}\boldsymbol{\mu}_\beta)' D_{(\lambda)}^{-1}(y - X_{(\lambda)}\boldsymbol{\mu}_\beta) \right]^{-(n+a)/2} \tag{6.38}$$

with

$$D_{(\lambda)} \equiv I_n + X_{(\lambda)} V_\beta X'_{(\lambda)}. \tag{6.39}$$

Since the prior for λ is discrete-valued, one can calculate the (unnormalized) ordinates above for $\lambda \in \{1, 2, \ldots, T-1\}$, normalize these by dividing through by the sum of all such values, and then obtain a draw from the resulting discrete distribution.[10] The posterior conditional $\sigma^2|\lambda, y$ is identical to that in (6.8), recognizing that X is now $X_{(\lambda)}$ and must be re-calculated at each iteration of the algorithm. Similarly, $\beta|\lambda, \sigma^2, y$ is given in (6.5) and (6.6) where X is, again, replaced with $X_{(\lambda)}$.

2.3.2 *Example with US annual temperature data*

In what follows we illustrate use of the changepoint model using a sample of annual US temperature data. Specifically, we obtain information on annual temperatures in the United States over the period 1895–2006, providing $n = 112$ data points.

In providing this example we confess to know little (if anything) about the science of climate change. We do not introduce this example to either support or cast doubt on theories of global warming, but simply include it with the hope that the reader may appreciate the generality and usefulness of the model considered in this section as well as the relative ease with which simulation methods can be used to estimate its parameters.

We suppose that temperature patterns over this period may have a single break date and seek to learn about the location of this break as well as its magnitude. Although the simplicity of this model likely discredits it as an accurate descriptor of the evolution of US temperature, it is worth noting that similar models with break points have been considered by others in the field, including Ivanov and Evtimov (2001) and Stockwell and Cox (2009) and that this issue has also been investigated by economists (e.g. Fomby and Vogelsang 2002) employing related models that potentially include breaks (Vogelsang and Franses 2005). We consider below a restricted version of the changepoint model discussed earlier in this section, tailored to our application, and specify:

$$y_t = \beta_0 + \beta_1 t + \beta_2 (t - \lambda)_+ + \epsilon_t, \quad t = 1, 2, \ldots, T \tag{6.40}$$

$$= x_{t,\lambda}\beta + \epsilon_t, \quad \epsilon_t|X, \lambda, \sigma^2 \stackrel{iid}{\sim} \mathcal{N}(0, \sigma^2) \tag{6.41}$$

or stacked over t, we have, identical to (6.35),

$$y = X_{(\lambda)}\beta + \epsilon, \quad \epsilon|X, \lambda, \sigma^2 \sim N(0, \sigma^2 I_n), \tag{6.42}$$

where

$$z_+ \equiv \max\{0, z\}, \ \ x_{t,\lambda} = [1 \ \ t \ \ (t-\lambda)_+], \ \ \beta = \begin{bmatrix} \beta_0 \\ \beta_1 \\ \beta_2 \end{bmatrix}, \ \text{ and } \ X_{(\lambda)} \equiv \begin{bmatrix} x_{1,\lambda} \\ x_{2,\lambda} \\ \vdots \\ x_{T,\lambda} \end{bmatrix}. \tag{6.43}$$

[10] To avoid calculating determinants and inverses of n-dimensional matrices in this step, note $D_{(\lambda)}^{-1} = I_n - X[X'X + V_\beta{}^{-1}]^{-1}X'$ and $|D_{(\lambda)}| = |V_\beta||V_\beta{}^{-1} + X'X|$.

This specification allows for different slopes before and after λ, but does not allow for a discrete jump in temperatures before and after the break. While such jumps may exist, we abstract from this possibility here and impose a smooth function relating year to expected temperature. Moreover, we do not consider the possibility of multiple breaks or potentially different variances across the regimes. Models of multiple breaks can be found, for example, in Chib (1998) and Koop and Potter (2007), among others. Finally, we restrict $\lambda \in \{3, 4, \ldots, T-3\}$, specify equal prior probability over each element of this set, and choose

$$\begin{bmatrix} \beta_0 \\ \beta_1 \\ \beta_2 \end{bmatrix} \sim \mathcal{N}\left[\begin{pmatrix} 52 \\ 0 \\ 0 \end{pmatrix}, \quad \sigma^2 \begin{pmatrix} 10 & 0 & 0 \\ 0 & 10 & 0 \\ 0 & 0 & 10 \end{pmatrix}\right], \tag{6.44}$$

$$\sigma^2 \sim IG(3, 1) \tag{6.45}$$

as our remaining priors. The sampling procedure of Section 2.3.1 is employed to generate 10,000 simulations from the joint posterior in (6.37), which are used to calculate the quantities in Figures 6.2 and 6.3.

Figure 6.2 plots the posterior mean of the regression function relating time to average temperature. To do this we calculate the conditional mean function $X_{(\lambda)}\boldsymbol{\beta}$ for each simulation from the joint posterior. The collection of these functions is then averaged to obtain the posterior mean, which is presented in the figure along with the scatterplot of

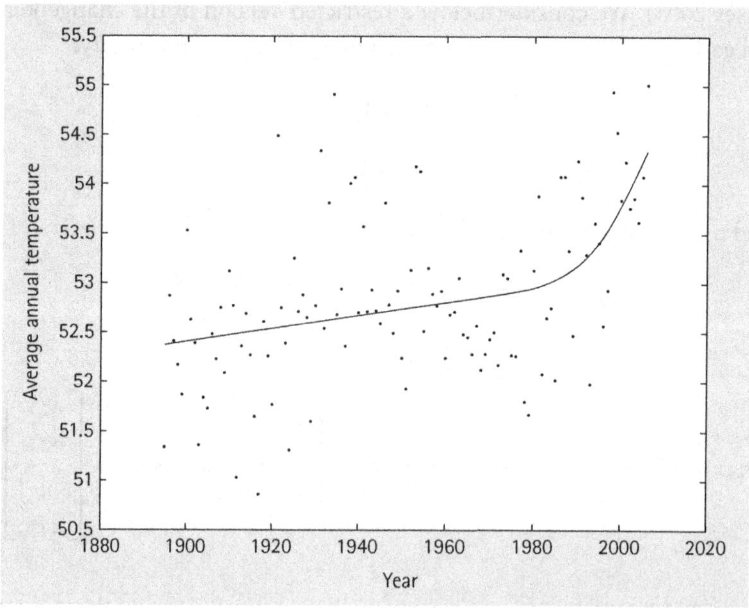

FIGURE 6.2 Raw temperature data and posterior mean

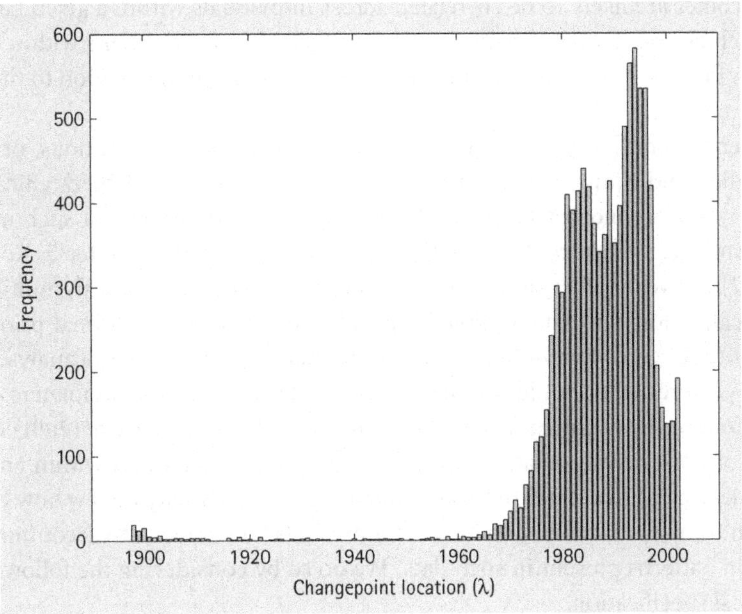

FIGURE 6.3 Posterior changepoint frequencies

the raw data. Importantly, note that this approach accounts for uncertainty regarding the location of the changepoint and thus, unlike a classical method that would condition on a point estimate of the changepoint's location, is smooth and not necessarily "kinked." Again, it is worthwhile to emphasize how uncertainty in the location of the changepoint is easily accounted for when using our posterior simulations to calculate quantities of interest.

Figure 6.3 plots posterior simulations associated with the changepoint λ. The figure clearly shows an update of our uniform prior to a posterior, suggesting that the changepoint has occurred since 1970, with a mode occurring in the late 1990s. This offers suggestive evidence that is broadly consistent with the global (or, at least US) warming message.

2.4 Hierarchical linear models

Many data sets commonly used in applied work, including the National Longitudinal Survey of Youth (NLSY), Panel Study of Income Dynamics (PSID), and the Survey of Income and Program Participation (SIPP) are *longitudinal* in nature, tracking behaviors, outcomes, and responses of a given set of individuals over a period of time. In a similar spirit, other data sets are characterized by (and the models employed should account for) *clustering*—where the outcomes of particular units are likely to be correlated with one another, given the sampling scheme or structure of the problem at hand. For example, wage outcomes are likely to be correlated across individuals within a given family, and student achievement scores are likely to be correlated across students within the same school. In this section we investigate hierarchical models for application to these types of data.

The literature on hierarchical models in Bayesian work is voluminous, originating with Lindley and Smith (1972) and Smith (1973) on the use of hierarchical priors. Recent Bayesian econometrics texts also highlight the importance of such models in applied work (e.g. Geweke 2005, section 3.1; Rossi et al. 2005, chapter 5; Koop 2007, chapter 12). Geweke (2005) notes the connection between models with multilevel (i.e. hierarchical) priors and latent variable specifications with conventional priors, while Rossi et al. (2005) note that individual-level parameters in these types of analyses may be of primary interest and should not be simply regarded as nuisance parameters and marginalized out of the problem. Later in this chapter, following Geweke (2001), we unite a variety of popular univariate and multivariate nonlinear models within an encompassing hierarchial structure. In this section our goal is to briefly review how the linear regression framework of the previous sections can be generalized to accommodate the correlation patterns present in such data. We do so by considering the following basic hierarchical specification:

$$y_{it} = \beta_{0i} + \boldsymbol{x}_{it}\boldsymbol{\beta}_{1i} + \epsilon_{it}, \quad i = 1, 2, \ldots, n, \ t = 1, 2, \ldots, T_i, \tag{6.46}$$

or

$$y_{it} = z_{it}\boldsymbol{\beta}_i + \epsilon_{it} \tag{6.47}$$

with $z_{it} = [1 \ \ \boldsymbol{x}_{it}]$ and $\boldsymbol{\beta}_i = [\beta_{0i} \ \ \boldsymbol{\beta}_{1i}']'$. In the above, i indexes outcomes for unit (or "individual") i and t is typically interpreted as time index. In this formulation we permit unit-level variation in both intercepts and slopes. This level of generality is seemingly reasonable yet somewhat uncommon, as much of the applied microeconometric literature finds it sufficient to impose homogeneity in slopes (i.e. $\boldsymbol{\beta}_{1i} = \boldsymbol{\beta}_1$) and to permit variation only through unit-level intercepts. Such analyses follow as a restricted case of the analysis presented here. Finally, we also consider the general case of an unbalanced panel, while simultaneously abstracting from related issues such as augmenting the model to include missing outcomes or covariate data.

We add structure to the model by supposing that the unit-level parameters are drawn from a common distribution. To this end, we specify a prior of the form:

$$\boldsymbol{\beta}_i|\boldsymbol{\beta}, \boldsymbol{\Sigma} \stackrel{ind}{\sim} G(\boldsymbol{\beta}_i|\boldsymbol{\beta}, \boldsymbol{\Sigma}), \tag{6.48}$$

where the common parameters $\boldsymbol{\beta}$ and $\boldsymbol{\Sigma}$ are of interest, and are objects we seek to learn about from the given data. The model is completed by adding priors for the common parameters $\boldsymbol{\beta}$ and $\boldsymbol{\Sigma}$ and a prior for the error variance parameter σ^2.

This formulation of the model appears rather similar to classical random effects approaches where a distribution, like that in (6.48), is specified yet is typically designated as a "population distribution" characterizing variation in tastes. Unlike the Bayesian approach to this model, however, the unit-level parameters β_i from the frequentist perspective are commonly regarded as nuisance parameters and are integrated out of the conditional likelihood. In many applications the β_i are, however, of primary interest and in such situations the Bayesian methodology seems particularly attractive, as the unit-level parameters are sampled in the course of implementing the posterior simulator. The adoption of the prior in (6.48) also imparts a form of shrinkage in the estimation of the β_i and helps to reduce concerns regarding overfitting in standard fixed effects modeling. Our representation of the model also assumes independence between the parameters of (6.48) and variables in x_{it}, although such correlations can be modeled in generalizations of this specification.

2.4.1 *Posterior simulation in the gaussian hierarchical model*

To fix ideas, let us suppose that $\epsilon_{it}|Z, \sigma^2 \overset{iid}{\sim} \mathcal{N}(0, \sigma^2)$. Extensions of the model to allow for unit-specific variance parameters or non-normality can also be handled, when desired. In addition, we employ priors of the forms:

$$\beta_i|\beta, \Sigma_\beta \overset{iid}{\sim} \mathcal{N}\left(\beta, \Sigma_\beta\right), \quad i = 1, 2, \ldots, n \tag{6.49}$$

$$\beta \sim \mathcal{N}\left(\mu_\beta, V_\beta\right) \tag{6.50}$$

$$\Sigma_\beta^{-1} \sim W\left([\kappa R]^{-1}, \kappa\right) \tag{6.51}$$

$$\sigma^2 \sim IG\left(\frac{a}{2}, b\right), \tag{6.52}$$

with W denoting a Wishart distribution.[11] The joint posterior distribution of all parameters of the model is then:

$$p\left(\{\beta_i\}_{i=1}^n, \beta, \Sigma_\beta^{-1}, \sigma^2|y\right) \propto p(\sigma^2)p(\beta)p(\Sigma_\beta^{-1}) \prod_{i=1}^n \left[\phi\left(y_i|Z_i\beta_i, \sigma^2 I_{T_i}\right)\phi(\beta_i|\beta, \Sigma_\beta)\right], \tag{6.53}$$

where $y_i = [y_{i1} \;\; y_{i2} \;\; \cdots \;\; y_{iT_i}]'$, $y = [y_1' \; y_2' \cdots y_n']'$, Z_i, in a similar manner, stacks the $\{z_{it}\}_{t=1}^{T_i}$ into a $T_i \times k$ matrix, and β_i is a $k \times 1$ vector of parameters.

We generate samples from this joint posterior by employing a blocking step, as described in Chib and Carlin (1999). That is, we propose a scheme to sample from the joint conditional $p(\{\beta_i\}_{i=1}^n, \beta|\Sigma_\beta^{-1}, \sigma^2, y)$ by first drawing from $p(\beta|\Sigma_\beta^{-1}, \sigma^2, y)$ and then drawing (independently) from the series of conditional posteriors: $p(\beta_i|\beta, \Sigma_\beta^{-1}, \sigma^2, y)$. As such, the sampling of β and $\{\beta_i\}$ makes use of the marginal-conditional decomposition, takes place in a single block, and, importantly, the sampling of $\beta_1, \beta_2, \ldots, \beta_n$ must occur immediately following the sampling of β, with no other simulation steps

[11] We parameterize the Wishart as follows: $H \sim W_k(A, \nu) \Rightarrow p(H) \propto |H|^{(\nu-k-1)/2} \exp[-(1/2)tr(A^{-1}H)]$ where H is a $k \times k$ matrix.

intervening. The sampler is completed by drawing from the complete posterior conditionals for the variance parameter and inverse covariance matrix.

Noting

$$y_i|\boldsymbol{\beta}, \boldsymbol{\Sigma}_{\beta}^{-1}, \sigma^2 \overset{ind}{\sim} \mathcal{N}\left(Z_i\boldsymbol{\beta}, \sigma^2 I_{T_i} + Z_i\boldsymbol{\Sigma}_{\beta}Z_i'\right), \quad i = 1, 2, \ldots, n, \tag{6.54}$$

it follows that

$$\boldsymbol{\beta}|\boldsymbol{\Sigma}_{\beta}^{-1}, \sigma^2, y \sim \mathcal{N}(D_{\beta}d_{\beta}, D_{\beta}), \tag{6.55}$$

where

$$D_{\beta} \equiv \left[\left(\sum_i Z_i'[\sigma^2 I_{T_i} + Z_i\boldsymbol{\Sigma}_{\beta}Z_i']^{-1}Z_i\right) + V_{\beta}^{-1}\right]^{-1} \tag{6.56}$$

and

$$d_{\beta} = \left(\sum_i Z_i'[\sigma^2 I_{T_i} + Z_i\boldsymbol{\Sigma}_{\beta}Z_i']^{-1}y_i\right) + V_{\beta}^{-1}\boldsymbol{\mu}_{\beta}. \tag{6.57}$$

A sample from the conditional density $p(\{\boldsymbol{\beta}_i\}|\boldsymbol{\beta}, \boldsymbol{\Sigma}_{\beta}^{-1}, \sigma^2, y)$ will then produce the desired draw from our joint conditional posterior distribution. Inspection of (6.53) shows that each of the $\boldsymbol{\beta}_i$ are conditionally independent a posteriori. Thus, we can independently sample from each conditional posterior, or specifically, we can independently draw, for $i = 1, 2, \ldots, n$:

$$\boldsymbol{\beta}_i|\boldsymbol{\beta}, \boldsymbol{\Sigma}_{\beta}^{-1}, \sigma^2, y \overset{ind}{\sim} \mathcal{N}\left(\left[Z_i'Z_i/\sigma^2 + \boldsymbol{\Sigma}_{\beta}^{-1}\right]^{-1}\left(Z_i'y_i/\sigma^2 + \boldsymbol{\Sigma}_{\beta}^{-1}\boldsymbol{\beta}\right), \left[Z_i'Z_i/\sigma^2 + \boldsymbol{\Sigma}_{\beta}^{-1}\right]^{-1}\right). \tag{6.58}$$

Finally, letting $T = \sum_{i=1}^{n} T_i$ we obtain:

$$\sigma^2|\boldsymbol{\beta}_1, \boldsymbol{\beta}_2, \cdots, \boldsymbol{\beta}_n, y \sim IG\left(\frac{T+a}{2}, \left[b + \frac{1}{2}\sum_{i=1}^{n}\sum_{t=1}^{T_i}(y_{it} - z_{it}\boldsymbol{\beta}_i)^2\right]\right) \tag{6.59}$$

and the conditional posterior density for the inverse covariance matrix $\boldsymbol{\Sigma}_{\beta}^{-1}$ is

$$\boldsymbol{\Sigma}_{\beta}^{-1}|\boldsymbol{\beta}, \boldsymbol{\beta}_1, \boldsymbol{\beta}_2, \cdots, \boldsymbol{\beta}_n, y \sim W\left(\left[\sum_{i=1}^{n}(\boldsymbol{\beta}_i - \boldsymbol{\beta})(\boldsymbol{\beta}_i - \boldsymbol{\beta})' + \kappa R\right]^{-1}, n + \kappa\right). \tag{6.60}$$

A posterior simulator for this normal hierarchical linear model proceeds by successively sampling from (6.55), (6.58), (6.59), and (6.60).

2.4.2 Two applications of hierarchical linear modeling

To show how hierarchical models can be estimated in practice we provide two illustrative examples. The first application has become something of a classic in the MCMC literature (though the application itself is, perhaps, rather unappealing), making use of

Table 6.3: Posterior quantities for a selection of parameters

Parameter	Post Mean	Post Std.
$\beta_{Intercept}$	106.6	2.33
β_{Slope}	6.18	0.108
$\Sigma_\beta(1,1)$	124.7	42.00
$\Sigma_\beta(2,2)$	0.277	0.087
$\Sigma_\beta(1,2)/\sqrt{\Sigma_\beta(1,1) \times \Sigma_\beta(2,2)}$	−0.126	0.210
$\beta_{0,5}$	90.73	5.50
$\beta_{0,30}$	106.62	5.15
$\beta_{1,5}$	6.43	0.229
$\beta_{1,30}$	6.13	0.214

the data set employed in the seminal study of Gelfand et al. (1990) that helped to illuminate the benefits afforded by Gibbs sampling in empirical work. The second application, hopefully more engaging, involves the impact of class size on student achievement.

Application No. 1 In our initial application, each of $n = 30$ rats is weighed at five different points in time, specifically 8, 15, 22, 29, and 36 days since birth. The outcome, y_{it}, denotes the weight of rat i in grams at date t, while x_{it} simply denotes the time of measurement, and as such, $x_{it} = x_{jt}$ for all i, j.

For our priors, we set

$$\boldsymbol{\mu}_\beta = \begin{bmatrix} 100 \\ 15 \end{bmatrix}, \quad V_\beta = \begin{bmatrix} 40^2 & 0 \\ 0 & 100 \end{bmatrix}, \quad a = 6, \quad b = 40, \quad \kappa = 5, \quad \text{and } R = \begin{bmatrix} 100 & 0 \\ 0 & .25 \end{bmatrix}. \tag{6.61}$$

Posterior means and standard deviations for a selection of parameters are provided in Table 6.3 above.

The results suggest that the birth weight of an "average" rat is about 106.6 grams, and the average weight gained per day is about 6.2 grams. The fifth entry in the table gives the correlation between the unit-level intercept and slope parameters. The posterior mean of this correlation is negative, suggesting a degree of "catching up"—rats that are large at birth tend to have lower growth rates than rats that are comparably small at birth. The last four entries of the table provide posterior means and standard deviations of parameters for the fifth and 30th rats. The results here are consistent with the general pattern in the "population": rat 5 is smaller at birth than rat 30, but also has a higher growth rate.

It is also worth noting that our posterior simulator produces draws for each $\boldsymbol{\beta}_i$ and therefore interesting quantities involving comparisons of unit-level parameters can be easily calculated. For example, we can state: $\Pr(\beta_{1,5} > \beta_{1,30}|y) \approx 0.84$, suggesting reasonably strong evidence that the fifth rat possesses a faster rate of growth than the 30th. Quantities like these can be quite useful in practice, particularly when using a hierarchical model for other, more interesting pursuits. For example, Geweke et al. (2003) use a hierarchical model and unit-level parameter estimates to evaluate and rank the performances of hospitals while Aitken and Longford (1986), Laird (1989), and Li and Tobias (2005) have used them to compare the performances of schools. Stochastic frontier models (e.g. Koop et al. 1997; Koop and Steel 2001) also share a very similar structure and goal, with one-sided distributions for unit-level parameters commonly employed to gauge the "efficiency" of cross-sectional units. In these applications, posterior simulations of the unit-level parameters are quite valuable and can be used to address interesting and relevant economic questions.

Application No. 2 In our second application we follow Krueger (1998) and Krueger and Whitmore (2001) and apply our model to analyze data from Project STAR (Student/Teacher Achievement Ratio). Project STAR was an experiment in Tennessee that randomly assigned students to one of three types of classes—small class, regular size class, and regular size class with a teacher's aide (regular/aide class). In order to be eligible for participation in the experiment, each school had to be large enough to have at least three classes per grade, thus enabling all three types of classes to be represented in every school. The panel used in our application is unbalanced, as some schools have more than three classes per grade (though all have at least three), and moreover, the number of students within a given class type is not always constant in the data (for example, some small classes have 15 students, while others have 16). The dependent variable we specify is a measure of student achievement and, specifically, is the average of a reading percentile score and math percentile score of a Project STAR student. There are two treatment variables—a dummy variable indicating whether a student is assigned to a small class and another indicating assignment to a regular/aide class. The default category, therefore, is assignment to a regular class.

The Project STAR data we use contains 79 participating schools with a total of 5,726 students who entered the project during kindergarten. The panel is unbalanced, as each school is not represented by the same number of students. We focus on the achievement measure taken at the end of the kindergarten year and consider heterogeneity of treatment impacts across schools. Therefore, in this application of the model in (6.47), i denotes the school and t no longer represents a time index but, instead, denotes the student within a school.

As one can see from the estimation results in Table 6.4, being in a small class is associated with an expected increase of 5.48 percentile points in the average test score. Furthermore, being assigned to a regular-sized class with a teacher's aide does not appear to provide any large improvement on average over assignment to a regular classroom. Importantly, the effects of class-size reductions appear to vary greatly across schools, as reflected in the posterior mean of the square root of the (2,2) element of $\boldsymbol{\Sigma}_\beta$ in (6.49), which is 10.6. As (6.49) suggests with these values, and our posterior simulations directly reveal, several schools even show a negative small class effect.

We also note that the correlation among elements of $\boldsymbol{\beta}_i$ are quite strong. The positive correlation between the small class and regular/aide parameters suggests that schools

Table 6.4: Posterior means, standard deviations, and probabilities of being positive of the parameters

Parameter	Post. Mean	Post. Std.	$\Pr(\cdot > 0 \mid y)$
β_0 (intercept)	51	1.82	1
β_1 (small class)	5.48	1.44	1
β_2 (regular/aide class)	0.311	1.26	0.596
$\sqrt{\sigma^2}$	22.9	0.221	1
$\sqrt{\Sigma_\beta(1,1)}$	15.2	1.32	1
$\sqrt{\Sigma_\beta(2,2)}$	10.6	1.24	1
$\sqrt{\Sigma_\beta(3,3)}$	8.93	1.14	1
$\Sigma_\beta(1,2)/\sqrt{\Sigma_\beta(1,1) \times \Sigma_\beta(2,2)}$	−0.454	0.111	0.000125
$\Sigma_\beta(1,3)/\sqrt{\Sigma_\beta(1,1) \times \Sigma_\beta(3,3)}$	−0.483	0.111	0.000125
$\Sigma_\beta(2,3)/\sqrt{\Sigma_\beta(2,2) \times \Sigma_\beta(3,3)}$	0.548	0.118	1

most inclined to benefit from smaller classes are also the ones with relatively large benefits to adding an aide to regular-sized classrooms. We also see a rather strong, negative correlation between the school-specific intercepts (regular-sized class parameters) and small and regular/aide parameters. One interpretation of this result, which seems to be sensible, is that schools whose students score low (high) in regular-sized classes are the ones that benefit the most (least) from class-size reductions. Adoption of the hierarchical specification to this data reveals not only a sizeable amount of heterogeneity across schools, but also sheds light on the schools that would be most impacted by changes to class size.

The foregoing examples and discussion were intended to introduce rather than fully describe Bayesian approaches to hierarchical linear models. Such methods can be easily extended to nonlinear models, including the binary and multiple choice models we will discuss in later sections. Moreover, recent work has sought to relax many of the distributional assumptions made, particularly in modeling the unit-level parameters (see e.g. Rossi and Allenby, Chapter 8 of this volume). Finally, we note that time-invariant covariates can be included in the middle stage of the hierarchy, or the modeling of $\boldsymbol{\beta}_i$, and more general error structures can be considered, for example, allowing for autocorrelation among the ϵ_{it} (see e.g. Chib and Jeliazkov 2006 on handling this and other issues in a more complex dynamic binary choice setting).

2.5 Endogeneity in linear models

The problem of endogeneity plays a central role in the practice of microeconometrics. While most textbook discussions of and applications involving endogeneity are classical in nature, centered upon or employing Instrumental Variables (IV), Two stage least squares (2SLS), or other approaches for estimation, studies such as Drèze (1976), Drèze and Richard (1983), Geweke (1996a), Kleibergen and Zivot (2003), Hoogerheide et al. (2007b), Sims (2007), and Conley et al. (2008) mark important Bayesian advances in this literature. The importance of this issue is also suggested by the rather prominent and detailed treatment it receives in many current Bayesian textbooks (Lancaster 2004: chapter 8; Rossi et al. 2005: chapter 7; Koop et al. 2007: chapter 14) and even elsewhere in this volume (e.g. Rossi and Allenby, Chapter 8 this volume). Furthermore, numerous applications have been tackled from a Bayesian point of view, often highlighting the ease with which MCMC methods can be adapted to deal with endogeneity problems in many different kinds of models (e.g. Li 1998; Geweke et al. 2003; Munkin and Trivedi 2003; Deb et al. 2006; Kline and Tobias 2008; Chib et al. 2009).

We frame our discussion of endogeneity within the context of a linear regression model, where one of the right-hand-side variables is endogenous. While this is somewhat restrictive, it is not terribly so, as simple generalizations can accommodate higher dimension endogeneity problems. Moreover, a recent study by Chernozhukov and Hansen (2008) suggests that this is the modal model entertained in the literature[12] and thus serves as a natural starting point for our analysis.

Consider the model:

$$y_i = \alpha_0 + \alpha_1 x_i + \boldsymbol{\alpha}_2 \mathbf{w}_i + \epsilon_i \tag{6.62}$$

$$x_i = \beta_0 + \boldsymbol{\beta}_1 \mathbf{z}_i + u_i, \tag{6.63}$$

where

$$\begin{bmatrix} \epsilon_i \\ u_i \end{bmatrix} \Bigg| W, Z \overset{iid}{\sim} \mathcal{N}\left[\begin{pmatrix} 0 \\ 0 \end{pmatrix}, \begin{pmatrix} \sigma_\epsilon^2 & \sigma_{\epsilon u} \\ \sigma_{\epsilon u} & \sigma_u^2 \end{pmatrix} \right] \equiv \mathcal{N}(\mathbf{0}, \boldsymbol{\Sigma}).$$

The exogenous variables $\mathbf{w}_i$ are covariates entering the y-outcome equation, while $\mathbf{z}_i$ enter the reduced form equation for x. As shown below, there can be (and always is) overlap between these two sets of variables, yet identification will require the appearance of at least one column of Z that is not contained in W.

Letting $\boldsymbol{\theta}$ denote all the parameters of the model, we can write

$$p(\epsilon_i, u_i|\boldsymbol{\theta}) = p(\epsilon_i|u_i, \boldsymbol{\theta})p(u_i|\boldsymbol{\theta}). \tag{6.64}$$

Noting that the Jacobian of the transformation from (ϵ_i, u_i) to (y_i, x_i) is unity, we obtain

$$p(y_i, x_i|\boldsymbol{\theta}) = \phi\left(y_i \left| \alpha_0 + \alpha_1 x_i + \boldsymbol{\alpha}_2 \mathbf{w}_i + \frac{\sigma_{\epsilon u}}{\sigma_u^2}(x_i - \beta_0 - \boldsymbol{\beta}_1 \mathbf{z}_i), \sigma_\epsilon^2(1 - \rho_{\epsilon u}^2) \right.\right)$$
$$\times \phi(x_i|\beta_0 + \boldsymbol{\beta}_1 \mathbf{z}_i, \sigma_u^2), \tag{6.65}$$

where $\rho_{\epsilon u} \equiv \sigma_{\epsilon u}/[\sigma_\epsilon \sigma_u]$.

[12] Chernozhukov and Hansen (2008) find 108 articles in the *American Economic Review* (AER), *Quarterly Journal of Economics* (QJE), and *Journal of Political Economics* (JPE) over the period 1999–2004 that employ linear IV, and 91 of these report results with one endogenous right-hand-side variable.

It is useful to pause and discuss identification in the context of this system of equations. To this end, first consider the case where the set of exogenous covariates is common to both equations, that is, $z_i = w_i$. In this case, (6.65) becomes:

$$p(y_i, x_i|\boldsymbol{\theta}) = \phi\left(y_i \left| \left[\alpha_0 - \beta_0 \frac{\sigma_{\epsilon u}}{\sigma_u^2}\right] + \left[\alpha_1 + \frac{\sigma_{\epsilon u}}{\sigma_u^2}\right] x_i + \left[\boldsymbol{\alpha}_2 - \boldsymbol{\beta}_1 \frac{\sigma_{\epsilon u}}{\sigma_u^2}\right] w_i, \sigma_\epsilon^2(1-\rho_{\epsilon u}^2)\right.\right) \quad (6.66)$$
$$\times \phi(x_i|\beta_0 + \boldsymbol{\beta}_1 z_i, \sigma_u^2).$$

Some quick accounting, then, shows that the likelihood is a function of just seven (blocks of) parameters:

$$\beta_0,\ \boldsymbol{\beta}_1,\ \sigma_u^2,\ \psi_0 = [\alpha_0 - \beta_0 \frac{\sigma_{\epsilon u}}{\sigma_u^2}],\ \psi_1 = [\alpha_1 + \frac{\sigma_{\epsilon u}}{\sigma_u^2}],$$
$$\boldsymbol{\psi}_2 = [\boldsymbol{\alpha}_2 - \boldsymbol{\beta}_1 \frac{\sigma_{\epsilon u}}{\sigma_u^2}],\ \text{and}\ \psi_3 = \sigma_\epsilon^2(1 - \rho_{\epsilon u}^2), \quad (6.67)$$

whereas we seek to recover the eight "structural" parameters of $\boldsymbol{\theta}$:

$$\alpha_0, \quad \alpha_1, \quad \boldsymbol{\alpha}_2, \quad \beta_0, \quad \boldsymbol{\beta}_1, \quad \sigma_u^2, \quad \sigma_\epsilon^2, \quad \text{and}\ \sigma_{\epsilon u}. \quad (6.68)$$

As a result, the quantities in (6.67) are identified by the likelihood, whereas the full set of structural parameters in (6.68) are not identifiable. Importantly, note that the "causal effect" α_1—the object that garners most attention in practice—is among the parameters that are not identifiable when the set of covariates appearing in (6.62) and (6.63) are the same.

While several assumptions regarding the model can be used to achieve identification in a specification like (6.62)–(6.63),[13] the most common one is to assume the presence of at least one element of Z that is not contained in W. That is, a careful understanding of the problem at hand leads to the determination of a set of variables (or "instruments") in z_i that are not contained in w_i and can be exploited for purposes of identification and estimation. Indeed, (6.65) shows how such exclusion restrictions can be exploited for identification purposes: The parameter $\boldsymbol{\beta}_1$ is identifiable from the marginal (reduced form) density of x_i, and the coefficient on the elements of z *not contained in* w in the conditional density $y|x$ becomes $-[\sigma_{\epsilon u}/\sigma_u^2]\boldsymbol{\beta}_1$. Together, these two pieces of information enable identification of the ratio $\sigma_{\epsilon u}/\sigma_u^2$, which is attributable to

[13] The "kitchen sink" approach represents such an alternative, where a host of covariates are included in (6.62), and the rich set of employed observables is argued to be sufficient to render ϵ and x uncorrelated, or at least approximately so. Common sense or an inspection of (6.65) reveals that (6.62) can then be estimated as a single equation when $\sigma_{\epsilon u} = 0$, leading to a recursive system. (The implications of this assumption were first noted by the Cowles Commission, with Christ (1994) offering a nice overview of their early econometric contributions in this (and other) settings. The restriction $\sigma_{\epsilon u} = 0$ and its implications remain relevant today, e.g. in identification of VAR models). While this identification strategy typically does not sit well with the majority of practitioners, who have come to view IV as *the* solution to the identification problem and *the* device enabling the extraction of causal impacts, it does occasionally find a sympathetic referee (or two or three). Dearden et al. (2002) is a prominent, well-crafted example. Other alternatives for identification, even less widely used in practice, include the imposition of cross-equation parameter restrictions.

the role of unobserved confounding. Once this ratio is known, the causal effect α_1, as well as the remaining parameters of the model, clearly become identifiable, as is evident from (6.65). This simple argument illustrates the value of instruments as vehicles for identification, and also suggests potential difficulties in separating α_1 from $\sigma_{\epsilon u}/\sigma_u^2$ when the instruments are poor (weak). We will revisit this issue in the analysis of Section 2.5.3.

2.5.1 *Posterior simulation*

Stack the variables into vectors and matrices by writing:

$$\begin{bmatrix} y_i \\ x_i \end{bmatrix} = \begin{bmatrix} 1 & x_i & w_i & 0 & 0 \\ 0 & 0 & 0 & 1 & z_i \end{bmatrix} \begin{bmatrix} \alpha_0 \\ \alpha_1 \\ \alpha_2 \\ \beta_0 \\ \beta_1 \end{bmatrix} + \begin{bmatrix} \epsilon_i \\ u_i \end{bmatrix} \tag{6.69}$$

or

$$\tilde{y}_i = \tilde{X}_i \boldsymbol{\beta} + \tilde{\epsilon}_i, \tag{6.70}$$

with $\tilde{y}_i$, $\tilde{X}_i$, $\boldsymbol{\beta}$, and $\tilde{\epsilon}_i$ defined in the obvious ways. Furthermore, suppose we continue to employ priors of the forms:

$$\boldsymbol{\beta} \sim \mathcal{N}(\boldsymbol{\mu}_\beta, V_\beta) \tag{6.71}$$

$$\boldsymbol{\Sigma}^{-1} \sim W\left[(\kappa R)^{-1}, \kappa\right]. \tag{6.72}$$

With this done, posterior simulation in our linear model with an endogeneity problem follows in a straightforward way. In particular, a simple two-block Gibbs algorithm can be employed that iteratively samples from the following two conditional posterior distributions:

$$\boldsymbol{\beta}|\boldsymbol{\Sigma}, y, x \sim \mathcal{N}(D_\beta d_\beta, D_\beta), \tag{6.73}$$

where

$$D_\beta = \left(V_\beta^{-1} + \sum_{i=1}^{n} \tilde{X}_i{}' \boldsymbol{\Sigma}^{-1} \tilde{X}_i\right)^{-1}, \quad d_\beta = V_\beta^{-1} \boldsymbol{\mu}_\beta + \sum_{i=1}^{n} \left(\tilde{X}_i{}' \boldsymbol{\Sigma}^{-1} \tilde{y}_i\right) \tag{6.74}$$

and

$$\boldsymbol{\Sigma}^{-1}|\boldsymbol{\beta}, y, x \sim W\left(\left[\sum_{i=1}^{n} \tilde{\epsilon}_i \tilde{\epsilon}_i{}' + \kappa R\right]^{-1}, n + \kappa\right). \tag{6.75}$$

A posterior simulator for this model proceeds by sampling from (6.73) and (6.75). The reader may note, and perhaps be puzzled by, the connection of the above sampling scheme to what one would obtain from a standard SUR analysis where no endogenous variables appear as right-hand-side covariates. That is, one may rightfully ask: why does the simulator for this model with an endogeneity problem reduce to essentially the same simulator for a bivariate SUR without an endogeneity concern? The connection here critically relies on the Jacobian of transformation being equal to one; such a result would not be obtained for a purely simultaneous equations model that is not triangular.

2.5.2 *Application: BMI data*

To illustrate how such methods are applied in practice, we consider a restricted application of the model of Kline and Tobias (2008), who employ data from the British Cohort study, a longitudinal survey of the cohort of all people born in Great Britain between April 5 and April 11, 1970. The data set contains the usual set of demographic variables and wage outcomes, along with heights and weights of the survey participants. Furthermore, one of the survey waves also obtains information on the heights and weights of the respondent's parents. These variables enable us to calculate the respondent's Body Mass Index (BMI), defined as weight (in kilograms) divided by the square of height (in meters), as well as the BMI of his/her parents.

We use hourly wages as our outcome of interest, which are observed when the respondents are approximately 29 years of age. Furthermore, we consider the analysis for males only. Our application is designed with the primary intent to estimate the "causal" impact of BMI on (log) hourly wages, a question that has received rather significant attention within the labor literature. As additional controls, we include family income (when the respondent was 10 years of age), and whether or not the respondent has a college degree. The constructed parental BMI variables, denoted MomBMI and DadBMI are used as our instruments (exclusion restrictions) for child BMI. Our final sample consists of $n = 2,561$ observations.[14]

Coefficient posterior means and standard deviations are reported in Table 6.5 below, setting $\boldsymbol{\mu}_\beta = 0$ $V_\beta = 10I_k$, $\kappa = 5$, and $\boldsymbol{R} = I_2$ as our prior hyperparameters.

The results presented in Table 6.5 are generally consistent with the findings of Kline and Tobias (2008). First, our instruments are important variables in explaining variation in BMI, clearly suggesting that higher parental BMI leads to higher child BMI, as our simulations would show $\Pr(\beta_{1,MomBMI} > 0, \beta_{1,DadBMI} > 0 | \boldsymbol{y}, \boldsymbol{x}) = 1$. Furthermore, the relationship between BMI and wages is negative, as a one-point increase in BMI leads to an approximate 4.1 reduction in hourly wages. Finally, the role of unobservables is also important and strong evidence is provided that $\rho_{\epsilon u} > 0$. Kline and Tobias (2008) argue that this is consistent with a tradeoff between work effort and health—individuals unobservably dedicated to their job (thus, presumably, earning higher wages) do so at the expense of investments in health (regular exercise, maintaining a well-balanced diet, etc.), leading to a positive correlation between ϵ and u.

2.5.3 *A few comments on weak instruments*

As the reader may be aware, there has been a great deal of attention given recently to the problem of weak/many instruments (an excellent recent treatment of this issue

[14] This data set is, unfortunately, restricted access and therefore can not be made available on the website accompanying this chapter.

Table 6.5: Parameter posterior means and standard deviations from BMI application

Variable	Post. Mean	Post Std.
Log Wage Equation		
Constant	2.96	0.215
BMI	−0.041	0.008
FamInc	0.001	0.0001
Degree	0.244	0.024
BMI Equation		
Constant	15.10	0.670
FamInc	0.0003	0.001
Degree	−0.599	0.172
MomBMI	0.176	0.018
DadBMI	0.259	0.020
Other Parameters		
σ_ϵ^2	0.200	0.011
σ_u^2	11.22	0.305
$\rho_{\epsilon u}$	0.342	0.057

from the Bayesian perspective is offered by Hoogerheide et al. 2007a). Much interest in this issue developed subsequent to Bound et al.'s (1995) critique of the study by Angrist and Krueger (1991), the latter of which paved the way for a host of instrumental variable-based studies and accounted for an increased emphasis on natural experiments in economics. While it is not our intent to review the history of this literature, or to document any of the recent frequentist developments within it, we do wish to note that Bayesian approaches are not immune to the weak instruments "problem" and that the presence of such instruments has potentially important consequences for posterior inference.

We demonstrate this point via two generated data experiments. Specifically, we first generate $n = 1,000$ observations from a simplified version of (6.62)–(6.63):[15]

$$y_i = \alpha_0 + \alpha_1 x_i + \epsilon_i \tag{6.76}$$

$$x_i = \beta_0 + \beta_1 z_i + u_i \tag{6.77}$$

where $z_i \overset{iid}{\sim} \mathcal{N}(0,1)$, $\sigma_\epsilon = \sigma_u = 1$, and $\rho_{xy} = 0.5$, to introduce a reasonable degree of unobserved confounding.[16] We generate two different data sets under two different values of β_1, setting $\beta_1 = 0.01$ or $\beta_1 = 1$, to investigate what happens to aspects of the

[15] The intention here is not to reproduce sampling properties of the procedure by generating numerous data sets of the same size. The points we seek to make can be illustrated with one realization of data from this (adequately large) sample.

[16] A complete description of the parameters used to generate the data is given in Table 6.6.

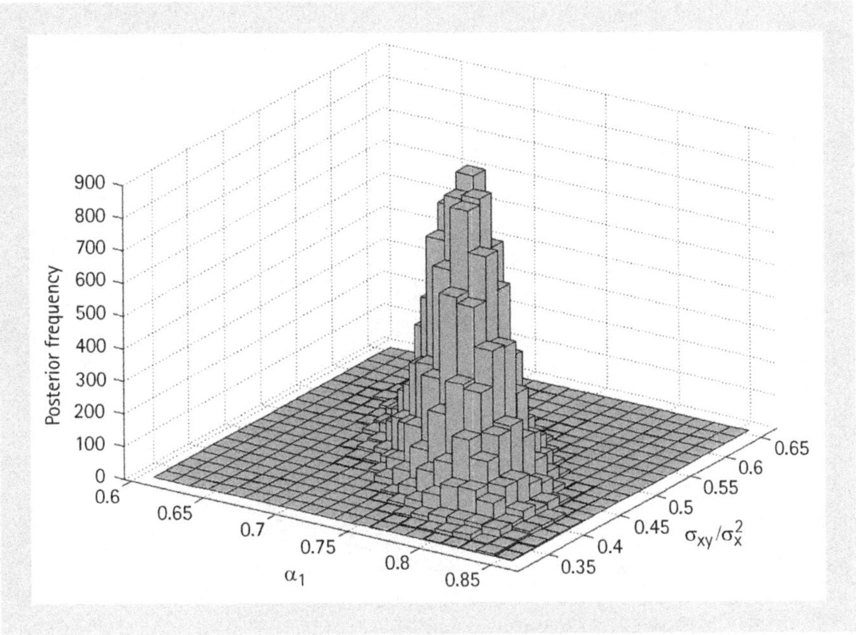

FIGURE 6.4 Joint posterior, strong instrument

joint posterior when the instrument is "weak" or "strong," respectively. To justify these labels, note that the population R-squared for the reduced form (marginal density for x) equation in (6.77), given that $\text{Var}(z) = 1$ and $\sigma_\epsilon = \sigma_u = 1$, is

$$\frac{\beta_1^2}{\beta_1^2 + 1}. \tag{6.78}$$

Thus, when the instrument is weak in this design, the population R-squared is (approximately) 0.0001[17] while the strong instrument gives a population R-squared value of 1/2.

Results from this experiment are provided in Figures 6.4–6.5. Before discussing these details, we first note that inference regarding the "total effect" of x on y, obtained from the conditional density $y|x$ in (6.67) as $\alpha_1 + \sigma_{\epsilon u}/\sigma_u^2$, is not affected by the quality of the instrument. To illustrate, we note that the posterior mean (and standard deviation) for this total effect parameter are 1.23 (0.027) and 1.26 (0.028) for the weak and strong instrument cases, respectively. Thus, with an equal sample size, our ability to assess the overall or total impact of x on y is independent of the strength of the instrument.

Figures 6.4 and 6.5 show how the strength of the instrument does, however, aid in separating the "causal" effect α_1 from the effect attributable to unobserved confounding,

[17] Though this seems small, it is very similar to the R-squared obtained from a regression of educational attainment on quarter of birth using the Angrist and Krueger (1991) data.

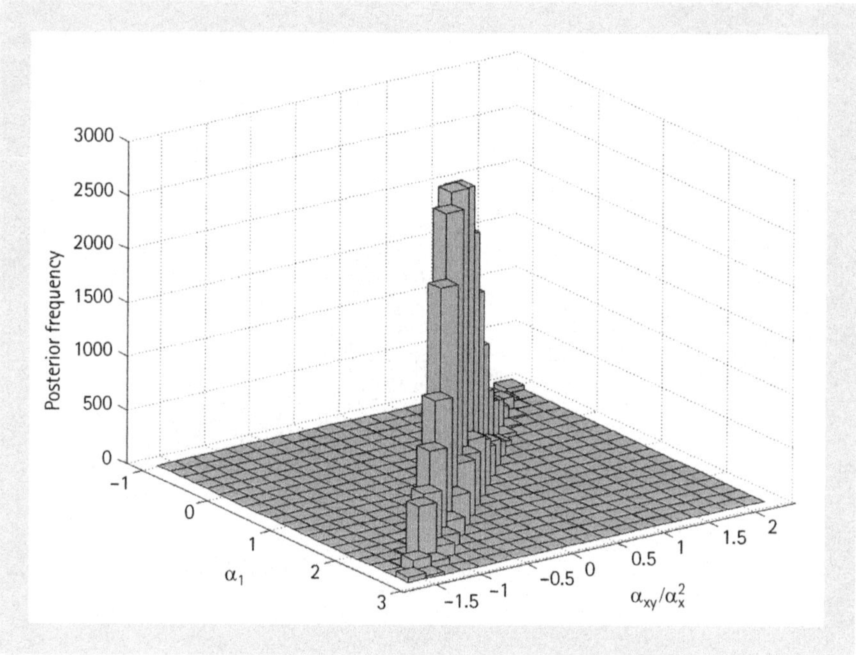

FIGURE 6.5 Joint posterior, weak instrument

$\sigma_{\epsilon u}/\sigma_u^2$. In Figure 6.4 results for the strong instrument case are presented. Importantly, note how this joint posterior has nearly collapsed around the parameter values $\alpha_1 = 0.75$ (left-side axis) and $\sigma_{\epsilon u}/\sigma_u^2 = 0.5$ (right-side axis) that were used to generate the data.

Figure 6.5 presents a similar set of results for the weak instruments case. First, we note the very diffuse axes over which this posterior surface is plotted, which are vastly more spread out than those of Figure 6.4. Second, we observe the ridge in the likelihood surface along the line (approximately) given by $\alpha_1 + \sigma_{\epsilon u}/\sigma_u^2 = 1.25$. In the presence of weak instruments, we fare equally well in identifying the total effect of x on y, but our ability to separate this impact into a "causal" effect and an effect arising from unobserved confounding suffers substantially.

Our final generated data experiment illustrates the role of the prior when weak instruments are present. For this purpose we generate two different data sets, each with $n = 200$ observations. The process used to generate each data set follows the same design as the one previously employed in this section, leading to separate data sets created for analysis of the "weak" and "strong" IV cases. Unlike the previous analysis, however, we also consider two different priors and employ both in the estimation of the weak IV and strong IV generated data sets. The hyperparameters $\kappa = 3$, $\boldsymbol{R} = \boldsymbol{I}_2$, and $\boldsymbol{V}_{\boldsymbol{\beta}} = \boldsymbol{I}_4$ are constant in all experiments. However, for one prior (denoted P1), we set the prior mean of $\boldsymbol{\beta}$ to be the zero vector: $\boldsymbol{\mu}_{\boldsymbol{\beta}} = [0\ 0\ 0\ 0]'$ and in the second (denoted P2), we set $\boldsymbol{\mu}_{\boldsymbol{\beta}} = [0\ -3\ 0\ 0]'$. Thus, the two priors alter the mean of α_1, with P1 centering the

Table 6.6: Posterior means from generated data experiment

	True Value	Strong, P1	Strong, P2	Weak, P1	Weak, P2
α_0	2.00	2.02	2.00	1.59	0.553
α_1	0.750	0.728	0.710	0.338	−0.725
β_0	−1.00	−1.07	−1.07	−0.984	−0.982
β_1	1.00 or 0.010	0.968	0.945	−0.016	0.004
σ_ϵ^2	1.00	1.05	1.08	1.79	4.53
σ_u^2	1.00	1.07	1.08	0.912	0.913
$\rho_{\epsilon u}$	0.500	0.500	0.514	0.601	0.886

α_1 prior over zero, and P2 centering it over -3. Our goal is to examine how this change in prior impacts our posterior results, and to assess its differential impact across the weak and strong IV data sets in particular. The fact that the prior should matter when the IV is weak was already suggested by Figure 6.5.

As shown in Table 6.6, with strong instruments, parameter posterior means are quite close to the values of the parameters used to generate the data. As expected, the shift in the prior mean of α_1 does lower the posterior mean of α_1 when the instruments are strong, though not tremendously so. On the other hand, when the instruments are weak, posterior means do not closely match the values of the parameters used to generate the data and the prior has a sizeable impact on our calculations, as the posterior mean of α_1 even changes sign and remains far away from 0.75.

Although not shown in the tables above, the mixing of the posterior simulations is also strongly affected by the quality of the instruments; in the strong IV case, inefficiency factors (see Chib, Chapter 5 of this volume for additional information on these factors) were less than four for all parameters, and approximately unity for some, suggesting that our Gibbs calculations are essentially of the same quality as those that would be obtained under iid sampling from the posterior. Furthermore, in the weak instrument case, inefficiency factors for regression and variance parameters of (6.76) as well as $\rho_{\epsilon u}$ were in excess of 1,000, suggesting that more than 1,000n Gibbs simulations would be required to achieve the numerical accuracy afforded by n iid posterior draws.

3 Nonlinear Hierarchical Models

In this section we review posterior simulation in several univariate nonlinear models that are linear in suitably defined latent data (Geweke and Keane (2001) and Geweke (2005) take up a wide range of latent variable models and offer a similar type of unifying treatment). The structure of and resulting posterior simulators for many simple and popular models of this type can be united with a hierarchical structure and we present such a general description here. Let $\boldsymbol{\theta} = [\boldsymbol{\beta}' \; \boldsymbol{\alpha}' \; \sigma^2]'$ and consider a representative *univariate latent linear model*, expressed as

$$p(\boldsymbol{\theta}) = p(\boldsymbol{\alpha})p(\boldsymbol{\beta})p(\sigma^2) \tag{6.79}$$

$$z_i|X, \boldsymbol{\theta} \overset{ind}{\sim} \mathcal{N}(x_i\boldsymbol{\beta}, \sigma^2), \quad i = 1, 2, \ldots, n \tag{6.80}$$

$$y_i = g(z_i, \boldsymbol{\alpha}), \quad i = 1, 2, \ldots, n. \tag{6.81}$$

Equation (6.79) specifies a prior for the model's parameters $\boldsymbol{\theta}$, and throughout we specify prior independence among these parameters. Equation (6.80) describes the generation of a latent variable, only partially observed by the econometrician. To fix ideas we specify that this latent variable is conditionally normally distributed throughout our discussion. The normality assumption can be relaxed (and frequently is in practice), and below we will reference sources that generalize this assumption in the context of particular models. Finally, y_i represents the observed outcome, connected to the latent data and parameters through the function $g(z_i, \boldsymbol{\alpha})$.

With the use of data augmentation (e.g. Tanner and Wong 1987; Albert and Chib 1993a), posterior simulation in these models typically proceeds by first characterizing the joint posterior distribution of latent data and parameters:

$$p(z, \boldsymbol{\theta}|y) \propto p(\boldsymbol{\theta})p(z|\boldsymbol{\theta})p(y|z, \boldsymbol{\theta}) \tag{6.82}$$

$$= p(\boldsymbol{\theta}) \prod_{i=1}^{n} \phi(z_i|x_i\boldsymbol{\beta}, \sigma^2) I[y_i = g(z_i, \boldsymbol{\alpha})], \tag{6.83}$$

with $z = [z_1 \; z_2 \; \cdots \; z_n]'$, $y = [y_1 \; y_2 \; \cdots \; y_n]'$, $I(\cdot) = 1$ if the statement in the parentheses is true and $I(\cdot) = 0$ otherwise. A posterior simulator produced via the Gibbs sampler, then, successively draws from complete posterior conditionals for $\boldsymbol{\alpha}$, σ^2, $\boldsymbol{\beta}$, and z. Assuming that the prior for $\boldsymbol{\beta}$ is of the form: $\boldsymbol{\beta} \sim \mathcal{N}(\boldsymbol{\mu}_\beta, V_\beta)$, $\sigma^2 \sim IG(a/2, b)$, and not making any further assumptions regarding the prior for $\boldsymbol{\alpha}$, we obtain:

$$\boldsymbol{\beta}|z, \sigma^2, y \sim \mathcal{N}\left(\left[X'X/\sigma^2 + V_\beta^{-1}\right]^{-1}\left[X'z/\sigma^2 + V_\beta^{-1}\boldsymbol{\mu}_\beta\right], \left[X'X/\sigma^2 + V_\beta^{-1}\right]^{-1}\right) \tag{6.84}$$

$$\sigma^2|\boldsymbol{\beta}, z, y \sim IG\left(\frac{n+a}{2}, \left[b + \frac{1}{2}\sum_{i=1}^{n}(z_i - x_i\boldsymbol{\beta})^2\right]\right) \tag{6.85}$$

$$p(z_i|\boldsymbol{\beta}, \boldsymbol{\alpha}, y) \propto \phi(z_i|x_i\boldsymbol{\beta}, \sigma^2) I[z_i \in \{z_i : y_i = g(z_i, \boldsymbol{\alpha})\}] \tag{6.86}$$

$$p(\boldsymbol{\alpha}|z, y) \propto p(\boldsymbol{\alpha}) \prod_{i=1}^{n} I[y_i = g(z_i, \boldsymbol{\alpha})]. \tag{6.87}$$

The computational value of the latent data becomes apparent from expressions (6.84) and (6.85), as the conditional posteriors for the parameters $\boldsymbol{\beta}$ and σ^2 closely mimic those in Section 2.1, given that the model is essentially a linear regression model in the latent data z. The third posterior conditional is also easily sampled, as it amounts to drawing each z_i, independently from an $\mathcal{N}(x_i\beta, \sigma^2)$ distribution, truncated to a region (interval) defined by α and y_i.

In the following sections we review how this structure unites Bayesian approaches to several popular econometric models, including the probit model, the tobit model, and the ordered probit. We begin with models for binary choice.

3.1 Models for binary choice

For models of binary choice, equations (6.79)–(6.81) apply, with α being null (empty) and σ^2 restricted to unity for identification purposes. Therefore, posterior simulation in binary choice problems only involves sampling from (6.84) and (6.86). Furthermore, equation (6.81) specializes to:

$$y_i = I(z_i > 0), \quad i = 1, 2, \ldots, n. \tag{6.88}$$

3.1.1 *The probit model*

The probit model emerges under the assumption of conditionally normally distributed latent data, as in (6.80). Therefore, posterior simulation proceeds, as noted in Albert and Chib (1993a), by first drawing β from the normal posterior conditional in (6.84) (with $\sigma^2 = 1$) and then independently sampling the latent data as follows:

$$z_i|y, \beta \sim \begin{cases} \mathcal{TN}_{(0,\infty)}(x_i\beta, 1) & \text{if} y_i = 1 \\ \mathcal{TN}_{(-\infty,0]}(x_i\beta, 1) & \text{if} y_i = 0 \end{cases}, \quad i = 1, 2, \ldots, n, \tag{6.89}$$

where, notationally, $x \sim \mathcal{TN}_{(a,b)}(\mu, \sigma^2)$ denotes that x is a normally distributed random variable with (untruncated) mean μ and (untruncated) variance σ^2 which is then truncated to the interval (a, b). This truncated density retains the shape of the normal density over (a, b), is zero outside this interval, and is simply scaled up to be proper. While one can generate draws from the truncated normal above by repeatedly drawing from a $\mathcal{N}(x_i\beta, 1)$ distribution and simply waiting for a draw that falls in the desired half-line, this process is quite inefficient, and sometimes prohibitively so. Draws from the desired truncated normals in (6.89) can, however, be *directly* produced using the method of inversion. To this end, let

$$u \sim U(0, 1)$$

be a draw from the uniform distribution on the unit interval. We can then form the variable w, where

$$w = \mu + \sigma\Phi^{-1}\left(\Phi\left(\frac{a-\mu}{\sigma}\right) + u\left[\Phi\left(\frac{b-\mu}{\sigma}\right) - \Phi\left(\frac{a-\mu}{\sigma}\right)\right]\right), \tag{6.90}$$

and simple derivations show that $w \sim \mathcal{TN}_{(a,b)}(\mu, \sigma^2)$.

When applying this result for posterior simulation of latent data in the probit model, note that when $y_i = 1$, $a = 0$ and $b = \infty$ and thus $\Phi([b - x_i\boldsymbol{\beta}]/\sigma) = 1$. Likewise, when $y_i = 0$, $a = -\infty$ and $b = 0$ so that $\Phi([a - x_i\boldsymbol{\beta}]/\sigma) = 0$. In this way a Gibbs sampler for the probit proceeds in two steps: multivariate normal sampling from the $\boldsymbol{\beta}$ posterior conditional and independent truncated normal sampling for the posterior conditional for the latent data.[18]

3.1.2 *The logit model*

The model that is (arguably) most commonly employed with binary data is the logit model, which specifies

$$\Pr(y_i = 1|\boldsymbol{x}_i, \boldsymbol{\beta}) = \frac{\exp(\boldsymbol{x}_i\boldsymbol{\beta})}{1 + \exp(\boldsymbol{x}_i\boldsymbol{\beta})}. \tag{6.91}$$

There are several Bayesian alternatives for estimating the logit model and we describe a few possibilities here.

For purposes of continuity, we should first review how the framework of (6.79)–(6.81) can be extended to accommodate the logit. This can be done by, again, first setting $\sigma^2 = 1$ and noting $\boldsymbol{\alpha}$ is null for the logit. Furthermore, we expand the parameter vector $\boldsymbol{\theta}$ to $\boldsymbol{\theta} = [\boldsymbol{\beta}'\ \boldsymbol{\lambda}']$. The new set of parameters $\boldsymbol{\lambda}$ will be regarded as *scale mixing variables*, and the addition of such variables to the error variance will aid in expanding the normal sampling model. To illustrate the role of these variables, we could consider the linear model

$$y_i = \boldsymbol{x}_i\boldsymbol{\beta} + \epsilon_i, \qquad \epsilon_i|X, \boldsymbol{\lambda}, \sigma^2, \overset{ind}{\sim} \mathcal{N}(0, \lambda_i\sigma^2),$$

where

$$\lambda_i|\boldsymbol{\lambda}_0 \overset{iid}{\sim} G(\boldsymbol{\lambda}_0)$$

for some prior distribution G and set of hyperparameters $\boldsymbol{\lambda}_0$. As demonstrated in previous work (e.g. Andrews and Mallows 1974; Carlin and Polson 1991; Geweke 1993; Koop et al. 2007, chapter 15), different choices of G give rise to sampling models (marginalized over $\boldsymbol{\lambda}$) other than the normal. Specifically, assuming $\lambda_i \sim IG(\nu/2, \nu/2)$ produces a Student-t sampling model for $y|\boldsymbol{\beta}, \sigma^2$, while assuming $\lambda_i \sim Exp(2)$ (an exponential distribution with mean 2) produces a double exponential sampling model for $y|\boldsymbol{\beta}, \sigma^2$.

A similar structure, with λ_i specified to follow the asymptotic distribution of the Kolmogorov distance statistic, produces a logistic distribution for $\boldsymbol{y}|\boldsymbol{\beta}, \sigma^2$. Applied to our latent variable representation of the binary choice model, we write:

[18] Holmes and Held (2006) actually suggest using a blocking step, first marginalizing $\boldsymbol{\beta}$ out of the latent variable equation, producing a multivariate normal for the latent data vector $\boldsymbol{z}$. Each element of $\boldsymbol{z}$ must then be sampled from a univariate truncated normal, whose mean depends on all other elements of $\boldsymbol{z}$ and must be updated each time a new element of $\boldsymbol{z}$ is sampled. While this may afford some improved mixing properties, its use remains rather uncommon in practice, as the simpler alternative in (6.84) and (6.89) displays adequate mixing performance.

$$z_i|\boldsymbol{\beta}, \lambda_i \overset{ind}{\sim} \mathcal{N}(\boldsymbol{x}_i\boldsymbol{\beta}, 4\lambda_i^2), \quad i = 1, 2, \ldots, n, \tag{6.92}$$

where the λ_i are independently distributed, with priors that follow the asymptotic distribution of the Kolmogorov distance statistic:

$$p(\lambda_i) = 8\sum_{k=1}^{\infty}(-1)^{k+1}k^2\lambda_i \exp(-2k^2\lambda_i^2), \quad \lambda_i > 0, \quad i = 1, 2, \ldots, n. \tag{6.93}$$

We sketch in general detail why this strategy reproduces the logit model.[19] We do so by obtaining the density for the latent z_i marginalized over the mixing variable λ_i. To this end, note that, provided it is permissible to interchange the order of integration and summation (and dropping the subscript i in λ_i for notational ease):

$$p(z_i|\boldsymbol{x}_i, \boldsymbol{\beta}) = \int_0^{\infty}(2\pi 4\lambda^2)^{-1/2} \exp\left(-\frac{1}{8\lambda^2}(z_i - \boldsymbol{x}_i\boldsymbol{\beta})^2\right) 8\sum_{k=1}^{\infty}(-1)^{k+1}k^2\lambda \exp(-2k^2\lambda^2)d\lambda \tag{6.94}$$

$$= 4(2\pi)^{-1/2}\sum_{k=1}^{\infty}(-1)^{k+1}k^2 \int_0^{\infty} \exp\left[-\frac{1}{2}\left(\frac{1}{4}(z_i - \boldsymbol{x}_i\boldsymbol{\beta})^2\lambda^{-2} + 4k^2\lambda^2\right)\right] d\lambda. \tag{6.95}$$

The integral above can be simplified by observing (e.g. Andrews and Mallows 1974: equation 2.2):

$$\int_0^{\infty} \exp\left(-\frac{1}{2}[a^2u^2 + b^2u^{-2}]\right) du = \left(\frac{\pi}{2a^2}\right)^{1/2} \exp(-|ab|). \tag{6.96}$$

Making use of the formula above, and then simplifying (6.95) gives the alternating series representation:

$$p(z_i|\boldsymbol{x}_i, \boldsymbol{\beta}) = \sum_{k=1}^{\infty}(-1)^{k+1}k \exp\left(-k|z_i - \boldsymbol{x}_i\boldsymbol{\beta}|\right). \tag{6.97}$$

To evaluate this quantity, recall that $(1+x)^{-1}$ can be represented in series form as $\sum_{k=0}^{\infty}(-1)^k x^k$ for $|x| < 1$. Thus, by differentiation,

$$(1+x)^{-2} = \sum_{k=1}^{\infty}(-1)^{k+1}kx^{k-1}. \tag{6.98}$$

Applying this result to our formula in (6.97) with $x = \exp(-|z_i - \boldsymbol{x}_i\boldsymbol{\beta}|)$, we obtain:

$$p(z_i|\boldsymbol{x}_i, \boldsymbol{\beta}) = \frac{\exp(-|z_i - \boldsymbol{x}_i\boldsymbol{\beta}|)}{[1 + \exp(-|z_i - \boldsymbol{x}_i\boldsymbol{\beta}|)]^2} = \frac{\exp[-(z_i - \boldsymbol{x}_i\boldsymbol{\beta})]}{(1 + \exp[-(z_i - \boldsymbol{x}_i\boldsymbol{\beta})])^2}, \tag{6.99}$$

producing a logistic density for the latent z_i.

The above shows how the logistic distribution can be represented as a scale mixture of normals and thus how MCMC methods can be employed to estimate the model

[19] See Andrews and Mallows (1974) and Stefanski (1991) for further details based on Laplace transforms.

using the general structure of (6.79)—(6.81). While sampling from the $\boldsymbol{\beta}$ and z posterior conditionals proceeds similarly to the probit model, calculations for the logit also require sampling from the conditional distribution of the mixing variables $\boldsymbol{\lambda}$. Chen and Dey (1998) propose to use a Student-t approximation to the logistic distribution and sample λ_i^2, $i = 1, 2, \ldots, n$ from an optimally chosen inverse gamma proposal density. Moreover, they discuss procedures for efficient calculation of the infinite sum in (6.93) that is required in the M-H step. Holmes and Held (2006) also pursue this approach for estimating the logit, using rejection sampling with a generalized inverse Gaussian proposal density to sample the mixing variables $\boldsymbol{\lambda}$. In either approach, however, the calculations involved remain reasonably non-trivial, and such techniques appear infrequently in practice.

A second approach for fitting the binary logit (as well as the multinomial logit) has been suggested by Frühwirth-Schnatter and Frühwirth (2007), with extensions for variable selection provided by Tüchler (2008). They begin by noting, as shown by McFadden (1974), that the logit likelihood can be derived from a latent variable framework based on Type I extreme value assumptions on the disturbances. Specifically, the utility afforded by the $y_i = 0$ choice (denoted z_{i0}) is assumed to follow a Type I extreme value distribution (with covariates omitted for identification purposes), while the latent utility afforded by the $y_i = 1$ option (which includes covariates) is given as

$$z_{i1} = \boldsymbol{x}_i\boldsymbol{\beta} + \epsilon_i, \quad p(\epsilon_i) = \exp\left[-\epsilon_i - \exp(-\epsilon_i)\right]. \tag{6.100}$$

The idea of Frühwirth-Schnatter and Frühwirth (2007), similar in spirit to that of Chib et al. (2002), is to replace the computationally troublesome Type I extreme value distribution in (6.100) with a nearly identical—yet computationally more appealing—normal mixture approximation (see e.g. Griffin et al., chapter 4 of this volume for more discussion of mixture models). Specifically, they write

$$p(\epsilon_i) \approx \sum_{r=1}^{10} w_r \phi(\epsilon_i; m_r, s_r^2), \tag{6.101}$$

where the weights $\{w_r\}_{r=1}^{10}$, component means $\{m_r\}_{r=1}^{10}$, and component variances $\{s_r^2\}_{r=1}^{10}$ are chosen to minimize the Kullback-Leibler distance between the mixture approximation and the extreme value distribution. The optimal values of these parameters are enumerated in Table 1 of Frühwirth-Schnatter and Frühwirth (2007: 3511) and are not repeated here for the sake of brevity.

Making this replacement, the (approximate) latent utility for the $y_i = 1$ choice becomes

$$p(z_{i1}|\boldsymbol{\beta}) = \sum_{r=1}^{10} w_r \phi(z_{i1}; \boldsymbol{x}_i\boldsymbol{\beta} + m_r, s_r^2). \tag{6.102}$$

When fitting mixture models like these, it is helpful to augment the mixture density with a set of component indicator variables, $\{r_i\}_{i=1}^n$ where $r_i = j$ denotes that z_{i1} is "drawn from" the jth component of the mixture (with mean $\boldsymbol{x}_i\boldsymbol{\beta} + m_j$ and variance s_j^2). In this case, $j = 1, 2, \ldots, 10$ given the ten component approximation to the Type I extreme value distribution. Formally, we write

$$z_{i1}|\boldsymbol{\beta}, r_i \overset{ind}{\sim} \mathcal{N}(\boldsymbol{x}_i\boldsymbol{\beta} + m_{r_i}, s_{r_i}^2), \quad \Pr(r_i = j) = w_j, \quad j = 1, 2, \ldots, 10.$$

The above pieces yield the following augmented posterior distribution for the logit

$$\begin{aligned} p(z_1, z_0, \boldsymbol{\beta}, \boldsymbol{r}|y) &\propto p(\boldsymbol{\beta}, \boldsymbol{r})p(z_1, z_0|\boldsymbol{\beta}, \boldsymbol{r})p(y|z_1, z0, \boldsymbol{\beta}, \boldsymbol{r}) \qquad (6.103) \\ &= p(\boldsymbol{\beta}) \prod_{i=1}^{n} \Bigg[\left(\sum_{j=1}^{10} I(r_i = j)w_j \right) \phi(z_{i1}; \boldsymbol{x}_i\boldsymbol{\beta} + m_{r_i}, s_{r_i}^2)p(z_{i0}) \\ &\quad \times \left[I(y_i = 0)I(z_{i0} \geq z_{i1}) + I(y_i = 1)I(z_{i0} < z_{i1}) \right] \Bigg], \end{aligned}$$

where $p(z_{i0})$ is the Type I extreme value and represents the latent utility of the $y_i = 0$ option. In practice, this latent variable does not need to be simulated in the course of the sampler, though its value does indirectly affect the sampling of z_1.

Under the normal prior $\boldsymbol{\beta} \sim \mathcal{N}(\boldsymbol{\mu}_\beta, \boldsymbol{V}_\beta)$, the sampling of $\boldsymbol{\beta}$ from the (approximate) conditional posterior follows immediately:

$$\boldsymbol{\beta}|z_1, z_0, \boldsymbol{r}, \boldsymbol{y} \sim \mathcal{N}(\boldsymbol{D}_\beta \boldsymbol{d}_\beta, \boldsymbol{D}_\beta), \qquad (6.104)$$

where

$$\boldsymbol{D}_\beta = \left(\boldsymbol{X}'\boldsymbol{\Sigma}^{-1}\boldsymbol{X} + \boldsymbol{V}_\beta^{-1}\right)^{-1} \quad \text{and} \quad \boldsymbol{d}_\beta = \boldsymbol{X}'\boldsymbol{\Sigma}^{-1}\tilde{\boldsymbol{y}} + \boldsymbol{V}_\beta^{-1}\boldsymbol{\mu}_\beta,$$

with $\boldsymbol{\Sigma} \equiv diag\{s_{r_i}^2\}$, $\tilde{\boldsymbol{y}} \equiv \boldsymbol{y} - \boldsymbol{m}$, $\boldsymbol{m} \equiv [m_{r_1} \ m_{r_2} \ \cdots \ m_{r_n}]'$.

In a similar way, the component indicator variables are sampled independently from their discrete conditional posterior distributions,

$$\Pr(r_i = j|z_1, z_0, \boldsymbol{\beta}, y) \propto \frac{w_j}{s_j}\phi\left(\frac{z_{i1} - \boldsymbol{x}_i\beta - m_j}{s_j}\right), \quad j = 1, 2, \ldots, 10. \qquad (6.105)$$

For the latent data z_1, Frühwirth-Schnatter and Frühwirth go back to the exact representation of the logit and note, by a simple change of variables, $\exp(-z_{i0}) \sim Exp(1)$ and likewise, $\exp(-z_{i1}) \sim Exp(\lambda_i)$ where "Exp" denotes an exponential distribution, $\lambda_i \equiv \exp(\boldsymbol{x}_i\boldsymbol{\beta})$ and $\exp(\cdot)$ denotes the exponential function.

When $y_i = 1$, the observed outcome imposes the restriction $z_{i0} < z_{i1}$ on the latent data or, equivalently, $\exp(-z_{i0}) > \exp(-z_{i1})$. In this instance, therefore, $\exp(-z_{i1})$ can be sampled as the minimum of two exponential random variables, which turns out to imply

$$\exp(-z_{i1}) \sim Exp(1 + \lambda_i), \quad \text{when } y_i = 1. \qquad (6.106)$$

When $y_i = 0$, we obtain the restriction $\exp(-z_{i0}) \leq \exp(-z_{i1})$. Similar algebra can be employed to verify that $\exp(-z_{i1})$ can be sampled as the sum of two exponential random variables in this case:

$$\exp(-z_{i1}) = x_{1i} + x_{2i}, \quad x_{1i} \sim Exp(1 + \lambda_i), \quad x_{2i} \sim Exp(\lambda_i), \text{when } y_i = 0. \tag{6.107}$$

Posterior simulation in the logit via auxiliary variable augmentation proceeds by sampling from (6.104) and (6.105) and then using (6.106) and (6.107) to sample the latent utility vector z_1. It is useful to note that each of the steps only requires sampling from standard distributions, making this an attractive algorithm for the practitioner.

Yet another approach for posterior simulation in the logit involves the M-H algorithm. To this end, we first note that the Hessian for the logit is obtained as

$$\mathcal{H} = -X'AX = -\sum_{i=1}^{n} x_i' \Lambda_i (1 - \Lambda_i) x_i, \tag{6.108}$$

where X is the $n \times k$ matrix of stacked covariate data, $\Lambda_i = \exp(x_i\beta)/(1 + \exp(x_i\beta))$, and A is an $n \times n$ diagonal matrix with $\Lambda_i(1 - \Lambda_i)$ assembled on the main diagonal. This Hessian can be used to scale the proposal density in the M-H step. A random-walk M-H algorithm, for example, would proceed by sampling

$$\beta^* \sim \mathcal{N}\left(\beta^{(r)}, -c^2\mathcal{H}^{-1}\right), \tag{6.109}$$

where c^2 is a tuning parameter chosen to minimize the relative inefficiency of the M-H procedure.

Given a current parameter vector $\beta^{(r)}$, and a β^* sampled from (6.109), the chain will move from $\beta^{(r)}$ to β^* with probability

$$\min\{1, p_r\} \tag{6.110}$$

where

$$p_r = \exp\left[\log p(\beta^*) - \log p(\beta^{(r)}) + \sum_{i=1}^{n}\left(y_i \log\left[\frac{\Lambda_i^*}{\Lambda_i^{(r)}}\right] + (1 - y_i)\log\left[\frac{1 - \Lambda_i^*}{1 - \Lambda_i^{(r)}}\right]\right)\right], \tag{6.111}$$

and Λ_i^* and $\Lambda_i^{(r)}$ denote the logit predicted probability for person i evaluated at the candidate and current value of the chain, respectively, and the first two terms in p_r denote the (log) difference in prior ordinates.

Implementation of the M-H algorithm requires an initial estimate of the parameter vector β in order to calculate A and thus the Hessian $\mathcal{H}$. One possibility in this regard is to simply perform Maximum Likelihood Estimation (MLE) of the logit, which is cheaply obtained and widely available in most software packages, and use the MLE estimate to calculate A and thus the Hessian.

An alternative that would not require MLE calculation is simply to start with a guess for β, perhaps setting $\beta = 0$, producing $\Lambda_i = 1/2\ \forall i$, and run the M-H algorithm above. Once a desired number of simulations has been produced, the algorithm can be terminated, a posterior mean of $\boldsymbol{\beta}$ calculated, and the matrix A and Hessian $\mathcal{H}$ can then be updated. This process could be repeated until the calculated posterior means have stabilized. We take this route in the example provided in this section. Since the likelihood function of the logit model is strictly concave, the above Metropolis-Hastings approach can work well, especially for samples sufficiently large.

3.1.3 *Other link functions*

While the probit and logit are the most widely used among the binary choice models, they are not the only possibilities, and indeed, can be inappropriately restrictive. The complementary log-log link model, for example, specifying

$$\Pr(y_i = 1|\boldsymbol{x}_i, \boldsymbol{\beta}) = 1 - \exp[-\exp(\boldsymbol{x}_i\boldsymbol{\beta})] \tag{6.112}$$

offers an asymmetric link, and can be estimated using methods similar to our final M-H algorithm for the logit. Other skewed link models, including skew-normal links, are described by Chen et al. (1999) and further possibilities are explored by Basu and Mukhopadhyay (2000). Geweke and Keane (2000) describe a binary choice model based on finite normal mixtures.

3.1.4 *Application*

Our application again makes use of the British Cohort Study data of Section 2.5.2. In this case our binary outcome of interest is whether or not the respondent is obese, whose clinical definition is having a BMI in excess of 30. The covariates we employ include parental BMI and indicators denoting whether or not the respondent is married, has a college degree, or exercises regularly. For our priors, we choose $\boldsymbol{\beta} \sim \mathcal{N}(0, 100I_6)$.

We estimate the probit model using the algorithm discussed in Section 3.1.1 and also estimate the logit and complementary log-log specifications for this data. For the logit, we start out with $\boldsymbol{\beta} = 0, c^2 = 2$, and calculate the Hessian at $\boldsymbol{\beta} = \mathbf{0}$. The posterior simulator is then run for 10,000 iterations and posterior means are calculated based on the final 5,000 simulations. The Hessian is then recalculated at the updated posterior mean, c is set to unity, and the simulator is run for an additional 25,000 iterations. This process is then repeated one final time, with final posterior statistics calculated from the last 24,000 iterations of this third run. We approach the complementary log-log model in the same way, sampling candidates from our proposal density as:

$$\boldsymbol{\beta}^* \sim \mathcal{N}\left(\boldsymbol{\beta}^{(r)}, c^2(X'DX)^{-1}\right), \tag{6.113}$$

where D is a diagonal matrix with

$$\left(y_i \frac{\exp(-\exp(\boldsymbol{x}_i\boldsymbol{\beta}))\exp(\boldsymbol{x}_i\boldsymbol{\beta})}{1 - \exp(-\exp(\boldsymbol{x}_i\boldsymbol{\beta}))} - (1 - y_i)\exp(\boldsymbol{x}_i\boldsymbol{\beta})\right)^2 \tag{6.114}$$

as the (i, i) entry. Therefore, for the complementary log-log model, the covariance matrix of our proposal density is chosen as a scaled Berndt, Hall, Hall, and Hausman (BHHH) estimate (Berndt et al. 1974) of the inverse information matrix.

Table 6.7: Marginal effect posterior means and posterior standard deviations from binary choice application

Variable	Probit		Logit		Complementary-Log-Log	
	Post. Mean	Post. Std.	Post. Mean	Post. Std.	Post. Mean	Post. Std
MomBMI	0.010	0.002	0.009	0.002	0.008	0.002
DadBMI	0.011	0.002	0.010	0.002	0.009	0.002
Married	0.022	0.012	0.022	0.011	0.021	0.010
Degree	−0.016	0.016	−0.017	0.016	−0.018	0.016
ExerciseReg	−0.003	0.016	−0.004	0.015	−0.003	0.014
Log ML	−928.93		−936.55		−936.22	

In Table 6.7 we provide posterior means and standard deviations associated with model-specific marginal effects for each of these variables. When required, we evaluate these at the sample average of the continuous parental BMI variables and set the marriage, college degree, and regular exercise variables to unity. For binary covariates, marginal effects are calculated as the difference in predicted probabilities upon setting the binary variable to zero, and the remaining covariates fixed at means (or unity). To compare these models, we also calculate log marginal likelihoods. For the probit model, these are calculated using the method of Chib (1995), while marginal likelihoods for the logit and complementary log-log models, which use the M-H algorithm, are calculated using Chib and Jeliazkov (2001).

The results in the table are sensible and operate in the direction that we might expect. A one point increase in either maternal or paternal BMI increases the likelihood of child obesity by about 1 percent; married individuals are about 2 percent more likely to be obese, and those with a college degree are nearly 2 percent less likely to be obese. The results obtained are quite consistent across models, and the data favor the probit specification among these three alternatives.

3.2 The tobit model

The tobit model is a widely used specification for censored data and Chib (1992) marks the first MCMC-based Bayesian procedure for inference in the tobit. The basic tobit specification, with a single censoring point at zero, can be mapped into the framework of (6.79)–(6.81) with $\boldsymbol{\alpha}$ being null and (6.81) specializing to:

$$y_i = \max\{0, z_i\}. \tag{6.115}$$

As such, a posterior simulator for the tobit is remarkably simple. The regression parameters $\boldsymbol{\beta}$ are sampled directly from (6.84) and the variance parameter σ^2 is drawn directly from (6.85). As for the latent data, let $D_i = I(y_i > 0)$. Equation (6.86) together with the rule in (6.115) then imply the latent z_i can be sampled by setting

$$z_i = D_i y_i + (1 - D_i) w_i, \tag{6.116}$$

where

$$w_i \overset{ind}{\sim} \mathcal{TN}_{(-\infty,0)}(\boldsymbol{x}_i\boldsymbol{\beta}, \sigma^2), i = 1, 2, \ldots, n. \tag{6.117}$$

In other words, w_i only needs to be simulated for the set of observations with $y_i = 0$. Other generalizations of the tobit, such as allowing for an unknown censoring point, or allowing for two-sided censoring, offer straightforward extensions of this basic model.

3.3 Models for ordinal outcomes

The ordered probit represents another commonly encountered microeconometric model that fits within the structure described by (6.79)–(6.81). For the ordered probit, $\sigma^2 = 1$, and the parameters $\boldsymbol{\alpha}$ are *threshold* or *cutpoint* parameters to be estimated within the model. Specifically, we assume $y_i \in \{1, 2, \ldots, J\}$, where the discrete outcomes have a natural ordinal interpretation, such as degrees of agreement/disagreement with a given statement.

For the ordered probit, (6.81) becomes

$$y_i = j \quad \text{if} \quad \alpha_j < z_i \leq \alpha_{j+1}, \quad j = 1, 2, \ldots, J. \tag{6.118}$$

An intercept parameter is presumed to be in $\boldsymbol{x}_i$, and standard identification conditions are imposed on the cutpoints, namely: $\alpha_1 = -\infty$, $\alpha_2 = 0$, and $\alpha_{J+1} = \infty$.

3.3.1 *Posterior simulation*

In terms of posterior simulation, a standard Gibbs sampler can be applied, as in Albert and Chib (1993a). The regression parameters $\boldsymbol{\beta}$ are simulated as in (6.84), with $\sigma^2 = 1$, the latent data are drawn from a truncated normal distribution implied by (6.86) and (6.118):

$$z_i | \boldsymbol{\beta}, \boldsymbol{\alpha}, \boldsymbol{y} \overset{ind}{\sim} \mathcal{TN}_{(\alpha_{y_i}, \alpha_{y_i+1}]}(\boldsymbol{x}_i\boldsymbol{\beta}, 1), \tag{6.119}$$

and the elements of the cutpoint vector α_j, under an improper prior of the form $p(\boldsymbol{\alpha}) \propto c$, can be sampled from their conditional posterior distributions:

$$\alpha_j | \boldsymbol{\alpha}_{-j}, \boldsymbol{z}, \boldsymbol{y} \sim U\left[\max\left\{\alpha_{j-1}, \{z_i : y_i = j-1\}\right\}, \min\left\{\alpha_{j+1}, \{z_i : y_i = j\}\right\}\right]. \tag{6.120}$$

Unfortunately the algorithm above does not mix well in practice. Cowles (1996) investigates this issue and suggests sampling $\boldsymbol{\alpha}$ and $\boldsymbol{z}$ in a blocking step by first integrating out the latent $\boldsymbol{z}$ (i.e. working directly with the ordered probit likelihood), sampling $\boldsymbol{\alpha}$, and then sampling from the complete posterior conditional distribution for the latent data.

This is done in an M-H step, where a series of truncated normal densities are used to sample the cutpoints. Nandram and Chen (1996) also investigate this issue and discuss posterior simulation based on a rescaling transformation.

To motivate their reparameterization, suppose $J = 3$ to fix ideas (so that there is only one unknown cutpoint, denoted as α) and let

$$\delta = \frac{\beta}{\alpha}, \quad \sigma = \frac{1}{\alpha}, \quad \text{and} \quad \tilde{z}_i = \frac{z_i}{\alpha}. \tag{6.121}$$

This reparameterization leads to an equivalent model:

$$\tilde{z}_i = x_i\delta + \nu_i, \quad \nu_i|X,\sigma \stackrel{iid}{\sim} \mathcal{N}(0,\sigma^2) \tag{6.122}$$

with

$$y_i = \begin{cases} 1 \text{ if } \tilde{z}_i \leq 0 \\ 2 \text{ if } 0 < \tilde{z}_i \leq 1 \, . \\ 3 \text{ if } \tilde{z}_i > 1. \end{cases} \tag{6.123}$$

If we additionally specify that a diffuse, improper prior on $\boldsymbol{\beta}, \boldsymbol{\alpha}$ is employed: $p(\boldsymbol{\beta}, \boldsymbol{\alpha}) \propto c$, we obtain the following joint posterior for the reparameterized model:

$$p(\delta, \sigma^2, \tilde{z}|y) \propto \sigma^{-n} \prod_{i=1}^{n} \exp\left(-\frac{1}{2\sigma^2}[\tilde{z}_i - x_i\delta]^2\right) I(\tilde{\alpha}_{y_i} < \tilde{z}_i \leq \tilde{\alpha}_{y_i+1}), \tag{6.124}$$

where all of the $\tilde{\alpha}_{y_i}$ are *known* upon reparameterization. The conditionals for $\boldsymbol{\beta}$ and $\tilde{z}$ are like those in (6.84) and (6.86), with $V_{\beta}^{-1} = 0$ and the conditional support in (6.86) defined by the intervals $I(\tilde{\alpha}_{y_i} < \tilde{z}_i^* \leq \tilde{\alpha}_{y_i+1})$, all of which do not depend on unknown parameters. The (reparameterized) variance parameter is sampled as:

$$\sigma^2|\delta, \tilde{z}, y \sim IG\left(\frac{n}{2}, \left[\frac{1}{2}(\tilde{z} - X\delta)'(\tilde{z} - X\delta)\right]\right). \tag{6.125}$$

For each post-convergence iteration, the original parameters α and $\boldsymbol{\beta}$ can be calculated. When the outcome variable takes on more than three possible values, Nandram and Chen (1996) suggest the use of an M-H algorithm to sample the unknown cutpoints where all parameters are drawn in a single step based on a Dirichlet proposal density for differences in cutpoint values. Other contributions to this literature include Chen and Dey (2000); Albert and Chib (2001); and Graves et al. (2008). The first and last of these references consider multivariate ordinal outcomes, departures from normality, and a series of related issues.

3.3.2 *Ordered probit: application*

To illustrate estimation of the ordered probit in practice, we revisit our data from the British Cohort Study. In this case we refine our classification of weight categories into "normal" weight ($y = 1$), "overweight" ($y = 2$), and "obese" ($y = 3$). The first of these is

Table 6.8: Posterior statistics from ordinal BMI application

	Parameter / Variable		Probability Change: Parental BMI		
	Post. Mean	Post. Std.	Category	Post. Mean.	Post. Std.
Constant	−2.89	0.220			
MomBMI	0.051	0.006	$y=1$	0.150	0.011
DadBMI	0.067	0.008			
Married	0.214	0.041	$y=2$	−0.097	0.008
Degree	−0.169	0.051			
ExerciseReg.	0.026	0.058	$y=3$	−0.053	0.005
α	1.29	0.034			

defined as a BMI less than 25,[20] the second represents a BMI between 25 and 30, and obesity denotes BMI in excess of 30.

We employ the same set of covariates as those used in Section 3.1.4 and make use of the reparameterization technique described above, employing improper priors for $\boldsymbol{\beta}$ and α. The sampler is run for 2,500 iterations, and the first 500 of these are discarded as the burn-in period.

In addition to coefficient posterior means and standard deviations, we also report posterior means and posterior standard deviations for a particular effect of interest, as summarized in the three right-hand columns of Table 6.8. In particular, we consider how probabilities associated with each BMI classification change in response to a one standard deviation decrease in parental BMI values. Specifically, we first calculate the predicted probability of each BMI category at sample means of MomBMI and DadBMI, with the remaining covariates fixed at unity. This process is repeated, but this time the three probabilities are calculated upon setting the MomBMI and DadBMI values at one standard deviation below their respective sample means (with the remaining covariates still fixed at unity). Posterior means and standard deviations of the probability changes resulting from these one standard deviation decreases in parental BMI are then reported in the final two columns of Table 6.8. The results show that such a reduction in parental BMI leads to a 15 increase in the probability that the child will be normal weight, a 9.7 decrease in the probability of being overweight, and a 5.3 decrease in the probability of obesity.

4 Multivariate Latent Models

We build upon the topics of the last section to now discuss multivariate latent variable models. We proceed in a similar fashion by first introducing a general latent multivariate

[20] While it is indeed possible to be "underweight," we abstract from this issue, and note that approximately 1% of our sample had a BMI less than 19.

framework and then discussing particular models that emerge from this specification. The basic model that we have in mind is a straightforward multivariate generalization of (6.79)–(6.81), where $\boldsymbol{\theta} = [\boldsymbol{\beta}' \; vec(\boldsymbol{\Sigma})']'$, and[21]

$$p(\boldsymbol{\theta}) = p(\boldsymbol{\beta})p(\boldsymbol{\Sigma}^{-1}) \tag{6.126}$$

$$z_i|X, \boldsymbol{\theta} \overset{ind}{\sim} \mathcal{N}(X_i\boldsymbol{\beta}, \boldsymbol{\Sigma}), \quad i = 1, 2, \ldots, n \tag{6.127}$$

$$y_i|z_i = g(z_i), \quad i = 1, 2, \ldots, n. \tag{6.128}$$

For our priors in (6.126), we continue to use a multivariate normal prior for $\boldsymbol{\beta}$: $\boldsymbol{\beta} \sim \mathcal{N}(\boldsymbol{\mu}_\beta, V_\beta)$ and a Wishart prior for $\boldsymbol{\Sigma}^{-1}$: $\boldsymbol{\Sigma}^{-1} \sim W([\kappa R]^{-1}, \kappa)$.

With an eye toward implementation of the Gibbs sampler in a model of this form, we obtain the following conditional posterior distributions:

$$\boldsymbol{\beta}|\boldsymbol{\Sigma}, Z, y \sim \mathcal{N}\left(D_\beta d_\beta, D_\beta\right) \tag{6.129}$$

where

$$D_\beta \equiv \left[\left(\sum_{i=1}^n X_i'\boldsymbol{\Sigma}^{-1}X_i\right) + V_\beta^{-1}\right]^{-1} \quad \text{and} \quad d_\beta \equiv \left(\sum_{i=1}^n X_i'\boldsymbol{\Sigma}^{-1}z_i\right) + V_\beta^{-1}\boldsymbol{\mu}_\beta, \tag{6.130}$$

$$\boldsymbol{\Sigma}^{-1}|\boldsymbol{\beta}, Z, y \sim W\left(\left[\sum_{i=1}^n (z_i - X_i\boldsymbol{\beta})(z_i - X_i\boldsymbol{\beta})' + \kappa R\right]^{-1}, n + \kappa\right) \tag{6.131}$$

and

$$p(z_i|\boldsymbol{\beta}, \boldsymbol{\Sigma}, y) \propto \phi(z_i|X_i\boldsymbol{\beta}, \boldsymbol{\Sigma})I[z_i \in \{z_i : y_i = g(z_i)\}], \quad i = 1, 2, \ldots, n. \tag{6.132}$$

Rather trivially, we note that this framework also describes a Gibbs algorithm for sampling in the Seemingly Unrelated Regressions (SUR) model. For the standard SUR specification, outcomes are fully observed so that there is no latent data (i.e. $y_i = z_i$) and posterior simulation simply involves the sampling of $\boldsymbol{\beta}$ from (6.129) and $\boldsymbol{\Sigma}^{-1}$ from (6.131). Though the SUR model is free of any latent data, it is useful nonetheless to note that a limiting version of this framework also describes posterior simulation within this system of linear equations.

As shown in the following discussion, the model above is also sufficiently general to include generalized tobit,[22] the multinomial probit, and the multivariate probit models as special cases. Each of these important microeconometric models, however, will impose different restrictions on $\boldsymbol{\Sigma}$ for identification purposes. Therefore, procedures for

[21] We do not discuss multivariate ordinal models here. See Graves et al. (2008), for example, for further discussion.

[22] Amemiya (1985) enumerates five different types of generalized tobit models and discusses classical estimation and inference for each. In what follows we discuss posterior simulation in Amemiya's Type 2 (hurdle model) and Type 5 (potential outcomes model) specifications, noting that similar methods apply to the estimation of all 5 generalized tobit variants.

sampling $\boldsymbol{\Sigma}^{-1}$ (or its constituent elements) will differ across the models. Furthermore, since the mapping in (6.128) will also change with the model, procedures for sampling the latent z_i will also differ among the specifications enumerated below. The sampling of $\boldsymbol{\beta}$ from its posterior conditional, however, will proceed as described in (6.129) in all cases, with the latent and covariate data suitably defined within the context of each model.

4.1 The hurdle/sample selection model

The simple tobit specification of Section 3.2 is often criticized for its inability to simultaneously account for the incidence of zeros and the density of non-zero outcomes. Such concerns can be mitigated, and the performance of the model generally improved, when elaborating the structure with a separate process for modeling the zero outcome. The following specification, commonly termed the *hurdle* or *sample selection model*, studied at length from a Bayesian perspective by van Hasselt (2008), adds this level of generality:

$$z_{i1} = \boldsymbol{r}_i\boldsymbol{\alpha} + u_{i1} \tag{6.133}$$

$$z_{i2} = \boldsymbol{w}_i\boldsymbol{\delta} + u_{i2} \tag{6.134}$$

where

$$\boldsymbol{u}_i = \begin{bmatrix} u_{i1} \\ u_{i2} \end{bmatrix} \Bigg| \boldsymbol{R}, \boldsymbol{W}, \boldsymbol{\Sigma} \overset{iid}{\sim} \mathcal{N}\left(0, \begin{bmatrix} 1 & \sigma_{12} \\ \sigma_{12} & \sigma_2^2 \end{bmatrix}\right) \equiv \mathcal{N}(0, \boldsymbol{\Sigma}) \tag{6.135}$$

and

$$y_i = \exp[z_{i2}]I(z_{i1} > 0). \tag{6.136}$$

The above specification contains two latent variable equations, unlike the single equation of the tobit model. Equation (6.136) establishes the connection between the latent and observed data and clarifies the roles of each latent variable in the hurdle model. Specifically, z_{i1} in (6.133) models the $y_i = 0$ or $y_i \neq 0$ event. If the latent z_{i1} is positive, then the observed non-zero outcome is presumed to be generated from (6.134) and is given as $\exp[z_{i2}]$.[23] Similar to the standard tobit, if z_{i1} is non-positive, then the observed y_i is set to zero.

The model above fits exactly within the multivariate framework described in (6.126)–(6.128) with $\boldsymbol{z}_i = [z_{i1}\ z_{i2}]'$, $\boldsymbol{\beta} = [\boldsymbol{\alpha}'\ \boldsymbol{\delta}']'$, and

$$\boldsymbol{X}_i = \begin{bmatrix} \boldsymbol{r}_i & 0 \\ 0 & \boldsymbol{w}_i \end{bmatrix}. \tag{6.137}$$

23 The exponential term is introduced to guarantee that the observed outcome is positive, and is also consistent with a majority of applied work, where the *potential* outcome z_{i2} in (6.134) is modeled log-linearly.

A Gibbs sampling algorithm, then, follows from (6.129)–(6.132), with the sampling of $\boldsymbol{\Sigma}^{-1}$ and z_i tailored to the hurdle model. As for the regression parameters, posterior simulation of $\boldsymbol{\beta}$ proceeds exactly as in (6.129), given our definitions of the covariate and latent data. As for the sampling of $\boldsymbol{\Sigma}^{-1}$, a slight complication is introduced, given a restriction on the (1,1) element of $\boldsymbol{\Sigma}$; the posterior conditional for $\boldsymbol{\Sigma}^{-1}$ conditioned on this prior restriction is no longer Wishart.

One alternative to the sampling of $\boldsymbol{\Sigma}^{-1}$ in this instance (and, in fact, to the sampling of the covariance matrix in all models is this section) is to ignore this restriction, implement a sampler that traverses through a non-identified parameter space, and simply post-process the posterior simulations to focus on the identifiable quantities of interest: $\boldsymbol{\alpha}/\boldsymbol{\Sigma}_{(1,1)}, \boldsymbol{\delta}, \rho_{12}$, and σ_2^2 (where ρ_{12} denotes the correlation between u_1 and u_2). This approach has been advocated by McCulloch and Rossi (1994) and Rossi et al. (2005), who argue that navigating through the non-identified parameter space simplifies the posterior computations and also improves mixing of the posterior simulations. Under this approach, sampling of $\boldsymbol{\Sigma}^{-1}$ proceeds identically to (6.131).

An alternate approach, which works directly with the identified parameters, is to first express u_{i2} conditionally on u_{i1} as:

$$u_{i2} = \sigma_{12}u_{i1} + \nu_i, \quad \nu_i \sim \mathcal{N}(0, \sigma_\nu^2), \tag{6.138}$$

where $\sigma_\nu^2 = \sigma_2^2 - \sigma_{12}^2$ and ν_i and u_{1i} are independent. Thus, we can re-write our model as

$$z_{i1} = \boldsymbol{r}_i\boldsymbol{\alpha} + u_{i1} \tag{6.139}$$

$$z_{i2} = \boldsymbol{w}_i\boldsymbol{\delta} + \sigma_{12}u_{i1} + \nu_i. \tag{6.140}$$

Aside from the latent data $\boldsymbol{z}$ (the sampling of which has not yet been addressed in either the identified or non-identified approaches), posterior simulation in the model with this parameterization cycles through three blocks of parameters: $\boldsymbol{\beta}, \sigma_{12}$, and σ_ν^2. To this end, we adopt the following priors for these quantities: $\sigma_\nu^2 \sim IG(a/2, b), \sigma_{12} \sim \mathcal{N}(\mu_{12}, V_{12})$, and $\boldsymbol{\beta} \sim \mathcal{N}(\boldsymbol{\mu}_\beta, \boldsymbol{V}_\beta)$. The first two of these effectively "replace" the Wishart prior for $\boldsymbol{\Sigma}^{-1}$ in (6.126). Finally, note that the inverse gamma prior on σ_ν^2 imposes $\sigma_\nu^2 > 0$ and thus $\boldsymbol{\Sigma}$ is restricted to be positive definite.

As stated previously, the regression parameters $\boldsymbol{\beta}$ are sampled as in (6.129). The covariance and variance parameters are then sampled by drawing:

$$\sigma_\nu^2|\boldsymbol{\beta}, \boldsymbol{z}, \sigma_{12}, \boldsymbol{y} \sim IG\left(\frac{n+a}{2}, \left[b + \frac{1}{2}\sum_{i=1}^{n}(z_{i2} - \boldsymbol{w}_i\boldsymbol{\delta} - \sigma_{12}u_{i1})^2\right]\right) \tag{6.141}$$

and

$$\sigma_{12}|\boldsymbol{\beta}, \boldsymbol{z}, \sigma_\nu^2, \boldsymbol{y} \sim \mathcal{N}(D_{12}d_{12}, D_{12}), \tag{6.142}$$

where

$$D_{12} = \left(\boldsymbol{u}_1'\boldsymbol{u}_1/\sigma_\nu^2 + V_{12}^{-1}\right)^{-1} \quad \text{and} \quad d_{12} = \boldsymbol{u}_1'\boldsymbol{u}_2/\sigma_\nu^2 + V_{12}^{-1}\mu_{12}. \tag{6.143}$$

In the expression above, $u_j = [u_{1j}\ u_{2j}\ \cdots\ u_{nj}]'$, $j = 1, 2$, denote the error vectors which are known given z and $\boldsymbol{\beta}$.

It remains to discuss the sampling of the latent data z_i, and the following describes how this is accomplished under either sampling scheme. First, suppose that $y_i > 0$. This observed outcome implies the restrictions $z_{i1} > 0$, $z_{2i} = \log(y_i)$. In this case, the sampling of z_{2i} is trivial (as its posterior is degenerate given y), and z_{1i} can be drawn from the univariate truncated normal:

$$z_{i1}|\boldsymbol{\beta}, \boldsymbol{\Sigma}, y \sim \mathcal{TN}_{(0,\infty)}\left[r_i\boldsymbol{\alpha} + \frac{\sigma_{12}}{\sigma_v^2 + \sigma_{12}^2}(\log y_i - w_i\boldsymbol{\delta}), \left(1 - \frac{\sigma_{12}^2}{\sigma_v^2 + \sigma_{12}^2}\right)\right], \ i \in \{i : y_i > 0\}. \tag{6.144}$$

On the other hand, consider the case when $y_i = 0$. This produces the restriction $z_{i1} \leq 0$, while no restriction is placed upon the potential (log) outcome z_{i2}. In this case we can sample directly from the bivariate conditional posterior distribution of the latent data $z_i = [z_{i1}\ z_{i2}]'$ by first drawing z_{i1} from its truncated normal conditional posterior:

$$z_{i1}|\boldsymbol{\beta}, \boldsymbol{\Sigma}, y \sim \mathcal{TN}_{(-\infty,0]}(r_i\alpha, 1), \quad i \in \{i : y_i = 0\}, \tag{6.145}$$

and then drawing z_{i2} from its conditional normal posterior distribution:

$$z_{i2}|\boldsymbol{\beta}, \boldsymbol{\Sigma}, y \sim \mathcal{N}\left[w_i\boldsymbol{\delta} + \sigma_{12}(z_{i1} - r_i\boldsymbol{\alpha}), \sigma_2^2 - \sigma_{12}^2\right], \quad i \in \{i : y_i = 0\}. \tag{6.146}$$

Posterior simulation in the hurdle model proceeds by sampling from (6.129), (6.144)–(6.146), and either (6.131) or (6.141)–(6.142), depending on whether one chooses to work in the identified or non-identified space. In this case, relatively little is lost in terms of the complexity of the algorithm, or its mixing properties, by working directly with identified parameters. Finally, we note that posterior simulations from the joint posterior of the hurdle model can be used to easily calculate policy-relevant parameters and therefore move beyond the narrow goal of parameter estimation. For example, these simulations can be used to summarize how hypothetical changes in the value of a covariate or set of covariates impact the probability that y_i is zero, or how such changes impact the entire distribution of y. Such calculations, as they involve nonlinear functions of the model parameters, are, in our view, comparably difficult to carry out from the classical perspective, perhaps allaying concerns that Bayesian approaches are "harder". It is worth noting, though potentially underemphasized in this chapter, that this point applies to all of the nonlinear models previously discussed as well as the multivariate nonlinear models that follow.

4.2 Endogeneity in nonlinear models

The analysis of Section 2.5 considered the endogeneity of a right-hand-side variable in a continuous (linear) framework. In practice, of course, endogeneity concerns are not limited to models with continuous variables and indeed, this problem often arises with discrete, censored, or ordinal outcome data.[24] In practice, unfortunately, researchers analyzing such data sometimes abandon nonlinear specifications in favor of linear models, shunning appropriate econometrics in favor of the familiarity and ease of linear methods such as IV or 2SLS.

In this section we review posterior simulation in a particular nonlinear model with an endogenous right-hand-side variable. As the reader will see, the posterior simulator for this model is only slightly more complicated than the one described in Section 2.5 for linear outcomes. As such, the techniques described here are really no more involved than those employed with linear models.

4.2.1 Posterior simulation with an endogenous binary variable

Though there are many different possibilities to consider here, let us fix ideas on a specific model, noting that the methods to follow clearly generalize to cases where the outcome is also latent or the endogenous variable is censored or ordered. Below, we consider a standard representation of a dummy endogenous variable model:

$$z_{i1} = \boldsymbol{r}_i \boldsymbol{\alpha} + u_{i1} \tag{6.147}$$

$$y_i = \alpha_0 + \alpha_1 D_i + \boldsymbol{s}_i \boldsymbol{\alpha}_2 + u_{i2}, \tag{6.148}$$

where

$$D_i = I(z_{i1} > 0). \tag{6.149}$$

The observed responses consist of a continuous outcome y_i and a binary "treatment" variable D_i, and the latter of these is specified to be generated by the latent variable in (6.147). In practice, α_1 is commonly the object of interest as the "causal" impact of the binary variable D_i on y_i (see Chamberlain, Chapter 1 of this volume for more on Bayesian estimation of treatment impacts). However, with observational data, determining this causal impact is not a trivial exercise, as individuals self-select into treatment regimes, thereby producing a correlation between u_1 and u_2. In frequentist parlance, the presence of this correlation leads to biased and inconsistent Ordinary Least Squares (OLS)-based estimation of α_1 using (6.148) only. Such theoretical concerns, as well as our understanding of the problem being studied, require that we allow for correlation among the unobservables. Therefore, we continue to make a bivariate normality assumption as in (6.135), with σ_{12} capturing the role of unobserved confounding in the model.

In terms of posterior simulation, the model in (6.147)–(6.149) is nearly identical to that for the hurdle model presented in the previous section. To make the connection between the two models explicit, simply define $\boldsymbol{w}_i = [1\ D_i\ \boldsymbol{s}_i]$ and $\boldsymbol{\delta} = [\alpha_0\ \alpha_1\ \boldsymbol{\alpha}_2]'$. The link between the latent and observed data, as in (6.128) for this model, reduces to:

$$y_i = z_{i2}, \qquad D_i = I(z_{i1} > 0). \tag{6.150}$$

[24] See e.g. Li (1998); Geweke et al. (2003); Chib (2003) for Bayesian examples.

Posterior sampling of $\boldsymbol{\beta}$ then proceeds as in (6.129). For a sampler that navigates through the identified parameter space, elements of the (reparameterized) $\boldsymbol{\Sigma}$ can be sampled as in (6.141)–(6.142). The latent variables z_{i1} are sampled independently, $i = 1, 2, \ldots, n$ from:

$$z_{i1}|\boldsymbol{\beta}, \boldsymbol{\Sigma}, y, D \sim \begin{cases} \mathcal{TN}_{(0,\infty)}\left(\boldsymbol{r}_i\boldsymbol{\alpha} + \frac{\sigma_{12}}{\sigma_\nu^2+\sigma_{12}^2}[y_i - \alpha_0 - \alpha_1 - \boldsymbol{s}_i\boldsymbol{\alpha}_2], 1 - \rho_{12}^2\right) & \text{if} D_i = 1 \\ \mathcal{TN}_{(-\infty,0]}\left(\boldsymbol{r}_i\boldsymbol{\alpha} + \frac{\sigma_{12}}{\sigma_\nu^2+\sigma_{12}^2}[y_i - \alpha_0 - \boldsymbol{s}_i\boldsymbol{\alpha}_2], 1 - \rho_{12}^2\right) & \text{if} D_i = 0 \end{cases}. \tag{6.151}$$

A posterior simulator for the dummy variable treatment effects model is given by (6.129), (6.141)–(6.142), and (6.151).

4.2.2 *Application: a count data model with endogeneity*

In practice, many models with endogeneity problems fit conveniently within the framework described by (6.126)–(6.128). One notable exception is in the analysis of count outcomes which, heretofore, has been ignored within this chapter, yet is an important specification in the analysis of microeconometric data. For this reason we pause to provide an application involving count data and choose to do so within the framework of a count outcome with an endogenous explanatory variable. Posterior simulation in such a case, unfortunately, does not proceed just by standard Gibbs steps, but instead makes use of several Metropolis-Hastings substeps to conduct the necessary sampling.

Our example comes from the study of Lakdawalla et al. (2006).[25] These authors study how the receipt of Highly Active AntiRetroviral Therapy (HAART) for HIV-positive patients impacts the subsequent number of sexual partners. The authors note that the presence of such treatment generally improves the health and longevity of its recipients, which might then, in turn, potentially impact the sexual behavior of the treated. Furthermore, if sexual activity increases significantly in response to treatment, the availability of HAART could even *reduce* social welfare, as the increased level of sexual activity upon receiving the health-improving treatment may leave the HIV-negative community at increased risk of infection.

We propose the following Bayesian framework, which is slightly different from the specification of Lakdawalla et al:

$$y_i|\boldsymbol{\beta}, \epsilon_i \overset{ind}{\sim} Po[\exp(d_i\beta_0 + \tilde{\boldsymbol{x}}_i\boldsymbol{\beta}_1 + \epsilon_i)] \tag{6.152}$$

$$z_i = \boldsymbol{w}_i\boldsymbol{\gamma} + u_i \tag{6.153}$$

$$d_i = I(z_i > 0) \tag{6.154}$$

$$\begin{pmatrix} \epsilon_i \\ u_i \end{pmatrix} \Bigg| \mathbf{X}, \boldsymbol{W} \overset{iid}{\sim} N\left[\begin{pmatrix} 0 \\ 0 \end{pmatrix}, \begin{pmatrix} \sigma_\epsilon^2 & \sigma_{\epsilon u} \\ \sigma_{\epsilon u} & \sigma_u^2 = 1 \end{pmatrix}\right] \equiv \mathcal{N}(\mathbf{0}, \boldsymbol{\Sigma}). \tag{6.155}$$

[25] We kindly thank the authors for supplying us with their data.

The model we employ specifies that, conditional on individual i's idiosyncratic term ϵ_i, the number of sexual partners y_i follows a Poisson distribution with mean $\exp(\boldsymbol{x}_i\boldsymbol{\beta} + \epsilon_i)$, $\boldsymbol{x}_i = [d_i\, \tilde{\boldsymbol{x}}_i]$, $\boldsymbol{\beta} = [\beta_0\, \boldsymbol{\beta}_1']'$. The covariates $\boldsymbol{x}_i$ help to explain variation in the number of sexual partners across individuals, and contains the binary d_i, denoting the decision to receive the HAART regimen, which is regarded as potentially endogenous. To motivate this potential endogeneity concern, it may be the case that people in failing or poor health will be more likely to seek out and receive the therapy but less likely to participate in risky sexual activities. This possibility is handled by permitting correlation among $\boldsymbol{u}$ and $\boldsymbol{\epsilon}$ through $\sigma_{\epsilon u}$. Furthermore, we note that the addition of ϵ_i relaxes the restrictive assumption of the Poisson that the variance and mean are the same, and thus we permit overdispersion through the adoption of a Poisson-lognormal mixture.

Since the receipt of the HAART treatment is a binary outcome, we augment the likelihood function by introducing a latent variable z_i such that $z_i > 0$ if $d_i = 1$ and $z_i \leq 0$ otherwise. Although most of the covariates affecting the decision to receive the therapy also affect the count outcome, we, following Lakdawalla et al. (2006), exploit state-level variation in the availability/generosity of public insurance for HIV-positive individuals. This includes accounting for two variables capturing the "medically needy threshold" set by the state, expressed as a percentage of the federal poverty line, and an indicator variable denoting whether the state's income eligibility threshold for Medicare through Supplemental Social Security Income (SSI) was less than 10 percentage points lower than the federal guideline. These two variables are included in $\boldsymbol{w}_i$ but omitted from $\boldsymbol{x}_i$. To complete the Bayesian analysis, we specify that $\boldsymbol{\beta} \sim \mathcal{N}(\boldsymbol{\mu}_\beta, \boldsymbol{V}_\beta)$, $\boldsymbol{\gamma} \sim \mathcal{N}(\boldsymbol{\mu}_\gamma, \boldsymbol{V}_\gamma)$, and $p(\boldsymbol{\Sigma}^{-1}) \propto f_W(\boldsymbol{\Sigma}^{-1}|[\kappa \boldsymbol{R}]^{-1}, \kappa) I(\sigma_u^2 = 1)$ where the indicator function notes that the $(2, 2)$ element of $\boldsymbol{\Sigma}$ is restricted to unity for identification purposes.

Following Chib et al. (1998) and Munkin and Trivedi (2003), we simulate from the joint posterior distribution of ϵ_i, $\boldsymbol{\beta}$, z_i, $\boldsymbol{\gamma}$, and $\boldsymbol{\Sigma}^{-1}$ by sampling these parameters iteratively from a Gibbs sampler, with Metropolis substeps used as needed. The conditional posterior density of ϵ_i is proportional to

$$p(\epsilon_i|\Xi_{-\epsilon_i}, \boldsymbol{y}, \boldsymbol{d}) \propto \exp[-\exp(\boldsymbol{x}_i\boldsymbol{\beta} + \epsilon_i)][\exp(\epsilon_i)]^{y_i} \times \exp\{-\frac{1}{2(\sigma_\epsilon^2 - \sigma_{\epsilon u}^2)}[\epsilon_i - \sigma_{\epsilon u}(z_i - \boldsymbol{w}_i\boldsymbol{\gamma})]^2\}, \tag{6.156}$$

where Ξ_{-x} denotes the parameters other than x. Although ϵ_i cannot be sampled directly, as the form of (6.156) is uncommon, an M-H step can be employed. Specifically, a candidate draw can be sampled from a t distribution centered around the mode of $\ln p(\epsilon_i|\Xi_{-\epsilon_i}, \boldsymbol{y}, \boldsymbol{d})$, with scale parameter and degrees of freedom parameter equal to $(\nu\omega V_{\hat{\epsilon}_i})^{-1}$ and ν, respectively. In practice, we choose $V_{\hat{\epsilon}_i}$ as the negative inverse Hessian of $\ln p(\epsilon_i|\Xi_{-\epsilon_i}, \boldsymbol{y}, \boldsymbol{d})$ evaluated at the mode and both ν and ω are tuning parameters. The candidate draw ϵ_i^* is then accepted with probability

$$\min\left\{\frac{p(\epsilon_i^*|\Xi_{-\epsilon_i}, \boldsymbol{y}, \boldsymbol{d})q(\epsilon_i^{(t-1)})}{p(\epsilon_i^{(t-1)}|\Xi_{-\epsilon_i}, \boldsymbol{y}, \boldsymbol{d})q(\epsilon_i^*)}, 1\right\},$$

where the $(t-1)$ superscript denotes the current value of the chain and $q(\cdot)$ denotes the proposal density. We use a similar Metropolis step to sample the parameter vector $\boldsymbol{\beta}$ whose conditional posterior is proportional to

$$p(\boldsymbol{\beta}|\Xi_{-\beta}, y, \boldsymbol{d}) \propto \exp[-\frac{1}{2}(\boldsymbol{\beta} - \boldsymbol{\mu}_\beta)' V_\beta^{-1}(\boldsymbol{\beta} - \boldsymbol{\mu}_\beta)] \prod_{i=1}^{n} \exp[-\exp(\boldsymbol{x}_i\boldsymbol{\beta} + \epsilon_i)]$$
$$\times [\exp(\boldsymbol{x}_i\boldsymbol{\beta} + \epsilon_i)]^{y_i}. \tag{6.157}$$

The proposal density used in the sampling of $\boldsymbol{\beta}$ is a multivariate t distribution with location parameter $\hat{\boldsymbol{\beta}} = \arg\max \ln p(\boldsymbol{\beta}|\Xi_{-\beta}, y, \boldsymbol{d})$, scale parameter of $(\mu\tau V_{\hat{\beta}})^{-1}$, and degrees of freedom parameter μ. Again, we select $V_{\hat{\beta}}$ as the negative inverse Hessian of $\ln p(\boldsymbol{\beta}|\Xi_{-\beta}, y, \boldsymbol{d})$ evaluated at the mode and both τ and μ are tuning parameters.

The latent data z are sampled independently from

$$z_i|\Xi_{-z_i}, y, \boldsymbol{d} \sim \begin{cases} \mathcal{TN}_{(-\infty,0]}\left(\boldsymbol{w}_i\boldsymbol{\gamma} + \sigma_{\epsilon u}\sigma_\epsilon^{-2}\epsilon_i, 1 - \sigma_{\epsilon u}^2\sigma_\epsilon^{-2}\right) & \text{if } d_i = 0 \\ \mathcal{TN}_{(0,\infty)}\left(\boldsymbol{w}_i\boldsymbol{\gamma} + \sigma_{\epsilon u}\sigma_\epsilon^{-2}\epsilon_i, 1 - \sigma_{\epsilon u}^2\sigma_\epsilon^{-2}\right) & \text{if } d_i = 1 \end{cases}. \tag{6.158}$$

The conditional posterior of the parameter vector $\boldsymbol{\gamma}$ is normal:

$$\boldsymbol{\gamma}|\Xi_{-\gamma}, y, \boldsymbol{d} \sim \mathcal{N}\left(D_\gamma d_\gamma, D_\gamma\right), \tag{6.159}$$

where

$$D_\gamma = [W'W(1 - \sigma_{\epsilon u}^2\sigma_\epsilon^{-2})^{-1} + V_\gamma^{-1}]^{-1}, \tag{6.160}$$
$$d_\gamma = [W'(z - \sigma_{\epsilon u}\sigma_\epsilon^{-2}\boldsymbol{\epsilon})(1 - \sigma_{\epsilon u}^2\sigma_\epsilon^{-2})^{-1} + V_\gamma^{-1}\boldsymbol{\mu}_\gamma], \tag{6.161}$$

and W, z, and $\boldsymbol{\epsilon}$ have been stacked over i in the obvious way.

In terms of the sampling of $\boldsymbol{\Sigma}^{-1}$ we could, again, employ the reparameterization as described in (6.141)–(6.142). In this instance, however, we use the algorithm of Nobile (2000), who provides a method for directly sampling from an inverse Wishart, conditional on a fixed diagonal element of $\boldsymbol{\Sigma}$. We express this as

$$p(\boldsymbol{\Sigma}^{-1}|\Xi_{-\Sigma}, y, \boldsymbol{d}) \propto f_W\left(\boldsymbol{\Sigma}^{-1}\middle|[\kappa R + [\boldsymbol{\epsilon}\ z - W\boldsymbol{\gamma}]'[\boldsymbol{\epsilon}\ z - W\boldsymbol{\gamma}]]^{-1}, n + \kappa\right) I(\sigma_u^2 = 1). \tag{6.162}$$

Estimation results using this algorithm are listed in Table 6.9. Non-whites, females, and less educated persons are less likely to receive the therapy and have fewer sexual partners. The HAART regimen is found to have a positive and strong impact on sexual behavior. Specifically, the results suggest that the receipt of the regimen increases the mean number of sexual partners by about $[\exp(1.31) - 1] \times 100\% = 271\%$. Since the mean number of partners in the sample is 2.16, the marginal effect suggests that treated individuals have 5.85 additional partners. Among the two instrumental variables

Table 6.9: Posterior means, standard deviations, and probabilities of being positive of the parameters

Variable	$E(\beta\|D)$	$Std(\beta\|D)$	$Pr(\beta > 0\|D)$
Partners equation			
Age	−0.0464	0.00549	0
Non-white	−0.133	0.1	0.0913
Female	−0.584	0.107	0
Less than HS degree	−0.608	0.154	0.00015
High school degree	−0.676	0.14	0
Some college or AA degree	−0.4	0.139	0.00321
State per capita income	0.063	0.035	0.965
Percent living in urban areas	−0.0225	0.0129	0.0411
Abortion rate	0.0228	0.00954	0.991
Percent thinking homosexuality wrong	−5.05	1.44	0.000513
Percent praying several times a week	7.03	1.96	1
HAART	1.31	0.313	0.999
HAART equation			
Age	0.000701	0.00413	0.567
Non-white	−0.212	0.0745	0.00206
Female	−0.15	0.0766	0.025
Less than HS degree	−0.263	0.119	0.0128
High school degree	−0.136	0.112	0.113
Some college or AA degree	−0.126	0.111	0.128
State per capita income	−0.0534	0.027	0.0234
Percent living in urban areas	0.0267	0.0098	0.997
Abortion rate	−0.0172	0.00731	0.00925
Percent thinking homosexuality wrong	2.64	1.4	0.969
Percent praying several times a week	−2.95	1.84	0.0546
Medically needy threshold	0.00416	0.00173	0.992
SSI threshold > 65% of FPL	0.115	0.156	0.772
Covariance matrix			
Variance σ_ϵ^2	1.74	0.228	1
Covariance $\sigma_{\epsilon u}$	−0.912	0.19	0

employed, the "medically needy threshold" proves to be empirically important, and the associated coefficient has a probability of being positive near one, indicating that individuals who are eligible for Medicaid through a medically needy program are more likely to receive the therapy. Finally, the variance of the error term ϵ_i is about 1.74, indicating some overdispersion for the conditionally Poisson-distributed number of partners outcome. The covariance estimate between ϵ_i and u_i also shows that unobservables affecting the number of partners and the treatment are negatively correlated, consistent with the notion that people who are less healthy are less involved in risky sexual behavior, but more active in seeking the treatment. These results are qualitatively quite similar to those reported in Lakdawalla et al. (2006), although our model and approach differ slightly from theirs. We conclude by noting an alternate approach to posterior simulation with count outcomes, based upon Gaussian mixture approximations, is described by Frühwirth-Schnatter et al. (2009).

4.3 Treatment effects models

A generalization of the model in the previous section is to explicitly consider the *counterfactual* or *potential* outcome. This represents the outcome the agent would have experienced had he/she made a different treatment decision than the one actually made. Consistent with the specification in (6.126)–(6.128), we write this model as a system of three latent variable equations:[26]

$$z_{i2} = \boldsymbol{w}_i\boldsymbol{\theta} + u_{i2} \tag{6.163}$$

$$z_{i1} = \boldsymbol{x}_i\boldsymbol{\beta}_1 + u_{i1} \tag{6.164}$$

$$z_{i0} = \boldsymbol{x}_i\boldsymbol{\beta}_0 + u_{i0} \tag{6.165}$$

where

$$D_i = I(z_{i2} > 0) \tag{6.166}$$

$$y_i = D_i z_{i1} + (1 - D_i) z_{i0} \tag{6.167}$$

and

$$\left.\begin{bmatrix} u_{i2} \\ u_{i1} \\ u_{i0} \end{bmatrix}\right| \mathbf{X}, \boldsymbol{W}, \boldsymbol{\Sigma} \sim \mathcal{N}\left(\begin{bmatrix} 0 \\ 0 \\ 0 \end{bmatrix}, \begin{bmatrix} 1 & \sigma_{21} & \sigma_{20} \\ \sigma_{21} & \sigma_1^2 & \sigma_{10} \\ \sigma_{20} & \sigma_{10} & \sigma_2^2 \end{bmatrix}\right) \equiv \mathcal{N}(0, \boldsymbol{\Sigma}). \tag{6.168}$$

Equations (6.166) and (6.167) represent the mapping between the observed and latent data in the potential outcomes model. Equation (6.163) describes the treatment decision, whose marginal analysis is identical to the probit analysis of Section 3.1.1. Equations (6.164) and (6.165) describe the outcome (or potential outcome) in each treatment regime. For example, if $D_i = 1$, then the treated outcome z_{i1} is observed, while the untreated outcome z_{i0} is not. Conversely, when $D_i = 0$, the untreated outcome z_{i0} is observed while the treated outcome is not.

This model, just like the previous models of this section, can be stacked into vector/matrix form for each individual, letting $\boldsymbol{z}_i = [z_{i2}\ z_{i1}\ z_{i0}]'$, $\boldsymbol{\beta} = [\boldsymbol{\theta}'\ \boldsymbol{\beta}_1'\ \boldsymbol{\beta}_0']'$, and

$$X_i = \begin{bmatrix} \boldsymbol{w}_i & 0 & 0 \\ 0 & \boldsymbol{x}_i & 0 \\ 0 & 0 & \boldsymbol{x}_i \end{bmatrix}. \tag{6.169}$$

Therefore, we find ourselves in a familiar situation when faced with the task of posterior simulation in the potential outcomes model. The parameter vector $\boldsymbol{\beta}$ will be sampled from (6.129) and the inverse covariance matrix $\boldsymbol{\Sigma}^{-1}$ can be sampled from (6.131) using the method of Nobile (2000) if the (1,1) element of $\boldsymbol{\Sigma}$ is set to unity. Alternatively, we can choose to work in the non-identified parameter space and post-process the draws to restrict our focus on identifiable parameters. In terms of the latent data, two

[26] Covariates can also change with the regime, though we do not consider this in the notation below.

latent quantities must be drawn for each individual. First, latent values of z_{i2} will be drawn for each individual from a univariate truncated normal, with conditional support restricted by the observed value of D_i. Second, the potential (missing) outcome will also be sampled for each individual from the corresponding conditional normal defined by (6.127). We omit the details of this procedure here, as it follows similarly to those described earlier, and complete details can be found in Koop, Poirier and Tobias (2007: 225-9).

In the potential outcomes framework, parameters of interest often center around the outcome gain (or loss) from receipt of treatment: $z_{i1} - z_{i0}$. Parameters that garner the most attention in this literature include the Average Treatment Effect (ATE):

$$ATE(\boldsymbol{\beta}, \boldsymbol{x}) = \boldsymbol{x}(\boldsymbol{\beta}_1 - \boldsymbol{\beta}_0), \tag{6.170}$$

the effect of Treatment on the Treated (TT):

$$TT(\boldsymbol{\beta}, x, z, D(z) = 1) = \boldsymbol{x}(\boldsymbol{\beta}_1 - \boldsymbol{\beta}_0) + (\rho_{21}\sigma_1 - \rho_{20}\sigma_0)\frac{\phi(z\boldsymbol{\theta})}{\Phi(z\boldsymbol{\theta})}, \tag{6.171}$$

and the Local Average Treatment Effect (LATE):

$$LATE(\boldsymbol{\beta}, x, z, \tilde{z}, D(z)=0, D(\tilde{z})=1) = \boldsymbol{x}(\boldsymbol{\beta}_1 - \boldsymbol{\beta}_0) + (\rho_{21}\sigma_1 - \rho_{20}\sigma_0)\left(\frac{\phi(\tilde{z}\boldsymbol{\theta}) - \phi(z\boldsymbol{\theta})}{\Phi(\tilde{z}\boldsymbol{\theta}) - \Phi(z\boldsymbol{\theta})}\right), \tag{6.172}$$

where ρ_{jk} denotes the correlation parameter between $\boldsymbol{u}_j$ and $\boldsymbol{u}_k$.

ATE summarizes the average gain (or loss) from treatment, TT represents the expected gain (or loss) from treatment for those actually taking the treatment (at a given set of characteristics z), and LATE denotes the expected gain (or loss) from treatment for those that would receive the treatment at $\tilde{z}$ but would not receive the treatment at z. Imbens and Angrist (1994) introduce the LATE parameter and interpret it as a treatment effect for a subgroup of "compliers"—individuals whose treatment behavior can be manipulated through the presence (or absence) of the instrument. For example, in the Angrist (1990) study of the Vietnam-era draft, LATE will recover the average earnings gain (or loss) from military service for those who are induced to join the military because of a low draft lottery number, but otherwise would not serve. When treatment effects differ across individuals, different instruments define different LATE parameters—in the Angrist example, the results would not speak to the impact of military service on the post-service earnings of those who joined the military voluntarily. Heckman et al. (2001 and 2003) provide further results, discuss mean treatment effect parameters that are not covariate-dependent, and provide asymptotic derivations under a variety of distributional assumptions. Chamberlain (Chapter 1 of this volume) also discusses more details relating to Bayesian approaches to treatment effect modeling.

The expressions above can be evaluated at particular values of $\boldsymbol{x}$ and z and the posterior simulations of $\boldsymbol{\beta}$ and $\boldsymbol{\Sigma}$ used to estimate and characterize the posterior uncertainty regarding these average treatment impacts. Alternatively, one can average over the covariates' values to eliminate the dependence of these expressions on x and z (e.g. Chib and Jacobi 2007).

The mean effects listed above are certainly interesting, but also rather limiting: they summarize various mean treatment impacts for different subpopulations. Other quantities, such as $\text{Var}(z_1 - z_0)$ or quantiles of $z_1 - z_0$, are also of interest, but receive minimal attention in this literature.

The reason motivating this restricted focus lies with the cross-regime covariance parameter σ_{10}. When we consider the likelihood function for this model,

$$L(\boldsymbol{\beta}, \boldsymbol{\Sigma}; y, D) = \prod_{\{i:D_i=1\}} p(D_i = 1, y_i^{(1)}) \prod_{\{i:D_i=0\}} p(D_i = 0, y_i^{(0)}), \tag{6.173}$$

with $y_i^{(j)} = z_{ij}$, it is clear that this parameter does not enter the likelihood and thus is not identified. That is, observations will *either* belong to regime 0 or regime 1, but never both. As such, the likelihood does not directly inform us about σ_{10}. However, many features of the outcome gain $z_1 - z_0$ will depend on the cross-regime covariance σ_{10}, leaving the researcher wanting to do and say more, but typically resigning herself to focus on identifiable quantities like the mean effects listed above.

When conducting simulation-based posterior inference using the model described above, however, posterior simulations regrading σ_{10} are produced, potentially enabling an expanded focus beyond conventional treatment effect parameters. Vijverberg (1993) first noticed the possibility of learning about σ_{10}. These ideas were refined and a Gibbs sampling algorithm for the normal model produced by Koop and Poirier (1997). Chib and Hamilton (2000) address this issue by setting the cross-regime parameter to zero, and derive and apply posterior simulators for a variety of non-normal sampling models under this restriction. Poirier and Tobias (2003) and Li et al. (2004) further describe the nature of learning that takes place regarding σ_{10}. Since $\boldsymbol{\Sigma}$ must be positive definite, they show that the *conditional* support of the non-identified correlation ρ_{10} is the interval:

$$\rho_{10}|\rho_{21}, \rho_{20} \in \left(\rho_{21}\rho_{20} - [(1-\rho_{21}^2)(1-\rho_{20}^2)]^{1/2}, \rho_{21}\rho_{20} + [(1-\rho_{21}^2)(1-\rho_{20}^2)]^{1/2}\right). \tag{6.174}$$

Thus, as the data pin down the values of the identified correlations ρ_{21} and ρ_{20}, learning about ρ_{10} takes place given the support restrictions above. The extent of this learning, however, is seriously limited, as the shape of the posterior within the bounds above is simply the conditional prior for the non-identified correlation. Nonetheless, the bounds above can be informative, particularly when unobserved confounding is large, and can serve to update our prior beliefs about the cross-regime correlation, potentially enabling the researcher to characterize something beyond mean treatment parameters. In the most recent statement on this issue, Chib (2007) suggests working with the likelihood for the observed data rather than the potential outcomes, noting that such an approach improves the mixing of the posterior simulations and also frees the researcher from dealing with the non-identified correlation parameter.

4.4 The multinomial probit model

The multinomial probit (MNP) model (see e.g. Geweke et al. (1994, 1997) or Train (2003, chapter 5) and the references cited therein) also maps directly into the framework given by (6.126)–(6.128). In the MNP model, an agent makes a single choice among J alternatives. We let y_i represent the observed choice made by agent i, and enumerate the alternatives so that $y_i \in \{0, 1, \ldots, J-1\}$.

The MNP model is derived from a random utility framework where a multivariate latent variable, generated as in (6.127), is specified to describe the utility afforded by each alternative. In practice, of course, utility needs to be normalized both for level and scale, as the observed choices made by agents would be unaffected by the addition of a common constant to each utility level or by multiplication of utility by a constant. The issue of level normalization is typically accomplished by considering differences in utility relative to some base alternative, which, here, we treat as alternative zero. This focus on utility differences reduces the dimension of the model to $J-1$ rather than J, and we assume (6.126)–(6.128) applies to the analysis of such differences in utility. Rossi and Allenby (Chapter 8 of this volume) provide more details on analysis of the MNP models as well as the multivariate probit model considered in the next section. Relatedly, multimomial logit (MNL) and mixed logit models are commonly used to analyze this type of data. We do not consider these models here, unfortunately, but refer the reader to Rossi et al. (2005: sections 3.11 and chapter 5) and Train (2003) for more details.

As for scale normalization in the MNP model, we again have several possibilities, which already have been discussed. First, we can normalize a diagonal element of the $(J-1) \times (J-1)$ covariance matrix $\mathbf{\Sigma}$. The posterior conditional distribution of $\mathbf{\Sigma}^{-1}$ is then a Wishart, with a diagonal entry restricted to unity. McCulloch et al. (2000) discuss a reparameterization of the restricted covariance matrix that enables sampling of the elements of $\mathbf{\Sigma}$ based on simple Gibbs steps. Nobile (2000) also provides an algorithm that enables direct sampling from a Wishart given such a diagonal restriction. Finally, Imai and van Dyk (2005) introduce marginal data augmentation as an alternate way to handle scale identification in the MNP and also to impove the mixing of the posterior simulations. All of these approaches can be applied to form a sampler that navigates through the identified parameter space.

Alternatively, the restriction can be ignored, a standard Wishart prior employed for $\mathbf{\Sigma}^{-1}$, leading to a standard posterior conditional for $\mathbf{\Sigma}^{-1}$. Identified functions of parameters can then be calculated from such a sampler. In this approach, "off-the-shelf" routines can be used to perform the sampling, yielding computational simplicity and improved mixing properties.

It remains to discuss the sampling of the latent data within the MNP model. To this end, let $z_i = [z_{i1}\ z_{i2}\ \cdots\ z_{iJ-1}]'$ represent the latent differenced utility vector in (6.127). The link in (6.128) for the multinomial probit reduces to:

$$y_i = \begin{cases} 0 \text{ if } \max\{z_{il}\}_{l=1}^{J-1} \leq 0 \\ j \text{ if } \max\{z_{il}\}_{l=1}^{J-1} = z_{ij} \end{cases}. \tag{6.175}$$

Therefore, the posterior conditional distributions of each z_i are independent across individuals, and the posterior conditional density for each latent vector z_i is a normal distribution, truncated to a "cone" defined by the restrictions above.

While it is not possible to draw directly from this multivariate truncated distribution, Geweke (1991) provides an alternative, specialized for use in the MNP model by McCulloch and Rossi (1994). They note that the posterior conditional distributions for each z_{ij} are univariate truncated normal, with conditional supports defined through the restrictions in (6.175). As such, we can apply methods like those described for the probit model to generate a series of univariate truncated normal draws for each element of the latent variable vector z_i. For example, if alternative 0 is chosen by agent i, then each of the z_{ij} are restricted to be non-positive. Similarly, if $j \neq 0$ is chosen by agent i, then z_{ij} is restricted to be positive and at least as large as all of the other z_{il}. Thus, sampling of the latent data involves first calculating the conditional mean and variance of each z_{ij} from the $J-1$ dimensional multivariate normal in (6.127), determining the support restrictions on z_{ij} given the observed choice made by agent i, and then sampling from the resulting univariate truncated normal. This process is repeated for each element of z_i (and then for all i), noting that the most recent simulations of the z_{il} are used when calculating the conditional mean and variance for successive elements of z_i. Finally, apart from the sampling mechanism for the MNP model discussed so far, it is worthwhile to note from Keane (1992) that identification of the MNP model can be quite fragile.

4.5 The multivariate probit model

The multivariate probit (MVP) model (e.g. Chib and Greenberg (1998)) is quite similar in structure to the multinomial probit of the previous section and shares the hierarchical, latent representation that unites the models in this section. In the MVP, agents continue to face a choice among J different alternatives, yet are not restricted to choosing a single element among the set. Furthermore, factors not observed by the econometrician may generate correlation among these choices, motivating the desire to consider outcomes jointly rather than individually.

For analysis of the MVP model, we let $\boldsymbol{y}_i = [y_{i1}\ y_{i2}\ \cdots\ y_{iJ}]'$, $y_{ij} \in \{0,1\}\ \forall\ i,j$, and

$$X_i = \begin{bmatrix} x_{i1} & 0 & \cdots & 0 \\ 0 & x_{i2} & \cdots & 0 \\ \vdots & \vdots & \ddots & \vdots \\ 0 & 0 & \cdots & x_{iJ} \end{bmatrix}, \quad \boldsymbol{\beta} = \begin{bmatrix} \boldsymbol{\beta}_1 \\ \boldsymbol{\beta}_2 \\ \vdots \\ \boldsymbol{\beta}_J \end{bmatrix}. \tag{6.176}$$

In the above notation we specify that the covariates vary both with the agent and the alternative, and we also allow for alternative-specific slope parameters. The former of these assumptions may or may not be true in practice, though such data differences do not significantly affect the development of the model or posterior simulator. The restrictions in (6.128) for the MVP model reduce to a series of probit-like restrictions:

$$y_{ij} = I(z_{ij} > 0), \quad j = 1, 2, \ldots, J. \tag{6.177}$$

The identification problem in the MVP model is slightly different from that in the MNP model, given the nature of the observed responses in (6.177). In particular, if we were to multiply the latent equation in (6.127) by a diagonal matrix C, then one can show that

$$\Pr(Y_i = y_i | \boldsymbol{\beta} = \boldsymbol{\beta}_0, \boldsymbol{\Sigma} = \boldsymbol{\Sigma}_0) = \Pr\big(Y_i = y_i | \boldsymbol{\beta} = \tilde{\boldsymbol{\beta}}, \boldsymbol{\Sigma} = C\boldsymbol{\Sigma}_0 C'\big), \tag{6.178}$$

where $\tilde{\boldsymbol{\beta}}$ is constructed by multiplying each $\boldsymbol{\beta}_{0j}$ by the (j, j) element of C. In other words, each latent variable equation can be rescaled yet leave the likelihood function for the observed data unchanged.

Chib and Winkelmann (1998) present a Bayesian analysis of the MVP model, working with the covariance matrix $\boldsymbol{\Sigma}$ in restricted correlation form (and thus work directly with identifiable parameters) and propose a tailored Metropolis-Hastings step for sampling this restricted correlation matrix. Alternatively, Edwards and Allenby (2003) and Rossi et al. (2005) advocate working in the non-identified parameter space and adopting a sampler that only requires simulation from standard distributions. Specifically, they suggest working with an unrestricted $\boldsymbol{\Sigma}$. The regression parameters $\boldsymbol{\beta}$ are sampled from (6.129), the inverse covariance matrix is sampled from (6.131), and each latent vector z_i is again multivariate truncated normal, with conditional support restrictions given by (6.177). As such, the algorithm of Geweke (1991) can be applied, and each component $z_{ij}, j = 1, 2, \ldots, J$ drawn from a univariate truncated normal.

To deal with the identification problem in the Edwards and Allenby (2003) approach, the posterior simulations are post-processed to report identifiable quantities. In the general case, this requires setting C to be a $J \times J$ diagonal matrix with diagonal entries $\{\sigma_{j,j}^{-1/2}\}$ and calculating $C\boldsymbol{\beta}$ and $C\boldsymbol{\Sigma}C'$ as the identifiable regression parameters and covariance matrix, respectively. This approach to posterior simulation of the MVP model is attractive in that it only requires sampling from standard distributions and offers improved mixing properties in practice.

5 Duration Models

Microeconometric applications often involve the analysis of duration data, with Bayesian applications including the investigation of unemployment duration (Lancaster 1979; Li 2006), employment duration (Campolieti 1997), and time spent in bankruptcy (Li 1999), among others. A particularly salient feature of economic applications is the possibility (or probability) that such variables exhibit state dependence, meaning that the probability of exiting a spell may depend on the length of time the person has remained within that spell.

One approach to duration modeling specifies that the duration random variable of interest, T, is continuous, with probability density function denoted as $f(t)$. In this case, the cumulative distribution function, denoted $F(t)$, is obtained as $F(t) = \text{Prob}(T < t) = \int_0^t f(u)du$, while the survivor function (or the probability that T continues at time t) is simply one minus the cumulative distribution function:

$$S(t) = \text{Prob}(T \geq t) = 1 - \text{Prob}(T < t) = 1 - F(t).$$

In many applications of duration modeling, interests center around the hazard function (Cox 1972), $\lambda(t) = f(t)/S(t)$. This is the instantaneous probability of T ending exactly at t, conditional on the event that it has lasted until t. The special interest in the hazard often leads researchers to embrace it as the "primitive" and from it the implied survivor and density functions are derived. Letting $\Lambda(t) = \int_0^t \lambda(u)du$ denote the integrated hazard, it can be easily shown that $S(t) = \exp[-\Lambda(t)]$ and $f(t) = \exp[-\Lambda(t)]\lambda(t)$.

To conduct a Bayesian duration analysis, we assume that we have n observations on the duration random variable T that are (conditionally) independent from one another, and denote these as $t_1, t_2, \cdots, t_n$. The likelihood function of the model is

$$p(y|\Xi) = \prod_{i=1}^{n} \exp[-\Lambda(t_i)]\lambda(t_i),$$

where $y = [t_1 \; t_2 \; \cdots \; t_n]'$ denotes the data and Ξ all the parameters. If we specify that the hazard function remains constant over time, that is, $\lambda(t) = \lambda$, the integrated hazard function reduces to $\Lambda(t) = \lambda t$, and the likelihood function becomes $p(y|\Xi) = \prod_{i=1}^{n} \exp(-\lambda t_i)\lambda$. In this case only one parameter, λ, appears in the likelihood function. Recognizing this as an exponential sampling likelihood, the gamma prior:

$$p(\lambda) = f_G(a, b) = b^{-a}\Gamma(a)^{-1}\lambda^{a-1}\exp(-\lambda b^{-1})$$

is known to be conjugate. Specifically, if this prior is employed, we obtain:

$$p(\lambda|y) = f_G(a + n, (b^{-1} + \sum_{i=1}^{n} t_i)^{-1}).$$

The foregoing approach, based on the assumption of a constant hazard, is quite restrictive. A more flexible alternative is to specify that the hazard is constant over suitably short intervals, but potentially different across intervals. To this end we divide the time horizon into K shorter periods and specify that the hazard function remains constant within each period, but varies across different periods (e.g. Holford 1976). In other words, $\lambda = \lambda_1$ within the first period, $\lambda = \lambda_2$ within the second period, and so on.

Correspondingly, we also divide duration t_i into K parts, $t_{i1}, t_{i2}, \cdots, t_{iK}$, and use $d_{i1}, d_{i2}, \cdots, d_{iK}$ to indicate whether t_i ends in a particular period. For example, if t_i ends in the middle of the fourth period, $t_{i1} = t_{i2} = t_{i3} = 1$, $t_{i4} = \frac{1}{2}$, $t_{i5} = t_{i6} = \cdots = t_{iK} = 0$, only $d_{i4} = 1$ and all other $d_{ik} = 0$. The likelihood function for the piecewise constant baseline hazard is

$$p(y|\Xi) = \prod_{i=1}^{n} \exp(-\sum_{k=1}^{K} \lambda_k t_{ik}) \prod_{k=1}^{K} \lambda_k^{d_{ik}}.$$

As with the constant hazard case, we can specify a common gamma prior for the piecewise hazards:

$$\lambda_k \overset{iid}{\sim} G(a, b), \quad k = 1, 2, \ldots, K,$$

producing

$$\lambda_k | y \overset{ind}{\sim} G(a + \sum_{i=1}^{n} d_{ik}, (b^{-1} + \sum_{i=1}^{n} t_{ik})^{-1}), \quad k = 1, 2, \ldots, K.$$

5.1 Discrete time approaches

Sometimes we do not know when duration t_i ends exactly, but know that it ends within one of the K periods, for example, $k = 4$. A discrete model can be used for this type of data (Campolieti 1997). Denote $\Phi(\gamma_k)$ as the probability t_i continues in period k, conditional on the fact that it lasts until period $k - 1$, where $\Phi(\cdot)$ stands for the standard normal cumulative distribution function and γ_k is a period specific parameter, similar to λ_k in the continuous time model. Let $s_{i1}, s_{i2}, \cdots, s_{iK}$ be indicator variables denoting whether a duration continues in period k. For instance, if duration t_i ends in the fourth period, $s_{i1} = s_{i2} = s_{i3} = 1$ and $s_{i4} = s_{i5} = \cdots = s_{iK} = 0$. The likelihood function of the discrete model is

$$p(y|\gamma) = \prod_{i=1}^{n} \prod_{k=1}^{K} \Phi(\gamma_k)^{s_{ik}} [1 - \Phi(\gamma_k)]^{d_{ik}},$$

where, as defined in the continuous model, d_{ik} indicates whether duration t_i ends in period k. A normal prior such as $\phi(\mu_\gamma, V_\gamma)$ is commonly used for the period-specific rate parameter γ_k.

Following Albert and Chib (1993a, 1993b) and Campolieti (1997), one can use a Gibbs sampler with data augmentation to simulate draws from the posterior distribution of the parameters. For each duration t_i, and for each period k within which duration t_i continues or ends, the likelihood function is augmented with a latent variable $y_{ik} = \gamma_k + \epsilon_{ik}$, where $\epsilon_{ik} \overset{iid}{\sim} \mathcal{N}(0, 1)$, such that $y_{ik} > 0$ if t_i continues in period k and $y_{ik} \leq 0$ if it ends in period k.

The Gibbs sampler consists of two steps. In the first step, y_{ik} is drawn from a $\mathcal{TN}_{(0,\infty)}(\gamma_k, 1)$ distribution if t_i continues in period k and from $\mathcal{TN}_{(-\infty,0]}(\gamma_k, 1)$ if it ends in period k. The second step draws γ_k from $\mathcal{N}(D_k d_k, D_k)$, where

$$D_k = [V_\gamma^{-1} + \sum_{i=1}^{n} I(s_{ik} = 1 \text{ or } d_{ik} = 1)]^{-1} \text{ and } d_k = V_\gamma^{-1} \mu_\gamma + \sum_{i=1}^{n} I(s_{ik} = 1 \text{ or } d_{ik} = 1) y_{ik}.$$

5.2 Other generalizations

Duration models can be extended in various directions to accommodate additional features. Sometimes it is reasonable to specify that the baseline hazards in neighboring periods are similar to each other, and therefore it is natural to impose a smoothing prior on the piecewise constant baseline hazards (see Campolieti (2000) for an application in the discrete time model). For example, we can impose the following prior on the first difference in the baseline hazards of adjacent periods: $\lambda_{k+1} - \lambda_k \sim \mathcal{N}(0, \eta)$. Smaller values of η place stronger prior information on the baseline hazards and make the estimates of baseline hazards smoother. The smoothness of the baseline hazard estimates also depends on the order of differencing, and it is possible to specify a prior using a higher order of differencing among the baseline hazards.

Right censoring represents another common feature of duration data. Assume that the censoring occurs at the end of period K so that we only observe duration t_i up to that point. If t_i ends in a period beyond K, the timing of the termination will not be observed. Importantly, the likelihood functions discussed previously automatically take into account this issue. Note that if duration t_i is censored at the end of period K and t_i continues beyond that point, the indicator variables $d_{i1}, d_{i2}, \cdots, d_{iK}$ will all be zero. For the continuous model, the likelihood function of t_i reduces to $\exp(-\sum_{k=1}^{K} \lambda_k t_{ik})$, corresponding to the probability of survival at the end of period K. In the discrete model, the likelihood function becomes $\prod_{k=1}^{K} \Phi(\gamma_k)^{s_{ik}}$, which is also the probability of surviving until period K.

Another well-established result in duration analysis is that the failure to account for the heterogeneity in hazards results in identification problems in duration dependence estimation. Variation in hazard rates across agents can be explained by observable characteristics that change over time. Following the proportional hazard analysis framework (Cox 1972), we incorporate a $1 \times j$ vector of time-varying covariates $\boldsymbol{x}_{ik}$ into the duration model. In the continuous time model, the hazard that t_i ends in period k is proportional to the baseline hazard λ_k: $\lambda_{ik} = \exp(\boldsymbol{x}_{ik}\boldsymbol{\beta})\lambda_k$, where $\boldsymbol{\beta}$ is a $j \times 1$ vector representing the impacts of covariates $\boldsymbol{x}_{ik}$ on the hazard rate. The likelihood function accommodating such time-varying covariates is

$$p(\boldsymbol{y}|\Xi) = \prod_{i=1}^{n} \exp[-\sum_{k=1}^{K} \exp(\boldsymbol{x}_{ik}\boldsymbol{\beta})\lambda_k t_{ik}] \prod_{k=1}^{K} [\exp(\boldsymbol{x}_{ik}\boldsymbol{\beta})\lambda_k]^{d_{ik}}.$$

In the discrete time model, time-varying covariates are incorporated by replacing $\Phi(\gamma_k)$ with $\Phi(\gamma_k + \boldsymbol{x}_{ik}\boldsymbol{\beta})$ in the likelihood function.

The modeling of time-varying covariates is an attempt to deal with the above identification problem, but it is unlikely that the heterogeneity in hazard can be captured entirely by observables. As such, it is also important to model the unobserved heterogeneity in hazard across individuals. Consistent with the proportional hazard specification, we add unobserved heterogeneity to the hazard function in the same way as we introduced observed heterogeneity in the hazard. In the continuous model we change the hazard function to $\lambda_{ik} = \exp(\boldsymbol{x}_{ik}\boldsymbol{\beta})\eta_i\lambda_k$, where η_i represents the individual level unobserved heterogeneity.

Researchers (e.g. Lancaster 1979) often specify that η_i follows a gamma distribution, $\eta_i|\nu \overset{iid}{\sim} G(\nu, \nu^{-1})$, so that it has unit mean and variance equal to ν^{-1}. In the discrete model, we change the continuation probability to $\Phi(\gamma_k + \boldsymbol{x}_{ik}\boldsymbol{\beta} + \alpha_i)$ to reflect the influence of the individual specific random effect on the hazard function. A standard, simple parametric assumption for the heterogeneity terms would be $\alpha_i \overset{iid}{\sim} \mathcal{N}(0, \sigma^2)$. Alternatively, we could be more flexible and allow a nonparametric specification of the unobserved heterogeneity through the use of a Dirichlet process prior as in Campolieti (2001). Finally, duration data sometimes appear in a hierarchical form (Guo and Rodriguez 1992; Sastry 1997; Bolstad and Manda 2001; Li 2007). For example, we may observe durations for individuals clustered within the same household, the same city, and so on. In such cases, we can capture unobserved heterogeneity in the hazard at the various levels via the proportional hazard approach. The following example provides an illustration.

5.3 An example

We modify the application in Li (2007), who studies the timing of high school dropout decisions, using data from the High School and Beyond Longitudinal survey. The full model estimated by Li accounts for the heterogeneity in hazard rates at the individual, school, and state levels. To simplify our discussions, we consider here a simpler version and model only sources of individual level heterogeneity, ignoring any possible correlations that may take place for individuals within the same school or state. Adopting the continuous time model, we define the hazard of dropping out of high school during month k for individual i as $\lambda_{ik} = \exp(\boldsymbol{x}_{ik}\boldsymbol{\beta})\eta_i\lambda_k$, where $\boldsymbol{x}_{ik}$ is a $j \times 1$ vector of individual level covariates, $\eta_i \overset{iid}{\sim} G(\nu, \nu^{-1})$ represents individual i's random effect in the hazard function, and λ_k corresponds to the piecewise constant baseline hazard in month k. The likelihood function for the model is

$$p(y|\Xi) = \prod_{i=1}^{n} \nu^{\nu}\Gamma(\nu)^{-1}\eta_i^{\nu-1}\exp(-\eta_i\nu)\exp[-\sum_{k=1}^{K}\exp(\boldsymbol{x}_{ik}\boldsymbol{\beta})\eta_i\lambda_k t_{ik}]\prod_{k=1}^{K}[\exp(\boldsymbol{x}_{ik}\boldsymbol{\beta})\eta_i\lambda_k]^{d_{ik}}.$$

We specify the following priors: $\boldsymbol{\beta} \sim \mathcal{N}(\boldsymbol{\mu}_\beta, \boldsymbol{V}_\beta)$, $\lambda_k \overset{iid}{\sim} G(a_\lambda, b_\lambda)$, $\nu \sim G(a_\nu, b_\nu)$, where $\boldsymbol{\beta}_0 = \boldsymbol{0}$, $\boldsymbol{V}_\beta = 1000\boldsymbol{I}_j$, $a_\lambda = a_\nu = 0.01$, and $b_\lambda = b_\nu = 100$.

A Metropolis-within-Gibbs algorithm is used to generate samples from the joint posterior distribution. The parameters $\{\lambda_k\}_{k=1}^K$, $\{\eta_i\}_{i=1}^n$ are sampled using Gibbs steps by drawing, in order, from:

Table 6.10: Posterior estimates and marginal effects of the coefficients

Variable/parameter	$E(\beta\|D)$	$Std(\beta\|D)$	$P(\beta > 0\|D)$	Marginal effect
Female	−0.14	0.0709	0.0201	−12.8
Minority	−0.186	0.0824	0.00962	−16.7
Family income ($10,000)	−0.0524	0.0368	0.0674	−5.04
Base year test score	−0.838	0.0446	0	−56.7
Father's education (year)	−0.0505	0.0107	0	−4.92
Mother's education (year)	−0.0771	0.0122	0	−7.41
Number of siblings	0.0947	0.0206	1	9.95
Dropout eligibility	0.654	0.112	1	93.6
Variance parameter (v^{-1})	0.929	0.13	1	

$$\lambda_k|y, \{\eta_i\}_{i=1}^n, \boldsymbol{\beta}) \overset{ind}{\sim} G(a_\lambda + \sum_{i=1}^n d_{ik}, [b_\lambda^{-1} + \sum_{i=1}^n \exp(\boldsymbol{x}_{ik}\boldsymbol{\beta})\eta_i t_{ik}]^{-1})$$

and

$$\eta_i|y, \{\lambda_k\}_{k=1}^K, v, \boldsymbol{\beta} \overset{ind}{\sim} G(v + \sum_{i=1}^n d_{ik}, [v + \sum_{i=1}^n \exp(\boldsymbol{x}_{ik}\boldsymbol{\beta})\lambda_k t_{ik}]^{-1}).$$

The conditional posterior distributions of v and $\boldsymbol{\beta}$ are not of a known form and therefore cannot be sampled directly. For these parameters, we employ M-H steps.

In Table 6.10 we list summary posterior statistics and also calculate the marginal effect of a covariate which corresponds to the percentage change in the dropout hazard due to a one-unit increase in the covariate x_j, or $[\exp(\beta_j) - 1] \times 100$. Our results show that being eligible to drop out of high school under compulsory schooling laws increases the dropout hazard of an individual by 93.6 percent. An increase of $10,000 in parental income decreases the dropout hazard by 5.04 percent while the variance parameter estimate v^{-1} indicates considerable unobserved variation across individuals in the dropout hazard.

6 Conclusion

We have reviewed Bayesian approaches to estimation in many models commonly encountered in microeconomics. While not exhaustive, the models considered in this chapter are among the most widely used in practice and can serve to accommodate many of the data types and some of the econometric problems that the practitioner will face. While not completely flexible, as nearly all the posterior simulators have been presented under conditionally normal sampling assumptions, we have provided references to the literature for extensions of the basic framework, and noted the "modularity" of MCMC methods. That is, existing computational techniques can be employed to expand the sampling window to the class of scale mixtures or finite mixtures of normals, for example, and implementation of these steps proceeds in largely the same way regardless of the model employed (Geweke 2001). Finally, examples using real data for many different models have been provided and code is made available to the interested practitioner for inspection, refinement, or further modification.

References

Aitken, M., and Longford, N. (1986). "Statistical Modeling Issues in School Effectiveness Studies (with discussion)". *Journal of the Royal Statistical Society, Series A*, 149: 1–42.

Albert, J., and Chib, S. (1993a). "Bayesian Analysis of Binary and Polychotomous Response Data". *Journal of the American Statistical Association*, 88: 669–79.

——— (1993b). "A Practical Bayes Approach for Longitudinal Probit Regression Models with Random Effects". Technical Report, Department of Mathematics and Statistics, Bowling Green State University.

——— (2001). "Sequential Ordinal Modeling with Applications to Survival Data". *Biometrics*, 57: 829–36.

Amemiya, T. (1985). *Advanced Econometrics*. Cambridge Mass: Harvard University Press.

Andrews, D. F., and Mallows, C. L. (1974). "Scale Mixtures of Normal Distributions". *Journal of the Royal Statistical Society, Series B*, 36: 99–102.

Angrist, J. D. (1990). "Lifetime Earnings and the Vietnam Era Draft Lottery: Evidence from Social Security Administrative Records". *American Economic Review*, 80: 313–36.

—— and Krueger, A. (1991). "Does Compulsory School Attendance Affect Schooling and Earnings?". *Quarterly Journal of Economics*, 106: 979–1014.

Basu, S., and Mukhopadhyay, S. (2000). "Bayesian Analysis of Binary Regression Using Symmetric and Asymmetric Links". *Sankhya*, 62, Series B, Pt. 3: 372–87.

Bernardo, J., and Smith, A. F. M. (1994). *Bayesian Theory*. Chichester: John Wiley & Sons.

Berndt, E., Hall, B., Hall, R., and Hausman, J. (1974). "Estimation and Inference in Nonlinear Structural Models". *Annals of Social Measurement*, 3:653–65.

Bolstad, W. M., and Manda, S. O. (2001). "Investigating Child Mortality in Malawi Using Family and Community Random Effects: A Bayesian Analysis". *Journal of the American Statistical Association*, 96: 12–19.

Bound, J., Jaeger, D., and Baker, R. (1995). "Problems with Instrumental Variables Estimation when the Correlation Between the Instruments and the Endogenous Regressors is Weak". *Journal of the American Statistical Association*, 90: 443–50.

Campolieti, M. (1997). "Bayesian Estimation of Duration Models: An Application of the Multiperiod Probit Model". *Empirical Economics*, 22: 461–80.

—— (2000). "Bayesian Estimation and Smoothing of the Baseline Hazard in Discrete Time Duration Models". *Review of Economics and Statistics*, 82/4: 685–701.

—— (2001). "Bayesian Semiparametric Estimation of Discrete Duration Models: An Application of the Dirichlet Process Prior". *Journal of Applied Econometrics*, 16/1: 1–22.

____ (2003). "On the Estimation of Hazard Models with Flexible Baseline Hazards and Non-parametric Unobserved Heterogeneity". *Economics Bulletin*, 3/24: 1–10.
Carlin, B. P., and Polson, N. G. (1991). "Inference for Nonconjugate Bayesian Models Using the Gibbs Sampler". *The Canadian Journal of Statistics*, 19: 399–405.
Chen, M-H. and Dey, D. (1998). "Bayesian Modeling of Correlated Binary Responses via Scale Mixture of Multivariate Normal Link Functions". *Sankhya*, 60, Series A, Pt. 3: 322–43.
____ ____ (2000). "Bayesian Analysis for Correlated Ordinal Data Models", in D. K. Dey, S. K. Ghosh, and B. K. Mallick (eds.), *Generalized Linear Models: A Bayesian Perspective*, New York: Marcel Dekker, 133–57.
____ ____ and Shao, Q. (1999). "A New Skewed Link Model for Dichotomous Quantal Response Data". *Journal of the American Statistical Association*, 94: 1172–86.
Chernozhukov, V., and Hansen, C. (2008). "The Reduced Form: A Simple Approach to Inference with Weak Instruments". *Economics letters*, 100: 68–71.
Chib, S. (1992), "Bayes Inference in the Tobit Censored Regression Model". *Journal of Econometrics*, 51: 79–99.
____ (1995). "Marginal Likelihood from the Gibbs Output". *Journal of the American Statistical Association*, 90: 1313–21.
____ (1998). "Estimation and Comparison of Multiple Change-Point Models". *Journal of Econometrics*, 86: 221–41.
____ (2003). "On Inferring Effects of Binary Treatments with Unobserved Confounders (with discussion)", in J. M. Bernardo, M. J. Bayarri, J. O. Berger, A. P. Dawid, D. Heckerman, A. F. M. Smith, and M. West (eds.), *Bayesian Statistics 7*, Oxford: Oxford University Press, 66–84.
____ (2007), "Analysis of Treatment Response Data without the Joint Distribution of Potential Outcomes". *Journal of Econometrics*, 140: 401–12.
____ and Carlin, B. P. (1999). "On MCMC Sampling in Hierarchical Longitudinal Models", *Statistics and Computing*, 9: 17–26.
____ and Greenberg, E. (1998). "Analysis of Multivariate Probit Models". *Biometrika*, 85: 347–61.
____ ____ (2007). "Semiparametric Modeling and Estimation of Instrumental Variable Models". *Journal of Computational and Graphical Statistics*, 16: 86–114.
____ ____ and Jeliazkov, I. (2009). "Estimation of Semiparametric Models in the Presence of Endogeneity and Sample Selection". *Journal of Computational and Graphical Statistics*, 18: 321–48.
____ and Winkelmann, R. (1998). "Posterior Simulation and Bayes Factors in Panel Count Data Models". *Journal of Econometrics*, 86: 33–54.
____ and B. Hamilton (2000). "Bayesian Analysis of Cross Section and Clustered Data Treatment Models". *Journal of Econometrics*, 97: 25–50.
Chib, S., and Jacobi, L. (2007). "Modeling and Calculating the Effect of Treatment at Baseline from Panel Outcomes". *Journal of Econometrics*, 140: 781–801.
____ and Jeliazkov, I. (2001). "Marginal Likelihood from the Metropolis-Hastings Output". *Journal of the American Statistical Association*, 96: 270–81.
____ and Jeliazkov, I. (2006). "Inference in Semiparametric Dynamic Models for Binary Longitudinal Data". *Journal of the American Statistical Association*, 101: 685–700.
____ Nardair, F., and N. Shephard (2002). "Markov Chain Monte Carlo Methods for Stochastic Volatility Models". *Journal of Econometrics*, 108: 281–316.
Chin Choy, J. H. and Broemeling, L. D. (1980). "Some Bayesian Inferences for a Changing Linear Model". *Technometrics*, 22/1: 71–8.

Christ, C. F. (1994). "The Cowles Commission's Contributions to Econometrics at Chicago, 1939–1955". *Journal of Economic Literature* 32: 30–59.

Cox, D. R. (1972). "Regression Models and Life-Tables". *Journal of the Royal Statistical Society, Series B*, 34/2: 187-220.

Conley, T., Hansen, C., McCulluch, R., and Rossi, P. (2008). "A Semi-Parametric Bayesian Approach to the Instrumental Variables Problem". *Journal of Econometrics*, 144: 276–305.

Cowles, M. K. (1996). "Accelerating Monte Carlo Markov Chain Convergence for Cumulative-link Generalized Linear Models". *Statistics and Computing*, 6: 101–111.

Dearden, L., Ferri, J., and Meghir, C. (2002). "The Effect of School Quality on Educational Attainment and Wages". *Review of Economics and Statistics*, 84: 1–20.

——— ——— ——— (2006). "Bayesian Analysis of the Two-Part Model with Endogeneity: Application to Health Care Expenditure". *Journal of Applied Econometrics*, 21: 1081–99.

Drèze, J. H. (1976). "Bayesian Limited Information Analysis of the Simultaneous Equations Model". *Econometrica*, 44: 1045–75.

——— and Richard, J.-F. (1983). "Bayesian Analysis of Simultaneous Equation Systems", in Z. Griliches and M.D. Intriligator (eds.), *Handbook of Econometrics*, vol. 1. Amsterdam: Narth-Holland.

Edwards, Y. D. and Allenby, G. M. (2003). "Multivariate Analysis of Multiple Response Data". *Journal of Marketing Research*, 40: 321–34.

Fomby, T. M., and Vogelsang, T. J. (2002). "The Application of Size Robust Trend Analysis to Global Warming Temperature Series". *Journal of Climate*, 15: 117–23.

Frühwirth-Schnatter, S. and Früwirth, R. (2007). "Auxiliary Mixture Sampling with Applications to Logistic Models." *Computational Statistics & Data Analysis*, 51: 3509–28.

——— ———, Held, L. and Rue, H. (2009). "Improved Auxiliary Mixture Sampling for Hierarchical Models of non-Gaussian Data". *Statistics and Computing*, 19: 479–492.

Gelfand, A. E., Hills, S. E., Racine-Poon, A., and Smith, A. F. M. (1990). "Illustration of Bayesian Inference in Normal Data Models Using Gibbs Sampling". *Journal of the American Statistical Association*, 412: 972–85.

Gelman, A., Roberts, G. O., and Gilks, W. R. (1996). "Efficient Metropolis Jumping Rules", in J. M. Bernardo, J. O. Berger, A. P. Dawid, and A. F. M. Smith (eds.), *Bayesian Statistics 5*, Oxford: Oxford University Press, 599–607.

Geweke, J. (1991). "Efficient Simulation from the Multivariate Normal and Student-*t* Distributions Subject to Linear Constraints", in E. M. Keramidas (ed.), *Computing Science and Statistics: Proceedings of the Twenty-Third Symposium on the Interface*, Fairfax, Va.: Interface Foundation of North America, Inc., 571-8, working paper version in PDF format at http://www.biz.uiowa.edu/faculty/jgeweke/papers.html.

——— (1993). "Bayesian Treatment of the Independent Student-*t* Linear Model". *Journal of Applied Econometrics*, 8: S19–S40.

——— (1996a). "Bayesian Reduced Rank Regression in Econometrics". *Journal of Econometrics*, 75: 121–46.

——— (1996b). "Bayesian Inference for Linear Models Subject to Linear Inequality Constraints", in W. O Johnson, J. C. Lee, and Z. Zellner (eds.), *Modeling and Prediction: Honoring Seymour Geisser*, New York: Springer-Verlag, 248–63.

——— (2005). *Contemporary Bayesian Econometrics and Statistics*, New York: Wiley.

——— Gowrisankaran, G., and Town, R. J. (2003). 'Bayesian Inference for Hospital Quality in a Selection Model'. *Econometrica*, 71: 1215–38.

Geweke, J. and M. Keane (2000). "An Empirical Analysis of Income Dynamics among Men in the PSID: 1968–1989". *Journal of Econometrics*, 96: 293–356.

——— (2001). "Computationally Intensive Methods for Integration in Econometrics", in J. J. Heckman and E. Leamer (eds.), *Handbook of Econometrics*, vol. 5, Amsterdam, North-Holland.

—— (2007). "Smoothly Mixing Regressions". *Journal of Econometrics*, 138: 252–91.

——— and Runkle, D. (1994). "Alternative Computational Approaches to Inference in the Multinomial Probit Model". *Review of Economics and Statistics*, 76: 609–32.

———— (1997). "Statistical Inference in the Multinomial Multiperiod Probit Model". *Journal of Econometrics*, 80: 125–66.

—— and Terui, N. (1993). "Bayesian Threshold Autoregressive Models for Nonlinear Time Series". *Journal of Time Series Analysis*, 14: 441–54.

Graves, J., Jeliazkov, I., and Kutzbach, M. (2008). "Fitting and Comparison of Models for Multivariate Ordinal Outcomes", in S. Chib, W. Griffith, G. Koop, and D. Terrell, (eds.), *Advances in Econometrics*, vol. 23, Bingley: Finerald, 115–56.

Guo, G., and Rodriguez, G. (1992). "Estimating a Multivariate Proportional Hazards Model for Clustered Data Using the EM Algorithm, with an Application to Child Survival in Guatemala". *Journal of the American Statistical Association*, 87: 969–76.

Harvey, A. C. (1976). "Estimating Regression Models with Multiplicative Heteroscedasticity". *Econometrica*, 44: 461–5.

Heckman, J. J., Tobias, J. L., and Vytlacil, E. (2001). "Four Parameters of Interest in the Evaluation of Social Programs". *Southern Economic Journal*, 68: 210–33.

———— (2003). "Simple Estimators for Treatment Parameters in a Latent Variable Framework". *Review of Economics and Statistics*, 85: 748–55.

Holford, T. R. (1976). "Life Tables with Concomitant Information". *Biometrics*, 32/3: 587–97.

Holmes, C. C., and Held, L. (2006). "Bayesian Auxiliary Variable Models for Binary and Multinomial Regression". *Bayesian Analysis*, 1: 146–68.

—— Kleibergen, F., and van Dijk, H. K. (2007). "Natural Conjugate Priors for the Instrumental Variables Regression Model Applied to the Angrist-Krueger Data". *Journal of Econometrics*, 138: 63–103.

Hoogerheide, L. F., Kaashoek J. F., and van Dijk, H. K. (2007). "On the Shape of Posterior Densities and Credible Sets in Instrumental Variable Regression Models with Reduced Rank: An Application of Flexible Sampling Methods Using Neural Networks". *Journal of Econometrics*, 139: 154–80.

Imai, K. and van Dyk, D. A. (2005). "A Bayesian analysis of the Multinomial Probit Model using Marginal Data Augmentation." *Journal of Econometrics*, 124: 311–334.

Imbens, G. W., and Angrist, J. D. (1994). "Identification and Estimation of Local Average Treatment Effects". *Econometrica*, 62: 467–75.

Ivanov, M. A., and Evtimov, S. N. (2001). "1963: The Break Point of the Northern Hemisphere Temperature Trend during the Twentieth Century". *International Journal of Climatology*, 30/11: 1738–46.

Keane, M. (1992). "A Note on Identification in the Multinomial Probit Model". *Journal of Business and Economics Statistics*, 10: 193–200.

Kleibergen, F., and Zivot, E. (2003). "Bayesian and Classical Approaches to Instrumental Variable Regression". *Journal of Econometrics*, 114: 29–72.

Kline, B. and Tobias, J. L. (2008). "The Wages of BMI: Bayesian Analysis of a Skewed Treatment Response Model with Nonparametric Endogeneity". *Journal of Applied Econometrics*, 23: 767–93.

Koop, G. (2003). *Bayesian Econometrics*, Chichester John Wiley and Sons.

—— Osiewalski, J., and Steel, M. (1997). "Bayesian Efficiency Analysis through Individual Effects: Hospital Cost Frontiers". *Journal of Econometrics*, 76: 77–105.

—— and Poirier, D. J. (1997). "Learning about the Across-Regime Correlation in Switching Regression Models". *Journal of Econometrics*, 78: 217–227.

—— and Steel, M. (2001). "Bayesian Analysis of Stochastic Frontier Models", in B. Baltagi (ed.), *A Companion to Theoretical Econometrics*, Malden, Mass. Blackwell Publishers, 520–37.

—— —— and Tobias, J. (2007). *Bayesian Econometric Methods*, Cambridge: Cambridge University Press.

—— and Potter, S. (2007). "Estimation and Forecasting in Models with Multiple Breaks". *Review of Economic Studies*, 74: 763–89.

Krueger, A. (1998). "Reassessing the View that American Schools are Broken". *FRBNY Economic Policy Review*, March, 29–43.

—— and Whitmore, D. (2001). "The Effect of Attending a Small Class in the Early Grades on College Test-Taking and Middle School Test Results: Evidence from Project STAR". *Economic Journal*, 111: 1–28.

Laird, N. M. (1989). "Empirical Bayes Ranking Methods". *Journal of Educational and Behavioral Statistics*, 14: 29–46.

Lakdawalla, D., Sood, N., and Goldman, D. (2006). "HIV Breakthroughs and Risky Sexual Behavior". *Quarterly Journal of Economics*, 121: 1063–102.

Lancaster, T. (1979). "Econometric Methods for the Duration of Unemployment". *Econometrica*, 47/4: 939–56.

—— (2003). "A Note on Bootstraps and Robustness", unpublished manuscript, Brown University.

—— (2004). *An Introduction to Modern Bayesian Econometrics*, Malden, Mass. Blackwell Publishing.

Leslie, D. S., Kohn, R., and Nott, D. J. (2007). "A General Approach to Heteroscedastic Linear Regression". *Statistics and Computing*, 17: 131–46.

Li, K. (1998). "Bayesian Inference in a Simultaneous Equations Model with Limited Dependent Variables". *Journal of Econometrics*, 85: 387–400.

—— (1999). "Bayesian Analysis of Duration Models: An Application to Chapter 11 Bankruptcy". *Economics Letters*, 63/3: 305–12.

—— (2006). "High School Completion and Future Youth Unemployment: New Evidence from High School and Beyond". *Journal of Applied Econometrics*, 21/1: 23–53.

—— (2007). "Bayesian Proportional Hazard Analysis of the Timing of High School Dropout Decisions". *Econometric Reviews*, 26/5: 529–56.

—— and Tobias, J. L. (2005). "Bayesian Modeling of School Effects Using Hierarchical Models with Smoothing Priors". *Studies in Nonlinear Dynamics and Econometrics*, 9/3, Article 4.

—— Poirier, D. J., and Tobias, J. L. (2004). "Do Dropouts Suffer from Dropping Out? Estimation and Prediction of Outcome Gains in Generalized Selection Models". *Journal of Applied Econometrics*, 19: 203–25.

Lindley, D. V. and Smith, A. F. M. (1972). "Bayes Estimates for the Linear Model". *Journal of the Royal Statistical Society, Series B*, 34: 1–41.

McCulloch, R. E., Polson, N. G., and Rossi, P. E. (2000). "A Bayesian Analysis of the Multinomial Probit Model with Fully Identified Parameters". *Journal of Econometrics*, 99: 173–93.

—— and Rossi, P. (1994). "An Exact Likelihood Analysis of the Multinomial Probit Model". *Journal of Econometrics*, 64: 207–40.

McFadden, D. (1974). "Conditional Logit Analysis of Qualitative Choice Behavior", in P. Zarembka, (ed.), *Frontiers of Econometrics*, New York: Academic Press, 105–142.

Munkin, M. K., and Trivedi, P. K. (2003). "Bayesian Analysis of Self-Selection Model with Multiple Outcomes Using Simulation-Based Estimation: An Application to the Demand for Healthcare". *Journal of Econometrics*, 114: 197–220.

———— (2008). "Bayesian Analysis of the Ordered Probit Model with Endogenous Selection". *Journal of Econometrics*, 143: 334–48.

Nandram, B., and Chen, M.-H. (1996). "Accelerating Gibbs Sampler Convergence in the Generalized Linear Models via a Reparameterization". *Journal of Statistical Computation and Simulation*, 54: 129–44.

Nobile, A. (2000). "Comment: Bayesian Multinomial Probit Models with a Normalization Constraint". *Journal of Econometrics*, 99: 335–45.

Percy, D. (1992). "Prediction for Seemingly Unrelated Regressions". *Journal of the Royal Statistical Society, Series B*, 54: 243–52.

Poirier, D. (1995). *Intermediate Statistics and Econometrics: A Comparative Approach*, Cambridge, Mass: MIT Press.

—— (2008). "Bayesian Interpretations of Heteroskedastic Consistent Covariance Estimators Using the Informed Bayesian Bootstrap", working paper, University of California, Irvine.

—— and Tobias, J. L. (2003). "On the Predictive Distributions of Outcome Gains in the Presence of an Unidentified Parameter". *Journal of Business and Economic Statistics*, 21: 258–68.

Rossi, P. E., Allenby, G. M., and McCulloch, R. (2005). *Bayesian Statistics and Marketing*, Chichester: Wiley.

Sastry, N. (1997). "A Nested Frailty Model for Survival Data, with an Application to the Study of Child Survival in Northeast Brazil". *Journal of the American Statistical Association*, 92: 426–35.

Sims, C. (2007). "Thinking about Instrumental Variables", available online at http://sims.princeton.edu/yftp/IV/.

Smith, A. F. M. (1973). "A General Bayesian Linear Model". *Journal of the Royal Statistical Society Series B*, 35: 67–75.

Stefanski, L. A. (1991). "A Normal Scale Mixture Representation of the Logistic Distribution". *Statistics and Probability Letters*, 11/1, 69–70.

Smith, M., and Kohn, R. (1996). "Nonparametric Regression Using Bayesian Variable Selection". *Journal of Econometrics*, 75: 317–43.

Stockwell, D. R. B., and Cox, A. (2009). "Structural Break Models of Climatic Regime-Shifts: Claims and Forecasts," working paper available at http://arxiv.org/abs/0907.1650.

Tanizaki, H., and Zhang, X. (2001). "Posterior Analysis of the Multiplicative Heteroscedasticity Model". *Communications in Statistics, Theory and Methods*, 30: 855–74.

Tanner, M., and Wong, W. (1987). "The Calculation of Posterior Distributions by Data Augmentation". *Journal of the American Statistical Association*, 82: 528–49.

Train, K. E. (2003). *Discrete Choice Methods with Simulation*, Cambridge: Cambridge University Press.

Tüchler, R. (2008). "Bayesian Variable Selection for Logistic Models using Auxiliary Mixture Sampling". *Journal of Computational and Graphical Statistics*, 17: 76–94.

van Hasselt, M. (2008). "Bayesian Inference in a Sample Selection Model", working paper, Department of Economics, University of Western Ontario.

Vijverberg, W. (1993). "Measuring the Unidentified Parameter of the Extended Roy Model of Selectivity". *Journal of Econometrics*, 57: 69–89.

Villani, M., Kohn, R., and Giordani, P. (2007). "Nonparametric Regression and Density Estimation Using Smoothly Varying Normal Mixtures", Sveriges Riksbank Working Paper Series, No. 211.

Vogelsang, T. J., and Franses, P. H. (2005). "Are Winters Getting Warmer?". *Environmental Modelling & Software*, 20: 1449–55.

White, H. (1980). "A Heteroscedasticity-Consistent Covariance Matrix Estimator and a Direct Test for Heteroscedasticity". *Econometrica*, 48: 817–38.

Yau, P., and Kohn, R. (2003). "Estimation and Variable Selection in Nonparametric Heteroscedastic Regression". *Statistics and Computing*, 13: 191–208.

Zellner, A. (1962). "An Efficient Method of Estimating Seemingly Unrelated Regressions and Test for Aggregation Bias". *Journal of the American Statistical Association*, 57: 348–68.

CHAPTER 7

BAYESIAN MACROECONOMETRICS

MARCO DEL NEGRO AND FRANK SCHORFHEIDE

1 Introduction

One of the goals of macroeconometric analysis is to provide quantitative answers to substantive macroeconomic questions. Answers to some questions, such as whether gross domestic product (GDP) will decline over the next two quarters, can be obtained with univariate time-series models by simply exploiting serial correlations. Other questions, such as what are the main driving forces of business cycles, require at least a minimal set of restrictions, obtained from theoretical considerations, that allow the identification of structural disturbances in a multivariate time-series model. Finally, macroeconometricians might be confronted with questions demanding a sophisticated theoretical model that is able to predict how agents adjust their behavior in response to new economic policies, such as changes in monetary or fiscal policy.

1.1 Challenges for inference and decision making

Unfortunately, macroeconometricians often face a shortage of observations necessary for providing precise answers. Some questions require high-dimensional empirical models. For instance, the analysis of domestic business cycles might involve processing

The views expressed in this chapter do not necessarily reflect those of the Federal Reserve Bank of New York or the Federal Reserve System. Ed Herbst and Maxym Kryshko provided excellent research assistance. We are thankful for the feedback received from the editors of the *Handbook*, John Geweke, Gary Koop, and Herman van Dijk, as well as for comments by Giorgio Primiceri, Dan Waggoner, and Tao Zha.

information from a large cross-section of macroeconomic and financial variables. The study of international co-movements is often based on highly parameterized multi-country vector autoregressive models. High-dimensional models are also necessary in applications in which it is reasonable to believe that parameters evolve over time, for instance, because of changes in economic policies. Thus, sample information alone is often insufficient to enable sharp inference about model parameters and implications. Other questions do not necessarily require a very densely parameterized empirical model, but they do demand identification restrictions that are not self-evident and that are highly contested in the empirical literature. For instance, an unambiguous measurement of the quantitative response of output and inflation to an unexpected reduction in the federal funds rate remains elusive. Thus, documenting the uncertainty associated with empirical findings or predictions is of first-order importance for scientific reporting.

Many macroeconomists have a strong preference for models with a high degree of theoretical coherence such as dynamic stochastic general equilibrium (DSGE) models. In these models, decision rules of economic agents are derived from assumptions about agents' preferences and production technologies and some fundamental principles such as intertemporal optimization, rational expectations, and competitive equilibrium. In practice, this means that the functional forms and parameters of equations that describe the behavior of economic agents are tightly restricted by optimality and equilibrium conditions. Thus, likelihood functions for empirical models with a strong degree of theoretical coherence tend to be more restrictive than likelihood functions associated with atheoretical models. A challenge arises if the data favor the atheoretical model and the atheoretical model generates more accurate forecasts, but a theoretically coherent model is required for the analysis of a particular economic policy.

1.2 How can Bayesian analysis help?

In Bayesian inference, a prior distribution is updated by sample information contained in the likelihood function to form a posterior distribution. Thus, to the extent that the prior is based on *nonsample* information, it provides the ideal framework for combining different sources of information and thereby sharpening inference in macroeconometric analysis. This combination of information sets is prominently used in the context of DSGE model inference in Section 4. Through informative prior distributions, Bayesian DSGE model inference can draw from a wide range of data sources that are (at least approximately) independent of the sample information. These sources might include microeconometric panel studies that are informative about aggregate elasticities or long-run averages of macroeconomic variables that are not included in the likelihood function because the DSGE model under consideration is too stylized to be able to explain their cyclical fluctuations.

Many macroeconometric models are richly parameterized. Examples include the vector autoregressions (VARs) with time-varying coefficients in Section 5 and the multicountry VARs considered in Section 6. In any sample of realistic size, there will be a shortage of information for determining the model coefficients, leading to very imprecise inference and diffuse predictive distributions. In the context of time-varying coefficient models, it is often appealing to conduct inference under the assumption that either coefficients change only infrequently, but by a potentially large amount, or that they change frequently, but only gradually. Such assumptions can be conveniently imposed by treating the sequence of model parameters as a stochastic process, which is of course nothing but a prior distribution that can be updated with the likelihood function.

To reduce the number of parameters in a high-dimensional VAR, one could of course set many coefficients equal to zero or impose the condition that the same coefficient interacts with multiple regressors. Unfortunately, such *hard* restrictions rule out the existence of certain spillover effects, which might be undesirable. Conceptually more appealing is the use of *soft* restrictions, which can be easily incorporated through probability distributions for those coefficients that are "centered" at the desired restrictions but that have a small, yet nonzero, variance. An important and empirically successful example of such a prior is the Minnesota prior discussed in Section 2.

An extreme version of lack of sample information arises in the context of structural VARs, which are studied in Section 2. Structural VARs can be parameterized in terms of reduced-form parameters, which enter the likelihood function, and an orthogonal matrix Ω, which does not enter the likelihood function. Thus, Ω is not identifiable based on the sample information. In this case, the conditional distribution of Ω given the reduced-form parameters will not be updated, and its conditional posterior is identical to the conditional prior. Identification issues also arise in the context of DSGE models. In general, as long as the joint prior distribution of reduced-form and nonidentifiable parameters is proper, meaning that the total probability mass is one, so is the joint posterior distribution. In this sense, the lack of identification poses no conceptual problem in a Bayesian framework. However, it does pose a challenge: it becomes more important to document which aspects of the prior distribution are not updated by the likelihood function and to recognize the extreme sensitivity of those aspects to the specification of the prior distribution.

Predictive distributions of future observations such as aggregate output, inflation, and interest rates are important for macroeconomic forecasts and policy decisions. These distributions need to account for uncertainty about realizations of structural shocks as well as uncertainty associated with parameter estimates. Since shocks and parameters are treated symmetrically in a Bayesian framework, namely as random variables, accounting for these two sources of uncertainty simultaneously is conceptually straightforward. To the extent that the substantive analysis requires a researcher to consider multiple theoretical and empirical frameworks, Bayesian analysis allows the researcher to assign probabilities to competing model specifications and update these probabilities in view of the data. Throughout this chapter, we will encounter a large number of variants of VARs (Sections 2 and 3) and DSGE models (Section 4) that potentially differ in their economic implications. With posterior model probabilities in hand, inference and decisions can be based on model averages (Section 7).

Predictions of how economic agents would behave under counterfactual economic policies never previously observed require empirical models with a large degree of theoretical coherence. The DSGE models discussed in Section 4 provide an example. As mentioned earlier, in practice posterior model probabilities often favor more flexible, nonstructural time-series models such as VARs. Nonetheless, Bayesian methods offer a rich toolkit for linking structural econometric models to more densely parameterized reference models. For instance, one could use the restrictions associated with the theoretically coherent DSGE model only loosely, to center a prior distribution on a more flexible reference model. This idea is explored in more detail in Section 4.

1.3 Outline of this Chapter

Throughout this chapter, we will emphasize multivariate models that can capture comovements of macroeconomic time series. We will begin with a discussion of vector autoregressive models in Section 2, distinguishing between reduced-form and structural VARs. Reduced-form VARs essentially summarize autocovariance properties of vector time series and can also be used to generate multivariate forecasts. More useful for substantive empirical work in macroeconomics are so-called structural VARs, in which the innovations do not correspond to one-step-ahead forecast errors but instead are interpreted as structural shocks. Much of the structural VAR literature has focused on studying the propagation of monetary policy shocks, that is, changes in monetary policy unanticipated by the public. After discussing various identification schemes and their implementation, we devote the remainder of Section 2 to a discussion of advanced topics such as inference in restricted or overidentified VARs. As an empirical illustration, we measure the effects of an unanticipated change in monetary policy using a four-variable VAR.

Section 3 is devoted to VARs with explicit restrictions on the long-run dynamics. While many macroeconomic time series are well described by stochastic trend models, these stochastic trends are often common to several time series. For example, in many countries the ratio (or log difference) of aggregate consumption and investment is stationary. This observation is consistent with a widely used version of the neoclassical growth model (King et al. 1988), in which the exogenous technology process follows a random walk. One can impose such common trends in a VAR by restricting some of the eigenvalues of the characteristic polynomial to unity. VARs with eigenvalue restrictions, written as so-called vector error correction models (VECM), have been widely used in applied work after Engle and Granger (1987) popularized the concept of cointegration. While frequentist analysis of nonstationary time-series models requires a different set of statistical tools, the shape of the likelihood function is largely unaffected by the presence of unit roots in autoregressive models, as pointed out by Sims and Uhlig

(1991). Nonetheless, the Bayesian literature has experienced a lively debate about how best to analyze VECMs. Most of the controversies are related to the specification of prior distributions. We will focus on the use of informative priors in the context of an empirical model for US output and investment data. Our prior is based on the balanced-growth-path implications of a neoclassical growth model. However, we also discuss an important strand of the literature that, instead of using priors as a tool to incorporate additional information, uses them to regularize or smooth the likelihood function of a cointegration model in areas of the parameter space in which it is very nonelliptical.

Modern dynamic macroeconomic theory implies fairly tight cross-equation restrictions for vector autoregressive processes, and in Section 4 we turn to Bayesian inference with DSGE models. The term *DSGE model* is typically used to refer to a broad class that spans the standard neoclassical growth model discussed in King et al. (1988), as well as the monetary model with numerous real and nominal frictions developed by Christiano et al. (2005). A common feature of these models is that the solution of intertemporal optimization problems determines the decision rules, given the specification of preferences and technology. Moreover, agents potentially face uncertainty with respect to total factor productivity, for instance, or the nominal interest rate set by a central bank. This uncertainty is generated by exogenous stochastic processes or shocks that shift technology or generate unanticipated deviations from a central bank's interest-rate feedback rule. Conditional on the specified distribution of the exogenous shocks, the DSGE model generates a joint probability distribution for the endogenous model variables such as output, consumption, investment, and inflation. Much of the empirical work with DSGE models employs Bayesian methods. Section 4 discusses inference with linearized as well as nonlinear DSGE models and reviews various approaches for evaluating the empirical fit of DSGE models. As an illustration, we conduct inference with a simple stochastic growth model based on US output and hours worked data.

The dynamics of macroeconomic variables tend to change over time. These changes might be a reflection of inherent nonlinearities of the business cycle, or they might be caused by the introduction of new economic policies or the formation of new institutions. Such changes can be captured by econometric models with time-varying parameters (TVP), discussed in Section 5. Thus, we augment the VAR models of Section 2 and the DSGE models of Section 4 with time-varying parameters. We distinguish between models in which parameters evolve according to a potentially nonstationary autoregressive law of motion and models in which parameters evolve according to a finite-state Markov-switching (MS) process. If time-varying coefficients are introduced in a DSGE model, an additional layer of complication arises. When solving for the equilibrium law of motion, one has to take into account that agents are aware that parameters are not constant over time and hence adjust their decision rules accordingly.

Because of the rapid advances in information technologies, macroeconomists now have access to and the ability to process data sets with a large cross-sectional as well as a large time-series dimension. The key challenge for econometric modeling is to avoid a proliferation of parameters. Parsimonious empirical models for large data sets can be obtained in several ways. We consider restricted large-dimensional vector autoregressive models as well as dynamic factor models (DFMs). The latter class of models assumes that the co-movement between variables is due to a relatively small number of common factors, which, in the context of a DSGE model, could be interpreted as the most important economic state variables. These factors are typically unobserved and follow some vector autoregressive law of motion. We study empirical models for so-called data-rich environments in Section 6.

Throughout the various sections of the chapter, we will encounter uncertainty about model specifications, such as the number of lags in a VAR, the importance of certain types of propagation mechanisms in DSGE models, the presence of time-variation in coefficients, or the number of factors in a dynamic factor model. A treatment of Bayesian model selection and, more generally, decision making under model uncertainty is provided in Section 7.

Finally, a word on notation. We use $Y_{t_0:t_1}$ to denote the sequence of observations or random variables $\{y_{t_0}, \ldots, y_{t_1}\}$. If no ambiguity arises, we sometimes drop the time subscripts and abbreviate $Y_{1:T}$ by Y. θ often serves as the generic parameter vector, $p(\theta)$ is the density associated with the prior distribution, $p(Y|\theta)$ is the likelihood function, and $p(\theta|Y)$ the posterior density. We use *iid* to abbreviate independently and identically distributed. A p-variate Normal distribution is denoted by $N_p(\mu, \sum)$. We say that a $p \times q$ matrix X is matricvariate Normal $MN_{p\times q}(M, Q \otimes P)$, meaning that $vec(X) \sim N_{pq}(vec(M), Q \otimes P)$ *if* $p(X|M, Q, P) \propto \exp\{-\frac{1}{2}tr[Q^{-1}(X - M)'P^{-1}(X - M)]\}$, where $\otimes$ is the Kronecker product, $vec(\cdot)$ stacks the columns of a matrix, and $tr[\cdot]$ is the trace operator. A $q \times q$ matrix $\sum$ has an Inverted Wishart distribution, denoted by $IW_q(S, \nu)$, if $p(\sum |S, \nu) \propto |\sum|^{-(\nu+q+1)/2} \exp\{-\frac{1}{2}tr[\sum^{-1} S]\}$. The p and q subscripts are omitted if no ambiguity arises. If $X|\Sigma \sim MN_{p\times q}(M, \Sigma \otimes P)$ is matricvariate Normal and $\Sigma \sim IW_q(S, \nu)$ has an Inverted Wishart distribution, we say that $(X, \Sigma) \sim MNIW(M, P, S, \nu)$. Here $\otimes$ is the Kronecker product. We use I to denote the identity matrix and use a subscript indicating the dimension if necessary. $tr[A]$ is the trace of the square matrix A, $|A|$ is its determinant, and $vec(A)$ stacks the columns of A. Moreover, we let $\|A\| = \sqrt{tr[A'A]}$. If A is a vector, then $\|A\| = \sqrt{A'A}$ is its length. We use $A_{(.j)}$ ($A_{(j.)}$) to denote the j'th column (row) of a matrix A. Finally, $\mathcal{I}\{x \geq a\}$ is the indicator function equal to one if $x \geq a$ and equal to zero otherwise.

2 Vector Autoregressions

At first glance, VARs appear to be straightforward multivariate generalizations of univariate autoregressive models. At second sight, they turn out to be one of the key empirical tools in modern macroeconomics. Sims (1980) proposed that VARs should replace large-scale macroeconometric models inherited from the 1960s, because the latter imposed *incredible* restrictions, which were largely inconsistent with the notion that economic agents take the effect of today's choices on tomorrow's utility into account.

Since then, VARs have been used for macroeconomic forecasting and policy analysis to investigate the sources of business-cycle fluctuations and to provide a benchmark against which modern dynamic macroeconomic theories can be evaluated. In fact, in Section 4 it will become evident that the equilibrium law of motion of many dynamic stochastic equilibrium models can be well approximated by a VAR. The remainder of this section is organized as follows. We derive the likelihood function of a reduced-form VAR in Section 2.1. Section 2.2 discusses how to use dummy observations to construct prior distributions and reviews the widely used Minnesota prior. In Section 2.3, we consider a reduced-form VAR that is expressed in terms of deviations from a deterministic trend. Section 2.4 is devoted to structural VARs in which innovations are expressed as functions of structural shocks with a particular economic interpretation, for example, an unanticipated change in monetary policy. Finally, Section 2.5 provides some suggestions for further reading.

2.1 A reduced-form VAR

Vector autoregressions are linear time-series models, designed to capture the joint dynamics of multiple time series. Figure 7.1 depicts the evolution of three important quarterly macroeconomic time series for the US over the period from 1964:Q1 to 2006:Q4: percentage deviations of real GDP from a linear time trend, annualized inflation rates computed from the GDP deflator, and the effective federal funds rate. These series are obtained from the FRED database maintained by the Federal Reserve Bank of St Louis. We will subsequently illustrate the VAR analysis using the three series plotted in Figure 7.1. Let y_t be an $n \times 1$ random vector that takes values in $\mathbb{R}^n$, where $n = 3$ in our empirical illustration. The evolution of y_t is described by the p'th order difference equation:

$$y_t = \Phi_1 y_{t-1} + \ldots + \Phi_p y_{t-p} + \Phi_c + u_t. \tag{7.1}$$

We refer to (7.1) as the reduced-form representation of a VAR(p), because the u_t's are simply one-step-ahead forecast errors and do not have a specific economic interpretation.

To characterize the conditional distribution of y_t given its history, one has to make a distributional assumption for u_t. We shall proceed under the assumption that the conditional distribution of y_t is Normal:

$$u_t \sim iidN(0, \Sigma). \tag{7.2}$$

We are now in a position to characterize the joint distribution of a sequence of observations $y_1, \ldots, y_T$. Let $k = np + 1$ and define the $k \times n$ matrix $\Phi = [\Phi_1, \ldots, \Phi_p, \Phi_c]'$. The joint density of $Y_{1:T}$, conditional on $Y_{1-p:0}$ and the coefficient matrices Φ and Σ, is called (conditional) likelihood function when it is viewed as a function of the parameters. It can be factorized as

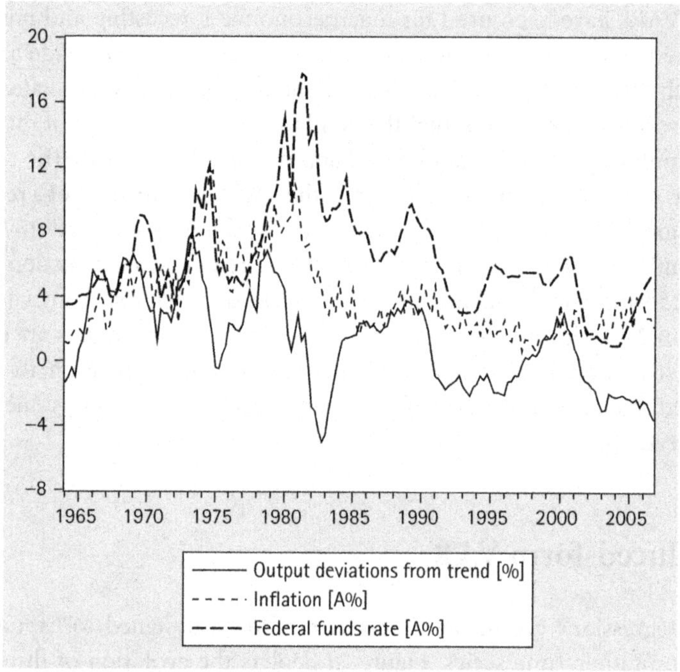

FIGURE 7.1 Output, inflation, and interest rates

Notes: The figure depicts US data from 1964:Q1 to 2006:Q4. Output is depicted in percentage deviations from a linear deterministic trend. Inflation and interest rates are annualized ($A\%$).

$$p(Y_{1:T}|\Phi,\Sigma,Y_{1-p:0}) = \prod_{t=1}^{T} p(y_t|\Phi,\Sigma,Y_{1-p:t-1}). \tag{7.3}$$

The conditional likelihood function can be conveniently expressed if the VAR is written as a multivariate linear regression model in matrix notation:

$$Y = X\Phi + U. \tag{7.4}$$

Here, the $T \times n$ matrices Y and U and the $T \times k$ matrix X are defined as

$$Y = \begin{bmatrix} y_1' \\ \vdots \\ y_T' \end{bmatrix}, \quad X = \begin{bmatrix} x_1' \\ \vdots \\ x_T' \end{bmatrix}, \quad x_t' = [y_{t-1}', \ldots, y_{t-p}', 1], \quad U = \begin{bmatrix} u_1' \\ \vdots \\ u_T' \end{bmatrix}. \tag{7.5}$$

In a slight abuse of notation, we abbreviate $p(Y_{1:T}|\Phi,\Sigma,Y_{1-p:0})$ by $p(Y|\Phi,\Sigma)$:

$$p(Y|\Phi,\Sigma) \propto |\Sigma|^{-T/2} \exp\left\{-\frac{1}{2}tr[\Sigma^{-1}\hat{S}]\right\} \tag{7.6}$$
$$\times \exp\left\{-\frac{1}{2}tr[\Sigma^{-1}(\Phi-\hat{\Phi})'X'X(\Phi-\hat{\Phi})]\right\},$$

where

$$\hat{\Phi} = (X'X)^{-1}X'Y, \quad \hat{S} = (Y - X\hat{\Phi})'(Y - X\hat{\Phi}). \tag{7.7}$$

$\hat{\Phi}$ is the maximum-likelihood estimator (MLE) of Φ, and $\hat{S}$ is a matrix with sums of squared residuals. If we combine the likelihood function with the improper prior $p(\Phi, \Sigma) \propto |\Sigma|^{-(n+1)/2}$, we can deduce immediately that the posterior distribution is of the form

$$(\Phi, \Sigma)|Y \sim MNIW\Big(\hat{\Phi}, (X'X)^{-1}, \hat{S}, T - k\Big). \tag{7.8}$$

Detailed derivations for the multivariate Gaussian linear regression model can be found in Zellner (1971). Draws from this posterior can be easily obtained by direct Monte Carlo sampling.

Algorithm 2.1. Direct Monte Carlo Sampling from Posterior of VAR Parameters
For $s = 1, \ldots, n_{sim}$:

(1) Draw $\Sigma^{(s)}$ from an $IW(\hat{S}, T - k)$ distribution.
(2) Draw $\Phi^{(s)}$ from the conditional distribution $MN(\hat{\Phi}, \Sigma^{(s)} \otimes (X'X)^{-1})$. □

An important challenge in practice is to cope with the dimensionality of the parameter matrix Φ. Consider the data depicted in Figure 7.1. Our sample consists of 172 observations, and each equation of a VAR with $p = 4$ lags has 13 coefficients. If the sample is restricted to the post-1982 period, after the disinflation under Fed Chairman Paul Volcker, the sample size shrinks to 96 observations. Now imagine estimating a two-country VAR for the US and the Euro Area on post-1982 data, which doubles the number of parameters. Informative prior distributions can compensate for lack of sample information, and we will subsequently discuss alternatives to the improper prior used so far.

2.2 Dummy observations and the Minnesota prior

Prior distributions can be conveniently represented by dummy observations. This insight dates back at least to Theil and Goldberger (1961). These dummy observations might be actual observations from other countries, observations generated by simulating a macroeconomic model, or observations generated from introspection. Suppose T^* dummy observations are collected in matrices Y^* and X^*, and we use the likelihood function associated with the VAR to relate the dummy observations to the parameters Φ and Σ. Using the same arguments that lead to (7.8), we deduce that up to a constant the product $p(Y^*|\Phi, \Sigma) \cdot |\Sigma|^{-(n+1)/2}$ can be interpreted as a $MNIW(\underline{\Phi}, (X^{*\prime}X^*)^{-1}, \underline{S}, T^* - k)$ prior for Φ and Σ, where $\underline{\Phi}$ and $\underline{S}$ are obtained from $\hat{\Phi}$ and $\hat{S}$ in (7.7) by replacing Y and X with Y^* and X^*. Provided that $T^* > k + n$ and $X^{*\prime}X^*$ is invertible, the prior distribution is proper. Now let $\bar{T} = T + T^*$, $\bar{Y} = [Y^{*\prime}, Y^\prime]^\prime$, $\bar{X} = [X^{*\prime}, X^\prime]^\prime$, and let $\bar{\Phi}$ and $\bar{S}$ be the analogue of $\hat{\Phi}$ and $\hat{S}$ in (7.7); then we deduce that the posterior of (Φ, Σ) is $MNIW(\bar{\Phi}, (\bar{X}^\prime\bar{X})^{-1}, \bar{S}, \bar{T} - k)$. Thus, the use of dummy observations leads to a conjugate prior. Prior and likelihood are conjugate if the posterior belongs to the same distributional family as the prior distribution.

A widely used prior in the VAR literature is the so-called Minnesota prior, which dates back to Litterman (1980) and Doan et al. (1984). Our exposition follows the more recent description in Sims and Zha (1998), with the exception that for now we focus on a reduced-form rather than on a structural VAR. Consider our lead example, in which y_t is composed of output deviations, inflation, and interest rates, depicted in Figure 7.1. Notice that all three series are fairly persistent. In fact, the univariate behavior of these series, possibly with the exception of post-1982 inflation rates, would be fairly well described by a random-walk model of the form $y_{i,t} = y_{i,t-1} + \eta_{i,t}$. The idea behind the Minnesota prior is to center the distribution of Φ at a value that implies a random-walk behavior for each of the components of y_t. The random-walk approximation is taken for convenience and could be replaced by other representations. For instance, if some series have very little serial correlation because they have been transformed to induce stationarity—for example log output has been converted into output growth—then an *iid* approximation might be preferable. In Section 4, we will discuss how DSGE model restrictions could be used to construct a prior.

The Minnesota prior can be implemented either by directly specifying a distribution for Φ or, alternatively, through dummy observations. We will pursue the latter route for the following reason. While it is fairly straightforward to choose prior means and variances for the elements of Φ, it tends to be difficult to elicit beliefs about the correlations between elements of the Φ matrix. After all, there are $nk(nk-1)/2$ of them. At the same time, setting all these correlations to zero potentially leads to a prior that assigns a lot of probability mass to parameter combinations that imply quite unreasonable dynamics for the endogenous variables y_t. The use of dummy observations provides a parsimonious way of introducing plausible correlations between parameters.

The Minnesota prior is typically specified conditional on several hyperparameters. Let $Y_{-\tau:0}$ be a presample, and let $\underline{y}$ and $\underline{s}$ be $n \times 1$ vectors of means and standard deviations. The remaining hyperparameters are stacked in the 5×1 vector λ with elements λ_i. In turn, we will specify the rows of the matrices Y^* and X^*. To simplify the exposition, suppose that $n = 2$ and $p = 2$. The dummy observations are interpreted as observations from the regression model (7.4). We begin with dummy observations that generate a prior distribution for Φ_1. For illustrative purposes, the dummy observations are plugged into (7.4):

$$\begin{bmatrix} \lambda_1\underline{s}_1 & 0 \\ 0 & \lambda_1\underline{s}_2 \end{bmatrix} = \begin{bmatrix} \lambda_1\underline{s}_1 & 0 & 0 & 0 & 0 \\ 0 & \lambda_1\underline{s}_2 & 0 & 0 & 0 \end{bmatrix} \Phi + \begin{bmatrix} u_{11} & u_{12} \\ u_{21} & u_{22} \end{bmatrix}. \tag{7.9}$$

According to the distributional assumption in (7.2), the rows of U are normally distributed. Thus, we can rewrite the first row of (7.9) as

$$\lambda_1 \underline{s}_1 = \lambda_1 \underline{s}_1 \phi_{11} + u_{11}, \quad 0 = \lambda_1 \underline{s}_1 \phi_{21} + u_{12}$$

and interpret it as

$$\phi_{11} \sim \mathcal{N}(1, \Sigma_{11}/(\lambda_1^2 \underline{s}_1^2)), \quad \phi_{21} \sim \mathcal{N}(0, \Sigma_{22}/(\lambda_1^2 \underline{s}_1^2)).$$

ϕ_{ij} denotes the element i, j of the matrix Φ, and Σ_{ij} corresponds to element i, j of Σ. The hyperparameter λ_1 controls the tightness of the prior.[1]

The prior for Φ_2 is implemented with the dummy observations

$$\begin{bmatrix} 0 & 0 \\ 0 & 0 \end{bmatrix} = \begin{bmatrix} 0 & 0 & \lambda_1 \underline{s}_1 2^{\lambda_2} & 0 & 0 \\ 0 & 0 & 0 & \lambda_1 \underline{s}_2 2^{\lambda_2} & 0 \end{bmatrix} \Phi + U, \tag{7.10}$$

where the hyperparameter λ_2 is used to scale the prior standard deviations for coefficients associated with y_{t-l} according to $l^{-\lambda_2}$. A prior for the covariance matrix Σ, centered at a matrix that is diagonal with elements equal to the presample variance of y_t, can be obtained by stacking the observations

$$\begin{bmatrix} \underline{s}_1 & 0 \\ 0 & \underline{s}_2 \end{bmatrix} = \begin{bmatrix} 0 & 0 & 0 & 0 & 0 \\ 0 & 0 & 0 & 0 & 0 \end{bmatrix} \Phi + U \tag{7.11}$$

λ_3 times.

The remaining sets of dummy observations provide a prior for the intercept Φ_c and will generate some a priori correlation between the coefficients. They favor unit roots and cointegration, which is consistent with the beliefs of many applied macroeconomists, and they tend to improve VAR forecasting performance. The *sums-of-coefficients* dummy observations, introduced in Doan et al. (1984), capture the view that when lagged values of a variable $y_{i,t}$ are at the level $\underline{y}_i$, the same value $\underline{y}_i$ is likely to be a good forecast of $y_{i,t}$, regardless of the value of other variables:

$$\begin{bmatrix} \lambda_4 \underline{y}_1 & 0 \\ 0 & \lambda_4 \underline{y}_2 \end{bmatrix} = \begin{bmatrix} \lambda_4 \underline{y}_1 & 0 & \lambda_4 \underline{y}_1 & 0 & 0 \\ 0 & \lambda_4 \underline{y}_2 & 0 & \lambda_4 \underline{y}_2 & 0 \end{bmatrix} \Phi + U. \tag{7.12}$$

The *co-persistence dummy observations*, proposed by Sims (1993), reflect the belief that when all lagged y_t's are at the level $\underline{y}$, y_t tends to persist at that level:

$$\begin{bmatrix} \lambda_5 \underline{y}_1 & \lambda_5 \underline{y}_2 \end{bmatrix} = \begin{bmatrix} \lambda_5 \underline{y}_1 & \lambda_5 \underline{y}_2 & \lambda_5 \underline{y}_1 & \lambda_5 \underline{y}_2 & \lambda_5 \end{bmatrix} \Phi + U. \tag{7.13}$$

The strength of these beliefs is controlled by λ_4 and λ_5. These two sets of dummy observations introduce correlations in prior beliefs about all coefficients, including the intercept, in a given equation.

VAR inference tends to be sensitive to the choice of hyperparameters. If $\lambda = 0$, then all the dummy observations are zero, and the VAR is estimated under an improper

[1] Consider the regression $y_t = \phi_1 x_{1,t} + \phi_2 x_{2,t} + u_t$, $u_t \sim iidN(0, 1)$, and suppose that the standard deviation of $x_{j,t}$ is s_j. If we define $\tilde{\phi}_j = \phi_j s_j$ and $\tilde{x}_{j,t} = x_{j,t}/s_j$, then the transformed parameters interact with regressors that have the same scale. Suppose we assume that $\tilde{\phi}_j \sim \mathcal{N}(0, \lambda^2)$, then $\phi_j \sim \mathcal{N}(0, \lambda^2/s_j^2)$. The s_j terms that appear in the definition of the dummy observations achieve this scale adjustment.

prior. The larger the elements of λ, the more weight is placed on various components of the Minnesota prior vis-á-vis the likelihood function. From a practitioner's view, an empirical Bayes approach of choosing λ based on the marginal likelihood function

$$p_\lambda(Y) = \int p(Y|\Phi, \Sigma)p(\Phi, \Sigma|\lambda)d(\Phi, \Sigma) \tag{7.14}$$

tends to work well for inference as well as for forecasting purposes. If the prior distribution is constructed based on T^* dummy observations, then an analytical expression for the marginal likelihood can be obtained by using the normalization constants for the MNIW distribution (see Zellner 1971):

$$p_\lambda(Y) = (2\pi)^{-nT/2} \frac{|\bar{X}'\bar{X}|^{-\frac{n}{2}}|\bar{S}|^{-\frac{\bar{T}-k}{2}}}{|X^{*\prime}X^*|^{-\frac{n}{2}}|S^*|^{-\frac{T^*-k}{2}}} \frac{2^{\frac{n(\bar{T}-k)}{2}} \prod_{i=1}^n \Gamma[(\bar{T}-k+1-i)/2]}{2^{\frac{n(T^*-k)}{2}} \prod_{i=1}^n \Gamma[(T^*-k+1-i)/2]}. \tag{7.15}$$

As before, we let $\bar{T} = T^* + T$, $\bar{Y} = [Y^{*\prime}, Y']'$, and $\bar{X} = [X^{*\prime}, X']'$. The hyperparameters $(\underline{y}, \underline{s}, \lambda)$ enter through the dummy observations X^* and Y^*. S^* ($\bar{S}$) is obtained from $\hat{S}$ in (7.7) by replacing Y and X with Y^* and X^* ($\bar{Y}$ and $\bar{X}$). We will provide an empirical illustration of this hyperparameter selection approach in Section 2.4. Instead of conditioning on the value of λ that maximizes the marginal likelihood function $p_\lambda(Y)$, one could specify a prior distribution for λ and integrate out the hyperparameter, which is commonly done in hierarchical Bayes models. A more detailed discussion of selection versus averaging is provided in Section 7.

A potential drawback of the dummy-observation prior is that one is forced to treat all equations symmetrically when specifying a prior. In other words, the prior covariance matrix for the coefficients in all equations has to be proportional to $(X^{*'}X^*)^{-1}$. For instance, if the prior variance for the lagged inflation terms in the output equation is ten times larger than the prior variance for the coefficients on lagged interest rate terms, then it also has to be ten times larger in the inflation equation and the interest rate equation. Methods for relaxing this restriction and alternative approaches of implementing the Minnesota prior (as well as other VAR priors) are discussed in Kadiyala and Karlsson (1997).

2.3 A second reduced-form VAR

The reduced-form VAR in (7.1) is specified with an intercept term that determines the unconditional mean of y_t if the VAR is stationary. However, this unconditional mean also depends on the autoregressive coefficients $\Phi_1, \ldots, \Phi_p$. Alternatively, one can use the following representation, studied, for instance, in Villani (2009):

$$y_t = \Gamma_0 + \Gamma_1 t + \widetilde{y}_t, \quad \widetilde{y}_t = \Phi_1 \widetilde{y}_{t-1} + \ldots + \Phi_p \widetilde{y}_{t-p} + u_t, \quad u_t \sim iidN(0, \Sigma). \tag{7.16}$$

Here Γ_0 and Γ_1 are $n \times 1$ vectors. The first term, $\Gamma_0 + \Gamma_1 t$, captures the deterministic trend of y_t, whereas the second part, the law of motion of $\widetilde{y}_t$, captures stochastic fluctuations around the deterministic trend. These fluctuations could either be stationary or nonstationary. This alternative specification makes it straightforward to separate beliefs about the deterministic trend component from beliefs about the persistence of fluctuations around this trend.

Suppose we define $\Phi = [\Phi_1, \ldots, \Phi_p]'$ and $\Gamma = [\Gamma_1', \Gamma_2']'$. Moreover, let $\widetilde{Y}(\Gamma)$ be the $T \times n$ matrix with rows $(y_t - \Gamma_0 - \Gamma_1 t)'$ and $\widetilde{X}(\Gamma)$ be the $T \times (pn)$ matrix with rows $[(y_{t-1} - \Gamma_0 - \Gamma_1(t-1))', \ldots, (y_{t-p} - \Gamma_0 - \Gamma_1(t-p))']$; then the conditional likelihood function associated with (7.16) is

$$p(Y_{1:T}|\Phi, \Sigma, \Gamma, Y_{1-p:0}) \tag{7.17}$$
$$\propto |\Sigma|^{-T/2} \exp\left\{-\frac{1}{2} tr\left[\Sigma^{-1}(\widetilde{Y}(\Gamma) - \widetilde{X}(\Gamma)\Phi)'(\widetilde{Y}(\Gamma) - \widetilde{X}(\Gamma)\Phi)\right]\right\}.$$

Thus, as long as the prior for Φ and Σ conditional on Γ is *MNIW*, the posterior of $(\Phi, \Sigma)|\Gamma$ is of the *MNIW* form.

Let L denote the temporal lag operator such that $L^j y_t = y_{t-j}$. Using this operator, one can rewrite (7.16) as

$$\left(I - \sum_{j=1}^{p} \Phi_j L^j\right)(y_t - \Gamma_0 - \Gamma_1 t) = u_t.$$

Now define

$$z_t(\Phi) = \left(I - \sum_{j=1}^{p} \Phi_j L^j\right) y_t, \quad W_t(\Phi) = \left[\left(I - \sum_{j=1}^{p} \Phi_j\right), \left(I - \sum_{j=1}^{p} \Phi_j L^j\right) t\right],$$

with the understanding that $L^j t = t - j$. Thus, $z_t(\Phi) = W_t(\Phi)\Gamma + u_t$ and the likelihood function can be rewritten as

$$p(Y_{1:T}|\Phi, \Sigma, \Gamma, Y_{1-p:0}) \tag{7.18}$$
$$\propto \exp\left\{-\frac{1}{2}\sum_{t=1}^{T}(z_t(\Phi) - W_t(\Phi)\Gamma)'\Sigma^{-1}(z_t(\Phi) - W_t(\Phi)\Gamma)\right\}.$$

Thus, it is straightforward to verify that as long as the prior distribution of Γ conditional on Φ and Σ is matricvariate Normal, the (conditional) posterior distribution of Γ is also Normal. Posterior inference can then be implemented via Gibbs sampling, which is an example of a so-called *Markov chain Monte Carlo* (MCMC) algorithm, discussed in detail in Chib (Chapter 5 in this volume).

Algorithm 2.2. Gibbs Sampling from Posterior of VAR Parameters
For $s = 1, \ldots, n_{sim}$:

(1) Draw $(\Phi^{(s)}, \Sigma^{(s)})$ from the MNIW distribution of $(\Phi, \Sigma)|(\Gamma^{(s-1)}, Y)$.
(2) Draw $\Gamma^{(s)}$ from the Normal distribution of $\Gamma|(\Phi^{(s)}, \Sigma^{(s)}, Y)$. □

To illustrate the subtle difference between the VAR in (7.1) and the VAR in (7.16), we consider the special case of two univariate AR(1) processes:

$$y_t = \phi_1 y_{t-1} + \phi_c + u_t, \quad u_t \sim iidN(0,1), \tag{7.19}$$

$$y_t = \gamma_0 + \gamma_1 t + \widetilde{y}_t, \quad \widetilde{y}_t = \phi_1 \widetilde{y}_{t-1} + u_t, \quad u_t \sim iidN(0,1). \tag{7.20}$$

If $|\phi_1| < 1$, both AR(1) processes are stationary. The second process, characterized by (7.20), allows for stationary fluctuations around a linear time trend, whereas the first allows only for fluctuations around a constant mean. If $\phi_1 = 1$, the interpretation of ϕ_c in model (7.19) changes drastically, as the parameter is now capturing the drift in a unit-root process instead of determining the long-run mean of y_t. Schotman and van Dijk (1991) make the case that the representation (7.20) is more appealing, if the goal of the empirical analysis is to determine the evidence in favor of the hypothesis that $\phi_1 = 1$.[2] Since the initial level of the latent process $\tilde{y}_0$ is unobserved, γ_0 in (7.20) is nonidentifiable if $\phi_1 = 1$. Thus, in practice it is advisable to specify a proper prior for γ_0 in (7.20).

In empirical work researchers often treat parameters as independent and might combine (7.19) with a prior distribution that implies $\phi_1 \sim U[0, 1-\xi]$ and $\phi_c \sim N(\underline{\phi}_c, \lambda^2)$. For the subsequent argument, it is assumed that $\xi > 0$ to impose stationarity. Since the expected value of $I\!E[y_t] = \phi_c/(1-\phi_1)$, this prior for ϕ_1 and ϕ_c has the following implication. Conditional on ϕ_c, the prior mean and variance of the population mean $I\!E[y_t]$ increases (in absolute value) as $\phi_1 \longrightarrow 1-\xi$. In turn, this prior generates a fairly diffuse distribution of y_t that might place little mass on values of y_t that appear a priori plausible.

Treating the parameters of model (7.20) as independent—for example, $\phi_1 \sim U[0, 1-\xi]$, $\gamma_0 \sim N(\underline{\gamma}_0, \lambda^2)$, and $\gamma_1 = 0$—avoids the problem of an overly diffuse data distribution. In this case $I\!E[y_t]$ has *a priori* mean $\underline{\gamma}_0$ and variance λ^2 for every value of ϕ_1. For researchers who do prefer to work with model (7.19) but are concerned about a priori implausible data distributions, the co-persistence dummy observations discussed in Section 2.2 are useful. With these dummy observations, the implied prior distribution of the population mean of y_t conditional on ϕ_1 takes the form $I\!E[y_t]|\phi_1 \sim N(\underline{y}, (\lambda_5(1-\phi_1))^{-2})$. While the scale of the distribution of $I\!E[y_t]$ is still dependent on the autoregressive coefficient, at least the location remains centered at $\underline{y}$ regardless of ϕ_1.

2.4 Structural VARs

Reduced-form VARs summarize the autocovariance properties of the data and provide a useful forecasting tool, but they lack economic interpretability. We will consider two ways of adding economic content to the VAR specified in (7.1). First, one can turn (7.1) into a dynamic simultaneous equations model by premultiplying it with a matrix A_0, such that the equations could be interpreted as, for instance, monetary policy rule,

[2] Giordani et al. (Chapter 3 in this volume) discuss evidence that in many instances the so-called centered parameterization of (7.20) can increase the efficiency of MCMC algorithms.

money demand equation, aggregate supply equation, and aggregate demand equation. Shocks to these equations can in turn be interpreted as monetary policy shocks or as innovations to aggregate supply and demand. To the extent that the monetary policy rule captures the central bank's systematic reaction to the state of the economy, it is natural to assume that the monetary policy shocks are orthogonal to the other innovations. More generally, researchers often assume that shocks to the aggregate supply and demand equations are independent of each other.

A second way of adding economic content to VARs exploits the close connection between VARs and modern dynamic stochastic general equilibrium models. In the context of a DSGE model, a monetary policy rule might be well defined, but the notion of an aggregate demand or supply function is obscure. As we will see in Section 4, these models are specified in terms of preferences of economic agents and production technologies. The optimal solution of agents' decision problems combined with an equilibrium concept leads to an autoregressive law of motion for the endogenous model variables. Economic fluctuations are generated by shocks to technology, preferences, monetary policy, or fiscal policy. These shocks are typically assumed to be independent of each other. One reason for this independence assumption is that many researchers view the purpose of DSGE models as that of generating the observed co-movements between macroeconomic variables through well-specified economic propagation mechanisms, rather than from correlated exogenous shocks. Thus, these kinds of dynamic macroeconomic theories suggest that the one-step-ahead forecast errors u_t in (7.1) are functions of orthogonal fundamental innovations in technology, preferences, or policies.

To summarize, one can think of a structural VAR either as a dynamic simultaneous equations model, in which each equation has a particular structural interpretation, or as an autoregressive model, in which the forecast errors are explicitly linked to such fundamental innovations. We adopt the latter view in Section 2.4.1 and consider the former interpretation in Section 2.4.2.

2.4.1 Reduced-form innovations and structural shocks

A straightforward calculation shows that we need to impose additional restrictions to identify a structural VAR. Let ϵ_t be a vector of orthogonal structural shocks with unit variances. We now express the one-step-ahead forecast errors as a linear combination of structural shocks

$$u_t = \Phi_\epsilon \epsilon_t = \Sigma_{tr} \Omega \epsilon_t. \tag{7.21}$$

Here, Σ_{tr} refers to the unique lower-triangular Cholesky factor of Σ with nonnegative diagonal elements, and Ω is an $n \times n$ orthogonal matrix. The second equality ensures that the covariance matrix of u_t is preserved; that is, Φ_ϵ has to satisfy the restriction $\Sigma = \Phi_\epsilon \Phi_\epsilon'$. Thus, our structural VAR is parameterized in terms of the reduced-form parameters Φ and Σ (or its Cholesky factor Σ_{tr}) and the orthogonal matrix Ω. The joint distribution of data and parameters is given by

$$p(Y, \Phi, \Sigma, \Omega) = p(Y|\Phi, \Sigma) p(\Phi, \Sigma) p(\Omega|\Phi, \Sigma). \tag{7.22}$$

Since the distribution of Y depends only on the covariance matrix Σ and not on its factorization $\Sigma_{tr}\Omega\Omega'\Sigma_{tr}'$, the likelihood function here is the same as the likelihood function of the reduced-form VAR in (7.6), denoted by $p(Y|\Phi, \Sigma)$. The identification problem arises precisely from the absence of Ω in this likelihood function.

We proceed by examining the effect of the identification problem on the calculation of posterior distributions. Integrating the joint density with respect to Ω yields

$$p(Y, \Phi, \Sigma) = p(Y|\Phi, \Sigma)p(\Phi, \Sigma). \tag{7.23}$$

Thus, the calculation of the posterior distribution of the reduced-form parameters is not affected by the presence of the nonidentifiable matrix Ω. The conditional posterior density of Ω can be calculated as follows:

$$p(\Omega|Y, \Phi, \Sigma) = \frac{p(Y, \Phi, \Sigma)p(\Omega|\Phi, \Sigma)}{\int p(Y, \Phi, \Sigma)p(\Omega|\Phi, \Sigma)d\Omega} = p(\Omega|\Phi, \Sigma). \tag{7.24}$$

The conditional distribution of the nonidentifiable parameter Ω does not get updated in view of the data. This is a well-known property of Bayesian inference in partially identified models; see, for instance, Kadane (1974), Poirier (1998), and Moon and Schorfheide (2009). We can deduce immediately that draws from the joint posterior distribution $p(\Phi, \Sigma, \Omega|Y)$ can in principle be obtained in two steps.

Algorithm 2.3. Posterior Sampler for Structural VARs
For $s = 1, \ldots, n_{sim}$:

(1) Draw $(\Phi^{(s)}, \Sigma^{(s)})$ from the posterior $p(\Phi, \Sigma|Y)$.
(2) Draw $\Omega^{(s)}$ from the conditional prior distribution $p(\Omega|\Phi^{(s)}, \Sigma^{(s)})$. □

Not surprisingly, much of the literature on structural VARs reduces to arguments about the appropriate choice of $p(\Omega|\Phi, \Sigma)$. Most authors use dogmatic priors for Ω such that the conditional distribution of Ω, given the reduced-form parameters, reduces to a point mass. Priors for Ω are typically referred to as identification schemes because, conditional on Ω, the relationship between the forecast errors u_t and the structural shocks ϵ_t is uniquely determined. Cochrane (1994), Christiano et al. (1999), and Stock and Watson (2001) provide detailed surveys.

To present various identification schemes that have been employed in the literature, we consider a simple bivariate VAR(1) without intercept; that is, we set $n = 2$, $p = 1$, and $\Phi_c = 0$. For the remainder of this subsection, it is assumed that the eigenvalues of Φ_1 are all less than one in absolute value. This eigenvalue restriction guarantees that the VAR can be written as infinite-order moving average (MA(∞)):

$$y_t = \sum_{j=0}^{\infty} \Phi_1^j \Sigma_{tr}\Omega\epsilon_t. \tag{7.25}$$

We will refer to the sequence of partial derivatives

$$\frac{\partial y_{t+j}}{\partial \epsilon_t} = \Phi_1^j \Sigma_{tr} \Omega, \quad j = 0, 1, \ldots \tag{7.26}$$

as the impulse-response function. In addition, macroeconomists are often interested in so-called variance decompositions. A variance decomposition measures the fraction that each of the structural shocks contributes to the overall variance of a particular element of y_t. In the stationary bivariate VAR(1), the (unconditional) covariance matrix is given by

$$\Gamma_{yy} = \sum_{j=0}^{\infty} \Phi_1^j \Sigma_{tr} \Omega \Omega' \Sigma_{tr}' (\Phi^j)'.$$

Let $\mathcal{I}^i$ be the matrix for which element i, i is equal to one and all other elements are equal to zero. Then we can define the contribution of the i'th structural shock to the variance of y_t as

$$\Gamma_{yy}^{(i)} = \sum_{j=0}^{\infty} \Phi_1^j \Sigma_{tr} \Omega \mathcal{I}^{(i)} \Omega' \Sigma_{tr}' (\Phi^j)'. \tag{7.27}$$

Thus, the fraction of the variance of $y_{j,t}$ explained by shock i is $[\Gamma_{yy}^{(i)}]_{(jj)}/[\Gamma_{yy}]_{(jj)}$. Variance decompositions based on h-step-ahead forecast error covariance matrices $\sum_{j=0}^{h} \Phi_1^j \Sigma (\Phi^j)'$ can be constructed in the same manner. Handling these nonlinear transformations of the VAR parameters in a Bayesian framework is straightforward, because one can simply postprocess the output of the posterior sampler (Algorithm 2.3). Using (7.26) or (7.27), each triplet $(\Phi^{(s)}, \Sigma^{(s)}, \Omega^{(s)})$, $s = 1, \ldots, n_{sim}$, can be converted into a draw from the posterior distribution of impulse responses or variance decompositions. Based on these draws, it is straightforward to compute posterior moments and credible sets.

For $n = 2$, the set of orthogonal matrices Ω can be conveniently characterized by an angle φ and a parameter $\xi \in \{-1, 1\}$:

$$\Omega(\varphi, \xi) = \begin{bmatrix} \cos\varphi & -\xi \sin\varphi \\ \sin\varphi & \xi \cos\varphi \end{bmatrix} \tag{7.28}$$

where $\varphi \in (-\pi, \pi]$. Each column represents a vector of unit length in $\mathbb{R}^2$, and the two vectors are orthogonal. The determinant of Ω equals ξ. Notice that $\Omega(\varphi) = -\Omega(\varphi + \pi)$. Thus, rotating the two vectors by 180 degrees simply changes the sign of the impulse responses to both shocks. Switching from $\xi = 1$ to $\xi = -1$ changes the sign of the impulse responses to the second shock. We will now consider three different identification schemes that restrict Ω conditional on Φ and Σ.

Example 2.1 (Short-Run Identification): Suppose that y_t is composed of output deviations from trend, $\tilde{y}_t$, and that the federal funds rate, R_t, and the vector ϵ_t consists of innovations to technology, $\epsilon_{z,t}$, and monetary policy, $\epsilon_{R,t}$. That is, $y_t = [\tilde{y}_t, R_t]'$ and $\epsilon_t = [\epsilon_{z,t}, \epsilon_{R,t}]'$. Identification can be achieved by imposing restrictions on the informational structure. For instance, following an earlier literature, Boivin and Giannoni (2006b) assume in a slightly richer setting that the private sector does not respond to monetary policy shocks contemporaneously. This assumption can be formalized by considering the following choices of φ and ξ in (7.28): (i) $\varphi = 0$ and $\xi = 1$; (ii) $\varphi = 0$ and $\xi = -1$; (iii) $\varphi = \pi$ and $\xi = 1$; and (iv) $\varphi = \pi$ and $\xi = -1$. It is common in the literature to normalize the direction of the impulse response by, for instance, considering responses to *expansionary* monetary policy and technology shocks. The former could be defined as shocks that lower interest rates upon impact. Since by construction $\Sigma_{22}^{tr} \geq 0$, interest rates fall in response to a monetary policy shock in cases (ii) and (iii). Likewise, since $\Sigma_{11}^{tr} \geq 0$, output increases in response to $\epsilon_{z,t}$ in cases (i) and (ii). Thus, after imposing the identification and normalization restrictions, the prior $p(\Omega|\Phi, \Sigma)$ assigns probability one to the matrix Ω that is diagonal with elements 1 and -1. Such a restriction on Ω is typically referred to as a short-run identification scheme. A short-run identification scheme was used in the seminal work by Sims (1980).

Example 2.2 (Long-Run Identification): Now suppose y_t is composed of inflation, π_t, and output growth: $y_t = [\pi_t, \Delta \ln \tilde{y}_t]'$. As in the previous example, we maintain the assumption that business-cycle fluctuations are generated by monetary policy and technology shocks, but now reverse the ordering: $\epsilon_t = [\epsilon_{R,t}, \epsilon_{z,t}]'$. We now use the following identification restriction: unanticipated changes in monetary policy shocks do not raise output in the long run. The long-run response of the log-level of output to a monetary policy shock can be obtained from the infinite sum of growth-rate responses $\sum_{j=0}^{\infty} \partial \Delta \ln \tilde{y}_{t+j} / \partial \epsilon_{R,t}$. Since the stationarity assumption implies that $\sum_{j=0}^{\infty} \Phi_1^j = (I - \Phi_1)^{-1}$, the desired long-run response is given by

$$[(I - \Phi_1)^{-1} \Sigma_{tr}]_{(2.)} \Omega_{(.1)}(\varphi, \xi), \tag{7.29}$$

where $A_{(.j)}$ ($A_{(j.)}$) is the j'th column (row) of a matrix A. This identification scheme has been used, for instance, by Nason and Cogley (1994) and Schorfheide (2000). To obtain the orthogonal matrix Ω, we need to determine the φ and ξ such that the expression in (7.29) equals zero. Since the columns of $\Omega(\varphi, \xi)$ are composed of orthonormal vectors, we need to find a unit length vector $\Omega_{(.1)}(\varphi, \xi)$ that is perpendicular to $[(I - \Phi_1)^{-1} \Sigma_{tr}]'_{(2.)}$. Notice that ξ does not affect the first column of Ω; it only changes the sign of the response to the second shock. Suppose that (7.29) equals zero for $\tilde{\varphi}$. By rotating the vector $\Omega_{(.1)}(\tilde{\varphi}, \xi)$ by 180 degrees, we can find a second angle φ such that the long-run response in (7.29) equals zero. Thus, similar to Example 2.1, we can find four pairs (φ, ξ) such that the long-run effect (7.29) of a monetary policy shock on output is zero. While the shapes of the response functions are the same for each of these pairs, the sign will be different.

We could use the same normalization as in Example 2.1 by considering the effects of expansionary technology shocks (the level of output rises in the long run) and expansionary monetary policy shocks (interest rates fall in the short run). To implement this normalization, one has to choose one of the four (φ, ξ) pairs. Unlike in Example 2.1, where we used $\varphi = 0$ and $\xi = -1$ regardless of Φ and Σ, here the choice depends on Φ and Σ. However, once the normalization has been imposed, $p(\Omega|\Phi, \Sigma)$ remains a point mass. A long-run identification scheme was initially used by Blanchard and Quah (1989) to identify supply and demand disturbances in a bivariate VAR. Since long-run effects of shocks in dynamic systems are intrinsically difficult to measure, structural VARs identified with long-run schemes often lead to imprecise estimates of the impulse response function and to inference that is very sensitive to lag length choice and prefiltering of the observations. This point dates back to Sims (1972) and a detailed discussion in the structural VAR context can be found in Leeper and Faust (1997). More recently, the usefulness of long-run restrictions has been debated in the papers by Christiano et al. (2007) and Chari et al. (2008).

Example 2.3 (Sign-Restrictions): As before, let $y_t = [\pi_t, \Delta \ln \tilde{y}_t]'$ and $\epsilon_t = [\epsilon_{R,t}, \epsilon_{z,t}]'$. The priors for $\Omega|(\Phi, \Sigma)$ in the two preceding examples were degenerate. Faust (1998), Canova and De Nicoló (2002), and Uhlig (2005) propose to be more agnostic in the choice of Ω. Suppose we restrict only the direction of impulse responses by assuming that monetary policy shocks move inflation and output in the same direction upon impact. In addition, we normalize the monetary policy shock to be expansionary; that is, output rises. Formally, this implies that $\Sigma_{tr}\Omega_{(.1)}(\varphi, \xi) \geq 0$ and is referred to as a sign-restriction identification scheme. It will become clear subsequently that sign restrictions only partially identify impulse responses in the sense that they deliver (nonsingleton) sets. Since by construction $\Sigma_{11}^{tr} \geq 0$, we can deduce from (7.28) and the sign restriction on the inflation response that $\varphi \in (-\pi/2, \pi/2]$. Since $\Sigma_{22}^{tr} \geq 0$ as well, the inequality restriction for the output response can be used to sharpen the lower bound:

$$\Sigma_{21}^{tr} \cos \varphi + \Sigma_{22}^{tr} \sin \varphi \geq 0 \quad \text{implies} \quad \varphi \geq \underline{\varphi}(\Sigma) = \arctan\big(- \Sigma_{21}^{tr} / \Sigma_{22}^{tr} \big).$$

The parameter ξ can be determined conditional on Σ and φ by normalizing the technology shock to be expansionary. To implement Bayesian inference, a researcher now has to specify a prior distribution for $\varphi|\Sigma$ with support on the interval $[\underline{\varphi}(\Sigma), \pi/2]$ and a prior for $\xi|(\varphi, \Sigma)$. In practice, researchers have often chosen a uniform distribution for $\varphi|\Sigma$ as we will discuss in more detail below. □

For short- and long-run identification schemes, it is straightforward to implement Bayesian inference. One can use a simplified version of Algorithm 2.3, in which $\Omega^{(s)}$ is calculated directly as a function of $(\Phi^{(s)}, \Sigma^{(s)})$. For each triplet (Φ, Σ, Ω), suitable generalizations of (7.26) and (7.27) can be used to convert parameter draws into draws of impulse responses or variance decompositions. With these draws in hand, one can approximate features of marginal posterior distributions such as means, medians, standard deviations, or credible sets. In many applications, including the empirical illustration provided below, researchers are interested only in the response of an n-dimensional vector y_t to one particular shock, say a monetary policy shock. In this case, one can simply replace Ω in the previous expressions by its first column $\Omega_{(.1)}$, which is a unit-length vector.

Credible sets for impulse responses are typically plotted as error bands around mean or median responses. It is important to keep in mind that impulse-response functions are multidimensional objects. However, the error bands typically reported in the literature have to be interpreted point-wise, that is, they delimit the credible set for the response of a particular variable at a particular horizon to a particular shock. In an effort to account for the correlation between responses at different horizons, Sims and Zha (1999) propose a method for computing credible bands that relies on the first few principal components of the covariance matrix of the responses.

Bayesian inference in sign-restricted structural VARs is more complicated because one has to sample from the conditional distribution of $p(\Omega|\Phi, \Sigma)$. Some authors, like Uhlig (2005), restrict their attention to one particular shock and parameterize only one column of the matrix Ω. Other authors, like Peersman (2005), construct responses for the full set of n shocks. In practice, sign restrictions are imposed not just on impact but also over longer horizons $j > 0$. Most authors use a conditional prior distribution of $\Omega|(\Phi, \Sigma)$ that is *uniform*. Any r columns of Ω can be interpreted as an orthonormal basis for an r-dimensional subspace of $\mathbb{R}^n$. The set of these subspaces is called Stiefel manifold and denoted by $\mathcal{G}_{r,n-r}$. Thus, specifying a prior distribution for (the columns of) Ω can be viewed as placing probabilities on a Stiefel manifold. A similar problem arises when placing prior probabilities on cointegration spaces, and we will provide a more extensive discussion in Section 3.3. A uniform distribution can be defined as the unique distribution that is invariant to orthonormal transformations of $\mathbb{R}^n$ (James 1954). For $n = 2$, this uniform distribution is obtained by letting $\varphi \sim U(-\pi, \pi]$ in (7.28) and, in the case of Example 2.3, restricting it to the interval $[-\underline{\varphi}(\Sigma), \pi/2]$. Detailed descriptions of algorithms for Bayesian inference in sign-restricted structural VARs for $n > 2$ can be found, for instance, in Uhlig (2005) and Rubio-Ramírez et al. (2010).

Illustration 2.1: We consider a VAR(4) based on output, inflation, interest rates, and real money balances. The data are obtained from the FRED database of the Federal Reserve Bank of St Louis. Database identifiers are provided in parentheses. Per capita output is defined as real GDP (GDPC96) divided by the civilian noninstitutionalized population (CNP16OV). We take the natural log of per capita output and extract a deterministic trend by OLS (ordinary least squares) regression over the period 1959:I to 2006:IV.[3] The deviations from the linear trend are scaled by 100 to convert them into percentages. Inflation is defined as the log difference of the GDP deflator (GDPDEF), scaled by 400 to obtain annualized percentage rates. Our measure of nominal interest rates corresponds to the average federal funds rate (FEDFUNDS) within a quarter. We

[3] This deterministic trend could also be incorporated into the specification of the VAR. However, in this illustration we wanted (i) to only remove a deterministic trend from output and not from the other variables and (ii) to use Algorithm 2.1 and the marginal likelihood formula (7.15) which do not allow for equation-specific parameter restrictions.

divide sweep-adjusted M2 money balances by quarterly nominal GDP to obtain inverse velocity. We then remove a linear trend from log inverse velocity and scale the deviations from trend by 100. Finally, we add our measure of detrended per capita real GDP to obtain real money balances. The sample used for posterior inference is restricted to the period from 1965:I to 2005:I.

We use the dummy-observation version of the Minnesota prior described in Section 2.2 with the hyperparameters $\lambda_2 = 4$, $\lambda_3 = 1$, $\lambda_4 = 1$, and $\lambda_5 = 1$. We consider five possible values for λ_1, which controls the overall variance of the prior. We assign equal prior probability to each of these values and use (7.15) to compute the marginal likelihoods $p_\lambda(Y)$. Results are reported in Table 7.1. The posterior probabilites of the hyperparameter values are essentially degenerate, with a weight of approximately one on $\lambda_1 = 0.1$. The subsequent analysis is conducted conditional on this hyperparameter setting.

Draws from the posterior distribution of the reduced-form parameters Φ and Σ can be generated with Algorithm 2.1, using the appropriate modification of $\hat{S}$, $\hat{\Phi}$, and X, described at the beginning of Section 2.2. To identify the dynamic response to a monetary policy shock, we use the sign-restriction approach described in Example 2.3. In particular, we assume that a contractionary monetary policy shock raises the nominal interest rate upon impact and for one period after the impact. During these two periods, the shock also lowers inflation and real money balances. Since we are identifying only one shock, we focus on the first column of the orthogonal matrix Ω. We specify a prior for $\Omega_{(.1)}$ that implies that the space spanned by this vector is uniformly distributed on the relevant Stiefel manifold. This uniform distribution is truncated to enforce the sign restrictions given (Φ, Σ). Thus, the second step of Algorithm 2.3 is implemented with an acceptance sampler that rejects proposed draws of Ω for which the sign restrictions are not satisfied. Proposal draws $\tilde{\Omega}$ are obtained by sampling $Z \sim N(0, I)$ and letting $\tilde{\Omega} = Z/\|Z\|$.

Posterior means and credible sets for the impulse responses are plotted in Figure 7.2. According to the posterior mean estimates, a one-standard deviation shock raises interest rates by 40 basis points upon impact. In response, the (annualized) inflation rate drops by 30 basis points, and real money balances fall by 0.4%. The posterior mean of the output response is slightly positive, but the 90% credible set ranges from -50 to about 60 basis points, indicating substantial uncertainty about the sign and magnitude of the real effect of unanticipated changes in monetary policy under our fairly agnostic prior for the vector $\Omega_{(.1)}$. □

Table 7.1: Hyperparameter choice for Minnesota prior

λ_1	0.01	0.10	0.50	1.00	2.00
$\pi_{i,0}$	0.20	0.20	0.20	0.20	0.20
$\ln p_\lambda(Y)$	−914.35	-868.71	-888.32	-898.18	−902.43
$\pi_{i,T}$	0.00	1.00	0.00	0.00	0.00

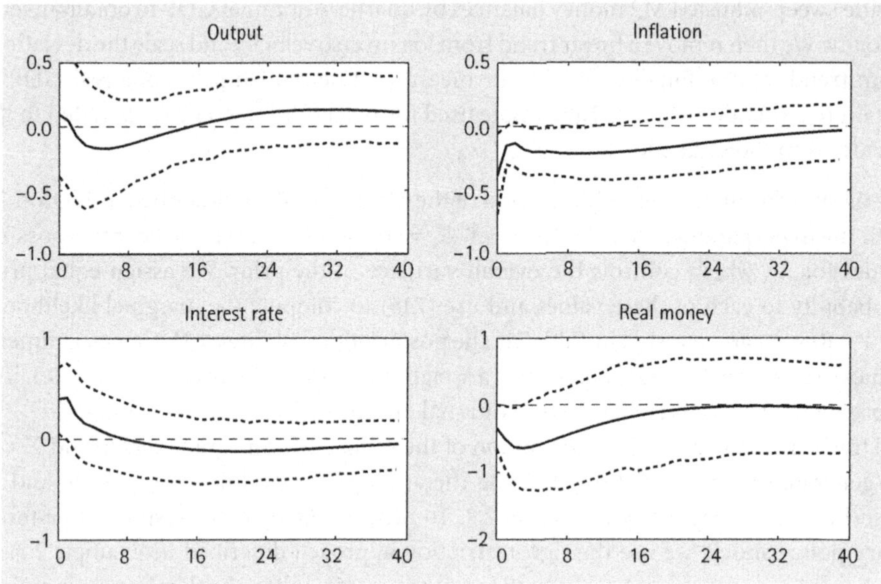

FIGURE 7.2 Response to a monetary policy shock

Notes: The figure depicts 90% credible bands and posterior mean responses for a VAR(4) to a one-standard-deviation monetary policy shock.

2.4.2 An alternative structural VAR parameterization

We introduced structural VARs by expressing the one-step-ahead forecast errors of a reduced-form VAR as a linear function of orthogonal structural shocks. Suppose we now premultiply both sides of (7.1) by $\Omega'\Sigma_{tr}^{-1}$ and define $A_0' = \Omega'\Sigma_{tr}^{-1}$, $A_j = \Omega'\Sigma_{tr}^{-1}\Phi_j$, $j = 1, \ldots, p$, and $A_c = \Omega'\Sigma_{tr}^{-1}\Phi_c$; then we obtain

$$A_0' y_t = A_1 y_{t-1} + \ldots A_p y_{t-p} + A_c + \epsilon_t, \quad \epsilon_t \sim iidN(0, I). \tag{7.30}$$

Much of the empirical analysis in the Bayesian SVAR literature is based on this alternative parameterization (see, for instance, Sims and Zha 1998). The advantage of (7.30) is that the coefficients have direct behaviorial interpretations. For instance, one could impose identifying restrictions on A_0 such that the first equation in (7.30) corresponds to the monetary policy rule of the central bank. Accordingly, $\epsilon_{1,t}$ would correspond to unanticipated deviations from the expected policy.

A detailed discussion of the Bayesian analysis of (7.30) is provided in Sims and Zha (1998). As in (7.5), let $x_t' = [y_{t-1}', \ldots, y_{t-p}', 1]$ and Y and X be matrices with rows y_t', x_t', respectively. Moreover, we use E to denote the $T \times n$ matrix with rows ϵ_t'. Finally, define $A = [A_1, \ldots, A_p, A_c]'$ such that (7.30) can be expressed as a multivariate regression of the form

$$YA_0 = XA + E \tag{7.31}$$

with likelihood function

$$p(Y|A_0, A) \propto |A_0|^T \exp\left\{-\frac{1}{2}tr[(YA_0 - XA)'(YA_0 - XA)]\right\}. \qquad (7.32)$$

The term $|A_0|^T$ is the determinant of the Jacobian associated with the transformation of E into Y. Notice that, conditional on A_0, the likelihood function is quadratic in A, meaning that under a suitable choice of prior, the posterior of A is matricvariate Normal.

Sims and Zha (1998) propose prior distributions that share the Kronecker structure of the likelihood function and hence lead to posterior distributions that can be evaluated with a high degree of numerical efficiency, that is, without having to invert matrices of the dimension $nk \times nk$. Specifically, it is convenient to factorize the joint prior density as $p(A_0)p(A|A_0)$ and to assume that the conditional prior distribution of A takes the form

$$A|A_0 \sim MN\left(\underline{A}(A_0), \lambda^{-1}I \otimes \underline{V}(A_0)\right), \qquad (7.33)$$

where the matrix of means $\underline{A}(A_0)$ and the covariance matrix $\underline{V}(A_0)$ are potentially functions of A_0 and λ is a hyperparameter that scales the prior covariance matrix. The matrices $\underline{A}(A_0)$ and $\underline{V}(A_0)$ can, for instance, be constructed from the dummy observations presented in Section 2.2:

$$\underline{A}(A_0) = (X^{*\prime}X^*)^{-1}X^{*\prime}Y^*A_0, \quad \underline{V}(A_0) = (X^{*\prime}X^*)^{-1}.$$

Combining the likelihood function (7.32) with the prior (7.33) leads to a posterior for A that is conditionally matricvariate Normal:

$$A|A_0, Y \sim MN\left(\bar{A}(A_0), I \otimes \bar{V}(A_0)\right), \qquad (7.34)$$

where

$$\bar{A}(A_0) = \left(\lambda\underline{V}^{-1}(A_0) + X'X\right)^{-1}\left(\lambda\underline{V}^{-1}(A_0)\underline{A}(A_0) + X'YA_0\right)$$
$$\bar{V}(A_0) = \left(\lambda\underline{V}^{-1}(A_0) + X'X\right)^{-1}.$$

The specific form of the posterior for A_0 depends on the form of the prior density $p(A_0)$. The prior distribution typically includes normalization and identification restrictions. An example of such restrictions, based on a structural VAR analyzed by Robertson and Tallman (2001), is provided next.

Example 2.4: Suppose y_t is composed of a price index for industrial commodities (PCOM), M2, the federal funds rate (R), real GDP interpolated to monthly frequency ($\tilde{y}$), the consumer price index (CPI), and the unemployment rate (U). The exclusion restrictions on the matrix A_0' used by Robertson and Tallman (2001) are summarized in

Table 7.2: Identification restrictions for A_0'

	Pcom	M2	R	Y	CPI	U
Inform	X	X	X	X	X	X
MP	0	X	X	0	0	0
MD	0	X	X	X	X	0
Prod	0	0	0	X	0	0
Prod	0	0	0	X	X	0
Prod	0	0	0	X	X	X

Notes: Each row in the table represents a behavioral equation labeled on the left-hand side of the row: information market (Inform), monetary policy rule (MP), money demand (MD), and three equations that characterize the production sector of the economy (Prod). The column labels reflect the observables: commodity prices (Pcom), monetary aggregate (M2), federal funds rate (R), real GDP (Y), consumer price index (CPI), and unemployment (U). A 0 entry denotes a coefficient set to zero.

Table 7.2. Each row in the table corresponds to a behavioral equation labeled on the left-hand side of the row. The first equation represents an information market, the second equation is the monetary policy rule, the third equation describes money demand, and the remaining three equations characterize the production sector of the economy. The entries in the table imply that the only variables that enter contemporaneously into the monetary policy rule (MP) are the federal funds rate (R) and M2. The structural VAR here is overidentified, because the covariance matrix of the one-step-ahead forecast errors of a VAR with $n = 6$ has in principle 21 free elements, whereas the matrix A_0 has only 18 free elements. Despite the fact that overidentifying restrictions were imposed, the system requires a further normalization. One can multiply the coefficients for each equation $i = 1, \ldots, n$ by -1, without changing the distribution of the endogenous variables. A common normalization scheme is to require that the diagonal elements of A_0 all be nonnegative. In practice, this normalization can be imposed by postprocessing the output of the posterior sampler: for all draws $(A_0', A_1, \ldots, A_p, A_c)$ multiply the i'th row of each matrix by -1 if $A_{0,ii} < 0$. This normalization works well if the posterior support of each diagonal element of A_0 is well away from zero. Otherwise, this normalization may induce bimodality in distributions of other parameters. □

Waggoner and Zha (2003) developed an efficient MCMC algorithm to generate draws from a restricted A_0 matrix. For expositional purposes, assume that the prior for $A|A_0$ takes the form (7.33), with the restriction that $\underline{A}(A_0) = \underline{M}A_0$ for some matrix $\underline{M}$ and that $\underline{V}(A_0) = \underline{V}$ does not depend on A_0, as is the case for our dummy-observation prior. Then the marginal likelihood function for A_0 is of the form

$$p(Y|A_0) = \int p(Y|A_0, A)p(A|A_0)dA \propto |A_0|^T \exp\left\{-\frac{1}{2}tr[A_0'\bar{S}A_0]\right\}, \tag{7.35}$$

where $\bar{S}$ is a function of the data as well as $\underline{M}$ and $\underline{V}$. Waggoner and Zha (2003) write the restricted columns of A_0 as $A_{0(.i)} = U_i b_i$ where b_i is a $q_i \times 1$ vector, q_i is the number of unrestricted elements of $A_{0(.i)}$, and U_i is an $n \times q_i$ matrix, composed of orthonormal column vectors. Under the assumption that $b_i \sim N(\underline{b}_i, \underline{\Omega}_i)$, independently across i, we obtain

$$p(b_1, \ldots, b_n | Y) \propto |[U_1 b_1, \ldots, U_n b_n]|^T \exp\left\{ -\frac{T}{2} \sum_{i=1}^{n} b_i' S_i b_i \right\}, \tag{7.36}$$

where $S_i = U_i'(\bar{S} + \underline{\Omega}_i^{-1})U_i$ and A_0 can be recovered from the b_i's. Now consider the conditional density of $b_i | (b_1, \ldots, b_{i-1}, b_{i+1}, \ldots, b_n)$:

$$p(b_i | Y, b_1, \ldots, b_{i-1}, b_{i+1}, \ldots, b_n) \propto |[U_1 b_1, \ldots, U_n b_n]|^T \exp\left\{ -\frac{T}{2} b_i' S_i b_i \right\}.$$

Since b_i also appears in the determinant, its distribution is not Normal. Characterizing the distribution of b_i requires a few additional steps. Let V_i be a $q_i \times q_i$ matrix such that $V_i' S_i V_i = I$. Moreover, let w be an $n \times 1$ vector perpendicular to each vector $U_j b_j$, $j \neq i$, and define $w_1 = V_i' U_i' w / \| V_i' U_i' w \|$. Choose $w_2, \ldots, w_{q_i}$ such that $w_1, \ldots, w_{q_i}$ form an orthonormal basis for $\mathbb{R}^{q_i}$ and we can introduce the parameters $\beta_1, \ldots, \beta_{q_i}$ and reparameterize the vector b_i as a linear combination of the w_j's:

$$b_i = V_i \sum_{j=1}^{q_i} \beta_j w_j. \tag{7.37}$$

By the orthonormal property of the w_j's, we can verify that the conditional posterior of the β_j's is given by

$$\begin{aligned} &p(\beta_1, \ldots, \beta_{q_i} | Y, b_1, \ldots, b_{i-1}, b_{i+1}, \ldots, b_n) \\ &\propto \left(\sum_{j=1}^{q_i} |[U_1 b_1, \ldots, \beta_j V_i w_j, \ldots, U_n b_n]| \right)^T \exp\left\{ -\frac{T}{2} \sum_{j=1}^{q_i} \beta_j^2 \right\} \\ &\propto |\beta_1|^T \exp\left\{ -\frac{T}{2} \sum_{j=1}^{q_i} \beta_j^2 \right\}. \end{aligned} \tag{7.38}$$

The last line follows because $w_2, \ldots, w_{q_i}$ by construction falls in the space spanned by $U_j b_j, j \neq i$. Thus, all β_j's are independent of each other, β_1 has a Gamma distribution, and $\beta_j, 2 \leq j \leq q_i$, are normally distributed. Draws from the posterior of A_0 can be obtained by Gibbs sampling.

Algorithm 2.4. Gibbs Sampler for Structural VARs
For $s = 1, \ldots, n_{sim}$:

(1) Draw $A_0^{(s)}$ conditional on $(A^{(s-1)}, Y)$ as follows. For $i = 1, \ldots, n$ generate $\beta_1, \ldots, \beta_{q_i}$ from (7.38) conditional on $(b_1^{(s)}, \ldots, b_{i-1}^{(s)}, b_{i+1}^{(s-1)}, \ldots, b_n^{(s-1)})$, define $b_i^{(s)}$ according to (7.37), and let $A_{0(.i)}^{(s)} = U_i b_i^{(s)}$.

(2) Draw $A^{(s)}$ conditional on $(A_0^{(s)}, Y)$ from the matricvariate Normal distribution in (7.34). □

2.5 Further VAR topics

The literature on Bayesian analysis of VARs is by now extensive, and our presentation is by no means exhaustive. A complementary survey of Bayesian analysis of VARs including VARs with time-varying coefficients and factor-augmented VARs can be found in Koop and Korobilis (2010). Readers who are interested in using VARs for forecasting purposes can find algorithms to compute such predictions efficiently, possibly conditional on the future path of a subset of variables, in Waggoner and Zha (1999). Rubio-Ramírez et al. (2010) provide conditions for the global identification of VARs of the form (7.30). Our exposition was based on the assumption that the VAR innovations are homoskedastic. Extensions to GARCH-type heteroskedasticity can be found, for instance, in Pelloni and Polasek (2003). Uhlig (1997) proposes a Bayesian approach to VARs with stochastic volatility. We will discuss VAR models with stochastic volatility in Section 5.

3 VARs with Reduced-Rank Restrictions

It is well documented that many economic time series such as aggregate output, consumption, and investment exhibit clear trends and tend to be very persistent. At the same time, it has long been recognized that linear combinations of macroeconomic time series (potentially after a logarithmic transformation) appear to be stationary. Examples are the so-called *Great Ratios*, such as the consumption-output or investment-output ratio (see Klein and Kosobud 1961). The left panel of Figure 7.3 depicts log nominal GDP and nominal aggregate investment for the United States over the period 1965–2006 (obtained from the FRED database of the Federal Reserve Bank of St Louis) and the right panel shows the log of the investment-output ratio. While the ratio is far from constant, it exhibits no apparent trend, and the fluctuations look at first glance mean-reverting. The observation that particular linear combinations of nonstationary economic time series appear to be stationary has triggered a large literature on cointegration starting in the mid 1980s; see, for example, Engle and Granger (1987), Johansen (1988), Johansen (1991), and Phillips (1991).

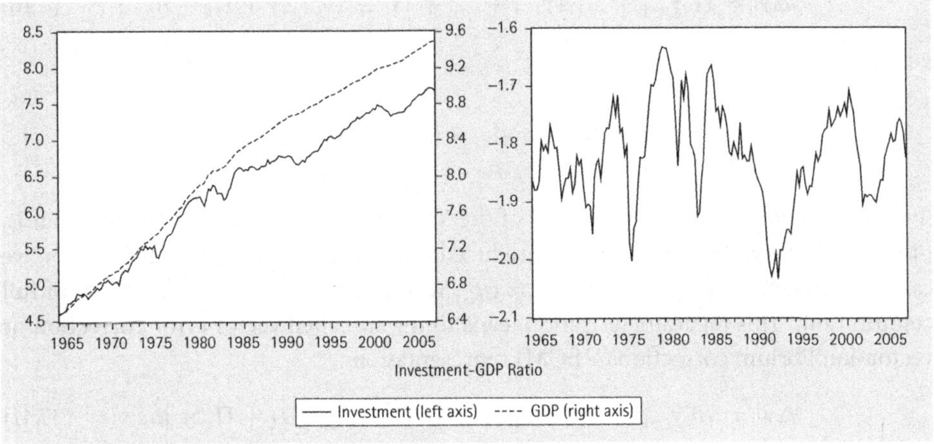

FIGURE 7.3 Log nominal output and investment

Notes: The figure depicts US data from 1964:Q1 to 2006:Q4.

More formally, the dynamic behavior of a univariate autoregressive process $\phi(L)y_t = u_t$, where $\phi(L) = 1 - \sum_{j=1}^{p} \phi_j L^p$ and L is the lag operator, crucially depends on the roots of the characteristic polynomial $\phi(z)$. If the smallest root is unity and all other roots are outside the unit circle, then y_t is nonstationary. Unit-root processes are often called integrated of order one, I(1), because stationarity can be induced by taking first differences $\Delta y_t = (1 - L)y_t$. If a linear combination of univariate I(1) time series is stationary, then these series are said to be cointegrated. Cointegration implies that the series have common stochastic trends that can be eliminated by taking suitable linear combinations. In Section 4, we will discuss how such cointegration relationships arise in a dynamic stochastic general equilibrium framework. For now, we will show in Section 3.1 that one can impose co-trending restrictions in a VAR by restricting some of the eigenvalues of its characteristic polynomial to unity. This leads to the so-called vector error correction model, which takes the form of a reduced-rank regression. Such restricted VARs have become a useful and empirically successful tool in applied macroeconomics. In Section 3.2, we discuss Bayesian inference in cointegration systems under various types of prior distributions.

3.1 Cointegration restrictions

Consider the reduced-form VAR specified in (7.1). Subtracting y_{t-1} from both sides of the equality leads to

$$\Delta y_t = (\Phi_1 - I)y_{t-1} + \Phi_2 y_{t-2} + \ldots + \Phi_p y_{t-p} + \Phi_c + u_t, \quad u_t \sim iidN(0, \Sigma). \quad (7.39)$$

For $j = 1, \ldots, p-1$ define $\Pi_j = -\sum_{i=j+1}^{p} \Phi_p$ and $\Pi_c = \Phi_c$. Then we can rewrite (7.39) as

$$\Delta y_t = \Pi_* y_{t-1} + \Pi_1 \Delta y_{t-1} + \ldots + \Pi_{p-1} \Delta y_{t-p+1} + \Pi_c + u_t, \tag{7.40}$$

where

$$\Pi_* = -\Phi(1) \quad \text{and} \quad \Phi(z) = I - \sum_{j=1}^{p} \Phi_j z^j.$$

$\Phi(z)$ is the characteristic polynomial of the VAR. If the VAR has unit roots —that is, $|\Phi(1)| = 0$—then the matrix Π_* is of reduced rank. If the rank of Π_* equals $r < n$, we can reparameterize the matrix as $\Pi_* = \alpha\beta'$, where α and β are $n \times r$ matrices of full column rank. This reparameterization leads to the so-called vector error correction or vector equilibrium correction (VECM) representation:

$$\Delta y_t = \alpha\beta' y_{t-1} + \Pi_1 \Delta y_{t-1} + \ldots + \Pi_{p-1} \Delta y_{t-p+1} + \Pi_c + u_t, \tag{7.41}$$

studied by Engle and Granger (1987).

A few remarks are in order. It can be easily verified that the parameterization of Π_* in terms of α and β is not unique: for any nonsingular $r \times r$ matrix A, we can define $\tilde{\alpha}$ and $\tilde{\beta}$ such that $\Pi_* = \alpha A A^{-1} \beta' = \tilde{\alpha}\tilde{\beta}'$. In addition to the matrices α and β, it is useful to define a matrix $\alpha_\perp$ and $\beta_\perp$ of full column rank and dimension $n \times (n-r)$ such that $\alpha'\alpha_\perp = 0$ and $\beta'\beta_\perp = 0$. If no root of $\Phi(z) = 0$ lies inside the unit circle and $\alpha'_\perp \beta_\perp$ has full rank, then (7.41) implies that y_t can be expressed as (Granger's Representation Theorem):

$$y_t = \beta_\perp (\alpha'_\perp \Gamma \beta_\perp)^{-1} \alpha'_\perp \sum_{\tau=1}^{t} (u_\tau + \Pi_c) + \Psi(L)(u_t + \Pi_c) + P_{\beta_\perp} y_0. \tag{7.42}$$

$\Gamma = I - \sum_{j=1}^{p-1} \Pi_j$, $P_{\beta_\perp}$ is the matrix that projects onto the space spanned by $\beta_\perp$, and $\Psi(L)u_t = \sum_{j=0}^{\infty} \Psi_j u_{t-j}$ is a stationary linear process. It follows immediately that the r linear combinations $\beta' y_t$ are stationary. The columns of β are called cointegration vectors. Moreover, y_t has $n-r$ common stochastic trends given by $(\alpha'_\perp \Gamma \beta_\perp)^{-1} \alpha'_\perp \sum_{\tau=1}^{t} (u_\tau + \Pi_c)$. A detailed exposition can be found, for instance, in the monograph by Johansen (1995).

If y_t is composed of log GDP and investment, a visual inspection of Figure 7.3 suggests that the cointegration vector β is close to $[1, -1]'$. Thus, according to (7.41), the growth rates of output and investment should be modeled as functions of lagged growth rates as well as the log investment-output ratio. Since in this example $\beta_\perp$ is 2×1 and the term $(\alpha'_\perp \Gamma \beta_\perp)^{-1} \alpha'_\perp \sum_{\tau=1}^{t} (u_\tau + \Pi_c)$ is scalar, Equation (7.42) highlights the fact that output and investment have a common stochastic trend. The remainder of Section 3 focuses on the formal Bayesian analysis of the vector error correction model. We will examine various approaches to specifying a prior distribution for Π_* and discuss Gibbs samplers to implement posterior inference. In practice, the researcher faces uncertainty about the number of cointegration relationships as well as the number of lags that should be included. A discussion of model selection and averaging approaches is deferred to Section 7.

3.2 Bayesian inference with Gaussian prior for β

Define $\Pi = [\Pi_1, \ldots, \Pi_{p-1}, \Pi_c]'$ and let $u_t \sim N(0, \Sigma)$. Inspection of (7.41) suggests that conditional on α and β, the VECM reduces to a multivariate linear Gaussian regression model. In particular, if $(\Pi, \Sigma)|(\alpha, \beta)$ is MNIW, then we can deduce immediately that the posterior $(\Pi, \Sigma)|(Y, \alpha, \beta)$ is also of the MNIW form and can easily be derived following the calculations in Section 2. A Gibbs sampler to generate draws from the posterior distribution of the VECM typically has the following structure:

Algorithm 3.1. Gibbs Sampler for VECM
For $s = 1, \ldots, n_{sim}$:

(1) Draw $(\Pi^{(s)}, \Sigma^{(s)})$ from the posterior $p(\Pi, \Sigma|\Pi_*^{(s-1)}, Y)$.
(2) Draw $\Pi_*^{(s)}$ from the posterior $p(\Pi_*|\Pi^{(s)}, \Sigma^{(s)}, Y)$. □

To simplify the subsequent exposition, we will focus on inference for $\Pi_* = \alpha\beta'$ conditional on Π and Σ for the remainder of this section (Step 2 of Algorithm 3.1). To do so, we study the simplified model

$$\Delta y_t = \Pi_* y_{t-1} + u_t, \quad \Pi_* = \alpha\beta', \quad u_t \sim iidN(0, \Sigma), \tag{7.43}$$

and treat Σ as known. As before, it is convenient to write the regression in matrix form. Let ΔY, X, and U denote the $T \times n$ matrices with rows $\Delta y_t'$, y_{t-1}', and u_t', respectively, such that $\Delta Y = X\Pi_*' + U$.

In this section, we consider independent priors $p(\alpha)$ and $p(\beta)$ that are either flat or Gaussian. Geweke (1996) used such priors to study inference in the reduced-rank regression model. Throughout this subsection we normalize $\beta' = [I_{r\times r}, B'_{r\times(n-r)}]$. The prior distribution for β is induced by a prior distribution for B. This normalization requires that the elements of y_t be ordered such that each of these variables appears in at least one cointegration relationship. We will discuss the consequences of this normalization later on.

In the context of our output-investment illustration, one might find it attractive to center the prior for the cointegration coefficient B at -1, reflecting either presample evidence on the stability of the investment-output ratio or the belief in an economic theory that implies that industrialized economies evolve along a balanced-growth path along which consumption and output grow at the same rate. We will encounter a DSGE model with such a balanced-growth-path property in Section 4. For brevity, we refer to this class of priors as balanced-growth-path priors. An informative prior for α could be constructed from beliefs about the speed at which the economy returns to its balanced-growth path in the absence of shocks.

Conditional on an initial observation and the covariance matrix Σ (both subsequently omitted from our notation), the likelihood function is of the form

$$p(Y|\alpha, \beta) \propto |\Sigma|^{-T/2} \exp\left\{ -\frac{1}{2} tr[\Sigma^{-1}(\Delta Y - X\beta\alpha')'(\Delta Y - X\beta\alpha')]\right\}. \tag{7.44}$$

In turn, we will derive conditional posterior distributions for α and β based on the likelihood (7.44). We begin with the posterior of α. Define $\tilde{X} = X\beta$. Then

$$p(\alpha|Y,\beta) \propto p(\alpha)\exp\left\{-\frac{1}{2}tr[\Sigma^{-1}(\alpha\tilde{X}'\tilde{X}\alpha' - 2\alpha\tilde{X}'\Delta Y)]\right\}. \tag{7.45}$$

Thus, as long as the prior of $vec(\alpha')$ is Gaussian, the posterior of $vec(\alpha')$ is multivariate Normal. If the prior has the same Kronecker structure as the likelihood function, then the posterior is matricvariate Normal.

The derivation of the conditional posterior of β is more tedious. Partition $X = [X_1, X_2]$ such that the partitions of X conform to the partitions of $\beta' = [I, B']$ and rewrite the reduced-rank regression as

$$\Delta Y = X_1\alpha' + X_2B\alpha' + U.$$

Now define $Z = \Delta Y - X_1\alpha'$ and write

$$Z = X_2B\alpha' + U. \tag{7.46}$$

The fact that B is right-multiplied by α' complicates the analysis. The following steps are designed to eliminate the α' term. Post-multiplying (7.46) by the matrix $C = [\alpha(\alpha'\alpha)^{-1}, \alpha_\perp]$ yields the seemingly unrelated regression

$$\left[\tilde{Z}_1,\ \tilde{Z}_2\right] = X_2\left[B,\ 0\right] + \left[\tilde{U}_1,\ \tilde{U}_2\right], \tag{7.47}$$

where

$$\tilde{Z}_1 = Z\alpha(\alpha'\alpha)^{-1}, \quad \tilde{Z}_2 = Z\alpha_\perp, \quad \tilde{U}_1 = U\alpha(\alpha'\alpha)^{-1}, \quad \tilde{U}_2 = U\alpha_\perp.$$

Notice that we cannot simply drop the $\tilde{Z}_2$ equations. Through $\tilde{Z}_2$, we obtain information about $\tilde{U}_2$ and hence indirectly information about $\tilde{U}_1$, which sharpens the inference for B. Formally, let $\tilde{\Sigma} = C'\Sigma C$ and partition $\tilde{\Sigma}$ conforming with $\tilde{U} = [\tilde{U}_1, \tilde{U}_2]$. The mean and variance of $\tilde{Z}_1$ conditional on $\tilde{Z}_2$ are given by $(\tilde{\Sigma}_{12}\tilde{\Sigma}_{22}^{-1}\tilde{Z}_2 + X_2B)$ and $\tilde{\Sigma}_{1|2} = \tilde{\Sigma}_{11} - \tilde{\Sigma}_{12}\tilde{\Sigma}_{22}^{-1}\tilde{\Sigma}_{21}$, respectively. Define $\tilde{Z}_{1|2} = \tilde{Z}_1 - \tilde{\Sigma}_{12}\tilde{\Sigma}_{22}^{-1}\tilde{Z}_2$. Then we can deduce

$$p(B|Y,\alpha) \propto p(\beta(B))\exp\left\{-\frac{1}{2}tr\left[\tilde{\Sigma}_{1|2}^{-1}(\tilde{Z}_{1|2} - X_2B)'(\tilde{Z}_{1|2} - X_2B)\right]\right\}. \tag{7.48}$$

Thus, if the prior distribution for B is either flat or Normal, then the conditional posterior of B given α is Normal.

Algorithm 3.2. Gibbs Sampler for Simple VECM with Gaussian Priors
For $s = 1, \ldots, n_{sim}$:

(1) Draw $\alpha^{(s)}$ from $p(\alpha|\beta^{(s-1)}, Y)$ given in (7.45).
(2) Draw $B^{(s)}$ from $p(B|\alpha^{(s)}, Y)$ given in (7.48) and let $\beta^{(s)} = [I, B^{(s)'}]'$. □

Illustration 3.1: We use the VECM in (7.41) with $p = 4$ and the associated moving-average representation (7.42) to extract a common trend from the US investment and GDP data depicted in Figure 7.3. We use an improper prior of the form

$$p(\Pi, \Sigma, \alpha, B) \propto |\Sigma|^{-(n+1)/2} \exp\left\{-\frac{1}{2\lambda}(B - (-1))^2\right\},$$

where $\lambda \in \{0.01, 0.1, 1\}$. The prior distribution for the cointegration vector $\beta = [1, B]'$ is centered at the balanced-growth-path values $[1, -1]'$. Draws from the posterior distribution are generated through a Gibbs sampler in which Step 2 of Algorithm 3.1 is replaced by the two steps described in Algorithm 3.2. The posterior density for B is plotted in Figure 7.4 for the three parameterizations of the prior variance λ. The posterior is similar for all three choices of λ, indicating that the data are quite informative about the cointegration relationship. For each prior, the posterior mean of B is about -1.07, with most of the mass of the distributions placed on values less than -1, indicating a slight violation of the balanced-growth-path restriction. Using posterior draws based on $\lambda = 0.10$, Figure 7.5 plots the decompositions of log nominal aggregate investment and log nominal GDP into common trends and stationary fluctuations around those trends. The plots in the left column of the figure display the common trend $\beta_\perp(\alpha'_\perp \Gamma \beta_\perp)^{-1}\alpha'_\perp \sum_{\tau=1}^{t}(u_t + \Pi_c)$ for each series, while the plots in the right column show the demeaned stationary component $\Psi(L)u_t$. The vertical bands indicate National Bureau of Economic Research (NBER) recession periods. □

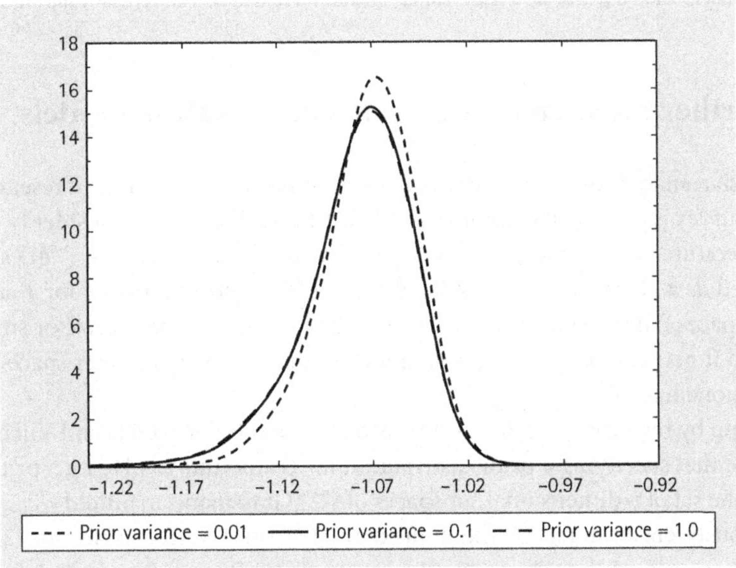

FIGURE 7.4 Posterior density of cointegration parameter

Notes: The figure depicts Kernel density approximations of the posterior density for B in $\beta = [1, B]'$ based on three different priors: $B \sim N(-1, 0.01)$, $B \sim N(-1, 0.1)$, and $B \sim N(-1, 1)$.

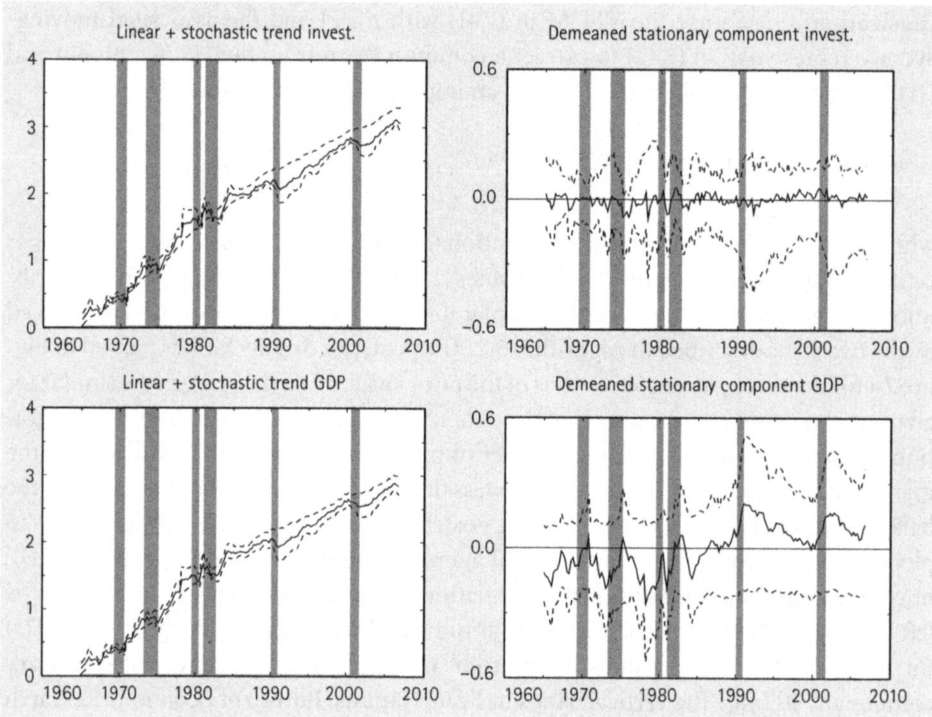

FIGURE 7.5 Trends and fluctuations

Notes: The figure depicts posterior medians (solid) and 90% credible intervals (dashed) for the common trends in log investment and output as well as deviations around these trends. The vertical bands indicate NBER recessions.

3.3 Further research on Bayesian cointegration models

The Bayesian analysis of cointegration systems has been an active area of research, and a detailed survey is provided by Koop et al. (2006). Subsequently, we consider two strands of this literature. The first strand points out that the columns of β in (7.41) should be interpreted as a characterization of a subspace of $\mathbb{R}^n$ and that priors for β are priors over subspaces. The second strand uses prior distributions to regularize or smooth the likelihood function of a cointegration model in areas of the parameter space in which it is very nonelliptical.

We begin by reviewing the first strand. Strachan and Inder (2004) and Villani (2005) emphasize that specifying a prior distribution for β amounts to placing a prior probability on the set of r-dimensional subspaces of $\mathbb{R}^n$ (Grassmann manifold $\mathcal{G}_{r,n-r}$), which we previously encountered in the context of structural VARs in Section 2.4.1. Our discussion focuses on the output-investment example with $n = 2$ and $r = 1$. In this case the Grassmann manifold consists of all the lines in $\mathbb{R}^2$ that pass through the origin. Rather than normalizing one of the ordinates of the cointegration vector β to one, we can alternatively normalize its length to one and express it in terms of polar coordinates.

For reasons that will become apparent subsequently, we let

$$\beta(\varphi) = [\cos(-\pi/4 + \pi(\varphi - 1/2)), \sin(-\pi/4 + \pi(\varphi - 1/2))]', \quad \varphi \in (0, 1].$$

The one-dimensional subspace associated with $\beta(\varphi)$ is given by $\lambda\beta(\varphi)$, where $\lambda \in \mathbb{R}$. In our empirical illustration, we used a balanced-growth-path prior that was centered at the cointegration vector $[1, -1]'$. This vector lies in the space spanned by $\beta(1/2)$. Thus, to generate prior distributions that are centered at the balanced-growth-path restriction, we can choose a Beta distribution for φ and let $\varphi \sim B(\gamma, \gamma)$. If $\gamma \gg 1$, then the prior is fairly dogmatic. As γ approaches 1 from above it becomes more diffuse. In fact, if $\gamma = 1$, then $\varphi \sim U(0, 1]$, and it turns out that the subspaces associated with $\beta(\varphi)$ are uniformly distributed on the Grassmann manifold (see James 1954). This uniform distribution is defined to be the unique distribution that is invariant under the group of orthonormal transformations of $\mathbb{R}^n$. For $n = 2$, this group is given by the set of orthogonal matrices specified in (7.28), which rotate the subspace spanned by $\beta(\varphi)$ around the origin. Villani (2005) proposes to use the uniform distribution on the Grassman manifold as a reference prior for the analysis of cointegration systems and, for general n and r, derives the posterior distribution for α and β using the ordinal normalization $\beta' = [I, B']$.

Strachan and Inder (2004) are very critical of the ordinal normalization, because a flat and apparently noninformative prior on B in $\beta' = [I, B']$ favors the cointegration spaces near the region where the linear normalization is invalid, meaning that some of the first r variables do not appear in any cointegration vector. Instead, these authors propose to normalize β according to $\beta'\beta = I$ and develop methods of constructing informative and diffuse priors on the Grassmann manifold associated with β.

We now turn to the literature on regularization. Kleibergen and van Dijk (1994) and Kleibergen and Paap (2002) use prior distributions to correct irregularities in the likelihood function of the VECM, caused by local nonidentifiability of α and B under the ordinal normalization $\beta' = [I, B']$. As the loadings α for the cointegration relationships $\beta' y_{t-1}$ approach zero, B becomes nonidentifiable. If the highly informative balanced-growth-path prior discussed previously were replaced by a flat prior for B—that is $p(B) \propto$ *constant*—to express diffuse prior beliefs about cointegration relationships, then the conditional posterior of B given $\alpha = 0$ is improper, and its density integrates to infinity. Under this prior, the marginal posterior density of α can be written as

$$p(\alpha|Y) \propto p(\alpha) \int p(Y|\alpha, B) dB.$$

Since $\int p(Y|B, \alpha = 0) dB$ determines the marginal density at $\alpha = 0$, the posterior of α tends to favor near-zero values for which the cointegration relationships are poorly identified.

Kleibergen and Paap (2002) propose the following alternative. The starting point is a singular-value decomposition of a (for now) unrestricted $n \times n$ matrix Π'_*, which takes the form:

$$\Pi'_* = VDW' = \begin{bmatrix} V_{11} & V_{12} \\ V_{21} & V_{22} \end{bmatrix} \begin{bmatrix} D_{11} & 0 \\ 0 & D_{22} \end{bmatrix} \begin{bmatrix} W'_{11} & W'_{21} \\ W'_{12} & W'_{22} \end{bmatrix}. \tag{7.49}$$

V and W are orthogonal $n \times n$ matrices, and D is a diagonal $n \times n$ matrix. The partitions V_{11}, D_{11}, and W_{11} are of dimension $r \times r$, and all other partitions conform. Regardless of the rank of Π'_*, it can be verified that the matrix can be decomposed as follows:

$$\begin{aligned} \Pi'_* &= \begin{bmatrix} V_{11} \\ V_{21} \end{bmatrix} D_{11} \begin{bmatrix} W'_{11} & W'_{21} \end{bmatrix} + \begin{bmatrix} V_{12} \\ V_{22} \end{bmatrix} D_{22} \begin{bmatrix} W'_{12} & W'_{22} \end{bmatrix} \\ &= \beta\alpha' + \beta_\perp \Lambda \alpha'_\perp, \end{aligned} \tag{7.50}$$

where

$$\beta = \begin{bmatrix} I \\ B \end{bmatrix}, \quad B = V_{21}V_{11}^{-1}, \quad \text{and} \quad \alpha' = V_{11}D_{11}[W'_{11}, W'_{21}].$$

The matrix Λ is chosen to obtain a convenient functional form for the prior density below:

$$\Lambda = (V'_{22}V_{22})^{-1/2}V_{22}D_{22}W'_{22}(W_{22}W'_{22})^{-1/2}.$$

Finally, the matrices $\beta'_\perp$ and $\alpha'_\perp$ take the form $\beta'_\perp = M'_\beta[V'_{12}\ V'_{22}]$ and $\alpha'_\perp = M'_\alpha[W'_{12}\ W'_{22}]$, respectively. Here M_α and M_β are chosen such that the second equality in (7.50) holds. For $\Lambda = 0$ the rank of the unrestricted Π'_* in (7.50) reduces to r and we obtain the familiar expression $\Pi'_* = \beta\alpha'$.

The authors start from a flat prior on Π_*: that is, $p(\Pi_*) \propto$ *constant*, ignoring the rank reduction generated by the r cointegration relationships. They proceed by deriving a conditional distribution for Π_* given $\Lambda = 0$, and finally use a change of variables to obtain a distribution for the parameters of interest, α and B. Thus,

$$p(\alpha, B) \propto |J_{\Lambda=0}(\Pi_*(\alpha, B, \Lambda))| \propto |\beta'\beta|^{(n-r)/2}|\alpha\alpha'|^{(n-r)/2}. \tag{7.51}$$

Here, $J_{\Lambda=0}(\Pi_*(\alpha, B, \Lambda))$ is the Jacobian associated with the mapping between Π_* and (α, B, Λ). This prior has the property that as $\alpha \longrightarrow 0$, its density vanishes and counteracts the divergence of $\int p(Y|\alpha, B)dB$. Details of the implementation of a posterior simulator are provided in Kleibergen and Paap (2002).

4 Dynamic Stochastic General Equilibrium Models

The term *DSGE model* is typically used to refer to a broad class of dynamic macroeconomic models that spans the standard neoclassical growth model discussed in King et al. (1988) as well as the monetary model with numerous real and nominal frictions developed by Christiano et al. (2005). A common feature of these models is that decision rules of economic agents are derived from assumptions about preferences and technologies by solving intertemporal optimization problems. Moreover, agents potentially face uncertainty with respect to total factor productivity, for instance, or the nominal interest rate set by a central bank. This uncertainty is generated by exogenous stochastic processes that shift technology, for example, or generate unanticipated deviations from a central bank's interest-rate feedback rule.

Conditional on distributional assumptions for the exogenous shocks, the DSGE model generates a joint probability distribution for the endogenous model variables such as output, consumption, investment, and inflation. In a Bayesian framework, this likelihood function can be used to transform a prior distribution for the structural parameters of the DSGE model into a posterior distribution. This posterior is the basis for substantive inference and decision making. DSGE models can be used for numerous tasks, such as studying the sources of business-cycle fluctuations and the propagation of shocks to the macroeconomy, generating predictive distributions for key macroeconomic variables, and analyzing the welfare effects of economic policies, taking both parameter and model uncertainty into account.

The remainder of this section is organized as follows. We present a prototypical DSGE model in Section 4.1. The model solution and state-space representation are discussed in Section 4.2. Bayesian inference on the parameters of a linearized DSGE model is discussed in Section 4.3. Extensions to models with indeterminacies or stochastic volatility, and to models solved with nonlinear techniques are discussed in Sections 4.4, 4.5, and 4.6, respectively. Section 4.7 discusses numerous methods of documenting the performance of DSGE models and comparing them to less restrictive models such as vector autoregressions. Finally, we provide a brief discussion of some empirical applications in Section 4.8. A detailed survey of Bayesian techniques for the estimation and evaluation of DSGE models is provided in An and Schorfheide (2007a).

4.1 A prototypical DSGE model

Figure 7.6 depicts postwar aggregate log output, hours worked, and log labor productivity for the US. Precise data definitions are provided in Ríos-Rull et al. (2009). Both output and labor productivity are plotted in terms of percentage deviations from a linear trend. The simplest DSGE model that tries to capture the dynamics of these series is the neoclassical stochastic growth model. According to this model, an important source of the observed fluctuations in the three series is exogenous changes in total factor productivity. We will illustrate the techniques discussed in this section with the estimation of a stochastic growth model based on observations on aggregate output and hours worked.

The model consists of a representative household and perfectly competitive firms. The representative household maximizes the expected discounted lifetime utility from consumption C_t and hours worked H_t:

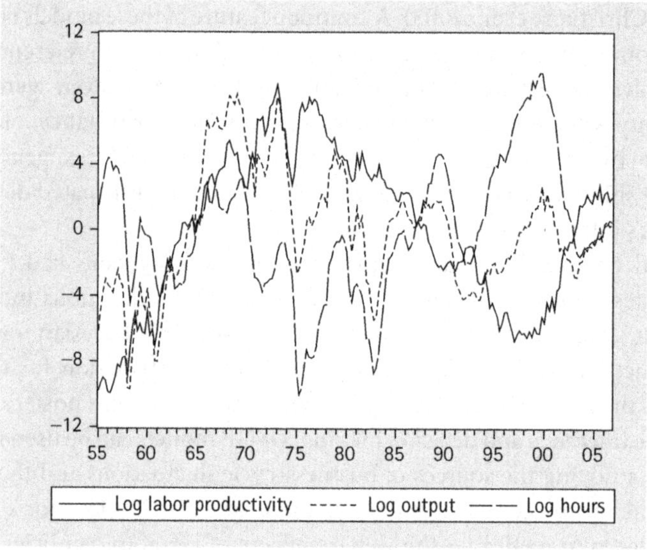

FIGURE 7.6 Aggregate output, hours, and labor productivity

Notes: Output and labor productivity are depicted in percentage deviations from a deterministic trend, and hours are depicted in deviations from its mean. Sample period is 1955:Q1 to 2006:Q4.

$$\mathbb{E}_t\left[\sum_{s=0}^{\infty}\beta^{t+s}\left(\ln C_{t+s}-\frac{(H_{t+s}/B_{t+s})^{1+1/\nu}}{1+1/\nu}\right)\right] \tag{7.52}$$

subject to a sequence of budget constraints

$$C_t + I_t \leq W_t H_t + R_t K_t.$$

The household receives the labor income $W_t H_t$, where W_t is the hourly wage. It owns the capital stock K_t and rents it to the firms at the rate R_t. Capital accumulates according to

$$K_{t+1} = (1-\delta)K_t + I_t, \tag{7.53}$$

where I_t is investment and δ is the depreciation rate. The household uses the discount rate β, and B_t is an exogenous preference shifter that can be interpreted as a labor supply shock. If B_t increases, then the disutility associated with hours worked falls. Finally, ν is the aggregate labor supply elasticity. The first-order conditions associated with the household's optimization problem are given by a consumption Euler equation and a labor supply condition:

$$\frac{1}{C_t} = \beta\mathbb{E}\left[\frac{1}{C_{t+1}}(R_{t+1}+(1-\delta))\right] \quad \text{and} \quad \frac{1}{C_t}W_t = \frac{1}{B_t}\left(\frac{H_t}{B_t}\right)^{1/\nu}. \tag{7.54}$$

Firms rent capital, hire labor services, and produce final goods according to the following Cobb-Douglas technology:

$$Y_t = (A_t H_t)^\alpha K_t^{1-\alpha}. \tag{7.55}$$

The stochastic process A_t represents the exogenous labor-augmenting technological progress. Firms solve a static profit maximization problem and choose labor and capital to equate marginal products of labor and capital with the wage and rental rate of capital, respectively:

$$W_t = \alpha \frac{Y_t}{H_t}, \quad R_t = (1-\alpha)\frac{Y_t}{K_t}. \tag{7.56}$$

An equilibrium is a sequence of prices and quantities such that (i) the representative house-hold maximizes utility and firms maximize profits taking the prices as given, and (ii) markets clear, implying that

$$Y_t = C_t + I_t. \tag{7.57}$$

To close the model, we specify a law of motion for the two exogenous processes. Log technology evolves according to

$$\ln A_t = \ln A_0 + (\ln \gamma)t + \ln \widetilde{A}_t, \quad \ln \widetilde{A}_t = \rho_a \ln \widetilde{A}_{t-1} + \sigma_a \epsilon_{a,t}, \quad \epsilon_{a,t} \sim iidN(0,1), \tag{7.58}$$

where $\rho_a \in [0,1]$. If $0 \leq \rho_a < 1$, the technology process is trend stationary. If $\rho_a = 1$, then $\ln A_t$ is a random-walk process with drift. Exogenous labor supply shifts are assumed to follow a stationary AR(1) process:

$$\ln B_t = (1-\rho_b)\ln B_* + \rho_b \ln B_{t-1} + \sigma_b \epsilon_{b,t}, \quad \epsilon_{b,t} \sim iidN(0,1), \tag{7.59}$$

and $0 \leq \rho_b < 1$. To initialize the exogenous processes, we assume that in period $t = -\tau$

$$\ln \widetilde{A}_{-\tau} = 0 \quad \text{and} \quad \ln B_{-\tau} = 0.$$

The solution to the rational expectations difference equations (7.53) to (7.59) determines the law of motion for the endogenous variables Y_t, C_t, I_t, K_t, H_t, W_t, and R_t.

The technology process $\ln A_t$ induces a common trend in output, consumption, investment, capital, and wages. Since we will subsequently solve the model by constructing a local approximation of its dynamics near a steady state, it is useful to detrend the model variables as follows:

$$\widetilde{Y}_t = \frac{Y_t}{A_t}, \ \widetilde{C}_t = \frac{C_t}{A_t}, \ \widetilde{I}_t = \frac{I_t}{A_t}, \ \widetilde{K}_{t+1} = \frac{K_{t+1}}{A_t}, \ \widetilde{W}_t = \frac{W_t}{A_t}. \tag{7.60}$$

The detrended variables are mean reverting. This bounds the probability of experiencing large deviations from the log-linearization point for which the approximate solution becomes inaccurate. According to our timing convention, K_{t+1} refers to capital at the end of period t/beginning of $t+1$, and is a function of shocks dated t and earlier. Hence, we are detrending K_{t+1} by A_t. It is straightforward to rewrite (7.53) to (7.57) in terms of the detrended variables:

$$\frac{1}{\widetilde{C}_t} = \beta \mathbb{E}\left[\frac{1}{\widetilde{C}_{t+1}} e^{-a_{t+1}}(R_{t+1} + (1-\delta))\right], \quad \frac{1}{\widetilde{C}_t}\widetilde{W}_t = \frac{1}{B_t}\left(\frac{H_t}{B_t}\right)^{1/\nu} \tag{7.61}$$
$$\widetilde{W}_t = \alpha \frac{\widetilde{Y}_t}{H_t}, \quad R_t = (1-\alpha)\frac{\widetilde{Y}_t}{\widetilde{K}_t} e^{a_t}$$
$$\widetilde{Y}_t = H_t^\alpha \left(\widetilde{K}_t e^{-a_t}\right)^{1-\alpha}, \quad \widetilde{Y}_t = \widetilde{C}_t + \widetilde{I}_t, \quad \widetilde{K}_{t+1} = (1-\delta)\widetilde{K}_t e^{-a_t} + \widetilde{I}_t.$$

The process a_t is defined as

$$a_t = \ln \frac{A_t}{A_{t-1}} = \ln \gamma + (\rho_a - 1)\ln \widetilde{A}_{t-1} + \sigma_a \epsilon_{a,t}. \tag{7.62}$$

This log ratio is always stationary, because if $\rho_a = 1$, the $\ln \widetilde{A}_{t-1}$ term drops out. Finally, we stack the parameters of the DSGE model in the vector θ:

$$\theta = [\alpha, \beta, \gamma, \delta, \nu, \ln A_0, \rho_a, \sigma_a, \ln B_*, \rho_b, \sigma_b]'. \tag{7.63}$$

If we set the standard deviations of the innovations $\epsilon_{a,t}$ and $\epsilon_{b,t}$ to zero, the model economy becomes deterministic and has a steady state in terms of the detrended variables. This steady state is a function of θ. For instance, the rental rate of capital, the capital-output, and the investment-output ratios are given by

$$R_* = \frac{\gamma}{\beta} - (1-\delta), \quad \frac{\widetilde{K}_*}{\widetilde{Y}_*} = \frac{(1-\alpha)\gamma}{R_*}, \quad \frac{\widetilde{I}_*}{\widetilde{Y}_*} = \left(1 - \frac{1-\delta}{\gamma}\right)\frac{\widetilde{K}_*}{\widetilde{Y}_*}. \tag{7.64}$$

In a stochastic environment, the detrended variables follow a stationary law of motion, even if the underlying technology shock is nonstationary. Moreover, if $\rho_a = 1$, the model generates a number of cointegration relationships, which according to (7.60) are obtained by taking pairwise differences of $\ln Y_t$, $\ln C_t$, $\ln I_t$, $\ln K_{t+1}$, and $\ln W_t$.

4.2 Model solution and state-space form

The solution to the equilibrium conditions (7.59), (7.61), and (7.62) leads to a probability distribution for the endogenous model variables, indexed by the vector of structural parameters θ. This likelihood function can be used for Bayesian inference. Before turning to the Bayesian analysis of DSGE models, a few remarks about the model solution are in order. In most DSGE models, the intertemporal optimization problems of economic agents can be written recursively, using Bellman equations. In general, the value and policy functions associated with the optimization problems are nonlinear in terms of both the state and the control variables, and the solution of the optimization problems requires numerical techniques. The solution of the DSGE model can be written as

$$s_t = \Phi(s_{t-1}, \epsilon_t; \theta), \tag{7.65}$$

where s_t is a vector of suitably defined state variables and ϵ_t is a vector that stacks the innovations for the structural shocks.

For now, we proceed under the assumption that the DSGE model's equilibrium law of motion is approximated by log-linearization techniques, ignoring the discrepancy between the nonlinear model solution and the first-order approximation. We adopt the convention that if a variable X_t ($\widetilde{X}_t$) has a steady state X_* ($\widetilde{X}_*$), then $\widehat{X}_t = \ln X_t - \ln X_*$ ($\widehat{X}_t = \ln \widetilde{X}_t - \ln \widetilde{X}_*$). The log-linearized equilibrium conditions of the neoclassical growth model (7.61) are given by the following system of linear expectational difference equations:

$$\begin{aligned}
&\widehat{C}_t = \mathbb{E}_t\left[\widehat{C}_{t+1} + \widehat{a}_{t+1} - \frac{R_*}{R_* + (1-\delta)}\widehat{R}_{t+1}\right] \\
&\widehat{H}_t = \nu\widehat{W}_t - \nu\widehat{C}_t + (1+\nu)\widehat{B}_t, \quad \widehat{W}_t = \widehat{Y}_t - \widehat{H}_t, \\
&\widehat{R}_t = \widehat{Y}_t - \widehat{K}_t + \widehat{a}_t, \quad \widehat{K}_{t+1} = \frac{1-\delta}{\gamma}\widehat{K}_t + \frac{\widetilde{I}_*}{\widetilde{K}_*}\widehat{I}_t - \frac{1-\delta}{\gamma}\widehat{a}_t, \\
&\widehat{Y}_t = \alpha\widehat{H}_t + (1-\alpha)\widehat{K}_t - (1-\alpha)\widehat{a}_t, \quad \widehat{Y}_t = \frac{\widetilde{C}_*}{\widetilde{Y}_*}\widehat{C}_t + \frac{\widetilde{I}_*}{\widetilde{Y}_*}\widehat{I}_t, \\
&\widehat{A}_t = \rho_a\widehat{A}_{t-1} + \sigma_a\epsilon_{a,t}, \quad \widehat{a}_t = \widehat{A}_t - \widehat{A}_{t-1}, \quad \widehat{B}_t = \rho_b\widehat{B}_{t-1} + \sigma_b\epsilon_{b,t}.
\end{aligned} \tag{7.66}$$

A multitude of techniques are available for solving linear rational expectations models (see, for instance, Sims 2002b). Economists focus on solutions that guarantee a nonexplosive law of motion for the endogenous variables that appear in (7.66), with the loose justification that any explosive solution would violate the transversality conditions associated with the underlying dynamic optimization problems. For the neoclassical growth model, the solution takes the form

$$s_t = \Phi_1(\theta)s_{t-1} + \Phi_\epsilon(\theta)\epsilon_t. \tag{7.67}$$

The system matrices Φ_1 and Φ_ϵ are functions of the DSGE model parameters θ, and s_t is composed of three elements: the capital stock at the end of period t, $\widehat{K}_{t+1}$, as well as the two exogenous processes $\widehat{A}_t$ and $\widehat{B}_t$. The other endogenous variables, $\widehat{Y}_t$, $\widehat{C}_t$, $\widehat{I}_t$, $\widehat{H}_t$, $\widehat{W}_t$, and $\widehat{R}_t$ can be expressed as linear functions of s_t.

Like all DSGE models, the linearized neoclassical growth model has some apparent counterfactual implications. Since fluctuations are generated by two exogenous disturbances, $\widehat{A}_t$ and $\widehat{B}_t$, the likelihood function for more than two variables is degenerate. The model predicts that certain linear combinations of variables, such as the labor share $\widehat{lsh} = \widehat{H}_t + \widehat{W}_t - \widehat{Y}_t$, are constant, which is clearly at odds with the data. To cope with this problem authors have added either so-called measurement errors (Sargent 1989; Altug 1989; and Ireland 2004), or additional shocks as in Leeper and Sims (1995) and more recently Smets and Wouters (2003). In the subsequent illustration, we restrict the dimension of the vector of observables y_t to $n = 2$, so that it matches the number of exogenous shocks. Our measurement equation takes the form

$$y_t = \Psi_0(\theta) + \Psi_1(\theta)t + \Psi_2(\theta)s_t. \tag{7.68}$$

Equations (7.67) and (7.68) provide a state-space representation for the linearized DSGE model. If the innovations ϵ_t are Gaussian, then the likelihood function can be obtained from the Kalman filter, which is described in detail in Giordani et al. (Chapter 3, this volume).

In the subsequent empirical illustration, we let y_t consist of log GDP and log hours worked. In this case, Equation (7.68) becomes

$$\begin{bmatrix} \ln GDP_t \\ \ln H_t \end{bmatrix} = \begin{bmatrix} \ln Y_0 \\ \ln H_* \end{bmatrix} + \begin{bmatrix} \ln \gamma \\ 0 \end{bmatrix} t + \begin{bmatrix} \widehat{Y}_t + \widehat{A}_t \\ \widehat{H}_t \end{bmatrix},$$

where $Y_o = Y_* A_o$ and H_* and Y_* are the steady states of hours worked and output, respectively. The variables $\widehat{A}_t$, $\widehat{Y}_t$, and $\widehat{H}_t$ are linear functions of s_t. Notice that even though the DSGE model was solved in terms of the detrended model variable $\widehat{Y}_t$, the trend generated by technology $(\ln \gamma)t + \widehat{A}_t$ is added in the measurement equation. Thus, we are able to use nondetrended log real GDP as an observable and to learn about the technology growth rate γ and its persistence ρ_a from the available information about the level of output.

Although we focus on the dynamics of output and hours in this section, it is instructive to examine the measurement equations that the model yields for output and investment. Suppose we use the GDP deflator to convert the two series depicted in Figure 7.3 from nominal into real terms. Then, we can write

$$\begin{bmatrix} \ln GDP_t \\ \ln I_t \end{bmatrix} = \begin{bmatrix} \ln Y_0 \\ \ln Y_0 + (\ln \widetilde{I}_* - \ln \widetilde{Y}_*) \end{bmatrix} + \begin{bmatrix} \ln \gamma \\ \ln \gamma \end{bmatrix} t + \begin{bmatrix} \widehat{A}_t + \widehat{Y}_t \\ \widehat{A}_t + \widehat{I}_t \end{bmatrix}.$$

This representation highlights the common trend in output and investment generated by the technology process $\widehat{A}_t$. If $\rho_a = 1$, then the last line of (7.66) implies that $\widehat{A}_t$ follows a random-walk process and hence induces nonstationary dynamics. In this case, the model implies the following cointegration relationship:

$$\begin{bmatrix} -1 & 1 \end{bmatrix} \begin{bmatrix} \ln GDP_t \\ \ln I_t \end{bmatrix} = \ln \left[\frac{(1-\alpha)(\gamma - 1 + \delta)}{\gamma/\beta - 1 + \delta} \right] + \widehat{I}_t - \widehat{Y}_t.$$

Recall that both $\widehat{Y}_t$ and $\widehat{I}_t$ are stationary, even if $\rho_a = 1$. We used this model implication in Section 3.2 as justification of our informative prior for the cointegration vector. In contrast, the posterior estimates of the cointegration vector reported in Illustration 3.1 suggest that the balanced-growth-path implication of the DSGE model is overly restrictive. In practice, such a model deficiency may lead to posterior distributions of the autoregressive coefficients associated with shocks other than technology that concentrate near unity.

4.3 Bayesian inference

Although most of the literature on Bayesian estimation of DSGE models uses fairly informative prior distributions, this should not be interpreted as "cooking up" desired results based on almost dogmatic priors. To the contrary, the spirit behind the prior elicitation is to use other sources of information that do not directly enter the likelihood function. To the extent that this information is indeed precise, the use of a tight prior distribution is desirable. If the information is vague, it should translate into a more dispersed prior distribution. Most important, the choice of prior should be properly documented.

For concreteness, suppose the neoclassical growth model is estimated based on aggregate output and hours data over the period 1955 to 2006. There are three important sources of information that are approximately independent of the data that enter the likelihood function and therefore could be used for the elicitation of prior distribution: (i) information from macroeconomic time series other than output and hours during the period 1955 to 2006; (ii) micro-level observations that are, for instance, informative about labor-supply decisions; and (iii) macroeconomic data, including observations on output and hours worked, prior to 1955. Consider source (i). It is apparent from (7.64) that long-run averages of real interest rates, capital-output ratios, and investment-output ratios are informative about α, β, and δ. Moreover, the parameter α equals the labor share of income in our model. Since none of these variables directly enters the likelihood function, it is sensible to incorporate this information through the prior distribution. The parameters ρ_a, ρ_b, σ_a, and σ_b implicitly affect the persistence and volatility of output and hours worked. Hence, prior distributions for these parameters can be chosen such that the implied dynamics of output and hours are broadly in line with presample evidence, that is, information from source (iii). Del Negro and Schorfheide (2008) provide an approach for automating this type of prior elicitation. Finally, microeconometric estimates of labor supply elasticities—an example of source (ii)—could be used to specify a prior for the Frisch elasticity ν, accounting for the fact that most of the variation in hours worked at the aggregate level is due to the extensive margin, that is, to individuals moving in and out of unemployment.

Because of the nonlinear relationship between the DSGE model parameters θ and the system matrices Ψ_0, Ψ_1, Ψ_2, Φ_1, and Φ_ϵ in (7.67) and (7.68), the marginal and conditional distributions of the elements of θ do not fall into the well-known families of probability distributions. Up to now, the most commonly used procedures for generating draws from the posterior distribution of θ are the Random-Walk Metropolis (RWM) Algorithm described in Schorfheide (2000) and Otrok (2001) or the Importance Sampler proposed in DeJong et al. (2000). The basic RWM Algorithm takes the following form

Algorithm 4.1. Random-Walk Metropolis (RWM) Algorithm for DSGE Model

(1) Use a numerical optimization routine to maximize the log posterior, which up to a constant is given by $\ln p(Y|\theta) + \ln p(\theta)$. Denote the posterior mode by $\tilde{\theta}$.

(2) Let $\tilde{\Sigma}$ be the inverse of the (negative) Hessian computed at the posterior mode $\tilde{\theta}$, which can be computed numerically.
(3) Draw $\theta^{(0)}$ from $N(\tilde{\theta}, c_0^2\tilde{\Sigma})$ or directly specify a starting value.
(4) For $s = 1, \ldots, n_{sim}$: draw ϑ from the proposal distribution $N(\theta^{(s-1)}, c^2\tilde{\Sigma})$. The jump from $\theta^{(s-1)}$ is accepted ($\theta^{(s)} = \vartheta$) with probability min $\{1, r(\theta^{(s-1)}, \vartheta|Y)\}$ and rejected ($\theta^{(s)} = \theta^{(s-1)}$) otherwise. Here,

$$r(\theta^{(s-1)}, \vartheta|Y) = \frac{p(Y|\vartheta)p(\vartheta)}{p(Y|\theta^{(s-1)})p(\theta^{(s-1)})}. \qquad \square$$

If the likelihood can be evaluated with a high degree of precision, then the maximization in Step 1 can be implemented with a gradient-based numerical optimization routine. The optimization is often not straightforward as the posterior density is typically not globally concave. Thus, it is advisable to start the optimization routine from multiple starting values, which could be drawn from the prior distribution, and then set $\tilde{\theta}$ to the value that attains the highest posterior density across optimization runs.

The evaluation of the likelihood typically involves three steps: (i) the computation of the steady state; (ii) the solution of the linear rational expectations system; and (iii) the evaluation of the likelihood function of a linear state-space model with the Kalman filter. While the computation of the steady states is trivial in our neoclassical stochastic growth model, it might require the use of numerical equation solvers for more complicated DSGE models. Any inaccuracy in the computation of the steady states will translate into an inaccurate evaluation of the likelihood function that makes use of gradient-based optimization methods impractical. Chib and Ramamurthy (2010) recommend using a simulated annealing algorithm for Step 1. In some applications we found it useful to skip Steps 1 to 3 by choosing a reasonable starting value, such as the mean of the prior distribution, and replacing $\tilde{\Sigma}$ in Step 4 with a matrix whose diagonal elements are equal to the prior variances of the DSGE model parameters and whose off-diagonal elements are zero.

Based on practitioners' experience, Algorithm 4.1 tends to work well if the posterior density is unimodal. The scale factor c_0 controls the expected distance between the mode and the starting point of the Markov chain. The tuning parameter c is typically chosen to obtain a rejection rate of about 50%. In this case, reasonable perturbations of the starting points lead to chains that after 100,000 to 1,000,000 iterations provide very similar approximations of the objects of interest, for example posterior means, medians, standard deviations, and credible sets. An and Schorfheide (2007b) describe a hybrid MCMC algorithm with transition mixture to deal with a bimodal posterior distribution. Most recently, Chib and Ramamurthy (2010) have developed a multiblock Metropolis-within-Gibbs algorithm that randomly groups parameters in blocks and thereby dramatically reduces the persistence of the resulting Markov chain and improves the efficiency of the posterior sampler compared to a single-block RWM algorithm. A detailed discussion can be found in Chib (Chapter 5 in this volume).

Illustration 4.1: The prior distribution for our empirical illustration is summarized in the first five columns of Table 7.3. Based on National Income and Product Account

Table 7.3: Prior and posterior distribution for DSGE model parameters

		Prior			Posterior			
					Det. Trend		Stoch. Trend	
Name	Domain	Density	Para (1)	Para (2)	Mean	90% Intv.	Mean	90% Intv.
α	[0,1)	Beta	0.66	0.02	0.65	[0.62, 0.68]	0.65	[0.63, 0.69]
ν	$\mathbb{R}^+$	Gamma	2.00	1.00	0.42	[0.16, 0.67]	0.70	[0.22, 1.23]
$4 \ln \gamma$	$\mathbb{R}$	Normal	0.00	0.10	.003	[.002, .004]	.004	[.002, .005]
ρ_a	$\mathbb{R}^+$	Beta	0.95	0.02	0.97	[0.95, 0.98]	1.00	
σ_a	$\mathbb{R}^+$	InvGamma	0.01	4.00	.011	[.010, .012]	.011	[.010, .012]
ρ_b	$\mathbb{R}^+$	Beta	0.80	0.10	0.98	[0.96, 0.99]	0.98	[0.96, 0.99]
σ_b	$\mathbb{R}^+$	InvGamma	0.01	4.00	.008	[.007, .008]	.007	[.006, .008]
$\ln H_*$	$\mathbb{R}$	Normal	0.00	10.0	−0.04	[−0.08, 0.01]	−0.03	[−0.07, 0.02]
$\ln Y_0$	$\mathbb{R}$	Normal	0.00	100	8.77	[8.61, 8.93]	8.39	[7.93, 8.86]

Notes: Para (1) and Para (2) list the means and the standard deviations for Beta, Gamma, and Normal distributions; the upper and lower bound of the support for the Uniform distribution; s and ν for the Inverted Gamma distribution, where $p_{IG}(\sigma|\nu, s) \propto \sigma^{-\nu-1} e^{-\nu s^2/2\sigma^2}$. To estimate the stochastic growth version of the model we set $\rho_a = 1$. The parameters $\beta = 0.99$ and $\delta = 0.025$ are fixed.

(NIPA) data, published by the Bureau of Economic Analysis, we choose the prior means for α, β, and δ to be consistent with a labor share of 0.66, an investment-to-output ratio of about 25%, and an annual interest rate of 4%. These choices yield values of $\underline{\alpha} = 0.66$, $\underline{\beta} = 0.99$, and $\underline{\delta} = 0.025$ in quarterly terms. As is quite common in the literature, we decided to use dogmatic priors for β and δ. Fixing these parameters is typically justified as follows. Conditional on the adoption of a particular data definition, the relevant long-run averages computed from NIPA data appear to deliver fairly precise measurements of steady-state relationships that can be used to extract information about parameters such as β and δ, resulting in small prior variances. The use of a dogmatic prior can then be viewed as a (fairly good) approximation of a low-variance prior. For illustrative purposes, we use such a low-variance prior for α. We assume that α has a Beta distribution with a standard deviation of 0.02.

An important parameter for the behavior of the model is the labor supply elasticity. As discussed in Ríos-Rull et al. (2009), a priori plausible values vary considerably. Micro-level estimates based on middle-age white males yield a value of 0.2, balanced-growth considerations under slightly different household preferences suggest a value of 2.0, and Rogerson's (1988) model of hours' variation along the extensive margin would lead to $\nu = \infty$. We use a Gamma distribution with parameters that imply a prior mean of 2 and a standard deviation of 1. Our prior for the technology shock parameters is fairly diffuse with respect to the average growth rate; it implies that the total factor productivity has a serial correlation between 0.91 and 0.99, and that the standard deviation of the shocks is about 1% each quarter. Our prior implies that the preference shock is slightly less persistent than the technology shock. Finally, we use fairly agnostic priors on the location parameters $\ln Y_0$ (which is a transformation of $\ln A_0$) and $\ln H_*$.

The distributions specified in the first columns of Table 7.3 are marginal distributions. A joint prior is typically obtained by taking the product of the marginals for all elements of θ, which is what we will do in the empirical illustration. Alternatively, one could replace a subset of the structural parameters by, for instance, R_*, lsh_*, $\widetilde{I}_*/\widetilde{K}_*$, and $\widetilde{K}_*/\widetilde{Y}_*$, and then regard beliefs about these various steady states as independent. Del Negro and Schorfheide (2008) propose to multiply an initial prior $\tilde{p}(\theta)$ constructed from marginal distributions for the individual elements of θ by a function $f(\theta)$ that reflects beliefs about steady-state relationships and autocovariances. This function is generated by interpreting long-run averages of variables that do not appear in the model and presample autocovariances of y_t as noisy measures of steady states and population autocovariances. For example, let $lsh_*(\theta)$ be the model-implied labor share as a function of θ and $\widehat{lsh}$ a sample average of postwar US labor shares. Then $\ln f(\theta)$ could be defined as $-(lsh_*(\theta) - \widehat{lsh})^2/(2\lambda)$, where λ reflects the strength of the belief about the labor share. The overall prior then takes the form $p(\theta) \propto \tilde{p}(\theta)f(\theta)$.

The prior distribution is updated based on quarterly data on aggregate output and hours worked ranging from 1955 to 2006. Unlike in Figure 7.6, we do not remove a deterministic trend from the output series. We apply the RWM Algorithm to generate 100,000 draws from the posterior distribution of the parameters of the stochastic growth model. The scale parameter in the proposal density is chosen to be $c = 0.5$, which leads to a rejection rate of about 50%. Posterior means and 90% credible intervals, computed from the output of the posterior simulator, are summarized in the last four columns of Table 7.3. We consider two versions of the model. In the deterministic trend version, the autocorrelation parameter of the technology shock is estimated subject to the restriction that it lie in the interval $[0, 1)$, whereas it is fixed at 1 in the stochastic trend version. Due to the fairly tight prior, the distribution of α is essentially not updated in view of the data. The posterior means of the labor supply elasticity are 0.42 and 0.70, respectively, which is in line with the range of estimates reported in Ríos-Rull et al. (2009). These relatively small values of ν imply that most of the fluctuations in hours worked are due to the labor supply shock. The estimated shock autocorrelations are around 0.97, and the innovation standard deviations of the shocks are 1.1% for the technology shock and 0.7% for the preference shock. We used a logarithmic transformation of γ, which can be interpreted as the average quarterly growth rate of the economy and is estimated to be 0.3% to 0.4%. The estimates of $\ln H_*$ and $\ln Y_0$ capture the level of the two series. Once draws from the posterior distribution have been generated, they can be converted into other objects of interest such as responses to structural shocks. □

4.4 Extensions I: indeterminacy

Linear rational expectations systems can have multiple stable solutions, and this is referred to as *indeterminacy*. DSGE models that allow for indeterminate equilibrium solutions have received a lot of attention in the literature, because this indeterminacy might arise if a central bank does not react forcefully enough to counteract deviations of inflation from its long-run target value. In an influential paper, Clarida et al. (2000) estimated interest rate feedback rules based on US postwar data and found that the policy rule estimated for pre-1979 data would lead to indeterminate equilibrium dynamics in a DSGE model with nominal price rigidities. The presence of indeterminacies raises a few complications for Bayesian inference, described in detail in Lubik and Schorfheide (2004).

Consider the following simple example. Suppose that y_t is scalar and satisfies the expectational difference equation

$$y_t = \frac{1}{\theta}\mathbb{E}_t[y_{t+1}] + \epsilon_t, \quad \epsilon_t \sim iidN(0,1), \quad \theta \in (0,2]. \tag{7.69}$$

Here, θ should be interpreted as the structural parameter, which is scalar. It can be verified that if, on the one hand, $\theta > 1$, the unique stable equilibrium law of motion of the endogenous variable y_t is given by

$$y_t = \epsilon_t. \tag{7.70}$$

If, on the other hand, $\theta \leq 1$, one obtains a much larger class of solutions that can be characterized by the ARMA(1,1) process

$$y_t = \theta y_{t-1} + (1+M)\epsilon_t - \theta\epsilon_{t-1}. \tag{7.71}$$

Here, the scalar parameter $M \in \mathbb{R}$ is used to characterize all stationary solutions of (7.69). M is completely unrelated to the agents' tastes and technologies characterized by θ, but it does affect the law of motion of y_t if $\theta \leq 1$. From a macroeconomist's perspective, M captures an indeterminacy: based on θ alone, the law of motion of y_t is not uniquely determined.

From an econometrician's perspective, one needs to introduce this auxiliary parameter M to construct the likelihood function. The likelihood function has the following features. According to (7.70), the likelihood function is completely flat (does not vary with θ and M) for $\theta > 1$ because all parameters drop from the equilibrium law of motion. If $\theta \leq 1$ and $M = 0$, the likelihood function does not vary with θ because the roots of the autoregressive and the moving-average polynomial in the ARMA(1,1) process (7.71) cancel. If $\theta \leq 1$ and $M \neq 0$, then the likelihood function exhibits curvature. In a Bayesian framework, this irregular shape of the likelihood function does not pose any conceptual challenge. In principle, one can combine proper priors for θ and M and obtain a posterior distribution. However, in more realistic applications the implementation of posterior simulation procedures require extra care. Lubik and Schorfheide (2004) divided the parameter space into Θ_D and Θ_I (for model (7.69), $\Theta_D = (1,2]$ and $\Theta_D = [0,1]$) along the lines of the determinacy-indeterminacy boundary, treated the subspaces as separate models, generated posterior draws for each subspace separately, and used marginal likelihoods to obtain posterior probabilities for Θ_D and Θ_I.

4.5 Extensions II: stochastic volatility

One of the most striking features of postwar US GDP data is the reduction in the volatility of output growth around 1984. This phenomenon has been termed the *Great Moderation* and is also observable in many other industrialized countries. To investigate the sources of this volatility reduction, Justiniano and Primiceri (2008) allow the volatility of the structural shocks ϵ_t in (7.67) to vary stochastically over time. The authors adopt a specification in which log standard deviations evolve according to an autoregressive process. An alternative approach would be to capture the Great Moderation with Markov-switching shock standard deviations (see Section 5).

In the context of the stochastic growth model, consider for instance the technology shock $\epsilon_{a,t}$. We previously assumed in (7.58) that $\epsilon_{a,t} \sim N(0,1)$. Alternatively, suppose that

$$\epsilon_{a,t} \sim N(0, v_t^2), \quad \ln v_t = \rho_v \ln v_{t-1} + \eta_t, \quad \eta_t \sim iidN(0, \omega^2). \tag{7.72}$$

Justiniano and Primiceri (2008) solved the linear rational expectational system obtained from the log-linearized equilibrium conditions of their DSGE model and then augmented the linear solution by equations that characterize the stochastic volatility of the exogenous structural shocks. Their approach amounts to using (7.67) and assuming that the element $\epsilon_{a,t}$ in the shock vector ϵ_t evolves according to (7.72). The following Gibbs sampler can be used to generate draws from the posterior distribution.

Algorithm 4.2. Metropolis-within-Gibbs Sampler for DSGE Model with Stochastic Volatility

For $s = 1, \ldots, n_{sim}$:

(1) Draw $\theta^{(s)}$ conditional on $(\theta | v_{1:T}^{(s-1)}, Y)$. Given the sequence $v_{1:T}^{(s-1)}$ the likelihood function of the state-space model can be evaluated with the Kalman filter. Consequently, the RWM step described in Algorithm 4.1 can be used to generate a draw $\theta^{(s)}$.

(2) Draw $\epsilon_{a,1:T}^{(s)}$ conditional on $(\theta^{(s)}, v_{1:T}^{(s-1)}, Y)$ using the simulation smoother of Carter and Kohn (1994), described in Giordani et al.(Chapter 3, this volume).

(3) Draw $(\rho_v^{(s)}, \omega^{(s)})$ conditional on $(v_{1:T}^{(s-1)}, Y)$ from the Normal-Inverse Gamma posterior obtained from the AR(1) law of motion for $\ln v_t$ in (7.72).

(4) Draw $v_{1:T}^{(s)}$ conditional on $(\epsilon_{a,1:T}^{(s)}, \rho_v^{(s)}, \omega^{(s)}, Y)$. Notice that (7.72) can be interpreted as a nonlinear state-space model, where $\epsilon_{a,t}$ is the observable and v_t is the latent state. Smoothing algorithms that generate draws of the sequence of stochastic volatilities have been developed by Jacquier et al. (1994) and Kim et al. (1998) and are discussed in Jacquier and Polson (Chapter 9, this volume) and Giordani et al. (Chapter 3, this volume). □

The empirical model of Justiniano and Primiceri (2008) ignores any higher-order dynamics generated from the nonlinearities of the DSGE model itself on grounds of computational ease. As we will see in the next subsection, Bayesian inference is more difficult to implement for DSGE models solved with nonlinear techniques.

4.6 Extension III: general nonlinear DSGE models

DSGE models are inherently nonlinear, as can be seen from the equilibrium conditions (7.61) associated with our stochastic growth model. Nonetheless, given the magnitude of the business-cycle fluctuations of a country like the United States or the Euro area, many researchers take the stand that the equilibrium dynamics are well approximated by a linear state-space system. However, this linear approximation becomes unreliable if economies are hit by large shocks, as is often the case for emerging market economies, or if the goal of the analysis is to study asset-pricing implications or consumer welfare. It can be easily shown that for any asset j, yielding a gross return $R_{j,t}$, the linearized consumption Euler equation takes the form

$$\widehat{C}_t = \mathbb{E}_t\left[\widehat{C}_{t+1} + \widehat{a}_{t+1} - \widehat{R}_{j,t+1}\right], \tag{7.73}$$

implying that all assets yield the same expected return. Thus, log-linear approximations have the undesirable feature (for asset-pricing applications) that risk premia disappear.

The use of nonlinear model solution techniques complicates the implementation of Bayesian estimation for two reasons. First, it is computationally more demanding to obtain the nonlinear solution. The most common approach in the literature on estimated DSGE models is to use second-order perturbation methods. A comparison of solution methods for DSGE models can be found in Aruoba et al. (2004). Second, the evaluation of the likelihood function becomes more costly because both the state transition equation and the measurement equation of the state-space model are nonlinear. Thus, (7.67) and (7.68) are replaced by (7.65) and

$$y_t = \Psi(s_t; \theta). \tag{7.74}$$

Fernández-Villaverde and Rubio-Ramírez (2007) and Fernández-Villaverde and Rubio-Ramírez (2008) show how a particle filter can be used to evaluate the likelihood function associated with a DSGE model. A detailed description of the particle filter is provided in Giordani et al. (Chapter 3, this volume).

Bayesian analysis of nonlinear DSGE models is currently an active area of research and faces a number of difficulties that have not yet been fully resolved. For the particle filter to work in the context of the stochastic growth model described above, the researcher has to introduce measurement errors in (7.74). Suppose that $\{s_{t-1}^{(i)}\}_{i=1}^N$ is a collection of particles whose empirical distribution approximates $p(s_{t-1}|Y_{1:t-1}, \theta)$. Without errors in the measurement equation, a proposed particle $\tilde{s}_t^{(i)}$ has to satisfy the following two equations:

$$y_t = \Psi(\tilde{s}_t^{(i)}; \theta) \tag{7.75}$$

$$\tilde{s}_t^{(i)} = \Phi(s_{t-1}^{(i)}, \epsilon_t^{(i)}; \theta). \tag{7.76}$$

If $\tilde{s}_t^{(i)}$ is sampled from a continuous distribution, the probability that (7.75) is satisfied is zero. Thus, in the absence of measurement errors, $\tilde{s}_t^{(i)}$ needs to be sampled from a discrete distribution. One can plug (7.76) into (7.75), eliminating $\tilde{s}_t^{(i)}$, and then find all real solutions $\tilde{\epsilon}$ of ϵ for the equation $y_t = \Psi(\Phi(s_{t-1}^{(i)}, \epsilon; \theta); \theta)$. Based on the $\tilde{\epsilon}$'s, one can obtain the support points for the distribution of $\tilde{s}_t^{(i)}$ as $\Phi(s_{t-1}^{(i)}, \tilde{\epsilon}; \theta)$. In practice, this calculation is difficult if not infeasible to implement, because the nonlinear equation might have multiple solutions.

If errors $\eta_t \sim N(0, \Sigma_\eta)$ are added to the measurement equation (7.74), which in the context of our stochastic growth model amounts to a modification of the DSGE model, then (7.75) turns into

$$y_t = \Psi(\tilde{s}_t^{(i)}; \theta) + \eta_t. \tag{7.77}$$

This equation can be solved for any $\tilde{s}_t^{(i)}$ by setting $\eta_t = y_t - \Psi(\tilde{s}_t^{(i)}; \theta)$. An efficient implementation of the particle filter is one for which a large fraction of the N $\tilde{s}_t^{(i)}$'s are associated with values of η_t that are small relative to Σ_η. Some authors—referring to earlier work by Sargent (1989), Altug (1989), or Ireland (2004)—make measurement errors part of the specification of their empirical model. In this case, it is important to realize that one needs to bound the magnitude of the measurement error standard deviations from below to avoid a deterioration of the particle filter performance as these standard deviations approach zero.

4.7 DSGE model evaluation

An important aspect of empirical work with DSGE models is the evaluation of fit. We will distinguish three approaches. First, a researcher might be interested in assessing whether the fit of a stochastic growth model improves if one allows for convex investment adjustment costs. Posterior odds of a model with adjustment costs versus a model without are useful for such an assessment. Second, one could examine to what extent a DSGE model is able to capture salient features of the data. For instance, in the context of the stochastic growth model we could examine whether the model is able to capture the correlation between output and hours worked that we observe in the data. This type of evaluation can be implemented with predictive checks. Finally, a researcher might want to compare one or more DSGE models to a more flexible reference model such as a VAR. We consider three methods of doing so. Such comparisons can be used to examine whether a particular DSGE model captures certain important features of the data. Alternatively, they can be used to rank different DSGE model specifications.

4.7.1 *Posterior odds*

The Bayesian framework allows researchers to assign probabilities to various competing models. These probabilities are updated through marginal likelihood ratios according to

$$\frac{\pi_{i,T}}{\pi_{j,T}} = \frac{\pi_{i,0}}{\pi_{j,0}} \times \frac{p(Y|\mathcal{M}_i)}{p(Y|\mathcal{M}_j)}. \tag{7.78}$$

Here, $\pi_{i,0}$ ($\pi_{i,T}$) is the prior (posterior) probability of model $\mathcal{M}_i$ (which has parameters $\theta_{(i)}$) and

$$p(Y|\mathcal{M}_i) = \int p(Y|\theta_{(i)}, \mathcal{M}_i)p(\theta_{(i)})d\theta_{(i)} \tag{7.79}$$

is the marginal likelihood function. The key challenge in posterior odds comparisons is the computation of the marginal likelihood that involves a high-dimensional integral. If posterior draws for the DSGE model parameters are generated with the RWM algorithm, the methods proposed by Geweke (1999) and Chib and Jeliazkov (2001) can be used to obtain numerical approximations of the marginal likelihood. Posterior odds-based model comparisons are fairly popular in the DSGE model literature. For instance, Rabanal and Rubio-Ramírez (2005) use posterior odds to assess the importance of price and wage stickiness in the context of a small-scale New Keynesian DSGE model, and Smets and Wouters (2007) use odds to determine the importance of a variety of real and nominal frictions in a medium-scale New Keynesian DSGE model. Section 7 provides a more detailed discussion of model selection and model averaging based on posterior probabilities.

Illustration 4.2: We previously estimated two versions of the neoclassical stochastic growth model: a version with a trend-stationary technology process and a version with a difference-stationary exogenous productivity process. The log-marginal data densities $\ln p(Y|\mathcal{M}_i)$ are 1392.8 and 1395.2, respectively. If the prior probabilities for the two specifications are identical, these marginal data densities imply that the posterior probability of the difference-stationary specification is approximately 90%. □

4.7.2 *Predictive checks*

A general discussion of the role of predictive checks in Bayesian analysis can be found in Lancaster (2004), Geweke (2005), and Geweke (2007). Predictive checks can be implemented based on either the prior or the posterior distribution of the DSGE model parameters θ. Let $Y^*_{1:T}$ be a hypothetical sample of length T. The predictive distribution for $Y^*_{1:T}$ based on the time t information set $\mathcal{F}_t$ is

$$p(Y^*_{1:T}|\mathcal{F}_t) = \int p(Y^*_{1:T}|\theta)p(\theta|\mathcal{F}_t)d\theta. \tag{7.80}$$

We can then use $\mathcal{F}_0$ to denote the prior information and $\mathcal{F}_T$ to denote the posterior information set that includes the sample $Y_{1:T}$. Draws from the predictive distribution can be obtained in two steps. First, generate a parameter draw $\tilde{\theta}$ from $p(\theta|\mathcal{F}_t)$. Second, simulate a trajectory of observations $Y^*_{1:T}$ from the DSGE model conditional on $\tilde{\theta}$. The simulated trajectories can be converted into sample statistics of interest, $\mathcal{S}(Y^*_{1:T})$, such as the sample correlation between output and hours worked, to obtain an approximation for predictive distributions of sample moments. Finally, one can compute the value of the statistic $\mathcal{S}(Y_{1:T})$ based on the actual data and assess how far it lies in the tails of its predictive distribution. If $\mathcal{S}(Y_{1:T})$ is located far in the tails, one concludes that the model has difficulties explaining the observed patterns in the data.

The goal of prior predictive checks is to determine whether the model is able to capture salient features of the data. Because the prior predictive distribution conveys the implications of models without having to develop methods for formal posterior inference, prior predictive checks can be very useful at an early stage of model development. Canova (1994) was the first author to use prior predictive checks to assess the implications of a stochastic growth model driven solely by a technology shock. Prior predictive distributions are closely related to marginal likelihoods. A comparison of (7.79) and (7.80) for $t = 0$ indicates that the two expressions are identical. The prior predictive check assesses whether the density that the Bayesian model assigns *a priori* to the observed data is high or low. One can make the procedure more easily interpretable by replacing the high-dimensional data matrix Y with a low-dimensional statistic $\mathcal{S}(Y)$.

In posterior predictive checks, the distribution of the parameters, $p(\theta|\mathcal{F}_T)$, is conditioned on the observed data $Y_{1:T}$. In its core, the posterior predictive check works like a frequentist specification test. If $\mathcal{S}(Y_{1:T})$ falls into the tails (or low-density region) of the predictive distribution derived from the estimated model, then the model is discredited. Chang et al. (2007) use posterior predictive checks to determine whether a stochastic growth model, similar to the one analyzed in this section, is able to capture the observed persistence of hours worked.

4.7.3 VARs as reference models

Vector autoregressions play an important role in the assessment of DSGE models, since they provide a more richly parameterized benchmark. We consider three approaches to using VARs for the assessment of DSGE models.

Models of Moments Geweke (2010) points out that many DSGE models are too stylized to deliver a realistic distribution for the data Y that is usable for likelihood-based inference. Instead, these models are designed to capture certain underlying population moments, such as the volatilities of output growth, hours worked, and the correlation between these two variables. Suppose we collect these population moments in the vector φ, which in turn is a function of the DSGE model parameters θ. Thus, a prior distribution for θ induces a model-specific distribution for the population characteristics, denoted by $p(\varphi|\mathcal{M}_i)$. At the same time, the researcher considers a VAR as reference model $\mathcal{M}_0$ that is meant to describe the data and at the same time delivers predictions about φ. Let $p(\varphi|Y,\mathcal{M}_0)$ denote the posterior distribution of population characteristics as obtained from the VAR. Geweke (2010) shows that

$$\frac{\pi_{1,0}\int p(\varphi|\mathcal{M}_1)p(\varphi|Y,\mathcal{M}_0)d\varphi}{\pi_{2,0}\int p(\varphi|\mathcal{M}_2)p(\varphi|Y,\mathcal{M}_0)d\varphi} \tag{7.81}$$

can be interpreted as the odds ratio of $\mathcal{M}_1$ versus $\mathcal{M}_2$ conditional on the reference model $\mathcal{M}_0$. The numerator in (7.81) is large if there is a strong overlap between the predictive densities for φ between DSGE model $\mathcal{M}_1$ and VAR $\mathcal{M}_0$. The ratio formalizes the confidence interval overlap criterion proposed by DeJong et al. (1996) and has been used, for instance, to examine the asset-pricing implications of DSGE models. In practice, the densities $p(\varphi|\mathcal{M}_i)$ and $p(\varphi|Y,\mathcal{M}_0)$ can be approximated by Kernel density estimates based on draws of φ. Draws of φ can be obtained by transforming draws of the DSGE model and VAR parameters, respectively.

Loss-Function-Based Evaluation Schorfheide (2000) proposes a Bayesian framework for a loss function-based evaluation of DSGE models. As in Geweke (2010)'s framework, the researcher is interested in the relative ability of two DSGE models to capture a certain set of population moments φ, which are transformations of model parameters θ. Unlike in Geweke (2010), the DSGE models are assumed to deliver a probability distribution for the data Y. Suppose there are two DSGE models, $\mathcal{M}_1$ and $\mathcal{M}_2$, and a VAR that serves as a reference model $\mathcal{M}_0$. The first step of the analysis consists of computing model-specific posterior predictive distributions $p(\varphi|Y,\mathcal{M}_i)$ and posterior model probabilities $\pi_{i,T}$, $i=0,1,2$. Second, one can form a predictive density for φ by averaging across the three models

$$p(\varphi|Y)=\sum_{i=0,1,2}\pi_{i,T}p(\varphi|Y,\mathcal{M}_i). \tag{7.82}$$

If, say, DSGE model $\mathcal{M}_1$ is well specified and attains a high posterior probability, then the predictive distribution is dominated by $\mathcal{M}_1$. If, however, none of the DSGE models fits well, then the predictive density is dominated by the VAR. Third, one specifies a loss function $L(\hat{\varphi},\varphi)$, for example $L(\hat{\varphi},\varphi)=\|\hat{\varphi}-\varphi\|^2$, under which a point prediction $\hat{\varphi}$ of φ is to be evaluated. For each DSGE model, the prediction $\hat{\varphi}_{(i)}$ is computed by minimizing the expected loss under the DSGE model-specific posterior:

$$\hat{\varphi}_{(i)}=\text{argmin}_{\tilde{\varphi}}\int L(\tilde{\varphi},\varphi)p(\varphi|Y,\mathcal{M}_i)d\varphi,\quad i=1,2.$$

Finally one can compare DSGE models $\mathcal{M}_1$ and $\mathcal{M}_2$ based on the posterior expected loss $\int L(\hat{\varphi}_{(i)},\varphi)p(\varphi|Y)d\varphi$, computed under the overall posterior distribution (7.82) that averages the predictions of the reference model and all DSGE models. In this procedure, if the DSGE models are poorly specified, the evaluation is loss-function dependent, whereas the model ranking becomes effectively loss-function independent if one of the DSGE models has a posterior probability that is close to one.

DSGE-VARs Building on work by Ingram and Whiteman (1994), Del Negro and Schorfheide (2004) link DSGE models and VARs by constructing families of prior distributions that are more or less tightly concentrated in the vicinity of the restrictions that a DSGE model implies for the coefficients of a VAR. We will refer to such a model as DSGE-VAR. The starting point is the VAR specified in Equation (7.1). Assuming that the data have been transformed such that y_t is stationary, let $\mathbb{E}^D_\theta[\cdot]$ be the expectation under the DSGE model conditional on parameterization θ and define the autocovariance matrices

$$\Gamma_{XX}(\theta) = \mathbb{E}^D_\theta[x_t x_t'], \quad \Gamma_{XY}(\theta) = \mathbb{E}^D_\theta[x_t y_t'].$$

A VAR approximation of the DSGE model can be obtained from the following restriction functions that relate the DSGE model parameters to the VAR parameters:

$$\Phi^*(\theta) = \Gamma^{-1}_{XX}(\theta)\Gamma_{XY}(\theta), \quad \Sigma^*(\theta) = \Gamma_{YY}(\theta) - \Gamma_{YX}(\theta)\Gamma^{-1}_{XX}(\theta)\Gamma_{XY}(\theta). \qquad (7.83)$$

To account for potential misspecification of the DSGE model, we now use a prior distribution that, while centered at $\Phi^*(\theta)$ and $\Sigma^*(\theta)$, allows for deviations of Φ and Σ from the restriction functions:

$$\Phi, \Sigma|\theta \sim MNIW\Big(\Phi^*(\theta), [\lambda T\Gamma_{XX}(\theta)]^{-1}, \lambda T\Sigma^*(\theta), \lambda T - k\Big). \qquad (7.84)$$

This prior distribution can be interpreted as a posterior calculated from a sample of $T^* = \lambda T$ artificial observations generated from the DSGE model with parameters θ. Here, λ is a hyperparameter, and T denotes the actual sample size.

The next step is to turn the reduced-form VAR into a structural VAR. According to the DSGE model, the one-step-ahead forecast errors u_t are functions of the structural shocks ϵ_t, that is $u_t = \Sigma_{tr}\Omega\epsilon_t$, see (7.21). Let $A_0(\theta)$ be the contemporaneous impact of ϵ_t on y_t according to the DSGE model. With a QR factorization, the initial response of y_t to the structural shocks can be uniquely decomposed into

$$\left(\frac{\partial y_t}{\partial \epsilon_t'}\right)_{DSGE} = A_0(\theta) = \Sigma^*_{tr}(\theta)\Omega^*(\theta), \qquad (7.85)$$

where $\Sigma^*_{tr}(\theta)$ is lower-triangular and $\Omega^*(\theta)$ is an orthogonal matrix. The initial impact of ϵ_t on y_t in the VAR, in contrast, is given by

$$\left(\frac{\partial y_t}{\partial \epsilon_t'}\right)_{VAR} = \Sigma_{tr}\Omega. \qquad (7.86)$$

To identify the DSGE-VAR, we maintain the triangularization of its covariance matrix Σ and replace the rotation Ω in (7.86) with the function $\Omega^*(\theta)$ that appears in (7.85). The rotation matrix is chosen such that, in absence of misspecification, the DSGE's and the DSGE-VAR's impulse responses to all shocks approximately coincide. To the extent that misspecification is mainly in the dynamics, as opposed to the covariance matrix of innovations, the identification procedure can be interpreted as matching, at least qualitatively, the posterior short-run responses of the VAR with those from the DSGE model.

The final step is to specify a prior distribution for the DSGE model parameters θ, which can follow the same elicitation procedure that was used when the DSGE model was estimated directly. Thus, we obtain the hierarchical model

$$p_\lambda(Y, \Phi, \Sigma, \theta) = p(Y|\Phi, \Sigma)p_\lambda(\Phi, \Sigma|\theta)p(\Omega|\theta)p(\theta), \tag{7.87}$$

with the understanding that the distribution of $\Omega|\theta$ is a point mass at $\Omega^*(\theta)$. Since Φ and Σ can be conveniently integrated out, we can first draw from the marginal posterior of θ and then from the conditional distribution of (Φ, Σ) given θ. This leads to the following algorithm.

Algorithm 4.3. Posterior Draws for DSGE-VAR

(1) Use Algorithm 4.1 to generate a sequence of draws $\theta^{(s)}$, $s = 1, \dots, n_{sim}$, from the posterior distribution of θ, given by $p_\lambda(\theta|Y) \propto p_\lambda(Y|\theta)p(\theta)$. The marginal likelihood $p_\lambda(Y|\theta)$ is obtained by straightforward modification of (7.15). Moreover, compute $\Omega^{(s)} = \Omega^*(\theta^{(s)})$.

(2) For $s = 1, \dots, n_{sim}$: draw a pair $(\Phi^{(s)}, \Sigma^{(s)})$ from its conditional MNIW posterior distribution given $\theta^{(s)}$. The MNIW distribution can be obtained by the modification of (7.8) described in Section 2.2. □

Since the empirical performance of the DSGE-VAR procedure crucially depends on the weight placed on the DSGE model restrictions, it is useful to consider a data-driven procedure to select λ. As in the context of the Minnesota prior, a natural criterion for the choice of λ is the marginal data density

$$p_\lambda(Y) = \int p_\lambda(Y|\theta)p(\theta)d\theta. \tag{7.88}$$

For computational reasons, it is convenient to restrict the hyperparameter to a finite grid Λ. If one assigns equal prior probability to each grid point, then the normalized $p_\lambda(Y)$'s can be interpreted as posterior probabilities for λ. Del Negro et al. (2007) emphasize that the posterior of λ provides a measure of fit for the DSGE model: high posterior probabilities for large values of λ indicate that the model is well specified and that a lot of weight should be placed on its implied restrictions. Define

$$\hat{\lambda} = \text{argmax}_{\lambda \in \Lambda}\, p_\lambda(Y). \tag{7.89}$$

If $p_\lambda(Y)$ peaks at an intermediate value of λ, say, between 0.5 and 2, then a comparison between DSGE-VAR($\hat{\lambda}$) and DSGE model impulse responses can potentially yield important insights about the misspecification of the DSGE model. The DSGE-VAR approach was designed to improve forecasting and monetary policy analysis with VARs. The framework has also been used as a tool for model evaluation and comparison in Del Negro et al. (2007) and for policy analysis with potentially misspecified DSGE models in Del Negro and Schorfheide (2009).

4.8 DSGE models in applied work

Much of the empirical analysis with DSGE models is conducted with Bayesian methods. Since the literature is fairly extensive and rapidly growing, we do not attempt to provide a survey of the empirical work. Instead, we will highlight a few important contributions and discuss how Bayesian analysis has contributed to the proliferation of estimated DSGE models. The first published papers that conduct Bayesian inference in DSGE models are DeJong et al. (2000), Schorfheide (2000), and Otrok (2001). Smets and Wouters (2003) document that a DSGE model that is built around the neoclassical growth model presented previously and enriched by habit formation in consumption, capital adjustment costs, variable factor utilization, nominal price and wage stickiness, behavioral rules for government spending and monetary policy, and numerous exogenous shocks could deliver a time-series fit and forecasting performance for a vector of key macroeconomic variables that is comparable to a VAR. Even though posterior odds comparison, literally taken, often favors VARs, the theoretical coherence and the ease with which model implications can be interpreted make DSGE models an attractive competitor.

One reason for the rapid adoption of Bayesian methods is the ability to incorporate nonsample information, meaning data that do not enter the likelihood function, through the use of prior distributions. Many of the priors used by Smets and Wouters (2003) as well as in subsequent work are fairly informative, and over the past five years the literature has become more careful about systematically documenting the specification of prior distributions in view of the available nonsample information. From a purely computational perspective, this kind of prior information often tends to smooth out the shape of the posterior density, which improves the performance of posterior simulators. Once parameter draws have been obtained, they can be easily converted into objects of interest. For instance, Justiniano et al. (2009) study the relative importance of investment-specific technology shocks and thereby provide posterior distributions of the fraction of the business-cycle variation of key macroeconomic variables explained by these shocks.

A large part of the literature tries to assess the importance of various propagation mechanisms that are useful for explaining observed business-cycle fluctuations. Bayesian posterior model probabilities are widely employed to compare competing model specifications. For instance, Rabanal and Rubio-Ramírez (2005) compare the relative importance of wage and price rigidities. Unlike standard frequentist likelihood ratio tests, posterior odds remain applicable, even if the model specifications under consideration are nonnested, for example, a DSGE model with sticky wages versus a DSGE model with sticky prices.

DSGE models with nominal rigidities are widely used to analyze monetary policy. This analysis might consist of determining the range of policy rule coefficients that guarantees a unique stable rational expectations solution and suppresses self-fulfilling expectations, of choosing interest-rate feedback rule parameters that maximize the welfare of a representative agent or minimizes a convex combination of inflation and output-gap volatility, or in finding a welfare-maximizing mapping between the underlying state variables of the economy and the policy instruments. The solution to these optimal policy problems always depends on the unknown taste and technology parameters. The Bayesian framework enables researchers and policy makers to take this parameter uncertainty into account by maximizing posterior expected welfare. A good example of this line of work is the paper by Levin et al. (2006). Several central banks have adopted DSGE models as tools for macroeconomic forecasting, for example, Adolfson et al. (2007) and Edge et al. (2009). An important advantage of the Bayesian methods described in this section is that they deliver predictive distributions for the future path of macroeconomic variables that reflect both parameter uncertainty and uncertainty about the realization of future exogenous shocks.

5 Time-Varying Parameters Models

The parameters of the models presented in the preceding sections were assumed to be time-invariant, implying that economic relationships are stable. In Figure 7.7, we plot quarterly US GDP-deflator inflation from 1960 to 2006. Suppose one adopts the view that the inflation rate can be decomposed into a target inflation, set by the central bank, and some stochastic fluctuations around this target. The figure offers three views of US monetary history. First, it is conceivable that the target rate was essentially constant between 1960 and 2006, but there were times, for instance, the 1970s, when the central bank let the actual inflation deviate substantially from the target. An alternative interpretation is that throughout the 1970s the Fed tried to exploit an apparent trade-off between unemployment and inflation and gradually revised its target upward. In the early 1980s, however, it realized that the long-run Phillips curve is essentially vertical and that the high inflation had led to a significant distortion of the economy. Under the chairmanship of Paul Volcker, the Fed decided to disinflate, that is, to reduce the target inflation rate. This time-variation in the target rate could be captured either by a slowly-varying autoregressive process or through a regime-switching process that shifts from a 2.5% target to a 7% target and back.

This section considers models that can capture structural changes in the economy. Model parameters either vary gradually over time according to a multivariate autoregressive process (Section 5.1), or they change abruptly as in Markov-switching or structural-break models (Section 5.2). The models discussed subsequently can be written in state-space form, and much of the technical apparatus needed for Bayesian inference can be found in Giordani et al. (Chapter 3 of this volume). We focus on placing the Time-Varying Parameters (TVP) models in the context of the empirical macroeconomics literature and discuss specific applications in Section 5.3. There are other

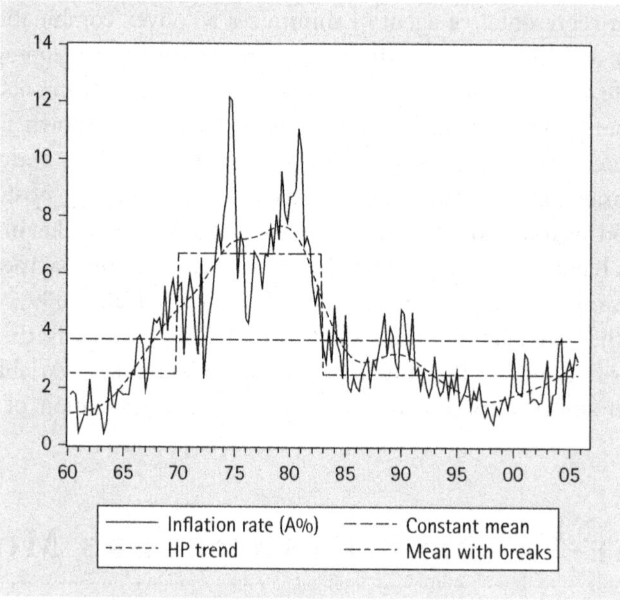

FIGURE 7.7 Inflation and measures of trend inflation

Notes: Inflation is measured as quarter-to-quarter changes in the log GDP deflator, scaled by 400 to convert it into annualized percentages (A%). The sample ranges from 1960:Q1 to 2005:Q4. HP trend refers to trend constructed with Hodrick-Prescott fitter (smoothing parameter $\lambda = 1600$).

important classes of nonlinear time-series models such as threshold vector autoregressive models (Geweke 1993; Koop and Potter 1999, for instance), in which the parameter change is linked directly to observables rather than to latent state variables. Due to space constraints, we are unable to discuss these models in this chapter.

5.1 Models with autoregressive coefficients

Most of the subsequent discussion is devoted to VARs with parameters that follow an autoregressive law of motion (Section 5.1.1). Whenever time-varying parameters are introduced into a DSGE model, an additional complication arises. For the model to be theoretically coherent, one should assume that the agents in the model are aware of the time-variation, say, in the coefficients of a monetary policy rule, and form their expectations and decision rules accordingly. Hence, the presence of time-varying parameters significantly complicates the solution of the DSGE model's equilibrium law of motion and requires the estimation of a nonlinear state-space model (Section 5.1.2).

5.1.1 Vector autoregressions

While VARs with time-varying coefficients were estimated with Bayesian methods almost two decades ago (see, for instance, Sims 1993), their current popularity in empirical macroeconomics is largely due to Cogley and Sargent (2002), who took advantage of the MCMC innovations in the 1990s. They estimated a VAR in which the coefficients follow unit-root autoregressive processes. The motivation for their work, as well as for the competing Markov-switching approach of Sims and Zha (2006) discussed in Section 5.2, arises from the interest in documenting time-varying features of business cycles in the United States and other countries.

Cogley and Sargent (2002) set out to investigate time-variation in US inflation persistence using a three-variable VAR with inflation, unemployment, and interest rates. The rationale for their reduced-form specification is provided by models in which the policy maker and/or agents in the private sector gradually learn about the dynamics of the economy and consequently adapt their behavior (see Sargent 1999). The central bank might adjust its target inflation rate in view of changing beliefs about the effectiveness of monetary policy, and the agents might slowly learn about the policy change. To the extent that this adjustment occurs gradually in every period, it can be captured by models in which the coefficients are allowed to vary in each period. Cogley and Sargent's (2002) work was criticized by Sims (2002a), who pointed out that the lack of time-varying volatility in their VAR may well bias the results in favor of finding changes in the dynamics. Cogley and Sargent (2005b) address this criticism of their earlier work by adding time-varying volatility to their model. Our subsequent exposition of a TVP VAR allows for drifts in both the conditional mean and the variance parameters.

Consider the reduced-form VAR in Equation (7.1), which we are reproducing here for convenience:

$$y_t = \Phi_1 y_{t-1} + \ldots + \Phi_p y_{t-p} + \Phi_c + u_t.$$

We defined $x_t = [y'_{t-1}, \ldots, y'_{t-p}, 1]'$ and $\Phi = [\Phi_1, \ldots, \Phi_p, \Phi_c]'$. Now let $X_t = I_n \otimes x_t$ and $\phi = vec(\Phi)$. Then we can write the VAR as

$$y_t = X'_t \phi_t + u_t, \tag{7.90}$$

where we replaced the vector of constant coefficients, ϕ, with a vector of time-varying coefficients, ϕ_t. We let the parameters evolve according to the random-walk process:

$$\phi_t = \phi_{t-1} + \nu_t, \quad \nu_t \sim iidN(0, Q). \tag{7.91}$$

We restrict the covariance matrix Q to be diagonal and the parameter innovations ν_t to be uncorrelated with the VAR innovations u_t. The u_t innovations are also normally distributed, but unlike in Section 2, their variance now evolves over time:

$$u_t \sim N(0, \Sigma_t), \quad \Sigma_t = B^{-1} H_t (B^{-1})'. \tag{7.92}$$

In the decomposition of Σ_t, the matrix B is a lower-triangular matrix with ones on the diagonal, and H_t is a diagonal matrix with elements $h^2_{i,t}$ following a geometric random walk:

$$\ln h_{i,t} = \ln h_{i,t-1} + \eta_{i,t}, \quad \eta_{i,t} \sim iidN(0, \sigma^2_i). \tag{7.93}$$

Notice that this form of stochastic volatility was also used in Section 4.5 to make the innovation variances for shocks in DSGE models time varying.

The prior distributions for Q and the σ_i's can be used to express beliefs about the magnitude of the period-to-period drift in the VAR coefficients and the changes in the volatility of the VAR innovations. In practice these priors are chosen to ensure that the shocks to (7.91) and (7.93) are small enough that the short- and medium-run dynamics of y_t are not swamped by the random-walk behavior of ϕ_t and H_t. If the prior distributions for ϕ_0, Q, B, and the σ_i's are conjugate, then one can use the following Gibbs sampler for posterior inference.

Algorithm 5.1. Gibbs Sampler for TVP VAR
For $s = 1, \ldots, n_{sim}$:

(1) Draw $\phi_{1:T}^{(s)}$ conditional on $(B^{(s-1)}, H_{1:T}^{(s-1)}, Q^{(s-1)}, \sigma_1^{(s-1)} \ldots \sigma_n^{(s-1)}, Y)$. Equations (7.90) and (7.91) provide a state-space representation for y_t. Thus, $\phi_{1:T}$ can be sampled using the algorithm developed by Carter and Kohn (1994), described in Giordani et al. (Chapter 3, this volume).

(2) Draw $B^{(s)}$ conditional on $(\phi_{1:T}^{(s)}, H_{1:T}^{(s-1)}, Q^{(s-1)}, \sigma_1^{(s-1)} \ldots \sigma_n^{(s-1)}, Y)$. Conditional on the VAR parameters ϕ_t, the innovations to equation (7.90) are known. According to (7.92), Bu_t is normally distributed with variance H_t:

$$Bu_t = H_t^{\frac{1}{2}} \epsilon_t, \tag{7.94}$$

where ϵ_t is a vector of standard normals. Thus, the problem of sampling from the posterior distribution of B under a conjugate prior is identical to the problem of sampling from the posterior distribution of A_0 in the structural VAR specification (7.30) described in detail in Section 2.4.2.

(3) Draw $H_{1:T}^{(s)}$ conditional on $(\phi_{1:T}^{(s)}, B^{(s)}, Q^{(s-1)}, \sigma_1^{(s-1)} \ldots \sigma_n^{(s-1)}, Y)$. Conditional on ϕ_t and B, we can write the i'th equation of (7.94) as $z_{i,t} = B_{(i.)}u_t \sim N(0, h_{i,t}^2)$, which is identical to (7.72). Thus, as in Section 4.5, one can use the algorithms of Jacquier et al. (1994) or Kim et al. (1998) to draw the sequences $h_{i,t:T}$.

(4) Draw $Q^{(s)}$ conditional on $(\phi_{1:T}^{(s)}, B^{(s)}, H_{1:T}^{(s)}, \sigma_1^{(s-1)} \ldots \sigma_n^{(s-1)}, Y)$ from the appropriate Inverted Wishart distribution derived from (7.91).

(5) Draw $\sigma_1^{(s)} \ldots \sigma_n^{s}$ conditional on $(\phi_{1:T}^{(s)}, B^{(s)}, H_{1:T}^{(s)}, Q^{(s)}, Y)$ from the appropriate Inverted Gamma distributions derived from (7.93). □

For the initial vector of VAR coefficients, ϕ_0, Cogley and Sargent (2002) and Cogley and Sargent (2005b) use a prior of the form $\phi_0 \sim N(\underline{\phi}_0, \underline{V}_0)$, where $\underline{\phi}_0$ and $\underline{V}_0$ are obtained by estimating a fixed-coefficient VAR with a flat prior on a presample. Del Negro (2003) advocates the use of a shrinkage prior with tighter variance than Cogley and Sargent's to partly overcome the problem of overfitting. Imposing the restriction that for each t, all roots of the characteristic polynomial associated with the VAR coefficients ϕ_t lie outside the unit circle introduces a complication that we do not explore here. Koop and Potter (2008) discuss how to impose such a restriction efficiently.

Primiceri (2005) extends the above TVP VAR by also allowing the nonzero off-diagonal elements of the contemporaneous covariance matrix B to evolve as random-walk processes. If one is willing to assume that the lower-triangular B_t's identify structural shocks, then this model generalizes the constant-coefficient structural SVAR discussed in Section 2.4 with $\Omega = I$ to a TVP environment. Primiceri (2005) uses a structural TVP VAR for interest rates, inflation, and unemployment to estimate a time-varying monetary policy rule for the postwar United States. Del Negro (2003) suggests an alternative approach, where time-variation is directly imposed on the parameters of the structural model—that is, the parameters of the VAR in equation (7.30). Finally, no cointegration restrictions are imposed on the VAR specified in (7.90). A Bayesian analysis of a TVP cointegration model can be found in Koop et al. (2008).

5.1.2 DSGE models with drifting parameters

Recall the stochastic growth model introduced in Section 4.1. Suppose that one changes the objective function of the household to

$$\mathbb{E}_t\left[\sum_{s=0}^{\infty}\beta^{t+s}\left(\ln C_{t+s} - \frac{(H_{t+s}/B)^{1+1/\nu}}{1+1/\nu}\right)\right]. \tag{7.95}$$

We can interpret our original objective function (7.52) as a generalization of (7.95), in which we have replaced the constant parameter B, which affects the disutility associated with working, by a time-varying parameter B_t. But in our discussion of the DSGE model in Section 4.1, we never mentioned time-varying parameters; we simply referred to B_t as a labor supply or preference shock. Thus, a time-varying parameter is essentially just another shock.

If the DSGE model is log-linearized, as in (7.66), then all structural shocks (or time-varying coefficients) appear additively in the equilibrium conditions. For instance, the preference shock appears in the labor supply function

$$\widehat{H}_t = \nu\widehat{W}_t - \nu\widehat{C}_t + (1+\nu)\widehat{B}_t. \tag{7.96}$$

Now imagine replacing the constant Frisch elasticity ν in (7.52) and (7.95) by a time-varying process ν_t. In a log-linear approximation of the equilibrium conditions, the time-varying elasticity will appear as an additional additive shock in (7.96) and therefore be indistinguishable in its dynamic effects from B_t; provided that the steady-state ratio $H_*/B_* \neq 1$. If $H_*/B_* = 1$, then ν_t has no effects on the first-order dynamics. Thus, for additional shocks or time-varying parameters to be identifiable, it is important that the log-linear approximation be replaced by a nonlinear solution technique. Fernández-Villaverde and Rubio-Ramírez (2008) take a version of the constant-coefficient DSGE model estimated by Smets and Wouters (2003) and allow for time variation in the coefficients that determine the interest-rate policy of the central bank and the degree of price and wage stickiness in the economy. To capture the different effects of a typical monetary policy shock and a shock that changes the central bank's reaction to deviations from the inflation target, for instance, the authors use a second-order perturbation method to solve the model and the particle filter to approximate its likelihood function. Thus, the topic of DSGE models with time-varying autoregressive parameters has essentially been covered in Section 4.6.

5.2 Models with Markov-switching parameters

Markov-switching (MS) models represent an alternative to drifting autoregressive coefficients in time-series models with time-varying parameters. MS models are able to capture sudden changes in time-series dynamics. Recall the two different representations of a time-varying target inflation rate in Figure 7.7. The piecewise constant path of the target can be generated by a MS model but not by the drifting-parameter model of the previous subsection. We will begin with a discussion of MS coefficients in the context of a VAR (Section 5.2.1) and then consider the estimation of DSGE models with MS parameters (Section 5.2.2).

5.2.1 *Markov-switching VARs*

MS models have been popularized in economics by the work of Hamilton (1989), who used them to allow for different GDP-growth-rate dynamics in recession and expansion states. We will begin by adding regime-switching to the coefficients of the reduced-form VAR specified in (7.1), which we write in terms of a multivariate linear regression model as

$$y_t' = x_t'\Phi(K_t) + u_t', \quad u_t \sim iidN(0, \Sigma(K_t)) \tag{7.97}$$

using the same definitions of Φ and x_t as in Section 2.1. Unlike before, the coefficient vector Φ is now a function of K_t. Here, K_t is a discrete M-state Markov process with time-invariant transition probabilities

$$\pi_{lm} = P[K_t = l \mid K_{t-1} = m], \quad l, m \in \{1, \ldots, M\}.$$

For simplicity, suppose that $M = 2$ and all elements of $\Phi(K_t)$ and $\Sigma(K_t)$ switch simultaneously, without any restrictions. We denote the values of the VAR parameter matrices in state $K_t = l$ by $\Phi(l)$ and $\Sigma(l)$, $l = 1, 2$, respectively. If the prior distributions of $(\Phi(l), \Sigma(l))$ are MNIW and the priors for the regime-switching probabilities π_{11} and π_{22} are independent Beta distributions, then posterior inference in this simple MS VAR model can be implemented with the following Gibbs sampler:

Algorithm 5.2. Gibbs Sampler for Unrestricted MS VARs

For $s = 1, \ldots, n_{sim}$:

(1) Draw $(\Phi^{(s)}(l), \Sigma^{(s)}(l))$ conditional on $(K_{1:T}^{(i-1)}, \pi_{11}^{(i-1)}, \pi_{22}^{(i-1)}, Y)$. Let $\mathcal{T}_l$ be a set that contains the time periods when $K_t = l$, $l = 1, 2$. Under a conjugate prior, the pos-

terior of $\Phi(l)$ and $\Sigma(l)$ is MNIW, obtained from the regression $y_t' = x_t'\Phi(l) + u_t$, $u_t \sim N(0, \Sigma(l)), t \in \mathcal{T}_l$.

(2) Draw $K_{1:T}^{(s)}$ conditional on $(\Phi^{(s)}(l), \Sigma^{(s)}(l), \pi_{11}^{(i-1)}, \pi_{22}^{(i-1)}, Y)$ using a variant of the Carter and Kohn (1994) approach, described in detail in Giordani et al. (Chapter 3, this volume).

(3) Draw $\pi_{11}^{(s)}$ and $\pi_{22}^{(s)}$ conditional on $(\Phi^{(s)}(s), \Sigma^{(s)}(s), K_{1:T}^{(s)}, Y)$. If one ignores the relationship between the transition probabilities and the distribution of K_1, then the posteriors of $\pi_{11}^{(s)}$ and $\pi_{22}^{(s)}$ take the form of Beta distributions. If K_1 is distributed according to the stationary distribution of the Markov chain, then the Beta distributions can be used as proposal distributions in a Metropolis step. □

If one imposes the condition that $\pi_{22} = 1$ and $\pi_{12} = 0$, then model (7.97) becomes a change-point model in which state 2 is the final state.[4] Alternatively, such a model can be viewed as a structural-break model in which at most one break can occur, but the time of the break is unknown. Kim and Nelson (1999a) use a changepoint model to study whether there has been a structural break in postwar US GDP growth toward stabilization. By increasing the number of states and imposing the appropriate restrictions on the transition probabilities, one can generalize the changepoint model to allow for several breaks. Chopin and Pelgrin (2004) consider a setup that allows the joint estimation of the parameters and the number of regimes that have actually occurred in the sample period. Koop and Potter (2007 and 2009) explore posterior inference in changepoint models under various types of prior distributions. Koop et al. (2009) consider a modification of Primiceri (2005)'s framework where parameters evolve according to a changepoint model and study the evolution over time of the monetary policy transmission mechanism in the United States.

In a multivariate setting, the unrestricted MS VAR in (7.97) with coefficient matrices that are a priori independent across states may involve a large number of coefficients, and parameter restrictions can compensate for lack of sample information. For instance, Paap and van Dijk (2003) start from the VAR specification used in Section 2.3 that expresses y_t as a deterministic trend and autoregressive deviations from this trend. The authors impose the restriction that only the trend is affected by the MS process:

$$y_t = y_t^* + \Gamma_0(K_t) + \widetilde{y}_t, \quad \widetilde{y}_t = \Phi_1\widetilde{y}_{t-1} + \ldots + \Phi_p\widetilde{y}_{t-p} + u_t, \quad u_t \sim iidN(0, \Sigma), \tag{7.98}$$

where

$$y_t^* = y_{t-1}^* + \Gamma_1(K_t).$$

This model captures growth-rate differentials between recessions and expansions and is used to capture the joint dynamics of U.S. aggregate output and consumption.

[4] More generally, for a process with M states, one would impose the restrictions $\pi_{MM} = 1$ and $\pi_{j+1,j} + \pi_{jj} = 1$.

Thus far, we have focused on reduced-form VARs with MS parameters. Sims and Zha (2006) extend the structural VAR given in (7.30) to a MS setting:

$$y_t' A_0(K_t) = x_t' A(K_t) + \epsilon_t', \quad \epsilon_t \sim iidN(0, I) \tag{7.99}$$

where ϵ_t is a vector of orthogonal structural shocks and x_t is defined as in Section 2.1. The authors reparameterize the $k \times n$ matrix $A(K_t)$ as $D(K_t) + GA_0(K_t)$, where G is a $k \times n$ with the $n \times n$ identity matrix in the first n rows and zeros elsewhere. Thus,

$$y_t' A_0(K_t) = x_t'(D(K_t) + GA_0(K_t)) + \epsilon_t'. \tag{7.100}$$

If $D(K_t) = 0$, then the reduced-form VAR coefficients are given by $\Phi = A(K_t)[A_0(K_t)]^{-1} = G$ and the elements of y_t follow random-walk processes, as implied by the mean of the Minnesota prior (see Section 2.2). Loosely speaking, if the prior for $D(K_t)$ is centered at zero, the prior for the reduced-form VAR is centered at a random-walk representation.

To avoid a proliferation of parameters, Sims and Zha (2006) impose constraints on the evolution of $D(K_t)$ across states. Let $d_{i,j,l}$ correspond to the coefficient associated with lag l of variable i in equation j. The authors impose that $d_{i,j,l}(K_t) = \delta_{i,j,l}\lambda_{i,j}(K_t)$. This specification allows for shifts in $D(K_t)$ to be equation or variable dependent but rules out lag dependency. The authors use their setup to estimate MS VAR specifications in which (i) only the coefficients of the monetary policy rule change across Markov states, (ii) only the coefficients of the private-sector equations switch, and (iii) only coefficients that implicitly control innovation variances (heteroskedasticity) change. The Gibbs sampler for the parameters of (7.100) is obtained by merging and generalizing Algorithms 2.4 and 5.2. Details are provided in Sims et al. (2008).

5.2.2 DSGE models with Markov-switching coefficients

A growing number of papers incorporate Markov-switching effects in DSGE models. Consider the nonlinear equilibrium conditions of our stochastic growth model in (7.61). The most rigorous and general treatment of Markov-switching coefficients would involve replacing the vector θ with a function of the latent state K_t, $\theta(K_t)$, and solving the nonlinear model while accounting for the time variation in θ. Since the implementation of the solution and the subsequent computation of the likelihood function are very challenging, the literature has focused on various short-cuts, which introduce Markov-switching in the coefficients of the linearized model given by (7.66).

Following Sims (2002b), we write the linearized equilibrium conditions of the DSGE model in the following canonical form:

$$\Gamma_0(\theta)x_t = C(\theta) + \Gamma_1(\theta)x_{t-1} + \Psi(\theta)\epsilon_t + \Pi(\theta)\eta_t. \tag{7.101}$$

For the stochastic growth model presented in Section 4, θ is defined in (7.63), and the vector x_t can be defined as follows:

$$x_t = \left[\widehat{C}_t, \widehat{H}_t, \widehat{W}_t, \widehat{Y}_t, \widehat{R}_t, \widehat{I}_t, \widehat{K}_{t+1}, \widehat{A}_t, \widehat{a}_t, \widehat{B}_t, \mathbb{E}_t[\widehat{C}_{t+1}], \mathbb{E}_t[\widehat{a}_{t+1}], \mathbb{E}_t[\widehat{R}_{t+1}]\right]'.$$

The vector η_t comprises the following one-step-ahead rational expectations forecast errors:

$$\eta_t = \left[(\widehat{C}_t - \mathbb{E}_{t-1}[\widehat{C}_t]), (\widehat{a}_t - \mathbb{E}_{t-1}[\widehat{a}_t]), (\widehat{R}_t - \mathbb{E}_{t-1}[\widehat{R}_t])\right]'$$

and ϵ_t stacks the innovations of the exogenous shocks: $\epsilon_t = [\epsilon_{a,t}, \epsilon_{b,t}]'$. With these definitions, it is straightforward, albeit slightly tedious, to rewrite (7.66) in terms of the canonical form (7.101). In most applications, including our stochastic growth model, one can define the vector x_t such that the observables y_t can, as in Section 4.2, be expressed simply as a linear function of x_t; that is:

$$y_t = \Psi_0(\theta) + \Psi_1(\theta)t + \Psi_2(\theta)x_t. \tag{7.102}$$

Markov-switching can be introduced into the linearized DSGE model by expressing the DSGE model parameters θ as a function of a hidden Markov process K_t, which we denote by $\theta(K_t)$.

Schorfheide (2005) considers a special case of this Markov-switching linear rational expectations framework, because in his analysis the process K_t affects only the target inflation rate of the central bank, which can be low or high. Using the same notation as in Section 5.2.1, the number of states is $M = 2$, and the state transition probabilities are denoted by π_{lm}. If we partition the parameter vector $\theta(K_t)$ into a component θ_1 that is unaffected by the hidden Markov process K_t and a component $\theta_2(K_t)$ that varies with K_t and takes the values $\theta_2(l)$, $l = 1, 2$, the resulting rational expectations system can be written as

$$\Gamma_0(\theta_1)x_t = C(\theta_1, \theta_2(K_t)) + \Gamma_1(\theta_1)x_{t-1} + \Psi(\theta_1)\epsilon_t + \Pi(\theta_1)\eta_t \tag{7.103}$$

and is solvable with the algorithm provided in Sims (2002b). The solution takes the special form

$$y_t = \Psi_0 + \Psi_1 t + \Psi_2 x_t, \quad x_t = \Phi_1 x_{t-1} + \Phi_\epsilon[\mu(K_t) + \epsilon_t] + \Phi_0(K_t), \tag{7.104}$$

where only Φ_0 and μ depend on the Markov process K_t (indirectly through $\theta_2(K_t)$), but not the matrices Ψ_0, Ψ_1, Ψ_2, Φ_1, and Φ_ϵ. Equation (7.104) defines a (linear) Markov-switching state-space model, with the understanding that the system matrices are functions of the DSGE model parameters θ_1 and $\theta_2(K_t)$. Following a filtering approach that simultaneously integrates over x_t and K_t, discussed in Kim and Nelson (1999b), Schorfheide (2005) constructs an approximate likelihood that depends only on θ_1, $\theta_2(1)$, $\theta_2(2)$, and the transition probabilities π_{11} and π_{22}. This likelihood function is then used in Algorithm 4.1 to implement posterior inference.

The analysis in Schorfheide (2005) is clearly restrictive. For instance, there is a large debate in the literature about whether the central bank's reaction to inflation and output deviations from target changed around 1980. A candidate explanation for the reduction of macroeconomic volatility in the 1980s is a more forceful reaction of central banks to inflation deviations. To capture this explanation in a Markov-switching rational expectations model, it is necessary that not just the intercept in (7.101) but also the slope coefficients be affected by the regime shifts. Thus, subsequent work by Davig and Leeper (2007) and Farmer et al. (2009) is more ambitious in that it allows for switches in all the matrices of the canonical rational expectations model:

$$\Gamma_0(\theta(K_t))x_t = C(\theta(K_t)) + \Gamma_1(\theta(K_t))x_{t-1} + \Psi(\theta(K_t))\epsilon_t + \Pi(\theta(K_t))\eta_t.$$

Characterizing the full set of solutions for this general MS linear rational expectations model and conditions under which a unique stable solution exists is the subject of ongoing research.

5.3 Applications of Bayesian TVP models

Bayesian TVP models have been applied to several issues of interest, including macroeconomic forecasting, for example, Sims (1993) and Cogley et al. (2005). Here, we shall focus on one specific issue, namely, the debate over whether the dynamics of US inflation changed over the last quarter of the 20th century and, to the extent that they have, whether monetary policy played a major role in affecting inflation dynamics. Naturally, this debate evolved in parallel to the debate over the magnitude and causes of the Great Moderation, that is, the decline in the volatility of business cycles around 1984 initially documented by Kim and Nelson (1999a) and McConnell and Perez-Quiros (2000). Whatever the causes of the changes in output dynamics were—shocks, monetary policy, or other structural changes—it is likely that these same causes affected the dynamics of inflation.

Bayesian inference in a TVP VAR yields posterior estimates of the reduced-form coefficients ϕ_t in (7.90). Conditioning on estimates of ϕ_t for various periods between 1960 and 2000, Cogley and Sargent (2002) compute the spectrum of inflation based on their VAR and use it as evidence that both inflation volatility and persistence have changed dramatically in the United States. Cogley and Sargent (2005b) find that their earlier empirical results are robust to time-variation in the volatility of shocks and argue that changes in the monetary policy rule are partly responsible for the changes in inflation dynamics. Based on an estimated structural TVP VAR, Primiceri (2005) argues that monetary policy has indeed changed since the 1980s but that the impact of these changes on the rest of the economy has been small. He claims that variation in the volatility of the shocks is the main cause for the lower volatility of both inflation and business cycles in the post-Volcker period. Sims and Zha (2006) conduct inference with a MS VAR and find no support for the hypothesis that the parameters of the monetary policy rule differed pre- and post-1980. To the contrary, they provide evidence that it was the behavior of the private sector that changed and that shock heteroskedasticity is important. Similarly, using an AR time-varying coefficients VAR identified with sign restrictions, Canova and Gambetti (2009) find little evidence that monetary policy has become more aggressive in responding to inflation since the early 1980s. Cogley and Sbordone (2008) use a TVP VAR to assess the stability of the New Keynesian Phillips curve during the past four decades.

Given the numerical difficulties of estimating nonlinear DSGE models, there currently exists less published empirical work based on DSGE models with time-varying coefficients. Two notable exceptions are the papers by Justiniano and Primiceri (2008) discussed in Section 4.5 and Fernández-Villaverde and Rubio-Ramírez (2008). The latter paper provides evidence that after 1980 the US central bank has changed interest rates more aggressively in response to deviations of inflation from the target rate. The authors also find that the estimated frequency of price changes has decreased over time. This frequency is taken as exogenous within the Calvo framework they adopt.

6 Models for Data-Rich Environments

We now turn to inference with models for data sets that have a large cross-sectional and time-series dimension. Consider the VAR(p) from Section 2:

$$y_t = \Phi_1 y_{t-1} + \ldots + \Phi_p y_{t-p} + \Phi_c + u_t, \quad u_t \sim iidN(0, \Sigma), \quad t = 1, \ldots, T,$$

where y_t is an $n \times 1$ vector. Without mentioning it explicitly, our previous analysis was tailored to situations in which the time-series dimension T of the data set is much larger than the cross-sectional dimension n. For instance, in Illustration 2.1 the time-series dimension was approximately $T = 160$ and the cross-sectional dimension was $n = 4$. This section focuses on applications in which the ratio T/n is relatively small, possibly less than 5.

High-dimensional VARs are useful for applications that involve large cross-sections of macroeconomic indicators for a particular country—for example, GDP and its components, industrial production, measures of employment and compensation, housing starts and new orders of capital goods, price indices, interest rates, consumer confidence measures, etc. Examples of such data sets can be found in Stock and Watson (1999 and 2002). Large-scale VARs are also frequently employed in the context of multicountry econometric modeling. For instance, to study international business cycles among OECD countries, y_t might be composed of aggregate output, consumption, investment, and employment for a group of 20 to 30 countries, which leads to $n > 80$.

In general, for the models considered in this section there will be a shortage of sample information to determine parameters, leading to imprecise inference and diffuse predictive distributions. Priors can be used to impose either hard or soft parameter restrictions and thereby to sharpen inference. Hard restrictions involve setting combinations of VAR coefficients equal to zero. For instance, Stock and Watson (2005), who study international business cycles using output data for the G7 countries, impose the restriction that in the equation for GDP growth in a given country enter only the trade-weighted averages of the other countries' GDP growth rates. Second, one could use very informative, yet nondegenerate, prior distributions for the many VAR coefficients, which is what is meant by soft restrictions. Both types of restrictions are discussed in Section 6.1. Finally, one could express y_t as a function of a lower-dimensional vector of variables called factors, possibly latent, that drive all the co-movement among the elements of y_t, plus a vector ζ_t of so-called idiosyncratic components, which evolve independently from one another. In such a setting, one needs only to parameterize the evolution of the factors, the impact of these on the observables y_t, and the evolution of the univariate idiosyncratic components, rather than the dynamic interrelationships among all the elements of the y_t vector. Factor models are explored in Section 6.2.

6.1 Restricted high-dimensional VARs

We begin by directly imposing hard restrictions on the coefficients of the VAR. As before, define the $k \times 1$ vector $x_t = [y'_{t-1}, \ldots, y'_{t-p}, 1]'$ and the $k \times n$ matrix $\Phi = [\Phi_1, \ldots, \Phi_p, \Phi_c]'$, where $k = np + 1$. Moreover, let $X_t = I_n \otimes x_t$ and $\phi = vec(\Phi)$ with dimensions $kn \times n$ and $kn \times 1$, respectively. Then we can write the VAR as

$$y_t = X_t' \phi + u_t, \quad u_t \sim iidN(0, \Sigma). \tag{7.105}$$

To incorporate the restrictions on ϕ, we reparameterize the VAR as follows:

$$\phi = M\theta. \tag{7.106}$$

θ is a vector of size $\kappa \ll nk$, and the $nk \times \kappa$ matrix M induces the restrictions by linking the VAR coefficients ϕ to the lower-dimensional parameter vector θ. The elements of M are known. For instance, M could be specified such that the coefficient in Equation i, $i = 1, .., n$, associated with the l'th lag of variable j is the sum of an equation-specific parameter, a variable-specific parameter, and a lag-specific parameter. Here, θ would comprise the set of all $n + n + p$ equation/variable/lag-specific parameters, and M would be an indicator matrix of zeros and ones that selects the elements of θ associated with each element of ϕ. The matrix M could also be specified to set certain elements of ϕ equal to zero and thereby exclude regressors from each of the n equations of the VAR. Since the relationship between ϕ and θ is linear, Bayesian inference in this restricted VAR under a Gaussian prior for θ and an Inverted Wishart prior for Σ is straightforward.

To turn the hard restrictions (7.106) into soft restrictions, one can construct a hierarchical model, in which the prior distribution for ϕ conditional on θ has a nonzero variance:

$$\phi = M\theta + \nu, \quad \nu \sim N(0, V), \tag{7.107}$$

where ν is an $nk \times 1$ vector with $nk \times nk$ covariance matrix V. The joint distribution of parameters and data can be factorized as

$$p(Y, \phi, \theta) = p(Y|\phi)p(\phi|\theta)p(\theta). \tag{7.108}$$

A few remarks are in order. First, (7.108) has the same form as the DSGE-VAR discussed in Section 4.7.3, except that the conditional distribution of ϕ given θ is centered at the simple linear restriction $M\theta$ rather than the rather complicated VAR approximation of a DSGE model. Second, (7.108) also nests the Minnesota prior discussed in Section 2.2, which can be obtained by using a degenerate distribution for θ concentrated at $\underline{\theta}$ with a suitable choice of M, $\underline{\theta}$, and V. Third, in practice the choice of the prior covariance matrix V is crucial for inference. In the context of the Minnesota prior and the DSGE-VAR, we expressed this covariance matrix in terms of a low-dimensional vector λ of hyperparameters such that $\|V(\lambda)\| \longrightarrow 0$ ($\|V(\lambda)\| \longrightarrow \infty$) as $\|\lambda\| \longrightarrow \infty$ ($\|\lambda\| \longrightarrow 0$) and recommended conditioning on a value of λ that maximizes the marginal likelihood function $p_\lambda(Y)$ over a suitably chosen grid.

Finally, since the discrepancy between the posterior mean estimate of ϕ and the restriction $M\theta$ can be reduced by increasing the hyperparameter λ, the resulting Bayes estimator of ϕ is often called a *shrinkage* estimator. De Mol et al. (2008) consider a covariance matrix V that in our notation takes the form $V = \Sigma \otimes (I_k/\lambda^2)$ and show that there is a tight connection between these shrinkage estimators and estimators of conditional mean functions obtained from factor models, which we will discuss below. They document empirically that with a suitably chosen shrinkage parameter the forecast performance of their Bayes predictor constructed from a large number of regressors is similar to the performance of a predictor obtained by regressing y_t on the first few principal components of the regressors x_t, as is often done in the factor model literature.

Canova and Ciccarelli (2009) allow the deviations of ϕ from the restricted subspace characterized by $M\theta$ to differ in each period t. Formally, they allow for time-variation in ϕ and let

$$\phi_t = M\theta + \nu_t, \quad \nu_t \sim iidN(0, V). \tag{7.109}$$

The deviations ν_t from the restriction $M\theta$ are assumed to be independent over time, which simplifies inference. In fact, the random deviations ν_t can be merged with the VAR innovations u_t, resulting in a model for which Bayesian inference is fairly straightforward to implement. Inserting (7.109) into (7.105), we obtain the system

$$y_t = (X_t'M)\theta + \zeta_t. \tag{7.110}$$

The $n \times \kappa$ matrix of regressors $X_t'M$ essentially contains weighted averages of the regressors, where the weights are given by the columns of M. The random vector ζ_t is given by $\zeta_t = X_t'\nu_t + u_t$ and, since x_t contains lagged values of y_t, forms a Martingale difference sequence with conditional covariance matrix $X_t'VX_t + \Sigma$. If one chooses a prior covariance matrix of the form $V = \Sigma \otimes (I_k/\lambda^2)$, then the covariance matrix of ζ_t reduces to $(1 + (x_t'x_t)/\lambda^2)\Sigma$. The likelihood function (conditional on the initial observations $Y_{-p+1:0}$) takes the convenient form

$$p(Y_{1:T}|\theta,\lambda) \propto \prod_{t=1}^{T} \Bigg[\big|(1 + (x_t'x_t)/\lambda^2)\Sigma\big|^{-1/2} \tag{7.111}$$
$$\times \exp\left\{ -\frac{1}{2(1 + (x_t'x_t)/\lambda^2)}(y_t - X_t'M\theta)'\Sigma^{-1}(y_t - X_t'M\theta) \right\} \Bigg],$$

and Bayesian inference under a conjugate prior for θ and Σ is straightforward.

Canova and Ciccarelli (2009) further generalize expression (7.109) by assuming that the vector θ is time-varying and follows a simple autoregressive law of motion. They discuss in detail how to implement Bayesian inference in this more general environment. The authors interpret the time-varying θ_t as a vector of latent factors. Their setting is therefore related to that of the factor models described in the next subsection. In multicountry VAR applications, M could be chosen such that y_t is a function of lagged country-specific variables and, say, average lagged output growth and unemployment across countries. If most of the variation in the elements of y_t is due to the cross-sectional averages, then the business cycles in the various countries are highly synchronized. Canova and Ciccarelli (2009) use their framework to study the convergence in business cycles among G7 countries.

6.2 Dynamic factor models

Factor models describe the dynamic behavior of a possibly large cross-section of observations as the sum of a few common components, which explain co-movements, and of series-specific components, which capture idiosyncratic dynamics of each series. While factor models have been part of the econometricians' toolbox for a long time—the *unobservable index* models by Sargent and Sims (1977) and Geweke (1977), for example—the contribution of Stock and Watson (1989) generated renewed interest in this class of models among macroeconomists. These authors use a factor model to exploit information from a large cross-section of macroeconomic time series for forecasting. While Stock and Watson (1989) employ maximum likelihood methods, Geweke and Zhou (1996) and Otrok and Whiteman (1998) conduct Bayesian inference with dynamic factor models (DFM). Our baseline version of the DFM is introduced in Section 6.2.1, and posterior inference is described in Section 6.2.2. Some applications are discussed in Section 6.2.3. Finally, Section 6.2.4 surveys various extensions of the basic DFM.

6.2.1 *Baseline specification*

A DFM decomposes the dynamics of n observables $y_{i,t}$, $i = 1, \ldots, n$, into the sum of two unobservable components:

$$y_{i,t} = a_i + \lambda_i f_t + \xi_{i,t}, \quad t = 1, \ldots, T. \tag{7.112}$$

Here, f_t is a $\kappa \times 1$ vector of factors that are common to all observables, and $\xi_{i,t}$ is an idiosyncratic process that is specific to each i. Moreover, a_i is a constant and λ_i is a $1 \times \kappa$ vector of loadings that links $y_{i,t}$ to the factor f_t. The factors follow a vector autoregressive process of order q:

$$f_t = \Phi_{0,1} f_{t-1} + \ldots + \Phi_{0,q} f_{t-q} + u_{0,t}, \quad u_{0,t} \sim iidN(0, \Sigma_0), \tag{7.113}$$

where Σ_0 and the $\Phi_{0,j}$ matrices are of dimension $\kappa \times \kappa$ and $u_{0,t}$ is a $\kappa \times 1$ vector of innovations. We use 0-subscripts to denote parameter matrices that describe the law of motion of the factors. The idiosyncratic components follow autoregressive processes of order p_i:

$$\xi_{i,t} = \phi_{i,1}\xi_{i,t-1} + \ldots + \phi_{i,p_i}\xi_{i,t-p_i} + u_{i,t}, \quad u_{i,t} \sim iidN(0, \sigma_i^2). \tag{7.114}$$

At all leads and lags, the $u_{i,t}$ innovations are independent across i and independent of the innovations to the law of motion of the factors $u_{0,t}$. These orthogonality assumptions are important to identifying the factor model, as they imply that all co-movements in the data arise from the factors.

Without further restrictions, the latent factors and the coefficient matrices of the DFM are not identifiable. One can premultiply f_t and its lags in (7.112) and (7.113) as well as $u_{0,t}$ by a $\kappa \times \kappa$ invertible matrix H and postmultiply the vectors λ_i and the matrices $\Phi_{0,j}$ by H^{-1}, without changing the distribution of the observables. There are several approaches to restricting the parameters of the DFM to normalize the factors and achieve identification. We will provide three specific examples in which we impose restrictions on Σ_0 and the first κ loading vectors stacked in the matrix

$$\Lambda_{1,\kappa} = \begin{bmatrix} \lambda_1 \\ \vdots \\ \lambda_\kappa \end{bmatrix}.$$

The loadings λ_i for $i > \kappa$ are always left unrestricted.

Example 6.1: Geweke and Zhou (1996) restrict $\Lambda_{1,\kappa}$ to be lower-triangular:

$$\Lambda_{1,\kappa} = \Lambda_{1,\kappa}^{tr} = \begin{bmatrix} X & 0 \cdots 0 & 0 \\ \vdots & \ddots & \vdots \\ X & X \cdots X & X \end{bmatrix}. \tag{7.115}$$

Here, X denotes an unrestricted element, and 0 denotes a zero restriction. The restrictions can be interpreted as follows. According to (7.115), factor $f_{2,t}$ does not affect $y_{1,t}$, factor $f_{3,t}$ does not affect $y_{1,t}$ and $y_{2,t}$, and so forth. However, these zero restrictions alone are not sufficient for identification because the factors and hence the matrices $\Phi_{0,j}$ and Σ_0 could still be transformed by pre- and postmultiplication of an arbitrary invertible lower-triangular $\kappa \times \kappa$ matrix H_{tr} without changing the distribution of the observables. Under this transformation, the factor innovations become $H_{tr}u_{0,t}$. Since Σ_0 can be expressed as the product of the unique lower-triangular Choleski factor $\Sigma_{0,tr}$ and its transpose, one can choose $H_{tr} = \Sigma_{0,tr}^{-1}$ such that the factor innovations reduce to a vector of independent standard Normals. To implement this normalization, we simply let

$$\Sigma_0 = I_\kappa. \tag{7.116}$$

Finally, the signs of the factors need to be normalized. Let $\lambda_{i,i}$, $i = 1, \ldots, \kappa$, be the diagonal elements of $\Lambda_{1,\kappa}$. The sign normalization can be achieved with a set of restrictions of the form

$$\lambda_{i,i} \geq 0, \quad i = 1, \ldots, \kappa. \tag{7.117}$$

Thus, (7.115), (7.116), and (7.117) provide a set of identifying restrictions. □

Example 6.2: Suppose we start from the normalization in the previous example and proceed with premultiplying the factors by the diagonal matrix H that is composed of the diagonal elements of $\Lambda_{1,\kappa}^{tr}$ in (7.115) and postmultiplying the loadings by H^{-1}. This transformation leads to a normalization in which $\Lambda_{1,\kappa}$ is restricted to be lower-triangular with ones on the diagonal and Σ_0 is a diagonal matrix with nonnegative elements. The one-entries on the diagonal of $\Lambda_{1,\kappa}$ also take care of the sign normalization. Since under the normalization $\lambda_{i,i} = 1$, $i = 1, \ldots, \kappa$, factor $f_{i,t}$ is forced to have a unit impact on $y_{i,t}$, there exists a potential pitfall. For instance, imagine that there is only one factor and that $y_{1,t}$ is uncorrelated with all other observables. Imposing $\lambda_{1,1} = 1$ may result in a misleading inference for the factor as well as for the other loadings. □

Example 6.3: Suppose we start from the normalization in Example 6.1 and proceed with premultiplying the factors by the matrix $H = \Lambda_{1,\kappa}^{tr}$ in (7.115) and postmultiplying the loadings by H^{-1}. This transformation leads to a normalization in which $\Lambda_{1,\kappa}$ is restricted to be the identity matrix and Σ_0 is an unrestricted covariance matrix. As in Example 6.2, the one-entries on the diagonal of $\Lambda_{1,\kappa}$ take care of the sign normalization. □

Finally, one might find it attractive to impose overidentifying restrictions. For concreteness, imagine that the factor model is used to study co-movements in output across US states, and let $y_{i,t}$ correspond to output in state i in period t. Moreover, suppose that the number of factors is $\kappa = 3$, where $f_{1,t}$ is interpreted as a national business cycle and $f_{2,t}$ and $f_{3,t}$ are factors that affect the Eastern and Western regions, respectively. In this case, one could impose the condition that $\lambda_{i,j} = 0$ if state i does not belong to region $j = 2, 3$.

6.2.2 *Priors and posteriors*

We now describe Bayesian inference for the DFM. To simplify the notation, we will discuss the case in which the lag length in (7.114) is the same for all i ($p_i = p$) and $q \leq p + 1$. As we did previously in this chapter, we adopt the convention that $Y_{t_0:t_1}$ and $F_{t_0:t_1}$ denote the sequences $\{y_{t_0}, \ldots, y_{t_1}\}$ and $\{f_{t_0}, \ldots, f_{t_1}\}$, respectively. Premultiply (7.112) by $1 - \phi_{i,1}L \cdots - \phi_{i,p}L^p$, where L here denotes the lag operator. The quasi-differenced measurement equation takes the form

$$\begin{aligned} y_{i,t} &= a_i + \lambda_i f_t + \phi_{i,1}(y_{i,t-1} - a_i - \lambda_i f_{t-1}) + \ldots \\ &\quad + \phi_{i,p}(y_{i,t-p} - a_i - \lambda_i f_{t-p}) + u_{i,t}, \quad \text{for} \quad t = p{+}1, .., T. \end{aligned} \tag{7.118}$$

Let $\theta_i = [a_i, \lambda_i, \sigma_i, \phi_{i,1}, .., \phi_{i,p}]'$ be the parameters entering (7.118) and θ_0 be the parameters pertaining to the law of motion of the factors (7.113). The joint distribution of data, parameters, and latent factors can be written as

$$\begin{aligned} & p(Y_{1:T}, F_{0:T}, \{\theta_i\}_{i=1}^n, \theta_0) \\ &= \left[\prod_{t=p+1}^{T} \left(\prod_{i=1}^{n} p(y_{i,t}|Y_{i,t-p:t-1}, F_{t-p:t}, \theta_i) \right) p(f_t|F_{t-q:t-1}, \theta_0) \right] \\ &\quad \times \left(\prod_{i=1}^{n} p(Y_{i,1:p}|F_{0:p}, \theta_i) \right) p(F_{0:p}|\theta_0) \left(\prod_{i=1}^{n} p(\theta_i) \right) p(\theta_0). \end{aligned} \tag{7.119}$$

To obtain the factorization on the right-hand side of (7.119), we exploited the fact that the conditional distribution of $y_{i,t}$ given $(Y_{1:t-1}, F_{0:t}, \theta_i)$ depends on lagged observables only through $Y_{i,t-p:t-1}$ and on the factors only through $F_{t-p:t}$. Moreover, the distribution of f_t conditional on $(Y_{1:t-1}, F_{0:t-1}, \theta_0)$ is a function only of $F_{t-q:t-1}$. The distributions $p(y_{i,t}|Y_{i,t-p:t-1}, F_{t-p:t}, \theta_i)$ and $p(f_t|F_{t-q:t-1}, \theta_0)$ can easily be derived from expressions (7.118) and (7.113), respectively.

The term $p(Y_{i,1:p}|F_{0:p}, \theta_i)$ in (7.119) represents the distribution of the first p observations conditional on the factors, which is given by

$$\begin{bmatrix} y_{i,1} \\ \vdots \\ y_{i,p} \end{bmatrix} \Bigg| (F_{0:p}, \theta_i) \sim N\left(\begin{bmatrix} a_i + f_1 \\ \vdots \\ a_i + f_p \end{bmatrix}, \ \Sigma_{i,1:p}(\theta_i) \right). \tag{7.120}$$

The matrix $\Sigma_{i,1:p}(\theta_i)$ is the covariance matrix of $[\xi_{i,1},\dots,\xi_{i,p}]'$, which can be derived from the autoregressive law of motion (7.114) by assuming that $\xi_{i,-(\tau+1)} = \dots = \xi_{i,-(\tau+p)} = 0$ for some $\tau > 0$. If the law of motion of $\xi_{i,t}$ is stationary for all θ_i in the support of the prior, one can set $\tau = \infty$, and $\Sigma_{i,1:p}$ becomes the covariance matrix associated with the unconditional distribution of the idiosyncratic shocks. Detailed derivations can be found in Otrok and Whiteman (1998). The initial distribution of the factors $p(F_{0:p}|\theta_0)$ can be obtained in a similar manner using (7.113).

The remaining terms, $p(\theta_i)$ and $p(\theta_0)$, represent the priors for θ_i and θ_0, which are typically chosen to be conjugate (see, for example, Otrok and Whiteman 1998). Specifically, the priors on the constant term a_i and the loadings λ_i are normal, namely, $N(\underline{a}_i, \underline{V}_{a_i})$ and $N(\underline{\lambda}_i, \underline{V}_{\lambda_i})$. If the $\lambda_{i,i}$, $i = 1,\dots,\kappa$ elements are restricted to be nonnegative to resolve the sign-indeterminacy of the factors as in Example 6.1, then the density associated with the prior for λ_i needs to be multiplied by the indicator function $\mathcal{I}\{\lambda_{i,i} \geq 0\}$ to impose the constraint (7.117). The autoregressive coefficients for the factors and the idiosyncratic shocks have a Normal prior. Define $\phi_0 = [vec(\Phi_{0,1})', .., vec(\Phi_{0,q})']'$ and assume that Σ_0 is normalized to be equal to the identity matrix. The prior for ϕ_0 is $N(\underline{\phi}_0, \underline{V}_{\phi_0})$. Likewise, the prior for $\phi_i = [\phi_{i,1}, .., \phi_{i,p}]'$ is $N(\underline{\phi}_i, \underline{V}_{\phi_i})$. In some applications, it may be desirable to truncate the prior for ϕ_0 (ϕ_i) to rule out parameters for which not all of the roots of the characteristic polynomial associated with the autoregressive laws of motion of f_t and $\xi_{i,t}$ lie outside the unit circle. Finally, the prior for the idiosyncratic volatilities σ_i can be chosen to be of the Inverted Gamma form.

A Gibbs sampler can be used to generate draws from the posterior distribution. The basic structure of the sampler is fairly straightforward though some of the details are tedious and can be found, for instance, in Otrok and Whiteman (1998). Conditional on the factors, Equation (7.112) is a linear Gaussian regression with AR(p) errors. The posterior density takes the form

$$p(\theta_i|F_{0:T},\theta_0,Y_{1:T}) \propto p(\theta_i)\left(\prod_{t=p+1}^{T} p(y_{i,t}|Y_{i,t-p:t-1},F_{t-p:t},\theta_i)\right) p(Y_{i,1:p}|F_{0:p},\theta_i). \quad (7.121)$$

Under a conjugate prior, the first two terms on the right-hand side correspond to the density of a Normal-Inverted Gamma distribution. The last term reflects the effect of the initialization of the AR(p) error process, and its log is not a quadratic function of θ_i. Draws from the distribution associated with (7.121) can be obtained with the procedure of Chib and Greenberg (1994).

If the prior for $\lambda_{i,i}$, $i = 1,\dots,\kappa$ includes the indicator function $\mathcal{I}\{\lambda_{i,i} \geq 0\}$, one can use an acceptance sampler that discards all draws of θ_i for which $\lambda_{i,i} < 0$. If the prior of the loadings does not restrict $\lambda_{i,i} \geq 0$, $i = 1,\dots,\kappa$, but is symmetric around zero, then one can resolve the sign indeterminacy by postprocessing the output of the (unrestricted) Gibbs sampler: for each set of draws $(\{\theta_i\}_{i=1}^n, \theta_0, F_{0:T})$ such that $\lambda_{i,i} < 0$, flip the sign of the i'th factor and the sign of the loadings of all n observables on the ith factor. Hamilton et al. (2007) discuss the sign normalization and related normalization issues in other models at length. Since the errors $\xi_{i,t}$ in equation (7.112) are independent across

i, the sampling can be implemented one i at a time, which implies that computational cost is linear in the size of the cross-section.

Conditional on the factors, the posterior for the coefficients θ_0 in (7.113) is obtained from a multivariate generalization of the preceding steps. Its density can be written as

$$p(\theta_0|F_{0:T},\{\theta_i\}_{i=1}^n,Y_{1:T}) \propto \left(\prod_{t=p+1}^{T} p(f_t|F_{t-p:t-1},\theta_0)\right) p(\theta_0)p(F_{0:p}|\theta_0). \tag{7.122}$$

The first term on the right-hand side corresponds to the conditional likelihood function of a VAR(q) and has been extensively analyzed in Section 2. If the prior for θ_0 is conjugate, the first two terms are proportional to the density of a MNIW distribution if Σ_0 is unrestricted and corresponds to a multivariate normal density if the DFM is normalized such that $\Sigma_0 = I$. The last terms capture the probability density function of the initial factors $f_0,\ldots,f_p$. Thus, θ_0 cannot be directly sampled from, say, a MNIW distribution. As in the case of θ_i, one can use a variant of the procedure proposed by Chib and Greenberg (1994).

In the third block of the Gibbs sampler, one draws the factors $F_{0:T}$ conditional on $(\{\theta_i\}_{i=1}^n,\theta_0,Y_{1:T})$. Two approaches exist in the Bayesian DFM literature. Otrok and Whiteman (1998) explicitly write out the joint Normal distribution of the observations $Y_{1:T}$ and the factors $F_{0:T}$, $p(Y_{1:T},F_{0:T}|\{\theta_i\}_{i=1,n},\theta_0)$ and derive the posterior distribution $p(F_{0:T}|\{\theta_i\}_{i=1,n},\theta_0,Y_{1:T})$ using the formula for conditional means and covariance matrices of a multivariate normal distribution.[5] Their approach involves inverting matrices of size T and hence becomes computationally expensive for data sets with a large time-series dimension. An alternative is to cast the DFM into a linear state-space form and apply the algorithm of Carter and Kohn (1994) for sampling from the distribution of the latent states, described in Giordani et al. (Chapter 3, this volume). To avoid the increase in the dimension of the state vector with the cross-sectional dimension n, it is convenient to exclude the AR(p) processes $\xi_{i,t}$ from the state vector and to use the quasi-differenced measurement equation (7.118) instead of (7.112).

We will now provide some more details on how to cast the DFM into state-space form with *iid* measurement errors and a VAR(1) state-transition equation. For ease of notation, we shall subsequently assume that the factor f_t is scalar ($\kappa = 1$). Stacking (7.118) for all i, one obtains the measurement equation

$$(I_n - \sum_{j=1}^{p}\tilde{\Phi}_j L^j)\tilde{y}_t = (I_n - \sum_{j=1}^{p}\tilde{\Phi}_j)\tilde{a} + \Lambda^*\tilde{f}_t + \tilde{u}_t, \quad t = p+1,\ldots,T, \tag{7.123}$$

[5] If $X = [X_1', X_2']$ is distributed $N(\mu,\Sigma)$ then $X_1|X_2$ is distributed $N\big(\mu_1 + \Sigma_{12}\Sigma_{22}^{-1}(X_2-\mu_2),\ \Sigma_{11} - \Sigma_{12}\Sigma_{22}^{-1}\Sigma_{21}\big)$, where the partitions of μ and Σ conform with the partitions of X.

where L is the temporal lag operator, $\tilde{y}_t = [y_{1,t}, \ldots, y_{n,t}]'$, $\tilde{a} = [a_1, \ldots, a_n]'$, $\tilde{u}_t = [u_{1,t}, \ldots, u_{n,t}]'$, the $\tilde{\Phi}_j$'s are diagonal $n \times n$ matrices with elements $\phi_{1,j}, \ldots, \phi_{n,j}$, and

$$\Lambda^* = \begin{bmatrix} \lambda_1 & -\lambda_1\phi_{1,1} & \ldots & -\lambda_1\phi_{1,p} \\ \vdots & & \ddots & \vdots \\ \lambda_n & -\lambda_n\phi_{n,1} & \ldots & -\lambda_n\phi_{n,p} \end{bmatrix}.$$

Due to the quasi-differencing, the random variables $\tilde{u}_t$ in the measurement equation (7.123) are *iid*. The $(p+1) \times 1$ vector $\tilde{f}_t$ collects the latent states and is defined as $\tilde{f}_t = [f_t, .., f_{t-p}]'$. The state-transition equation is obtained by expressing the law of motion of the factor (7.113) in companion form

$$\tilde{f}_t = \tilde{\Phi}_0 \tilde{f}_{t-1} + \tilde{u}_{0,t}, \tag{7.124}$$

where $\tilde{u}_{0,t} = [u_{0,t}, 0, .., 0]'$ is an *iid* $(p+1) \times 1$ random vector and $\tilde{\Phi}_0$ is the $(p+1) \times (p+1)$ companion form matrix

$$\tilde{\Phi}_0 = \begin{bmatrix} [\Phi_{0,1}, & \ldots, & \Phi_{0,q}, & 0_{1\times(p+1-q)}] \\ & I_p & & 0_{p\times 1} \end{bmatrix}. \tag{7.125}$$

Since (7.123) starts from $t = p+1$ as opposed to $t = 1$, one needs to initialize the filtering step in the Carter and Kohn (1994) algorithm with the conditional distribution of $p(F_{0:p}|Y_{1:p}, \{\theta_i\}_{i=1}^n, \theta_0)$. As mentioned above, this conditional distribution can be obtained from the joint distribution $p(F_{0:p}, Y_{1:p}|\{\theta_i\}_{i=1}^n, \theta_0)$ by using the formula for conditional means and covariance matrices of a multivariate normal distribution. Del Negro and Otrok (2008) provide formulas for the initialization. The Gibbs sampler can be summarized as follows:

Algorithm 6.1. Sampling from the Posterior of the DFM

For $s = 1, \ldots, n_{sim}$:

(1) Draw $\theta_i^{(s)}$ conditional on $(F_{0:T}^{(s-1)}, \theta_0^{(s-1)}, Y_{1:T})$ from (7.121). This can be done independently for each $i = 1, \ldots, n$.
(2) Draw $\theta_0^{(s)}$ conditional on $(F_{0:T}^{(s-1)}, \{\theta_i^{(s)}\}_{i=1}^n, Y_{1:T})$ from (7.122).
(3) Draw $F_{0:T}^{(s)}$, conditional on $(\{\theta_i^{(s)}\}_{i=1}^n, \theta_0^{(s)}, Y_{1:T})$. □

We have omitted the details of the conditional posterior distributions. The exact distributions can be found in the references given in this section. Last, we have not discussed the issue of determining the number of factors κ. In principle, one can regard DFMs with different κ's as individual models and treat the determination of the number of factors as a model selection or a model averaging problem, which will be discussed in more detail in Section 7. In practice, the computation of marginal likelihoods for DFMs, which are needed for the evaluation of posterior model probabilities, is numerically challenging. Lopes and West (2004) discuss the computation of marginal likelihoods for a static factor model in which the factors are *iid*. The authors also consider a MCMC approach where the number of factors is treated as an unknown parameter and is drawn jointly with all the other parameters.

6.2.3 *Applications of dynamic factor models*

How integrated are international business cycles? Are countries more integrated in terms of business-cycle synchronization within a region (say, within Europe) than across regions (say, France and the United States)? Has the degree of co-movement changed significantly over time as trade and financial links have increased? These are all natural questions to address using a dynamic factor model, which is precisely what Kose et al. (2003) do. The authors estimate a DFM on a panel of annual data on output, investment, and consumption for 60 countries and about 30 years. The model includes a world factor that captures the world business cycle, regional factors that capture region-specific cycles (say, Latin America), and country-specific cycles. These factors are assumed to evolve independently from one another. The authors find that international business-cycle co-movement is significant. In terms of the variance decomposition of output in the G7 countries, for instance, world cycles are on average as important as country-specific cycles, in the sense that world and country-specific cycles explain a similar share of the variance of output growth. For the average country in the world, country-specific cycles are, not surprisingly, much more important than world cycles. Regional cycles are not particularly important at all, suggesting that integration is no higher within regions than across regions.

The study of house prices is another interesting application of factor models. House prices have both an important national and regional component, where the former is associated with nationwide conditions (for example, stance of monetary policy and the national business cycle), while the latter is associated with regional business cycles and other region-specific conditions (for example, migration and demographics). Del Negro and Otrok (2007) apply dynamic factor models to study regional house prices in the US.

In a Bayesian framework, estimating models where regional or country-specific factors are identified by imposing the restriction that the respective factors have zero loadings on series that do not belong to that region or country is quite straightforward. Models with such restrictions are harder to estimate using nonparametric methods such as principal components. Moreover, using Bayesian methods, we can conduct inference on the country factors even if the number of series per country is small, as is the case in Kose et al. (2003), while nonparametric methods have a harder time characterizing the uncertainty that results from having a small cross-section.

6.2.4 *Extensions and alternative approaches*

We briefly discuss four extensions of the basic DFM presented above. These extensions include Factor Augmented VARs, DFMs with time-varying parameters, hierarchical DFMs, and hybrid models that combine a DSGE model and a DFM.

Factor Augmented VARs Bernanke et al. (2005) propose a class of models called factor augmented VARs (or FAVARs), which modify the standard factor model in two dimensions. First, the FAVAR allows for additional observables $y_{0,t}$, for example, the federal funds rate, to enter the measurement equation, which becomes

$$y_{i,t} = a_i + \gamma_i y_{0,t} + \lambda_i f_t + \xi_{i,t}, \quad i = 1, \dots, n, \quad t = 1, \dots, T, \tag{7.126}$$

where $y_{0,t}$ and γ_i are $m \times 1$ and $1 \times m$ vectors, respectively. Second, the observable vector $y_{0,t}$ and the unobservable factor f_t are assumed to jointly follow a vector autoregressive process of order q:

$$\begin{bmatrix} f_t \\ y_{0,t} \end{bmatrix} = \Phi_{0,1} \begin{bmatrix} f_{t-1} \\ y_{0,t-1} \end{bmatrix} + \dots + \Phi_{0,q} \begin{bmatrix} f_{t-q} \\ y_{0,t-q} \end{bmatrix} + u_{0,t}, \quad u_{0,t} \sim iidN(0, \Sigma_0), \tag{7.127}$$

which is the reason for the term *factor augmented* VAR. The $\Phi_{0,j}$ matrices are now of size $(\kappa + m) \times (\kappa + m)$. The innovation vector $u_{0,t}$ is still assumed to be normally distributed with mean 0 and variance Σ_0, with the difference that the variance-covariance matrix Σ_0 is no longer restricted to be diagonal. The idiosyncratic components $\xi_{i,t}$ evolve according to (7.114), and the innovations to their law of motion $u_{i,t}$ are subject to the distributional assumptions $u_{i,t} \sim N(0, \sigma_i^2)$. Moreover, we maintain the assumption that the innovations $u_{i,t}$ are independent across i and independent of $u_{0,t}$ at all leads and lags. In order to achieve identification, Bernanke et al. (2005) assume that (i) the $\kappa \times \kappa$ matrix obtained by stacking the first κ λ_i's equals the identity I_κ (as in Example 6.3), and (ii) the $\kappa \times m$ matrix obtained by stacking the first κ γ_i's is composed of zeros.

The appeal of the FAVAR is that it affords a combination of factor analysis with the structural VAR analysis described in Section 2.4. In particular, one can assume that the vector of reduced-form shocks $u_{0,t}$ relates to a vector of structural shocks $\epsilon_{0,t}$ as in (7.21):

$$u_{0,t} = \Sigma_{0,tr} \Omega_0 \epsilon_{0,t}, \tag{7.128}$$

where Σ_0^{tr} is the unique lower-triangular Cholesky factor of Σ_0 with nonnegative diagonal elements, and Ω_0 is an arbitrary orthogonal matrix. Bernanke et al. (2005) apply their model to study the effects of monetary policy shocks in the United States. They identify monetary policy shocks by imposing a short-run identification scheme where Ω_0 is diagonal as in Example 2.1. This identification implies that the central bank responds contemporaneously to the information contained in the factors. In contrast, unanticipated changes in monetary policy only affect the factors with a one-period lag.

At least in principle, conducting inference in a FAVAR is a straightforward application of the tools described in Section 6.2.2. For given factors, obtaining the posterior distribution for the parameters of (7.126) and (7.127) is straightforward. Likewise, the factors can be drawn using expressions (7.126) and the first κ equations of the VAR in (7.127), as the measurement and transition equations, respectively, in a state-space representation.

Time-Varying Parameters For the same reasons that it may be useful to allow parameter variation in a VAR as we saw in Section 5, we may want to allow for time-variation in the parameters of a factor model. For instance, co-movements across countries may have changed as a result of increased financial or trade integration, or because of monetary arrangements (monetary unions, switches from fixed to flexible exchange rates, and so forth). Del Negro and Otrok (2008) accomplish that by modifying the standard factor model in two ways. First, they make the loadings vary over time. This feature allows for changes in the sensitivity of individual series to common factors. The second innovation amounts to introducing stochastic volatility in the law of motion of the factors and the idiosyncratic shocks. This feature accounts for changes in the relative importance of common factors and of idiosyncratic shocks. Both loadings and volatilities evolve according to a random walk without drift as in Cogley and Sargent (2005b). Del Negro and Otrok (2008) apply this model to study the time-varying nature of international business cycles, in an attempt to determine whether the Great Moderation has country-specific or international roots. Mumtaz and Surico (2008) introduce time-variation in the law of motion of the factors (but not in any of the other parameters) and use their model to study cross-country inflation data.

Hierarchical factors Ng et al. (2008) pursue a modeling strategy different from the one outlined in Section 6.2.1. Their approach entails building a hierarchical set of factor models, where the hierarchy is determined by the level of aggregation. For concreteness, in the study of international business cycles—the application discussed in the previous section—the three levels of aggregation are country, regional, and world. Only the most disaggregated factors—the country-level factors—would appear in the measurement equation (7.112). In turn, the country factors evolve according to a factor model in which the common components are the factors at the next level of aggregation (the regional factors). Similarly, the regional factors evolve according to a factor model in which the common components are the the world factors. This approach is more parsimonious than the one used by Kose et al. (2003).

Combining DSGE Models and Factor Models Boivin and Giannoni (2006a) estimate a DSGE-DFM that equates the latent factors with the state variables of a DSGE model. Accordingly, the factor dynamics are therefore subject to the restrictions implied by the DSGE model and take the form

$$f_t = \Phi_1(\theta_{DSGE})f_{t-1} + \Phi_\epsilon(\theta_{DSGE})\epsilon_t, \tag{7.129}$$

where the vector f_t now comprises the minimal set of state variables associated with the DSGE model and θ_{DSGE} is the vector of structural DSGE model parameters. In the context of the simple stochastic growth model analyzed in Section 4, this vector would contain the capital stock as well as the two exogenous processes. Equation (7.129) is then combined with measurement equations of the form (7.112). Since in the DSGE-DFM the latent factors have a clear economic interpretation, it is in principle much easier to elicit prior distributions for the loadings λ_i. For instance, suppose $y_{i,t}$ corresponds to log GDP. The solution of the stochastic growth model delivers a functional relationship between log GDP and the state variables of the DSGE model. This relationship can be used to center a prior distribution for λ_i. Details of how to specify such a prior can be found in Kryshko (2010).

As before, define $\theta_i = [a_i, \lambda_i, \sigma_i, \phi_{i,1}, \ldots, \phi_{i,p}]'$, $i = 1, \ldots, n$. Inference in a DSGE-DFM can be implemented with a Metropolis-within-Gibbs sampler that iterates over (i) the conditional posterior distributions of $\{\theta_i\}_{i=1}^n$ given $(F_{1:T}, \theta_{DSGE}, Y_{1:T})$; (ii) the conditional distribution of $F_{1:T}$ given $(\{\theta_i\}_{i=1}^n, \theta_{DSGE}, Y_{1:T})$; and (iii) the distribution of θ_{DSGE} given $(\{\theta_i\}_{i=1}^n, Y_{1:T})$. Steps (i) and (ii) resemble Steps 1 and 3 in Algorithm 6.1, whereas Step (iii) can be implemented with a modified version of the Random-Walk-Metropolis step described in Algorithm 4.1. Details are provided in Boivin and Giannoni (2006a) and Kryshko (2010).

Boivin and Giannoni (2006a) use their DSGE-DFM to relate DSGE model variables such as aggregate output, consumption, investment, hours worked, wages, inflation, and interest rates to multiple observables, that is, multiple measures of employment and labor usage, wage rates, price inflation, and so forth. Using multiple (noisy) measures implicitly allows a researcher to obtain a more precise measure of DSGE model variables—provided the measurement errors are approximately independent—and thus sharpens inference about the DSGE model parameters and the economic state variables, as well as the shocks that drive the economy. Kryshko (2010) documents that the space spanned by the factors of a DSGE-DFM is very similar to the space spanned by factors extracted from an unrestricted DFM. He then uses the DSGE-DFM to study the effect of unanticipated changes in technology and monetary policy, which are elements of the vector ϵ_t in (7.129), on a large cross-section of macroeconomic variables.

7 Model Uncertainty

The large number of vector autoregressive and dynamic stochastic general equilibrium models encountered thus far, combined with great variation in the implications for policy across models, makes the problem of model uncertainty a compelling one in macroeconometrics. More specifically, in the context of VARs, there is uncertainty about the number of lags and cointegration relationships as well as appropriate restrictions for identifying policy rules or structural shocks. In the context of a DSGE model, a researcher might be uncertain whether price stickiness, wage stickiness, informational frictions, or monetary frictions are quantitatively important for the understanding of business-cycle fluctuations and should be accounted for when designing monetary and fiscal policies. In view of the proliferation of hard-to-measure coefficients in time-varying parameter models, there is uncertainty about the importance of such features in empirical models. Researchers working with dynamic factor models are typically uncertain about the number of factors necessary to capture the co-movements in a cross-section of macroeconomic or financial variables.

In a Bayesian framework, a model is formally defined as a joint distribution of data and parameters. Thus, both the likelihood function $p(Y|\theta_{(i)}, \mathcal{M}_i)$ and the prior density $p(\theta_{(i)}|\mathcal{M}_i)$ are part of the specification of a model $\mathcal{M}_i$. Model uncertainty is conceptually not different from parameter uncertainty, which is illustrated in the following example.

Example 7.1: Consider the two (nested) models:

$$\mathcal{M}_1: \; y_t = u_t, \quad u_t \sim iidN(0,1),$$
$$\mathcal{M}_2: \; y_t = \theta_{(2)}x_t + u_t, \quad u_t \sim iidN(0,1), \quad \theta_{(2)} \sim N(0,1).$$

Here $\mathcal{M}_1$ restricts the regression coefficient $\theta_{(2)}$ in $\mathcal{M}_2$ to be equal to zero. Bayesian analysis allows us to place probabilities on the two models, denoted by $\pi_{i,0}$. Suppose we assign prior probability $\pi_{1,0} = \lambda$ to $\mathcal{M}_1$. Then the mixture of $\mathcal{M}_1$ and $\mathcal{M}_2$ is equivalent to a model $\mathcal{M}_0$

$$\mathcal{M}_0: \quad y_t = \theta_{(0)}x_t + u_t, \quad u_t \sim iidN(0,1), \quad \theta_{(0)} \sim \begin{cases} 0 & \text{with prob. } \lambda \\ N(0,1) & \text{with prob. } 1-\lambda \end{cases}. \quad \square$$

In principle, one could try to construct a prior distribution on a sufficiently large parameter space such that model uncertainty can be represented as parameter uncertainty. However, as evident from the example, this prior distribution would have to assign nonzero probability to certain lower-dimensional subspaces, which complicates the computation of the posterior distribution. Thus, in most of the applications considered in this chapter, such an approach is impractical, and it is useful to regard restricted versions of a large encompassing model as models themselves, for example VARs of lag length $p = 1, \ldots, p_{max}$ and cointegration rank $r = 1, \ldots, n$ or a collection of linearized DSGE models, which can all be nested in an unrestricted state-space model.

The remainder of this section is organized as follows. Section 7.1 discusses the computation of posterior model probabilities and their use in selecting among a collection of models. Rather than first selecting a model and then conditioning on the selected model in the subsequent analysis, it may be more desirable to average across models and to take model uncertainty explicitly into account when making decisions. We use a stylized optimal monetary policy example to highlight this point in Section 7.2. In many macroeconomic applications, in particular those that are based on DSGE models, posterior model probabilities are often overly decisive, in that one specification essentially attains posterior probability one and all other specifications receive probability zero. These decisive probabilities found in individual studies are difficult to reconcile with the variation in results and model rankings found across different studies and therefore are in some sense *implausible*. In view of potentially implausible posterior model probabilities, a decision maker might be inclined to robustify her decisions. These issues are discussed in Section 7.3.

7.1 Posterior model probabilities and model selection

Suppose we have a collection of M models denoted by $\mathcal{M}_1$ through $\mathcal{M}_M$. Each model has a parameter vector $\theta_{(i)}$, a proper prior distribution $p(\theta_{(i)}|\mathcal{M}_i)$ for the model parameters, and prior probability $\pi_{i,0}$. The posterior model probabilities are given by

$$\pi_{i,T} = \frac{\pi_{i,0}p(Y_{1:T}|\mathcal{M}_i)}{\sum_{j=1}^{M}\pi_{j,0}p(Y_{1:T}|\mathcal{M}_j)}, \quad p(Y_{1:T}|\mathcal{M}_i) = \int p(Y_{1:T}|\theta_{(i)},\mathcal{M}_i)p(\theta_{(i)}|\mathcal{M}_i)d\theta_{(i)}, \tag{7.130}$$

where $p(Y_{1:T}|\mathcal{M}_i)$ is the marginal likelihood or data density associated with model $\mathcal{M}_i$. As long as the likelihood functions $p(Y_{1:T}|\theta_{(i)},\mathcal{M}_i)$ and prior densities $p(\theta_{(i)}|\mathcal{M}_i)$ are properly normalized for all models, the posterior model probabilities are well defined. Since for any model $\mathcal{M}_i$

$$\ln p(Y_{1:T}|\mathcal{M}_i) = \sum_{t=1}^{T}\ln\int p(y_t|\theta_{(i)},Y_{1,t-1},\mathcal{M}_i)p(\theta_{(i)}|Y_{1,t-1},\mathcal{M}_i)d\theta_{(i)}, \tag{7.131}$$

log marginal likelihoods can be interpreted as the sum of one-step-ahead predictive scores. The terms on the right-hand side of (7.131) provide a decomposition of the one-step-ahead predictive densities $p(y_t|Y_{1,t-1},\mathcal{M}_i)$. This decomposition highlights the fact that inference about the parameter $\theta_{(i)}$ is based on time $t-1$ information, when making the prediction for y_t. The predictive score is small whenever the predictive distribution assigns a low density to the observed y_t. It is beyond the scope of this chapter to provide a general discussion of the use of posterior model probabilities or odds ratios for model comparison. A survey is provided by Kass and Raftery (1995). In turn, we shall highlight a few issues that are important in the context of macroeconometric applications.

We briefly mentioned in Sections 2.2 (hyperparameter choice for Minnesota prior) and 4.3 (prior elicitation for DSGE models) that in practice priors are often based on presample (or training sample) information. Since in time-series models observations have a natural ordering, we could regard observations $Y_{1:T^*}$ as presample and $p(\theta|Y_{1:T^*})$ as a prior for θ that incorporates this presample information. Conditional on $Y_{1:T^*}$, the marginal likelihood function for subsequent observations $Y_{T^*+1:T}$ is given by

$$p(Y_{T^*+1:T}|Y_{1:T^*}) = \frac{p(Y_{1:T})}{p(Y_{1:T^*})} = \int p(Y_{T^*+1:T}|Y_{1:T^*},\theta)p(\theta|Y_{1:T^*})d\theta. \tag{7.132}$$

The density $p(Y_{T^*+1:T}|Y_{1:T^*})$ is often called predictive (marginal) likelihood and can replace the marginal likelihood in (7.130) in the construction of posterior model probabilities, provided the prior model probabilities are also adjusted to reflect the presample information $Y_{1:T^*}$. As before, it is important that $p(\theta|Y_{1:T^*})$ be a proper density. In the context of a VAR, a proper prior could be obtained by replacing the dummy observations Y^* and X^* with presample observations. Two examples of papers that use predictive marginal likelihoods to construct posterior model probabilities are Schorfheide (2000), who computes posterior odds for a collection of VARs and

DSGE models, and Villani (2001), who uses them to evaluate lag length and cointegration rank restrictions in vector autoregressive models. A more detailed discussion of predictive likelihoods can be found in Geweke (2005). An application of predictive likelihoods to forecast combination and model averaging is provided by Eklund and Karlsson (2007).

While the calculation of posterior probabilities is conceptually straightforward, it can be computationally challenging. There are only a few instances, such as the VAR model in (7.1) with conjugate MNIW prior, in which the marginal likelihood $p(Y) = \int p(Y|\theta)p(\theta)d\theta$ can be computed analytically. In fact, for priors represented through dummy observations the formula is given in (7.15). We also mentioned in Section 4.7.1 that for a DSGE model, or other models for which posterior draws have been obtained using the RWM Algorithm, numerical approximations to marginal likelihoods can be obtained using Geweke's (1999) modified harmonic mean estimator or the method proposed by Chib and Jeliazkov (2001). A more detailed discussion of numerical approximation techniques for marginal likelihoods is provided in Chib (Chapter 5, this volume). Finally, marginal likelihoods can be approximated analytically using a so-called Laplace approximation, which approximates $\ln p(Y|\theta) + \ln p(\theta)$ by a quadratic function centered at the posterior mode or the maximum of the likelihood function. The most widely used Laplace approximation is the one due to Schwarz (1978), which is known as Schwarz Criterion or Bayesian Information Criterion (BIC). Phillips (1996) and Chao and Phillips (1999) provide extensions to nonstationary time-series models and reduced-rank VARs.

Schorfheide (2000) compares Laplace approximations of marginal likelihoods for two small-scale DSGE models and bivariate VARs with two to four lags to numerical approximations based on a modified harmonic mean estimator. The VARs were specified such that the marginal likelihood could be computed exactly. The approximation error of the numerical procedure was at most 0.02 for log densities, whereas the error of the Laplace approximation was around 0.5. While the exact marginal likelihood was not available for the DSGE models, the discrepancy between the modified harmonic mean estimator and the Laplace approximation was around 0.1 on a log scale. While the results reported in Schorfheide (2000) are model and data specific, the use of numerical procedures to approximate marginal likelihood functions is generally preferable for two reasons. First, posterior inference is typically based on simulation-based methods, and the marginal likelihood approximation can often be constructed from the output of the posterior simulator with very little additional effort. Second, the approximation error can be reduced to a desired level by increasing the number of parameter draws upon which the approximation is based.

Posterior model probabilities are often used to select a model specification upon which any subsequent inference is conditioned. While it is generally preferable to average across all model specifications with nonzero posterior probability, a model selection approach might provide a good approximation if the posterior probability of one model is very close to one, the probabilities associated with all other specifications are very small, and the loss of making inference or decisions based on the highest posterior probability model is not too large if one of the low probability models is in fact correct. We shall elaborate on this point in Example 7.2 in Section 7.2. A rule for selecting one out of M models can be formally derived from the following decision problem. Suppose that a researcher faces a loss of zero if she chooses the "correct" model and a loss of $\alpha_{ij} > 0$ if she chooses model $\mathcal{M}_i$ although $\mathcal{M}_j$ is correct. If the loss function is symmetric in the sense that $\alpha_{ij} = \alpha$ for all $i \neq j$, then it is straightforward to verify that the posterior expected loss is minimized by selecting the model with the highest posterior probability. A treatment of model selection problems under more general loss functions can be found, for instance, in Bernardo and Smith (1994).

If one among the M models $\mathcal{M}_1, \dots, \mathcal{M}_M$ is randomly selected to generate a sequence of observations $Y_{1:T}$, then under fairly general conditions the posterior probability assigned to that model will converge to one as $T \longrightarrow \infty$. In this sense, Bayesian model selection procedures are consistent from a frequentist perspective. An early version of this result for general linear regression models was proved by Halpern (1974). The consistency result remains valid if the marginal likelihoods that are used to compute posterior model probabilities are replaced by Laplace approximations (see, for example, Schwarz 1978 and Phillips and Ploberger 1996). These Laplace approximations highlight the fact that log marginal likelihoods can be decomposed into a goodness-of-fit term, comprising the maximized log likelihood function $\max_{\theta_{(i)} \in \Theta_{(i)}} \ln p(Y_{1:T}|\theta_{(i)}, \mathcal{M}_i)$ and a term that penalizes the dimensionality, which in case of Schwarz's approximation takes the form of $-(k_i/2) \ln T$, where k_i is the dimension of the parameter vector $\theta_{(i)}$. Moreover, the consistency is preserved in nonstationary time-series models. Chao and Phillips (1999), for instance, prove that the use of posterior probabilities leads to a consistent selection of cointegration rank and lag length in vector autoregressive models.

7.2 Decision making and inference with multiple models

Economic policy makers are often confronted with choosing policies under model uncertainty.[6] Moreover, policy decisions are often made under a fairly specific loss function that is based on some measure of welfare. This welfare loss function might either be fairly ad hoc—for example, the variability of aggregate output and inflation—or micro-founded albeit model-specific—for instance, the utility of a representative agent in a DSGE model. The optimal decision from a Bayesian perspective is obtained by minimizing the expected loss under a mixture of models. Conditioning on the highest posterior probability model can lead to suboptimal decisions. At a minimum, the decision maker should account for the loss of a decision that is optimal under $\mathcal{M}_i$, if in fact one of the other models $\mathcal{M}_j, j \neq i$, is correct. The following example provides an illustration.

[6] Chamberlain (Chapter 4, this volume) studies the decision problem of an individual who chooses between two treatments from a Bayesian perspective.

Example 7.2: Suppose that output y_t and inflation π_t are related to each other according to one of the two Phillips curve relationships

$$\mathcal{M}_i: \; y_t = \theta(\mathcal{M}_i)\pi_t + \epsilon_{s,t}, \quad \epsilon_{s,t} \sim iidN(0,1), \quad i = 1, 2, \tag{7.133}$$

where $\epsilon_{s,t}$ is a cost (supply) shock. Assume that the demand side of the economy leads to the following relationship between inflation and money m_t:

$$\pi_t = m_t + \epsilon_{d,t}, \quad \epsilon_{d,t} \sim iidN(0,1), \tag{7.134}$$

where $\epsilon_{d,t}$ is a demand shock. Finally, assume that up until period T monetary policy was $m_t = 0$. All variables in this model are meant to be in log deviations from some steady state.

In period T, the central bank is considering a class of new monetary policies, indexed by δ:

$$m_t = -\epsilon_{d,t} + \delta\epsilon_{s,t}. \tag{7.135}$$

δ controls the strength of the central bank's reaction to supply shocks. This class of policies is evaluated under the loss function

$$\widetilde{L}_t = (\pi_t^2 + y_t^2). \tag{7.136}$$

If one averages with respect to the distribution of the supply shocks, the expected period loss associated with a particular policy δ under model $\mathcal{M}_i$ is

$$L(\mathcal{M}_i, \delta) = (\delta\theta(\mathcal{M}_i) + 1)^2 + \delta^2. \tag{7.137}$$

To provide a numerical illustration, we let

$$\theta(\mathcal{M}_1) = 1/10, \quad \theta(\mathcal{M}_2) = 1, \quad \pi_{1,T} = 0.61, \quad \pi_{2,T} = 0.39.$$

Here, $\pi_{i,T}$ denotes the posterior probability of model $\mathcal{M}_i$ at the end of period T. We will derive the optimal decision and compare it with two suboptimal procedures that are based on a selection step.

First, from a Bayesian perspective it is optimal to minimize the posterior risk (expected loss), which in this example is given by

$$\mathcal{R}(\delta) = \pi_{1,T}L(\mathcal{M}_1, \delta) + \pi_{2,T}L(\mathcal{M}_2, \delta). \tag{7.138}$$

A straightforward calculation leads to $\delta^* = \text{argmin}_\delta \, \mathcal{R}(\delta) = -0.32$ and the posterior risk associated with this decision is $\mathcal{R}(\delta^*) = 0.85$. Second, suppose that the policy maker had proceeded in two steps: (i) select the highest posterior probability model; and (ii) conditional on this model, determine the optimal choice of δ. The highest posterior probability model is $\mathcal{M}_1$, and, conditional on $\mathcal{M}_1$, it is optimal to set $\delta^*(\mathcal{M}_1) = -0.10$. The risk associated with this decision is $\mathcal{R}(\delta^*(\mathcal{M}_1)) = 0.92$, which is larger than $\mathcal{R}(\delta^*)$ and shows that it is suboptimal to condition the decision on the highest posterior prob-

Table 7.4: Expected losses

Decision	$\mathcal{M}_1$	$\mathcal{M}_2$	Risk $\mathcal{R}(\delta)$
$\delta^* = -0.32$	1.04	0.56	0.85
$\delta^*(\mathcal{M}_1) = -0.1$	0.99	0.82	0.92
$\delta^*(\mathcal{M}_2) = -0.5$	1.15	0.50	0.90

ability model. In particular, this model-selection-based procedure completely ignores the loss that occurs if in fact $\mathcal{M}_2$ is the correct model.

Third, suppose that the policy maker relies on two advisors $\mathcal{A}_1$ and $\mathcal{A}_2$. Advisor $\mathcal{A}_i$ recommends that the policy maker implement the decision $\delta^*(\mathcal{M}_i)$, which minimizes the posterior risk if only model $\mathcal{M}_i$ is considered. If the policy maker implements the recommendation of advisor $\mathcal{A}_i$, taking into account the posterior model probabilities $\pi_{i,T}$, then Table 7.4 provides the matrix of relevant expected losses. Notice that there is a large loss associated with $\delta^*(\mathcal{M}_2)$ if in fact $\mathcal{M}_1$ is the correct model. Thus, even though the posterior odds favor the model entertained by $\mathcal{A}_1$, it is preferable to implement the recommendation of advisor $\mathcal{A}_2$ because $\mathcal{R}(\delta^*(\mathcal{M}_2)) < \mathcal{R}(\delta^*(\mathcal{M}_1))$. However, while choosing between $\delta^*(\mathcal{M}_1)$ and $\delta^*(\mathcal{M}_2)$ is preferable to conditioning on the highest posterior probability model, the best among the two decisions, $\delta^*(\mathcal{M}_2)$, is inferior to the optimal decision δ^*, obtained by minimizing the overall posterior expected loss. In fact, in this numerical illustration, the gain from averaging over models is larger than the difference between $\mathcal{R}(\delta^*(\mathcal{M}_1))$ and $\mathcal{R}(\delta^*(\mathcal{M}_2))$. □

In more realistic applications, the two simple models would be replaced by more sophisticated DSGE models. These models would themselves involve unknown parameters. Cogley and Sargent (2005a) provide a nice macroeconomic illustration of the notion that one should not implement the decision of the highest posterior probability model if it has disastrous consequences in case one of the other models is correct. The authors consider a traditional Keynesian model with a strong output and inflation trade-off versus a model in which the Phillips curve is vertical in the long run. According to Cogley and Sargent's analysis, the posterior probability of the Keynesian model was already very small by the mid-1970s, and the natural rate model suggested implementing a disinflation policy. However, the costs associated with this disinflation were initially very high if, in fact, the Keynesian model provided a better description of the US economy. The authors conjecture that this consideration may have delayed the disinflation until about 1980.

Often, loss depends on future realizations of y_t. In this case, predictive distributions are important. Consider, for example, a prediction problem. The h-step-ahead predictive density is given by the mixture

$$p(y_{T+h}|Y_{1:T}) = \sum_{i=1}^{M} \pi_{i,T} p(y_{T+h}|Y_{1:T}, \mathcal{M}_i). \tag{7.139}$$

Thus, $p(y_{T+h}|Y_{1:T})$ is the result of the Bayesian averaging of model-specific predictive densities $p(y_{T+h}|Y_{1:T})$. Notice that only if the posterior probability of one of the models is essentially equal to one, conditioning on the highest posterior probability leads to approximately the same predictive density as model averaging. There exists an extensive literature on applications of Bayesian model averaging. For instance, Min and Zellner (1993) use posterior model probabilities to combine forecasts, and Wright (2008) uses Bayesian model averaging to construct exchange rate forecasts. If the goal is to generate point predictions under a quadratic loss function, then it is optimal to average posterior mean forecasts from the M models, using the posterior model probabilities as weights. This is a special case of Bayesian forecast combination, which is discussed in more general terms in Geweke and Whiteman (2006). Strachan and van Dijk (2006) average across VARs with different lag lengths and cointegration restrictions to study the dynamics of the Great Ratios.

If the model space is very large, then the implementation of model averaging can be challenging. Consider the empirical Illustration 2.1, which involved a four-variable VAR with four lags, leading to a coefficient matrix Φ with 68 elements. Suppose one constructs submodels by restricting VAR coefficients to zero. Based on the exclusion of parameters, one can in principle generate $2^{68} \approx 3 \cdot 10^{20}$ submodels. Even if one restricts the set of submodels by requiring that a subset of the VAR coefficients is never restricted to be zero and one specifies a conjugate prior that leads to an analytical formula for the marginal likelihoods of the submodels, the computation of posterior probabilities for all submodels can be a daunting task. As an alternative, George et al. (2008) develop a stochastic search variable selection algorithm for a VAR that automatically averages over high posterior probability submodels. The authors also provide detailed references to the large literature on Bayesian variable selection in problems with large sets of potential regressors. In a nutshell, George et al. (2008) introduce binary indicators that determine whether a coefficient is restricted to be zero. An MCMC algorithm then iterates over the conditional posterior distribution of model parameters and variable selection indicators. However, as is typical of stochastic search applications, the number of restrictions actually visited by the MCMC simulation is only a small portion of all possible restrictions.

Bayesian model averaging has also become popular in growth regressions following the work of Fernandez et al. (2001), Sala-i Martin et al. (2004), and Masanjala and Papageorgiou (2008). The recent empirical growth literature has identified a substantial number of variables that potentially explain the rate of economic growth in a cross-section or panel of countries. Since there is uncertainty about exactly which explanatory variables to include in a growth regression, Bayesian model averaging is an appealing procedure. The paper by Sala-i Martin et al. (2004) uses a simplified version of Bayesian model averaging, in which marginal likelihoods are approximated by Schwarz's (1978) Laplace approximation and posterior means and covariances are replaced by maxima and inverse Hessian matrices obtained from a Gaussian likelihood function.

7.3 Difficulties in decision making with multiple models

While Bayesian model averaging is conceptually very attractive, it very much relies on the notion that the posterior model probabilities provide a plausible characterization of model uncertainty. Consider a central bank deciding on its monetary policy. Suppose that a priori the policy makers entertain the possibility that either wages or prices of intermediate goods producers are subject to nominal rigidities. Moreover, suppose that—as is the case in New Keynesian DSGE models—these rigidities have the effect that wage (or price) setters are not able to adjust their nominal wages (prices) optimally, which distorts relative wages (prices) and ultimately leads to the use of an inefficient mix of labor (intermediate goods). The central bank could use its monetary policy instrument to avoid the necessity of wage (price) adjustments and thereby nullify the effect of the nominal rigidity.

Based on the tools and techniques in the preceding sections, one could now proceed by estimating two models, one in which prices are sticky and wages are flexible and one in which prices are flexible and wages are sticky. Results for such an estimation, based on a variant of the Smets and Wouters (2007) models, have been reported, for instance, in Table 5 of Del Negro and Schorfheide (2008). According to their estimation, conducted under various prior distributions, US data favor the sticky price version of the DSGE model with odds that are greater than e^{40}. Such odds are not uncommon in the DSGE model literature. If these odds are taken literally, then under relevant loss functions we should completely disregard the possibility that wages are sticky. In a related study, Del Negro et al. (2007) compare versions of DSGE models with nominal rigidities in which those households (firms) that are unable to reoptimize their wages (prices) are indexing their past price either by the long-run inflation rate or by last period's inflation rate (dynamic indexation). According to their Figure 4, the odds in favor of the dynamic indexation are greater than e^{20}, which again seems very decisive.

Schorfheide (2008) surveys a large number of DSGE model-based estimates of price and wage stickiness and the degree of dynamic indexation. While the papers included in this survey build on the same theoretical framework, variations in some details of the model specification as well as in the choice of observables lead to a significant variation in parameter estimates and model rankings. Thus, posterior model odds from any individual study, even though formally correct, appear to be overly decisive and in this sense implausible from a meta-perspective.

The problem of implausible odds has essentially two dimensions. First, each DSGE model corresponds to a stylized representation of a particular economic mechanism, such as wage or price stickiness, augmented by auxiliary mechanisms that are designed to capture the salient features of the data. By looking across studies, one encounters several representations of essentially the same basic economic mechanism, but each representation attains a different time-series fit and makes posterior probabilities appear fragile across studies. Second, in practice macroeconometricians often work with incomplete model spaces. That is, in addition to the models that are being formally analyzed, researchers have in mind a more sophisticated structural model, which may be too complicated to formalize or too costly (in terms of intellectual and computational resources) to estimate. In some instances, a richly parameterized vector autoregression that is only loosely connected to economic theory serves as a stand-in. In view of these reference models, the simpler specifications are potentially misspecified. For illustrative purposes, we provide two stylized examples in which we explicitly specify the sophisticated reference model that in practice is often not spelled out.

Example 7.3: Suppose that a macroeconomist assigns equal prior probabilities to two stylized models $\mathcal{M}_i$: $y_t \sim iidN(\mu_i, \sigma_i^2)$, $i = 1, 2$, where μ_i and σ_i^2 are fixed. In addition, there is a third model $\mathcal{M}_0$ in the background, given by $y_t \sim iidN(0, 1)$. For the sake of argument, suppose it is too costly to analyze $\mathcal{M}_0$ formally. If a sequence of T observations were generated from $\mathcal{M}_0$, the expected log posterior odds of $\mathcal{M}_1$ versus $\mathcal{M}_2$ would be

$$\begin{aligned}
\mathbb{E}_0\left[\ln \frac{\pi_{1,T}}{\pi_{2,T}}\right] &= \mathbb{E}_0\left[-\frac{T}{2}\ln \sigma_1^2 - \frac{1}{2\sigma_1^2}\sum_{t=1}^{T}(y_t-\mu_1)^2\right. \\
&\quad \left. -\left(-\frac{T}{2}\ln \sigma_2^2 - \frac{1}{2\sigma_2^2}\sum_{t=1}^{T}(y_t-\mu_2)^2\right)\right] \\
&= -\frac{T}{2}\left[\ln \sigma_1^2 + \frac{1}{\sigma_1^2}(1+\mu_1^2)\right] + \frac{T}{2}\left[\ln \sigma_2^2 + \frac{1}{\sigma_2^2}(1+\mu_2^2)\right],
\end{aligned}$$

where the expectation is taken with respect to $y_1, \ldots, y_T$ under $\mathcal{M}_0$. Suppose that the location parameters μ_1 and μ_2 capture the key economic concept, such as wage or price stickiness, and the scale parameters are generated through the various auxiliary assumptions that are made to obtain a fully specified DSGE model. If the two models are based on similar auxiliary assumptions, that is, $\sigma_1^2 \approx \sigma_2^2$, then the posterior odds are clearly driven by the key economic contents of the two models. If, however, the auxiliary assumptions made in the two models are very different, it is possible that the posterior odds and hence the ranking of models $\mathcal{M}_1$ and $\mathcal{M}_2$ are dominated by the auxiliary assumptions, σ_1^2 and σ_2^2, rather than by the economic contents, μ_1 and μ_2, of the models. □

Example 7.4: This example is adapted from Sims (2003). Suppose that a researcher considers the following two models. $\mathcal{M}_1$ implies $y_t \sim iidN(-0.5, 0.01)$ and model $\mathcal{M}_2$ implies $y_t \sim iidN(0.5, 0.01)$. There is a third model, $\mathcal{M}_0$, given by $y_t \sim iidN(0, 1)$, that is too costly to be analyzed formally. The sample size is $T = 1$. Based on equal prior probabilities, the posterior odds in favor of model $\mathcal{M}_1$ are

$$\frac{\pi_{1,T}}{\pi_{2,T}} = \exp\left\{-\frac{1}{2\cdot 0.01}[(y_1+1/2)^2 - (y_1-1/2)^2]\right\} = \exp\left\{-100y_1\right\}.$$

Thus, for values of y_1 less than -0.05 or greater than 0.05 the posterior odds are greater than $e^5 \approx 150$ in favor of one of the models, which we shall term *decisive*. The models $\mathcal{M}_1$ ($\mathcal{M}_2$) assign a probability of less than 10^{-6} outside the range $[-0.55, -0.45]$ ($[0.45, 0.55]$). Using the terminology of the prior predictive checks described in Section 4.7.2, for observations outside these ranges one would conclude that the models have severe difficulties explaining the data. For any observation falling into the intervals $(-\infty, -0.55]$, $[-0.45, -0.05]$, $[0.05, 0.45]$, and $[0.55, \infty)$, one would obtain decisive posterior odds and at the same time have to conclude that the empirical observation is difficult to reconcile with the models $\mathcal{M}_1$ and $\mathcal{M}_2$. At the same time, the reference model $\mathcal{M}_0$ assigns a probability of almost 0.9 to these intervals. □

As illustrated through these two stylized examples, the problems in the use of posterior probabilities in the context of DSGE models are essentially twofold. First, DSGE models tend to capture one of many possible representations of a particular economic mechanism. Thus, one might be able to find versions of these models that preserve the basic mechanisms but deliver very different odds. Second, the models often suffer from misspecification, which manifests itself through low posterior probabilities in view of more richly parameterized vector autoregressive models that are less tightly linked to economic theory. Posterior odds exceeding e^{50} in a sample of 120 observations are suspicious (to us) and often indicate that we should compare different models or consider a larger model space.

Sims (2003) recommends introducing continuous parameters such that different submodel specifications can be nested in a larger encompassing model. The downside of creating these encompassing models is that it is potentially difficult to properly characterize multimodal posterior distributions in high-dimensional parameter spaces. Hence, a proper characterization of posterior uncertainty about the strength of various competing decision-relevant economic mechanisms remains a challenge. Geweke (2010) proposes to deal with incomplete model spaces by pooling models. This pooling amounts essentially to creating a convex combination of one-step-ahead predictive distributions, which are derived from individual models. The time-invariant weights of this mixture of models are then estimated by maximizing the log predictive score for this mixture (see (7.131)).

In view of these practical limitations associated with posterior model probabilities, a policy maker might find it attractive to robustify her decision. In fact, there is a growing literature in economics that studies the robustness of decision rules to model misspecification (see Hansen and Sargent 2008). Underlying this robustness is often a static or dynamic two-person zero-sum game, which we illustrate in the context of Example 7.2.

Example 7.2, Continued Recall the monetary policy problem described at the beginning of this section. Suppose scepticism about the posterior probabilities $\pi_{1,T}$ and $\pi_{2,T}$ generates some concern about the robustness of the policy decision to perturbations of these model probabilities. This concern can be represented through the following game between the policy maker and a fictitious adversary, called nature:

Table 7.5: Nash equilibrium as a function of risk sensitivity τ

τ	0.00	1.00	10.0	100
$q^*(\tau)$	1.00	1.10	1.43	1.60
$\delta^*(\tau)$	-0.32	-0.30	-0.19	-0.12

$$\min_{\delta} \max_{q \in [0, 1/\pi_{1,T}]} \quad q\pi_{1,T} L(\mathcal{M}_1, \delta) + (1 - q\pi_{1,T}) L(\mathcal{M}_2, \delta) \qquad (7.140)$$
$$+ \frac{1}{\tau} \Big[\pi_{1,T} \ln(q\pi_{1,T}) + (1 - \pi_{1,T}) \ln(1 - q\pi_{1,T}) \Big].$$

Here, nature uses q to distort the posterior model probability of model $\mathcal{M}_1$. To ensure that the distorted probability of $\mathcal{M}_1$ lies in the unit interval, the domain of q is restricted to $[0, 1/\pi_{1,T}]$. The second term in (7.140) penalizes the distortion as a function of the Kullback-Leibler divergence between the undistorted and distorted probabilities. If τ is equal to zero, then the penalty is infinite and nature will not distort $\pi_{1,T}$. If, however, $\tau = \infty$, then conditional on a particular δ nature will set $q = 1/\pi_{1,T}$ if $L(\mathcal{M}_1, \delta) > L(\mathcal{M}_2, \delta)$ and $q = 0$ otherwise. For selected values of τ, the Nash equilibrium is summarized in Table 7.5. In our numerical illustration, $L(\mathcal{M}_1, \delta) > L(\mathcal{M}_2, \delta)$ in the relevant region for δ. Thus, nature has an incentive to increase the probability of $\mathcal{M}_1$, and in response the policy maker reduces (in absolute terms) her response δ to a supply shock. □

The particular implementation of robust decision making in Example 7.2 is very stylized. While it is our impression that in actual decision making a central bank is taking the output of formal Bayesian analysis more and more seriously, the final decision about economic policies is influenced by concerns about robustness and involves adjustments of model outputs in several dimensions. These adjustments may reflect some scepticism about the correct formalization of the relevant economic mechanisms as well as the availability of information that is difficult to process in macroeconometric models such as VARs and DSGE models.

References

Adolfson, M., Lindé, J., and Villani, M. (2007). "Forecasting Performance of an Open Economy Dynamic Stochastic General Equilibrium Model," *Econometric Reviews*, 26(2–4): 289–328.

Altug, S. (1989). "Time-to-Build and Aggregate Fluctuations: Some New Evidence," *International Economic Review*, 30(4): 889–920.

An, S., and Schorfheide, F. (2007a). "Bayesian Analysis of DSGE Models," *Econometric Reviews*, 26(2–4): 113–72.

——— (2007b). "Bayesian Analysis of DSGE Models—Rejoinder," *Econometric Reviews*, 26(2–4): 211–19.

Aruoba, S. B., Fernández-Villaverde, J., and Rubio-Ramírez, J. F. (2004). "Comparing Solution Methods for Dynamic Equilibrium Economies," *Journal of Economic Dynamics and Control*, 30(12): 2477–508.

Bernanke, B. S., Boivin, J., and Eliasz, P. (2005). "Measuring the Effects of Monetary Policy," *Quarterly Journal of Economics*, 120(1): 387–422.

Bernardo, J. E., and Smith, A. F. (1994). *Bayesian Theory*. Hoboken, NJ: John Wiley & Sons.

Blanchard, O. J., and Quah, D. (1989). "The Dynamic Effects of Aggregate Demand and Supply Disturbances," *American Economic Review*, 79(4), 655–73.

Boivin, J., and Giannoni, M. P. (2006a). "DSGE Models in a Data Rich Enviroment," NBER Working Paper, 12772.

——— (2006b). "Has Monetary Policy Become More Effective," *Review of Economics and Statistics*, 88(3): 445–62.

Canova, F. (1994). "Statistical Inference in Calibrated Models," *Journal of Applied Econometrics*, 9: S123–44.

—— and Ciccarelli, M. (2009). "Estimating Multi-country VAR Models," *International Economic Review*, 50(3): 929–59.

—— and De Nicoló, G. (2002). "Monetary Disturbances Matter for Business Fluctuations in the G-7," *Journal of Monetary Economics*, 49(4): 1131–59.

—— and Gambetti, L. (2009). "Structural Changes in the US Economy: Is There a Role for Monetary Policy?," *Journal of Economic Dynamics and Control*, 33(2): 477–90.

Carter, C., and Kohn, R. (1994). "On Gibbs Sampling for State Space Models," *Biometrika*, 81(3): 541–53.

Chang, Y., Doh, T., and Schorfheide, F. (2007). "Non-stationary Hours in a DSGE Model," *Journal of Money, Credit, and Banking*, 39(6): 1357–73.

Chao, J., and Phillips, P. C. (1999). "Model Selection in Partially-Nonstationary Vector Autoregressive Processes with Reduced Rank Structure," *Journal of Econometrics*, 91(2): 227–71.

Chari, V. V., Kehoe, P. J., and McGrattan, E. R. (2008). "Are Structural VARs with Long-Run Restrictions Useful in Developing Business Cycle Theory?," *Journal of Monetary Economics*, 55(8): 1337–152.

Chib, S., and Greenberg, E. (1994). "Bayes Inference in Regression Models with ARMA(p,q) Errors," *Journal of Econometrics*, 64(1–2): 183–206.

—— and Jeliazkov, I. (2001). "Marginal Likelihoods from the Metropolis Hastings Output," *Journal of the American Statistical Association*, 96(453): 270–81.

—— and Ramamurthy, S. (2010). "Tailored Randomized Block MCMC Methods with Application to DSGE Models," *Journal of Econometrics*, 155(1): 19–38.

Chopin, N., and Pelgrin, F. (2004). "Bayesian Inference and State Number Determination for Hidden Markov Models: An Application to the Information Content of the Yield Curve about Inflation," *Journal of Econometrics*, 123(2): 327–44.

Christiano, L. J., Eichenbaum, M., and Evans, C. L. (1999). "Monetary Policy Shocks: What Have We Learned and to What End," in J. B. Taylor and M. Woodford (eds.), *Handbook of Macroeconomics*, vol. 1a. Amsterdam: North-Holland, 65–148.

————— (2005). "Nominal Rigidities and the Dynamic Effects of a Shock to Monetary Policy," *Journal of Political Economy*, 113(1): 1–45.

——— and Vigfusson, R. (2007). "Assessing Structural VARs," in D. Acemoglu, K. Rogoff, and M. Woodford (eds.), *NBER Macroeconomics Annual 2006*, vol. 21. Cambridge, Mass.: MIT Press, 1–72.

Clarida, R., Gali, J., and Gertler, M. (2000). "Monetary Policy Rules and Macroeconomic Stability: Evidence and Some Theory," *Quarterly Journal of Economics*, 115(1): 147–80.

Cochrane, J. H. (1994). "Shocks," *Carnegie Rochester Conference Series on Public Policy*, 41(4): 295–364.

Cogley, T., Morozov, S., and Sargent, T. J. (2005). "Bayesian Fan Charts for U.K. Inflation: Forecasting Sources of Uncertainty in an Evolving Monetary System," *Journal of Economic Dynamics and Control*, 29(11): 1893–925.

—— and Sargent, T. J. (2002). "Evolving Post-World War II U.S. Inflation Dynamics," in B. S. Bernanke, and K. Rogoff (eds.), *NBER Macroeconomics Annual 2001*, vol. 16. Cambridge, Mass.: MIT Press, 331–88.

—— —— (2005a). "The Conquest of US Inflation: Learning and Robustness to Model Uncertainty," *Review of Economic Dynamics*, 8(2): 528–63.

—— —— (2005b). "Drifts and Volatilities: Monetary Policies and Outcomes in the Post-WWII US," *Review of Economic Dynamics*, 8(2): 262–302.

—— and Sbordone, A. M. (2008). "Trend Inflation, Indexation, and Inflation Persistence in the New Keynesian Phillips Curve," *American Economic Review*, 98(5): 2101–26.

Davig, T., and Leeper, E. M. (2007). "Generalizing the Taylor Principle," *American Economic Review*, 97(3): 607–35.

De Mol, C., Giannone, D., and Reichlin, L. (2008). "Forecasting Using a Large Number of Predictors: Is Bayesian Shrinkage a Valid Alternative to Principal Components?," *Journal of Econometrics*, 146(2): 318–28.

DeJong, D. N., Ingram, B. F., and Whiteman, C. H. (1996). "A Bayesian Approach to Calibration," *Journal of Business Economics and Statistics*, 14(4): 1–9.

—— —— —— (2000). "A Bayesian Approach to Dynamic Macroeconomics," *Journal of Econometrics*, 98(2): 203–23.

Del Negro, M. (2003). "Discussion of Cogley and Sargent's 'Drifts and Volatilities: Monetary Policy and Outcomes in the Post WWII US'," Federal Reserve Bank of Atlanta Working Paper, 2003-06.

—— and Otrok, C. (2007). "99 Luftballoons: Monetary Policy and the House Price Boom Across the United States," *Journal of Monetary Economics*, 54(7): 1962–85.

—— —— (2008). "Dynamic Factor Models with Time-Varying Parameters. Measuring Changes in International Business Cycles," Federal Reserve Bank of New York Staff Report, 325.

—— and Schorfheide, F. (2004). "Priors from General Equilibrium Models for VARs," *International Economic Review*, 45(2): 643–73.

—— —— (2008). "Forming Priors for DSGE Models (and How it Affects the Assessment of Nominal Rigidities)," *Journal of Monetary Economics*, 55(7): 1191–208.

—— —— (2009). "Monetary Policy with Potentially Misspecified Models," *American Economic Review*, 99(4): 1415–50.

—— —— Smets, F., and Wouters, R. (2007). "On the Fit of New Keynesian Models," *Journal of Business and Economic Statistics*, 25(2): 123–62.

Doan, T., Litterman, R., and Sims, C. A. (1984). "Forecasting and Conditional Projections Using Realistic Prior Distributions," *Econometric Reviews*, 3(4): 1–100.

Edge, R., Kiley, M., and Laforte, J.-P. (2009). "A Comparison of Forecast Performance between Federal Reserve Staff Forecasts, Simple Reduced-Form Models, and a DSGE Model," Federal Reserve Board of Governors Finance and Economics Discussion Paper Series, 2009-10.

Eklund, J., and Karlsson, S., (2007). "Forecast Combination and Model Averaging Using Predictive Measures," *Econometric Reviews*, 26(2–4): 329–63.

Engle, R. F., and Granger, C. W. (1987). "Co-integration and Error Correction: Representation, Estimation, and Testing," *Econometrica*, 55(2): 251–76.

Farmer, R., Waggoner, D., and Zha, T. (2009). "Understanding Markov Switching Rational Expectations Models," *Journal of Economic Theory*, 144(5): 1849–67.

Faust, J. (1998). "The Robustness of Identified VAR Conclusions about Money," *Carnegie Rochester Conference Series on Public Policy*, 49(4): 207–44.

Fernandez, C., Ley, E., and Steel, M. F. J. (2001). "Model Uncertainty in Cross-Country Growth Regressions," *Journal of Applied Econometrics*, 16(5): 563–76.

Fernández-Villaverde, J., and Rubio-Ramírez, J. F. (2007). "Estimating Macroeconomic Models: A Likelihood Approach," *Review of Economic Studies*, 74(4): 1059–87.

——— ——— (2008). "How Structural are Structural Parameters?," in D. Acemoglu, K. Rogoff, and M. Woodford (eds.), *NBER Macroeconomics Annual 2007*, vol. 22. University of Chicago Press, Chicago: University of Chicago Press.

George, E. I., Ni, S., and Sun, D. (2008). "Bayesian Stochastic Search for VAR Model Restrictions," *Journal of Econometrics*, 142(1): 553–80.

Geweke, J. (1977). "The Dynamic Factor Analysis of Economic Time Series," in D. J. Aigner and A. S. Goldberger, (eds.), *Latent Variables in Socio-Economic Models*. Amsterdam: North-Holland, chapter 19.

——— (1996). "Bayesian Reduced Rank Regression in Econometrics," *Journal of Econometrics*, 75(1): 121–46.

——— (1999). "Using Simulation Methods for Bayesian Econometric Models: Inference, Development, and Communication," *Econometric Reviews*, 18(1): 1–126.

——— (2005). *Contemporary Bayesian Econometrics and Statistics*. Hoboken, NJ: John Wiley & Sons.

——— (2007). "Bayesian Model Comparison and Validation," *American Economic Review Papers and Proceedings*, 97: 60–4.

——— (2010). *Complete and Incomplete Econometric Models*. Princeton: Princeton University Press.

——— and Terui, N. (1993). "Bayesian Threshold Autoregressive Models for Nonlinear Time Series," *Journal of Time Series Analysis*, 14(5): 441–54.

——— and Whiteman, C. H. (2006). "Bayesian Forecasting," in G. Elliott, C. W. Granger, and A. Timmermann (eds.), *Handbook of Economic Forecasting*, vol. 1. Amsterdam: North-Holland, 3–80.

——— and Zhou, G. (1996). "Measuring the Pricing Error of the Arbitrage Pricing Theory," *Review of Financial Studies*, 9(2): 557–87.

Halpern, E. F. (1974). "Posterior Consistency for Coefficient Estimation and Model Selection in the General Linear Hypothesis," *Annals of Statistics*, 2(4): 703–12.

Hamilton, J. D. (1989). "A New Approach to the Economic Analysis of Nonstationary Time Series and the Business Cycle," *Econometrica*, 57(2): 357–84.

——— Waggoner, D., and Zha, T. (2007). "Normalization in Econometrics," *Econometric Reviews*, 26(2–4): 221–52.

Hansen, L. P., and Sargent, T. J. (2008). *Robustness*. Princeton: Princeton University Press.

Ingram, B., and Whiteman, C. (1994). "Supplanting the Minnesota Prior— Forecasting Macroeconomic Time Series Using Real Business Cycle Model Priors," *Journal of Monetary Economics*, 49(4): 1131–59.

Ireland, P. N. (2004). "A Method for Taking Models to the Data," *Journal of Economic Dynamics and Control*, 28(6): 1205–26.

Jacquier, E., Polson, N. G., and Rossi, P. E. (1994). "Bayesian Analysis of Stochastic Volatility Models," *Journal of Business & Economic Statistics*, 12(4): 371–89.

James, A. T. (1954). "Normal Multivariate Analysis and the Orthogonal Group," *Annals of Mathematical Statistics*, 25(1): 40–75.

Johansen, S. (1988). "Statistical Analysis of Cointegration Vectors," *Journal of Economic Dynamics and Control*, 12(2–3): 231–54.

—— (1991). "Estimation and Hypothesis Testing of Cointegration Vectors in Gaussian Vector Autoregressive Models," *Econometrica*, 59(6): 1551–80.

—— (1995). *Likelihood-Based Inference in Cointegrated Vector Autoregressive Models*. New York: Oxford University Press.

Justiniano, A., and Primiceri, G. E. (2008). "The Time-Varying Volatility of Macroeconomic Fluctuations," *American Economic Review*, 98(3): 604–41.

—— —— and Tambalotti, A. (2009). "Investment Shocks and Business Cycles," NBER Working Paper, 15570.

Kadane, J. B. (1974). "The Role of Identification in Bayesian Theory," in S. E. Fienberg and A. Zellner (eds.), *Studies in Bayesian Econometrics and Statistics*. Amsterdam: North-Holland, 175–91.

Kadiyala, K. R., and Karlsson, S. (1997). "Numerical Methods for Estimation and Inference in Bayesian VAR-Models," *Journal of Applied Econometrics*, 12(2): 99–132.

Kass, R. E., and Raftery, A. E. (1995). "Bayes Factors," *Journal of the American Statistical Association*, 90(430): 773–95.

Kim, C., and Nelson, C. R. (1999a). "Has the U.S. Economy Become More Stable? A Bayesian Approach Based on a Markov-Switching Model of the Business Cycle," *Review of Economics and Statistics*, 81(4): 608–18.

—— (1999b). *State-Space Models with Regime Switching*. Cambridge, Mass.: MIT Press.

Kim, S., Shephard, N., and Chib, S. (1998). "Stochastic Volatility: Likelihood Inference and Comparison with ARCH Models," *Review of Economic Studies*, 65(3): 361–93.

King, R. G., Plosser, C. I., and Rebelo, S. (1988). "Production, Growth, and Business Cycles: I The Basic Neoclassical Model," *Journal of Monetary Economics*, 21(2–3): 195–232.

Kleibergen, F., and Paap, R. (2002). "Priors, Posteriors and Bayes Factors for a Bayesian Analysis of Cointegration," *Journal of Econometrics*, 111(2): 223–49.

—— and van Dijk, H. K. (1994). "On the Shape of the Likelihood/Posterior in Cointegration Models," *Econometric Theory*, 10(3–4): 514–51.

Klein, L. R., and Kosobud, R. F. (1961). "Some Econometrics of Growth: Great Ratios of Economics," *Quarterly Journal of Economics*, 75(2): 173–98.

Koop, G., and Korobilis, D. (2010). "Bayesian Multivariate Time Series Methods for Empirical Macroeconomics," in *Foundations and Trends in Econometrics*, 3(4): 267–358.

—— Leon-Gonzalez, R., and Strachan, R. (2008). "Bayesian Inference in the Time Varying Cointegration Model," Rimini Center for Economic Analysis Working Paper, 23-08.

—— —— —— (2009). "On the Evolution of the Monetary Policy Transmission Mechanism," *Journal of Economic Dynamics and Control*, 33(4): 997–1017.

—— and Potter, S. M. (1999). "Bayes Factors and Nonlinearity: Evidence from Economic Time Series," *Journal of Econometrics*, 88(2): 251–81.

—— —— (2007). "Estimation and Forecasting in Models with Multiple Breaks," *Review of Economic Studies*, 74(3): 763–89.

——— (2008). "Time-Varying VARs with Inequality Restrictions," Manuscript, University of Strathclyde and FRB New York.

——— (2009). "Prior Elicitation in Multiple Change-point Models," *International Economic Review*, 50(3): 751–72.

—— Strachan, R., van Dijk, H. K., and Villani, M. (2006). "Bayesian Approaches to Cointegration," in ed. by T. C. Mills and K. P. Patterson (eds.), *Palgrave Handbook of Econometrics*, vol. 1. Basingstoke: Palgrave Macmillan, 871–98.

Kose, M. A., Otrok, C., and Whiteman, C. H. (2003). "International Business Cycles: World, Region, and Country-Specific Factors," *American Economic Review*, 93(4): 1216–39.

Kryshko, M. (2010). "Data-Rich DSGE and Dynamic Factor Models," Manuscript, University of Pennsylvania.

Lancaster, T. (2004). *An Introduction to Modern Bayesian Econometrics*. Malden, Mass.: Blackwell Publishing.

Leeper, E. M., and Faust, J. (1997). "When do Long-Run Identifiying Restrictions Give Reliable Results?," *Journal of Business & Economic Statistics*, 15(3): 345–53.

—— and Sims, C. A. (1995). "Toward a Modern Macroeconomic Model Usable for Policy Analysis," in S. Fischer and J. J. Rotemberg (eds.), *NBER Macroeconomics Annual 1994*. Cambridge, Mass.: MIT Press, 81–118.

Levin, A., Onatski, A., Williams, J. C., and Williams, N. (2006). "Monetary Policy under Uncertainty in Micro-founded Macroeconometric Models," in M. Gertler and K. Rogoff (eds.), *NBER Macroeconomics Annual 2005*, vol. 20. Cambridge, MIT Press, 229–287.

Litterman, R. B. (1980). "Techniques for Forecasting with Vector Autoregressions," Ph.D. thesis, University of Minnesota.

Lopes, H. F., and West, M. (2004). "Bayesian Model Assessment in Factor Analysis," *Statistica Sinica*, 14(1): 41–67.

Lubik, T. A., and Schorfheide, F. (2004). "Testing for Indeterminancy: An Application to U.S. Monetary Policy," *American Economic Review*, 94(1): 190–217.

Masanjala, W. H., and Papageorgiou, C. (2008). "Rough and Lonely Road to Prosperity: A Reexamination of the Sources of Growth in Africa Using Bayesian Model Averaging," *Journal of Applied Econometrics*, 23(5): 671–82.

McConnell, M. M., and Perez-Quiros, G. (2000). "Output Fluctuations in the United States: What Has Changed since the Early 1980's?," *American Economic Review*, 90(5): 1464–76.

Min, C.-K., and Zellner, A. (1993). "Bayesian and Non-Bayesian Methods for Combining Models and Forecasts with Applications to Forecasting International Growth Rates," *Journal of Econometrics*, 56(1–2): 89–118.

Moon, H. R., and Schorfheide, F. (2009). "Bayesian and Frequentist Inference in Partially-Identified Models," NBER Working Paper, 14882.

Mumtaz, H., and Surico, P. (2008). "Evolving International Inflation Dynamics: World and Country Specific Factors," CEPR Discussion Paper, 6767.

Nason, J. M., and Cogley, T. (1994). "Testing the Implications of Long-Run Neutrality for Monetary Business Cycle Models," *Journal of Applied Econometrics*, 9: S37–70.

Ng, S., Moench, E., and Potter, S. M. (2008). "Dynamic Hierarchical Factor Models," Manuscript, Columbia University and FRB New York.

Otrok, C. (2001). "On Measuring the Welfare Costs of Business Cycles," *Journal of Monetary Economics*, 45(1): 61–92.

—— and Whiteman, C. H. (1998). "Bayesian Leading Indicators: Measuring and Predicting Economic Conditions in Iowa," *International Economic Review*, 39(4): 997–1014.

Paap, R., and van Dijk, H. K. (2003). "Bayes Estimates of Markov Trends in Possibly Cointegrated Series: An Application to U.S. Consumption and Income," *Journal of Business Economics & Statistics*, 21(4): 547–63.

Peersman, G. (2005). "What Caused the Millenium Slowdown? Evidence Based on Vector Autoregressions," *Journal of Applied Econometrics*, 20(2): 185–207.

Pelloni, G., and Polasek, W. (2003). "Macroeconomic Effects of Sectoral Shocks in Germany, the U.K. and, the U.S.: A VAR-GARCH-M Approach," *Computational Economics*, 21(1): 65–85.

Phillips, P. C. B. (1991). "Optimal Inference in Cointegrated Systems," *Econometrica*, 59(2): 283–306.

____ (1996). "Econometric Model Determination," *Econometrica*, 64(4): 763–812.

____ and Ploberger, W. (1996). "An Asymptotic Theory of Bayesian Inference for Time Series," *Econometrica*, 64(2): 318–412.

Poirier, D. (1998). "Revising Beliefs in Nonidentified Models," *Econometric Theory*, 14(4): 483–509.

Primiceri, G. E. (2005). "Time Varying VARs and Monetary Policy," *Review of Economic Studies*, 72(3): 821–52.

Rabanal, P., and Rubio-Ramírez, J. F. (2005). "Comparing New Keynesian Models of the Business Cycle: A Bayesian Approach," *Journal of Monetary Economics*, 52(6): 1151–66.

Ríos-Rull, J.-V., Schorfheide, F., Fuentes-Albero, C., Kryshko, M., and Santaeulalia-Llopis, R. (2009). "Methods versus Substance: Measuring the Effects of Technology Shocks," NBER Working Paper, 15375.

Robertson, J. C., and Tallman, E. W. (2001). "Improving Federal Funds Rate Forecasts in VAR Models Used for Policy Analysis," *Journal of Business & Economic Statistics*, 19(3): 324–30.

Rogerson, R. (1988). "Indivisible Labor Lotteries and Equilibrium," *Journal of Monetary Economics*, 21(1): 3–16.

Rubio-Ramírez, J. F., Waggoner, D., and Zha, T. (2010). "Structural Vector Autoregressions: Theory of Identification and Algorithms for Inference," *Review of Economic Studies*, 77(2): 665–96.

Sala-i Martin, X., Doppelhofer, G., and Miller, R. I. (2004). "Determinants of Long-Term Growth: A Bayesian Averaging of Classical Estimates (BACE) Approach," *American Economic Review*, 94(4): 813–35.

Sargent, T. J. (1989). "Two Models of Measurements and the Investment Accelerator," *Journal of Political Economy*, 97(2): 251–87.

____ (1999). *The Conquest of American Inflation*. Princeton: Princeton University Press.

____ and Sims, C. A. (1977). "Business Cycle Modeling without Pretending to Have Too Much a Priori Economic Theory," in *New Methods in Business Cycle Research*. Minneapolis: Federal Reserve Bank of Minneapolis.

Schorfheide, F. (2000). "Loss Function-Based Evaluation of DSGE Model," *Journal of Applied Econometrics*, 15(6): 645–70.

____ (2005). "Learning and Monetary Policy Shifts," *Review of Economic Dynamics*, 8(2): 392–419.

____ (2008). "DSGE Model-Based Estimation of the New Keynesian Phillips Curve," *FRB Richmond Economic Quarterly*, Fall Issue, 397–433.

Schotman, P. C., and van Dijk, H. K. (1991). "On Bayesian Routes to Unit Roots," *Journal of Applied Econometrics*, 6(4): 387–401.

Schwarz, G. (1978). "Estimating the Dimension of a Model," *Annals of Statistics*, 6(2): 461–4.

Sims, C. A. (1972). "The Role of Approximate Prior Restrictions in Distributed Lag Estimation," *Journal of the American Statistical Association*, 67(337): 169–75.

—— (1980). "Macroeconomics and Reality," *Econometrica*, 48(4): 1–48.

—— (1993). "A 9 Variable Probabilistic Macroeconomic Forecasting Model," in J. H. Stock and M. W. Watson (eds.), *Business Cycles, Indicators, and Forecasting*, vol. 28 of *NBER Studies in Business Cycles*. Chicago: University of Chicago Press, 179–214.

—— (2002a). "Comment on Cogley and Sargent's 'Evolving post World War II U.S. Inflation Dynamics'," in B. S. Bernanke and K. Rogoff (eds.), *NBER Macroeconomics Annual 2001*, vol. 16. Cambridge, Mass.: MIT Press, 373–9.

—— (2002b). "Solving Linear Rational Expectations Models," *Computational Economics*, 20(1–2): 1–20.

—— (2003). "Probability Models for Monetary Policy Decisions," Manuscript, Princeton University.

—— and Uhlig, H. (1991). "Understanding Unit Rooters: A Helicopter Tour," *Econometrica*, 59(6): 1591–9.

—— Waggoner, D., and Zha, T. (2008). "Methods for Inference in Large Multiple-Equation Markov-Switching Models," *Journal of Econometrics*, 146(2): 255–74.

—— and Zha, T. (1998). "Bayesian Methods for Dynamic Multivariate Models," *International Economic Review*, 39(4): 949–68.

—— —— (1999). "Error Bands for Impulse Responses," *Econometrica*, 67(5): 1113–55.

—— —— (2006). "Were there Regime Switches in U.S. Monetary Policy?," *American Economic Review*, 96(1): 54–81.

Smets, F., and Wouters, R. (2003). "An Estimated Dynamic Stochastic General Equilibrium Model of the Euro Area," *Journal of the European Economic Association*, 1(5): 1123–75.

—— —— (2007). "Shocks and Frictions in US Business Cycles: A Bayesian DSGE Approach," *American Economic Review*, 97(3): 586–606.

Stock, J. H., and Watson, M. W. (1989). "New Indices of Coincident and Leading Economic Indicators," in O. J. Blanchard and S. Fischer (eds.), *NBER Macroeconomics Annual 1989*, vol. 4. Cambridge, Mass.: MIT Press, 351–94.

—— —— (1999). "Forecasting Inflation," *Journal of Monetary Economics*, 44(2): 293–335.

—— —— (2001). "Vector Autoregressions," *Journal of Economic Perspectives*, 15(4): 101–15.

—— —— (2002). "Macroeconomic Forecasting Using Diffusion Indexes," *Journal of Business and Economic Statistics*, 20(2): 147–62.

—— —— (2005). "Understanding Changes in International Business Cycle Dynamics," *Journal of the European Economic Association*, 3(5): 968–1006.

Strachan, R., and Inder, B. (2004). "Bayesian Analysis of the Error Correction Model," *Journal of Econometrics*, 123(2): 307–25.

—— and van Dijk, H. K. (2006). "Model Uncertainty and Bayesian Model Averaging in Vector Autoregressive Processes," Manuscript, Tinbergen Institute, 06/5.

Theil, H., and Goldberger, A. S. (1961). "On Pure and Mixed Estimation in Economics," *International Economic Review*, 2(3): 65–78.

Uhlig, H. (1997). "Bayesian Vector Autoregressions with Stochastic Volatility," *Econometrica*, 65(1): 59–73.

—— (2005). "What are the Effects of Monetary Policy on Output? Results from an Agnostic Identification Procedure," *Journal of Monetary Economics*, 52(2): 381–419.

Villani, M. (2001). "Fractional Bayesian Lag Length Inference in Multivariate Autoregressive Processes," *Journal of Time Series Analysis*, 22(1): 67–86.

——(2005). "Bayesian Reference Analysis of Cointegration," *Econometric Theory*, 21(2): 326–57.

——(2009). "Steady State Priors for Vector Autoregressions," *Journal of Applied Econometrics*, 24(4): 630–50.

Waggoner, D., and Zha, T. (1999). "Conditional Forecasts in Dynamic Multivariate Models," *Review of Economics and Statistics*, 81(4): 639–51.

—— ——(2003). "A Gibbs Sampler for Structural VARs," *Journal of Economic Dynamics and Control*, 28(2): 349–66.

Wright, J. (2008). "Bayesian Model Averaging and Exchange Rate Forecasting," *Journal of Econometrics*, 146: 329–41.

Zellner, A. (1971). *An Introduction to Bayesian Inference in Econometrics*. Hoboken, NJ: John Wiley & Sons.

CHAPTER 8

BAYESIAN APPLICATIONS IN MARKETING

PETER ROSSI AND GREG ALLENBY

1 Introduction

Our approach to the application of Bayesian methods in marketing has been influenced by aspects of marketing data and the decision problems confronting both consumers and firms. While there are compelling arguments for the adoption of the Bayesian paradigm by all econometricians (see the examples and models considered by Li and Tobias, chapter 6, this volume), we believe that the characteristics of marketing applications make for an especially good fit with the Bayesian approach.

Marketing data originate in the decisions of individual consumers or survey respondents. Consumer data is generated by purchases of products and is often collected at the point of sale. At this level, the data is fundamentally discrete with a modal value of 0 in the sense that consumers select only a tiny subset of the available products on any one purchase occasion. Some survey methods confront consumers with a choice from among a set of products as a way of indirectly measuring consumer preferences. This data is less sparse than actual purchase data but is still discrete. Other surveys ask consumers to reflect on their use of products or exposure to media and have questions that ask consumers which of a large set of products or media they "regularly purchase" or "regularly view." Still other survey methods collect ordinal data by using questions on a discrete rating scale. Thus, modeling of consumer-level purchase or survey data requires models that allow for sparse and discrete outcome variables. Demand models that give rise to a mixture of corner and interior solutions are discussed in Section 2.

Peter Rossi would like to acknowledge the Kilts Center for Marketing, Booth School of Business, University of Chicago, for providing research funds. Greg Allenby thanks the Fisher College of Business at Ohio State University for generous research support.

Not all marketing data is available at the consumer level. Purchase data is frequently aggregated up to a store or market level. This removes some of the discreteness from the data, though even at the store level many products are sold only infrequently. However, this poses the question of what models are appropriate for aggregated data. An approach championed by some is to take the aggregation seriously by starting from a disaggregated model of sales and adding up or integrating over a distribution of consumer types. In Section 2, we consider models of aggregate market shares which are derived from individual choice.

Although much data in marketing is fundamentally discrete, standard models of choice between mutually exclusive alternatives are not always appropriate. Consumers may not regard products, even in a narrowly defined product class, as close substitutes. For example, we often see consumers simultaneously purchasing multiple varieties of the same product. We also see consumers "trading-up" to higher quality products in response to price discounts or changes in budget allocation. Standard linear or homothetic models of choice cannot capture either phenomenon.

When consumers are confronted with a very large number of choice alternatives, they adopt decision rules to narrow the set of products under consideration. In some situations, this can be modeled formally by some sort of search process. In others, the set of products under consideration can be determined by more informal heuristics. In either case, we might adapt a more standard choice model to include a screening rule process.

Our focus on developing non-standard models for consumer purchase data is driven by the need to accommodate not just important aspects of the data itself but by the need to evaluate marketing actions. For the evaluation and improvement of marketing policies, we must postulate a model of the decision process rather than simply a descriptive statistical model for the data. Much of our research has been to explore alternative specifications of the consumer decision process, including not only the utility function over consumption of products but also the context of the decision.

In Section 3, we consider more standard statistical approaches that generate discreteness by applying a censoring function to underlying continuous latent variables. This approach generates models that can be employed in situations where more descriptive models are required. In addition, the MCMC methods appropriate for models with latent variables have general usefulness for models that are derived from demand theory.

Most of marketing is predicated on the assumption that consumers differ in their evaluation of products and in their reaction to the marketing environment. Our own experience has been that this finding of large differences between consumers is pervasive. Thus, any model of purchase and consumer behavior must accommodate a rich specification for heterogeneity. Models of heterogeneity are discussed in Section 4.

If the firm wants to customize its actions to specific customers or groups of customers, models of heterogeneity are doubly important. When we began our research program in marketing in the late 1980s, customization at a low level of aggregation was mostly of academic interest. However, it is now widely recognized as a potential source of value for the firm. Incorporating consumer heterogeneity requires inference for parameters at the lowest level of aggregation. This poses a challenge to standard non-Bayesian econometric methods which are focused mostly on common parameters and view individual-level parameters as incidental. Another implication of the fact that we want to include parameters at the lowest level of aggregation (which we term the "unit level") is that we are unlikely to ever have a great deal of information for the unit-level parameters. This provides a strong motivation for the use of Bayesian methods and informative priors.

As firms become increasingly sophisticated in monitoring the environment, the exogeneity assumption for marketing mix variables can be compromised. Most of the sales response or demand models are built to assume marketing mix variables are like any other covariate. It is common to condition on these variables and view them as chosen independent of the marketing environment. If a marketing mix variable (such as price) is set by the firm with partial knowledge of the unobserved portion of demand, then this assumption of independence is violated. In these situations, the conditional model of sales response must be augmented with a model of how the x variables are determined. The unobserved portion of demand can include common demand shocks, unobserved advertising or promotional activities, omitted variables capturing dynamic considerations, and unobserved product or quality characteristics. An equally important complication occurs when the firm is setting the level of the marketing mix variables with partial information about the responsiveness of the consumer to the x variables (that is when x is a function not of some portion of the error term but of the response coefficients). This latter situation not only has the potential to bias the analysis but introduces a new source of additional information regarding the parameters of the purchase or sales model. We will explore both of these issues in Section 5.

The need for non-standard models which accommodate discreteness and consumer heterogeneity is met by a particular set of Bayesian computational methods and models. We emphasize the need for proper, informative priors. As discussed in Section 4, hierarchical models embody a form of informative prior. Bayes estimators based on informative priors display well-known shrinkage properties which ensure excellent sampling properties and numerical stability in computing. In some contexts, the use of informative priors is essential for the development of Bayesian procedures with desirable computational and convergence properties. We will see examples of this with various probit models in Section 3. In these models, it can be advantageous to work in the unidentified parameter space. This is an option that is available to the Bayesian but not the frequentist. That is, we can set up computational methods that navigate the unidentified space but report on the distribution of identified parameters only. This approach requires a proper prior, however, and illustrates yet another advantage that is available with informative priors. From a purely computational point of view, proper priors modify likelihoods with singularities or near singularities, producing well-behaved posteriors. We do not require numerical linear algebra methods which are robust to ill-conditioned matrices as all posterior computations are done with properly conditioned matrices.

All of the methods and models discussed in this chapter are implemented in our contributed R (R 2009) package, `bayesm` (Rossi and McCulloch 2008). As required, we will cite the appropriate functions that implement a specific model. To obtain the package, install R (search for "CRAN" on the web) and use the "install packages" menu item to install `bayesm`.

2 Demand Models

In this section, we will outline several utility specifications that incorporate discreteness and other important aspects of consumer decisions. We start with a specification of the direct utility function over product consumption and a set of random utility error terms. We prefer to derive models that are consistent with these primitives rather than simply specifying an ad hoc statistical model.

When faced with discrete (but not necessarily multinomial data), many researchers attempt to adapt a standard multinomial logit model (MNL) to the problem. Covariates such as price, product characteristics, and demographic variables are added as explanatory variables in the MNL model without a discussion of how these variables affect the consumer decision problem. There is some justification in adding price through an appeal to an indirect utility specification, but it is not clear how to enter product characteristics. Certainly, product characteristics may ultimately affect demand, but it is an open question as to how this occurs. Demand might be derived from preferences defined over characteristics or product characteristics could influence the decision process. For example, a product characteristic might be used as the basis of a screening rule to determine which products enter into consideration for purchase (Gilbride and Allenby 2004). If utility is defined over product characteristics only, this will give rise to a very different model of demand than a standard logit model.[1]

For example, consider the situation in which some consumers purchase multiple varieties of the same product, such as a soft drink. The standard MNL is a model of mutually exclusive choices in which products are assumed to be highly substitutable. Clearly, purchase of soft drink varieties does not conform to the assumptions made by the MNL model. Some researchers might simply delete "troublesome" consumers or purchase occasions on which multiple products are purchased. Others might redefine the products by aggregation so as to remove the problem; for example, one might aggregate all of the colas into one product and all of the lemon-lime drinks into another. Still others might simply ignore the problem and fit the MNL model by a non-likelihood based method such as the Generalized Method of Moments (GMM). These researchers never realize they are applying a model with zero likelihood to their data.

On the other hand, our approach is to think carefully about the decision process and utility formulation. Demand for variety might stem from multiple consumption occasions (Dubé 2004) or simply from a non-standard utility function which allows

[1] For an extensive discussion of formulating economically consistent models of demand, see Chandukala et al. (2007).

varieties of soft drinks to be imperfect substitutes. Such a utility function can give rise to multiple varieties being purchased with others at zero demand (Kim et al. (2002)); that is, the vector of demand in the product category can have zero entries and more than one non-zero value.

We start with a specification of the generic demand problem. In most marketing applications, attention is restricted to a subset of goods. Usually this set of products is considered to have interrelated demand and is sometimes called a product category. Here we will refer to the set of products as a demand group. In most cases, the products can be thought of as reasonably close substitutes, but we might also consider the possibility that there are complementarities. We recognize that consumers are deciding how much to consume or purchase not only from this set of products but also for other products outside this group for which we have little or no data or are unwilling to model explicitly. We can think of the set of products not explicitly modeled as a composite good or outside alternative and view the consumers as choosing both among the products in the category and also between this product group and the outside good.

For most marketing applications, it is not useful to take the outside alternative as literally all other products and services or even all other products within a store or shopping outlet. This would imply that the reason a consumer is not observed to purchase from the demand group at a given occasion is that the utility that can be attained from purchase in the demand group is less than that which can be obtained from the outside alternative. In most applications, a narrower definition of the outside good is appropriate. For example, we might consider a subset of soft drinks for demand modeling. The outside good could be soft drink products outside this set or, more generally, beverages that might be regarded as potential substitutes. Defining the outside good as all of a very broad class of products puts a burden on the model to capture patterns of purchase incidence that are motivated by factors outside the model. In many applications in marketing, the analysis conditions on expenditures in the product category and there is no outside good. The limitation of the conditional approach is that the effect of changes made in the product set or marketing mix on category demand cannot be measured.

If x denotes a vector of consumption amounts for K products and z represents the outside alternative, we can formulate the consumer problem as:

$$\max_{x,z} U\left(x, z|\theta_h\right) \quad \text{subject to } p'x + z \leq E \tag{8.1}$$

Here we normalize so that the price of the outside good is 1 or that all prices are relative to the outside good. E denotes the expenditure allocation for the demand group. The utility function, $U()$, is indexed by possibly household-specific parameters, θ_h. The model in (8.1) does not provide an explicit role for any marketing mix variable other than price. In particular, product attributes are not explicitly incorporated into the model. For many consumer products, it is difficult to measure more than a small subset of product attributes. Again, the soft drink example serves us well. We could define a cola attribute but we don't expect to be able to differentiate between Pepsi and Coke using product attributes. In many instances, it may be useful to think of each product as having a unique set of attributes. Other researchers partition the attributes into those which are observed by the econometrician and those that are unobservable (see, for example, Berry et al. 1995). Conjoint analyses (Orme 2009) define product explicitly in terms of attributes and seek to direct measures of utility over attributes. The influence of promotional and advertising variables requires additional assumptions about how these variables are incorporated into consumer decisions. A simple model of advertising would be that advertising exposure enhances the marginal utility of the product.

The problem in (8.1) is deterministic if the U function is known. Clearly, decisions by consumers are not perfectly predictable given only prices. For this reason, unobservables or errors are introduced into the model. The standard random utility interpretation assumes that these errors represent an unobservable utility component—consumers make deterministic demand decisions but that this is unobservable to the econometrician. The interpretation of these unobservables depends in part upon their specification. We could introduce errors into utility as follows:

$$U_{i,t}^{h} = \overline{U}_{i,t}^{h} e^{\epsilon_{ijt}}. \tag{8.2}$$

$U_{i,t}^{h}$ is the marginal utility associated with good i for consumer j on purchase occasion t. $\bar{U}$ is the deterministic part of the utility function and typically would be parameterized by (possibly) consumer-specific parameters, θ_h. $\{\epsilon_{1ht}, \ldots, \epsilon_{Kht}\}$ represents the unobservable component of utility for each of the K products in the demand group on a specific purchase occasion. The functional form of (8.2) insures that marginal utility is always positive. These errors reconcile the observed demand with that predicted given knowledge of the utility parameters and prices and form the basis for the likelihood function or the observed joint distribution of demand.

Consumer heterogeneity can be viewed as an error component that is constant across purchase occasions for the same consumer. This would create what appears to be correlation between observations for the same consumer. Our approach is different. We will assume that, conditional on consumer-specific utility parameters, θ_h, the error terms are independent across consumers. From this point on, we will suppress the individual h subscripts. We will return to the modeling of consumer differences in Section 4.

The likelihood for the model is derived by considering the mapping from the error terms to the quantity demanded. If we substitute the marginal utility errors into the demand problem in (8.1), then demand, $y_t^* = \left(x_t^*, z_t^*\right)$, is a function of the marginal utility given the vector of prices and E:

$$y_t^* = f\left(\epsilon_t | \theta, p_t, E\right). \tag{8.3}$$

If the utility function is of a form which allows for corner solutions, then the quantity demanded can have a mixture of discrete and continuous distributions. The point masses in the quantity demanded must be computed by integrating over the appropriate region of the error term space which is consistent with a particular configuration of zero and non-zero demand. For example, if we observed a positive quantity of one of the brands purchased, the likelihood would receive a contribution from the density of continuous demand as well as a point mass for the probability of non-zero demand for this good. Evaluation of the likelihood would involve evaluation of the Jacobian of the transformation from ϵ to y^* as well as the computation of the probabilities of various sets in the error space (see discussion in section on the demand for variety below).

Specification of the model involves choices for the functional form of U and assumptions regarding the joint distribution of the error terms. The simplest possible assumption is that the error terms are independent across consumers, purchase occasions, and products (see, for example, Guadagni and Little 1983). There are good reasons to doubt whether the assumption of independence is appropriate. For example, if there exists an unobservable product attribute, then there is a component of the error term that varies across products but is common across consumers and time periods. This induces correlation of errors across products. Aggregate demand shocks might be common across all consumers but vary from period to period, again creating a source of dependence.

Choices of the utility functional form reflect important aspects of the marketing problem. A useful simplification is to write the utility function as nesting a sub-utility function for the products in the demand group and a bivariate utility over the sub-utility function and the outside good:

$$U(x, z) = V(u(x), z). \tag{8.4}$$

This is known as a separable utility function. Under these conditions, the utility maximization problem breaks into two parts. A decision is made as to how to allocate expenditure between the outside good and the demand group. If a non-zero allocation of expenditure is made to the demand group, then a further decision is made as to how to allocate this expenditure among the products.

2.1 Linear utility

One simple case of the separable utility function in (8.4) is a linear utility:

$$U(x, z) = \psi' x + \psi_z z. \tag{8.5}$$

The linear utility assumption means that only one good (including the outside good) will be purchased as there can be no tangencies of the budget set with the indifference curves. Thus, this specification produces a mutually exclusive choice model. We should never see both the outside good and one or more products from the demand group being chosen. However, in many applications this is ignored and observations of a purchase from the demand group and the outside good are coded as only a purchase from the demand group.

Demand models based on the linear utility in (8.5) have an especially simple role for the expenditure variable. As long as there is sufficient budget for the purchase of the goods, the quantity demanded will be E/p and the product chosen will be the product

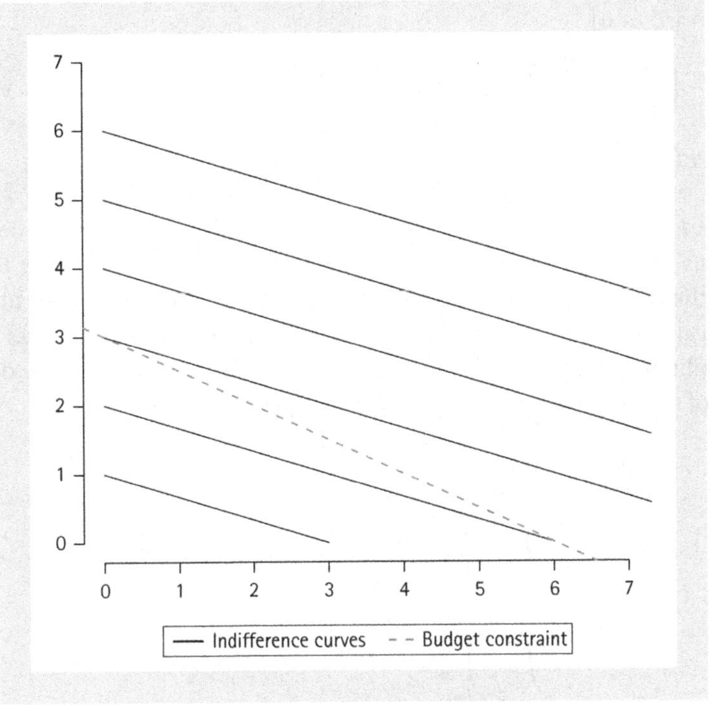

FIGURE 8.1 Homothetic linear utility

with the highest ratio of marginal utility to price, ψ_j/p_j. As E increases, the product chosen will not change (see Allenby and Rossi 1991). This property is illustrated in Figure 8.1. Linear utility is an example of a homothetic utility function. A homothetic utility function is a monotone transformation of a function that is homogeneous of degree one. This means that the slope of the indifference curves is constant along any ray through the origin. As shown in Allenby et al. (2010), the assumption of homotheticity implies that the ratio of demand for any two products is independent of E.

The likelihood for demand derived from the linear utility model is derived via a standard random utility argument as discussed above for the general case. We assume that marginal utility has an unobservable or "random" component. Assumptions regarding this component yield various possible likelihood functions. For the linear utility model, the likelihood is simply the probability of purchase of the observed product choice. Quantity demanded does not provide any more information unless E is regarded as an unknown parameter. The probability of choice is derived from the distribution of the error terms which represent the unobservable component of utility. For expositional simplicity, we will fold the outside good into the argument of the utility function and denote this vector as, y. $U\left(y\right) = \psi' y$. If we introduce the errors into marginal utility as in $\psi_{jt} = \psi_j e^{\epsilon_{jt}}$, then the first-order conditions for choice of brand i are given by:

$$Pr\,(i) = Pr\left[y_i^* > 0\right] \tag{8.6}$$

$$= Pr\left(\frac{\psi_{i,t}}{p_{it}} > \frac{\psi_{j,t}}{p_{j,t}}\right) = Pr\left(ln\psi_i - lnp_{it} + \epsilon_{it} > ln\psi_j - lnp_{jt} + \epsilon_{ij}\right)\ \forall j \neq i \tag{8.7}$$

$$= Pr\left(\epsilon_{jt} < V_{it} - V_{jt} + \epsilon_{it}\right)\ \forall j \neq i. \tag{8.8}$$

Here $V_{jt} = ln\psi_j - lnp_{jt}$. y_i^* denotes the quantity demanded. In order to compute the probabilities defined by the inequalities in (8.6), some assumptions have to be made regarding the distribution of the errors. If we assume that the errors are independent and identically distributed over each of the goods and independent across time, then the probabilities can be expressed in terms of integrals of the cumulative distribution functions of the errors (suppressing the t subscript).

$$Pr\,(i) = Pr\left(y_i^* > 0\right) \tag{8.9}$$

$$= \int_{-\infty}^{+\infty}\left(\prod_{j\neq i}\int_{-\infty}^{V_i - V_j + \epsilon_i} \pi\left(\epsilon_j\right) d\epsilon_j\right) \pi\left(\epsilon_i\right) d\epsilon_i \tag{8.10}$$

$$= \int_{-\infty}^{+\infty}\prod_{j\neq i} F\left(V_i - V_j + \epsilon_i\right) \pi\left(\epsilon_i\right) d\epsilon_i, \tag{8.11}$$

where $F(\cdot)$ is the CDF of the error distribution and $\pi\,(\cdot)$ is the density of the error terms.

The error terms are introduced to accommodate the fact that consumers do not make perfectly predictable demand decisions. The error terms can also be interpreted as a model of horizontal differentiation between products. If we consider only the deterministic part of the utility function, then the linear form implies that products are perfect substitutes. The assumption of perfect substitutability between products mean that consumers are always willing to exchange two goods at a constant rate given by the ratio of the linear coefficients. Some interpret this as perfectly substituable products having identical sources of utility but that they merely differ in the units of utility obtained from each product. A simple example would be different package sizes of the same product. The error term introduces a source of differentiation between the products so that consumers do not view them as identical up to a scale factor. The error terms create a demand for a product even if all consumers agree that it is dominated in terms of expected value (expected marginal utility divided by price). Because the error terms have unbounded support, there is always a non-zero probability that the consumer will purchase the product. Some criticize this assumption as unrealistic. For models involving product positioning and new products, this is particularly worrisome as it implies that all new products, however redundant given existing products, will enhance consumer welfare. These arguments tend to favor the notion that all products are valued in some sort of characteristic space which is finite but which may not be observable. This can motivate interest in models with non iid (independent and identically distributed) error terms.

If the errors have an extreme value type I distribution with scale parameter σ, then the CDF given by $F(t) = \exp\left(-\frac{1}{\sigma}\exp\left(-\frac{t}{\sigma}\right)\right)$ and (8.9) has a simple closed-form expression (McFadden 1981).

$$Pr(i) = \frac{\exp\left(\frac{ln\psi_i - lnp_i}{\sigma}\right)}{\sum_{j=1}^{K+1}\exp\left(\frac{ln\psi_j - lnpj_i}{\sigma}\right)} = \frac{\exp\left(\beta_{0,i} + \beta_p lnp_i\right)}{\sum_{j=1}^{K+1}\exp\left(\beta_{0,j} + \beta_p lnp_j\right)}. \tag{8.12}$$

We note here that the price coefficient is the reciprocal of the extreme value error scale parameter. In many applications of MNL models, the price coefficient is used to convert the other coefficients into a monetary value for different values of the associated explanatory variables. Sonnier et al. (2007) demonstrate the importance of careful consideration of the prior in these computations. In particular, it may be more reasonable to assess the prior on the ratio of a product attribute to the price coefficient rather than separately on the price coefficient and other coefficients.

In (8.12), there are redundant parameters as we can simply normalize with respect to any of the goods. If we normalize with respect to the $K + 1$st (outside good), we obtain an expression whose parameters are identified. We have used the fact that we set the price of the outside good to 1 to derive (8.13).

$$\begin{aligned} Pr(i) &= \frac{\exp\left(\beta_{0,i} + \beta_p lnp_i\right)}{\sum_{j=1}^{K+1}\exp\left(\beta_{0,j} + \beta_p lnp_j\right)} \times \frac{\exp\left(-\beta_{0,kK+1} - \beta_p lnp_{K+1}\right)}{\exp\left(-\beta_{0,kK+1} - \beta_p lnp_{K+1}\right)} \\ &= \frac{\exp\left(\tilde{\beta}_{0,i} + \tilde{\beta}_p lnp_i\right)}{1 + \sum_{j=1}^{K}\exp\left(\tilde{\beta}_{0,j} + \tilde{\beta}_p lnp_j\right)}. \end{aligned} \tag{8.13}$$

The MNL model is the only model which displays the Independence of Irrelevant Alternatives (IIA) property (McFadden 1981). The ratio of choice probabilities for products i and j depends only on variables and parameters for these two alternatives and *not* on the characteristics of any other choice alternative as the denominators in the choice probabilities will cancel out.

$$\frac{Pr(i)}{Pr(j)} = \frac{\exp\left(\tilde{\beta}_{0,i} + \tilde{\beta}_p lnp_i\right)}{\exp\left(\tilde{\beta}_{0,j} + \tilde{\beta}_p lnp_j\right)}. \tag{8.14}$$

It is well known that this same IIA property imposes severe restrictions on the cross-price elasticities of demand of product i with respect to product j (see, for example, Train 2003, section 3.6).

$$\frac{\partial Pr(i)}{\partial p_j}\frac{p_j}{Pr(i)} = \frac{\partial Pr(i)}{\partial lnp_j}\frac{1}{Pr(i)} = -\beta_p Pr(j). \tag{8.15}$$

This manifestation of the IIA property is often called the "proportional draw" property. If the price of product j is reduced, then it will draw increased demand proportionate to its choice probability. Often this property is applied at the market level. If we observe a market consisting of a large number of identical customers, then, by the law of large numbers, market shares will be similar to the choice probabilities conditional on price. To return to our soft drink example, suppose we consider a market with Coke, RC Cola, and 7-Up. Coke and RC Cola are both cola drinks with a similar taste, while 7-Up is a lemon-lime soft drink. 7-Up is a strong national brand, while RC Cola is a weaker brand with only pockets of strong regional demand. For this reason, we expect that 7-Up will have a larger share than RC Cola. The logit model would imply that the cross-price elasticity between Coke and 7-Up would be larger than that between Coke and RC Cola, even though we might expect Cola soft drinks to be more interdependent in demand.

Relaxing the IIA property has spawned interest in choice models derived using linear utility but with non-independent and non-extreme value errors. In Section 3, we consider the model with correlated normal errors. However, the fundamental weakness of the logit model for many marketing applications is the use of a linear utility structure.

2.2 Non-homothetic utility for multinomial data

Consider the problem of formulating a demand model for mutually exclusive choices, but where the choice options differ in quality. For example, consumers may purchase only one of a variety of offerings in categories such as cars, vacations, and electric razors. Choice is still characterized as a strict corner solution where just one of the alternatives has non-zero demand. As demonstrated earlier, this can only be ensured when indifference curves are linear. However, as the the budget allocated to the product category increases, we expect a higher demand for higher qualty goods. That is, consumers achieve higher utility by purchasing higher quality goods rather than simply consuming more of lower quality goods. We can define goods whose demand increases as expenditure increases as goods that are relatively superior to goods of lower quality for which demand declines as expenditure allocation increases. The lower quality goods are termed "relatively inferior."

Allenby and Rossi (1991) and Allenby et al. (2010) propose an implicitly defined utility function with linear indifference curves but non-constant marginal utility.

$$
\begin{aligned}
ln\,U(x, z) &= ln\,(u(x)) + \tau\,ln\,(z) \\
u(x) &= \sum_{k=1}^{K} \psi_k(\bar{u})\,x_k \\
\psi_k(\bar{u}) &= \exp\left[\alpha_k - \kappa_k \bar{u}(x, z)\right].
\end{aligned}
\tag{8.16}
$$

In this specification, marginal utility increases with attainable utility, $\bar{u}$. As consumers allocate more expenditure to the product class, attainable utility increases and relatively superior products increase their marginal utility relative to the inferior products. The utility function has valid linear indifference curves if $\kappa_k > 0$. Relatively smaller values of

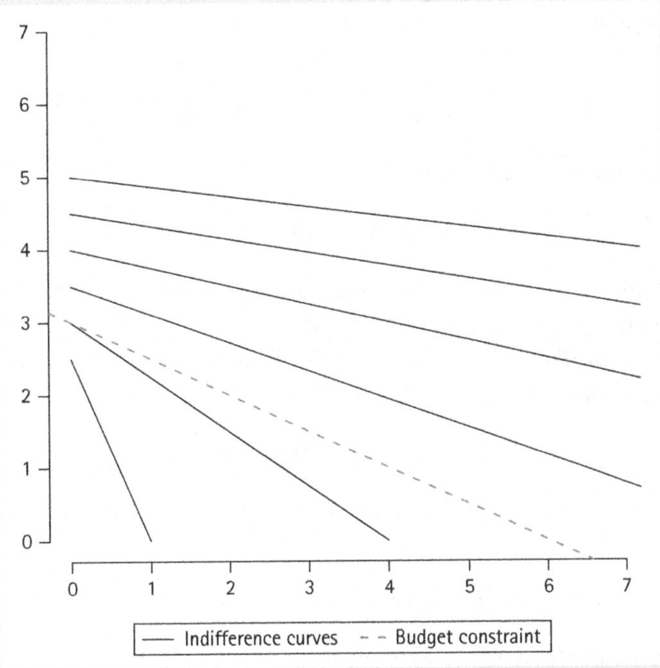

FIGURE 8.2 Non-homothetic linear utility

κ are associated with superior goods. Figure 8.2 shows the rotating indifference curves associated with this utility function. As the budget constraint is relaxed, the product chosen can shift as the relatively superior product becomes more highly valued given that the ratio of marginal utilities is not constant and increasing in attainable utility for the relatively superior products.

The non-homothetic utility function specified in (8.16) overcomes a number of the limitations of homothetic utility functions. In many situations, we observe that consumers are willing to "trade up" from lower-priced and lower-quality products to higher-priced and higher-quality products. For any homothetic utility system, product choice will not be altered by increases in E. This is an important consideration both across consumers and for the same consumer observed over time. Wealthier consumers may have greater E, but, more importantly, price reductions in a demand group can stimulate a demand for higher quality products in the group. This effect can be captured in the non-homothetic choice model discussed here, but not in the standard, linear utility, logit formulation.

In (8.16) a standard bivariate utility over the product class and the outside good ensures an interior solution, with an inside good purchased as long as the expenditure allocation is sufficient to allow for purchase. Given an assumption on marginal utility errors, we can derive the probability of choice of a brand by recognizing that only one brand will be purchased and, therefore, $E - p_i$ will be allocated to the outside alternative if brand i is chosen.

The log of utility associated with choice of brand i is:

$$ln\bar{u}^i = \alpha_i - \kappa_i \bar{u}^i + \tau ln\left(E - p_i\right), \tag{8.17}$$

where $\bar{u}^i$ is the root of the equation:

$$lnx + \kappa_i x - \alpha_i - \tau ln\left(E - p_i\right) = 0. \tag{8.18}$$

The root of (8.18) can be found by Newton's method. We note that Newton's method can be shown to converge on the unique root of (8.18).

We can derive the likelihood or choice probabilities for this model by the usual device of introducing errors into the marginal utilities.

$$\psi_{i,t}\left(\bar{u}\right) = \psi_i\left(\bar{u}\right)\exp\left(\epsilon_{it}\right).$$

The probability of selecting product i, given the computation of $\bar{u}^i$ for all choice alternatives, is:

$$Pr\left(i\right) = Pr\left(\alpha_i - \kappa_i \bar{u}^i + \tau ln\left(E - p_i\right) + \epsilon_k > \alpha_j - \kappa_j \bar{u}^j + \tau ln\left(E - p_j\right) + \epsilon_j \ \forall j \ni p_j \leq E\right).$$

If the error terms are the standard extreme value type I, we get a MNL with a non-linear regression function and the restriction that a non-zero probability of choice obtained only for products that are in the feasible consumption set.

$$Pr\left(i\right) = \frac{\exp\left(\alpha_i - \kappa_i \bar{u}^i + \tau ln\left(E - p_i\right)\right)}{\sum_{j \ni p_j < E} \exp\left(\alpha_j - \kappa_j \bar{u}^j + \tau ln\left(E - p_j\right)\right)}. \tag{8.19}$$

The non-homothetic choice model in (8.19) builds on the simple extreme value and independent errors but gives rise to a much richer pattern of demand with non-trivial income effects. It should be emphasized that income effects occur not only across households but for the same household when there are price changes in the demand group. During sale periods, the feasible level of utility can rise and this can increase the marginal utility of higher quality brands, inducing consumers to trade up to these offerings.

2.3 Multiple discreteness, satiation and the demand for variety

While variants of the multinomial choice model (any model in which the outcome is a multinomial random variable like the MNL or MNP models) are immensely popular both in marketing and in the Industrial Organization literature, we frequently observe non-mutually exclusive choice behavior. For example, consumers are observed to buy more than one variety of yogurt or movies or CDs, while it is still true that consumers

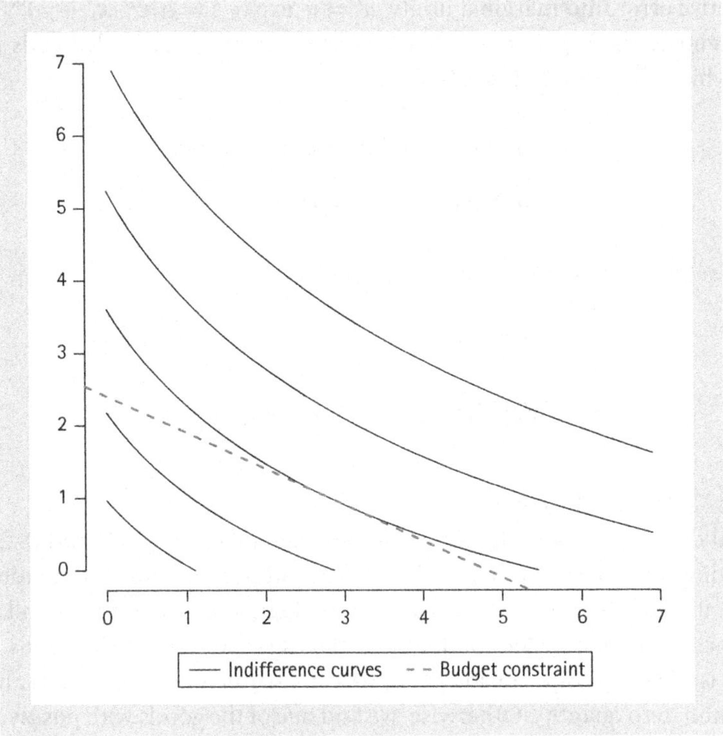

FIGURE 8.3 Non-linear utility

rarely buy more than a tiny fraction of the available products. For this reason, some have called this type of demand, multiple discreteness. We will need a utility function which is capable of a mixture of interior and corner solutions. Figure 8.3 displays a non-linear utility function that is capable of both interior and corner solutions as the indifference curves intersect axes instead of the more typical case where the indifference curves are tangential to the axes. In modeling the demand for variety, we might also consider the possibility of satiation or declining marginal utility. A simple utility function which achieves these goals is the translated power utility, as proposed by Kim et al. (2002).

$$u(x) = \sum_{k=1}^{K} \psi_k (x_k + \gamma_k)^{\alpha_k}. \tag{8.20}$$

In this model, the γ parameters serve to translate the utility so that the indifference curves can intersect the axes and result in corner solutions. The α parameters result in diminishing marginal utility. Marginal utility can be calculated from (8.20) as $u^i = \alpha_i \psi_i (x_i + \gamma_i)^{\alpha_i - 1}$.

We can derive the likelihood for this model from the Kuhn-Tucker (K-T) conditions (see, for example, Avriel 1976) for the consumer problem (Pudney 1989). We introduce a multiplicative error into marginal utility, $u^i = \bar{u}^i \exp(\epsilon_i) = \alpha_i \psi_i (x_i + \gamma_i)^{\alpha_i - 1} \exp(\epsilon_i)$, and differentiate the Lagrangian. x_j^* denotes the quantity demanded (this is optimal solution which obeys the K-T conditions).

$$\bar{u}^i \exp(\epsilon_i) - \lambda p_j = 0 \ \text{ if } x_j^* > 0$$

$$\bar{u}^i \exp(\epsilon_i) - \lambda p_j < 0 \ \text{ if } x_j^* = 0$$

Dividing by price and taking the logs, we obtain:

$$V_j\left(x_j^* | p_j\right) + \epsilon_j = ln\lambda \quad \text{if } x_j^* > 0 \tag{8.21}$$

$$V_j\left(x_j^* | p_j\right) + \epsilon_j < ln\lambda \quad \text{if } x_j^* = 0, \tag{8.22}$$

where $V_j\left(x_j^* | p_j\right) = ln\left(\bar{u}^j\right) - ln\left(p_j\right)$.

Optimal demand satisfies the K-T conditions in equations (8.21) and (8.22) as well as the "adding-up" constraint that $p'x^* = E$. The "adding-up" constraint induces a singularity in the distribution of x^*. To handle this singularity, we use the standard device of differencing the first-order conditions with respect to one of the goods. If one of the goods is the composite outside good, we can assume that this good is always consumed in non-zero quantity. Otherwise, we find one of the goods with positive demand. Without loss of generality assume that this is good 1. The K-T conditions can now be written.

$$v_j = h_j\left(x^*, p\right) \quad \text{if } x_j^* > 0$$

$$v_j < h_j\left(x^*, p\right) \quad \text{if } x_j^* = 0,$$

where $v_j = \epsilon_j - \epsilon_1$ and $h_j\left(x^*, p\right) = V_1 - V_j$ and $j = 2, \ldots, m$.

The likelihood for a given vector of demands can be constructed given an assumed distribution of the differenced errors, $\nu = \nu_2, \ldots, \nu_m$. If we assume that $\nu \sim N(0, \Omega)$, then the distribution of quantity demanded can be derived as a mixed discrete-continuous distribution. If we observe a corner (namely, zero consumption of one or more goods), then a discrete lump of probability is introduced by the fact that there is an entire region (a subset of R^{m-1}) of the marginal utility errors consistent with this corner solution. For non-zero quantities demanded, there will be a continuous density derived by change-of-variable methods. Suppose the first n goods have non-zero demand. The likelihood of quantity demanded has a continuous component for the first n goods, combined with the probability that the last $n+1, \ldots, m$ goods have zero demand.

$$\begin{aligned} &Pr\left(x_i^* > 0,\ i = 2, \ldots, n;\ x_i^* = 0,\ i = n+1, \ldots, m\right) \\ &= \int_{-\infty}^{h_m} \cdots \int_{-\infty}^{h_{n+1}} \phi\left(h_2, \ldots, h_n, \nu_{n+1}, \ldots, \nu_m | 0, \Omega\right) |J| d\nu_{n+1} \ldots d\nu_m, \end{aligned} \tag{8.23}$$

where $\phi(\cdot)$ is the multivariate normal density, $h_j = h_j(x^*, p)$, and J is the Jacobian with elements given by

$$J_{ij} = \frac{\partial h_{i+1}(x^*, p)}{\partial x^*_{j+1}} \quad i, j = 1, \ldots, n-1. \tag{8.24}$$

Kim et al. (2002) explain how to evaluate the likelihood using the GHK method (see Keane 1994 and Hajivassiliou et al. 1996) to compute the required integrals (see Bhat 2005, 2008 for the case of extreme value errors). R source code for this likelihood is available on the website for Rossi et al. (2005).

2.4 Models for aggregate shares

In many marketing research contexts, individual consumer-level data is not available. Rather, data is aggregated over consumers such as store-level or account or market-level data. In particular, aggregate data is often summarized by market shares along with some market size variable. The modeling of market share data is important for the practice of marketing. One reasonable point of view is that the models for aggregate share data should be *consistent* with those postulated at the individual level even if individual consumer data is not available. For example, it is possible to take the standard multinomial logit model as the model governing consumer choice. In a market with a very large number of consumers, the market shares are the expected probabilities of purchase which would be derived by integrating the individual model over the distribution of heterogeneity. The problem is that with a continuum of consumers, all of the choice model randomness will be averaged out and the market shares will be a deterministic function of the included choice model covariates. To overcome this problem, Berry et al. (1995) introduced an additional error term into consumer-level utility which reflects a market-wide unobservable. For their model, the utility of brand j for consumer i and time period t is given by

$$U_{ijt} = X_{jt}\theta^i_j + \eta_{jt} + \epsilon_{ijt}, \tag{8.25}$$

where X_{jt} is a vector of brand attributes, θ^i_j is a $k \times 1$ vector of coefficients, η_{jt} is an unobservable common to all consumers, and ϵ_{ijt} is the standard idiosyncratic shock (iid extreme value type I). If we normalize the utility of the outside good to zero, then market shares (denoted by s_{jt}) are obtained by integrating the multinomial logit model over a distribution of consumer parameters, $f(\theta^i|\delta)$, $\theta^i = [\theta^i_1, \ldots, \theta^i_J]$. δ is the vector of hyperparameters which govern the distribution of heterogeneity:

$$s_{jt} = \int \frac{\exp\left(X_{jt}\theta^i_j + \eta_{jt}\right)}{1 + \sum_{k=1}^{J} \exp\left(X_{kt}\theta^i_k + \eta_{kt}\right)} f(\theta^i|\delta)\, d\theta^i = \int s_{ijt}\left(\theta^i|X_t, \eta_t\right) f(\theta^i|\delta)\, d\theta^i.$$

While it is not necessary to assume that consumer parameters are normally distributed, most applications assume a normal distribution. In some cases, difficulties in estimating the parameters of the mixing distribution force investigators to further restrict the covariance matrix of the normal distribution to a diagonal matrix (see Jiang et al. 2009). Assume that $\theta^i \sim N\left(\bar{\theta}, \Sigma\right)$, then the aggregate shares can be expressed as a function of aggregate shocks and the preference distribution parameters.

$$s_{jt} = \int \frac{\exp\left(X_{jt}\theta^i + \eta_{jt}\right)}{1 + \sum_{k=1}^{J} \exp\left(X_{kt}\theta_k^i + \eta_{kt}\right)} \phi\left(\theta^i | \theta, \Sigma\right) d\theta^i = h\left(\eta_t | X_t, \bar{\theta}, \Sigma\right), \tag{8.26}$$

where η_t is the $J \times 1$ vector of common shocks.

If we make an additional distributional assumption regarding the aggregate shock, η_t, we can derive the likelihood. Given that we have already made specific assumptions regarding the form of the utility function, the distribution of the idiosyncratic choice errors, and the distribution of heterogeneity, this does not seem particularly restrictive. However, the recent literature on GMM methods for aggregate share models does emphasize the lack of distributional assumptions regarding the aggregate shock. We will assume that the aggregate shock is iid across both products and time periods and follows a normal distribution, $\eta_{jt} \sim N\left(0, \tau^2\right)$. The normal distribution assumption is not critical to the derivation of the likelihood; however, as Bayesians we must make some specific parametric assumptions. In theory, the GMM estimator should be robust to autocorrelated and heteroskedastic errors of an unknown form. Jiang et al. (2009) propose a Bayes estimator based on a normal likelihood and document that this estimator has excellent sampling properties even in the presence of misspecification and, in all cases considered, has better sampling properties than a GMM approach (see Chen and Yang 2007 and Musalem et al. 2009 for other Bayesian approaches).

The joint density of shares at "time" t (in some applications of aggregate share models, shares are observed over time for one market and in others, shares are observed for a cross-section of markets. In the latter case, the "t" index would index markets) can be obtained by using standard change of variable arguments:

$$\begin{aligned} \pi\left(s_{1t}, \ldots, s_{Jt} | X, \bar{\theta}, \Sigma, \tau^2\right) &= \phi\left(h^{-1}\left(s_{1t}, \ldots, s_{Jt} | X, \bar{\theta}, \Sigma\right) | 0, \tau^2 I_J\right) J_{(\eta \to s)} \\ &= \phi\left(h^{-1}\left(s_{1t}, \ldots, s_{Jt} | X, \bar{\theta}, \Sigma\right) | 0, \tau^2 I_J\right) \left(J_{(s \to \eta)}\right)^{-1}, \end{aligned} \tag{8.27}$$

where $\phi\left(\cdot\right)$ is the multivariate normal density. The Jacobian is given by

$$J_{(s \to \eta)} = \left\| \frac{\partial s_j}{\partial \eta_k} \right\| \tag{8.28}$$

$$\frac{\partial s_j}{\partial \eta_k} = \begin{cases} \int -s_{ij}\left(\theta^i\right) s_{ik}\left(\theta^i\right) \phi\left(\theta^i | \bar{\theta}, \Sigma\right) & k \neq j \\ \int s_{ij}\left(\theta^i\right)\left(1 - s_{ik}\left(\theta^i\right)\right) \phi\left(\theta^i | \bar{\theta}, \Sigma\right) & k = j. \end{cases} \tag{8.29}$$

It should be noted that, given the observed shares, the Jacobian is a function of Σ only (see Jiang et al. 2009 for details).

To evaluate the likelihood function based on (8.27), we must compute the h^{-1} function and evaluate the Jacobian. The share inversion function can be evaluated using the iterative method of BLP (see Berry et al. 1995). Both the Jacobian and the share inversion require a method for approximation of the integrals required to compute "expected share" as in (8.26). Typically, this is done by direct simulation; that is, averaging over draws from the normal distribution of consumer-level parameters. It has been noted that the GMM methods can be sensitive to simulation error in the evaluation of the integral as well as errors in computing the share inversion. Since the number of integral estimates and share inversions is of the order of magnitude of the number of likelihood or GMM criterion evaluations, it would desirable, from a strictly numerical point of view, that the inference procedure exhibit little sensitivity to the number of iterations of the share inversion contraction or the number of simulation draws used in the integral estimates. Our experience is that the Bayesian methods that use stochastic search as opposed to optimization are far less sensitive to these numerical errors. For example, Jiang et al. (2009) show that the sampling properties of Bayes estimates are virtually identical when 50 or 200 simulation draws are used in the approximation of the share integrals; this is not true of GMM estimates.

2.5 MCMC suggestions

In this section, we have introduced a variety of models designed to capture aspects of the discrete decision process at the consumer level. Even the simplest linear utility models give rise to a likelihood which is not amenable to conjugate analysis (compare the standard linear models in Li and Tobias (Chapter 6, this volume)). The non-homothetic model (8.19), variety models (8.23), and aggregate share models (8.27) define likelihoods that must be evaluated by using numerical approximations to various integrals and, possibly, roots of equations that implicitly define the utility function (8.18). RW Metropolis methods (Chib, Chapter 5, this volume) are ideal for these non-conjugate problems of modest dimension. For satisfactory performance, some tuning will be required for the Metropolis method. In particular, the random walk covariance matrix must be chosen with care. Recall that a general strategy is to propose candidates as follows

$$\theta^c = \theta + \epsilon \quad \epsilon \sim N\left(0, s^2 C\right). \tag{8.30}$$

For the linear utility, multinomial logit model, C can be chosen as any reasonable Hessian estimate and the Roberts and Rosenthal (2001) suggestion that $s = {}^{2.93}/_{dim(\theta)}$ will work well. The non-homothetic utility function can be tuned successfully using either Hessian estimates from an optimizer or the covariance matrix of a shorter "tuning" run. The log-concavity of the standard MNL model and the near log-concavity of the non-homothetic model ensure adequate performance of an initial optimizer. However, the variety model and the aggregate share model have far less regular likelihoods and should be tuned with shorter initial runs using a diagonal or identity RW increment co-variance matrices.

If the elements of the variance-covariance matrix of the normal distribution of individual parameters in the aggregate logit model (8.26) are included in the parameter vector used in an RW Metropolis step, then we must impose positive definiteness. We reparameterize so as to impose positive definiteness and use a standard RW metropolis on an unrestricted parameter space. Positive definiteness can be imposed by writing Σ in terms of its Cholesky root:

$$\Sigma = U'U$$

$$U = \begin{bmatrix} e^{r_{11}} & r_{12} & \cdots & r_{1K} \\ 0 & e^{r_{22}} & \ddots & \vdots \\ \vdots & \ddots & \ddots & r_{K-1,K} \\ 0 & \cdots & 0 & e^{r_{KK}} \end{bmatrix}, \tag{8.31}$$

where K is the number of coefficients in the micro-level choice model. The prior is assessed on the r vector which induces a prior on Σ. The relationship between the Cholesky root and the elements of Σ is order dependent. Jiang et al. (2009) discuss an assessment procedure that induces a prior on the variance elements of Σ, which has approximately the same diffusion for each element. It should be emphasized that, if diffuse priors are desired, it is a simple matter to assess a normal prior on r as long as different priors are used for the diagonal versus off-diagonal Cholesky elements.

$$r_{jj} \sim N\left(0, \sigma^2_{r_{jj}}\right) \quad j = 1, \ldots, K \tag{8.32}$$

$$r_{jk} \sim N\left(0, \sigma^2_{off}\right) \quad k = 1, \ldots, K; \; j > k. \tag{8.33}$$

Jiang et al. (2009) show how to choose the parameters of the priors in (8.32) and (8.33) so as to achieve approximately the same prior dispersion for all elements in Σ.

3 Statistical Models for Discrete Data

In this section, we will discuss various models for discrete data that are motivated primarily by descriptive aspects of the outcome measure. In particular, we will consider multinomial and multivariate probit models based on a correlated normal error structure and a generalized model for count data (see also, Li and Tobias, Chapter 6, this volume).

3.1 Multinomial probit

The Multinomial Logit Model (8.13) can be derived from linear utility and extreme value errors that are independent across choice alternatives. A natural generalization of this model would be to allow for correlation between the error terms. These correlated error terms would allow for more flexible substitution between alternatives as explanatory variables such as price vary. The proportional draw or IIA property of the logit model means that elasticities are driven entirely by one parameter. Correlation between errors allows for products that are positively correlated to have higher cross-elasticities or greater substitutability (see, for example, Hausman and Wise 1978). One interpretation of the correlation is that it might arise from some sort of unobservable characteristic. Choice alternatives that have similar levels of this characteristic are more highly correlated. To allow for correlation in the utility errors, we move to an underlying normal latent regression model. Consider the situation in which we choose between p alternatives:

$$
\begin{aligned}
y_i &= f(z_i) \\
f(z_i) &= \sum_{j=1}^{p} jI\left(max(z_i) = z_{ij}\right) \\
z_i &= X_i\delta + v_i \quad v_i \sim N(0, \Omega).
\end{aligned}
\tag{8.34}
$$

X_i contains explanatory variables which can be thought of as of two types: (i) alternative specific information such a price or other marketing mix variables, and (ii) covariate or "demographic" information characterizing the respondents or consumers whose choices are being observed. In many applications, we also include an alternative specific intercept term that can be interpreted as some sort of vertical quality measure:

$$X_i = \left[(1, d_i) \bigotimes I_p \; A_i \right],$$

where d_i is a vector of covariates (for example, demographic variables) and A_i contains observations on the alternative specific variables such as product attributes.

The model in (8.34) has both a location and a scale invariance identification problem. Location invariance means that we can add a scalar random variable u to z and not affect the alternatives chosen, that is, $f(z_i + u\iota) = f(z_i)$. With a full-covariance matrix, the models are observationally equivalent, as $Var(z_i + u\iota|X_i, \delta) = \Omega + \sigma_u^2 I$ and $Var(z_i|X_i, \delta) = \Omega$; both are unrestricted covariance matrices. This identification problem can be restated as that all latent comparisons are relative and there has to be some sort of normalization. With a full covariance structure, the most convenient way is to difference the latent system by subtracting one of the alternatives from all of the others. With a restricted covariance structure such as a diagonal Ω, it is possible to achieve identification simply by fixing one of the alternatives to have a zero intercept and fixing one of the diagonal elements of Ω.

The differenced system is written

$$w_i = X_i^d \beta + \epsilon_i \quad \epsilon_i \sim N(0, \Sigma), \tag{8.35}$$

where

$$w_{ij} = z_{ij} - z_{ip}, X_i^d = \begin{bmatrix} x'_{ij} - x'_{ip} \\ \vdots \\ x'_{i,p-1} - x'_{ip} \end{bmatrix}, \epsilon_{ij} = \nu_{ij} - \nu_{ip}. \tag{8.36}$$

The differenced system is now $p - 1$ dimensional; $y_i = k, k = 1, \ldots, p - 1$ if $max(w_i) = w_{ik}$ and $y_i = p$ if $w_i < 0$. The *bayesm* function, `createX`, can be used to automatically configure X matrices using information on alternative specific and non-alternative specific explanatory variables, to include intercepts, set the base alternative, and to difference.

Even the differenced system in (8.35) is not identified, as the system still exhibits scale invariance. If we scale the vector of differenced latents, w_i, by multiplying by a positive constant, then we still leave the observed choice unchanged. In the classical literature, this is typically handled by normalizing an element of Σ to be one. The identified parameters in (8.35) are $\tilde{\beta} = {}^{\beta}/_{\sigma_{ii}}$ and $\tilde{\Sigma} = {}^{\Sigma}/_{\sigma_{11}}$.

However, in the Bayesian approach, it is not necessary to impose identification restrictions prior to the analysis of the posterior. One approach is to put informative priors on the unidentified parameter space and recognize that certain functions of the parameters have a posterior that is influenced by both the prior and the likelihood and other functions are only influenced by the prior. There are two advantages of this approach: (i) standard normal/inverted Wishart priors can be used for the unidentified parameters, (ii) the Markov chain Monte Carlo (MCMC) method that navigates the unidentified space has superior mixing properties as discussed in Rossi et al. (2005), Section 4.2. The standard priors are given by

$$\beta \sim N\left(\overline{\beta}, \underline{A}^{-1}\right) \quad \Sigma \sim IW\left(\underline{V}, \underline{\nu}\right). \tag{8.37}$$

The priors in (8.37) are on the unidentified parameter space. These can either be regarded as a legitimate statement of prior beliefs or as a device to induce a prior on the space of identifed parameters $\tilde{\beta}, \tilde{\Sigma}$. The user of the MCMC algorithm with priors on the non-identified parameters must check this induced prior to see that it is reasonable. In many applications, all that is desired is a relatively diffuse but proper prior. It is a simple matter to check the induced prior by simulating from (8.37) and transforming to the identified parameters. Marginals of the prior on the identified prior can be inspected to see if they represent the investigator's beliefs. In Figure 8.4, we plot the prior distribution for the identified parameters in the MNP model using the defaults for the *rmnpGibbs* procedure in *bayesm*. The top panel displays the prior induced on an identified regression coefficient, the middle panel shows a representative covariance element of the identified covariance matrix $\tilde{\Sigma}$, and the bottom panel shows

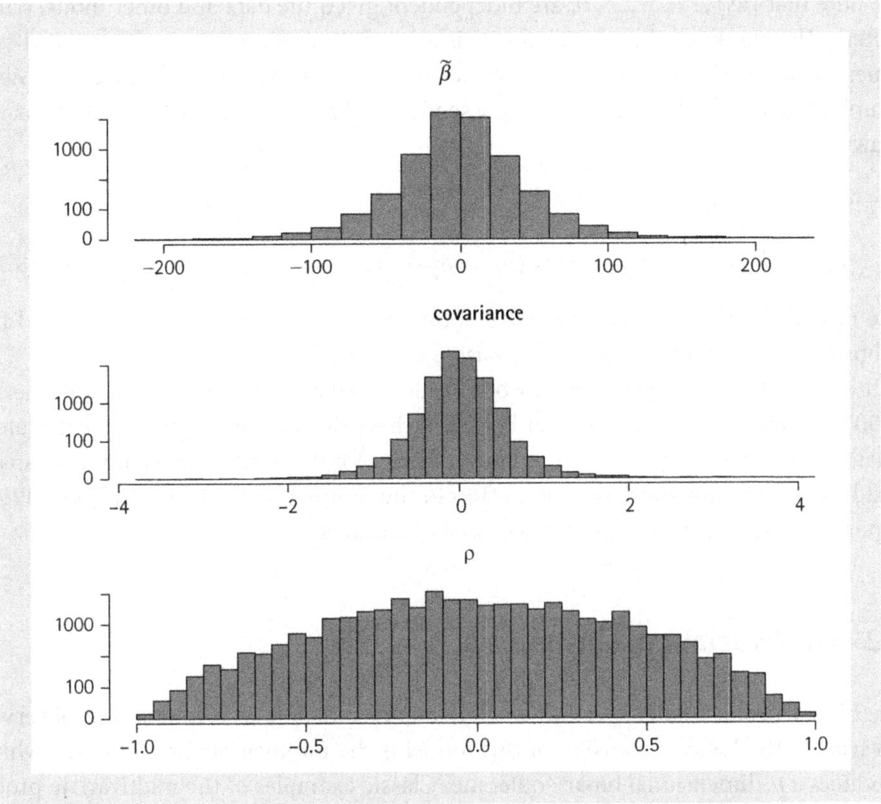

FIGURE 8.4 Default prior for MNP model

the prior for a representative correlation. It is a simple matter to verify that these priors are adequate to represent diffuse or vague beliefs. In particular, the implied prior for the identified regression coefficient, $\tilde{\beta}$, is symmetric and puts prior mass over a very large range of possible values. An approach which uses priors on the non-identified space to induce priors over the identified parameters is very useful in situations where a diffuse prior is desired. This approach could become cumbersome for situations in which very informative priors are desired. However, situations in which informative priors are needed may require priors which are not conjugate and this renders the entire Gibbs sampler proposed unusable. For example, if you have strong prior information about the correlations between some, but not all, of the choice errors, this information will be impossible to encode using standard conjugate Inverted Wishart priors.

Given these conditionally conjugate priors, a standard Gibbs sampler can be constructed as in McCulloch and Rossi (1994):

$$\begin{aligned} w_i | \beta, \Sigma, y_i, X_i^d \quad & i = 1, \ldots, n \\ \beta | \Sigma, w & \\ \Sigma | \beta, w. & \end{aligned} \tag{8.38}$$

We note that $\{w_i\}, i = 1, \ldots, n$, are independent given the data and other model parameters. The conditional posterior for w_i is a $p-1$ dimensional normal truncated to a cone. The insight of Geweke (1991) and McCulloch and Rossi (1994) is to create a Gibbs sampler that breaks the draw of w_i into a sequence of $p-1$ univariate truncated normal draws.

$$w_{ij}|w_{i,-j} \sim N\left(\mu_{ij}, \tau_{jj}^2\right) \\ \times \left[I(j = y_i)\, I\left(w_{ij} > max\left(w_{i,-j}, 0\right)\right) + I(j \neq y_i)\, I\left(w_{ij} < max\left(w_{i,-j}, 0\right)\right)\right]. \quad (8.39)$$

The moments of the truncated normal above are given in Rossi et al. (2005) and the Gibbs sampler is implemented in the *bayesm* function, `rmnpGibbs`.

It is possible to put a prior directly on the identified parameters (see McCulloch et al. 2000). However, the Gibbs sampler based on this prior is more highly autocorrelated. Imai and van Dyk (2005) propose a modified prior for the unidentified parameter space that has similar autocorrelation properties to the original McCulloch and Rossi (1994) paper, but is less sensitive to extreme initial conditions.

3.2 Multivariate probit model

The binary probit model specifies a single binary outcome as a function of observed covariates. The logical extension of this model is the multivariate probit model which produces a p-dimensional binary outcome. Classic examples of the multivariate probit model include purchases in multiple categories such as in Manchanda et al. (1999). In this application, households are observed to purchase in related categories of products, for example, pasta and pasta sauce, and there is the possibility that there are correlations between the latent "attractiveness" or utility of related categories. Another common situation arises in survey market research where respondents can select 0 to p items from a list of p items. Typically, these questions provide lists of products and the respondent is asked which products she purchases on a regular basis. Again, the choices of items can be viewed as revealing an underlying pattern of similarity between products.

The multivariate probit is based on a latent p-variate normal regression model. The censoring mechanism is that we only observe the sign of the latent response vector.

$$w_i = X_i\beta + \epsilon_i \quad \epsilon_i \sim N(0, \Sigma) \\ y_{ij} = \begin{cases} 1 & \text{if } w_{ij} > 0 \\ 0 & \text{otherwise.} \end{cases} \quad (8.40)$$

Edwards and Allenby (2003) view this latent representation as the problem of conducting a standard multivariate analysis of binary outcome data. Clustering in the "1" outcome in the observed dependent variable (conditional on covariates) reveals a correlation between items. The identification problem in the multivariate probit is that arbitrary scaling of the underlying latent variables is possible without changing the outcome variable. This means that in many applications only the correlation structure of the latent variables is identified. Chib and Greenberg (1998) present an MCMC algorithm for the identified space of parameters; however, this algorithm requires tuning and has not been shown to work in problems with a high-dimensional covariance matrix. The algorithm of Edwards and Allenby (2003) can work in 20-plus dimensional problems with no tuning.

The identification problem in the multivariate probit depends on the structure of the X array. In the general case, X will include intercepts for each of the p choice alternatives and covariates that are allowed to have different coefficients for each of the p outcomes:

$$X_i = \left(z_i' \otimes I_p\right),$$

where z_i is a $d \times 1$ vector of observations on the covariates. Thus, X is a $p \times k$ matrix and $k = p \times d$. We interpret β as a stacked vector of coefficients representing the impact of each of the variables in z on the p latent outcomes:

$$\beta = \begin{bmatrix} \beta_1 \\ \vdots \\ \beta_d \end{bmatrix}.$$

β_d represents the impact of z_{id} on the mean latent utilities for each of the p possible outcomes. If z is measured income, then there can be different effects of income on the probability of each of the p outcomes. We might expect that this would be true for a category with a wide range of product qualities. Higher income consumers might have a greater probability of purchasing higher quality products. For this X structure, the identification problem is most severe. Each element of the latent w vector can be scaled by a different positive constant without altering the binary outcomes. Thus, the identified parameters for this model are the correlation matrix of the errors and appropriately scaled regression coefficients. That is, we can define a transformation from the unidentified to identified parameters by

$$\begin{aligned} \tilde{B} &= \Lambda B \\ R &= \Lambda \Sigma \Lambda, \end{aligned} \tag{8.41}$$

where

$$B = \left[\beta_1, \ldots, \beta_p\right]$$

$$\Lambda = \begin{bmatrix} 1/\sqrt{\sigma_{11}} & & \\ & \ddots & \\ & & 1/\sqrt{\sigma_{pp}} \end{bmatrix}.$$

If the coefficients on a given covariate are restricted to be equal across all p choices, then there are fewer unidentified parameters. We cannot scale each equation by a *different* positive constant. For example, if z were to contain an attribute of a set of product offerings, then we might consider restricting the impact of variation in this attribute to be the same across outcomes or impose the restriction, $\beta_{j1} = \ldots = \beta_{jp}$ for covariate j. In this case, we cannot scale each element of the latent vector by a different scale factor and the identification problem is identical to the one in the Multinomial Probit Model.

Edwards and Allenby (2003) implement a Gibbs sampler for the Multivariate Probit model using the non-identified approach in which a proper prior is imposed on the non-identified parameter space and only the posterior distribution of identified parameters (8.41) is reported. The Gibbs sampler is the same as in the MNP model (8.38) except that the truncation points for the draw of the latent utilities (as in 8.39) are 0 as in the binary probit. This sampler is implemented in the *bayesm* function, `rmvpGibbs`. Some care should be exercised in the prior setting for the IW prior on Σ. Very diffuse priors on Σ are informative on the prior distribution of correlation coefficients. In particular, very diffuse priors imply a "U" shaped prior distribution for the correlation coefficients.

3.3 Count regression models

In some marketing applications, the outcome variable is best viewed as a count variable with a potentially large number of values. For example, if we observe physicians writing prescriptions for a specific drug at a given period of time, we might observe zeros but also rather large numbers as well. Marketing actions such as visits by salespeople presumably increase the expected number of prescriptions. Given the truncation at zero and the integer aspects of the data, standard regression models are not appropriate. The Poisson regression model is often used for count data, but suffers from the restrictive assumption that the conditional mean and variance are required to be the same. In many applications, the data exhibit "over-dispersion," that is, the conditional variance exceeds the conditional mean. The negative binomial regression model provides a natural generalization of the Poisson model in the sense that it provides for any degree of over-dispersion (see also Morrison and Schmittlein 1988).

$$Pr\left(y_i = k|\lambda_i, \alpha\right) = \frac{\Gamma\left(\alpha + k\right)}{\Gamma\left(\alpha\right)\Gamma\left(k+1\right)}\left(\frac{\alpha}{\alpha + \lambda_i}\right)^{\alpha}\left(\frac{\lambda_i}{\alpha + \lambda_i}\right)^{k}. \tag{8.42}$$

In this parameterization of the negative-binomial, λ is the mean and α is the over-dispersion parameter (as $\alpha \to \infty$, the negative binomial approaches the Poisson distribution). A standard log-link function provides a way of incorporating covariates:

$$ln\left(\lambda_i\right) = x_i'\beta. \tag{8.43}$$

Priors for β and α can be conveniently chosen as

$$\begin{aligned} p\left(\beta, \alpha\right) &= p\left(\beta\right)p\left(\alpha\right) \\ \beta &\sim N\left(\underline{\beta}, \underline{A}^{-1}\right) \\ \alpha &\sim G\left(\underline{a}, \underline{b}\right). \end{aligned} \tag{8.44}$$

An MCMC algorithm for the model in (8.42), (8.43), and (8.44) can be defined by a "Gibbs-style" combination of two Random Walk Metropolis methods to draw first from the posterior of $\beta|\alpha$ and then from the univariate posterior of $\alpha|\beta$. This sampler is implemented in the *bayesm* function, *rnegbinRw*. The random walk increment density can be chosen based on an estimated Hessian evaluated at the posterior mode or MLE. The *bayesm* function uses the Roberts and Rosenthal (2001) scaling suggestion.

4 Hierarchical Models

A fundamental premise of marketing is that customers differ in both their preferences for product features as well as their sensitivities to marketing variables. Observable characteristics such as psycho-demographics can only be expected to explain a limited portion of the variation in tastes and responsiveness. Disaggregated data is required in order to measure customer heterogeneity. Typically, disaggregated data is obtained for a relatively large number of cross-sectional units but with a relatively short history of activity. In the consumer packaged goods industry, store-level panel data is common, especially for retailers. There is also increased availability of customer-level purchase data from specialized panels of consumers or from detailed purchase histories assembled from firm records. As the level of aggregation decreases, discrete features of sales data become magnified. The short time span of panel data, coupled with the comparatively sparse information in discrete data, means that we are unlikely to have a great deal of sample information about any one cross-sectional unit. If inference about unit-level parameters is important, then the prior will matter and assessing informative priors will be important. Increasingly, firms want to make decentralized marketing decisions that exploit more detailed disaggregated information. Examples include store- or zone-level pricing, targeted electronic couponing, and sales force activities in the pharmaceutical industry. This contrasts markedly with applications in microeconomics where the average response to a variable is often deemed more important. However, even the evaluation of policies which are uniform across some set of consumers will require information about the distribution of preferences in order to evaluate the effect on social welfare.

From a Bayesian perspective, modeling panel data is about the choice of a prior over a high-dimensional parameter space. The hierarchical approach is one convenient way of specifying the joint prior over unit-level parameters. Clearly, this prior will be informative and must be in order to produce reasonable inferences. However, it is reasonable to ask for flexibility in the form of this prior distribution. In this section, we will introduce hierarchical models for general unit-level models. Recognizing the need for flexibility in the prior, we will expand the set of priors to include mixtures of normal distributions.

4.1 A Generic hierarchical approach

Consider a cross-section of H units, each with a likelihood, $p\left(y_h|\theta_h\right), h = 1, \ldots, H, \theta_h$ with a $k \times 1$ vector. y_h generically represents the data on the hth unit and θ_h is a vector of unit-level parameters. While there is no restriction on the model for each unit, common examples include a multinomial logit or standard regression model at the unit level. The parameter space can be very large and consists of the collection of unit-level parameters, $\{\theta_h, h = 1, \ldots, H\}$. Our goal will be to conduct a posterior analysis of this joint set of parameters. It is common to assume that units are independent conditional on θ_h. More generally, if the units are *exchangeable* (see Bernardo and Smith 1994), then we require a prior distribution which is the same no matter what the ordering of the units are. In this case, we can write down the posterior for the panel data as

$$p\left(\theta_1, \ldots, \theta_H|y_1, \ldots, y_H\right) \propto \prod_{h=1}^{H} p\left(y_h|\theta_h\right) p(\theta_1, \ldots, \theta_H|\tau), \tag{8.45}$$

where τ is a vector of prior parameters. The prior assessment problem posed by this model is daunting as it requires specifying a potentially very high-dimensional joint distribution. One simplification would be to assume that the unit-level parameters are independent and identically distributed, a priori. In this case, the posterior factors and inference can be conducted independently for each of the H units:

$$p\left(\theta_1, \ldots, \theta_H|y_1, \ldots, y_H\right) \propto \prod_{h=1}^{H} p\left(y_h|\theta_h\right) p(\theta_h|\tau). \tag{8.46}$$

Given τ, the posterior in (8.46) is the Bayesian analogue of the classical *fixed effects* estimation approach. However, there are still advantages to the Bayesian approach in that an informative prior can be used. The informative prior will impart important shrinkage properties to Bayes estimators. In situations in which the unit-level likelihood may not be identified, a proper prior will regularize the problem and produce sensible inferences. The real problem is a practical one in that some guidance must be provided to assessing the prior parameters, τ.

The specification of the conditionally independent prior can be very important due to the scarcity of data for many of the cross-sectional units. Both the form of the prior and the values of hyperparameters are important and can have pronounced effects on the unit-level inferences. For example, consider a normal prior, $\theta_h \sim N\left(\bar{\theta}, V_\theta\right)$. Just the use of a normal prior distribution is highly informative regardless of the value of the hyperparameters. The thin tails of the prior distribution will reduce the influence of the likelihood when the likelihood is centered far away from the prior. For this reason, the choice of the normal prior is far from innocuous. For many applications, the shrinkage of outliers is a desirable feature of the normal prior. The prior results in very stable estimates, but at the same time this prior might mask or attenuate differences in consumers. It will, therefore, be important to consider more flexible priors.

If we accept the normal form of the prior as reasonable, a method for assessing the prior hyperparameters is required (Allenby and Rossi 1999). It may be desirable to adapt the shrinkage induced by use of an informative prior to the characteristics of both the data for any particular cross-sectional unit as well as the differences between units. Both the location and spread of the prior should be influenced by both the data and our prior beliefs. For example, consider a cross-sectional unit with little information available. For this unit, the posterior should shrink toward some kind of "average" or representative unit. The amount of shrinkage should be influenced by both the amount of information available for this unit as well as the amount of variation across units. A hierarchical model achieves this result by putting a prior on the common parameter, τ. The hierarchical approach is a model specified by a sequence of conditional distributions, starting with the likelihood and proceeding to a two-stage prior:

$$\begin{aligned} &p\left(y_h|\theta_h\right)\\ &p\left(\theta_h|\tau\right)\\ &p\left(\tau|\underline{h}\right). \end{aligned} \tag{8.47}$$

The prior distribution on $\theta_h|\tau$ is sometimes called the first-stage prior. In non-Bayesian applications, this is often called a random effect or random coefficient model and is regarded as part of the likelihood. The prior on τ completes the specification of a joint prior distribution on all model parameters:

$$p\left(\theta_1,\ldots,\theta_H,\tau|\underline{h}\right)=p\left(\theta_1,\ldots,\theta_H|\tau\right)p\left(\tau|h\right)=\prod_{h=1}^{H}p\left(\theta_h|\tau\right)p\left(\tau|\underline{h}\right). \tag{8.48}$$

One way of regarding the hierarchical model is just as a device to induce a joint prior on the unit-level parameters, that is, we can integrate out τ to inspect the implied prior:

$$p\left(\theta_1,\ldots,\theta_H|\underline{h}\right)=\int\prod_{h=1}^{H}p\left(\theta_h|\tau\right)p\left(\tau|\underline{h}\right)d\tau. \tag{8.49}$$

It should be noted that, while $\{\theta_h\}$ are independent conditional on τ, the implied joint prior can be highly dependent, particularly if the prior on τ is diffuse (note: it is sufficient that the prior on τ should be proper in order for the hierarchical model to specify a valid joint distribution). To illustrate this, consider a linear model, $\theta_h=\tau+\nu_h$. τ acts as a common variance component and the correlation between any two θs is

$$Corr\left(\theta_h,\theta_k\right)=\frac{\sigma_\tau^2}{\sigma_\tau^2+\sigma_\nu^2}.$$

As the diffusion of the distribution of τ relative to ν increases, this correlation tends toward one.

4.2 MCMC schemes

Given the independence of the units conditional θ_h, all MCMC algorithms for a hierarchical model will contain two basic groups of conditional distributions:

$$\begin{array}{c} p\left(\theta_h|y_h,\tau\right) \quad h=1,\ldots,H \\ p\left(\tau|\left\{\theta_h\right\},\underline{h}\right). \end{array} \tag{8.50}$$

As is well known, the second part of this scheme exploits the conditional independence of y_h and τ. The first part of (8.50) is dependent on the form of the unit-level likelihood, while the second part depends on the form of the first-stage prior. Typically, the priors in the first and second stages are chosen to exploit some sort of conjugacy and the $\{\theta_h\}$ are treated as "data" with respect to the second stage.

4.3 Fixed versus random effects

In classical approaches, there is a distinction made between a "fixed effects" specification in which there are different parameters for every cross-sectional unit and random effects models in which the cross-sectional unit parameters are assumed to be draws from a super-population. Advocates of the fixed effects approach explain that the approach does not make any assumption regarding the form of the distribution or the independence of random effects from included covariates in the unit-level likelihood. The Bayesian analogue of the fixed effects classical model is an independence prior with no second-stage prior on the random effects parameters as in (8.46). The Bayesian hierarchical model is the Bayesian analogue of a random effects model. The hierarchical model assumes that each cross-sectional unit is exchangeable (possibly conditional on some observable variables). This means that a key distinction between models (Bayesian or classical) is what sort of predictions can be made for a new cross-sectional unit. In either the classical or Bayesian "fixed effects" approach, no predictions can be made about a new member of the cross-section as there is no model linking units. Under the random effects view, all units are exchangeable and the predictive distribution for the parameters of a new unit is given by

$$p\left(\theta_{h*}|y_1,\ldots,y_H\right) = \int p\left(\theta_{h*}|\tau\right)p\left(\tau|y_1,\ldots,y_H\right)d\tau. \tag{8.51}$$

4.4 First stage priors

4.4.1 *Normal prior*

A straightforward model to implement is a normal first stage prior with possible covariates:

$$\theta_h = \Delta' z_h + v_h, \quad v_h \sim N(0, V_\theta), \tag{8.52}$$

where z_h is a $d \times 1$ vector of observable characteristics of the cross-sectional unit. Δ is a $d \times k$ matrix of coefficients. The specification in (8.52) allows the mean of each of the elements of θ_h to depend on the z vector. For ease of interpretation, we find it useful to subtract the mean and use an intercept.

$$z_h = (1, x_h - \bar{x}).$$

In this formulation, the first row of Δ can be interpreted as the mean of θ_h.

Equation (8.52) specifies a multivariate regression model and it is convenient, therefore, to use the conjugate prior for the multivariate regression model:

$$\begin{gathered} V_\theta \sim IW\left(\underline{V}, \underline{\nu}\right) \\ \delta = vec(\Delta) \,|\, V_\theta \sim N\left(\underline{\bar{\delta}}, V_\theta \otimes \underline{A}^{-1}\right), \end{gathered} \tag{8.53}$$

where $\underline{A}$ is a $d \times d$ precision matrix. This prior specification allows for direct one-for-one draws of the common parameters, δ and V_θ. In *bayesm*, these draws can be achieved using the utility function, `rmultireg`.

4.4.2 *Mixture of normals prior*

While the normal distribution is flexible, there is no particular reason to assume a normal first-stage prior. For example, if the observed outcomes are choices among products, some of the coefficients might be brand-specific intercepts. Heterogeneity in tastes for a product might be more likely to assume the form of clustering by brand. That is, we might find "clusters" of consumers who prefer specific brands over other brands. The distribution of tastes across consumers might then be multi-modal. We might want to shrink different groups of consumers in different ways or shrink to different group means. A multi-modal distribution will achieve this goal. For other coefficients, such as a price-sensitivity coefficient, we might expect a skewed distribution centered over negative values. Mixtures of multivariate normals are one way of achieving a great deal of flexibility (see, for example, Griffin et al., Chapter 4 in this volume, and the references therein). Multi-modal, thick-tailed, and skewed distributions are easily achieved from mixtures of a small number of normal components. For larger numbers of components, virtually any joint continuous distribution can be approximated. The mixture of normals model for the first-stage prior is given by

$$\begin{gathered} \theta_h = \Delta' z_h + v_h \\ v_h \sim N(\mu_{ind}, \Sigma_{ind}) \\ ind \sim MN(\pi), \end{gathered} \tag{8.54}$$

where π is a $K \times 1$ vector of multinomial probabilities. This is a latent version of a mixture of K normals model in which a multinomial mixture variable, denoted here by *ind*, is used. In the mixture of normal specification, we remove the intercept term from z_h and allow v_h to have a non-zero mean. This allows the normal mixture components to mix on the means as well as on scale, introducing more flexibility. As before, it is convenient to demean the variables in z. A standard set of conjugate priors can be used for the mixture probabilities and component parameters, coupled with a standard conjugate prior on the Δ matrix:

$$\begin{aligned} \delta = vec\left(\Delta\right) &\sim N\left(\bar{\underline{\delta}}, \underline{A}_{\delta}^{-1}\right) \\ \pi &\sim D\left(\underline{\alpha}\right) \\ \mu_k &\sim N\left(\bar{\underline{\mu}}, \Sigma_k \otimes \underline{a}_{\mu}^{-1}\right) \\ \Sigma_k &\sim IW\left(\underline{V}, \underline{\nu}\right). \end{aligned} \tag{8.55}$$

Assessment of these conjugate priors is relatively straightforward for diffuse settings. Given that the θ vector can be of moderately large dimension (>5) and the θ_h parameters are not directly observed, some care must be exercised in the assessment of prior parameters. In particular, it is customary to assess the Dirichlet portion of the prior by using the interpretation that the $K \times 1$ hyperparameter vector, $\underline{\alpha}$, is an observed classification of a sample of size, $\sum \underline{\alpha}_k$, into the K components. Typically, all components in $\underline{\alpha}$ are assessed equal. When a large number of components are used, the elements of α should be scaled down in order to avoid inadvertently specifying an informative prior with equal prior probabilities on a large number of components. We suggest a setting of $\underline{\alpha}_k = 0.5/K$.

As in the single component normal model, we can exploit the fact that, given the $H \times k$ matrix, Θ, whose columns consist of each θ_h values and standard conditionally conjugate priors in (8.55), the mixture of normals model in (8.54) is easily handled by a standard unconstrained Gibbs Sampler augmented with the latent vector of component indicators (see Rossi et al. 2005, Section 5.5.1). The latent draws can be used for clustering as discussed below. We should note that any label-invariant quantity, such as a density estimate or clustering, is not affected by the "label-switching" identification problem (see Frühwirth-Schnatter 2006 for a discussion). In fact, the unconstrained Gibbs sampler is superior to various constrained approaches in terms of mixing.

A tremendous advantage of Bayesian methods when applied to mixtures of normals is that, with proper priors, Bayesian procedures do not overfit the data and provide reasonable and smooth density estimates. In order for a component to obtain appreciable posterior mass, there must be enough structure in the "data" to favor the component in terms of a Bayes factor. As is standard in Bayesian procedures, the existence of a prior puts an implicit penalty on models with a larger number of components. It should also be noted that the prior for the mixture of normals puts positive probability on models with less than K components. In other words, this is really a prior on models of different dimensions. In practice, it is common for the posterior mass to be concentrated on a set of components of much smaller size than K.

The posterior distribution of any ordinate of the joint (or marginal densities) of the mixture of normals can be constructed from the posterior draws of component parameters and mixing probabilities. In particular, a Bayes estimate of a density ordinate can be constructed:

$$\hat{d}(\theta) = \frac{1}{R}\sum_{r=1}^{R}\sum_{k=1}^{K}\pi_k^r \phi\left(\theta|\mu_k^r, \Sigma_k^r\right). \tag{8.56}$$

Here the superscript r refers to an MCMC posterior draw, with $\phi(\cdot)$ the k-variate multivariate normal density. If marginals of sub-vectors of θ are required, then we simply compute the required parameters from the draws of the joint parameters. The *bayesm* plot method for normal mixtures, `plot.bayesm.nmix`, will automatically compute and plot univariate and bivariate marginals for general normal mixtures.

4.4.3 Dirichlet process priors

While it can be argued that a finite mixture of normals is a very flexible prior, it is true that the number of components must be pre-specified by the investigator. Given that Bayes methods are being used, a practical approach would be to assume a very large number of components and allow the proper priors and natural parsimony of Bayes inference to produce reasonable density estimates. For large samples, it might be reasonable to increase the number of components in order to accommodate greater flexibility. The Dirichlet Process (DP) approach can, in principle, allow the number of mixture components to be as large as the sample size and potentially increase with the sample size. This allows for a claim that a DP prior can facilitate general non-parametric density estimation. Griffin et al. (Chapter 4, this volume) provide a discussion of the DP process approach to density estimation. We review only that portion of this method necessary to fix notation for use within a hierarchical setting.

Consider a general setting in which each θ_h is drawn from a possibly different multivariate normal distribution:

$$\theta_h \sim N(\mu_h, \Sigma_h).$$

The DP process prior is a hierarchical prior on the joint distribution of $\{(\mu_1, \Sigma_1), \ldots, (\mu_H, \Sigma_H)\}$. The DP prior has the effect of grouping together cross-section units with the same value of (μ, Σ) and specifying a prior distribution for these possible "atoms."

The DP process prior is denoted $G(\alpha, G_0(\lambda))$. $G(\cdot)$ specifies a distribution over distributions that is centered on the base distribution, G_0, with tightness parameter, α. Under the DP prior, G_0 is the marginal prior distribution for the parameters for any one cross-sectional unit. α specifies the prior distribution on the clustering of units to a smaller number of unique (μ, Σ) values. Given the normal base distribution for the cross-sectional parameters, it is convenient to use a natural conjugate base prior:

$$G_0(\lambda): \quad \mu_h|\Sigma_h \sim N\left(\bar{\mu}, \frac{1}{\underline{a}} \times \Sigma_h\right), \quad \Sigma_h \sim IW\left(\underline{V}, \underline{\nu}\right), \tag{8.57}$$

where λ is the set of prior parameters in (8.57), $\bar{\mu}, \underline{a}, \underline{\nu}, \underline{V}$.

In our approach to a DP model, we also put priors on the DP process parameters, α and λ. The Polya Urn representation of the DP model can be used to motivate the choice of prior distributions on these process parameters. α influences the number of unique values of (μ, Σ) or the probability that a new set of parameter values will be "proposed" from the base distribution, G_0. λ governs the distribution of proposed values. For example, if we set λ to put high prior probability on small values of Σ, then the DP prior will attempt to approximate the density of parameters with normal components of small variance. It is also important that the prior on μ should put support on a wide enough range of values to locate normal components at wide enough spacing to capture the structure of the distribution of parameters. On the other hand, if we set very diffuse values of λ then this will reduce the probability of the "birth" of a new component via the usual Bayes Factor argument.

For each value of α there is a distribution on the number of distinct values of (μ, Σ) as shown in Antoniak (1974).

$$Pr\left(I^* = k\right) = \left\|S_n^{(k)}\right\| \alpha^k \frac{\Gamma(\alpha)}{\Gamma(n+\alpha)}, \tag{8.58}$$

where $S_n^{(k)}$ are Sterling numbers of the first kind and I^* is the number of clusters or unique values of the parameters in the joint distribution of $(\mu_h, \Sigma_h, h = 1, \ldots, H)$. It is common in the literature to set a Gamma prior on α. Our approach is to propose a simple and interpretable distribution for α:

$$p(\alpha) \propto \left(1 - \frac{\alpha - \underline{\alpha}_l}{\underline{\alpha}_u - \underline{\alpha}_l}\right)^{\underline{\phi}}, \tag{8.59}$$

where $\alpha \in \left(\underline{\alpha}_l, \underline{\alpha}_u\right)$. We assess the support of α by setting the expected minimum and maximum number of components, I^*_{min} and I^*_{max}. We then invert to obtain the bounds of support for α. It should be noted that this device does not restrict the support of the number of components but merely assesses an informative prior that puts most of the mass of the distribution of α on values which are consistent with the specified range in the number of unique components. A draw from the posterior distribution of α can easily be accomplished as I^* is sufficient and we can use a griddy Gibbs sampler as this is simply a univariate draw.

Priors on λ (8.57) can be also be implemented by setting $\bar{\mu} = 0$ and letting $V = \nu v I_k$. If $\Sigma \sim IW(\nu v I_k, \nu)$, then $mode(\Sigma) = \frac{\nu}{\nu+2} v I_k$. This parameterization helps separate the choice of a location for the Σ matrix (governed by v) from the choice of the tightness on the prior for Σ (ν). In this parameterization, there are three scalar parameters that govern the base distribution, (a, v, ν). We take them to be a priori independent with the following distributions:

$$\begin{aligned} p(a, v, \nu) &= p(a)\, p(v)\, p(\nu) \\ a &\sim U\left(\underline{a}_l, \underline{a}_u\right) \\ v &\sim U\left(\underline{v}_l, \underline{v}_u\right) \\ \nu &= dim(\theta_h) - 1 + \exp(z), \; z \sim U\left(\underline{z}_l, \underline{z}_u\right), \; z_l > 0. \end{aligned} \tag{8.60}$$

It is a simple matter to write down the conditional posterior given that the unique set of (μ, Σ) is sufficient. The set of I^* unique parameter values is denoted $\Delta^* \left\{ \left(\mu_i^*, \Sigma_j^*\right), j = 1, \ldots, I^* \right\}$. The conditional posterior is given by

$$p\left(a, \nu, v | \Delta^*\right) \propto \prod_{i=1}^{I^*} \left|a^{-1}\Sigma_i^*\right|^{-1/2} \exp\left(-\frac{a}{2}\left(\mu_i^*\right)'\left(\Sigma_i^*\right)^{-1}\mu_i^*\right)$$

$$\left|\nu v I_k\right|^{\nu/2}\left|\Sigma_i^*\right|^{-(\nu+k+1)/2} \operatorname{etr}\left(-\frac{1}{2}\nu v \Sigma_i^*\right) p\left(a, \nu, v\right). \quad (8.61)$$

We note that the conditional posterior factors and, conditional on Δ^*, a and (ν, v) are independent.

4.5 Examples

4.5.1 Linear hierarchical model

The linear hierarchical model with a normal first-stage prior is covered in Koop (2003) and Geweke (2005). An implementation is available in the *bayesm* routine, `rhierLinearModel`. Given the modularity of the MCMC approach, it is a simple matter to extend the model to include finite mixtures of normals or DP process priors. An implementation for finite normal mixtures is available in the *bayesm* routine, `rhierLinearMixture`.

4.5.2 Multinomial logit models

If the cross-sectional model is a multinomial logit (8.13), then finite mixtures of normals or DP process priors can be used. An implementation for finite normal mixtures is available in the *bayesm* routine, `rhierMnlMixture`, and for DP process priors in `rhierMnlDP`.

4.5.3 Multivariate ordinal probit with scale-usage heterogeneity

Many surveys ask a battery of questions which are on a K-point ratings scale. This data is ordinal and there is some question as to whether there is also interval information in the responses. Typically, a battery of M questions is administered to each of N respondents. The data for the survey can the represented as an $N \times M$ array, $X = \left[x_{ij}\right]$. An example of this sort of survey might be a customer satisfaction survey with M questions about service delivery or product quality. One useful approach to this problem is to assume that the responses are from an underlying M-dimensional latent system, a natural generalization of the univariate ordinal probit.

Assume there are $K+1$ common and ordered cut-off points $\{c_k : c_{k-1} \leq c_k, k = 1, \ldots K\}$, with $c_0 = -\infty$, $c_K = \infty$, such that for all i, j, and k,

$$x_{ij} = k \text{ if } c_{k-1} \le y_{ij} \le c_k$$
$$y_i \sim N\left(\mu_i^*, \Sigma_i^*\right), \tag{8.62}$$

where y_i is an $M \times 1$ vector. This can be interpreted as implying that each respondent has their own underlying covariate structure for the M survey questions. As a special case, all respondents have the same latent variable distribution and we would obtain a multivariate ordinal probit. We introduce respondent-specific parameters to accommodate what we have termed scale-usage heterogeneity. That is, we see that some respondents have a tendency to use only a portion of the ratings scale. For example, some respondents tend to use either the middle, low, or high end of the scale. Experts in survey research have noted this for years and have noted systematic cultural differences in scale usage as well. Scale-usage heterogeneity obscures the relationships in the data and must be adjusted for. Inferences about scale usage are only possible if multiple questions are administered to the same respondent. Rossi et al. (2001) consider a hierarchical approach to incorporating scale-usage heterogeneity.

Scale-usage patterns can be created by a respondent-specific location and scale shift in the latent continuous variables. For example, a respondent who uses the top end of the scale can be modeled as someone who has a positive shift in the mean of the latent variables (across all questions) and who has a lower variance. The location scale model is a parsimonious way of creating heterogeneity between respondents. The model does assume, however, that there is a meaningful common latent scale between all respondents:

$$y_i = \mu + \tau_i \iota + \sigma_i z_i, \quad z_i \sim N(0, \Sigma). \tag{8.63}$$

We employ a hierarchical model for the distribution of the location and scale parameters over respondents.

$$\begin{bmatrix} \tau_i \\ ln\sigma_i \end{bmatrix} \sim N(\phi, \lambda). \tag{8.64}$$

The scale-usage translation must be restricted so that the model is identifed. Conditional on the cut-offs, we cannot allow for arbitrary translation and scaling of the latents. To avoid this identification problem, we set $E[\tau_i] = 0$ and Mode $(\sigma_i) = 1$. This can be achieved by specifying that

$$\phi_1 = 0$$
$$\phi_2 = \lambda_{22}. \tag{8.65}$$

Even with these restrictions to achieve identification of the (τ_i, σ_i) parameters, there are still identification restrictions that must be imposed on the cut-off parameters. The cut-off parameters exhibit a location and scale-invariance problem. We fix the sum of the cut-offs and the sum of the squared cut-offs to remove the location/scale invariance problem:

$$\sum_k c_k = m_1$$
$$\sum_k c_k^2 = m_2. \tag{8.66}$$

In order to reduce the number of cut-off parameters, particularly for seven or larger point scales, we introduce a quadratic parameterization of the cut-off parameters:

$$c_k = a + bk + ek^2. \tag{8.67}$$

Given the parameterization in (8.67) and the identification restrictions (8.66), there is only one free parameter, e.

The priors for this model are given by

$$\begin{aligned}\pi\left(\mu,\Sigma,\phi,\Lambda,e\right) &= \pi\left(\mu\right)\pi\left(\Sigma\right)\pi\left(\phi\right)\pi\left(\Lambda\right)\pi\left(e\right)\\ \pi\left(\mu\right) &\propto \text{constant}\\ e &\sim U\left(-0.2, 0.2\right)\\ \Sigma &\sim IW\left(\underline{V}_{\Sigma}, \underline{\nu}_{\Sigma}\right)\\ \Lambda &\sim IW\left(\underline{V}_{\Lambda}, \underline{\nu}_{\Lambda}\right).\end{aligned} \tag{8.68}$$

The range of the prior on e is chosen to provide an adequate range of possible patterns of cut-offs. We note that given the identification restrictions (8.65), the prior on Λ induces a prior on ϕ. Rossi et al. (2001) define a Gibbs sampler for this model that uses a method of collapsing for acceleration by integrating out the latents, $\{y_i\}$, from one of the draws (see the appendix for details). An implementation is available in the *bayesm* routine, `rscaleUsage`.

4.5.4 *Computational notes*

Customized Metropolis-Hastings for the General Hierarchical Problem In the generic hierarchical model (8.47), a likelihood is postulated for each cross-sectional "unit" and this is coupled with a two-stage hierarchical prior. If a Metropolis-Hastings random walk step is used for the draw of $\theta_h|y_h,\tau,h$, then, in principle, any model can be used for the unit likelihood. Given the flexibility of mixture of normals priors and Dirichlet Process priors, a Gibbs sampler can usually be constructed for the draws of $\tau|\{\theta_h\}$.

The only limitation is that the M-H random walk methods only work well if the random walk increments can be tuned to conform as closely as possible to the curvature in the conditional posterior

$$p\left(\theta_h|y_h,\tau\right) \propto p\left(y_h|\theta_h\right)p\left(\theta_h|\tau\right). \tag{8.69}$$

Therefore, for all except the most regular models, it will be necessary to customize the Metropolis chains for each cross-sectional unit. Without prior information on highly probable values of the first-stage prior parameters, τ, it will be difficult to use the strategy of trial runs to tune the Metropolis chains, given that a large fraction of cross-sectionals have limited information about the model parameters. One other possibility that is often employed is to use the pooled likelihood for all units and scale the Hessian from this pooled likelihood for the number of observations in any one unit (see Allenby and Rossi 1993). Define $\bar{\ell}(\theta) = \prod_{h=1}^{H} \ell(\theta_h | y_h)$ as the pooled likelihood. The scaled Hessian is given by

$$\bar{H}_h = \frac{n_h}{N} \frac{\partial^2 log \bar{\ell}}{\partial \theta_h \partial \theta_h'} |_{\theta = \hat{\theta}_{MLE}}, \tag{8.70}$$

where $N = \sum_{h=1}^{H} n_h$ and n_h is the number of observations for cross-sectional unit h. The scaled Hessian is a curvature estimate for each cross-sectional unit but it is based on a mixture across units. While this will get the scaling or units approximately correct for each element of θ, there is no guarantee that this curvature estimate will approximate the correlation structure in each individual unit. The virtue of the use of a Hessian based on the pooled sample is that the pooled MLE is often easy to find and has a non-singular Hessian.

The opposite extreme from the use of the pooled MLE would be to use Hessian estimates constructed from each unit likelihood. This would require that the MLE exist and that the Hessian is non-singular for each cross-sectional unit likelihood. For choice model applications, this would require, at a minimum, that each cross-sectional unit be observed to choose at least once from all choice alternatives (sometimes termed a "complete" purchase history). If a unit does not choose a particular alternative and if an alternative-specific intercept is included in the model, then the MLE will not be defined for this unit. There would exist a direction of recession in which an intercept will drift off to $-\infty$ with an increasing likelihood. What is required is a regularization of the unit-level likelihood for that sub-sample of units with singular Hessians or non-existent MLEs. Our proposal is to borrow from the "fractional" likelihood literature for the purpose of computing an estimate of the unit-level Hessian. This is only used for the Random Walk Metropolis increment covariance matrix and is *not* used to replace the unit-level likelihood in posterior computations.

To compute the Hessian, we form a fractional combination of the unit-level likelihood and the pooled likelhood:

$$\ell_h^*(\theta) = \ell_h(\theta)^{(1-w)} \bar{\ell}(\theta)^{w\beta}. \tag{8.71}$$

The fraction, w, should be chosen to be a rather small number so that only a "fraction" of the pooled likelihood, $\bar{\ell}$, is combined with the unit likelihood, ℓ_h, to form the regularized likelihood. β is chosen to properly scale the pooled likelihood to the same order as the unit likelihood. $\beta = \frac{n_h}{N}$ (8.71) is maximized to estimate the Hessian at the "modified" MLE. This Hessian can be combined with the normal covariance matrix from the unit-level conditionally normal prior (note: if the prior is of the mixture of normal form, we are conditioning on the indicator for this unit). If the RW Metropolis increments are $N(0, s^2\Omega)$, then

$$\Omega = \left(H_h + V_\theta^{-1}\right)^{-1} \tag{8.72}$$

$$H_h = -\frac{\partial^2 log\ell_h^*}{\partial\theta\partial\theta'}|_{\theta=\hat{\theta}_h}, \tag{8.73}$$

where $\hat{\theta}_h$ is the maximum of the modified likelihood in (8.71). This customized MH method is illustrated in the *bayesm* routine, `rhierMnlRwMixture`.

Clustering Using a Mixture of Normals In many marketing applications, some sort of clustering method is desired to group "observations" or units that exhibit some sort of similarity. Most clustering methods are based on distance metrics that are related to the normal distribution. If a mixture of normals is used, a very general clustering method can be developed. "Observations" are grouped into various normal sub-populations. The only caveat is that there is no restriction that variance of each normal mixture component be "smaller" than the variation across components. For example, a thick-tailed distribution across units can be approximated by the mixture of a small variance normal with a very large variance normal. Observations that get clustered into the large variance component should be interpreted as "similar" only to the extent that they are outliers.

In addition to the metric by which similarity is gauged, there is also a question as to what variables should be used as the basis of clustering. Traditional methods cluster units on the basis of observables such as psycho-graphics. However, if unit-level behavioral data is available, it is now possible to cluster units on the basis of unit-level parameters. In some applications, these parameters can be interpreted as representing unit-level tastes. This form of clustering on the basis of inference about the unit-level parameters, θ_h, can be termed "behavioral" clustering. Given that psycho-graphics is not very predictive of brand preferences or sensitivity to marketing variables, it is likely that behavioral clustering will be very useful in marketing applications.

To cluster based on a mixture of normals model (8.54), we use the latent indicators of component "assignment". We note that this can apply either when a mixture of normals approach is applied directly to data (density estimation) or as the random coefficient distribution. There can be a fixed number of normal components or a random number of components as in the DP models. All that is required is that we have draws from the posterior distribution of the indicator variables. These draws of the indicator variables, *ind*, can be used to form a similarity matrix,

$$S = \left[s_{i,j}\right] \tag{8.74}$$

$$s_{i,j} = \begin{cases} 0 & if\ ind_i \neq ind_j \\ 1 & if\ ind_i = ind_j. \end{cases}$$

We note that the similarity matrix is invariant to label-switching. (8.74) defines a function from a given partition or classification of the observations to the similarity matrix. To emphasize this dependence, we will denote this function as $S(ind)$. That is, for any clustering of the observations defined in an indicator vector, we can compute the associated similarity matrix. We can also find, for any similarity matrix, a classification or indicator vector consistent with the given similarity matrix. This function we denote by $ind = g(S)$.

By simply averaging over the draws from the marginal posterior of the indicator variables, we can estimate the posterior expectation of the similarity matrix:

$$S^* = E_{ind|data}\left[S(ind)\right]$$
$$\hat{S^*} = \frac{1}{R}\sum_{r=1}^{R} S\left(ind^r\right). \tag{8.75}$$

Given the expected similarity matrix, the clustering problem involves the assignment or partition of the units so as to minimize some sort of loss function. Let *ind* be an assignment of units to groups and $L(S^*, S(ind))$ be a loss function, then we can define the clustering algorithm as the solution to the following problem:

$$min_{ind} L\left(S^*, S(ind)\right). \tag{8.76}$$

In general, this problem is a difficult optimization problem involving non-continuous choice variables. One could adopt two heuristics for the solution of the problem: (1) simply "classify" two observations as in the same group if the posterior expectation of similarity is greater than a cut-off value; (2) find the posterior draw which minimizes loss. A simple loss function would be the sum of the absolute values of the differences between estimated posterior similarity and the implied similarity for a given value of the indicator or classification variable:

$$ind_{opt} = argmin_{\{ind^r\}}\left[\sum_i\sum_j\left|\hat{S}_{ij} - S\left(ind^r\right)[i,j]\right|\right]. \tag{8.77}$$

The second heuristic uses the MCMC chain as a stochastic search process. The `bayesm` routine, `clusterMix`, implements both heuristics.

Data Structures for Panel Data and Normal Mixture Draws Both generic panel data and normal mixture MCMC output require data structures that are somewhat different from standard arrays. A generalized vector or list is an appropriate structure. That is, we require that the panel data be indexed by panelist or cross-sectional unit, but the data for each unit might consist of groups of objects of different types, such as vectors and arrays. One might want to append information for customized MCMC draws to the panel data itself. This would facilitate retrieval for an MCMC method based on a hierarchical structure. Similarly, a set of draws from a normal mixture consists of a set of *R* objects, each one of which is a set of objects of different type and dimension. In *R*, the list data structure is ideally suited for this purpose. A list is a generalized vector, each element of which can be any valid type of *R* object including a vector, array, function, or list itself. Lists can be nested, therefore, to any desired level. For example, it is possible to have a list of lists.

Panel data can be stored as a list of lists. In *R* notation, we could store a regression-style panel data set as the object `panel_data` which is a list of H panelists. The hth panelist would be indexed by `panel_data[[h]]`, which is a list of two elements y, and X (the *R* syntax for indexing a list is the double square bracket). That is, `panel_data[[h]][[1]]`$=y_h$ and `panel_data[[h]][[2]]`$=X_h$. This approach avoids storage of indices in arrays or the use of ragged arrays. Given the pairwise list structure in *R*, it is a simple matter to add in new elements. For example, suppose you wish to add a customized Hessian (see (8.73)) to the panel data, it is a simple matter to define

```
panel_data[[h]]=c(panel_data[[h]],hess),
```

where "`c()`" is the *R* function for concatenation.

The list structure is even more useful for storage of MCMC draws for normal components. A mixture of K multivariate normals can be represented as a list of K lists, `mix_norm[[k]][[1]]`$=\mu$, `mix_norm[[k]][[2]]`$=\Sigma$ (in practice, of course, we might store the inverse of the Cholesky root of Σ for ease of use in density evaluation). The MCMC draws would then be stored as a list of length R (R draws) of lists of K lists. This is the structure used in both DP and Finite Mixture functions in *bayesm*.

5 Non-random Marketing Mix Variables

All of the models considered so far are motivated by a regression-style or conditional response model. That is, we model the distribution of some response variable (such as choice or sales) conditional on a set of covariates which include marketing mix variables:

$$\begin{aligned} &p\left(y|x,\theta\right) \\ &p\left(x|\tau\right). \end{aligned} \tag{8.78}$$

Typically, we assume that the marginal distribution of the x variables is not related to the conditional distribution of $y|x$. However, we must recognize that the market mix variables in x are not set at random or independently of the sales response equation. Classic examples might include price setting where managers set prices on the basis of predictions of y. For example, suppose a retailer is aware that a manufacturer is going to issue a rebate or coupon in the next period and this will affect sales of an item. It is entirely possible that the retailer will set price taking this "demand shock" into account. However, the statistician observing price and sales data might not observe the coupon or rebate events and might fail to take account of the strategic price-setting behavior. Suppose that the coupon drop made demand more inelastic and the retailer raised prices in response. This could have the effect of making prices appear to have less effect on demand.

In the hierarchical setting, Manchanda et al. (2004) consider the situation in which the x variable is set with partial knowledge of the response parameter, θ, at the unit level. The application considered is the allocation of the sales force to various accounts. If the cost of sales force visits is roughly equal across accounts, then we would assume that the sales manager would allocate a budget-constrained sales force to the most responsive accounts. This means that the level of x is related to the cross-sectional unit value, θ_h.

One approach to the problem of strategically determined x values or non-random x is to model the choice of x as a function of the sales response equation as well as of cost considerations of the firm. This would provide a model for the joint distribution of both x and y. The problem with this approach is that it is usually based on the assumption that the firm behaves optimally in the determination of the x values. This gives rise to an optimality conundrum in that if we assume optimality we can only estimate demand and firm parameters and have little to say to firms as to how to improve profitability. One way out of the optimality conundrum is to assume that firms set prices optimally with respect to some information set that does not have complete information about the model parameters. In this manner, improved profitability can be obtained from a richer information set (see, for example, Rossi et al. 1996). We will not take this approach here, but instead consider the possibility that there exists what econometricians call an instrumental variable.

5.1 Bayesian instrumental variables

If we want to avoid making assumptions about precisely how the x variables are set, one approach is to assume that there is some portion of the variation in x that is *exogeneous* or determined by factors independent of y (analogous to true experimental variation). It will be useful to introduce the notion of an error term or driving variable to the determination of y. The sales response model can now be written:

$$y = f_y\left(x, \epsilon_y|\theta\right). \tag{8.79}$$

This equation is sometimes termed the "structural equation," but it does not represent the conditional distribution of $y|x$ as x is not independent of ϵ_y. We postulate the existence of an "instrumental variable" that is independent of ϵ_y. That is, we assume that x is driven in part by the instrument and another error term that is correlated or dependent on ϵ_y:

$$x = f_x\left(z, \epsilon_x|\omega\right). \tag{8.80}$$

Classical instrumental variable (IV) methods merely exploit the fact that ϵ_y and z are assumed to be uncorrelated. In a Bayesian approach, a fully specified likelihood function must be used. Given a joint distribution on $\left(\epsilon_y, \epsilon_x\right)$, we can derive the joint distribution of $\left(y, x\right)$, which is the "reduced form,"

$$p\left(x, y|z, \theta, \omega\right). \tag{8.81}$$

An important special case of (8.81) is the case of linear equations:

$$\begin{aligned} x &= \delta' z + \epsilon_x \\ y &= \beta x + \epsilon_y. \end{aligned} \tag{8.82}$$

Note that, for ease of exposition, we have not included intercepts in the equation or other "exogenous" variables in the y equation (see Rossi et al. 2005 for the general case). Our discussion includes the most common case, in which there is only one potentially "endogenous" variable and an arbitrary number of instruments. We should note that while the first equation in (8.82) is a regression equation, the second equation is not if the error terms are dependent. That is, $p\left(\epsilon_y|x\right) \neq p\left(\epsilon_y\right)$ (see Lancaster 2004).

5.1.1 *Normal errors*

We will start our discussion of the linear instrumental variables model using bivariate normal errors. This will provide the basic intuition for Bayesian inference and can easily be extended if the errors have a mixture of normals or DP process errors:

$$\begin{pmatrix} \epsilon_x \\ \epsilon_y \end{pmatrix} \sim N\left(0, \Sigma\right). \tag{8.83}$$

With normal errors, it is a simple matter to derive the likelihood function for the linear model. To derive the joint distribution of $y, x|z$, we simply substitute into the structural equation from the instrumental variables equation:

$$\begin{aligned} x &= \pi_x' z + v_x \\ y &= \pi_y' z + v_y, \end{aligned} \tag{8.84}$$

with

$$\begin{pmatrix} v_x \\ v_y \end{pmatrix} \sim N\left(0, \Omega\right), \; \Omega = A\Sigma A', \; A = \begin{bmatrix} 1 & 0 \\ \beta & 1 \end{bmatrix} \tag{8.85}$$

and

$$\pi_x = \delta, \; \pi_y = \beta\delta.$$

Our view is that it is best to put priors directly on (β, δ, Σ) rather than on the reduced-form coefficients and reduced-form error covariance matrix. In particular, it would be inappropriate to assume that Ω and π_y are a priori independent, since both sets of parameters depend on β. A useful starting point is to use conditionally conjugate and independent priors for the linear system:

$$\delta \sim N\left(\bar{\underline{\delta}}, \underline{A}_\delta^{-1}\right), \; \beta \sim N\left(\bar{\underline{\beta}}, \underline{a}_\beta^{-1}\right), \; \Sigma \sim IW\left(\underline{V}, \underline{\nu}\right). \tag{8.86}$$

It is easy to define a Gibbs sampler for the system (8.82) and (8.83). The Gibbs sampler contains three sets of conditional posterior distributions:

$$\begin{aligned} &\beta \mid \delta, \Sigma, y, x, Z \\ &\delta \mid \beta, \Sigma, y, x, Z \\ &\Sigma \mid \beta, \delta, y, x, Z. \end{aligned} \tag{8.87}$$

The intuition for the Gibbs sampler is the same intuition that motivates the "endogeneity" problem in the first place. We know that the linear structural equation for y is not a valid regression equation because the error term is a non-zero mean which depends on x. However, the first distribution in the Gibbs sampler conditions on δ, which means that we can "observe" ϵ_x and the conditional distribution of $\epsilon_y|\epsilon_x$ can be derived. This distribution can be used to convert the structural equation into an equation with an $N(0,1)$ error term:

$$\left(y - \frac{\sigma_{xy}}{\sigma_x^2}\epsilon_x\right) = \beta x + u, \; u \sim N\left(0, \sigma_y^2 - \frac{\sigma_{xy}}{\sigma_x^2}\right). \tag{8.88}$$

Dividing through by σ_u converts the first Gibbs sampler draw into a Bayes regression with a unit variance error term. The second conditional in the Gibbs sampler is simply a restricted two-variate regression which can be achieved easily by "doubling" the observations with rows of z_i and βz_i. The final Gibbs sampler conditional is a standard Inverted Wishart draw. This Gibbs sampler is implemented in the *bayesm* routine, `rivGibbs`.

5.1.2 *Mixture of normals and DP errors*

A legitimate concern about the Bayesian "IV" procedure is the additional specification of normal error terms in both the structural and "first-stage" instrument equation. This is not required for classical IV estimators. Usually, this is a concern about the possible inconsistency of an estimator based on a misspecified likelihood. Equally important, but rarely appreciated, is the possibility for improved inference if it is possible to detect and model the non-normal structure in the error term. For example, suppose that the error terms are a mixture of a normal error with small variance and another normal error with a very large variance. The single component normal error model may be sensitive to the outliers and will treat the outlying error terms inefficiently. In principle, it should be possible to detect and down-weight observations that appear to have errors drawn from the outlying component. The classical IV approach sacrifices efficiency for the sake of consistency. In a semi-parametric Bayesian approach, it is theoretically possible to be robust to misspecification while not reducing efficiency. That is, in the normal case we might not lose much or any efficiency, but in the non-normal case we exploit the structure and construct an efficient procedure.

A logical place to start a departure from normality is the mixture of normals model. Intuitively, if we condition on the latent indicator variable for the membership in normal components, we should be able to reuse the Gibbs sampler for the normal model as we can adjust and properly normalize for different variances. If we use mixture of normals to approximate any unknown bivariate density of the error terms in the linear system (8.82), we need to be careful to allow the means of each component to be non-zero. A mixture of normals with zero or equal means is simply a scale mixture and cannot approximate skewed or multi-modal distributions. For this reason, we will allow non-zero means for the error terms and remove the intercepts from the model:

$$\begin{aligned} x &= Z\delta + \epsilon_x^* \\ y &= \beta x + \epsilon_y^* \\ \begin{pmatrix} \epsilon_x^* \\ \epsilon_y^* \end{pmatrix} &\sim N\left(\mu_{ind}, \Sigma_{ind}\right) \end{aligned} \tag{8.89}$$

To complete this model, we need to put a prior over the number of values of normal components. In the standard finite mixture of normals, we assume that there up to K possible unique values. As discussed in Griffin et al. (Chapter 4, this volume), a DP prior can be used which puts positive prior probability on up to N unique components. The DP process, $G(\alpha, G_0)$, defines this prior. We assess a prior on α (8.59) and directly set the hyperparameters for the base prior distribution, G_0 (see 8.57). We use the following parameterization of G_0:

$$G_0 : \mu|\Sigma \sim N\left(0, \underline{a}^{-1}\Sigma\right), \; \Sigma \sim IW\left(\underline{c}I_2, \underline{\nu}\right). \tag{8.90}$$

To assess G_0, we center and scale both y and x. For centered and scaled dependent variables, we would expect that the bivariate distribution of the errors terms is concentrated on the region $[-2, 2] \times [-2, 2]$. In order to achieve full flexibility, we want the possibility of locating normal components over a "wide" range of values and with a reasonable range of small and large variances (see Conley et al. 2008 for details on the prior assessment). Our default values are very diffuse:

$$\underline{a} = 0.016, \; \underline{c} = 0.17, \; \underline{\nu} = 2.004.$$

We assess the prior on α to put prior mass on values of the number of unique components from 1 to at least 10 or more, though we note that the DP prior puts positive prior probability on up to N (the sample size) unique values or components.

In the Polya Urn method for drawing from the posterior distribution distribution in DP models, $\theta_i = (\mu_i, \Sigma_i)$ components are drawn for each observation. However, these values are clustered to a smaller number of unique values. The indicator variable can be formed from the set of draws of the errors distribution parameters and the set of unique values. This means that we can form a Gibbs sampler for the linear IV model with a DP process prior on the errors from the following steps:

$$\begin{gathered} \beta|\delta, ind, \{\theta_i\}, x, y, Z \\ \delta|\beta, ind, \{\theta_i\}, x, y, Z \\ \{\theta_i\}|\beta, \delta, x, y, Z \\ \alpha|I^*. \end{gathered} \tag{8.91}$$

Given a set of draws of $\{\theta_i, i = 1, \ldots, N\}$, we can define the I^* unique values as $\left\{\theta_j^*, j = 1, \ldots, I^*\right\}$. The indicator vector, *ind*, is defined by $ind_i = j$ if $\theta_i = \theta_j^*$. The draws of β and δ in (8.91) are basically the same as for the normal model except that adjustments must be made for the means of the error terms and there are different means and variance terms depending on which unique value is associated with each observation. The *bayesm* routine, `rivDP`, implements the full Gibbs sampler, including a so-called "remix" step that is not documented in (8.91).

Conley et al. (2008) consider the performance of the Bayesian IV procedure with DP errors under conditions of both normal and non-normal errors and weak and strong instruments. Performance is measured by the efficiency of a point estimator as well as the coverage of HPD intervals. There is virtually no loss to the use of the DP prior in the sense that, under normal errors, the inference on the structural parameters, β, is the same under DP or normal priors. However, under non-normal errors, the DP prior adapts to the non-normality and outperforms Bayes IV based on a single component normal prior. Comparisons with state-of-the-art classical methods for non-normal errors and weak instruments show that the Bayes procedure extracts much more information from the sample.

5.2 Strategically determined X values in a hierarchical setting

In some marketing situations, marketing variables are customized at the cross-sectional unit level. Examples include customizing trade promotions or wholesale prices in specific markets, targeting and customization of coupons for specific consumers, and allocation of sales force differentially across accounts. In a typical hierarchical setting, we start with a conditional response model of the general form:

$$p\left(y_{ht}|x_{ht}, \theta_h\right). \tag{8.92}$$

Implicitly, the standard analyses of this situation consider the distribution of x_{ht} to be independent of θ_h. However, a more general approach would be to simultaneously model the sales response model and the determination of the marketing mix, taking into account that the distribution of x_{ht} may depend on θ_h:

$$\begin{gathered} p\left(y_{ht}|x_{ht}, \theta_h\right) \\ p\left(x_{ht}|\theta_h, \tau\right). \end{gathered} \tag{8.93}$$

This approach is a generalization of the models developed by Chamberlain (1980) and Chamberlain (1984) and applied in a marketing context by Bronnenberg and Mahajan (2001). Chamberlain considers situations in which the x variables are correlated with random intercepts in a variety of standard linear and logit/probit models. Our random effects apply to all of the response model parameters and we can handle non-standard and non-linear models. However, the basic results of Chamberlain regarding consistency of the conditional modeling approach apply. Unless T grows, any likelihood-based estimator for the conditional model will be inconsistent. The severity of this asymptotic bias will depend on model, data, and T. For small T, these biases have been documented to be very large.

The general data-augmentation and Metropolis-Hasting MCMC approach is ideally suited to exploit the conditional structure of (8.93). That is, we can alternate between draws of $\theta_h|\tau$ (here we recognize that the $\{\theta_h\}$ are independent conditional on τ) and $\tau | \{\theta_h\}$. With some care in the choice of the proposal density, this MCMC approach can handle a very wide range of specific distributional models for both the conditional and marginal distributions.

To further specify the model in (8.93), it is useful to think about the interpretation of the parameters in the θ vector. We might postulate that in the marketing mix application, the important quantities are the level of sales given some "normal" settings of x (e.g. baseline sales) and the derivative of sales with respect to various marketing mix variables. In many situations, decision makers are setting marketing mix variables proportional to the baseline level of sales. More sophisticated decision makers might recognize that the effectiveness of the marketing mix is also important in the allocation of marketing resources. This means that the specification of the marginal distribution of x should make the level of x a function of the baseline level of sales and the derivatives of sales with respect to the elements of x.

Manchanda et al. (2004) consider a special case of (8.93) in which the sales response model is a Negative Binomial Regression for the counts of prescriptions made by physicians. x includes the number of sales calls during the same period of time that prescriptions are monitored. The number of sales calls is modeled as strategically determined as a function of the sales call ("detail") responsiveness. This means that both the level and changes in the number of sales calls are informative regarding the effect of this variable. The additional information that is available from the modeling of the x variable as a function of θ_h is considerable and is a more important aspect of the problem than possible biases from the fact that x is dependent on the random coefficients (see Yang et al., 2003).

6 Conclusions

In this chapter, we have reviewed applications of Bayesian methods and models in marketing. Marketing applications highlight two under-emphasized aspects of the Bayesian paradigm. Due to the low information content and discreteness of disaggregate marketing data, informative priors are essential and require careful assessment. Flexibility in the specification of prior distributions, particularly in the hierarchical setting is very important. Finally, marketing applications require that models of the consumer decision process be implemented. This gives rise to non-standard likelihoods. The simulation-based methods, now dominant in Bayesian work, free the investigator from reliance on standard models and priors. We regard marketing applications as a stimulating source of new models and a severe stress test for existing models and methods.

References

Allenby, G. M., Garratt, M. J., and Rossi, P. E. (2010). "A Model for Trade-Up and Change in Considered Brands," *Marketing Science*, 29(1): 40–56.

—— and Rossi, P. E. (1991). "Quality Preceptions and Asymmetric Switching Between Brands," *Marketing Science*, 10(3): 185–204.

—— —— (1993). "A Bayesian Approach to Estimating Household Parameters," *Journal of Marketing Research*, 30(2): 171–82.

—— —— (1999). "Marketing Models of Consumer Heterogeneity," *Journal of Econometrics*, 89: 57–78.

Antoniak, C. E. (1974). "Mixtures of Dirichlet Processes with Applications to Bayesian Non-parametric Problems," *The Annals of Statistics*, 2(6): 1152–74.

Avriel, M. (1976). *Nonlinear Programming: Analysis and Methods*. Prentice-Hall.

Bernardo, J. M., and Smith, A. F. M. (1994). *Bayesian Theory*. John Wiley & Sons.

Berry, S., Levinsohn, J., and Pakes, A. (1995). "Automobile Prices in Market Equilibrium," *Econometrica*, 63(4): 841–90.

Bhat, C. R. (2005). "A Multiple Discrete-Continuous Extreme Value Model: Formulation and Application to Discretionary Time-Use Decisions," *Transportation Research Part B*, 39: 679–707.

—— (2008). "The Multiple Discrete-Continuous Extreme Value Model: Role of Utility Function Parameters, Identification Considerations, and Model Extensions," *Transportation Research Part B*, 42: 274–303.

Bronnenberg, B. J., and Mahajan, V. (2001). "Multimarket Data: Joint Spatial Dependence in Market Shares and Promotional Variables," *Marketing Science*, 20(3): 284–99.

Chamberlain, G. (1980). "Analysis of Covariance with Qualitative Data," *Review of Economic Studies*, 47: 225–38.

—— (1984). "Panel Data," in Z. Griliches, and M. Intriligator, (eds.), *Handbook of Econometrics*, vol. 2. North-Holland.

Chandukala, S. R., Kim, J., Otter, T., Rossi, P. E., and Allenby, G. M. (2007). "Choice Models in Marketing: Economic Assumptions, Challenges and Trends," *Foundations and Trends in Marketing*, 2(2): 97–184.

Chen, Y., and Yang, S. (2007). "Estimating Disaggregate Models Using Aggregate Data through Augmentation of Individual Choice," *Journal of Marketing Research*, 44; 613–21.

Chib, S., and Greenberg, E. (1998). "Analysis of Multivariate Probit Models," *Biometrika*, 85(2): 347–61.

Conley, T. G., Hansen, C. B., McCulloch, R. E., and Rossi, P. E. (2008). "A Semi-parametric Bayesian Apporach to the Instrumental Variable Problem," *Journal of Econometrics*, 144: 276–305.

Dubé, J.-P. (2004). "Multiple Discreteness and Product Differentiation: Demand for Carbonated Soft Drinks," *Marketing Science*, 23(1): 66–81.

Edwards, Y., and Allenby, G. M. (2003). "Multivariate Analysis of Multiple Response Data," *Journal of Marketing Research*, 40(3): 321–34.

Fruhwirth-Schnatter, S. (2006). *Finite Mixture and Markov Switching Models*. Springer.

Geweke, J. (1991). "Efficient Simulation from the Multivariate Normal and Student-*t* Distributions Subject to Linear Constraints," in (ed.), E. M. Keramidas, *Computing Science and Statistics: Proceedings of the 23rd Symposium*, 571–78.

____ (2005). *Contemporary Bayesian Econometrics and Statistics*. Chichester: John Wiley & Sons.

Gilbride, T. J., and Allenby, G. M. (2004). "A Choice Model with Conjunctive, Disjunctive, and Compensatory Screening Rules," *Marketing Science*, 23(3): 391–406.

Guadagni, P. M., and Little, J. D. C. (1983). "A Logit Model of Brand Choice Calibrated on Scanner Data," *Marketing Science*, 2(3): 203–38.

Hajivassiliou, V., McFadden, D. L., and Ruud, P. (1996). "Simulation of Multivariate Normal Rectangle Probabilities and their Derivatives," *Journal of Econometrics*, 72: 85–134.

Hausman, J., and Wise, D. A. (1978). "A Conditional Probit Model for Qualitative Choice: Discrete Decisions Recognizing Interdependence and Heterogeneous Preferences," *Econometrica*, 46(2): 403–426.

Imai, K., and D. A. van Dyk (2005). "A Bayesian Analysis of the Multinomial Probit Model using Marginal Data Augmentation," *Journal of Econometrics*, 124: 311–34.

Jiang, R., Manchanda, P., and Rossi, P. E. (2009). "Bayesian Analysis of Random Coefficient Logit Models Using Aggregate Data," *Journal of Econometrics*, 149: 136–48.

Keane, M. P. (1994). "A Computationally Practical Simulation Estimator for Panel Data," *Econometrica*, 62(1): 95–116.

Kim, J., Allenby, G. M., and Rossi, P. E. (2002). "Modeling Consumer Demand for Variety," *Marketing Science*, 21(3): 229–50.

Koop, G. (2003). *Bayesian Econometrics*. John Wiley & Sons.

Lancaster, T. (2004). *An Introduction to Modern Bayesian Econometrics*. Blackwell.

Manchanda, P., Ansari, A., and Gupta, S. (1999). "The 'Shopping Basket': A Model for Multicategory Purchase Incidence Decisions," *Marketing Science*, 18(2): 95–114.

____ Rossi, P. E., and Chintagunta, P. K. (2004). "Response Modeling with Nonrandom Marketing-Mix Variables," *Journal of Marketing Research*, 41: 467–78.

McCulloch, R. E., Polson, N. G., and Rossi, P. E. (2000). "A Bayesian Analysis of the Multinomial Probit Model with Fully Identified Parameters," *Journal of Econometrics*, 99: 173–93.

____ Rossi, P. E. (1994). "An Exact Likelihood Analysis of the Multinomial Probit Model," *Journal of Econometrics*, 64: 207–40.

McFadden, D. L. (1981): "Econometric Models of Probabilistic Choice," in M. Intriligator, and Z. Griliches (eds), *Structural Analysis of Discrete Choice*, North-Holland, 1395–457.

Morrison, D. G., and Schmittlein, D. C. (1988). "Generalizing the NBD Model of Customer Purchases: What Are the Implications and is it Worth the Effort?," *Journal of Business and Economic Statistics*, 6(2): 145–59.

Musalem, A., Bradlow, E. T., and Raju, J. S. (2009). "Bayesian Estimation of Random-Coefficients Choice Models Using Aggregate Data," *Journal of Applied Econometrics*, 24: 490–516.

Orme, B. K. (2009). *Getting Started with Conjoint Analysis*. Research Publishers, LLC.

Pudney, S. E. (1989). *Modeling Individual Choice: The Econometrics of Corners, Kinks, and Holes*. Basil Blackwell.

R (2009). *R: A Language and Environment for Statistical Computing*. R Foundation for Statistical Computing.

Roberts, G. O., and J. S. Rosenthal (2001). "Optimal Scaling for Various Metropolis-Hastings Algorithms," *Statistical Science*, 16(4): 351–367.

Rossi, P. E., Allenby, G. M., and McCulloch, R. E. (2005). *Bayesian Statistics and Marketing*. John Wiley & Sons.

—— Gilula, Z., and Allenby, G. M. (2001). "Overcoming Scale Usage Heterogeneity: A Bayesian Hierarchical Approach," *Journal of the American Statistical Association*, 96(453): 20–31.

—— McCulloch, R. E. (2008). *bayesm: Bayesian Inference for Marketing/Micro-Econometrics* 2.2-3 edn.

—— —— Allenby, G. M. (1996). "The Value of Purchase History Data in Target Marketing," *Marketing Science*, 15(4): 321–40.

Sonnier, G., Ainslie, A., Otter, T. (2007). "Heterogeneity Distributions of Willingness-to-Pay in Choice Models," *Quantitative Marketing and Economics*, 5: 313–31.

Train, K. E. (2003): *Discrete Choice Methods with Simulation*. Cambridge University Press.

Yang, S., Chen, Y., and Allenby, G. M. (2003). "Bayesian Analysis of Simultaneous Demand and Supply," *Quantitative Marketing and Economics*, 1: 251–75.

CHAPTER 9

BAYESIAN METHODS IN FINANCE

ERIC JACQUIER AND NICHOLAS POLSON

1 Introduction

This chapter discusses the use of Bayesian methods in finance. A first fundamental aspect of modern finance is that it asks questions of predictability. Discussions on the efficiency of markets center on the degree of predictability, if any, of financial series. This maps directly onto the Bayesian use of the predictive density. Further, as one must compare multiple competing models of predictability, the Bayesian perspective on testing, namely odds ratios for model comparison or averaging, is well suited. Second, the quantities of interest in many finance applications, for example the period of a cycle, hedge ratios, option prices, correlations between portfolios, and Sharpe ratios, are non-linear functions of the base parameters, used to write the likelihood function. For example, the period of a cycle in autocorrelation is a function of the autoregressive (AR) parameters. Bayesian methods, especially when posteriors are simulated, easily deliver the exact posterior density of such a non-linear function of the parameters. Third, in recent years, models of time-varying volatility have become increasingly complex, and Bayesian methods, in conjunction with Markov chain Monte Carlo techniques, have produced highly effective estimation and prediction algorithms for these models.

Eric Jacquier acknowledges financial support from HEC research funds. The chapter has benefited from comments from the *Handbook* editors, discussions with Shirley Miller and Maïa Cullen, and editing by Linda Tracey of Inkslingers. The authors are especially grateful to John Geweke and Herman Van Dijk for their innumerable insights and support. There is a rich body of Bayesian work in finance, and, as this chapter has no encyclopedic ambitions, a number of excellent papers are not discussed, with no implications as to their quality; apologies where they are due. A general acknowledgement is owed to Arnold Zellner whose foundational work and mentoring are at the source of nearly everything discussed in this chapter.

Finally, rationally based financial decision-making contains a vast normative aspect. Following Bayes' rule, an agent updates her beliefs on the predictive distribution of asset returns, possibly via the optimal averaging of competing models, none of which she holds to be true. She then devises a portfolio to maximize the expected utility of her predictive wealth.

With this in mind, Section 2 addresses the classic portfolio optimization introduced by Markowitz (1952) and Merton (1969). We first show how estimation error is addressed in the Bayesian framework. Even within the restrictive framework of one single model, for example, one period as in Markowitz or independently identically distributed (iid) log-normal as in Merton, expected-utility is now random since it is a function of parameters that are themselves random for the Bayesian.[1] Decision theory shows that conditioning on point estimates, no matter how *good*, does not yield an optimal strategy. One needs to integrate out the parameters using their posterior density, which yields the predictive density of future returns. This point is made early, for example, in Zellner and Chetty (1962) and Brown (1978). While the Bayesian methodology is optimal given the information available to the agent, diffuse priors alone offer limited improvement over the classical approach. Therefore, Section 2.2 discusses a remedy, empirical Bayes. This refers to the use of proper priors calibrated from the sample itself, rather than subjective priors reflecting actual views. We discuss the relation between these priors and the James and Stein (1961) shrinkage estimators, and how to calibrate both the mean vector and the covariance matrix as in Frost and Savarino (1986). Perhaps because the numerical effect did not appear too large at the time, for the one-period framework, the ideas in Brown (1978) and others did not get immediate widespread use. We show in Section 2.3 that the impact of uncertainty in the mean increases dramatically with the investment horizon; we discuss Jacquier (2006) and Barberis (2000). Section 2.4 discusses how the Bayesian econometrician can use priors to incorporate beliefs in asset-pricing models, as in Black and Litterman (1991) and Pastor (2000). We complete the section with a discussion of further issues.

Section 3 discusses the predictability of the mean of asset returns, central to finance, as it relates to the efficiency of financial markets. Predictability can be analyzed in a rather classic statistical time-series approach or from the viewpoint of its economic relevance. We start with the time series approach. Here the benefits of Bayesian analysis reside in the use of posterior odds, which allow the ranking of multiple models. The initial literature on predictability typically analyzed the ability of one or more variables to predict stock returns with classical statistical tools such as t-statistics, R-squares, or root mean-squared errors. The standard classical framework with one null hypothesis nested in an alternative does not allow the ranking of multiple, possibly non-nested models of predictability. In contrast, model odds ratios are perfectly fitted for that task, and we

[1] This is even before accounting for model uncertainty. Especially in Bayesian econometrics, there is no sense in which a given model is seen as true. Models are, hopefully, convenient windows through which to view the data, and make needed inference, prediction, or decision. See Poirier, Chapter 2 in this *Handbook*.

discuss Avramov (2002) and Cremers (2002), who contribute to the understanding of predictability by using Bayesian model comparison and, more importantly, averaging in this context. Predictability is often assessed by a measure that is a non-linear function of the basic parameters used to write the likelihood function. Classical estimation techniques are ill-equipped for this situation because of the approximations inherent in the asymptotic theory. We show such an example with the analysis of cyclicality in stock returns, and with Lamoureux and Zhou's (1996) Bayesian approach to the long-horizon return predictability.

Section 3.2 discusses the economic relevance of predictability, namely its impact on optimal allocation. A classic first paper that initiated this way of thinking is Kandel and Stambaugh (1996). They analyze predictability through the classic regression of stock returns on the dividend yield, specifically its impact on asset allocation, when parameter uncertainty is properly accounted for in the predictive density. Recognizing the stochastic nature of the predictor, they formulate the predictive regression as a bivariate vector autoregressive (VAR) process. Stambaugh (1999) provides a thorough analysis of this predictive regression. We conclude with a discussion of Barberis (2000) who pays special attention to the multi-period case.

Section 4 discusses some major contributions of Bayesian econometrics to the literature on empirical asset pricing. First we show how McCulloch and Rossi (1990, 1991) implement a Bayesian test of Ross's (1976) arbitrage pricing theory (APT) from statistical and economic perspectives. Second, a major issue in tests of latent factor models is the needed preliminary estimation of the factor scores and loadings. In contrast, for the CAPM and the index models, one usually only worries about the estimations of the loadings (betas). Classical approaches typically assume asymptotics in the time series or in the cross-section of assets. Geweke and Zhou (1995) show that neither assumption is necessary. They jointly estimate the scores and the factors with a simple MCMC algorithm. Third, within the CAPM world, it has long been established that tests of asset-pricing models were akin to testing whether the index at hand was ex-post efficient. This has led to a rich Bayesian literature tackling tests of asset-pricing models this way, which we discuss. Another perspective on the efficiency of markets is whether managed portfolios can beat passive indexes. We discuss Baks et al. (2001) and others who study mutual fund performance from a Bayesian perspective. We contrast with the approach in Jones and Shanken (2005), who study the funds jointly.

Section 5 discusses volatility and covariance modeling. It starts with a review of Bayesian Generalized Autoregressive Conditional Heteroskedasticity (GARCH), and continues with Stochastic Volatility (SV) modeling. MCMC algorithms have resulted in a tremendous growth in the use of SV models in financial econometrics, because they make possible the estimation of complex non-linear latent variable models for which the Kalman filter is not optimal. For example, the MCMC algorithms in Jacquier, Polson, and Rossi (1994, 2004) obtain the posterior densities of both the latent variables, here the volatilities, and the parameters. While MCMC methods can be applied to the maximization of the likelihood function, the Bayesian approach does not require this complicated step since it only needs to draw from the posterior distribution. We review a Bayesian MCMC algorithm for classic SV models with both leverage effects and fat tails. We show first how to design and diagnose the algorithm, then how to conduct model comparison by looking at the predictions of the model and by computing odds ratios. We show simple ways to obtain the odds ratios that only rely on the readily available posterior draws, thus bypassing the specific integration needed for the computation of the marginal likelihood. We then mention extensions to the model. We complete this section by discussing Bayesian strategies for estimating covariance matrices. We discuss two different approaches to the matrix, first where the individual volatilities and the correlation matrix are modeled separately; second, where factor models are allowed to constrain the covariance matrix. We discuss Bayesian estimation of the factor loadings, the β's. Cosemans et al. (2009) model jointly the cross-sectional and time-series dynamics of betas and show that it results in improved portfolio performance. Jostova and Philipov (2004) implement an MCMC algorithm for latent betas.

Section 6 reviews the area of empirical option pricing. We first discuss simulation based methods to compute the option price on the basis of draws of the uncertain volatility. Early methods only reflect the uncertainty in volatility. We then discuss the explicit addition of a pricing error to the model entertained, so that the likelihood incorporates model error. We discuss Jacquier and Jarrow (2000), who model the Black-Scholes pricing error as a function of observable variables. While their likelihood exclusively follows from the pricing error, they incorporate the historical returns via a prior on σ. In the same spirit, Eraker (2004) implements a vastly more general model where volatility is stochastic and can jump. Jones (2003b) links implied and historical volatilities by a linear relationship, allowing for errors. This in fact incorporates both the historical and risk-neutral process in the likelihood function

Section 7 discusses a promising recent development in finance: filtering with parameter learning. Filtering techniques have gained recognition over the past few years (see Giondani et al., Chapter 3 in this *Handbook* for classic filtering algorithms). MCMC methods allow inference for complex models with parameters θ and latent variables h by breaking their joint posterior distribution into conditionals, $(h|\theta)$ and $(\theta|h)$. This produces the joint distribution of the smoothed estimates of the latent variables, for example $(h_t|y_1, \ldots y_T)$. However, one often wants the distribution of the filtered values of the latent variable, $(h_t|y_1, \ldots, y_t)$ $\forall t \in [1, T]$. A feasible solution is to repeat an MCMC smoother for all desired subsamples $[1, t]$. It is, however, not attractive computationally. Particle filters deliver the desired filtered densities of the latent variables, but until recently, conditioned on a parameter value $(h_t|y_1, \ldots, y_t, \theta)$, which was not very interesting. In contrast, the more recent algorithms which we discuss allow for parameter learning. That is, at any time $t \in [1, T]$, the algorithm produces the density of both latent variables and parameters using only the data until time t, $(h_t|y_1, \ldots, y_t, \theta)$ and $(\theta_t|y_1, \ldots, y_t)$. We discuss implementations from Jacquier and Miller (2010).

2 Optimal Portfolio Design

2.1 The basic optimal portfolio setup with parameter uncertainty

Before introducing parameter uncertainty, we briefly review some key results of one-period optimal portfolio theory. See Markowitz (1952), Merton (1972), Roll (1977), Brandt (2009), or classic graduate finance textbooks for derivations. Markowitz's (1952) one-period framework assumes N jointly normal asset returns **R** with known mean vector $\boldsymbol{\mu}$ and covariance matrix Σ. A portfolio with weights w in the N assets has mean $\mu = w'\boldsymbol{\mu}$ and variance $\sigma^2 = w'\Sigma w$. This yields the well-known efficient frontier in the mean versus variance space, customarily plotted versus standard deviation. In brief, with short sales allowed, the locus of expected returns versus standard deviation of optimal portfolios that minimize variance subject to a desired expected return, is a hyperbola. Its vertex is the global minimum variance portfolio (MVP) whose vector of weights is $\Sigma^{-1}i/i'\Sigma^{-1}i$, where i is a vector of ones. Note that the weights sum to one due to the denominator. Without a risk-free asset, investors select a portfolio on this frontier, so as to maximize their expected utility, or certainty equivalent (CE), which represents the trade-off between mean and variance. For investors with constant relative risk aversion, the CE is $\mu - \frac{\gamma}{2}\sigma^2$. The weights maximizing this CE are equal to $\frac{1}{\gamma}\Sigma^{-1}(\boldsymbol{\mu} - \mu_0 i)$, where μ_0 is also a function of Σ^{-1} and $\boldsymbol{\mu}$.

The combinations of a risk-free asset with a risky asset on this frontier occur on a straight line, known as the capital allocation line (CAL), in this mean versus standard deviation space. The slope of this line is the Sharpe ratio, the ratio of the expected return in excess of the risk-free rate over the standard deviation, which investors seek to maximize. The resulting tangency portfolio of the N risky assets is located where the CAL is tangent to the frontier of risky assets. Its vector of weights is:

$$\frac{\Sigma^{-1}(\boldsymbol{\mu} - R_f i)}{i'\Sigma^{-1}(\boldsymbol{\mu} - R_f i)}. \tag{9.1}$$

Investors allocate their wealth between this tangency portfolio and the risk free rate according to their risk aversion. The optimal allocation, the weight in the risky portfolio which maximizes this certainty equivalent is:

$$w^{\star} = \frac{\mu - R_f}{\gamma\sigma^2}, \tag{9.2}$$

where μ, σ are the mean and standard deviation of the tangency portfolio found in (9.1), and $1 - w^*$ is allocated to the risk-free rate.

Parameters are unknown in actual implementations. The early practice was to substitute point estimates of the parameters $\boldsymbol{\mu}$ and Σ into the standard optimal portfolio formulas, or into an optimizer. However, decision theory shows that conditioning the problem on point estimates, as good as they may be, of model parameters leads to suboptimal portfolios. As pointed out by Zellner and Chetty (1965), accounting properly for estimation error requires the computation of the predictive density. The predictive density, an essentially Bayesian concept, is the joint density of future data, conditional only on the model used and the data already observed, **R**. In our case, the joint predictive density of the N asset returns for time T+1 is:

$$p(\mathbf{R}_{T+1}|\mathbf{R}) = \int p(\mathbf{R}_{T+1}|\mathbf{R}, \boldsymbol{\mu}, \Sigma)\, p(\boldsymbol{\mu}, \Sigma|\mathbf{R})\, d\boldsymbol{\mu}\, d\Sigma. \tag{9.3}$$

Note how the posterior density of the parameters is used to integrate them out of the density of the future returns $p(\mathbf{R}_{T+1}|\mathbf{R}, \boldsymbol{\mu}, \Sigma)$. Similarly, the predictive density of the return on a portfolio with weights w, follows by integrating its mean $\mu = w'\boldsymbol{\mu}$ and variance $\sigma^2 = w'\Sigma w$, out of the conditional density of its return.

Klein and Bawa (1976) demonstrate that computing, and then optimizing, expected utility around the predictive density is the optimal strategy. The intuition is clear in the Bayesian framework: the Sharpe ratio and the expected utility (or CE), $\mu - \frac{\gamma}{2}\sigma^2$ are random due to parameter uncertainty. How can one maximize a random function and hope to find a fixed answer? Also, going forward and substituting point estimates of μ, Σ in the CE or Sharpe ratio clearly omits an uncertainty that should be accounted for, especially by risk-averse investors. In this spirit, Brown (1976, 1978) and Bawa et al. (1979) incorporate parameter uncertainty into the optimal portfolio problem. They (mostly) use improper priors $p(\boldsymbol{\mu}, \Sigma) \propto |\Sigma|^{-(N+1)/2}$ to compute the predictive density of the parameters, and maximize expected utility for that predictive density.

The multivariate predictive density of returns is shown to be a student-t with mean $\hat{\boldsymbol{\mu}}$, degrees of freedom $T - N$, and covariance matrix $k\widehat{\Sigma}$, where the variance inflation factor k is $(1 + \frac{1}{T})\frac{T+1}{T-N-2}$. This modifies optimal allocation, especially when N is sizable relative to T. Relative to the portfolio based on point estimates, Bayesian optimal portfolios take smaller positions on the assets with higher risk, for example those with high $\widehat{\mu}$. If Σ is known, k reduces to $1 + \frac{1}{T}$, and the correction is far less dramatic. Consider, for example, the risky versus risk-free asset allocation. With an improper prior, the posterior density of μ is $N(\hat{\mu}, \frac{\sigma^2}{T})$, where $\hat{\mu}$ is the sample mean. The predictive density of the future return is $N(\hat{\mu}, \sigma^2(1 + \frac{1}{T}))$. Intuitively, the future variance faced by the investor is the sum of the return's variance given the mean and the variance of the uncertain mean. Computing the Merton allocation with respect to this predictive density of returns lowers the allocation on the tangency portfolio in (9.2) by the factor $1 + \frac{1}{T}$. However, it does not affect the weights of the risky assets in the tangency portfolios in (9.1).

Initially, these corrections did not appear important for the one-period model, when N was deemed small enough relative to T. The practice of substituting point estimates of $\boldsymbol{\mu}$ and Σ in the theoretical solutions remained common with both practitioners and academic researchers. However, practitioners eventually recognized that this *plug-in* approach was sensitive to estimation error (see for example Michaud 1989). Consider an investor who minimizes variance subject to a given desired mean return, and uses a point estimate of the mean vector. The highest individual point estimates are such because the corresponding mean may be high, and the sample of data used may lead to a positive estimation error. The next sample, corresponding to the investment period, will likely lead to lower point estimates for these means. This investor will then be over-invested in these estimation errors.

Jobson and Korkie (1980), and a following literature, discuss the sampling variability of the optimal portfolio weights due to the sampling variability of the vector of means and covariance matrix. The major problem with this approach is that, for an investor at decision time, the weights are not a random variable; they are a decision variable. Therefore, the statistical exercise of characterizing their sampling variability offers little insight to the investor, who needs to optimize the predictive utility on the basis of the sample at hand, as decision theory stipulates. A second problem is that the relationship between the portfolio weights and the mean and variance is non-linear. It can be shown that large variations in weights can result in small variations in portfolio mean and variance. Therefore, the frequentist degree of uncertainty in the weights is a poor indicator of the uncertainty in the future returns of optimized portfolios.

Another approach proposed computes the "resampled" frontier. One simulates returns data from the sampling distribution of the estimators of $\boldsymbol{\mu}$ and Σ, and then computes a frontier for each simulated data set. The resampled frontier is an average of these simulated frontiers. This frequentist simulation is very different from the Bayesian decision theory approach, which computes one frontier on the basis of the predictive density of returns obtained from the data at hand. The two methods are qualitatively similar in that both penalize the mean estimates of the more variable assets. The extreme mean estimates in the actual sample are averaged out in the simulated data sets, leading to smaller weights on these assets in the resampled frontier. Bayesian optimization based on the predictive density leads to smaller weights on these same assets, to the extent that they have a large variance. Harvey et al. (2008) compare the two approaches and conclude that the Bayesian method dominates.

Stambaugh (1997) generalizes the problem to the case where a subset of the assets has a shorter history, as when new assets are introduced. Consider N_1 assets with returns $\mathbf{R}_1$ on $[1, T]$, and N_2 assets with returns $\mathbf{R}_2$ on $[s, T]$. Earlier methods either used only the truncated common sample $[s, T]$, foregoing the information in $[1, s-1]$, or estimated separately subsets of μ, Σ, using the relevant subsamples. In the second case, μ_1, Σ_{11} were based upon $[1, T]$, while μ_2, Σ_{22}, $\Sigma_{1,2}$, were based on $[s, T]$. The second approach can produce singular estimates of Σ and still does not use all the information in the likelihood. Stambaugh rewrites the joint density $p(\mathbf{R}_1, \mathbf{R}_2|\boldsymbol{\mu}, \Sigma)$ as $p(\mathbf{R}_2|\mathbf{R}_1)\mathrm{p}(\mathbf{R}_1)$, and parameterizes it in terms of the regression of R_2 on R_1.

Using this full-sample likelihood function has two effects; first, μ_1 and Σ_{11} benefit from the added precision of the full sample; second, and less obvious, μ_2, Σ_{12}, Σ_{22} also benefit from the longer sample because the covariance between R_1 and R_2 is fully exploited. For example, with diffuse priors, the posterior mean of μ_2 is not just the unconditional $\widehat{\mu}_2$, it also uses information from the discrepancy in $\widehat{\mu}_1$ between $[1, s-1]$ and $[s, T]$. Similar results follow for Σ_{12} and Σ_{22}. The key intuition is that inference on the shorter assets differs from the truncated method if the two samples $[1, s-1]$ and $[s, T]$ produce different inferences on the longer assets. Stambaugh then derives the predictive density of returns and implements the method on a portfolio of longer developed market indices and a shorter index of emerging markets. For these data, the two methods produce drastically different tangency portfolios and optimal allocations in the tangency portfolio. Posterior analysis shows that the two methods produce very different inferences on the mean of the emerging market, but basically identical covariance matrices.

2.2 Shrinkage and empirical Bayes for the portfolio problem

The mean vector of financial assets is particularly difficult to estimate precisely, even with calendar spans of data as long as many decades. This is due to the magnitude of the standard deviation relative to the mean for typical financial returns. Further, due to the low autocorrelation of financial returns, sampling them at a higher frequency does not reduce the uncertainty in the mean, because mean and variance time-aggregate at the same rate for iid returns. For example, the posterior distribution of the annualized mean obtained from $252T$ daily returns is not tighter than the posterior distribution of the annual mean obtained from T annual returns. Econometricians and investors have to live with this fact. In contrast, one can reduce the uncertainty on the variance by increasing the sampling frequency. This is why, in the Merton world with constant variance and continuous time trading, the agent can be assumed to know the variance. This makes uncertainty in the mean the first-order effect to address in portfolio optimization.

The optimization process tends to put higher (lower) weights on the assets with higher (lower) mean. Due to parameter uncertainty, the extreme point estimates in the mean vector for the estimation period, are likely to be closer to the central estimates in the next period, the investment period. An optimizer which merely uses point estimates takes positions that are too extreme, and experiences poor performance during the investment period. The phenomenon is more serious for the more risk tolerant investors who load up more on the extreme mean returns. Jobson and Korkie (1981) use 25 years of monthly returns and show that the realized Sharpe ratios of a portfolio that optimizes on the basis of point estimates of μ, Σ is 0.08, versus 0.34 for a portfolio using the true quantities. The substitution approach is clearly costly. Frost and Savarino (1986) show that Bayesian optimization based on diffuse priors indeed improve over this classical substitution approach, but the amount of uncertainty in the mean is still too high to make the Markowitz framework appealing over passive strategies such as value or equal weighting. For example, the estimates and resulting portfolio weights still vary too much from period to period. We now discuss how portfolio performance can be improved with informative priors.

James and Stein (1961) prove the inadmissibility of the maximum likelihood estimator (MLE) of a multivariate mean, of dimension larger than two, by showing that it is dominated by a shrinkage, and therefore biased, estimator. Their shrinkage estimator is:

$$\hat{\mu}_{JS} = (1 - w)\hat{\mu} + w\mu_0 i, \tag{9.4}$$

where w is a data-based scalar weight, μ_0 is the scalar central value in the direction of which shrinkage occurs, and i is a vector of ones. w, formula omitted here, is inversely proportional to a quadratic form in $(\hat{\mu} - \mu_0 i)$ and Σ^{-1}. This estimator shrinks the original mean estimate to a common value μ_0.

Shrinkage is a natural approach to reduce the effect of parameter uncertainty in the mean. It counters the tendency of the optimizer to load on extreme value by bringing it closer to the center, replacing the MLE of the mean vector with a linear combination of that estimate and a chosen central mean. This reduces the cross-sectional dispersion of the vector of means. This effect is achieved in the Bayesian framework with the use of a prior. With normal conjugate priors, the posterior mean is a linear combination of the prior mean and the MLE. The weights are the respective precisions of these two components. Therefore, a given shrinkage estimation is consistent with some Bayesian prior. Note that individual prior means need not be equal, and the shrinkage does not have to occur toward a vector of equal values such as $\mu_0 i$ in (9.4). However, classic shrinkage corresponds to "empirical Bayes", where the prior parameters are based on the data, convenient for reducing parameter uncertainty, rather than representing the econometrician's subjective prior views.

An important question is whether there is a *better* central value toward which to shrink the initial estimate. Initial work proposed shrinking toward the grand mean. Jorion (1986) makes the important point that, under basic assumptions, μ_0 should be the mean of the global minimum variance portfolio (MVP). The intuition for this is clear. First, the MVP is robust to uncertainty in the mean because we do not require the mean vector to identify it. Second, the mean of the MVP is subject to the least uncertainty, since it has, by definition, the smallest variance of all portfolios. Shrinking toward a mean with the smallest possible uncertainty is precisely the desired objective. Jorion writes an empirical Bayes estimator where the prior on μ is $N(\eta, \lambda\Sigma)$. The hyperparameter λ calibrates the tightness of the prior, where η is the prior mean. Jorion puts a diffuse prior on η. Integrating out μ, η, one finds that the mean of the predictive density of the returns r is:

$$E(r|\mathbf{R}) = (1 - w)\ \hat{\mu} + w\mu_0 \mathrm{i},$$

where μ_0 is the mean of the MVP and $w = \lambda/(\lambda + T)$, showing that λ has the intuition of a notional sample size for the prior. As λ increases relative to T, the cross-sectional dispersion of $E(r|\mathbf{R})$ vanishes and the means shrink toward the global minimum variance portfolio. Jorion (1985) implements optimal portfolio selection on international assets with this empirical Bayes method. He shows that it dominates those approaches based upon the basic sample estimates. The portfolio weights are more stable through time as they do not take large bets on point estimates.

Dumas and Jacquillat (1990) implement a similar empirical approach to currency portfolios. They use logarithmic utility and lognormal returns, while Jorion was assuming normal returns. They argue that shrinking to the MVP introduces country-specific behavior they regard as undesirable because they want to model the asset allocation of a universal investor. This country-specific behavior arises if one admits deviations from purchasing power parity. Instead, they engineer an empirical Bayes prior which produces a shrinkage toward an equal weighted portfolio of currencies.

Frost and Savarino (1986) assume normal returns and exponential utility, and also shrink the covariance matrix by empirical Bayes. They formulate a conjugate Normal Inverse Wishart prior for (μ, Σ), centered on equal means, variances, and covariances. The prior on the mean is $p(\mu) \sim N(\mu_0 i, \frac{1}{\tau}\Sigma)$, where μ_0 is the MLE of the grand mean assuming equal means for the N returns, and τ is a notional sample size representing the strength of prior belief. The prior on Σ is an Inverse Wishart whose prior mean is a covariance matrix Ω with equal variances δ and correlations ρ. A parameter ν with the interpretation of a notional sample size models the prior strength of belief. Frost and Savarino estimate all prior parameters, including ν and τ by maximum likelihood, a strong use of empirical Bayes. To do this, they write the likelihood of the data, modeled by this prior, and maximize it.

The posterior mean vector is the weighted average seen above. The covariance matrix of the predictive density of returns is a weighted average of three quantities, the prior mean Ω, the sample covariance $\widehat{\Sigma}$, and an outer-product of the vector of discrepancies between prior and sample means $(\hat{\mu} - \mu_0)$. This latter term is typical of posterior covariance matrices when proper priors are used on means or regression coefficients. In term of optimization, this amounts to a shrinkage toward the equal weighted portfolio since no asset has preferred characteristics in the prior. With an investment universe of 25 randomly selected securities, Frost and Savarino compare the realized returns of optimized portfolios based on the classical point estimates, the Bayesian predictive densities with diffuse priors, and their empirical Bayes priors. Their results show that while the use of the predictive density with diffuse priors does improve on the classical method, the empirical Bayes estimator leads to a vast additional improvement over the diffuse prior.

2.3 Parameter uncertainty and long-run asset allocation

We will now see that parameter uncertainty compounds over time, becoming very important in the long run. Namely, we discuss inference on the compound excess return of the market index over the risk-free rate, and its impact on long-run asset allocation.

Merton (1969) derives the optimal asset allocation between one risky and one riskless asset in continuous time, generalizing the one-period result in (9.2). Consider an iid lognormal risky asset, where $\log(1 + R_t) \sim N(\mu, \sigma^2)$, its compound return over H periods, is:

$$\exp\,(\mu H + \sigma \sum_{i=1}^{H} \epsilon_{t+i}), \quad \epsilon_t \sim N(0, 1).$$

This H-period compound return is lognormal $(\mu H, \sigma^2 H)$; its expectation is therefore:

$$\exp\,(H\mu + \frac{1}{2}H\sigma^2). \tag{9.5}$$

Consider a risk-free return r_0, and a power utility of final wealth per dollar invested, $U(V_H) = \frac{1}{1-\gamma}\exp[(1-\gamma)\log(1+R_H)]$, where γ is the constant relative risk aversion. One of Merton's key assumptions is continuous rebalancing. It guarantees that the portfolio of the two assets is lognormal (see Dumas and Jacquillat 1990 for a discussion of the approximation to lognormality). Then, by Ito's lemma, the multi-period compound return for a constantly rebalanced allocation w is shown to be:

$$\log(V_H|\alpha,\sigma) \sim N\left[(r_0(1-w) + w\alpha - 0.5w^2\sigma^2)H, w^2\sigma^2 H\right], \tag{9.6}$$

where $\alpha = \mu + 0.5\sigma^2$. The expected utility is:

$$E[U(V_H)] = \frac{1}{1-\gamma}\exp\left[(1-\gamma)H(r_0 + w(\alpha - r_0) - 0.5w^2\sigma^2 + 0.5(1-\gamma)w^2\sigma^2)\right]. \tag{9.7}$$

The maximization of (9.7) over w gives the well-known Merton allocation:

$$w^* = \frac{\alpha - r_0}{\gamma\sigma^2}. \tag{9.8}$$

The allocation in (9.8) offers an added insight over its one-period counterpart in (9.2), even though they appear similar. Merton's iid lognormal framework is a multi-period problem. Yet, the horizon H present in the expected utility (9.7) drops out of the optimal solution in (9.8). This is the well-known irrelevance of the horizon in the optimal asset allocation, when returns are iid.

In contrast, most of the subsequent intertemporal portfolio literature entertains the predictability of risky asset returns, with predominantly negative autocorrelations. Then, the variance grows with the horizon at a slower rate than in the mean. One, therefore, optimally allocates more to the risky asset in the long than in the short run. Additionally, in a dynamic strategy, the investor can reallocate her optimal weight within the investment horizon, reaping a further benefit from the long-run horizon. See Brandt (2009) for a survey of intertemporal portfolio strategies.

There is an ongoing debate in the finance literature between those who consider that there is strong evidence of predictability and those who are unconvinced. However, one fact that is not up for debate is that mean returns are estimated with large errors. It is, therefore, curious that most of the finance literature has spent much more energy on predictability assuming known parameters, rather than the opposite. We now incorporate uncertainty in the mean into the optimal allocation problem.

For both classical and Bayesian frameworks, the sample mean, $\hat{\mu}$, computed from T years of data is a key sample statistic. For long-term forecasts, practitioners choose a point estimate by compounding the sample geometric return $G = \frac{1}{T}\log(\frac{P_T}{P_1})$. This amounts to estimating $E(V_H)$ by $e^{\hat{\mu}H}$. Academics, however, tend to substitute $\widehat{\mu}, \widehat{\sigma}$ in the theoretical expectation (9.5), possibly because of the maximum likelihood justification, where the estimator of a function is approximated by the function of the estimator. The difference in these point estimates becomes very large in the long run. Using Siegel's (1994) geometric and arithmetic averages of 7% and 8.5%, the two approaches grow \$1 to \$160 versus \$454 over 75 years.

Even in the classical framework, a solution that does not invoke asymptotic approximation can be found. Jacquier et al. (2005) assume that σ is known and show that, for this problem, the uncertainty in σ is secondary to the uncertainty in μ. They derive a minimum mean squared error classical estimator of $E(V_h)$:

$$M = e^{H(\widehat{\mu} - \frac{\sigma^2}{2}(1 - 3\frac{H}{T})}.$$

The penalty for estimation error in μ increases with the horizon. The MLE estimator obtains as $T/H \to \infty$. Even with 100 years of data, as in the most mature market, one is never close to asymptotic assumptions for the purpose of long-term forecasts. Panel (b) in Figure 9.1 plots the compounding factor in M versus H as the dashed line, for realistic values of μ and σ, a sample of $T = 50$ years, and horizon H from 1 to 40 years. It decreases linearly with $\frac{H}{T}$. The penalty in Figure 9.1 is so severe that one may wonder if it is even reasonable. For a very long horizon, it implies negative estimates of the compounding excess return, which does not make economic sense.

Let us see how the rational Bayesian investor incorporates uncertainty in the mean into her long horizon asset allocation. To do this, we repeat the asset allocation, with estimation error as in Bawa et al. (1979), but for the long run. The density of V_H in (9.6) is now conditional on μ, which must be integrated out to produce the predictive density of V_H. Then, the expected utility can be computed. Jacquier (2006) does this for a normal conjugate prior on μ. Consider for simplicity a diffuse prior, so that the posterior on μ is $N(\hat{\mu}, \frac{\sigma^2}{T})$. Because the integrations over the parameter and over the distribution of returns can be exchanged, one can also view this as integrating μ out of the conditional expected utility in (9.7). The expected (predictive) utility becomes:

$$E[U(V_H)] = \frac{1}{1-\gamma} \exp\left[(1-\gamma)H[r_0 + w(\hat{\alpha} - r_0) - 0.5w^2\sigma^2 + 0.5 \right.$$
$$\left. (1-\gamma)w^2\sigma^2(1 + \frac{H}{T})\right]\Bigg]. \tag{9.9}$$

Recall that $\alpha = \mu + 0.5\sigma^2$, it is replaced by its posterior mean $\hat{\alpha}$, and there is a new term in H/T at the end. Maximizing the expected utility in (9.9), Jacquier (2006) finds the optimal asset allocation:

$$w^* = \frac{\widehat{\alpha} - r_0}{\sigma^2\left[\gamma(1 + \frac{H}{T}) - \frac{H}{T}\right]}. \tag{9.10}$$

It is a function of the horizon H relative to the sample size T. It is in the spirit of Bawa et al. (1979), but the numerical effect is very large for long horizons. Panel (a) in

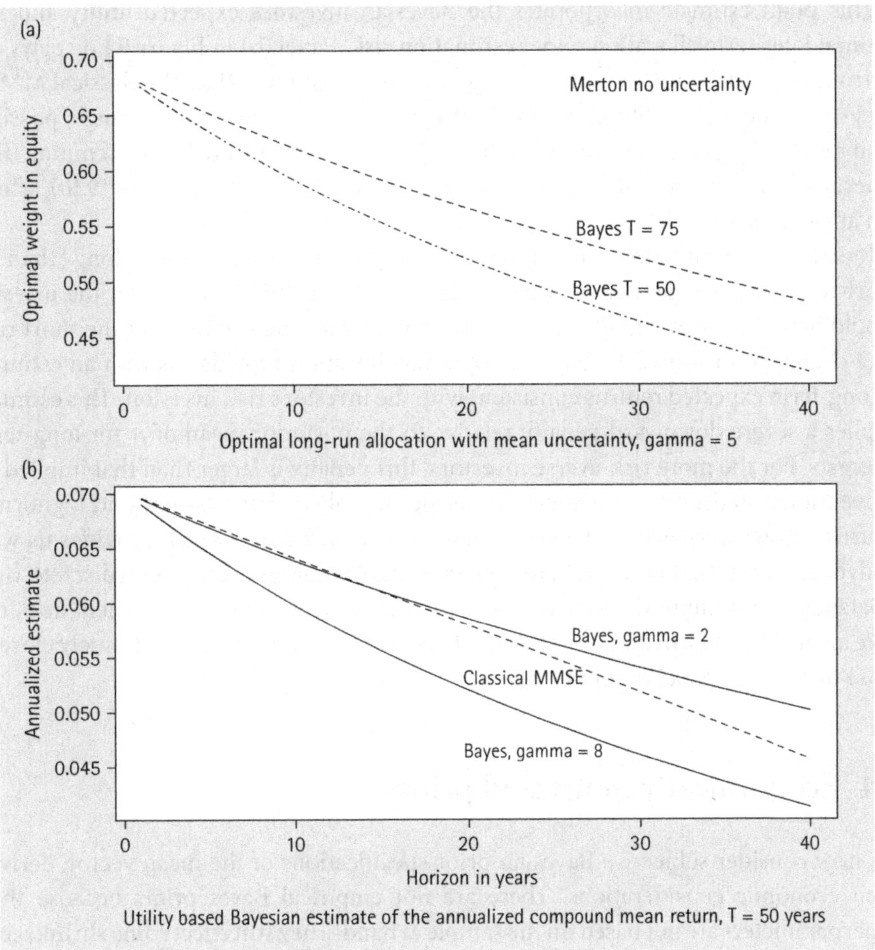

FIGURE 9.1 Bayesian long-term asset allocation and implied mean estimate

Notes: Diffuse prior on $\mu, R_f = 0.03, \hat{\mu} = 0.09, \sigma = 0.143$.

Figure 9.1 compares this Bayesian optimal allocation with Merton's. As the horizon H increases, the Bayesian allocation decreases drastically, even for a moderate risk aversion of $\gamma = 5$.

This allocation is consistent with an implicit point estimate of $E(V_H)$, optimal for the Bayesian investor given her risk aversion, the sample size T, and the horizon H. Equation (9.10) can be used to find this implicit point estimate of α, denoted α^*. This is, in essence, a change of measure to find the estimation risk-adjusted estimate of α. In the new measure where expected returns are risk-adjusted, Merton's optimal allocation (9.8) applies, that is, $w^* = \frac{\alpha^* - r_0}{\gamma \sigma^2}$. Equating this and (9.10) solves for α^*:

$$\alpha^* - r_0 = \frac{\widehat{\alpha} - r_0}{1 + \frac{H}{T}(1 - \frac{1}{\gamma 1})}.$$

This point estimate incorporates the Bayesian investor's expected utility and her optimal long-term allocation under estimation risk. Panel (b) in Figure 9.1 displays α^*. It strongly penalizes uncertainty for long horizons, even more than the classical MMSE for $\gamma = 8$. The finance literature points at typical risk aversions in this range, possibly even greater. Unlike M, α^* never implies negative estimates of the risk premium. This is because it is the implication of the investor's optimal asset allocation in (9.10), which can at worst be 0.

In summary, estimation error in the mean has a far greater effect on long- than on short-term optimal allocation. A Bayesian optimal allocation shows that the investor should have drastically smaller optimal weights for the long run than for the short run. By a change of measure, the Bayesian optimal allocation provides us with an estimate of long-term expected returns consistent with the investor's risk-aversion. This estimate implies a severe downward penalty relative to the posterior mean of μ for long-term forecasts. For the more risk-averse investors, this penalty is larger than that implied by conventional statistical estimators. The set-up described above assumes iid lognormal returns, known variance, and a continuous time rebalancing, which provides us with analytical results. Barberis (2000) implements this optimal allocation with discrete-time rebalancing and unknown variance. The predictive density of returns, then, does not have an analytical form and must be simulated. Barberis finds results extremely close to those pictured in panel (a) of Figure 9.1.

2.4 Economically motivated priors

We now consider subjective Bayesian prior specifications of the mean vector, derived from economic considerations. These are not empirical Bayes priors because their hyperparameters are not based on the sample at hand. They still effect some shrinkage in the sense that the cross-sectional dispersion of the resulting posterior means is generally much smaller than for the sample means.

Consider incorporating in the prior views on the mean vector the implications of an equilibrium model of expected returns such as the capital asset pricing model (CAPM). Portfolio weights consistent with the CAPM are the relative capitalization weights, as in the market portfolio. In the absence of additional information on specific returns, these are good weights to start from. Alternatively, one can simply replace expected returns by β's, since the CAPM states that expected excess returns are proportional to the asset beta. The uncertainty in the mean would be the uncertainty in betas, still an improvement as inference on the β's is more precise than inference on the mean. This, however, is not convenient for an investor who wants to incorporate private information on some of the assets, arising from proprietary analysis. This investor views the CAPM prediction for expected returns as prior information. She may have an econometric model to predict abnormal expected returns in excess of the CAPM, the so-called Jensen α. That will be the source of the likelihood function. In realistic settings it will be more sophisticated than the mere computation of average returns for a given sample period.

Black and Litterman (1991) (BL) is in this spirit. It specifically accounts for the fact that even active managers do not have private information on every asset in their investment universe. They notice that portfolio managers often modify only a few elements of the vector of means, for which they have private information. BL show that this practice has a large and undesirable impact on the entire vector of weights; rather, they combine investor views and market equilibrium, in the spirit of shrinkage. The originality of BL is that they do not write the prior expected returns from the asset-pricing model. Instead, they reverse engineer it from the observed weights of the different assets, assuming that these weights arise from the market's optimization of these expected returns. This amounts to inverting the well-known formula for the optimal weights, $w^* = \frac{1}{\gamma}\Sigma^{-1}\mu$, where γ is the representative investor's risk aversion. The remainder $(1 - w)$ is invested in the risk-free rate. The mean μ consistent with the observed capitalization weights w^* is BL's prior mean for the mean vector. They use a prior covariance matrix proportional to the data, $\frac{1}{T_0}\lambda\Sigma$, where T_0 is a notional prior sample size. BL are primarily concerned with uncertainty in the mean vector; in their implementation they use the sample covariance matrix.

BL combine this economic-based prior view with the investor's private views on μ. These private views are formulated as a set of linear combinations of the mean vectors, where normal error terms allow one to model the precision of the view. Essentially, they can be written as a multivariate normal distribution on μ. By assumption, these views come from some data analysis, but they do not need to. The posterior views, in BL's sense, result from combining the prior, asset-pricing-based view, with the private view. BL's formulation is conjugate, and the posterior mean is a simple weighted average of the economic and private means. This is a Bayesian learning scheme but curiously absent a formal likelihood function.

Zhou (2008) proposes to formally incorporate the data into the BL framework. He allows for three sources of information, the views from the economic model, the private views that may not use data, and the data. To do this, Zhou considers the final BL estimate of the mean as a prior. He then multiplies this prior by the likelihood to obtain a posterior mean. Zhou's motivation is that the data provide valuable information in the likely case that the economic model is inaccurate. This motivation runs a bit against the mainstream view, which, as we have seen, worries that it is the noisy data that lead to erratic estimation of the mean and, therefore, need to be restrained by shrinkage or an economic-based prior. Yet, Zhou's implementation shows how to easily blend the above three fundamental sources of information in the Bayesian framework. Also, in quantitative portfolio optimization, the private views most certainly come from the estimation of some structure on the data, for example, a predictive regression. Then, the problem simplifies as the prior can model the degree of belief in the departure from the equilibrium asset-pricing model.

Pastor (2000) demonstrates a natural approach to incorporating an asset-pricing model in the portfolio allocation by using the prior to reflect the strength of belief in the model. This encompasses the two extremes of an investor with complete disregard for the model, and one with total confidence in the model. Reasonable investors have beliefs somewhere in between. Pastor determines the predictive density of returns and the resulting maximum Sharpe portfolio. Pastor's methodology can incorporate modern multi-factor asset-pricing models, where the efficient frontier is spanned by a set of benchmark portfolios that mimic the realizations of factors. In these models, expected returns in excess of the risk-free rate are typically of the form $E(R_i) = \beta_i' E(F)$, where β_i is the vector of k factor loadings of asset i, and $E(F)$ is the vector of k factor expected excess returns. In the case of the CAPM, the single benchmark portfolio is the capitalization-weighted market portfolio.

Pastor considers a one-period set-up with normal returns and a risk-free asset where the investor maximizes the Sharpe ratio. The investment universe includes N ordinary assets and K benchmark, factor-mimicking, portfolios. These $N + K$ assets have mean vector E and covariance matrix V. The likelihood function, consistent with the existing literature, comes from the multivariate regression of the N assets excess returns on the K portfolio excess returns. Let R be the $T \times N$ matrix of asset returns, $X = [i_T, F]$, which includes a vector of ones and a $T \times K$ matrix of benchmark excess returns. Then, the multivariate regression of the assets on the benchmark returns is:

$$R = XB + U, \quad vec(U) \sim N(0, \Sigma \otimes I),$$

where $B' = [\alpha', B_2']$ includes the vector of abnormal returns, α and the factor loadings, B_2. This can also be written using Zellner's (1962) seemingly unrelated regressions framework. It helps to write one observation of the multivariate regression above, for asset i at time t:

$$R_{it} = \alpha_i + \beta_i' F_t + u_{it}.$$

α represents the deviation from the asset-pricing model, Jensen's alpha for the CAPM. If the asset-pricing model holds, α is zero. On the other hand, if the model is useless, α is unconstrained and the above regression delivers inference on $E(R)$.

The benchmark returns F are assumed to be iid $N(E_F, V_F)$. The likelihood function $p(R, F|B, \Sigma, E_F, V_F)$ is multivariate normal and decomposed as $p(R|F, .)p(F|.)$. As a technical aside, Pastor uses the results in Stambaugh (1997) to allow a longer history for the benchmark portfolios than for the N assets. The priors on E_F, V_F are left diffuse. The prior on B, Σ is normal for $B|\Sigma$ and Inverted Wishart for Σ, where $E(\Sigma) = s^2 I$, it is left largely non-informative for B_2 and Σ. The key prior for modeling the degree of belief in the model is that on α. Recall that α and B_2 are subsets of B. The prior on $\alpha|\Sigma$ is modeled as $N(0, \sigma_\alpha^2 \frac{\Sigma}{s^2})$. The zero mean centers the prior on the asset-pricing model; σ_α reflects the investor's degree of skepticism toward the model. The prior mean could also be centered on a non-zero value if the investor practiced some fundamental analysis; σ_α would then reflect the precision of the analyst's views.

The predictive density of returns $p(R_{T+1}|R, F)$ is simulated by drawing in sequence from $p(F_{T+1}|F)$ a multivariate student-t the posterior $(B, \Sigma|R, F)$, and the conditional density $p(R_{T+1}|B, \Sigma, F_{T+1})$. This integrates out the parameters and future benchmark returns from the conditional density of future returns. The draw of B, Σ can be done with a very effective Gibbs sampling. A large sample of draws allows the computation of the predictive mean and variance up to an arbitrary degree of precision. These two moments are then used to compute the maximum Sharpe ratio portfolio as per (9.1).

Intuitively, the predictive mean of returns is $\tilde{\alpha} + \tilde{\beta}\hat{E}_F$, where $\tilde{\alpha}$ is the posterior mean of α. This posterior mean is a linear combination of the prior mean, here zero, and the sample estimate. The posterior mean of β is almost always very close to the sample estimate as the prior on B_2 is diffuse. Therefore, the predictive mean is shrunk to the asset-pricing model prediction $\tilde{\beta}E(F)$, away from the sample estimate $\hat{\alpha} + \tilde{\beta}E(F)$. As σ_α increases, the predictive mean of returns tilts toward $\hat{\alpha}$, showing that the investor pays more attention to the sample estimate $\hat{\alpha}$ of mispricings.

An interesting use of the analysis is to document the effect of variations in σ_α on the optimal portfolio. Pastor implements the model to study the home bias effect. He uses one benchmark asset, the US market, and one other asset, an international index. He finds that an investor would require very strong belief in the global validity of the domestic CAPM, $\sigma_\alpha < 1\%$ annually, to justify holding as little in the foreign stock as is commonly observed. A second application sheds light on the Fama-French factors, especially the book-to-market benchmark portfolio. Pastor finds that even an investor with very strong prior beliefs in the CAPM would hold a sizable fraction of her portfolio in the book-to-market portfolio.

As a portfolio paper, Pastor (2000) shows how a rational Bayesian investor naturally incorporates her degree of belief in asset-pricing models into her optimal investment strategy. Possibly more strikingly, the paper recasts empirical asset-pricing in terms of the usefulness and impact of asset-pricing models on investing decisions. For a given sample and prior belief in the CAPM, we can see how optimal choice differs from that implied by the asset-pricing model.[2] This is in contrast with the earlier classical literature which argues whether an asset-pricing model, such as the CAPM, can or cannot be rejected by the data, with no obviously useful implication for the investor.

2.5 Other aspects of parameter and model uncertainty

While some of the work discussed so far integrates out Σ to obtain the predictive density, for example, Frost and Savarino (1986), it is mostly done assuming normal returns. This yields a multivariate Student-t predictive density of returns. The assumption of lognormal returns, coupled with a power utility, is often preferred in finance, especially for multi-period problems. The lognormal distribution is preserved under time aggregation, as seen in Section 2.3. However, the integration of the variance results in a log-Student-t predictive density. Geweke (2001) shows that expected utility then ceases to exist. The common practice has been, for asset allocation, to arbitrarily constrain the

[2] As such, the paper could have been discussed in the asset-pricing section below. It is not the first paper to use this approach; we discuss Kandel and Stambaugh (1996) later.

weight in the risky asset to be below one. Alternatively, a truncation of the log-Student-t distribution eliminates the problem.

Pastor (2000) assumes normal returns and ignores the fat-tailness inherent in the predictive density. This allows him to use an analytical formula for the optimum Sharpe ratio. In addition, one may want to model skewness and kurtosis in the conditional distribution of returns. Such generalizations can quickly render the maximization of expected utility intractable. One can use simulation methods or one can expand the utility function beyond the second moment of the distribution of returns. Harvey et al. (2010) allow for skewness and co-skewness in returns, with a skew-normal distribution, and formulate a utility function linear in skewness as well as mean and variance. This may be important because, while individual stocks may not exhibit strong skewness, portfolios of these stocks can have skewed returns. Therefore, portfolio weights should also be judged on their ability to increase skewness, since rational investors like skewness.

De Miguel et al. (2009) run a horse-race of 13 portfolio optimization models against a basic equal-weighted portfolio, named *one-over-N*. They use several combinations of the classic domestic and international portfolios encountered in the literature. Their sample period goes as far as 1963; they roll windows of ten years of monthly data. The 13 models include several of those mentioned so far. De Miguel et al. conclude that these models would have generated lower Sharpe ratios and certainty equivalent returns than the naive one-over-N rule over the past several decades. Their approach is based on a comparison of realized Sharpe ratios. Tu and Zhou (2009) revisit the results, using priors that incorporate, not only parameter uncertainty, but also the economic objective, here Sharpe ratio maximization. Their prior on the parameters is derived from a prior weight vector. Tu and Zhou document utility improvement over other prior specifications and also over the the one-over-N portfolio.

Finally, the presence of multiple competing models raises the issue of model uncertainty. Posterior odds can be used for model comparison, but also for optimal model averaging. The optimal model is a (normalized) posterior odds weighted average of the competing models. It would be interesting to revisit studies, such as De Miguel et al's. by incorporating the optimal combination model.

3 Predictability of Returns

A large finance literature has studied the predictability, or lack thereof, of stock returns. The ability to predict future returns is at the core of the debate on market efficiency. See Campbell, Lo, and MacKinlay (1997) (CLM), chapter 2, for a review of key classical results and techniques. Past returns, as well as firm and economy characteristics, have been used as predictors in time-series regressions or cross-sectional regressions where the returns lag the right-hand variables. The horizon may be short, a month or less, or long, up to business cycle horizons. First, predictability can be studied through its statistical significance. We will show examples that highlight some pitfalls of classical analysis when the econometrician is concerned with non-linear functions of the base parameters used in the likelihood function. Second, predictability can be studied through its core economic implications, for example its impact on optimal portfolio design. This is conveniently done in a Bayesian framework.

3.1 Statistical analysis of predictability

3.1.1 *Long-run predictability*

In the study of long-run predictability, Bayesian methods can lead to conclusions very different from classical methods. Consider the popular permanent-transitory component:

$$\begin{aligned} p_t &= q_t + z_t \\ q_t &= \mu + q_{t-1} + u_t, \; u_t \sim N(0, \sigma_u^2) \\ z_t &= \phi z_{t-1} + \epsilon_t, \; \epsilon_t \sim N(0, \sigma_\epsilon^2), \end{aligned} \tag{9.11}$$

where the log-price p_t is the sum of a random walk and a stationary AR(1). It generates the long-term negative autocorrelations observed in asset returns (but fails to generate the intermediate term positive autocorrelations; see CLM, chapter 2). A common approach has been to estimate directly the autocorrelation of long-term returns by the regressions:

$$r_{t,k} = \alpha_k + \beta_k r_{t-k,k} + \epsilon_{t,k}, \quad t = 1, \ldots .T, \tag{9.12}$$

where $r_{t,k}$ is the k-period return from $t - k$ to t. These regressions are run for k's between one and up to eight years. One can also compute the ratio $Var(r_{t,k})/(k\, Var(r_t))$. If log-prices follow a pure random walk, regression slopes should be zero and variance ratios should be one. These constitute typical null hypotheses for the classical approach (see CLM, chapter 2). It can be shown that, under the model in (9.11), β can tend to -0.5 as k increases.

In standard asymptotic analysis T goes to infinity, but the ratio K/T affects the computations. With $K/T \to 0$, the estimator of the ratio converges to 1 if the true ratio is 1. However, Richardson and Stock (1989) assume that $K/T \to c > 0$. This may reflect the fact that as the sample size increases, the investigator may explore larger k's. They show that the classical estimator of the variance ratio converges then to a value smaller than 1, and its variance does not vanish asymptotically. This alternative asymptotic limit under the hypothesis of no predictability is, in fact, consistent with the typical estimates in the literature (see CLM, chapter 2). These conflicting asymptotic limits make the interpretation of results for a given fixed sample difficult. Which asymptotic limit is the empiricist who uses one given sample size supposed to adopt?

In contrast, the Bayesian approach delivers the optimal posterior inference for the given sample of size T studied by the econometrician. Lamoureux and Zhou (1996) (LZ) implement Bayesian inference for the model in (9.11). The likelihood is a function of the parameters $(\phi, \sigma_u, \sigma_\epsilon)$. The posterior densities for functions of interest, such as β_k, do not obtain analytically, but can be simulated.

LZ use data augmentation to generate convenient conditional densities that are the basis for a Gibbs sampler. They add the vector $v = u/\sigma_u$ to the parameter space, and consider the joint data (v, r). The contemporaneous covariance between v and r is σ_u^2; the covariance matrix of r is a function of ϕ, σ_u. The joint posterior distribution of the parameters is intractable, but it can now be broken into a set of conditional distributions from which one can draw directly. Specifically, LZ show how to cycle between direct draws of $(v|\phi, \sigma_u, \sigma_\epsilon, r)$ and $(\phi, \sigma_u, \sigma_\epsilon|v, r)$, where the second distribution is further broken down into three univariate conditional posteriors. The key here is not only that one can draw from the conditional $(v|r, .)$, but also that the densities of the original parameters are greatly simplified by the conditioning on v. LZ extend the AR(1) in (9.11) to an AR(4) for quarterly data. An essential identification of the model is that the vector of AR coefficients must imply stationarity. In a Monte Carlo algorithm, this is enforced by rejection of the posterior draws that fail the requirement. For every draw of the AR(4) parameters, one computes the roots of the characteristic equation and rejects the draw if they are inside the unit circle.

These draws of the model parameters yield, by direct computation, draws of the nonlinear functions of interest, for example, the ratio of the variances of the random walk shock u_t to the total return r_t, σ_u^2/σ_r^2. The persistence of shocks to the stationarity of z_t is of interest, and LZ compute the posterior distribution of its half-life. One can also compute the long-run autocorrelation, the β_ks from (9.12), directly, as implied by the model. Each draw of the parameters yields a draw of these functions of interest; therefore we obtain their exact posterior distribution for our sample size.

Classical analysis for these long-term models yielded mixed results. The point estimates of β_k were deemed large enough to warrant attention; however, the power of these regressions against the null of no predictability was known to be weak (see CLM chapter 2). The results of the Bayesian analysis are very different. LZ study the inference on β_3, the three-year β in (9.12). For two different proper priors on the parameters $\phi, \sigma_u, \sigma_\epsilon$, they simulate the implied prior on β_3 simply by drawing from these two priors. Both priors allow for sizable probabilities of large negative β, and allow for a high fraction of the returns variance to come from the predictable component. They reflect the prior views of an investor who believes that a departure from the random walk hypothesis is quite possible. Strikingly, the resulting posteriors on β_3 are tightly centered on 0. Despite the initial priors, the data clearly speak loudly against the presence of a transitory component in stock returns.

Why then does frequentist analysis find large negative estimates of β_k? LZ make the case that, frequentist analysis is akin to a flat prior on the parameters $(\phi, \sigma_u, \sigma_v)$ in (9.11). They show that, with this prior, $p(\phi, \sigma_u, \sigma_\epsilon) \propto \frac{1}{\sigma_u \sigma_\epsilon}$, the posterior density for β has a mean and standard deviation similar to the point estimates in the classical results.

They also show that this flat prior implies a very odd prior on β_3, with two large spikes at 0 and -0.5. The key here is that diffuse priors on both variances allow the ratio of stationary to random walk variance, to be very large or very small, implying in turn, about equal probabilities of either a nearly pure random walk, or a very strong transitory component. Note here that, since the base prior is improper, LZ must have truncated or approximated it with a proper prior in order to draw from it. One should make sure that the shape of the implied prior is robust to the truncation or approximation chosen.

This result shows that the notion of a flat prior on the base parameters of a model, those used to write the likelihood, here $(\phi, \sigma_u, \sigma_\epsilon)$, can imply very informative priors on non-linear functions of these parameters. One must, therefore, be aware of the prior implied on functions of interest, by the prior chosen for the base parameters. This is easily done in a Bayesian framework. If necessary, the prior on the base parameters can be modified to imply a reasonable prior on the functions of interest. A small sample analysis in classical econometrics is possible but complicated and rarely seen in the empirical literature. In standard maximum likelihood analysis, functions of an MLE estimator are assumed to be asymptotically normal, their variance typically approximated via the Delta method. A careful Monte Carlo simulation of the sampling properties of the estimator of the function could detect departures from asymptotic approximations. It would then be clear to the careful classical statistician that, as shown in LZ, the classical analysis did input some undesirable prior views on the function of interest. This point is important, since an advantage often put forth by the proponents of classical analysis is that they do not need to put prior information into the analysis.

3.1.2 Predictability and cyclicality

We continue with another example where it is easy to understand that flat priors on the regression slope coefficients imply tight priors on a function of interest. A simple AR(1) in the stationary component as in (9.11) can generate the observed long-term negative autocorrelations; however, it can not also generate the shorter-term positive autocorrelations discussed in CLM, chapter 2. A model allowing for cyclical autocorrelation is required, that is, at least an AR(2). Geweke (1988a) shows the posterior probabilities of a cycle and posterior densities of the cycle periods for GDP. Such macroeconomic variables can be state variables for the investment opportunity set, and their cyclicality could permeate to the process of stock returns.

Jacquier (1991) studies the cyclicality of AR(3) models of stock returns. He shows that flat priors on the AR(3) parameters result in an undesirably informative prior for the two main functions of interest: the probability of existence of a cycle and the period of the cycle. As is well known, cyclicality obtains when the roots of the characteristic equations are complex. Consider an AR(2) and flat priors for (ϕ_1, ϕ_2) in the stationary region, known to be a triangle. Cyclicality occurs when $\phi_1^2 + 4\phi_2 < 0$, an area between a parabola and the base of the triangle (see Zellner 1971). For flat priors, the probability of being in this region is exactly two-thirds; therefore, flat priors on (ϕ_1, ϕ_2) in the region of stationarity imply a two-thirds probability of a cycle. For an AR(3), Jacquier (1991) shows that flat priors on ϕ_1, ϕ_2, ϕ_3 in the stationary region imply a probability of 0.934 of existence of a cycle. For the Bayesian econometrician, posterior probabilities of a cycle of up to two-thirds for an AR(2), and 0.93 for an AR(3) represent no evidence whatsoever of cyclicality.

Given that a cycle exists, its period is of interest. Flat priors on ϕ inside the cyclical domain also imply quite an informative prior on the distribution of this period. It is centered at 3 with about 50% of its mass between 2 and 5. The Bayesian econometrician naturally spots the inference problem by inspecting these implied priors, comparing them to the corresponding posteriors. As for possible remedies, one can easily modify the priors on ϕ to produce, if desired, a flatter-looking prior on the period of the cycle, and a prior probability of existence of the cycle closer to 0.5. Setting flat priors on the roots of the characteristic equation, rather than the AR parameters themselves, goes a long way to resolving the issue. In contrast, both detection and remedy for this situation are not practical in the classical framework. The ordinary least squares point estimate of ϕ matches numerically the Bayesian posterior mean resulting from diffuse priors on the ϕ; therefore, the classical analysis can not escape from this problem uncovered in the Bayesian framework.

3.1.3 *Model choice and predictability*

Studies of the predictability of stock returns can involve a number of competing regressions of stock returns on firm-specific or economy-wide variables. The number of variables and alternative models makes this an ideal ground for model comparison and, better, model averaging, via odds ratios. In contrast, classical analysis is ill-equipped for multiple model comparison. As early as 1991, Connolly (1991) reports odds ratios on the well-known week-end effect. Odds ratios also provide a more natural sample-based metric than the potentially severely misleading use of the p-value. See Berger (1985) for extensive discussions. The odds ratio of model 1 to model 2 is the posterior probability that 1 is true relative to 2, given the sample just observed.

Classically motivated criteria, such as the Akaike information criterion (AIC), allow model ranking. The Schwartz information criterion (SIC) is proposed as a large sample approximation of the odds ratio. Zellner (1978) shows that the AIC can be seen as a truncation of the posterior odds ratio, which omits many important terms. Jacquier (1991) shows that the approximation in the SIC can also be unsatisfactory in small samples even for simple AR models. Using these criteria, Bossaerts and Hillion (1999) find evidence of in-sample predictability, but no such evidence remains out of sample. It is unclear to what extent this contradiction between the criteria and the out-of-sample evidence is due to a possible over-fitting by these criteria. Even if the approximation was satisfactory, SIC and AIC could only be used for model ranking, not directly for model averaging.

Posterior odds ratios can of course serve to rank competing models, but, more interestingly, they determine the weight of each model for the purpose of model averaging, the optimal combination of all models. Avramov (2002) studies the predictability for monthly stock returns. He considers 14 widely studied candidate predictors, for example, dividend and earnings yields, momentum, default and term spreads, inflation, and size and value premiums. These 14 candidates define 2^{14} mutually exclusive models for which Avramov computes posterior odds ratios. Model j is a multivariate regression with normal errors:

$$r_t = B_j X^j_{t-1} + \epsilon_t, \quad \epsilon \sim N(0, \Sigma), \tag{9.13}$$

where r_t is a vector of six asset returns. Avramov models a vector of 6 portfolio returns, B_j includes the intercept and the slope coefficients for model j, and X^j includes ones and the candidate predictors z_j, as in Zellner's (1962) seemingly unrelated regression framework.

Avramov uses normal-inverse Wishart priors for B_j, Σ_j: the prior mean of B_j is zero for the slopes and $\bar{r}$ for the intercepts. Now consider a hypothetical sample with the same sample statistics as the one studied: $\bar{r}, \bar{z}_j$, and $\hat{V}_r, \hat{V}_{zj}$, the sample covariances matrices of the returns and predictors. Avramov sets the variance covariance matrix of B_j proportional to that which would arise in the multivariate regression in (9.13). The proportionality coefficient is in effect a notional sample size T_0 that can be used to tighten the prior against predictability. It is a multivariate generalization of the prior used by Kandel and Stambaugh (1996). This is essentially a version of Zellner's (1986) g-prior. Following K&S, Avramov uses a T_0 equal to 50 times the number of predictors. His sample size is $T = 540$. He finds analytical expressions for the posterior odds.

Avramov reports which predictors appear in the highest posterior odds model. He notes that it is easy to add up the posterior probabilities of the mutually exclusive models where each candidate predictor appears. The contrast between the two measures is striking. The best models use at most two predictors. However, far more than two predictors appear in many models. For example, the best model to predict the returns of a portfolio of large firms with medium book-to-market values has only the term premium as regressor, which appears in 54% of all possible models. Yet, four other candidate predictors appear in more than 20% of all models. The best model for another portfolio only includes inflation and earnings, present in 31% and 39% respectively of all models. But T-bill (Treasury bill), lagged index returns and a dummy variable for the month of January, present in respectively 28%, 48%, and 21% of the models, are not in the best model. Clearly the common practice in standard model identification and classical studies of predictability to choose and work only with the best model, passes by a lot of information. Odds ratios, while they properly rank models, similarly appear to omit essential information when they are used solely for model comparison.

A composite model can be built, using the posterior odds as weights. For each predictor, the posterior mean of its slope coefficient is the odds-weighted average of the posterior means for each model. The posterior variance can be shown to incorporate the within-model posterior variance for each model, as well as the measure of cross-model variability. The composite model defines a weighted predictive distribution for future stock returns. This distribution appropriately integrates out both model and within-model parameter uncertainties. Avramov shows that for his six portfolios, from 1953 to

1998, the composite model dominates the models chosen as best by any known model selection criterion.

In Avramov, all 2^{14} models have the same prior probability; however, as Cremers (2002) points out, there is a link between the probability of a variable being in the model and the probability of that model. His reasoning is as follows: assume that all variables have equal and independent prior probabilities p of entering the model, then the probability of any one model is $p^k(1-p)^{14-k}$. The only way that models can be equiprobable is if $p = 0.5$. However, this implies a prior probability of no predictability of 0.0001, and a joint probability of having more than four variables of 0.91. This is a lot of prior model mass on predictability. The issue of the choice of prior on parameters and on model size is non-trivial, and the subject of a rich literature. See Ley and Steel (2009) for recent work on the issue.

Therefore, Cremers's priors are different from Avramov. He also makes the point that diffuse priors imply higher prior R^2's for the models with more regressors. He controls this by tightening to zero the priors of the larger models so that the implied R^2's are the same. On this issue, Avramov does something similar, since he keeps the notional sample size in the prior equal to T_0 times the number of predictors. This does tighten the slope prior towards zero for the larger models, and he shows that his results are robust to values of T_0 between 25 and 100. Another difference is that Cremers predicts a univariate series, a value-weighted index, while Avramov runs a six-variate model. In contrast with Avramov, Cremers finds that his best models have more variables, but less out-of-sample evidence of predictability.

3.2 Economic relevance of predictability

We now turn to the economic relevance of predictability, measured by the impact of the competing models on optimal allocation. Performance is measured by the realized out-of-sample Sharpe ratios or certainty equivalent. We first discuss Kandel and Stambaugh (1996) (K&S), whose set-up is now standard and has been used and generalized. K&S consider the predictive regression of monthly returns on the dividend yield:

$$r_t = x'_{t-1}b + \epsilon_t. \tag{9.14}$$

They evaluate the relevance of predictability through its effect on a Bayesian investor's optimal allocation between the market and the T-Bill. Typical R^2's for this regression are below 5%; therefore, by statistical standards predictability does not appear formidable. Clearly though, as x_t varies through time, an investor may want to vary her optimal asset allocation since the conditional mean forecast of returns $x'_{t-1}b$ changes as well. This is also related to the inherent noise in the regression as well as the conditional mean at the time. Despite the low R^2's, K&S show that the typical monthly variations in the value of the regressors imply notable changes in the optimal asset allocation. They compute certainty equivalent returns to argue that these allocation changes are worth a lot to the investor.

Returns are lognormal and the investor solves for her optimal allocation by using power utility. K&S allow for stochastic regressors in (9.14), modeling them as a vector autoregression. The system of the VAR and (9.14) involves a slope coefficient and an error covariance matrix (B, Σ). The R^2 is a non-linear function of this covariance matrix and slopes. To each possible value of (B, Σ) there corresponds a value for the R^2. Hence, a distribution of (B, Σ) implies a distribution of the R^2. K&S consider two priors for (B, Σ), one diffuse and one denoted "no-predictability", centered on zero. This second prior is that described above for Avramov (2002). The notional sample size T_0 is proportional to the number of predictive variables, so that the implied prior R^2 stays about the same for a different number of predictors.

As the variances are unknown, the predictive density is Student-t. K&S constrain the optimal allocation w to be below 0.99 so that expected utility remains defined. Further, as they work in a discrete time set-up, the exact w^* would need to be obtained numerically. Instead, they use the continuous time-analytical optimum as an approximation. Their results are striking. Even for very low sample R^2's, the optimal asset allocation can vary a lot with the current level of the predictor. K&S compute the increase in expected utility due to the ability to change asset allocation: they compute the difference in optimal expected utility between a position where the regressors are at their unconditional mean and typical low or high values of the regressors. They find that the differences between these allocations amount to notable differences in certainty equivalent, sometimes more than 3% a year, despite the small R^2's of the regressions.

Avramov (2002) also conducts an optimization. His initial set-up in (9.13) is incomplete as he wants to look more than one step ahead. In order to draw several steps ahead, he formulates an AR(1) process for the regressors. Consequently, the predictive density $p(r_{T+K}|R)$ does not have an analytical expression for $K > 1$, due to the need to integrate out the returns at times $T+1, \ldots T+K-1$. In turn, the expected utility does not have an analytical integral either; even though he only optimizes a K-steps-ahead buy-and-hold portfolio, he needs to simulate the expected utility, and optimize these simulated values. Avramov looks at up to ten periods ahead. He notes that the asset allocation should be less sensitive to the current value of the predictor as the horizon increases, since the predictor is stationary.

The classic framework for predictability in returns includes a regression of the returns r on stochastic regressors x, which themselves follow an AR(1) with strong autocorrelation:

$$\begin{aligned} r_t &= \alpha + \beta x_{t-1} + u_t, \\ x_t &= \theta + \rho x_{t-1} + v_t. \end{aligned} \tag{9.15}$$

The shocks u_t, v_t have a non-diagonal covariance matrix Σ. Stambaugh (1999) undertakes a detailed Bayesian study of this predictive regression with lagged stochastic regressors, typically the dividend-price ratio or the corporate yield spread. The system is written as a large multivariate regression, and one formulates priors on $(\alpha, \beta, \theta, \rho, \Sigma)$. Stambaugh uses flat priors on the slope coefficients and Σ, and studies posterior inference and asset allocation. A key result is that the posterior mean of β is linearly related to the posterior mean of ρ through the covariance σ_{uv} which is negative. He describes the impact on inference and asset allocation of two key aspects of the modeling; whether ρ is allowed to be in the non-stationary regions, and whether the first observation is considered known or stochastic, which modifies the likelihood function. He then implements these alternative specifications on four subsamples of the data between 1927 and 1996. The ordering of the posterior means for the various specifications varies with the subsamples; consequently, there is no clear evidence that a given specification produces systematically higher, or lower, posterior means, apart from the naive ordinary least squares (OLS) which always produces the lowest β and highest ρ. Stambaugh then shows that these posterior differences lead to sizable differences in Merton allocation.

Barberis (2000) analyzes the effect of predictability and parameter uncertainty on the investor's asset allocation, especially for long horizons. He uses the same classic model as in Stambaugh (1999) or K&S, as in (9.15) where x_{t-1} is the dividend yield, $(d/p)_{t-1}$. After K&S, we suspect that predictability will have a strong impact on asset allocation. However, Section 2.3 has shown that parameter uncertainty compounds enormously as the horizon grows. Without predictability, but with parameter uncertainty on both mean and variance, Barberis finds results similar to Figure 9.1, panel a). Even though he integrates out variance and rebalances discretely, he finds optimal allocations very close to those in Jacquier (2006).

Because he rebalances discretely, and does not know variance, Barberis does not have an analytical solution to the Merton optimal allocation problem, such as in (9.10). For each draw of the posterior parameters, he draws from the multi-period predictive density of returns. Then for a number of candidate values of $w \in [0, 0.99]$, he computes and averages the utility of the asset allocation over the predictive draws. This is feasible since w is univariate and bounded. The optimal allocation is the w that yielded the highest (Monte Carlo estimate of) expected utility.

Barberis then considers predictability. As in Stambaugh (1999), the normal errors are negatively correlated, with the following effect on long-term allocation. Suppose that the dividend yield falls unexpectedly. The negative correlation implies that this is likely to be accompanied by a contemporaneous positive shock to stock returns. However, since the dividend yield is lower, stock returns are forecast to be lower in the future since $\beta > 0$. This contemporaneous rise, followed by a fall in future returns, causes variance to aggregate slower than for iid returns, leading the investor with a longer time horizon to allocate more to stocks. Assuming known parameters, Barberis confirms this intuition. However, when Barberis allows for parameter uncertainty as well as predictability, a very strong negative demand, as seen in Section 2.3, sets in to counter the positive demand due to predictability alone.

Wachter and Warusawitharana (2009) model predictability with a regression of returns on the dividend-price ratio and the corporate yield spread. They model the investor's degree of confidence in predictability via a prior on the coefficients of this regression. A small prior variance for these coefficients implies high skepticism about predictability since the prior mean is 0. As in Stambaugh (1999) and Barberis (2000), the predictors follow an AR(1), and the shocks to the predictors and returns can be correlated. They conclude that the data would convince even a skeptical investor to time the market. Modeling the prior degree of belief in predictability allows them to determine which types of investors would or would not be swayed by the data.

What matters in these studies is how incorporating predictability in returns affects the predictive density, and in turn the optimal asset allocation of a rational investor, not whether autocorrelations or slope coefficients are statistically significant.

4 Asset Pricing

This section surveys the finance literature that directly tests the validity of asset pricing models. Since Roll (1977), it has been understood that tests of the various versions of the CAPM are often equivalent to testing whether some index portfolio was ex-post mean-variance efficient; therefore, we first discuss the Bayesian approach to tests of portfolio efficiency.

Multi-factor models, whether from economic arguments or data-mining, have become a popular way to remedy the shortcomings of the CAPM. Some empirical analysis is based on latent factors, which requires the estimation of the factor as well as the actual test of the model pricing. We discuss some unique contributions of Bayesian methods to this aspect of the literature.

4.1 Asset pricing tests are portfolio efficiency tests

Typical one-pass tests of the CAPM have often used likelihood ratios, Lagrange multiplier, or Wald tests, whose small sample distributions are not the same (see CLM, chapter 5). The econometrician selects a number of assets to be priced, and a market index portfolio, and tests whether the index prices the assets properly according to the CAPM. Consistent with Roll's (1977) argument, these tests can be written as functions of a measure of the efficiency of the index chosen as the market portfolio with respect to the frontier spanned by the portfolios and the index (see CLM, chapter 5).

Shanken (1987) solves and generalizes the problem in a Bayesian framework. First he tests the efficiency, not of a single index, but of the most efficient linear combination of a set of portfolios. This is still with respect to the frontier spanned by N assets and the portfolios. Assume that the correlation between the highest Sharpe ratio portfolio on this frontier and the benchmark portfolio tested is 0.98. With enough data one will still reject the null of efficiency, even if the difference between 0.98 and 1 is meaningless.

This is a standard critique of the tests of point null hypotheses. The critique is even more warranted here, because, as Roll (1977) points out, we do not have the exact market portfolio, only a proxy with hopefully high, but not perfect, correlation with the market portfolio. For a given imperfect correlation between the chosen proxy and the portfolio with maximum Sharpe ratio, how much of the distance to 1 comes from the fact that we do not use the true market portfolio? Shanken formalizes this issue of proxy imperfection. It involves an added parameter, the correlation between the proxy and the true portfolio, on which he posits a prior distribution. He then tests the efficiency of the index by computing odds ratios that take into account the fact that we are using a proxy of the market portfolio.

Harvey and Zhou (1990) address the same problem by formulating priors on the mean and covariances of the assets; they do not incorporate beliefs about the imperfection of the proxy. In their crucial paper, Kandel et al. (1995) derive the posterior distribution of the maximum correlation between the portfolio tested and any portfolio on the efficient frontier. This posterior distribution is shown to be very sensitive to the choice of prior. As in Shanken (1987), they incorporate the fact that the portfolio tested is not a perfect proxy for a theoretical portfolio. This in effect makes the sharp null hypothesis of perfect correlation uninteresting. Their approach works for both cases, with and without a risk-free asset. They find that, especially in the presence of a risk-free asset, the choice of priors affects the results. For conventional sample sizes, a diffuse prior on the mean vector of the assets makes it very hard for the posterior of ρ to concentrate close to 1, the value implied by *efficiency*, even if the sample estimate of ρ is close to 1. This is another case where the parameter of interest, the maximized ρ, is a non-linear function of the base parameters μ, Σ, which has perverse effects on the prior distribution of ρ.

In related work, Pastor (2000) discusses how to incorporate into the portfolio optimization the investor's degree of belief in an asset-pricing model. Assume that expected returns are a linear combination of K factors, a generalization of the CAPM which centers on the efficiency of a single portfolio. If these factors can be replicated by K *benchmark* portfolios, then the frontier is spanned by these portfolios. The degree of belief is modeled by the tightness of the prior of the deviation from the model's prediction, for example, Jensen's α for the CAPM. Pastor and Stambaugh (2000) use this framework to compare the CAPM, the Fama-French three-factor model, and a third model, in a one-period, buy-and-hold mean-variance optimization framework. Portfolios are optimized using the predictive density implied by a model, and a degree of margin requirements. To compare models, they compute the loss in certainty equivalent for an investor who believes in one model but is forced to use weights that are optimal under another one. The result is that for realistic margin requirements and prior model uncertainty, the perceived differences between models are far smaller than classical testing lead us to believe. Note also that, from the viewpoint of portfolio optimization, the best strategy would be a composite model according to the posterior odds ratios of each model, an interesting avenue of research.

4.2 Bayesian tests of the APT and factor models

The Arbitrage Pricing Theory (APT) builds on the assumption that returns are generated by a statistical model with latent factors f_t:

$$R_t = E(R_t) + Bf_t + \epsilon_t, \quad \epsilon_t \sim N(0, D), \tag{9.16}$$

where R_t is the N vector of asset returns, and B is an N (stocks) $\times$ K (factors) matrix of factor loadings. The crucial assumption is that D, the covariance matrix of the idiosyncratic risks ϵ, is diagonal; exposures to the common factors explain all of the stock covariances. The number of free parameters in the $N \times N$ covariance matrix is constrained since it is modeled with the $K \times K$ factor covariance matrix, the $N \times K$ coefficient matrix, and the N error variances. McCulloch and Rossi (1990) show that at most five factors suffice to explain the covariances between returns. Therefore, the factor model is by itself a very effective device for inference on large covariance matrices.

In the absence of arbitrage, the APT model follows from (9.16). Expected returns are linearly related to the factor exposures B:

$$E(R_t) = r_{ft} i + B\gamma_t. \tag{9.17}$$

Here, γ is a k-vector of factor premia. McCulloch and Rossi (1990, 1991) are the first to implement a Bayesian test of the APT with latent variables. The first step of their procedure, by which they obtain the factor scores f_t, is, however, more classical in spirit. They use the method of asymptotic principal components (see Connor and Korajczyk 1986) to estimate the factor scores from a cross-section of more than $N = 1,500$ stock returns. The standard principal component methodology extracts the factor loadings from the sample covariance matrix, with precision increasing with the length of the time series. In contrast, Connor and Korajczyk show how to extract the factor scores from the $T \times T$ cross-product matrix of returns, with precision increasing in the number of stocks N. For the typical stock-market asset-pricing application, with very large N and not so large T, Connor and Korajczyk show that the f_t's are incredibly precisely estimated. McCulloch and Rossi (1990, 1991) essentially consider these scores f_t as known, when they implement the cross-sectional regression in (9.16). Therefore, they concentrate on a Bayesian implementation of (9.16), assured that it is not subject to issues of errors in the variables.

If both the factor model (9.16) and the APT (9.17) are correct, the intercept vector α in the multivariate regression

$$R = \alpha i' + BF + E, E \sim N(0, \Sigma),$$

must be zero. McCulloch and Rossi (1990) produce the posterior distributions for α. They use normal-Wishart priors for α, B, Σ. If the APT in (9.17) is correct, then α is zero. Second, they compare the certainty equivalent returns for a rational investor optimizing her portfolio with and without the constraint of the APT. For tractability, they assume normal returns and exponential utility. Their work represents the first utility-based evaluation of an asset-pricing model.

As this is a simple case of nested hypotheses, McCulloch and Rossi (1990) can use the Savage density ratio method to compute posterior odds for the null hypothesis of the APT model versus the hypothesis of mis-pricing ($\alpha \neq 0$). The Savage density ratio method allows odds ratios to be written without actually performing the integration necessary to obtain the marginal likelihood. Instead, the odds ratio is simply the ratio of a posterior to a prior ordinate, at the value specified under the constrained model, here $\alpha = 0$ (see Dickey 1971).

In small-small (cross-section and time-series) sample situations, even the N-asymptotic of Connor and Korajzyk might be inadequate, and suffer from errors in the variables. The standard principal components methods, in which sampling precision increases with T, will also be affected by severe problems of errors in the variables. A pure Bayesian framework, optimal for the T and N used by the econometrician, is going to be very useful. Geweke and Zhou (1995) show how to estimate latent factors and their loadings with a pure Gibbs sampler. The intuition is straightforward since both conditional posterior densities $B|F$ and $F|B$ represent a regression, whether time-series or cross-sectional. Upon convergence of their algorithm, Geweke and Zhou can produce analysis similar to Mc Culloch and Rossi, but bypassing any reliance on large N or large T.

4.3 Performance evaluation

One can view performance evaluation as a form of asset-pricing test where managed funds, rather than individual stocks or portfolios, are investigated for mis-pricing. Performance evaluation is also tied to predictability as the issue of persistence in performance inevitably arises (see for example, Avramov and Wermers 2006 for mutual funds).

Baks et al. (2001) approach performance evaluation via its impact on an investor who optimizes a portfolio of the index and one actively managed fund. Most importantly, they propose an innovative prior on a manager's Jensen α. The prior has a point mass on a slightly negative $\underline{\alpha}$, with probability $1 - q$ that the manager is unskilled. The performance $\underline{\alpha} = a - \text{fee} - \text{cost}$ is slightly negative because one subtracts from the raw performance a the fees and transaction costs due to active management. a is argued to be slightly negative because the unskilled manager trades with skilled managers. Then, the manager is skilled with probability q. Given skill, α is modeled by a normal truncated at the mode $\underline{\alpha}$. Baks et al. effectively remove possibly large negative values from the prior on α, as unskilled managers are not expected to display systematically large negative performance. Baks et al. show how to elicit the prior by specifying q, the fees and costs, and the probability that the manager's α will be above a specific level, for example 25 basis points. An important result is that, unless the investor is a priori extremely skeptical toward the possibility of skill, she would invest a non-negligible fraction of her wealth in actively managed funds. In contrast, for many of these same funds, the classical approach would fail to reject the null hypothesis of no skill, which would likely be followed by the decision not to invest in the fund. First, Baks et al.'s careful modeling of the prior on α affords them much needed precision in the estimation of α. Second, this application shows that even though two alternatives, here skill and no skill, may appear statistically close, they can still lead to very different investment decisions.

Baks et al. study each of 400 fund managers separately, and do not allow for interactions or learning across funds. They compute each α over a Fama-French three-factor model, and assume that the correlation matrix of idiosyncratic noises is diagonal. Jones and Shanken (2005) maintain this latter assumption but concentrate on learning across funds. The performance α_j of each fund is considered to be a random draw from a general distribution with cross-sectional mean μ_α and variance σ_α^2. Intuitively, consider that the prior on α_j draws from the average and variance of the sample α's of the other funds in the sample. Jones and Shanken point out that this shrinkage approach counters the undesirable unboundedness of the maximum posterior α when the number of funds increases. Also, in contrast with Baks et al. and others, they model different prior beliefs for each fund. The parameter space includes the α_j's (considered to be random draws of $\mu_\alpha, \sigma_\alpha$), as well as the individual fund β and standard deviations. Since μ_α and σ_α are unknown as well, the posterior densities of the parameters are not known analytically. Therefore, Jones and Shanken write a Gibbs algorithm which updates all parameters, especially the α_j's, μ_α, and σ_α. Their empirical results confirm that incorporating learning across funds dramatically reduces the highest posterior means.

5 Volatilities, Covariances, and Betas

Estimating and forecasting (co)variances is crucial in just about every area of finance, including risk management, option pricing, and portfolio optimization. At least in the univariate case, the literature has moved very quickly to the modeling of the time variation of volatility for a few reasons. The time variation of volatility has been taken for granted in finance since Officer (1973), and, because of its high autocorrelation, volatility is more successfully predicted than time-varying expected returns. The modeling of time-varying volatility goes a long way to help match the fat-tailness of the unconditional density of financial series. In brief, the research has shown that a good parsimonious model of time-varying volatility must have three key ingredients: (1) an autoregressive structure, (2) the ability to model asymmetries in returns where negative returns are associated with a greater volatility than same size positive returns, and (3) some additional modeling of fat-tailness for the conditional distribution of returns.

For a long time researchers used ad-hoc time-moving windows to allow for time-varying volatility. Engle's ARCH, a quantum jump in variance modeling, triggered a huge literature (see Bollerslev et al. 1994 for a survey). However, while the time-series ARCH literature was mushrooming, theoretical finance was already exploring the more general stochastic volatility (SV) for modeling purpose. One reason for the resilient success of GARCH models may be that they are viewed as good filters of unobserved volatility. For example, Nelson (1994) shows that, as one converges to continuous time records, GARCH models dominate Kalman filters in terms of mean squared errors. Another reason is their ease of implementation, at least in the univariate set-up; the multivariate case is far more complicated. While the ML framework works well computationally for the GARCH framework, classical methods can not handle the SV model well. The reason is that the SV model is non-linear and the volatility is a latent variable.

With the advent of Markov chain Monte Carlo (MCMC) algorithms, Bayesian methods have been able to deliver the optimal estimation for a large class of SV models (see for example Jacquier et al. (1994, 2004).[3] Further, Geweke (1994) and Kim et al. (1998) show that a lot can be gained from the added flexibility of the SV over the GARCH model. This section, therefore, first discusses some Bayesian GARCH algorithms. Then we show how to design, implement, and diagnose a simple MCMC Bayesian algorithm for a general univariate SV model with fat tails and asymmetric returns.

Precise inference for large covariance matrices is difficult even if they are assumed to be constant. Realistic finance applications often have many assets relative to the time period; therefore, parsimonious modeling requires some reasonable constraints on the matrix. One such constraint very well adapted to financial modeling is the factor model. We have already discussed the Bayesian estimation of a constant-parameter factor model in the asset-pricing section. We complete this discussion here with the implementation of time-varying factor models and betas.

5.1 Bayesian GARCH modeling

In a basic GARCH model, returns and their variance are as follows:

$$\begin{aligned} r_t &= \sqrt{h_t}\epsilon_t, \quad \epsilon_t \sim N(0,1), \\ h_t &= \omega + \alpha r_{t-1}^2 + \beta h_{t-1}. \end{aligned} \tag{9.18}$$

The model can be extended to allow for fat tails in the shock ϵ_t. A so-called *leverage effect* can be added to allow for variance to be higher when the return is negative. Glosten et al. (1992) add a sign dummy to the variance equation. In contrast, Nelson (1991) introduces the exponential GARCH model (EGARCH), based upon a logarithm formulation. This allows for negative right-hand-side variables in the variance equation,

[3] Jacquier et al. (2007) show that a simple adjustment of the Bayesian algorithm delivers the ML estimate and its asymptotic covariance matrix.

and eliminates the need for positivity constraints. For example, an EGARCH(1,1,) can be written as:

$$\log h_t = \omega + \theta \epsilon_{t-1} + \gamma(\epsilon_{t-1}^2 - E(\epsilon_{t-1}^2)) + \beta \log h_{t-1}. \tag{9.19}$$

Typically, one uses several years of daily returns to estimate a GARCH model. This often leads to precise reported standard errors of estimation for the simplest models. The prevalent technique has been the maximization of the likelihood function, which is conveniently done for the simplest models; however, experience shows that the maximization can be difficult for the more complex models. See Bollerslev et al. (1994) for a survey.

Bayesian estimation of the GARCH model requires MCMC methods as one can not draw directly from the posterior distribution of the parameters. To see this, consider the posterior density of the parameters $\theta = (\omega, \alpha, \beta)$ in equation (9.19), a simple GARCH(1,1) model with normal errors:

$$p(\theta|R) \propto p(\theta) \prod \frac{1}{\sqrt{h_t(\theta)}} \exp - \frac{y_t^2}{2h_t(\theta)}.$$

Even breaking θ into its individual components does not permit a simple Gibbs sampler. The model can be extended with a regression function γx_t in the returns equation, which does not pose any further difficulty. One then introduces an added conditional $p(\gamma|\theta)$ to the MCMC sampler, from which direct draws can be made. Geweke (1989) uses importance sampling to draw from the posterior distribution of the parameters, and, in turn, the h_t's for the pure-ARCH model, with no lagged h_t in the variance equation. Kleibergen and Van Dijk (1993) use importance sampling to estimate a GARCH with Student-t errors. Their approximation function for θ is a multivariate Student-t with very low degrees of freedom.

The priors used in Bayesian GARCH estimation are usually diffuse, but one wants to impose the positivity $(\omega, \alpha, \beta) > 0$, and, if desired, stationarity $\alpha + \beta < 1$ conditions. Note that Bayesian analysis, unlike maximum likelihood or the method of moments, does not require the existence of unconditional moments such as the variance of r_t. This is done by rejecting posterior draws which do not meet the conditions, which amounts to using a truncated prior since an indicator variable transfers directly to the posterior via Bayes theorem. Consider, for example, a possibly diffuse but proper density $p(\theta)$ defined on the real line. The econometrician wants to use this shape of density as a prior while imposing the condition $\theta \in [a, b]$. The prior is then $\pi(\theta) \propto p(\theta)\mathcal{I}_{[a,b]}$ where $\mathcal{I}$ is the indicator function. By Bayes theorem, the posterior is then $(\theta|D) \propto p(D|\theta)p(\theta)\mathcal{I}_{[a,b]}$.

Depending on the domain restriction, both prior and posterior may require a complicated integration to find the normalization constant due to the truncation. However, if one only needs to draw from the posterior, as in a direct MC or MCMC algorithm, this integration is done by drawing from $p(D|\theta)p(\theta)$, and then rejecting draws that do not belong to $[a, b]$. This truncation by rejection is one of the appealing practicalities of

Monte Carlo simulation of posterior and predictive densities. Clearly, the effectiveness of this practice, related to the fraction of draws rejected, depends on the amount of information in the likelihood about the domain of θ. An alternative prior strategy is to use a prior which does not require truncation, for example, a scaled Beta prior; however, such priors may not always lead to simple posterior densities. In Bayesian GARCH estimation, positivity and stationarity conditions are, therefore, enforced by rejecting the inadequate posterior draws. It turns out that only a very small fraction of the draws is rejected.

Bauwens and Lubrano (1998) estimate a GARCH where ϵ_t in (9.19) is Student-t, with ν degrees of freedom. They note that the posterior of ν does not integrate if the prior is on $(0, \infty)$. Precisely, $p(\nu)$ needs to decrease at a rate faster than $1/\nu$ for large ν's. It also needs to be well behaved at $\nu = 0$. Truncation away from zero solves the problem and may even be desirable for modeling purposes; recall that the unconditional variance is infinite for $\nu \leq 2$. Bauwens and Lubrano choose the prior $p(\nu) \propto 1/(1|\nu^2)$. An alternative specification could be Geweke's (1993) exponential prior $p(\nu) \propto \psi \exp -\psi\nu$. Bauwens and Lubrano use a griddy Gibbs to draw from each element of the conditional posterior. For each element of the parameter vector, the griddy Gibbs computes posterior ordinates on a grid of carefully selected points, and the cumulative distribution function (CDF) between these points by numerical integration (see Ritter and Tanner 1992). The inverse CDF method is then used to draw from the parameter. This is conceptually straightforward but numerically intensive, and requires a fair number of functional evaluations. Also, as Bauwens and Lubrano note, one needs to choose the grid carefully.

Muller and Pole (1998), in contrast, use a Metropolis-Hastings (MH) algorithm to estimate GARCH models with regressions or AR parameters in the mean. They first break the parameter vector (θ, γ) into its individual elements. Then they make an MH independence draw for each element. Nakatsuma (2000) extends the model, also using an MH algorithm. He allows for an ARMA in the errors, making use of Chib and Greenberg (1994), who estimate the ARMA model with an MH algorithm.

Nakatsuma's algorithm cycles the ARMA and GARCH parameters, respectively δ_1 and δ_2. The conditional $\delta_1|\delta_2$ uses an ARMA likelihood with heteroskedastic but known variances h_t, a minor modification of the MH algorithm in Chib and Greenberg (1994). The conditional $\delta_2|\delta_1$ uses the well-known ARMA representation of the GARCH model introduced by Bollerslev (see Bollerslev et al. 1994). For a GARCH(1,1), we have:

$$\epsilon_t^2 = \alpha_0 + (\alpha_1 + \beta_1)\epsilon_{t-1}^2 + \nu_t - \beta_1 \nu_{t-1}, \quad \nu_t = \epsilon_t^2 - h_t. \tag{9.20}$$

Note that ν_t is non-normal with variance $2h_t^2$. Nakatsuma uses (9.20) as the basis for the conditional posterior of $\delta_2|\delta_1$. As a direct draw is not available, a feasible proposal density for an independence MH draw of δ_2 obtains by replacing the true distribution of ν_t by a normal. The parameter vector draws are, in fact, further broken down, for both the ARMA and the GARCH, into the autoregressive and the moving average parameters. Accounting for the possible regression parameters, these are five major blocks of MH independence draws. However, Nakatsuma's method does not extend to the asymmetric GARCH of Glosten et al. (1992) and Nelson's (1991) EGARCH because they do not have an ARMA representation.

Vrontos et al. (2000) propose a random-walk MH algorithm. The algorithm is easy to apply since it does not require the fine tuning of a proposal density. The candidate draw is simply made by adding an increment $N(0, \sigma)$ to the current value; σ is tuned to generate no more than 50% repeats. Small moves generate lower repeat probability, but they do not travel enough in the parameter space. Large moves on the other hand may visit very low probability areas and cause too many repeats. Vrontos et al. initially break the parameter vector into univariate MH draws; however, they show that the numerical efficiency can be increased if one draws jointly the most highly correlated parameters. One should, in general, be cautious with Metropolis draws of high-dimensional vectors, and make sure that they do not lead to a high repeat rate.[4] In their case, however, the dimension is low. The entire parameter space for a GARCH(2,2) is five parameters plus the regression or mean parameter.

Possibly the most interesting contribution in Vrontos et al. is their use of the reversible jump algorithm, which allows them to simulate simultaneously a number of competing GARCH or EGARCH models. In addition to the parameter draws, the algorithm jumps to another candidate model with a certain probability. The MCMC algorithm effectively generates the posterior probabilities of the models, as well as the parameter draws of each model (see Green 1995). So their algorithm produces the posterior odds for each model, as well as the model averaging. A direct by-product of their method may be the posterior distribution of in-sample volatilities and the predictive distribution of future volatilities, for the optimal combination model that is the average of the models considered, with weights being the posterior probabilities of each model. For the Greek stock market, Vrontos et al. compare eight EGARCH models. The best model has a posterior probability of 0.47, but the next three models have posterior probabilities summing up to 0.43. This highlights the potential benefits of model averaging over the practice of selecting the best model.

These methods do not produce parameter posterior means drastically different from the MLE point estimate for very long series; however, if inference is needed for the parameters, one worries about the use of the Hessian matrix for standard errors, and the asymptotic normality assumption. In contrast, the Bayesian simulation methods produce the expected non-normal posterior distributions. Another, more important, issue is the difference in inference on in-sample and future volatilities (see Geweke 1989). The MLE estimates the volatilities h_ts at the MLE point estimate of the parameters. The Bayes methods delivers, by simulation, the entire posterior density of each h_t as well as of the parameters. The Bayesian econometrician can then choose the posterior mean as a point estimate optimal under quadratic loss. But having the entire posterior distribution allows proper inference, beyond the use of the posterior mean as a location estimate.

[4] One may decrease the repeat rate by reducing the dispersion of the proposal draws, but there may be a risk that the entire domain is not covered properly, especially in a high-dimensional multivariate setting.

A similar potential problem arises with multi-step ahead forecasting. Again, the MLE simply substitutes parameters estimates, running the variance equation sequentially to compute $\widehat{h}_{t+K}$, replacing r^2_{T+K-1} on its RHS by its forecast $\widehat{h}_{t+K-1}$. In contrast, a simulation-based Bayesian algorithm produces draws from the exact predictive density by running draws of the future shocks and volatilities to time $T+K$ through the volatility equation, for each draw of the parameters. This naturally produces the correct predictive density of future, time $T+K$ volatilities, which integrate out intermediate volatilities at $T+1, \ldots, T+K-1$, and parameters. See Geweke and Whiteman (2006) for discussions of Bayesian forecasting.

5.2 Stochastic volatility by MCMC

Consider the basic SV model below:

$$\begin{aligned} y_t &= \sqrt{h_t}\,\epsilon_t, \\ \log h_t &= \alpha + \delta \log h_{t-1} + \sigma_v v_t, \quad t = 1, \ldots, T \\ (\epsilon_t, v_t) &\sim N(0, I_2). \end{aligned} \tag{9.21}$$

The key difference with the GARCH model resides in the shock v_t to volatility, which makes it an unobservable latent variable; knowledge of the parameters, unlike the GARCH model, does not deliver the volatilities. Let $\omega = (\alpha, \delta, \sigma_v)$; the likelihood function $p(y|\omega)$ requires the integration of the T-dimensional vector of volatilities, that is, $p(y|\omega) = \int p(y|h, \omega)p(h|\omega)dh$.

The early literature used the method of moments to estimate the parameters, and the Kalman filter to obtain smoothed or filtered estimates of the volatilities given the parameters. Another approach, the quasi maximum likelihood (QML), was to approximate the SV model by a normal-linear state space model, assuming the normality of $\log \epsilon_t^2$. The likelihood of this approximate model could then be written in terms of the Kalman-filtered volatilities and maximized to obtain the parameters. These methods have been shown to perform poorly, (see Jacquier, Polson, and Rossi (1994), hereafter JPR). JPR develop a Bayesian MCMC algorithm to draw from the posterior densities of the parameters and the volatilities, as well as the predictive densities of the future volatilities. The algorithm uses Metropolis-Hastings independence sampling.

5.2.1 *A Metropolis-Hastings independence algorithm*

Given a prior for the parameters $p(\omega)$, one needs to draw from the posterior density $p(\omega, \mathbf{h}|\mathbf{y})$. Consider first a Gibbs cycle of the two conditional densities, $p(\mathbf{h}|\mathbf{y}, \omega)$ and $p(\omega|\mathbf{y}, \mathbf{h})$. The second is a draw of the posterior distribution of regression parameters. The prior used in JPR is the conjugate normal-gamma prior, with variances large enough to render it flat over the relevant parameter domain (see JPR). A simple joint draw of the high-dimensional $p(\mathbf{h}|\mathbf{y}, \omega)$ is not convenient, so one further breaks it into univariate densities $p(h_t|h_{-t}, y, \omega)$. JPR show that, by successive applications of Bayes's rule, it can be written as:

$$p(h_t|h_{t-1}, h_{t+1}, \omega, \mathbf{y}) \propto p(y|h_t)\, p(h_{t+1}|h_t, \omega)\, p(h_t|h_{t-1}, \omega),$$
$$\propto \frac{1}{h_t^{\frac{3}{2}}} \exp\left(\frac{-y_t^2}{2h_t} - \frac{(\log h_t - \mu_t)^2}{2\sigma_v^2/(1+\delta^2)}\right). \tag{9.22}$$

One can not draw directly from (9.22), but it is well approximated by an inverse gamma density. This is the basis for an MH independence draw. Therefore, the overall MCMC algorithm cycles through the elements of $(\omega, h_1, \ldots, h_T)$. One draws h_t from the inverse gamma density, and accepts the draw with the acceptance probability shown in JPR; otherwise the previous draw is repeated. This is referred to as a single-move algorithm, because it draws the latent variables h_t one at time. Since these volatilities are correlated together, the sequence of draws in this algorithm can exhibit high autocorrelation, especially for σ_v.

Large scale sampling experiments, for example, demonstrate the behavior of the algorithm. In repeated simulations, as the sample size increases, the Monte Carlo estimate of the posterior mean converges to the true parameters. For example, for the parameters $\delta = 0.95, \sigma_v = 0.26$, and $E(\sqrt{h_t}) = 3.2\%$, JPR simulate 500 samples of $T = 1500$ observations, and compute the posterior means for parameters and volatilities with 50000 draws of the algorithm. They find that the posterior mean of δ is 0.94 on average, with a root mean squared errors (RMSE) of 0.02, while that of σ_v is 0.279 on average with an RMSE of 0.04. Over the 750,000 $\sqrt{h_t}$s of this simulation, the posterior mean exhibits a mean absolute error (MAE) of 18.4%. By any standard, the posterior mean is very close to the true value as shown by the absence of bias and the very low RMSE. We also get an idea of the relative precision expected from the smoothed posterior mean of the volatilities, about 18%. For a given sample size, the posterior mean is not necessarily an unbiased estimator of the true parameter. Consequently, some Bayesians may find limited interest in a simulation of the sampling performance of the MCMC estimate of the posterior mean. The question here is whether the MCMC average is a good estimate of the posterior mean. If we find that its sampling behavior exhibits bias or high RMSE, how can we know if this is because of some failure of the algorithm or if we are actually seeing the sampling behavior of the true posterior mean? Recall that the posterior mean is optimal for a quadratic loss over the posterior distribution of the parameter, for the sample at hand.

Practically, in our case, the MCMC estimates of the posterior means do a great job of coming close to the actual parameters, by any intuitive measure. Second, JPR show that the sampling RMSE of the MCMC estimate of the posterior mean decreases with the sample size. Therefore, it reproduces the behavior expected from the posterior mean as the sample size increases. That is, the posterior mean converges to the MLE estimate as the sample size increases, and the MLE estimator converges to the true parameter. This is consistent with convergence of the algorithm. Another way that sampling experiments can be used is in comparing two algorithms in the same situation. If they both converge, they should produce the same results over and over.

An alternative algorithm has been proposed (see Kim et al. 1998, hereafter KSC) for the basic SV model. KSC model $\log \epsilon_t^2$, as a discrete mixture of normals, augmenting the state space accordingly, which allows them to draw directly from the multivariate distribution of **h**. While the computational burden at each draw is higher, the resulting draws are markedly less autocorrelated, notably for σ_v, than for the single-move sampler. In comparing the two algorithms, KSC and others misinterpret the high autocorrelation of the draws in the single-move algorithm as *slow convergence*. One should not confuse a high autocorrelation with a sign that the algorithm does not converge. It is a sign that the algorithm may accumulate information at a slower rate than if the autocorrelations were lower. One then takes the usual precautions of assessing the number of draws needed to obtain a desired precision for the MC estimate of, say, the posterior mean. This is done simply by computing standard errors robust to autocorrelation (see Geweke 1992). In fact, low autocorrelation may not even be a sign that an algorithm has converged; it may be stuck in a region of the parameter space while exhibiting low autocorrelation in that region. With lower autocorrelation, a given desired precision for Monte Carlo estimates requires fewer draws, but this has to be weighted by the required control processing unit (CPU) time per draw. In this case, the single-move algorithm is very fast; on a 2.8 Ghz Duo CPU, one generates 100,000 draws in seven minutes for a sample of $T = 1,500$ observations.

Sampling experiments can be used to compare different algorithms, for the same model. Jacquier and Miller (2010) show that the single and multi-move algorithms. produce the same output. Table 9.1 reproduces some results for 500 samples of 1,500 observations of the following SV model:

These performances are nearly identical, especially for the volatilities. Jacquier and Miller run both these algorithms on 809 days of the daily UK pound to US dollar exchange rate from January 2, 2006, to February 26, 2009. Table 9.2 shows the posterior analysis, where the two models produce nearly the same inference.

Table 9.1: Comparison of single-move and multi-move MCMC algorithms

	δ	σ_v	$\sqrt{h_t}$
True	0.960	0.210	
Single-move			
Mean	0.948	0.229	
RMSE	0.021	0.041	0.00219
%MAE			16.27
Multi-move			
Mean	0.952	0.221	
RMSE	0.017	0.037	0.00219
%MAE			16.19

Table 9.2: UK pound to US dollar, SV posterior analysis

	δ	σ_v
Single-move		
Mean	0.992	0.108
5%, 95%	0.983, 0.999	0.075, 0.146
Multi-move		
Mean	0.993	0.097
5%, 95%	0.988, 0.998	0.077, 0.122

Possibly, the multi-move will result in different posterior densities for the volatilities h_t? The sampling analysis in Table 9.1 only showed the sampling behavior of the posterior mean of h_t; what about the entire posterior distribution? Figure 9.2 plots the posterior mean and the fifth and 95th quantiles of the posterior distribution of $\sqrt{h_t}$, for both algorithms. They are in fact identical.

To conclude, SV models estimated by single-move or multi-move MCMC can deliver, period after period, posterior distributions of smoothed volatilities with a very satisfactory degree of precision, such as below 17% for the posterior mean of $\sqrt{h_t}$. Further results in section 7.2 confirm this for an extended SV model which exploits realized volatility.

5.2.2 SV with correlated errors and fat-tailed conditional returns

This section shows how to extend the basic SV to allow for correlated return and volatility errors, as well as fat-tailed conditional returns. We pay close attention to potential problems arising for the design of the proposal density.

A benefit of the basic single-move algorithm is that it extends readily, without further computing time burden, to the two most desired additional features: fat tails in the distribution of ϵ_t and correlated errors to generate the so-called leverage effect. We use Student-t errors as with the GARCH, and we introduce a correlation ρ between ϵ_t and v_t. This correlation is in line with the use of SV models in option pricing theory (see Heston 1993). The general SV model is:

$$
\begin{aligned}
y_t &= \sqrt{h_t}\epsilon_t = \sqrt{h_t}\sqrt{\lambda_t}z_t, \qquad (9.23)\\
\log h_t &= \alpha + \delta \log h_{t-1} + \sigma_v v_t, \quad t = 1, \ldots, T,\\
\nu/\lambda_t &\sim \chi^2_\nu,\\
(z_t, v_t) &\sim \mathcal{N}\left(0, \begin{pmatrix} 1 & \rho \\ \rho & 1 \end{pmatrix}\right).
\end{aligned}
$$

The shock to returns ϵ_t is modeled as a Student-$t(\nu)$ by setting a prior on λ_t as iid inverse gamma, that is $\nu/\lambda_t \sim \chi^2_\nu$. Explicitly modeling λ_t allows for a convenient simulation-based diagnostic for each observation. The prior on ν is integer uniform,

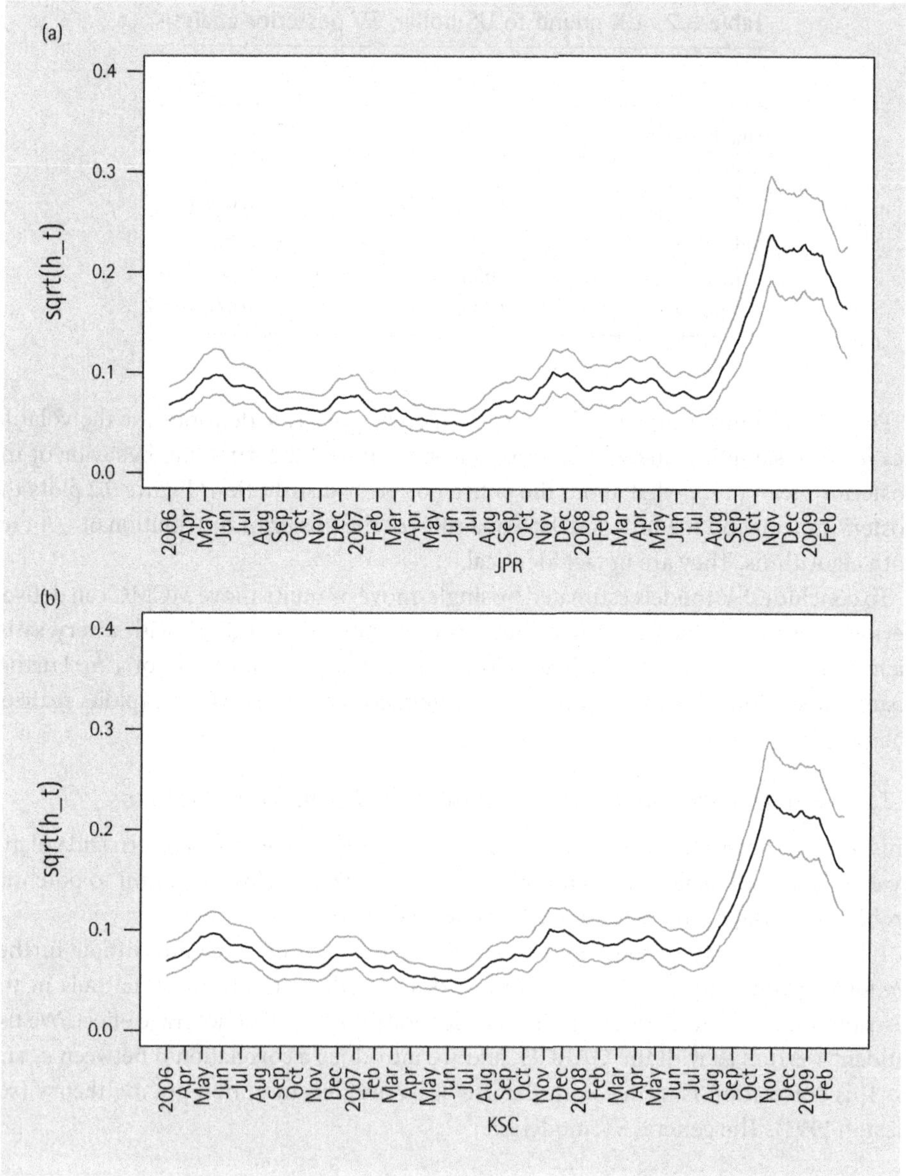

FIGURE 9.2 Posterior distribution of $\sqrt{h_t}$, mean, and 5%, 95% quantiles

for example on [5,60], if one wishes to rule out infinite conditional kurtosis. This discreteness of ν is not a problem since it would take a huge sample to deliver precise information for intervals smaller than 1. See Geweke (1993) for a continuous prior for ν. The parameter ω now includes $(\alpha, \delta, \sigma_v, \rho)$. We consider the conditional posterior distributions for the MCMC cycle:

(1) $p(\mathbf{h}|\omega, \boldsymbol{\lambda}, \mathbf{y})$, where the conditioning on ν is subsumed by $\boldsymbol{\lambda}$
(2) $p(\rho, \sigma_v|\mathbf{h}, \alpha, \delta, \boldsymbol{\lambda}, \mathbf{y})$
(3) $p(\alpha, \delta|\sigma_v, \mathbf{h}, \boldsymbol{\lambda}, \mathbf{y}) \equiv p(\alpha, \delta|\sigma_v, \mathbf{h})$
(4) $p(\boldsymbol{\lambda}, \nu|\mathbf{h}, \mathbf{y})$, where the conditioning on ω is subsumed by $\mathbf{h}$.

The fourth distribution is the extension for fat tails. It is straightforward and does not increase the computing burden measurably. Given a draw of ($\mathbf{h}$), the model simplifies by considering $y_t^* = y_t/\sqrt{h_t} = \lambda_t z_t$. A direct draw of the posterior $p(\boldsymbol{\lambda}, \nu|.) = p(\boldsymbol{\lambda}|\nu, .)\, p(\nu|.)$ can be made, where $p(\boldsymbol{\lambda}|\mathbf{y}^*, \nu,) = \prod_t p(\lambda_t \mid y_t^*, \nu)$. Jacquier et al. (2004) (JPR2) show that each $(\lambda_t|\nu, y_t^*)$ is a direct draw of an inverse gamma draw, and each $(\nu|\mathbf{y}^*)$ is a direct draw from a discrete multinomial distribution.

The third conditional is the posterior distribution of the slope coefficients of the AR(1) regression for $\log h_t$, conditional on the error standard deviation σ_v. We now consider the first two conditionals which contain the correlated errors extension. Their implementation provides a nice example of the care required to design the proposal density for an independence MH algorithm.

We will now see that care must be exercised in choosing the blanket of a Metropolis-Hastings independence algorithm. Given a draw of λ, the model in (9.23) simplifies by considering $y_t^{**} = y_t/\sqrt{\lambda_t}$. For $\mathbf{y}^{**}$, it is a SV model with correlated normal errors. The correlation ρ is modeled via the regression of $u_t = \sigma_v v_t$ on $z_t = y_t/\sqrt{h_t \lambda_t}$, specifically:

$$u_t = \psi z_t + \Omega \eta_t, \quad (\eta_t, \epsilon_t) \sim N(0, I), \tag{9.24}$$

where $\psi = \rho\sigma_v$ and $\Omega = \sigma_v^2(1 - \rho^2)$. This reparameterization of (ρ, σ_v) allows direct draws from the regression parameters $(\psi, \Omega|\mathbf{h})$. As the transformation is one-to-one, this yields direct draws for $(\rho, \sigma_v|\mathbf{h})$. Attempts to model ρ directly may require a Metropolis step, an unnecessary complication. JPR2 show how to model the prior on ψ, Ω, so as to have the desired prior on ρ, σ_v. The correlation ρ modifies the conditional posterior of $(h_t|\mathbf{y}, \omega, \mathrm{h}_{t-1}, \mathrm{h}_{t+1})$. JPR2 shows that it becomes:

$$p(h_t|h_{t-1}, h_{t+1}, \psi, \Omega, \mathbf{y}) \propto \frac{1}{\mathrm{h}_t^{\frac{3}{2}+\frac{\delta\psi \mathrm{y}_{t+1}}{\Omega\sqrt{\mathrm{h}_{t+1}}}}} \exp\left(\frac{-\mathrm{y}_t^2}{2\mathrm{h}_t}(1+\frac{\psi^2}{\Omega}) - \frac{(\log \mathrm{h}_t - \mu_t)^2}{2\Omega/(1+\delta^2)} + \frac{\psi \mathrm{y}_t \mathrm{u}_t}{\Omega\sqrt{\mathrm{h}_t}}\right), \tag{9.25}$$

which modifies (9.22) for $\psi \neq 0$, mostly by adding a third term in the exponent.[5]

As with the basic model, JPR2 initially approximate and merge the first two terms in the exponent of (9.25), to design an inverse gamma proposal density, denoted $q_1(h_t)$. They omit the third term in the exponent. Convergence theory, however, suggests that this should not be lost; it will naturally be accounted for when computing the ratio (p/q) needed for the repeat/accept probability. This should, therefore, not affect the theoretical capability of the algorithm to produce draws with invariant distribution p; at worst, one would think that it might affect the rate of convergence.

[5] ρ is the contemporaneous correlation between ϵ_t and v_t. It implies that $E(y_t) \neq 0$; however, the effect is small. Alternatively, ρ can be defined as $\mathrm{Cor}(\epsilon_t, v_{t+1})$, with a minor modification of (9.25).

In fact, JPR2 report that practical convergence did not happen; q_1 produced a very inefficient algorithm that would not close in on ρ no matter how long it ran or where it started from. If the issue was only about the rate of convergence, it was still too severe for us to wait for it to happen. Autocorrelations in the sequence of draws were not abnormally high, revealing nothing pathological. Recall that a key to performance in accept/reject and Hastings-Metropolis is how well the blanket approximates the desired posterior p. Specifically, if the ratio p/q is unbounded, the algorithm cannot be uniformly ergodic. It turns out that, in this model, a little extra work on q dramatically improves performance. JPR2 approximate $\frac{u_t}{\sqrt{h_t}}$ in (9.25) as a linear function in $\frac{1}{h_t}$, which can then be incorporated in the inverse gamma kernel. This yields a new proposal density, q_2, also inverse gamma.

A key diagnostic tool here and for any independence HM algorithm, is a plot of p/q for a wide range of values of h_t as the algorithm evolves. Figure 9.3 demonstrates this for a given h_t. The right plot shows that the ratio p/q_2 is much more stable than p/q_1 over a wide range of h_t. The left plot, where the kernels are normalized so as to be plotted together, shows that q_2 is right over p, while q_1 misses it. It is worse than q_1 not approximating the shape of p as well as q_2; it is that q_1 is in the wrong place. This is because the third term in the exponent of (9.25) often does not not have a mode; so it modifies the distribution kernel in the first two terms by shifting them. For independence MH algorithms, one should make sure that the ratio p/q is stable, specifically that it is not unbounded (see Mengersen and Tweedie 1994).

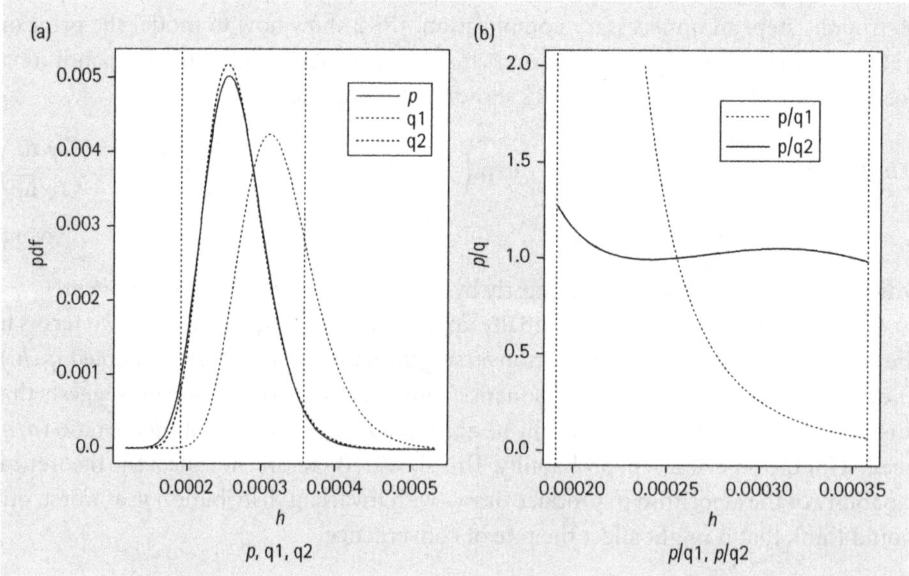

FIGURE 9.3 Improving the blanket density for the correlated model

5.2.3 *Volatility predictions for different models*

The literature is replete with simulation studies documenting parameter estimation. This is a good first step, but we are especially interested in the volatility densities produced by different models, especially future volatilities. Volatility forecasts are vehicles for risk management and option pricing. Do different models produce different forecasts, and in what circumstances? Bayesian MCMC algorithms deliver the marginal posterior density of the vector in-sample volatilities **h**. One draws the predictive densities of future volatilities, by simply drawing the future shocks v_{T+k}s, and using the AR(1) equation to obtain the future h_{T+k}s, for each draw of $(\mathbf{h}, \omega)$.

While the posterior odds (see below) provide one summary diagnostic, we can use these posterior and predictive densities to compare the outputs of competing models. In this case, we want to know whether differences between the models matter in their economic magnitudes. For the weekly US NYSE index return, JPR2 estimate the following SV models: basic, with correlated errors, with fat tails, and with both. A first important question is if and when these models produce different posterior densities for volatilities. We concentrate here on the posterior means. Figure 9.4, left-hand plot, shows the ratio of posterior means of h_t produced by the fat-tail and basic SV models, $E(h_{t,Fat})/E(h_{t,basic})$ versus the posterior mean of the mixing variable, $\sqrt{E(\lambda_t)}$. It clearly matters which model we choose. The model allowing for fat tails predicts markedly lower volatilities, especially for a number of observations where it estimates larger lambdas.

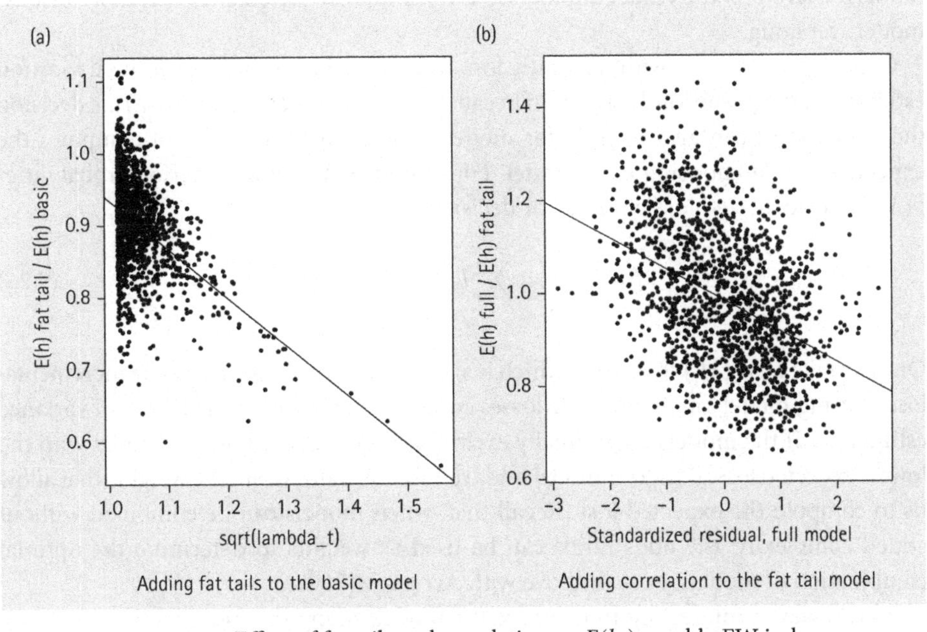

FIGURE 9.4 Effect of fat tails and correlation on $E(h_t)$; weekly EW index

Consider now adding correlated errors to the SV models with fat tails. The posterior mean of ρ for these data is -0.4. Figure 9.4, right-hand side, plots the ratio of posterior means of h_t for the full versus the fat-tailed model versus the posterior mean of ϵ_t (for the full model). Again, the choice of model appears to matter greatly. Observations with negative ϵ_t have larger volatility. The average ratio on the vertical axis is 1.09 for the first decile of ϵ, and only 0.9 for the tenth decile (right tail), a 20% difference.

Returning to the fat tails; does it matter if, as Figure 9.4 shows, the model with fat tails allocates some of the h_t into λ_t? The top plot in Figure 9.5 shows the daily change in the UK Pound to dollar ratio in 1985. An agent can implement the basic or the fat-tailed model. The thick line in the middle plot shows $E(\sqrt{h_t})$ for the basic model, the dashed line shows $E(\sqrt{h_t})$ for the fat-tailed model. The ragged line is $E(\sqrt{h_t\lambda_t})$; it shows that λ_t is far more than just a device to implement the Student-t errors. The model allocates a large λ_t mostly to the days that have a high h_t under the basic model. Then, the fat-tailed model will predict lower future volatility than the basic model, because λ_t does not have any persistence. These high volatility days are those when getting the best possible volatility prediction is crucial for a risk manager. The bottom plot shows out-of-sample forecasts originating from September 23, confirming this intuition. The two models can make very different volatility predictions, especially for high volatility days.

5.2.4 *The cost of a model*

The loss function approach allows an agent to summarize the cost of making the wrong decision. Our purpose here is illustrative, possibly more than normative, because with actual data, even the best inference will rarely lead to certainty as to the right and wrong models. Therefore, the reader should see the sections of the chapter where we discuss model averaging.

Consider an investor with quadratic loss. The posterior mean is an optimal location estimate on the posterior distribution because it minimizes expected loss. This decision theoretic aspect can also be used for model choice, whereby the agent computes the expected loss of choosing each model. For J models M_j with posterior probabilities $p(M_j|.)$, the expected loss of model or decision i is:

$$EL(M_i|.) = \sum_j L(M_i|M_j)p(M_j|.). \tag{9.26}$$

One can take $L(M_i|M_i)$ to be zero, which is a way of writing $L(M_i|M_j)$ as the incremental loss of using model i if j is true. The losses could, for example, be the RMSE of variance estimation. If the models are mutually exclusive, then one chooses the model with the lowest expected loss. Posterior model odds ratios, normalized, are the weights that allow us to compute the expected loss. Recall that, when models can be combined without added complexity, the odds ratios can be used as weights to determine the optimal combination of models, as seen above with Avramov (2002).

It is, however, interesting to compare the models along the loss function in (9.26). Consider an agent contemplating incorporating fat tails into a basic SV model. She

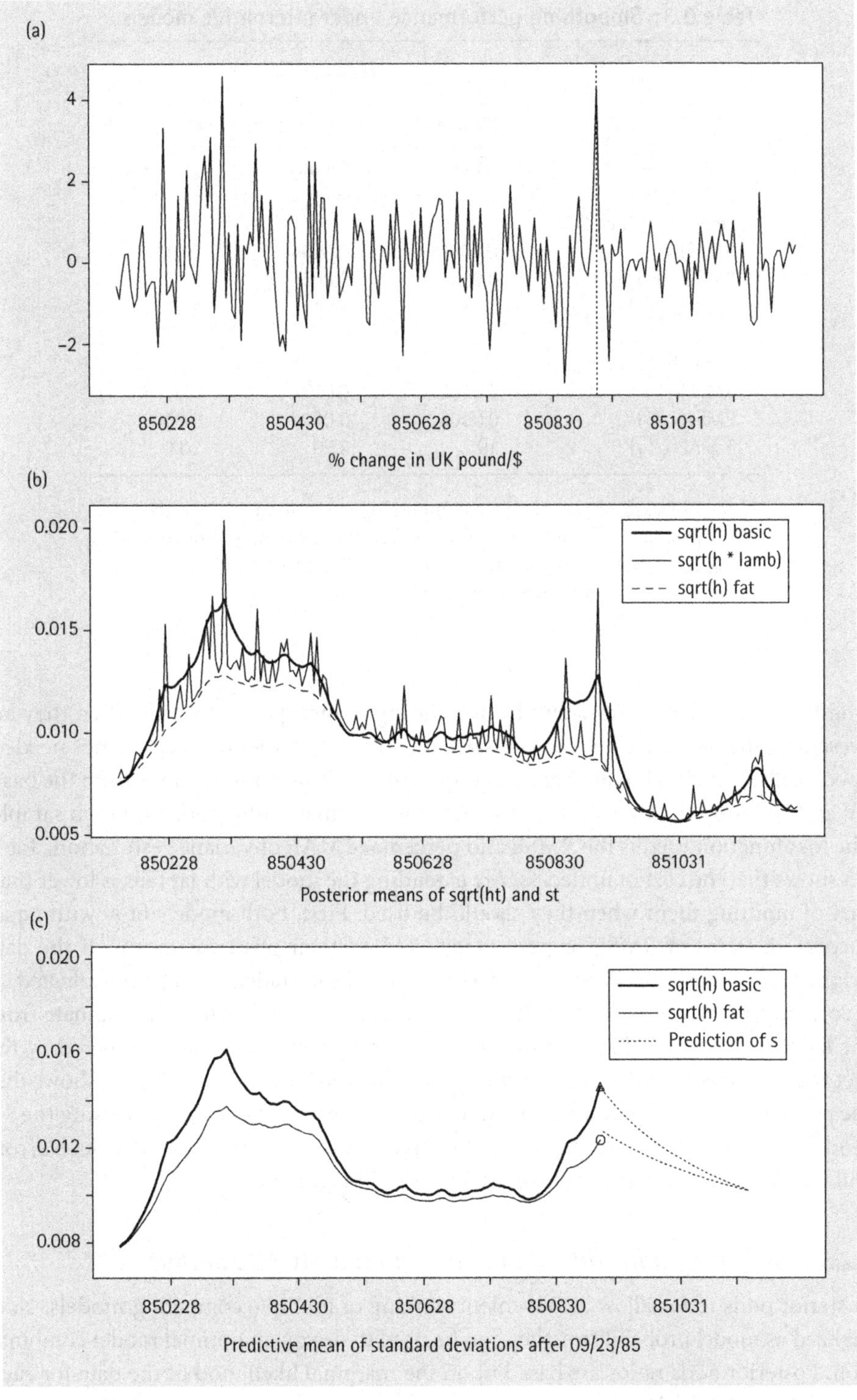

FIGURE 9.5 Differences between fat-tail and basic SV volatility forecasts

Table 9.3: Smoothing performance under alternative models

	Data generated by		
	Basic model	Fat-tailed model $\nu = 10$	
	All obs.	All obs	$\lambda_t > \lambda_{.9}$
Estimate fat-tailed SV			
RMSE(s_t)	0.0066	0.0104	0.0198
RMSE($\sqrt{h_t}$)	0.0066	0.0071	0.0076
%MAE($\sqrt{h_t}$)	18.3	21.4	23.7
Estimate basic SV			
RMSE(s_t)	0.0066	0.0107	0.0198
RMSE($\sqrt{h_t}$)	0.0066	0.0082	0.0098
%MAE($\sqrt{h_t}$)	19.2	25.9	30.6

Notes: For each observation, we compute the estimation error of the posterior mean of $\sqrt{h_t}$ and $s_t = \sqrt{h_t \lambda_t}$. When the data are generated by the fat-tailed SV, we also report RMSE and %MAE for the observations with a λ_t larger than the 90th percentile of $p(\lambda \mid \nu = 10)$.

wonders what penalty may result from omitting to incorporate fat tails when they are present in the data, or from unnecessarily incorporating them if they are not needed. Specifically, JPR (2004) simulate 500 samples of $T = 1,000$ observations from the basic SV and 500 from the SV with fat tails. They then estimate both models on each sample. The loss function used is the RMSE and percentage MAE of variance estimation. Table 9.3 shows that the cost of unnecessarily extending the model with fat tails is lower than that of omitting them when they should be used. First, both models fit s_t with equal success, in terms of RMSE or percentage MAE of their posterior means. If the data originate from the basic SV model, inference from the fat-tailed model is not affected, as it correctly allocates very little volatility to the λ_t's. However, if the data originate from the fat-tailed model, inference from the basic SV model is seriously hampered by the fact that it lumps λ_t and h_t into its view of h_t. The third column in Table 9.3 shows that the problem becomes quite severe on days when there was a large λ_t, while using the SV model results in a 24% MAE for $\sqrt{h_t}$, compared to 31% for the basic model. Such errors will transfer into volatility forecasts, as was seen in Figure 9.5.

5.2.5 Computing odds ratios directly from the MCMC output

Posterior odds ratios allow a convenient ranking of multiple competing models. Normalized as model probabilities, they can be used to design an optimal model combination. Posterior odds ratios are based upon the marginal likelihood of the data for each model. For a model M_0, we have:

$$p(y|M_0) = \int p(y|\theta_0, M_0)\, p(\theta_0|M_0)\, d\theta_0.$$

This marginal likelihood can be a source of computational difficulties; for any reasonably complex model, it does not have an analytical integral. In addition, with latent variables such as $\mathbf{h}$, even the conditional likelihood $p(y|\theta_0, M_0)$ itself does not have an analytical integral. Therefore, as much as possible, one should avoid computing this integral directly. Note also that the integral in the marginal likelihood requires proper priors. For the SV class of models, Jacquier and Polson (2000) follow Newton and Raftery (1994) and show how to compute the odds ratios directly from the MCMC posterior output of $(\mathbf{h}, \omega, \boldsymbol{\lambda}, \nu|\mathbf{y})$, without resorting to a direct evaluation of the marginal likelihood. They use the Savage density ratio method for an odds ratio on correlated errors, and Student's formula for an odds ratio on fat-tailed errors. Quantities are computed at each iteration of the MCMC posterior simulator; their Monte Carlo average delivers the odds ratios. This is fast because the posterior draws are already available from the posterior parameter and volatility sampler. We now review this methodology.

Odds for correlated errors In the SV model with correlated errors, the density of ρ follows by direct draw from that of ψ, Ω. Posterior analysis is intuitive, especially since we can formulate a very flat, but proper, prior for ρ. Since the basic SV, where $\rho = 0$, is nested in the correlated errors SV, we can use the efficient Savage density ratio method (see Dickey 1971). Consider two models $\mathcal{M}_1$: (ϕ, ω) and $\mathcal{M}_0$: $\omega = \omega_0$. If $p_1(\phi|\omega = \omega_0) = p_0(\phi)$, then:

$$\text{BF}_{0/1} = \frac{p_1(\omega_0|y)}{p_1(\omega_0)}.$$

The computation is done under the nesting model, and only requires ordinates of the posterior and prior densities of the parameter to be restricted. If the posterior ordinate of $p_1(\omega)$ at ω_0 is larger than the prior ordinate, the Bayes factor favors the restricted model.

The ratio requires the exact ordinates, so that it can't be applied to parameters drawn by Metropolis for which we only know the kernel of the density. This is another reason why algorithms that do not draw ρ or ν directly would be problematic. JPR (2004) use the Savage density ratio method on ψ, the slope coefficient in the regression (9.24). We have $\psi = 0$ for the basic SV model denoted B, the correlated model is denoted C, and the Bayes factor is the ratio of ordinates:

$$BF_{B|C} \frac{p_C(\psi = 0|\mathbf{y})}{p_C(\psi = 0)}.$$

The marginal posterior ordinate $p_C(\psi = 0|\mathbf{y})$ is obtained by integrating out all the other parameters and state variables. The density of ψ conditional on the other parameters is normally distributed, the slope of a regression; Ω can be integrated analytically, which yields a Student-t for $p_C(\psi|\mathbf{h}, \alpha, \delta, \mathbf{y})$. The integration of the other parameters is done by averaging the Student-t ordinate over the draws of the MCMC sampler. The Bayes factor can be approximated by

$$\widehat{\mathcal{BF}}_{B/C} = \frac{\Gamma(\frac{\nu_0+T}{2})\Gamma(\frac{\nu_0}{2})}{\Gamma(\frac{\nu_0+T-1}{2})\Gamma(\frac{\nu_0+1}{2})} \frac{1}{G} \sum_{g=1}^{G} \sqrt{\frac{1+a_{11}^{(g)}/p_0}{1+a_{22.1}^{(g)}/\nu_0 t_0^2}} \left[1+\frac{\tilde{\psi}^2}{\nu_1 t_1^2/p_1}^{(g)}\right]^{-\frac{\nu_0+T}{2}}, \quad (9.27)$$

where a_{11} and $a_{22.1}$, vary with the parameter draw (g) (see JPR2 for details). Note the averaging over the G draws of the MCMC sampler. The odds ratio only requires computing and cumulating the quantity on the right of the summation sign at each iteration of the sampler.

Odds for normal versus fat-tailed errors The posterior for ν is not a convenient vehicle for a formal odds ratio between the SV models with fat-tailed and normal errors. Since ν has a finite upper bound in JPR 2, $\nu \in [5, 60]$, the model with fat-tailed errors does not nest the one with normal errors. The fat-tailed model could nest the basic model with Geweke's (1994) parameterization in $1/\nu$; however, another condition necessary to the application of the Savage density ratio, $0 < p(\omega = \omega_0|D)$, would not be met, because the posterior goes to zero as $1/\nu \to 0$.

The following method helps circumvent the direct computation of the marginal likelihood. By Bayes theorem, with simple rearrangement of terms, the marginal likelihood for model $\mathcal{M}_1$ can be written as:

$$p_1(\mathrm{y}) = \frac{\mathrm{p}_1(\mathrm{y}|\omega,\psi)\mathrm{p}_1(\omega,\psi)}{\mathrm{p}_1(\omega,\psi|\mathrm{y})}. \quad (9.28)$$

This holds for any (ω, ψ) in the parameter space and is known as Student's formula (see Besag 1989). Chib (1995) proposes to use (9.28) directly to compute the marginal likelihood, by averaging the right-hand side over the Monte Carlo draws. It might be computationally unstable as it involves a high-dimension likelihood. Jacquier and Polson (2000) show instead that (9.28) can be incorporated into the computation of the Bayes factor, as follows:

$$BF_{0|1} = \int \frac{p_0(\mathrm{y}|\omega)\mathrm{p}_0(\omega)\mathrm{d}\omega}{p_1(\mathrm{y})} = \int \left[\int \frac{p_0(\mathrm{y}|\omega)\mathrm{p}_0(\omega)\mathrm{d}\omega}{p_1(\mathrm{y})}\right] p_1(\psi)d\psi$$
$$= \int\int \frac{p_0(\mathrm{y}|\omega)\mathrm{p}_0(\omega)}{p_1(\mathrm{y}|\omega,\psi)\mathrm{p}_1(\omega|\psi)} p_1(\omega,\psi|\mathrm{y})\mathrm{d}\psi\,\mathrm{d}\omega,$$

which is:

$$BF_{0|1} = E_{\omega,\psi|\mathrm{y}}\left[\frac{p_0(\mathrm{y}|\omega)}{p_1(\mathrm{y}|\omega,\psi)} \frac{p_0(\omega)}{p_1(\omega|\psi)}\right]. \quad (9.29)$$

The expectation is taken with respect to the posterior draws of ω, ψ in the larger model. In this general formulation, the domain for ψ in the larger model does not need to contain the values which represent the smaller model. For example, an SV model with Student-t errors with fixed degrees of freedom can be compared with the basic SV model, even though the latter corresponds to infinite degrees of freedom. Jacquier and Polson (2000) and JPR2 apply (9.29) to compute the Bayes factor for the fat-tailed versus the basic SV model:

$$BF_{B|F} = E_{\theta,\nu}\left[\frac{p_B(\mathbf{y}|\theta)\, p_B(\theta)}{p_F(\mathbf{y}|\theta,\nu)\, p_F(\theta|\nu)}\right],$$

where $\theta = (\alpha, \delta, \sigma_v, \mathbf{h})$, and E refers to the expectation over the joint posterior of (θ, ν) in the fat-tailed model. The choice of priors allows us to further simplify the result; with ν independent from the other parameters, we have $p_F(\theta|\nu) = p_F(\theta)$, and $p_F(\theta) = p_B(\theta)$. Therefore, the Bayes factor is only the ratio:

$$BF_{B|F} = E\left[\frac{p_B(\mathbf{y}|\theta)}{p_F(\mathbf{y}|\theta,\nu)}\right]. \tag{9.30}$$

Given an MCMC sample $\{\theta^g, \nu^g\}_{g=1}^G$ from the joint posterior $p_1(\theta, \nu|y)$, a Monte Carlo estimate of (9.30) is:

$$\widehat{BF}_{B|F} = \frac{1}{G}\sum_{g=1}^{G}\frac{p_B(\mathbf{y}|\theta^{(g)})}{p_F(\mathbf{y}|\theta^{(g)},\nu^{(g)})}. \tag{9.31}$$

Under M_B, $y_t \sim \sqrt{h_t}N(0,1)$, and under M_F, $y_t \sim \sqrt{h_t}$ Student-$t(\nu)$. Because we condition on $\mathbf{h}$, the likelihoods in the Bayes factors (9.30) are simple products of independent univariate densities. Since we only need a ratio of likelihoods conditional on the parameters at every draw, and not the likelihood of each model, their magnitude does not cause computational problems.

Further, (9.30) easily extends to the computation of $BF_{C|FC}$, the Bayes factor of the model with correlated errors over the full model. A draw of $(\alpha, \delta, \sigma_v, \mathbf{h})$, implies a draw for all v_ts. In the presence of correlation, it also provides information on the ϵ_ts, specifically, $\epsilon_t|v_t \sim N(\rho v_t, 1-\rho^2)$. One, therefore, extends (9.30) to the computation of $BF_{C|CF}$, by replacing y_t with $y_t^* = (y_t - \rho v_t)/\sqrt{1-\rho^2}$.

Empirical results JPR (2004) apply this method to compute odds ratios among the models for a number of financial series. They report odds that largely favor the general SV model with fat tails and correlated errors against the basic SV, for all stock indices and most exchange rates. For all exchange rates but the Canadian to US one, the odds, between three and ten to one, moderately favor the model with fat-tailed errors for weekly data. For daily data, the odds overwhelmingly favor the fat-tailed errors. For most indices, the odds very strongly favor the model with correlated errors. The full model is overwhelmingly favored over the basic SV model for all indices and exchange rates.

We report here some additional results on the leverage effect, contrasting indices, and individual stocks. Table 9.4 shows the posterior means of ν and ρ for the full model, and the Bayes factors. For individual stocks, the posterior distributions of ρ are centered very close to zero. The odds ratios moderately favor the models with no correlation. Yet, JPR

Table 9.4: Odds ratios for leverage effect, daily stock returns 1978–1998

	1978–1998			1989–1998
Company	ν	ρ	$BF_{F/FC}$	$BF_{F/FC}$
Merck	10	−0.05	5.3	1.5
Boeing	8	−0.02	7.1	4.1
Dole Food	6	0.02	3.8	1.7
H.P.	8	−0.07	4.4	2.3
Fedex	6	0.08	5.4	0.6
Ford	12	−0.01	8.9	7.1
Sony	8	0.11	1.2	0.4
Fleet Bank	10	0.03	4.3	3.5
Exxon	11	0.01	6.6	3.6
Merrill Lynch	9	0.00	9.3	2.5
Average	9	0.01		
Portfolio	10	−0.23	0.22	1.E−03

Notes:F: fat-tail, FC: full model, 25,000 posterior draws.

(2004) report strong odds in favor of correlated errors for all the indices studied. The last row in Table 9.4 estimates the SV models and odds ratios for a portfolio of the ten stocks above. There is now a negative correlation, and the odds ratio is in favor of the correlated errors. However, leverage can not be the cause of this effect since it does not appear with the individual stocks that exhibit as much variation in leverage as the portfolio. It is sometimes proposed that the correlation ρ can be driven by a small number of exceptional days in the sample. October 19, 1987, comes to mind. The last column of Table 9.4 shows the Bayes factors for the 1989–98 period. The result is the opposite to what is expected. Again, the odds are moderately against the correlated model for most stocks; however, they very strongly favor the correlated model for the portfolio; in fact, far more strongly than for the period that contains October 19.

The hypothesis of volatility feedback, often advanced as an alternative to the leverage effect, could not affect portfolios but not the stocks that constitute these portfolios. The negative correlation between return and volatility shocks of indices must be the result of a portfolio effect; arising from a time-variation in the correlation matrix of the stocks. A two-regime model for the correlation matrix of individual stock returns could be a fruitful avenue of research.

5.3 Estimating continuous time models

The theoretical option-pricing literature uses continuous-time processes, mainly because of their ability to produce tractable option-pricing models. Data are however observed at discrete times. To estimate a continuous-time model from discrete data, one uses its Euler discretization, which approximates the continuous trajectory of the process into a discrete one between the successive data intervals. For example, the following continuous-time constant elasticity of variance (CEV) model of the short rate:

$$dY_t = (\theta + \kappa Y_t)dt + \sigma Y_t^{\beta} dw_t,$$

is approximated by the discrete time process:

$$Y_t = \theta + (1 + \kappa)Y_{t-1} + \sigma Y_{t-1}^{\beta} w_t, w_t \sim N(0, 1).$$

This introduces a bias in the drift and diffusion parameters. We now discuss Bayesian methods that alleviate this discretization bias. Eraker (2001) concentrates on the specification of the diffusion process; Jones (2003a) develops independently a very similar technique, and studies the specification of the drift of the short-term rate.

The discretization bias disappears as the time between observations becomes shorter. This is the motivation for the Bayesian approach in Eraker (2001). He introduces $m - 1$ missing data between each observation. Consider the process $Y_i = (X_i, Z_i)$, where X_i is observed every m periods and Z_i can be a latent variable such as stochastic volatility; both X and Y can be multidimensional. If we knew the missing data, the discretization bias would be diminished as we would be converging to continuous time. Given these missing data, denoted $\widehat{X}$, the model is a standard discrete time model. Posterior analysis can be conducted with known Bayesian techniques; that is, we can draw from $p(\theta|\widehat{Y})$, where θ is the vector of parameters.

The final intuition comes from Gibbs sampling: if we can draw from the missing data given θ and the observed data X, we have a complete model to improve upon the discretization bias. Eraker (2001) shows how to do this for the CEV or stochastic volatility models. His method also applies to other processes. Let $\widehat{Y}_i$ be the time i element of the matrix $\hat{Y}$, where X_i is observed or is a missing value $\widehat{X}_i$. Given a draw of θ, Eraker updates $\widehat{Y}_i$ sequentially, drawing from $p(\widehat{Y}_i|\widehat{Y}_{i-1}, \widehat{Y}_{i+1}, \theta)$ for $i \in [1, \ldots, mT]$. Of course one does not update the observed values. By Bayes theorem, this update is shown to be:

$$p(\widehat{Y}_i|\widehat{Y}_{i-1}, \widehat{Y}_{i+1}, \theta) \;\propto\; p(\widehat{Y}_i|\widehat{Y}_{i-1}, \theta)\, p(\widehat{Y}_{i+1}|\widehat{Y}_i, \theta). \tag{9.32}$$

Both conditional discretized densities on the right-hand side are simple Gaussians given θ. Eraker characterizes (9.32) for a number of underlying processes. For constant drift and diffusion, we obtain $\widehat{Y}_i \sim N(\frac{1}{2}(\widehat{Y}_{i-1} + \widehat{Y}_{i+1}), \frac{1}{2}\frac{\sigma^2}{m})$, from which one can draw directly. For other processes, Eraker uses this density as the proposal for a Metropolis-Hastings draw.

As the number of missing data increases, one converges to the continuous time model; however as one converges to continuous time, the MCMC algorithm slows down due to the larger number of observations. Eraker (2001) shows by simulation that the algorithm still works fairly well even with 20 filled-in data. For actual data, posterior densities stabilize quickly as one keeps filling in missing data. Eraker (2001) estimates a CEV model with 2,288 weekly T-bill yields from 1954 to 1997. He finds that the three parameter posterior densities are unchanged after filling in four missing data between each observed data. Remarkably, his posterior mean for the CEV parameter is 0.76. He then estimates an SV model with CEV, and again, the parameter posterior densities only require four filled-in data to stabilize. An estimation with eight filled-in data does not show any change in the posteriors. See also Elerian et al. (2001) who study the diffusion case.

Jones (2003a), with a very similar approach, estimates the drift of a continuous time model for the short rate. He also finds that posterior distributions stabilize after the introduction of a few missing data. His posterior characterization of the drift is very different from that obtained with maximum likelihood analysis.

He incorporates this approach in Jones (2003b), where he examines the ability of generalized CEV models of stochastic volatility to generate the necessary features of the conditional returns distribution in periods of high variance. An interesting feature of Jones (2003b) is that he incorporates the information on volatility contained in option prices. First, he notes that expected average variance over the remaining life of an option is approximately linear in current variance for the processes used: $E^{Q}[V_{t,T}] \approx A + BV_t$. The coefficients A, B are known parametric functions of the variance process and the price of volatility risk. Second, he notes that Black-Scholes implied volatility is a proxy for $E^{Q}[V_{t,T}]$, the better when the option is close to the money. He, therefore, incorporates into the modeling the following link:

$$IV_t = A + BV_t + \epsilon_t, \quad \epsilon_t \sim N(0, \xi^2 V_t^2),$$

where IV_t is obtained from the VIX index. The ensuing MCMC algorithm requires a non-trivial draw for most blocks, because the posterior distributions are complicated by the link between implied and current volatilities, and the fact that A, B are non-linear functions of the process parameters. This is, however, an interesting way to bring information from the option prices into the estimation of the volatility process, without estimating option prices themselves.

5.4 Jumps

Chib et al. (2002) model an additive jump process in the returns equation of the discrete time SV model. This can be seen as an alternative to the fat-tailed conditional returns seen in Section 5.2.2.

Eraker et al. (2003), hereafter EJP, compare SV models with additive jump components in both the returns and variance equations. They discretize the continuous time models for daily US index returns, and do not implement the improvement discussed in section 5.3, making the case that the discretization bias is small for these daily returns. EJP start from existing results in the literature, which show how SV models with jumps in returns do not account well for the features of historical returns or option prices. They argue that jumps in volatility create a dynamic for both returns and volatility that is far different from added diffusion factors or jumps in returns. EJP consider several models nested within the general (discretized) specification:

$$R_{t+1} = \mu + \sqrt{V_t}\epsilon^r_{t+1} + \xi^r_{t+1}J^r_{t+1}$$
$$V_{t+1} = \kappa\theta + (1-\kappa)V_t + \sigma_v\epsilon^v_{t+1} + \xi^v_{t+1}J^v_{t+1}$$

The jump density is modeled as $J_t\xi_t$, where a jump occurs when $J_t = 1$. The jump intensities are λ^r, λ^v. Relative to the SV model, the parameter domain is extended to the vectors of jump states J^v, J^r and the jump intensity parameters λ^r, λ^v. EJP distinguish the following nested models: SV is the basic stochastic volatility model; SVJ adds the jumps in returns $\xi^r \sim N(\mu_r, \sigma_r)$; SVJC allows for correlated jumps: $\xi^v \sim \exp(\mu_v)$ for volatility; and $\xi^r|\xi^v \sim N(\mu_r + \rho_J\xi^v, \sigma_r^2)$ for returns. In SVIJ, the jumps are independent.

Bayesian inference allows the use of priors to impose constraints on the parameter space, without which the likelihood could be unbounded. The useful priors are those of jump size, intensity, and volatility. Here the prior is used to model large and rare movements in returns, with a low λ^r and a large σ^r. EJP's prior places low probability of jump standard deviation below 1%, and on more than a 10% chance of a daily jump. The priors of the other parameters are left uninformative. The MCMC algorithm draws iteratively from the following blocks of the posterior density of parameters and state variables:

(1) parameters: $p(\theta_i|\theta_{-i}, J, \xi, V, R) i = 1, .., K$
(2) jump times: $p(J_t = 1|\theta, \xi, V, R), t = 1, .., T$
(3) jump sizes: $p(\xi^r|\theta, \xi^v, J, V, R) : p(\xi^r|\theta, \xi^v, J, V, R)$
(4) volatilities: $p(V|\theta, J, \xi, R)$

Blocks 1, 2, and 3, the extensions of the basic SV model, can be drawn directly. The ability to analyze models of this level of complexity testifies to the flexibility of the hierarchical formulation used together with Bayesian MCMC methods. If there are concerns that the data may contain little information about some features of such a complex model, recall that the posterior draws will simply reflect this uncertainty. This is in contrast with the potential computational difficulties in attempting to numerically maximize the likelihood (unavailable analytically) of such a model. See Jacquier et al. (2007) for a maximum likelihood approach that exploits the simplicity of the Bayesian MCMC algorithm.

EJP also compute odds ratios for the various jump extensions. They avoid the computation of the marginal likelihood, which is not readily available for these complex models. Instead, they are able to rewrite the odds ratios in terms of posterior quantities. For example, the odds ratio of SVJ versus SV is a function of the probability that the entire vector of jumps J is equal to zero. The MCMC posterior simulator draws from this known probability (block 2 above). The odds ratios, therefore, involve only a minor additional computation at each step of the MCMC simulator. This extension of the Savage density ratio method is possible because the conditional density of the vectors J^r, J^v is available analytically. For the daily NASDAQ 100 and SP500, the Bayes factors show that the data strongly favor jumps in the volatility rather than in the return equations.

5.5 Estimating covariance matrices and betas

5.5.1 *Modeling the covariance matrix*

Even when it is not time varying, the estimation of the covariance matrix of a large vector of stock returns poses serious problems. It is full rank mathematically as long as the number of periods T is equal to or larger than N; however, it takes a sample far larger than N to obtain sufficient information on, for instance, the smallest Eigen value. Optimal portfolio weights are often functions of the inverse of the covariance matrix; therefore, in small samples, a lot of uncertainty on the smaller Eigen value will result in possible instability for the inverse of the matrix, in turn, affecting the optimal portfolio weights.

The factor model is a unique way of reducing dimensionality. It is also tightly related to finance modeling, for example, the APT. When factors are latent, Gibbs sampling makes it possible to draw the factors and their loadings, as shown in Geweke and Zhou (1995). The constraint is effective when the residual covariance matrix is assumed to be diagonal. The factor model is a very effective way to constrain the covariance matrix since it replaces $N(N+1)/2$ parameters by $K(K+1)/2 + (N+1)K$. Aguilar and West (2000) implement an algorithm, suggested in Jacquier et al. (1995), that extends the factor model to allow for stochastic volatility in the factors. See also Chib et al. (2006) for discussions of multivariate SV algorithms.

Another approach is the variance/correlation decomposition, where the covariance matrix is written as $D^{0.5}CD^{0.5}$ (see Barnard et al. 2000 and Engle's dynamical conditional correlations DCC model). The individual variances in D can follow univariate GARCH or SV models. The correlation matrix can then be modeled separately from the variances, perhaps with regimes. Regime switching models are conveniently estimated by Bayesian methods, most of the time requiring no more than direct Gibbs draws. See McCulloch and Tsay (1993) and Ghysels et al. (1998) for Bayesian estimation of univariate switching models in means and variances.

5.5.2 *Modeling betas*

Recall the factor model from the APT section. Geweke and Zhou (1995), McCulloch and Rossi (1990, 1991), and many others, assume that B, the matrix of factor loadings, is constant. It may, indeed, be too much to ask from the data, in latent variables models, to deliver precise inference on both time-varying betas and factor scores.

In many cases, however, the factors are considered observable, and it may become practical to allow for time-varing betas. In fact, modern intertemporal asset-pricing models imply that betas time-vary and are related to economy-wide or firm-specific state variables. Empirical work has so far mostly used basic rolling window filters to estimate betas. Also, even if one maintains that firm betas are constant, this assumption may be less tenable if one studies managed portfolios. Finally, with very few observable factors, time-varying betas may provide a more flexible specification for a time-varying covariance matrix. Jostova and Philipov (2005) use an MCMC algorithm to draw the betas, considered as unobservable latent state variables.

Cosemans et al. (2009) design a Bayesian estimator of betas that combines the cross-section and the time series. Within this framework, they show that the fit is improved by the cross-section, and the resulting out-of-sample forecasts improve portfolio performance. Cosemans et al. is a very interesting example where the simultaneous use of the time series and the cross-section yields predictive improvements. Their criterion is economic-based, as they assess competing models through their impact on optimal portfolio design.

6 Bayesian Inference in Option Pricing

Option prices depend on a number of factors. Some are known, such as the strike price and the time to maturity, and some are assumed to be known in most models, for example, interest rates, future dividend yields. Volatility, assumed to be known to the investor in the Black-Scholes and other earlier models, is unknown to the econometrician. Volatility over the remaining life of the option is assumed to be unknown to the investor in most modern models. Modeling the uncertainty in volatility is, therefore, a crucial aspect of the econometrics option pricing.

Econometric methods in option pricing take three main approaches. First, one can obtain information from the historical return process and use it to infer the option price; the likelihood comes from the historical return and variance process. Second, one can use option prices to draw inference directly on the risk-neutral process. In this case, the likelihood is formed from the pricing errors. This approach generally uses panels of options spanning a range of moneyness and maturity. A third segment of the literature attempts to combine the historical and pricing information in the likelihood. In this case, it is generally assumed that the historical and risk-neutral processes, of volatility for example, are of the same family, differing only by a drift shift due to the price of volatility risk.

Another strategic choice to be made is how to compute the option price itself. A relatively easily computed, semi-analytical option-pricing formula may be available, based on the model parameters, in the simpler cases, for example with deterministic volatility. In the more complex cases, the flexibility of the Monte Carlo method pays off. It extends the risk-neutral pricing methodology where the option price of a call of maturity T and exercise price K is:

$$C_T = e^{-r_f(T-t)} E_t^Q \left[Max(S_T - K, 0) \right], \tag{9.33}$$

where r_f is the appropriate risk-free rate, and E^Q is the risk-neutral expectation (see Cox and Ross 1976). For example, one simulates from the predictive density of the state variables, such as volatility, until maturity, each time computing the option payoff at maturity. The average of these discounted payoffs is the Monte Carlo estimate of the option price. This approach is generally referred to as predictive option pricing. This predictive approach is more effective for the latter class of option-pricing models, especially with stochastic volatility or jumps. The Bayesian implementation of (9.33) naturally incorporates in the predictive draws the posterior uncertainty on the parameter. This is in contrast with a conditional predictive implementation of (9.33) which would condition on a value of the parameters.

6.1 Likelihood based on underlying return only

Early empirical practice has been to substitute point estimates of σ, either historical or implied, into the Black-Scholes formula. However, even the simplest option-pricing model is a non-linear function of σ. Due to the non-linearity and the uncertainty in σ, the substitution of a point estimate into the option formula may lead to biases, in addition to failing to reflect the effect of the uncertainty of σ on the price. Karolyi (1993), the first Bayesian empirical option paper, addresses both issues. It adopts an empirical Bayes approach to reduce the uncertainty in σ_i, which is estimated from the history of the underlying stock return R_i, itself assumed to be lognormally distributed (μ, σ_i) in the model. Precision comes from cross-sectional shrinkage: Karolyi chooses a common conjugate prior for σ_i with location parameter τ and dispersion parameter ν (see Zellner 1971, appendix B). This yields the posterior density for σ_i given the history of underlying returns R_i:

$$p(\sigma_i|R_i) \propto \left(\frac{1}{\sigma_i^2}\right)^{\frac{\nu_i+\nu+2}{2}+1} \exp\left(-\frac{\nu_i s_i^2 + \nu\tau}{2\sigma_i^2}\right),$$

where $\nu_i = T_i - 1$, T_i is the sample size for the returns of asset i, and $\nu_i s_i^2$ is the sum of squared deviations of the R_i's from their sample mean. He obtains τ by the method of moments, where τ is essentially an average of the individual sample variances. Given τ, he assumes that the individual returns series R_i's are uncorrelated, and obtains ν by maximizing the log-likelihood $\log L(\nu, \tau)$. It can be seen that ν increases as the cross-sectional dispersion of the sample estimates of variance s_i^2 decreases. Here, empirical Bayes is used to obtain tighter posterior densities for the σ_i's by shrinkage.

Karolyi then points out that substituting a point estimate of σ_i into the Black-Scholes formula is inappropriate. He computes the Black-Scholes price as the expectation of Black-Scholes prices over the posterior density of σ_i, using the Monte Carlo average of the draws as the Black-Scholes estimate. This approach takes into account the non-linearity of the Black-Scholes formula with respect to σ. Note that Karolyi's approach is consistent with a model with stochastic volatility and no premium for volatility risk. In such a case, the option price can be shown to be the expectation of the Black-Scholes price over the distribution of unknown volatility, (see Hull and White 1987). Volatility is stochastic for Karolyi because he only observes its posterior distribution.

This Bayesian Monte Carlo approach extends to draw from the predictive density of volatility over the maturity horizon of the option, for more general option pricing models. In fact, in Hull and White (1987), volatility follows an AR(1). A Bayesian implementation by MCMC will make posterior draws of the model parameters and in-sample volatilities, and will, for each draw, make a predictive draw of volatility up to the maturity of the option. Each draw will then yield a corresponding draw of the option price. The MCMC estimate of the Hull and White price is the average of these draws. The method generalizes to the Heston (1993) model, where volatility and return shocks are correlated. In that case, one needs to make joint draws of future returns and volatilities, which is a minor increase in complexity of the algorithm. The option price computed for each draw makes use of the final underlying asset value for each MC draw.

6.2 Risk-neutral predictive option pricing

When the option-pricing model has a non-zero price of volatility risk, the predictive method must take this into account, by simulating from the risk-neutral predictive density rather than the historical-based density. Bauwens and Lubrano (2002), hereafter BL, price options with risk-neutral GARCH volatility forecasts. Their risk-neutral process is given by:

$$r_t = r_f + v_t; \quad v_t \sim N(0, h_t), \qquad (9.34)$$

$$h_t = \omega + \alpha(v_{t-1} - \mu_{t-1} + r_f)^2 + \beta h_{t-1},$$

where returns earn the risk-free rate r_f. Consequently, the squared error in the GARCH equation is modified. BL use $\mu_t = \mu + \rho r_{t-1}$ for the historical return conditional expectation. It is important to note that this risk-neutral process, while theoretically motivated, will not be estimated through option prices, but from the historical returns.

The starting point in BL's analysis is a Bayesian estimation of GARCH models from returns data (see also Section 5.1 in this chapter). They report that the posterior means of the GARCH parameters imply considerably less persistence than the ML estimates. Being closer to the boundary of the parameter space, the ML estimates, especially their standard errors, are unreliable.

BL implement a Bayesian predictive pricing as per (9.33). For a maturity of K, this requires drawing returns $r_{t+k} \sim N(r, \omega + \alpha(r_{t+k-1} - \mu_{t-1}) + \beta h_{t+k-1})$, and computing the GARCH risk-neutral volatility h_{t+k}, for $k \in [1, K]$. These draws of the compounded returns yield prices at maturity that allow the computation of a Monte Carlo estimate of (9.33). BL make the important point that the convergence of the Monte Carlo estimate to the price occurs if the returns process is stationary; draws in the non-stationary region must, therefore, be rejected. In the GARCH analysis, such draws occur about 2% of the time.

The Bayesian implementation of (9.33) allows for the integration of parameter uncertainty because each new predictive draw is made given a new draw of the posterior distribution of the parameters, here $(\rho, \alpha, \beta, \mu)$. This is in contrast with alternative approaches that would condition on a point estimate of the parameters. BL make N posterior draws and M predictive draws for each posterior draw. They justify it by the computational cost of a posterior relative to a predictive draw. However, with the computational power now available, one can as well set $M = 1$ and N large (see Geweke 1989).

There is, however, a distinction between posterior and predictive draws. As per most models, the agent is assumed to know the parameters of the volatility process. Consequently, the N predictive draws reflect the Monte Carlo implementation of (9.33), but not an uncertainty about the option price. The price *is* the expectation of the payoff along this predictive density. The only use of the spread of these N predictive draws would be to make sure that the Monte Carlo estimate has the desired precision. In contrast, the econometrician does not know the parameters, and draws from the predictive density by mixing the posterior draws of the parameters. Due to the posterior uncertainty, the econometrician faces an option price uncertainty, which she might want to document. Then, setting $M > 1$, finding the option price by Monte Carlo averaging over N predictive draws for each posterior draw, would allow one to characterize the posterior uncertainty.

Eraker et al. (2003), discussed in Section 5.4, decompose the uncertainty on simulated option prices into their predictive and posterior components, but in a different manner. They characterize posterior uncertainty by conditioning the draws on the mean of predictive volatility, and volatility uncertainty by conditioning the draws on the posterior mean of the parameters. Their Figure 8 shows that parameter uncertainty has the largest impact for the longer-term options, and for extreme moneyness in shorter-term options.

6.3 Likelihood based upon pricing errors

6.3.1 Deterministic volatility functions

In the Black-Scholes model, the return standard deviation σ is assumed to be constant, and is known to the investor, who observes prices in continuous time. The theoretical price is obtained by a no-arbitrage argument, whereby the option can be exactly replicated, in continuous time, by a hedge portfolio of the underlying asset and a riskless bill. A family of extensions of the Black-Scholes model allows σ to vary as a deterministic function of the underlying price. This preserves the possibility of forming a hedge portfolio, since σ is still perfectly predictable conditional on the underlying asset price. These are still pure no-arbitrage option pricing models, where any deviation between model and market price can only be an arbitrage possibility. For example, consider the practice of fitting flexible deterministic volatility functions of the stock price $\sigma = f(S)$ to panels of options, with trees, in a manner consistent with no-arbitrage. This is, however, viewed as over-fitting by the econometrician; using this method, Dumas et al. (1998) report large out-of-sample pricing errors contrasting with quasi-perfect in-sample fit.

One clearly needs to explicitly allow for model error to obtain a likelihood function from option price data. This is done in Jacquier and Polson (2000) for the Black-Scholes model and its deterministic extensions. The pricing error yields the likelihood function and, in turn the posterior distribution of option parameters and prices. Jacquier and Jarrow model option prices as:

$$\log C_i = \beta_1 \log b_i(x_{1i}, \sigma) + \beta_2 x_{2i} + \eta_i, \quad \eta_i \sim N(0, \sigma_\eta), \tag{9.35}$$

where (x_1, x_2) are known data including the stock price. The prior density for σ comes from the historical data observed prior to the panel of options. It, therefore, incorporates information from the historical returns, but not in the likelihood function. The logarithm formulation eliminates the potential for negative prices while keeping a tractable likelihood.

Jacquier and Jarrow produce the posterior densities of $\beta_1, \beta_2, \sigma, \sigma_\eta$, where σ_η is the standard deviation of the pricing error. They break down the joint posterior density into two Gibbs steps. First, one draws directly from $p(\beta, \sigma_\eta | \sigma, C)$, as (9.35) is a linear regression given σ. Second, $p(\sigma | \beta, \sigma_\eta)$ is obtained by a univariate Hastings-Metropolis step, using a truncated normal as proposal density. Jacquier and Jarrow implement the model on panels of individual US stock options.

The results show that the econometric specification has a great impact, in a way the model itself can not suggest. Allowing for heteroskedasticity in the error η_i greatly improves the pricing performance. Unlike the calibration methods used in Dumas et al., the likelihood-based approach allows the econometrician to assess in-sample potential problems with the model and its implementation. The posterior distributions of σ_η, β_2 give clear warning of the potential ineffectiveness of the extensions as the dimension of x_2 increases. As more variables are added in x_2, the posterior mean of σ_η decreases for out-of-the-money options, but does not improve for the other options. At the same time, the spread of the posterior distribution of the other parameters (β, σ) increases drastically.

A joint draw from the parameters yields a draw for the model price, model prediction, and hedge ratio. The uncertainty in prices and hedge ratios increases with the model size and becomes quite large. Consequently, even before engaging into prediction, the Bayesian econometrician knows that the larger models may not be effective. Having introduced pricing error, the econometrician faces an uncertain option price, which is at odds with the theoretical foundation of the model. We do not address this tension, the resolution of which goes well beyond the scope of this chapter. It involves theoretical modeling, no doubt resulting in a model more complex than the one being implemented. From the econometric viewpoint, we believe that the benefit of incorporating the imperfection of the model at hand far outweighs the cost of the contradiction with the model being implemented.

Jacquier and Jarrow then show that the out-of-sample performance of the extended models is not superior to the basic Black-Scholes model. However, the decrease in performance from in- to out-of-sample is not catastrophic as in Dumas et al. This is because, in contrast to the fitting criteria used in Dumas et al., the Bayesian method does not explicitly find parameters to minimize in-sample pricing errors. Such methods will exacerbate the potential for over-fitting, and are more likely to result in seriously degraded out-of-sample performance. The Bayesian method, in a first step, produces the uncertainty in the posterior density of parameters, and functions such as the option price. One expects therefore its out-of-sample performance to be more robust to over-fitting.

We conclude with two observations. First, in the formulation in (9.35) one can use the Savage density ratio method to compute model odds since direct draws of β are available. Second, the formulation in (9.35) would be more effective if the extensions were modeled on σ itself, rather than outside of the Black-Scholes model, as for example in $C_i = BS(x_{1,i}, \sigma(\beta_2 x_{2,i} + \eta_i))$. This parameterization would be more consistent with most generalizations of the Black-Scholes model. Having the error inside the Black-Scholes formula would guarantee the no-arbitrage conditions. It would, however, lead to a more complicated MCMC algorithm.

6.3.2 *Option pricing with stochastic volatility and jumps*

Eraker et al. (2003), discussed in Section 5.4, estimate historical processes allowing for jumps in volatility as well as in returns. Using odds ratios and the fraction of volatility explained by jumps and diffusion, they conclude that jumps in volatility are a crucial extension to the SV model. Then they adjust their historical densities for a plausible price of volatility risk to generate option prices as per (9.38). They conclude that jumps in volatility have the potential to create a very realistic smile in implied volatilities.

Eraker et al. (2003) do not estimate the price of risk from option data; this is done in Eraker (2004) who derives the likelihood from explicit option pricing errors, as Jacquier and Jarrow (2000), but for the vastly more complex model of Eraker et al. (2003). Recall the process on the stock price S and its volatility V:

$$\begin{aligned} dS_t &= aS_t dt + \sqrt{V_t} S_t dw_t^s + S_t dJ_t^s \\ dV_t &= \kappa(\theta - V_t)dt + \sigma_v \sqrt{V_t} dw_t^v + dJ_t^v, \end{aligned} \tag{9.36}$$

where the volatility and return shocks can be correlated, and both dS and dV can have jumps. To the SV, SVJ, and SVCJ models seen in Section 5.4, Eraker (2004) adds a model in which the jump intensity depends on volatility, that is, $\lambda = \lambda_0 + \lambda_1 V_t$. He uses the discretized versions of these models. Jump components Z are assumed to be exponential for variance and normally distributed for stocks. Consistent with the option-pricing literature, the risk-neutral processes corresponding to the above historical processes incorporate drift adjustments for the prices of jump and volatility risk. Specifically, the return and volatility drifts, and the mean jump, are adjusted for these prices.

Given the option prices Y_t with known characteristics χ_t, the model prices these options with error ϵ_t:

$$Y_t = F(S_t, V_t, \chi_t, \Theta) + \epsilon_t, \tag{9.37}$$

where Θ is the vector of parameters of the risk-neutral processes of S_t, V_t. Times between transactions can vary. To compute the price F, Eraker uses Fourier inversion methods available due to the affine structure of the model.

Equation (9.37) yields the density of the options data Y conditional on the relevant parameters, observable inputs, and state variables V and S needed for pricing, $p(Y|S, V, \Theta)$. However, these state variables must be integrated out in order to obtain the posterior densities of the parameters and option prices. The formulation of S, V in (9.36) is conditional on the state vectors of jumps J; those must also, therefore, be integrated out. Consequently, the joint density of options data and all state variables $p(Y, S, V, J, Z, \Theta)$ involves the parameters of the process in (9.36). This joint density multiplied by the priors on all parameters yields the desired posterior density $p(V, J, Z, \Theta|Y)$. Eraker breaks this posterior into MCMC conditional blocks of volatilities V, jump states J, jump components Z, and parameters Θ.

Eraker estimates the model with 3,000 option prices on S&P500 contracts recorded over 1,000 days from 1987 to 1990. Due to the computational demands of the model, he uses a small number of randomly selected contracts daily, on average three contracts per day. At the same time, the underlying return is recorded daily. The posterior analysis reveals the following. The jump-size parameters are hard to estimate precisely, because option data do not contain information about them. Given the posterior jump intensity which implies very rare jumps, two or three per 1,000 days, one clearly can not have much information in jump size. In contrast, volatility parameters are very precisely estimated. This in turn helps the state-dependent model, in which the jump intensity is linked to the current volatility. Eraker concludes that the jump in volatility dominates the other extensions to the SV model in terms of explaining returns. For these models, return and volatility jumps are negatively correlated. That is, a negative jump in returns is associated with a positive jump in volatility.

The posterior mean of the option-pricing function F in (9.37) is used as the estimate of the option price. Based on this, the in-sample pricing errors of the larger models do not show much improvement over the simpler ones. Eraker notes that this result is in contrast with most of the previous literature. Recall that, unlike least squares, the Bayesian method does not compute estimates to minimize pricing errors. It optimally describes the uncertainty about the parameters; the posterior mean then minimizes a squared error loss along that posterior uncertainty. In contrast, least squares methods are geared at fitting better with larger models. This is why an out-of-sample analysis is a very interesting complement. Eraker's out-of-sample results reveals some performance for the larger jump model, but the results are at best mixed.

Overall, the larger models in Eraker (2004) appear to perform better with respect to features of the time series of the stock return than pricing options. Eraker (2004) is an example of the degree of complexity that can be handled by Bayesian MCMC algorithms. It would be interesting to revisit the features of the model with a larger cross-section of options data as computing power allows. Using a small panel of randomly selected data means that only very rough information on the smile is available at any given time, possibly affecting the precision of estimation. Inference on rare and large jumps is definitely a difficult problem, to which option prices do not contribute much information.

7 Particle Filters with Parameter Learning

We conclude the chapter with a methodological approach that appears very promising for Bayesian econometrics in finance: the joint filtering of the latent state variables parameters.

MCMC methods for models with latent variables generally produce the posterior density of the parameters and of the smoothed state variable. For example, the MCMC algorithms for the SV models discussed in Section 5, produce $p(h_t|y^T)$ and $p(\theta|y^T)$, where $y^T \equiv (y_1, \ldots, y_T)$, and θ, h_t are the model parameters and the variance at time t. For a given sample of data, however, one may want, for each time t in the sample, the posterior density of both filtered volatilities and parameters $p(h_t|y^t)$ and $p(\theta|y^t)$. Running again the MCMC sampler, each time a new observation (y^{t+1}) becomes available, is a feasible but computationally unattractive solution. Recent research has, therefore, been devoted to filtering algorithms for non-linear state space models. Early filtering algorithms solve the problem conditional on a value of θ. This is unattractive for two reasons. First, they do not incorporate the uncertainty on θ into the predictive density of h_t. Second, the most likely value of θ on which to condition, comes from the posterior distribution of a single MCMC algorithm run on the whole sample. However, conditioning on the information from the entire sample is precisely what one wants to avoid when drawing from $p(h_t|y^t)$. Incorporating learning about θ in the filtering algorithm turned out to be quite difficult. Let x_t be the state variable in a general model; earlier attempts to draw from $p(\theta, x_t|y^t)$ suffered from degeneracy problems. Section 8 of the Kohn chapter discusses these earlier methods. Carvalho et al. (2010), hereafter CJLP, resolve the problem. In this Section, we briefly outline their method and present an application demonstrating the potential of particle filtering with parameter learning.

7.1 Methodology

Consider a model with observable y_t and latent state variable x_t. The goal is to update the current distribution $p(x_t, \theta|y^t)$ to $p(x_{t+1}, \theta|y^{t+1})$ after observing y_{t+1}. For notational convenience, ignore in a first step the parameter θ. Classic filtering algorithms proceed by first predicting and then updating, as follows:

$$p(x_{t+1}|y^t) = \int p(x_{t+1}|x_t)p(x_t|y^t)dx_t$$

$$p(x_{t+1}|y^{t+1}) \propto p(y_{t+1}|x_{t+1})p(x_{t+1}|y^t).$$

The distribution $p(x_t|y^t)$ is usually not known analytically. Particle filters approximate it by a discrete density $p^N(x_t|y^t)$, consisting of N *particles*, or draws, $x_t^{(i)}$ with weights $w_t^{(i)}$:

$$p^N\left(x_t|y^t\right) = \sum_{i=1}^{N} w_t^{(i)} \delta_{x_t^{(i)}} \to p(x_t|y^t) \text{ as } N \to \infty,$$

where δ is the Dirac function. In earlier algorithms, the weights are typically $1/N$. This discretization allows us to replace the integral in the prediction step with a sum. We now have:

$$p^N(x_{t+1}|y^{t+1}) \propto \sum_{i=1}^{N} p(y_{t+1}|x_{t+1})p(x_{t+1}|x_t^{(i)})w_t^{(i)},$$

where $p^N(x_{t+1}|y^{t+1})$ is a finite mixture. There are several classic particle filters to draw from this mixture, such as the exact, the sampling importance resampling (SIR), and the auxiliary particle (APF) filters. The SIR algorithm, for example, relies only on two steps given N samples from $p^N\left(x_t|y^t\right)$:

(1) (Propagate) Draw $x_{t+1}^{(i)} \sim p\left(x_{t+1}|x_t^{(i)}\right)$ for $i = 1, \ldots, N$;

(2) (Resample) Draw $x_{t+1}^{(i)} \sim Mult_N\left(\left\{w_{t+1}^{(i)}\right\}_{i=1}^{N}\right)$.

Note how the first step uses the transition density of the state variable, but no information about y_{t+1}. The transition density can be seen as the simplest and most convenient importance density to use in the propagation step. The weights are then based upon the information in y_{t+1}, and a multinomial draw is made from the N x_{t+1}'s obtained from the propagation step. In their auxiliary particle filter, Pitt and Shephard (1999) improve the importance density, and show that the optimal weights are $w_{t+1} \propto p(y_{t+1}|x_t)$. Possible problems with particle filters include degeneracy or sample impoverishment, where the number of particles from which one draws degenerates due to the inability of the transition density to cover the high probability states. This can happen, for example, around extreme values, if the propagation step does not use the information in y_{t+1}. Then the resampling step leads to sample impoverishment as most draws have nearly zero weights. See Giordani et al., Chapter 3 in this *Handbook* and CJLP for details.

Consider now extending this framework to parameter learning, where one needs to move from $p(\theta, x_t|y^t)$ to $p(\theta, x_{t+1}|y^{t+1})$. CJLP's algorithm combines two contributions.

First, they reverse the prediction-updating order, and instead follow a smoothing-prediction sequence:

$$p(x_t|y^{t+1}) \propto p(y_{t+1}|x_t)p(x_t|y^t);$$
$$p(x_{t+1}|y^{t+1}) = \int p(x_{t+1}|x_t)p(x_t|y^{t+1})dx_t.$$

For the discretized distribution used, this sequence leads to a resample-propagate particle algorithm:

(1) Resample particles with weights $w_t^{(i)} \propto p\left(y_{t+1}|x_t^{(i)}\right)$:
Draw an index $z(i) \sim Mult_N\left(\{w_t^{(i)}\}\right)$, and set $x_t^{(i)} = x_t^{z(i)}$ for $i = 1, \ldots, N$;

(2) Propagate state particles with $x_{t+1}^{(i)} \sim p\left(x_{t+1}|x_t^{(i)}, y_{t+1}\right)$, for $i = 1, \ldots, N$.

By resampling first, the compounding of approximation errors is reduced because the propagation of the states uses the information in y_{t+1}. The second contribution addresses the issue of parameter learning. Rather than attempting to update $p(\theta|y^t)$ directly, CJLP extend the state with a vector of conditional sufficient statistics s_t, and instead update $p(s_t|y^t)$. The sufficient statistics satisfy the conditions:

$$p(\theta|x^t, y^t) = p(\theta|s_t) \text{ where } s_{t+1} = \mathcal{S}\left(s_t, x_{t+1}, y_{t+1}\right).$$

CJLP show how to use particle methods to find the joint filtering distribution $p(x_t, s_t|y^t)$; the parameter θ is then simulated by $\theta^{(i)} \sim p(\theta|s_t)$. The sufficient statistics s_t are essentially the parameters of the posterior distribution $p(\theta|y_t)$.

Given a particle filtering algorithm with parameter learning, dynamic model comparison or averaging can be performed at each time t via sequential odds ratios. A Bayesian investor can then evaluate the economic benefits of predicting out-of-sample returns by learning about the models, parameters, and state variables sequentially in real time. Bayes' rule naturally revises beliefs as new return data are available.

7.2 Incorporating realized volatility into the SV model

We now discuss an application to the SV models. The MCMC algorithms seen in Section 5.2 produce draws from $p(h_t|y^T)$, the smoothed posterior density of the volatilities, which uses the entire information in the sample. This smoothed density coincides with the filtered volatility, $p(h_t|\mathrm{y}^t)$, only for the last observation of the sample. An MCMC algorithm, such as in JPR, makes 50,000 draws in four minutes for $T = 1,500$ observations on a dual-core 2.8 Ghz CPU. Computing draws of the filtered posterior densities $p(h_t, \omega_t|\mathrm{y}^t)$ by running the MCMC algorithm for every subsample y^t for $t \in [500, 1,500]$ would require about 45 hours of CPU time. This is not an issue for academics, but practitioners who may want to update many such models everyday would find themselves a bit more pressed for time. Another reason why the filtered density of the latent variables is of interest is that they allow for the computation of the likelihood function. This is convenient if one can not write posterior odds directly through the MCMC algorithm as in Section 5.

Jacquier and Miller (2010), JM hereafter, apply both the MCMC and the CJLP algorithm to an extended SV model for the logarithm of variance h_t:

$$\log h_t = \alpha + \delta \log h_{t-1} + \gamma RV_{t-1} + \sigma_v v_t, \tag{9.38}$$

where RV_{t-1} is a realized volatility measure (see also Brandt and Jones 2005). The addition of exogenous variables to the volatility equation is a technically simple but potentially very useful extension of the SV model. Other variables of interest can be incorporated in the SV equation, such as implied volatility or the number of non-trading days between observations.

The basic RV measure is computed as the sum of squared intra-day returns: $RV_t = \sum_{j=1}^{m} r_{t,j}^2$. Under ideal assumptions, it is shown to converge on the day's integrated volatility $IV_t = \int_{t-1}^{t} \sigma_\tau^2 d\tau$, as m goes to infinity. However, measurement errors in prices, microstructure effects, and the possibility of jumps have to be taken into account. Therefore, several variations of this basic realized volatility now exist to address these issues (see, for example Patton 2008). The realized volatility literature typically attempts to evaluate these competing measures by their ability to predict integrated volatility, IV_{t+1}. However, since IV_{t+1} is never exactly known, it is typically replaced by a RV_{t+1} measure in predictability regressions.

In contrast, equation (9.38) takes the view that the daily volatility h_t is the latent variable to be predicted, and that RV_{t-1} is only an observable with information on this latent variable, not the object to be predicted. JM conduct simulations to document what reduction in volatility uncertainty can be expected by incorporating RV_{t-1} in (9.38). Using the root-mean-squared error of the posterior mean, they show that, for simulated data, RV measures only improve out-of-sample volatility forecasts up to four days ahead at the most. They also propose an alternate econometric specification to improve upon (9.38), which models the fact that RV_t is a noisy estimate of $\log h_t$, and allows for its error η_t to be correlated with v_t. Therefore, instead of having RV_t in the volatility equation as in (9.38), an additional measurement equation is introduced:

$$\log RV_t = \beta_0 + \beta_1 \log h_t + \eta_t. \tag{9.39}$$

Competing volatility measures can be introduced, via seemingly unrelated measurement equations, as in (9.39).

JM apply MCMC to the SV model with and without RV, on the UK pound, euro, and yen daily exchange rate changes, and country index returns over 2006–2009. They find that 90% posterior confidence intervals on $\sqrt{h_t}$ have average widths of 47% on the pound and 41% on the euro, relative to $E(\sqrt{h_t})$ when RV is not used. The introduction of RV, as in (9.38), reduces these to 27% and 32%. However, RV brings no such

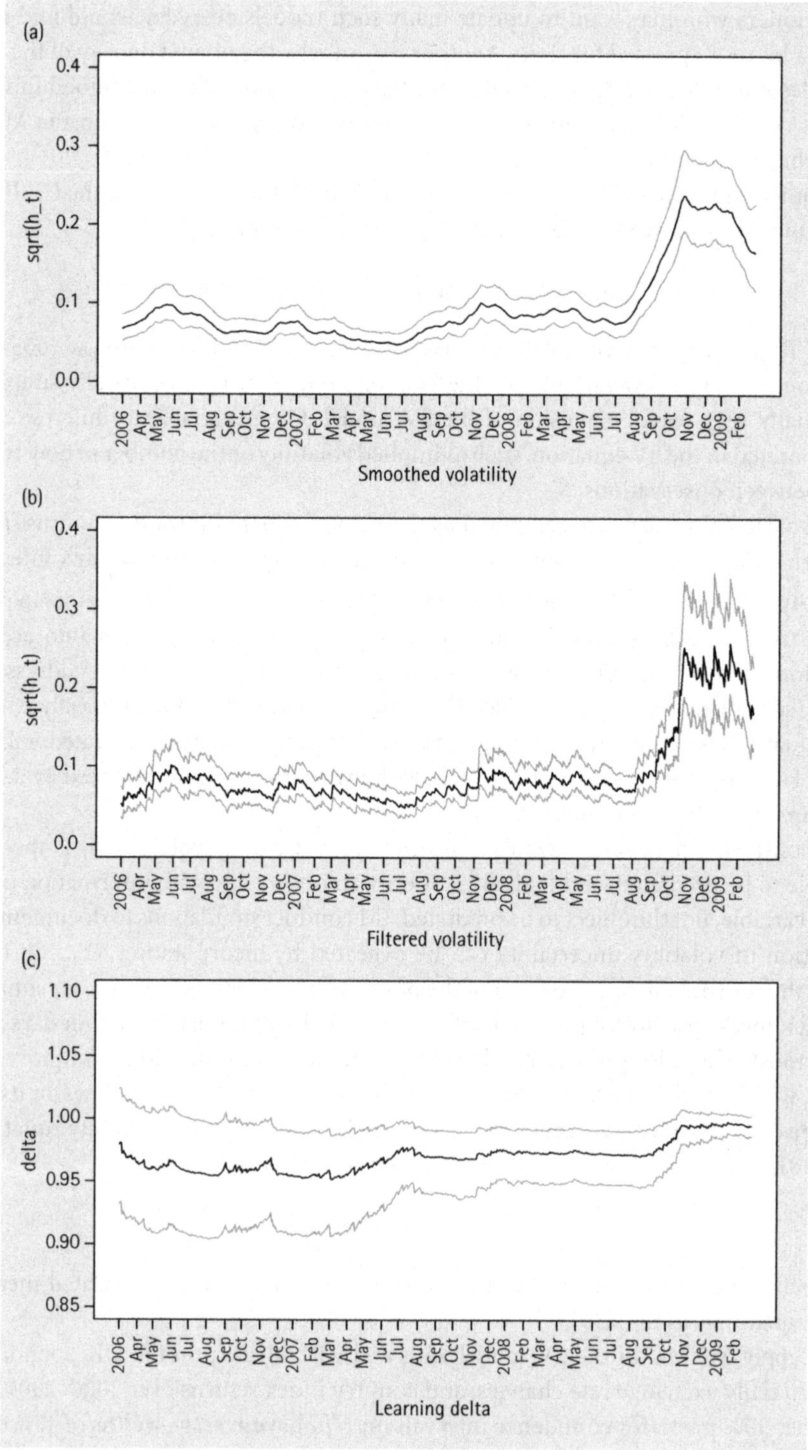

FIGURE 9.6 Smoothed and filtered $\sqrt{h_t}|R^T$, learning $\delta|R^t$,

Notes: SV model, £/\$, Jan. 2, 2006 to Feb. 26, 2009, Mean and 5%, 95% quantiles.

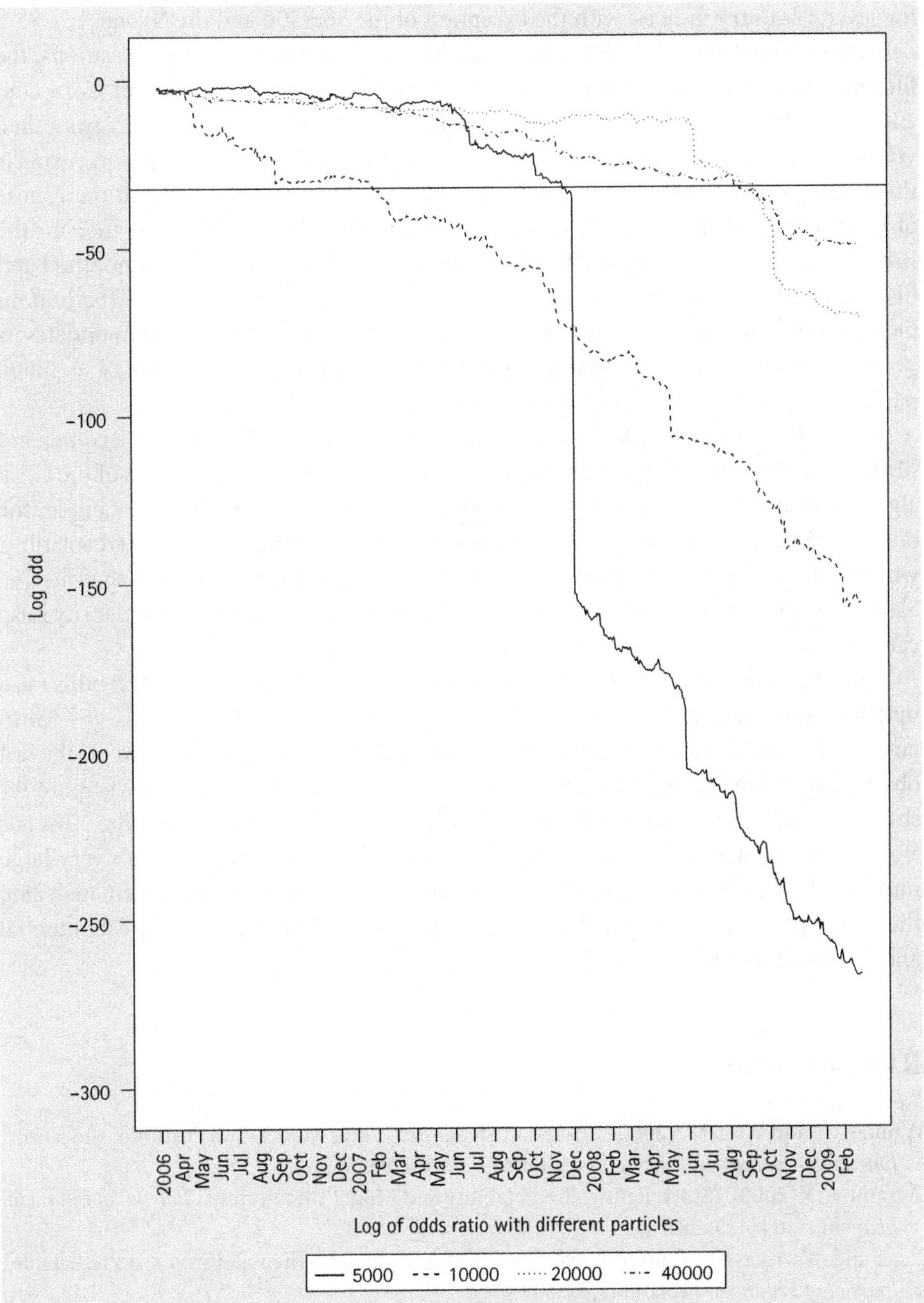

FIGURE 9.7 Log of odds ratios for basic SV versus SV with RV

Notes: Horizontal line: MCMC odds ratio. Particle filtering based odds ratios for 5K, 10K, 20K, and 40K particles. SV model, £/\$, Jan. 2, 2006 to Feb. 26, 2009.

improvement for the yen. They report similar improvements due to realized volatility for several country indices, with the exception of the S&P500 and the Nikkei.

JM then implement the CJLP algorithm. For these samples of 800 observations, the filtering algorithm with parameter learning requires about 25 minutes of Core-Duo 2.8 Ghz CPU time with 40,000 particles. Compared to filtered volatilities, smoothed volatilities benefit from the information contained in future y's; one, therefore, expects the posterior distributions of smoothed volatilities to have a tighter spread than those of filtered volatilities. Figure 9.6 demonstrates the magnitude of the difference for the British pound. The top and middle plots show the 90% intervals for the smoothed and filtered volatility densities obtained by MCMC and the CJLP algorithm. The bottom plot demonstrates the evolution of the parameter δ as the filtering algorithm updates its posterior distribution. The filtering algorithm for Figure 9.6 was run with $N = 40000$ particles.

A note of caution is in order with respect to the number of particles used. Jacquier and Miller note that, unless the number of particles is quite large, different runs of the CJLP algorithm can produce very different posterior densities. Consider, for example, the odds ratios for the basic SV model versus the model augmented with realized volatility, which is based on the parameter α_1 in (9.38). Since both MCMC and the filtering algorithms draw directly from the posterior density of α_1, a simple Savage density ratio can be used.

Figure 9.7 shows the MCMC odds ratios as a horizontal line, and the CJLP odds ratio updated every period for 5,000 to 40,000 particles. The MCMC log odds is -35, in favor of the model with realized volatility. The dynamic odds ratio obtained on the last observation from the particle filters should equal the MCMC odds ratios. Figure 9.7 shows that this only happens when the number of particles used is very large. This is a sign that the posterior distributions in the filtering algorithm may require a very large number of particles to be deemed reliable. Care needs to be exercised when analyzing the output of this type of algorithm. Nevertheless, these algorithms have great potential and are definitely worth exploring.

References

Aguilar, O., and West, M. (2000). “Bayesian Dynamics Factor Models and Portfolio Allocation”, *Journal of Business and Economics Statistics*, 18, July: 338–57.

Avramov, D. (2002). “Stock Return Predictability and Model Uncertainty”, *Journal of Financial Economics*, 64: 423–58.

—— and Wermers, R. (2006). “Investing in Mutual Funds when Returns are Predictable”, *Journal of Financial Economics*, 81: 339–77.

Baks, K., Metrick, A., and Wachter, J. (2001). “Should Investors Avoid all Actively Managed Mutual Funds? A study in Bayesian Performance Evaluation”, *Journal of Finance*, 56: 45–85.

Barberis, N. (2000). “Investing for the Long Run when Returns are Predictable”. *Journal of Finance*, 55: 225–64.

Barnard, J., McCulloch, R., and Meng Xiao-Li (2000)."Modeling Covariance Matrices in Terms of Standard Deviations and Correlations, with Application to Shrinkage", *Statistica Sinica*, 2000, 10(4): 1281–311.

Bauwens, L., and Lubrano, M. (1998). "Bayesian Inference on GARCH Models using Gibbs Sampler", *Econometrics Journal*, 1: 23–46.

—— —— (2002). "Bayesian Option Pricing Using Asymmetric GARCH Models", *Journal of Empirical Finance*, 9: 321–42.

Bawa, V., Brown S., and Klein, R. (1979). *Estimation Risk and Optimal Portfolio Choice*. Amsterdam: North-Holland.

Berger, J. (1985). *Statistical Decision Theory and Bayesian Analysis*, New York: Springer, Verlag.

Besag, J. (1989). "A Candidate's Formula: Curious Result in Bayesian Prediction", *Biometrika*, 76: 183.

Black, F., and Litterman, R. (1991). "Asset Allocation: Combining Investor Views with Market Equilibrium", *Journal of Fixed Income*, 1, September: 7–18.

Bollerslev, T., Engle, R. F., and Nelson, D. B. (1994). "ARCH Models", in R. F. Engle and D. McFadden (eds.), *Handbook of Econometrics*, IV. Amsterdam: North-Holland, 2959–3038.

Bossaerts, P., and Hillion, P. (1999). "Implementing Statistical Criteria to Select Return Forecasting Models: What do we learn?" *Review of Financial Studies*, 12: 405–28.

Brandt, M. W. (2009). "Portfolio Choice Problems", in Y. Ait-Sahalia and L. P. Hansen (eds.), *Handbook of Financial Econometrics*, Amsterdam: North-Holland.

—— and Jones, C. S. (2005). "Bayesian Range-Based Estimation of Stochastic Volatility Models", *finance Research Letters*, 2: 201–9.

Brown, S. (1976). "Optimal Portfolio Choice under Uncertainty: A Bayesian Approach". Ph.D Dissertation, University of Chicago.

—— (1978). "The Portfolio Choice Problem: Comparison of Certainty Equivalent and Optimal Bayes Portfolios", *Communications in Statistics: Simulation and Computation B7*, 321–34.

Campbell, J. Y., Lo, A. W., and MacKinlay, A. C. (1997). *The Econometrics of Financial Markets*. Princeton: Princeton University Press.

Carvalho, C., Johannes, M., Lopes, H., and Polson, N. G (2010). "Particle Learning and Smoothing", *Statistical Science*, 25(1): 88–106.

Chib, S. (1995). "Marginal Likelihood from the Gibbs Output". *Journal of the American Statistical Association*, 90(432): 1313–21.

—— and Greenberg, E. (1994), "Bayes Inference for Regression Models with ARMA(p, q) Errors", *Journal of Econometrics*, 64: 183–206.

—— and Nardari, F., and Shephard, N. (2002). "Markov Chain Monte Carlo Methods for Stochastic Volatility Models", *Journal of Econometrics*, 108: 281–316.

—— —— and Shephard, N. (2006). "Analysis of High Dimensional Multivariate Stochastic Volatility Models", *Journal of Econometrics*, 134: 341–71.

Connolly, R. A. (1991). "A Posterior Odds Analysis of the Weekend Effect", *Journal of Econometrics*, 49: 51–104.

Connor, G., and Korajczyk, R. A. (1986). "Performance Measurement with the Arbitrage Pricing Theory: A New Framework for Analysis", *Journal of Financial Economics*, 15: 373–94.

Cosemans, M., Frehen, R. G. P., Schotman, P. C., and Bauer, R. (2009). "Efficient Estimation of Firm-Specific Betas and its Benefits for Asset Pricing Tests and Portfolio Choice", SSRN: <http://ssrn.com/abstract=1342326>.

Cox, J. C., and Ross, S. A. (1976). "The Valuation of Options for Alternative Stochastic Processes", *Journal of Financial Economics*, 3: 145–66.
Cremers, M. (2002). "Stock Return Predictability: A Bayesian Model Selection Procedure", *Review of Financial Studies*, 15: 1223–49.
DeMiguel, V., Garlappi, L., and Uppal, R. (2009). "Optimal versus Naive Diversification: How Inefficient is the 1/N Portfolio Strategy", *Review of Financial Study*, 22(6): 2303–30.
Dickey, J. (1971)."The Weighted Likelihood Ratio, Linear Hypotheses on Normal Location Parameters", *Annals of Mathematical Statistics*, 42: 204–24.
Dumas, B., Fleming, J., and Whaley, R. (1998). "Implied Volatility Functions: Empirical Tests", *Journal of Finance*, 53: 2059–106.
—— and Jacquillat, B. (1990), "Performance of Currency Portfolios Chosen by a Bayesian Technique: 1967–1985", *Journal of Banking and Finance*, 14: 539–58.
Elerian, O., Chib, S., and Shephard, N. (2001). "Likelihood Inference for Discretely Observed Nonlinear Diffusions", *Econometrica*, 69: 959–94.
Eraker, B. (2001). "MCMC Analysis of Diffusion Models with Applications to Finance", *Journal of Business and Economic Statistics*, 19(2): 177–91.
—— (2004). "Do Stock Prices and Volatility Jump? Reconciling Evidence from Spot and Option Prices", *Journal of Finance*, 59(3), June, 1367–403.
—— Johannes, M., and Polson, N. G. (2003). "The Impact of Stochastic Volatility and Jumps in Returns". *Journal of Finance*, 58: 1269–300.
Frost, P. A., and Savarino, J. E. (1986). "An Empirical Bayes Approach to Efficient Portfolio Selection", *Journal of Financial and Quantitative Analysis*, 21: 293–305.
Geweke, J. (1988a). "The Secular and Cyclical Behavior of Real GDP in 19 OECD Countries, 1957–1983", *Journal of Business and Economic Statistics*, 6(4): 479–86.
—— (1988b). "Antithetic Acceleration of Monte Carlo Integration in Bayesian Inference", *Journal of Econometrics*, 38(1–2): 73–89.
—— (1989). "Exact Predictive Density for Linear Models with ARCH Disturbances", *Journal of Econometrics*, 40: 63–86.
—— (1992). "Evaluating the Accuracy of Sampling-Based Approaches to the Calculation of Posterior Moments", in J. O. Berger, J. M. Bernardo, A. P. Dawid, and A. F. M. Smith (eds.), *Bayesian Statistics 4*. Oxford: Oxford University Press, 169–94.
—— (1993). "Bayesian Treatment of the Student-*t* Linear Model", *Journal of Applied Econometrics*, 8: S19–S40.
—— (1994) "Bayesian Comparison of Econometric Models", Working Paper 532, Research Department, Federal Reserve Bank of Minneapolis.
—— (2001). "A Note on Some Limitations of CRRA Utility", *Economics Letters*, 71: 341–46.
—— and Whiteman, C. (2006). "Bayesian Forecasting", in G. Elliott, C. W. Granger, and A. Timmermann (eds.), *Handbook of Economic Forecasting*, vol. 1. Amsterdam: North-Holland, 4–80.
—— and Zhou, G. (1995). "Measuring the Pricing Error of the Arbitrage Pricing Theory", *Review of Financial Studies*, 9(2): 553–83.
Ghysels, E., McCulloch, R. E., and Tsay, R. S. (1998), "Bayesian Inference for Periodic Regime-Switching Models", *Journal of Applied Econometrics*, 13(2): 129–43.
Glosten, L. R., Jagannathan, R., and Runkle, D. E. (1992). "On the Relation between the Expected Value and the Volatility of the Nominal Excess Return on Stocks", *Journal of Finance*, 48: 1779-801.

Green, P. (1995). "Reversible Jump Markov Chain Monte Carlo Computation and Bayesian Model Determination", *Biometrika*, 82: 711–32.

Harvey, C. R., Liechty, J. C., and Liechty, M. W. (2008), "Bayes vs. Resampling: A Rematch", *Journal of Investment Management*, 6(1).

——— ——— ——— and Mueller, P. (2010). "Portfolio Selection with Higher Moments: A Bayesian Decision Theoretic Approach", *Quantitative Finance*, 10(5): 469–85.

——— and Zhou, G. (1990). "Bayesian Inferance in Asset Pricing Tests", *Journal of Financial Economics*, 26: 221–54.

Heston, S. (1993). "Closed-Form Solution of Options with Stochastic Volatility with Application to Bond and Currency Options", *Review of Financial Studies*, 6: 327–43.

Hull, J., and White, A. (1987). "The Pricing of Options on Assets with Stochastic Volatility", *Journal of Finance*, 42(2): 281–300.

Jacquier, E. (1991). "Predictability of Long Term Stock Returns and the Business Cycle", Ph.D. dissertation, Univercity of Chicago.

——— (2006). "Long-Term Forecasts of Mean Returns: Statistical vs. Economic Rationales", HEC Montreal Working Paper.

——— and Jarrow, R. A. (2000). "Bayesian Analysis of Contingent Claim Model Error", *Journal of Econometrics*, 94(1): 145–80.

——— Johannes, M., and Polson, N. G. (2007). "MCMC Maximum Likelihood for Latent State Models", *Journal of Econometrics*, 137(2): 615–40.

——— Marcus, A., and Kane, A. (2005). "Optimal Estimation of the Risk Premium for the Long-Term and Asset Allocation", *Journal of Financial Econometrics*, 3, winter: 37–56.

——— and Miller, S. (2010). "The Information Content of Realized Volatility", Working Paper HEC Montreal.

——— and Polson, N. (2000). "Odds Ratios for Non-nested Models: Application to Stochastic Volatility Models", Boston College manuscript.

——— ——— and Rossi, P. (1994). "Bayesian Analysis of Stochastic Volatility Models (with discussion)", *Journal of Business and Economic Statistics*, 12: 371–89.

——— ——— ——— (1995). "Models and Priors for Multivariate Stochastic Volatility Models", Working Paper, University of Chicago.

——— ——— ——— (2004). "Bayesian Analysis of Stochastic Volatility Models with Fat-Tails and Correlated Errors", *Journal of Econometrics*, 122: 185–212.

James, W., and Stein, C. (1961). "Estimation with Quadratic Loss", in J. Neyman (ed.), *Proceedings of the Fourth Berkeley Symposium on Mathematical Statistics and Probability*, vol. 1, Berkeley, Calif: University of California Press, 361–79.

Jobson, J. D., and Korkie, R. (1980). "Estimation for Markowitz Efficient Portfolios", *Journal of the American Statistical Association*, 75: 544–54.

——— ——— (1981). "Putting Markowtiz Theory to Work", *Journal of Portfolio Management*, summer: 70–4.

Johannes, M., Polson, N. G., and Stroud, J. R. (2010). "Optimal Filtering of Jump-Diffusions: Extracting Latent States from Asset Prices", *Review of Financial Studies*, 22(7): 2759–99.

Jones, C. (2003a). "Nonlinear Mean Reversion in the Short-Term Interest Rates", *Review of Financial Studies*, 16: 793–843.

——— (2003b). "The Dynamics of Stochastic Volatility: Evidence from Underlying and Options Markets", *Journal of Econometrics*, 116: 181–224.

——— and Shanken, J. (2005). "Mutual Fund Performance with Learning across Funds", *Journal of Financial Economics*, 78: 507–52.

Jorion, P. (1985), "International Portfolio Diversification with Estimation Risk", *Journal of Business*, 58: 259–78.

——(1986). "Bayes-Stein estimation for Portfolio Analysis", *Journal of Financial and Quantitative Analysis*, 21: 279–92.

Jostova, G., and Philipov, A. (2005). "Bayesian Analysis of Stochastic Betas", *Journal of Financial and Quantitative Analysis*, 40(4): 747–78.

Kandel, S., McCulloch, R., and Stambaugh, R. F. (1995). "Bayesian Inference and Portfolio Efficiency," *Review of Financial Studies*, 8: 1–53.

——and Stambaugh, R. F. (1996). "On the Predictability of Stock Returns: An Asset Allocation Perspective", *Journal of Finance*, 51: 385–424.

Karolyi, A. (1993), "A Bayesian Approach to Modeling Stock Return Volatility for Option Valuation", *Journal of Financial and Quantitative Analysis*, 28, December, 579–94.

Kim, S., Shephard, N., and Chib, S. (1998), "Stochastic Volatility: Likelihood Inference and Comparison with ARCH Models", *Review of Economic Studies*, 65: 361–93.

Kleibergen, F., and Van Dijk, H. K. (1993). "Non-stationarity in GARCH Models: A Bayesian Analysis", *Journal of Applied Econometrics*, 8: 41–61.

Klein, R. W., and Bawa, V. S. (1976). "The Effect of Estimation Risk on Optimal Portfolio Choice", *Journal of Financial Economics*, 3: 215–31.

Lamoureux, C., and Zhou, G. (1996). "Temporary Components of Stock Returns: What do the Data Tell us?" *Review of Financial Studies*, winter, 1033–59.

Ley, E., and Steel, M. F. J. (2009). "On the Effect of Prior Assumptions in Bayesian Model Averaging with Applications to Growth Regression", *Journal of Applied Econometrics*, 24(4): 651–74.

Markowitz, H. M. (1952). "Portfolio Selection", *Journal of Finance* 7: 77–91.

McCulloch, R., and Rossi, P. E. (1990). "Posterior, Predictive and Utility Based Approaches to Testing Arbitrage Pricing Theory", *Journal of Financial Economics*, 28: 7–38.

——(1991). "A Bayesian Approach to Testing the Arbitrage Pricing Theory", *Journal of Econometrics*, 49: 141–68.

——and Tsay, R. (1993). "Bayesian Inference and Prediction for Mean and Variance Shifts in Autoregressive Time Series", *Journal of the American Statistical Association*, 88(423): 968–78.

Mengersen, K. L., and Tweedie, R. L. (1996). "Rates of Convergence of the Hastings and Metropolis Algorithms", *The Annals of Statistics*, 24(1), February: 101–21.

Merton, R. C. (1969). "Lifetime Portfolio Selection under Uncertainty: The Continuous Time Case", *Review of Economics and Statistics*, 51: 247–57.

——(1972). "An Analytical Derivation of the Efficient Portfolio Frontier", *Journal of Financial and Quantitative Analysis*, 7(4): 1851–72.

Michaud, R. O. (1989). "The Markowitz Optimization Enigma: Is Optimized Optimal", *Financial Analysts Journal*, January: 31–42.

Muller, P., and Pole, A. (1998). "Monte Carlo Posterior Integration in GARCH Models", *Sankhya*, 60: 127–44.

Nakatsuma, T. (2000). "Bayesian Analysis of ARMA-GARCH Models: A Markov Chain Sampling Approach", *Journal of Econometrics*, 95: 57–69.

Nelson, D. B. (1991). "Conditional Heteroskedasticity in Asset Returns: A New Approach", *Econometrica*, 59: 347–70.

——(1994). "Comment on Bayesian Analysis of Stochastic Volatility Models", *Journal of Business and Economic Statistics*, 11: 406–10.

Newton, M., and Raftery, A. (1994). "Approximate Bayesian Inference with the Weighted Likelihood Bootstrap", *Journal of the Royal Statistical Society Series B*, 57: 3–48.
Officer, R. (1973). "The Variability of the Market Factor of the NYSE", *Journal of Business*, 46(3): 434–53.
Pastor, L. (2000). "Portfolio Selection and Asset Pricing Models", *Journal of Finance*, 50: 179–223.
—— and Stambaugh, R. F. (2000). "Comparing Asset Pricing Models: An Investment Perspective", *Journal of Financial Economics*, 56: 335–81.
Patton, A. (2008). "Data-Based Ranking of Realised Volatility Estimators", Working Paper, University of Oxford.
Pitt, M., and Shephard, M. (1999), "Filtering via Simulation: Auxiliary Particle Filters", *Journal of the American Statistical Association*, 94(446): 590–9.
Richardson, M., and Stock, J. H. (1989). "Drawing Inferences from Statistics Based on Multiyear Asset Returns", *Journal of Financial Economics*, 25(2), 323–348.
Ritter, C., and Tanner, M. (1992). "Facilitating the Gibbs Sampler: The Gibbs Stopper and the Griddy-Gibbs Sampler", *Journal of the American Statistical Association*, Vol. 87, No. 419 (Sep.), pp. 861-868.
Roll, R. (1977). "A Critique of the Asset Pricing Theory's Tests Part I: On Past and Potential Testability of the Theory", *Journal of Financial Economics*, 4(2), March: 129–76.
Ross, S. A. (1976), "The Arbitrage Theory of Capital Asset Pricing", *Journal of Economic Theory*, 13: 341–60.
Shanken, J. (1987). "A Bayesian Approach to Testing Portfolio Efficiency", *Journal of Financial Economics*, 19: 195–215.
Sharpe, W. (1963). "A Simplified Model for Portfolio Analysis", *Management Science*, 9: 277–93.
Siegel, J. (1994). *Stocks for the Long Run*. Newyork: McGraw-Hill.
Stambaugh, R. F. (1997). "Analyzing Investments whose Histories Differ in Length", *Journal of Financial Economics*, 45: 285–331.
—— (1999). "Predictive Regressions", *Journal of Financial Economics*, 54: 375–421.
Stein, C. (1955). "Inadmissibility of the Usual Estimator for the Mean of a Multivariate Normal Distribution", in *3rd Berkeley Symposium on Probability and Statistics*, vol. 1, Berkeley. Calif.: University of California Press, 197–206.
Tu, J., and Zhou, G. (2009). "Incorporating Economic Objectives into Bayesian Priors: Portfolio Choice under Parameter Uncertainty", *Journal of Financial and Quantitative Analysis*, 959–86.
Vrontos, I. D., Dellaportas, P., and Politis, D. (2000). "Full Bayesian Inference for GARCH and EGARCH Models", *Journal of Business and Economic Statistics*, 18: 187–98.
Wachter, J. A., and Warusawitharana, M. (2009). "Predictable Returns and Asset Allocation: Should a Skeptical Investor Time the Market?" *Journal of Econometrics*, 148, 162–78.
Zellner, A. (1962). "An Efficient Method of Estimating Seemingly Unrelated Regression Equations and Tests for Aggregation Bias", *Journal of the American Statistical Association*, 57: 348–68.
—— (1971). *An Introduction to Bayesian Inference in Econometrics*. New York: Wiley.
—— (1978). "Jeffreys-Bayes Posterior Odds Ratio and the Akaike Information Criterion for Discriminating between Models", *Economics Letters*, 1(4): 337–42.

—— (1986), "On Assessing Prior Distributions and Bayesian Regression Analysis with G-prior Distributions", In A. Zellner, *Bayesian Inference and Decision Techniques*, vol. 6 of Studies in Bayesian Econometrics and Statistics, Amsterdam: North-Holland, 233–43.

—— and Chetty, V. K. (1965). "Prediction and Decision Problems in Regression Models from the Bayesian Point of View", *Journal of the American Statistical Association*, 60: 608–15.

Zhou, G. (2008). "An Extension of the Black-Litterman Model: Letting the Data Speak", Working Paper, Olin Business School.

Index of Names

Index of Subjects

Made in the USA
Las Vegas, NV
07 December 2024

13397483R00313